A Practitioner's Guide to
THE CITY CODE ON TAKEOVERS AND MERGERS 2006/2007

A Practitioner's Guide to
THE CITY CODE ON TAKEOVERS AND MERGERS 2006/2007

Introduced by
Mark Warham
Director General
The Panel on Takeovers and Mergers

Edited by
Maurice Button

City & Financial Publishing

City & Financial Publishing
8 Westminster Court, Hipley Street
Old Woking
Surrey GU22 9LG
United Kingdom
Tel: 00 44 (0)1483 720707 Fax: 00 44 (0)1483 727928
Web: www.cityandfinancial.com

This book has been compiled from the contributions of the named authors. The views expressed herein do not necessarily reflect the views of their respective firms. Further, since this book is intended as a general guide only, its application to specific situations will depend upon the particular circumstances involved and it should not be relied upon as a substitute for obtaining appropriate professional advice.

This book is current as at 20 May 2006. Whilst all reasonable care has been taken in the preparation of this book, City & Financial Publishing and the authors do not accept responsibility for any errors it may contain or for any loss sustained by any person placing reliance on its contents.

All rights reserved. Neither the whole nor any part of this publication may be copied or otherwise reproduced without the prior written permission of the copyright holders.

ISBN 1 905121 11 3
(from Jan 2007: 978 1905 121 113)
© 2006 City & Financial Publishing and the authors.

Takeover Code © The Takeover Panel.

The Code is extant at 20 May 2006 but is revised from time-to-time.

British Library Cataloguing-in-Publication Data. A catalogue record for this book is available from the British Library.

Typeset by Cambrian Typesetters, Camberley and printed and bound in Great Britain by Biddles Ltd, King's Lynn.

Biographies

Mark Warham was appointed Director General of The Takeover Panel with effect from December 2005 on secondment from Morgan Stanley, where he is a Managing Director. Prior to joining Morgan Stanley in 2000 he was a Director of Schroders, which he joined in 1986 after having previously worked with 3i.

Simon Marchant is a partner at Freshfields Bruckhaus Deringer. He specialises in domestic and cross-border M&A and securities work, acting for corporate and investment banking clients.

Andy Ryde became a partner at Slaughter and May in 1996. He specialises in corporate law and works on UK and international M&A deals and securities offerings.

Roland Turnill became a partner at Slaughter and May in 2004. He specialises in public takeovers and mergers, private acquisitions and disposals, and joint ventures.

Christopher Pearson is a partner at Norton Rose. He qualified as a solicitor in 1984 and joined Norton Rose in 1986. From 1988 to 1991 he practised in Hong Kong. He became a partner of Norton Rose in 1992 and specialises in public company work. In recent years he has worked on a number of high-profile transactions including the Guinness/GrandMet merger; Mannesmann/Orange; Texas Utilities/The Energy Group; Ciba Specialty Chemicals/Allied Colloids; Trinity/Mirror Group; Deutsche Börse/London Stock Exchange; and Brascan/Canary Wharf.

Nick Adams is a partner at Norton Rose, specialising in corporate finance. Nick has extensive experience of public company takeovers and transactions. In recent years, deals Nick has worked on include Mannesmann/Orange; Mannesmann/Vodafone; Texas Utilities/The Energy Group; Trinity/Mirror Group; and Siemens Financial Services/Broadcastle. During 2000, Nick spent a year working as an investment banker at Schroder Salomon Smith Barney, where he worked on a number of takeovers, including Barclays/Woolwich.

Mark Gearing is a partner at Allen & Overy LLP. He has been a partner in the corporate department since 1992. His practice covers all types of corporate and commercial transactions, including domestic and international corporate finance and securities work. He has particular experience of public company takeovers having been seconded as joint secretary to the Takeover Panel between 1992 and 1994.

Carlton Evans has been a corporate partner at Linklaters since 1997 and is experienced in a wide range of corporate transactions. He was Secretary of the Takeover Panel for the two years ending June 1998 and has particular expertise in UK and international M&A and private equity.

David Pudge is a partner in the corporate finance practice at Clifford Chance LLP. He specialises in domestic and cross-border mergers and acquisitions, corporate finance transactions and stock exchange matters, with a particular focus on public takeover offers. Recent significant transactions include advising BPB on its defence against the unsolicited offer from Saint-Gobain, and Banco Santander on the acquisition of Abbey National plc by way of a scheme of arrangement. David also advised GKN plc on the demerger of its support services activities and their combination with Brambles Industries Limited of Australia by way of a dual listed companies structure.

Ursula Newton is a partner in the London Capital Markets Group at PricewaterhouseCoopers LLP where she specialises in advising on listing and public company transactions. She regularly lectures on the Listing Rules and City Code reporting issues.

Annabel Sykes is a partner at Freshfields Bruckhaus Deringer. She specialises in regulatory work for the financial services and insurance sectors. She was heavily involved in the successful restructuring of the Lloyd's insurance market advising, in particular, on the UK and overseas regulatory aspects. She also advises the Takeover Panel on regulatory matters. Annabel is a member of the Financial Services Authority's Lawyers' Consultative Group which meets regularly to discuss legal issues emerging from the Financial Services and Markets Act 2000 and the FSA's Handbook and consultation papers. She is leader of the Law Society's Company Law Committee Financial Services Working Party. Annabel is also a member of the Investment Management Association's (IMA) Legal Advisory Group.

Umesh Kumar is a senior associate in the financial institutions group at Freshfields Bruckhaus Deringer. He has a broad range of financial services and regulatory experience and regularly advises investment managers, banks, investment banks and securities houses on financial services and regulatory issues. Umesh spent six months on secondment to the legal department of Goldman Sachs Asset Management International in 2002 and earlier this year was on secondment to the equity compliance team at Merrill Lynch International.

Julian Francis joined Freshfields Bruckhaus Deringer in 1980 and became a partner in 1987. He worked in Frankfurt for four years, from 1990 to 1994. He has a wide ranging practice which includes IPOs, public and private M&A and corporate finance. He is advising the Takeover Panel on the implementation of the Takeover Directive.

Table of Contents

Biographies   v

1   The Takeover Panel   1
Mark Warham
Director General
The Takeover Panel

1.1	Introduction	1
1.2	Implementation of the Directive	3
1.3	Flexibility of the Code: application according to underlying purpose	4
1.4	Code amendment and recent Rule changes	4
1.5	Exempt status and recognised intermediary status	13
1.6	Some key Rules	15
1.7	The Panel and its Committees	19
1.8	The Panel Executive	21
1.9	Takeover Appeal Board	23
1.10	Relationship between the Panel and the Courts	23
1.11	Enforcement of the Code	25
1.12	Disciplinary Powers	27
1.13	Confidentiality, information sharing and cooperation	28

2   The Approach, Announcements and Independent Advice   29
Simon Marchant
Partner
Freshfields Bruckhaus Deringer

2.1	General considerations	29
2.2	Companies and transactions to which the Code applies	31
2.3	The approach	37
2.4	Announcing the offer	39
2.5	Secrecy	44
2.6	Pre-bid announcements	46

	2.7	Bid announcements	57
	2.8	Independent advice	64

3 Share Dealings – Restrictions and Disclosure Requirements 69
Andy Ryde and Roland Turnill
Partners
Slaughter and May

	3.1	Introduction	69
	3.2	Applicability of the rules	71
	3.3	Fundamental concepts	75
	3.4	Restrictions on the freedom to deal	83
	3.5	Disclosure of share dealings	116
	3.6	Miscellaneous	128

4 Mandatory and Voluntary Offers and their Terms 135
Christopher Pearson and Nick Adams
Partners
Norton Rose

	4.1	Introduction	135
	4.2	The mandatory offer and its terms	136
	4.3	The voluntary offer and its terms	150
	4.4	Competition law issues	164

5 Provisions Applicable to all Offers, Partial Offers and Redemption or Purchase by a Company of its own Securities 167
Mark Gearing
Partner
Allen & Overy

	5.1	Introduction	167
	5.2	Provisions applicable to all offers	167
	5.3	Partial offers	191
	5.4	Redemption or purchase of own securities	196

Contents

6   Documents from the Offeror and the Offeree   203
Carlton Evans
Partner
Linklaters

6.1	Introduction	203
6.2	General obligations in respect of documents	204
6.3	Offer document contents	210
6.4	Offeree Circular contents – Rule 25	218
6.5	Criminal Liability for non-compliant documents	221
6.6	Publication of Documents	222
6.7	Circulation of Documents	223
6.8	Specific issues	224
6.9	Other documents	227
6.10	Offers to holders of convertible securities and options – Rule 15	229
6.11	The Listing Rules	230
6.12	Financial Services and Markets Act 2000	232
6.13	Companies Act 1985	233
6.14	The use of websites in takeovers	234

7   Conduct During the Offer; Timing and Revision; and Restrictions Following Offers   237
David Pudge
Partner
Clifford Chance LLP

7.1	Introduction	237
7.2	Conduct during the offer	239
7.3	Timing and revision	256
7.4	Extensions of the offer	268
7.5	Revisions and increases	269
7.6	Alternative offers	271
7.7	Restrictions following offers and possible offers	273

8   Profit Forecasts and Asset Valuations   279
Ursula Newton
Partner
PricewaterhouseCoopers LLP

8.1	Profit forecasts	279
8.2	Asset valuations	291

9 Application of the Market Abuse Regime to Takeovers — 295
Annabel Sykes
Partner
Umesh Kumar
Senior Associate
Freshfields Bruckhaus Deringer

9.1	Introduction	295
9.2	Controversial aspects of market abuse	296
9.3	Background to the market abuse regime	297
9.4	Market abuse explained	299
9.5	Relevant powers of the Financial Services Authority	304
9.6	Impact on takeovers	307

10 The Takeover Directive — 313
Julian Francis
Partner
Freshfields Bruckhaus Deringer

10.1	Background	313
10.2	The Takeover Directive	313
10.3	Impact of the Directive on EU takeover rules	327
10.4	The future	329

THE CITY CODE ON TAKEOVERS AND MERGERS

INTRODUCTION

1	OVERVIEW	331
2	THE CODE	331
3	COMPANIES, TRANSACTIONS AND PERSONS SUBJECT TO THE CODE	332
4	THE PANEL AND ITS COMMITTEES	337
5	THE EXECUTIVE	340
6	INTERPRETING THE CODE	340
7	HEARINGS COMMITTEE	342
8	TAKEOVER APPEAL BOARD	345
9	PROVIDING INFORMATION AND ASSISTANCE TO THE PANEL AND THE PANEL'S POWERS TO REQUIRE DOCUMENTS AND INFORMATION	347
10	ENFORCING THE CODE	348
11	DISCIPLINARY POWERS	349

Contents

12	CO-OPERATION AND INFORMATION SHARING	351
13	FEES AND CHARGES	352

GENERAL PRINCIPLES 353

DEFINITIONS 355

RULES 371

SECTION D. THE APPROACH, ANNOUNCEMENTS AND INDEPENDENT ADVICE

RULE 1.		THE APPROACH	371
RULE 2.		SECRECY BEFORE ANNOUNCEMENTS; THE TIMING AND CONTENTS OF ANNOUNCEMENTS	372
	2.1	Secrecy	372
		Notes on Rule 2.1	
		1. Warning clients	372
		2. Proof printing	372
	2.2	When an announcement is required	372
		Notes on Rule 2.2	
		1. Panel to be consulted	373
		2. Clear statements	374
	2.3	Responsibilities of offerors and the offeree company	374
	2.4	The announcement of a possible offer	374
		Notes on Rule 2.4	
		1. Pre-conditions	375
		2. Announcement of a potential competing offer	376
		3. Period for clarification	376
		4. Extension of time limit	376
		5. Reservation of right to set statements aside	376
		6. Duration of restriction	376
		7. Statements by the offeree company	376
	2.5	The announcement of a firm intention to make an offer	377
		Notes on Rule 2.5	
		1. Unambiguous language	378
		2. Interests of a group of which an adviser is a member	378
		3. Subjective conditions	379
		4. New conditions for increased or improved offers	379
		5. Pre-conditions	379
		6. Financing conditions and pre-conditions	379

	2.6	Obligation on the offeror and the offeree company to circulate announcements	379
		Notes on Rule 2.6	
		1. Full text of announcement under Rule 2.5 to be made available	380
		2. Shareholders, employee representatives and employees outside the EEA	380
	2.7	Consequences of a "firm announcement"	380
		Note on Rule 2.7	
		When there is no need to post	380
	2.8	Statements of intention not to make an offer	380
		Notes on Rule 2.8	
		1. Prior consultation	381
		2. Rule 2.4(b)	381
		3. Concert parties	381
		4. Media reports	382
	2.9	Publication of an announcement about an offer or possible offer	382
		Notes on Rule 2.9	
		1. Distribution and availability of announcements	382
		2. Rules 6, 7, 9, 11, 17, 30, 31, 32, Appendix 1.6 and Appendix 5	382
	2.10	Announcement of numbers of relevant securities in issue	383
		Notes on Rule 2.10	
		1. Options to subscribe	383
		2. Treasury shares	383
RULE 3.		INDEPENDENT ADVICE	384
	3.1	Board of the offeree company	384
		Notes on Rule 3.1	
		1. Management buy-outs and offers by controllers	384
		2. When there is uncertainty about financial information	384
		3. When no recommendation is given or there is a divergence of views	384
	3.2	Board of an offeror company	384
		Notes on Rule 3.2	
		1. General	385
		2. Reverse takeovers	385
		3. Conflicts of interest	385

3.3	Disqualified advisers		385
	Notes on Rule 3.3		
	1.	*Independence of adviser*	385
	2.	*Investment trusts*	385
	3.	*Success fees*	386

SECTION E. RESTRICTIONS ON DEALINGS

RULE 4.			387
4.1	Prohibited dealings by persons other than the offeror		387
4.2	Restriction on dealings by the offeror and concert parties		387
	Notes on Rules 4.1 and 4.2		
	1.	*Other circumstances in which dealings may not take place*	388
	2.	*Consortium offers and joint offerors*	388
	3.	*No-profit arrangements*	388
	4.	*When an offer will not proceed*	389
	5.	*No dealing contrary to published advice*	389
	6.	*Discretionary fund managers and principal traders*	389
4.3	Gathering of irrevocable commitments		389
	Note on Rule 4.3		
	Irrevocable commitments		389
4.4	Dealings in offeree securities by certain offeree company associates		389
	Note on Rule 4.4		
	Irrevocable commitments and letters of intent		390
4.5	Restriction on the offeree company accepting an offer in respect of treasury shares		390
4.6	Restriction on securities borrowing and lending transactions by offerors, the offeree company and certain other parties		390
	Notes on Rule 4.6		
	1.	*Return of borrowed relevant securities*	391
	2.	*Pension funds*	391
	3.	*Disclosure or notice where consent is given*	391
	4.	*Discretionary fund managers and principal traders*	391

RULE 5.		TIMING RESTRICTIONS ON ACQUISITIONS	392
	5.1	Restrictions	392
		Notes on Rule 5.1	
		1. When more than 50% is held	392
		2. New shares, subscription rights, convertibles and options	392
		3. Allotted but unissued shares	392
		4. "Whitewashes"	393
		5. Maintenance of the percentage of the shares in which a person is interested	393
		6. Discretionary fund managers and principal traders	393
		7. Gifts	393
	5.2	Exceptions to restrictions	393
		Notes on Rule 5.2	
		1. Single shareholder	394
		2. Rule 9	395
		3. Revision	395
		4. After an offer lapses	395
	5.3	Acquisitions from a single shareholder – consequences	395
		Notes on Rule 5.3	
		1. If a person's interests are reduced	395
		2. Rights or scrip issues and "whitewashes"	395
	5.4	Acquisitions from a single shareholder – disclosure	395
		Note on Rule 5.4	
		Disclosure of the identity of the person dealing	396
RULE 6.		ACQUISITIONS RESULTING IN AN OBLIGATION TO OFFER A MINIMUM LEVEL OF CONSIDERATION	397
	6.1	Acquisitions before a Rule 2.5 announcement	397
	6.2	Acquisitions after a Rule 2.5 announcement	397
		Notes on Rule 6	
		1. Adjusted terms	398
		2. Acquisitions prior to the three month period	398
		3. No less favourable terms	398
		4. Highest price paid	399
		5. Cum dividend	400
		6. Convertible securities, warrants and options	400

	7.	Unlisted securities	400
	8.	Discretionary fund managers and principal traders	400
	9.	Offer period	400
	10.	Competition reference period	400
RULE 7.		CONSEQUENCES OF CERTAIN DEALINGS	401
7.1		Immediate announcement required if the offer has to be amended	401
		Note on Rule 7.1	
		Potential offerors	401
7.2		Dealings by connected discretionary fund managers and principal traders	401
		Notes on Rule 7.2	
	1.	Dealings prior to a concert party relationship arising	402
	2.	Qualifications	403
	3.	Dealings by principal traders	403
	4.	Dealings by discretionary fund managers	404
	5.	Rule 9	404
	6.	Disclosure of dealings in offer documentation	404
	7.	Consortium offers	405
7.3		Partial offers and "whitewashes"	405
RULE 8.		DISCLOSURE OF DEALINGS DURING THE OFFER PERIOD; ALSO INDEMNITY AND OTHER ARRANGEMENTS	406
8.1		Dealings by parties and by associates for themselves or for discretionary clients	406
8.2		Dealings by parties and by associates for non-discretionary clients	406
8.3		Dealings by persons with interests in securities representing 1% or more	406
8.4		Irrevocable commitments and letters of intent	407
		Notes on Rule 8	
	1.	Consultation with the Panel	407
	2.	Dealings in relevant securities of the offeror	408
	3.	Timing of disclosure	408
	4.	Method of disclosure (public or private)	408
	5.	Details to be included in disclosures (public or private)	408
	6.	Indemnity and other arrangements	411

7.	Time for calculating a person's interests	412
8.	Discretionary fund managers	412
9.	Recognised intermediaries	413
10.	Responsibilities of intermediaries	413
11.	Unquoted public companies and relevant private companies	413
12.	Potential offerors	414
13.	Companies Act 1985	414
14.	Irrevocable commitments and letters of intent	414

SECTION F. THE MANDATORY OFFER AND ITS TERMS

RULE 9 — 415

9.1 When a mandatory offer is required and who is primarily responsible for making it — 415

Notes on Rule 9.1
Persons acting in concert

1.	Coming together to act in concert	416
2.	Collective shareholder action	416
3.	Directors of a company	418
4.	Acquisition of interests in shares by members of a group acting in concert	419
5.	Employee Benefit Trusts	420

Other general interpretations

6.	Vendor of part only of an interest in shares	421
7.	Placings and other arrangements	421
8.	The chain principle	422
9.	Triggering Rule 9 during an offer period	422
10.	Convertible securities, warrants and options	423
11.	The reduction or dilution of a shareholding	424
12.	Gifts	425
13.	Discretionary fund managers and principal traders	425
14.	Allotted but unissued shares	425
15.	Treasury shares	425
16.	Aggregation of holdings across a group and recognised intermediaries	426
17.	Borrowed or lent shares	426
18.	Changes in the nature of a person's interest	426

9.2	Obligations of other persons	427
	Note on Rule 9.2	
	Prime responsibility	427
9.3	Conditions and consents	427
	Notes on Rule 9.3	
	1. When more than 50% is held	428
	2. Acceptance condition	428
	3. When dispensations may be granted	429
9.4	The Competition Commission and the European Commission	429
	Notes on Rule 9.4	
	1. If an offer lapses pursuant to Rule 12.1(a) or (b)	429
	2. Further acquisitions	430
9.5	Consideration to be offered	430
	Notes on Rule 9.5	
	1. Nature of consideration	431
	2. Calculation of the price	431
	3. Adjustment of highest price	432
	4. Cum dividend	433
9.6	Obligations of directors	433
9.7	Restrictions on exercise of control by an offeror	433
	Notes on Dispensations from Rule 9	
	1. Vote of independent shareholders on the issue of new securities ("Whitewash")	434
	2. Enforcement of security for a loan	435
	3. Rescue operations	435
	4. Inadvertent mistake	436
	5. Shares carrying 50% or more of the voting rights	436
	6. Enfranchisement of non-voting shares	437

SECTION G. THE VOLUNTARY OFFER AND ITS TERMS

RULE 10.	THE ACCEPTANCE CONDITION	439
	Notes on Rule 10	
	1. Waiver of 50% condition	439
	2. New shares	439
	3. Information to offeror during offer period and extension of offer to new shares	439
	4. Acceptances	440
	5. Purchases	442

	6.	Offers becoming or being declared unconditional as to acceptances before the final closing date	442
	7.	Offeror's receiving agent's certificate	442
	8.	Borrowed shares	443

RULE 11.	NATURE OF CONSIDERATION TO BE OFFERED	444
11.1	When a cash offer is required	444
	Notes on Rule 11.1	
	1. Price	444
	2. Gross acquisitions	445
	3. When the obligation is satisfied	445
	4. Equality of treatment	446
	5. Acquisitions for securities	446
	6. Revision	446
	7. Discretionary fund managers and principal traders	446
	8. Allotted but unissued shares	446
	9. Cum dividend	447
	10. Convertible securities, warrants and options	447
	11. Offer period	447
	12. Competition reference period	447
11.2	When a securities offer is required	447
	Notes on Rule 11.2	
	1. Basis on which securities are to be offered	448
	2. Equality of treatment	448
	3. Vendor placings	448
	4. Management retaining an interest	448
	5. Acquisition for a mixture of cash and securities	449
	6. Acquisitions in exchange for securities to which selling restrictions are attached	449
	7. Applicability of the Notes on Rule 11.1 to Rule 11.2	449
11.3	Dispensation from highest price	449
	Note on Rule 11.3	
	Relevant factors	449

RULE 12.	THE COMPETITION COMMISSION AND THE EUROPEAN COMMISSION	450
12.1	Requirement for appropriate term in offer	450
	Note on Rule 12.1	
	The effect of lapsing	450

	12.2	Offer period ceases during competition reference period	451
		Note on Rule 12.2	
		After a reference or initiation of proceedings	451
RULE 13.		PRE-CONDITIONS IN FIRM OFFER ANNOUNCEMENTS AND OFFER CONDITIONS	452
	13.1	Subjectivity	452
	13.2	The Competition Commission and the European Commission	452
	13.3	Acceptability of pre-conditions	452
		Note on Rules 13.1 and 13.3	
		Financing conditions and pre-conditions	453
	13.4	Invoking conditions and pre-conditions	453
	13.5	Invoking offeree protection conditions	454
		Notes on Rule 13.5	
		1. When an offeree protection condition may be invoked	454
		2. Availability of withdrawal rights	454

SECTION H. PROVISIONS APPLICABLE TO ALL OFFERS

RULE 14.		WHERE THERE IS MORE THAN ONE CLASS OF SHARE CAPITAL	455
	14.1	Comparable offers	455
		Notes on Rule 14.1	
		1. Comparability	455
		2. Offer for non-voting shares only	455
		3. Treatment of certain classes of share capital	455
	14.2	Separate offers for each class	455
RULE 15.		APPROPRIATE OFFER FOR CONVERTIBLES ETC.	456
		Notes on Rule 15	
		1. When conversion rights etc. are exercisable during an offer	456
		2. Rules 9 and 14	456
RULE 16.		SPECIAL DEALS WITH FAVOURABLE CONDITIONS	457
		Notes on Rule 16	
		1. Top-ups and other arrangements	457

A Practitioner's Guide to The City Code on Takeovers and Mergers 2006/2007

	2.	Offeree company shareholders' approval of certain transactions – eg disposal of offeree company assets	457
	3.	Finders' fees	458
	4.	Management retaining an interest and other management incentivisation	458

RULE 17. ANNOUNCEMENT OF ACCEPTANCE LEVELS — 459
   17.1 Timing and contents — 459
       Notes on Rule 17.1
       1. Acceptances of cash underwritten alternatives — 459
       2. General statements about acceptance levels — 459
       3. Alternative offers — 460
       4. Publication of announcements — 460
       5. Statements about withdrawals — 460
       6. Incomplete acceptances and offeror purchases — 460
   17.2 Consequences of failure to announce — 460

RULE 18. THE USE OF PROXIES AND OTHER AUTHORITIES IN RELATION TO ACCEPTANCES — 461

SECTION I. CONDUCT DURING THE OFFER

RULE 19. INFORMATION — 463
   19.1 Standards of care — 463
       Notes on Rule 19.1
       1. Financial advisers' responsibility for release of information — 463
       2. Unambiguous language — 463
       3. Sources — 463
       4. Quotations — 464
       5. Diagrams etc. — 464
       6. Use of television, videos, audio tapes etc. — 464
       7. Financial Services and Markets Act 2000 — 464
       8. Merger benefits statements — 464
   19.2 Responsibility — 465
       Notes on Rule 19.2
       1. Delegation of responsibility — 465
       2. Expressions of opinion — 466
       3. Quoting information about another company — 466
       4. Exclusion of directors — 466
       5. When an offeror is controlled — 466

19.3		Unacceptable statements	467
		Notes on Rule 19.3	
	1.	Holding statements	467
	2.	Statements of support	467
19.4		Advertisements	467
		Notes on Rule 19.4	
	1.	Clearance	468
	2.	Verification	468
	3.	Source	468
	4.	Use of alternative media	468
	5.	Forms	469
19.5		Telephone campaigns	469
		Notes on Rule 19.5	
	1.	Consent to use other callers	469
	2.	New information	469
	3.	Gathering of irrevocable commitments	469
	4.	Statutory and other regulatory provisions	470
19.6		Interviews and debates	470
19.7		Distribution and availability of documents and announcements	470
19.8		Information released following the ending of an offer period pursuant to Rule 12.2	471

RULE 20.		EQUALITY OF INFORMATION	472
20.1		Equality of information to shareholders	472
		Notes on Rule 20.1	
	1.	Furnishing of information to offerors	472
	2.	Press, television and radio interviews	472
	3.	Meetings	472
	4.	Information issued by associates (eg brokers)	473
	5.	Shareholders outside the EEA	474
20.2		Equality of information to competing offerors	474
		Notes on Rule 20.2	
	1.	General enquiries	474
	2.	Conditions attached to the passing of information	474
	3.	Management buy-outs	475
	4.	Mergers and reverse takeovers	475
	5.	The Competition Commission and the European Commission	475
20.3		Information to independent directors in management buy-outs	475

RULE 21.		RESTRICTIONS ON FRUSTRATING ACTION	476
21.1		When shareholders' consent is required	476
		Notes on Rule 21.1	
	1.	Consent by the offeror	477
	2.	"Material amount"	477
	3.	Interim dividends	478
	4.	The Competition Commission and the European Commission	478
	5.	When there is no need to post	478
	6.	Service contracts	478
	7.	Established share option schemes	479
	8.	Pension schemes	479
	9.	Redemption or purchase by an offeree company of its own securities	479
	10.	Shares carrying more than 50% of the voting rights	479
21.2		Inducement fees	479
		Notes on Rule 21.2	
	1.	Arrangements to which the Rule applies	480
	2.	Statutory provisions	480
	3.	"Whitewashes"	480
RULE 22.		RESPONSIBILITIES OF THE OFFEREE COMPANY REGARDING REGISTRATION PROCEDURES	481
		Note on Rule 22	
		Qualifying periods	481

SECTION J. DOCUMENTS FROM THE OFFEROR AND THE OFFEREE BOARD

RULE 23.		THE GENERAL OBLIGATION AS TO INFORMATION	483
		Notes on Rule 23	
	1.	Material changes	483
	2.	Offers conditional on shareholder action	483
	3.	Shareholders outside the EEA	483
RULE 24.		OFFEROR DOCUMENTS	484
24.1		Intentions regarding the offeree company, the offeror company and their employees	484
24.2		Financial and other information on the offeror, the offeree company and the offer	484

Contents

		Notes on Rule 24.2	
		1. Where the offeror is a subsidiary company	489
		2. Further information requirements	489
		3. Partial offers	489
		4. Persons acting in concert with the offeror	489
		5. Offers made under Rule 9	490
	24.3	Interests and dealings	490
		Notes on Rule 24.3	
		1. Directors	491
		2. Aggregation	491
		3. Discretionary fund managers and principal traders	491
	24.4	Directors' emoluments	492
		Note on Rule 24.4	
		Commissions etc.	492
	24.5	Special arrangements	492
	24.6	Incorporation of obligations and rights	492
		Notes on Rule 24.6	
		1. Incorporation by reference	493
		2. Rule 31.6(c)	493
	24.7	Cash confirmation	493
	24.8	Ultimate owner of securities acquired	493
	24.9	Admission to listing and admission to trading conditions	493
	24.10	Estimated value of unquoted paper consideration	494
	24.11	No set-off of consideration	494
	24.12	Arrangements in relation to dealings	494
	24.13	Cash underwritten alternatives which may be shut off	494
RULE 25.		OFFEREE BOARD CIRCULARS	495
	25.1	Views of the board on the offer, including the offeror's plans for the company and its employees	495
		Notes on Rule 25.1	
		1. When a board has effective control	495
		2. Split boards	495
		3. Conflicts of interest	496
		4. Management buy-outs	496
	25.2	Financial and other information	496
		Notes on Rule 25.2	
		1. Offeree board circular combined with offer document	496
		2. Offeree board circular posted after offer document	496

A Practitioner's Guide to The City Code on Takeovers and Mergers 2006/2007

25.3	Interests and dealings	497
	Notes on Rule 25.3	
	1. *When directors resign*	498
	2. *Pension funds*	498
25.4	Directors' service contracts	499
	Notes on Rule 25.4	
	1. *Particulars to be disclosed*	499
	2. *Recent increases in remuneration*	499
25.5	Arrangements in relation to dealings	500
25.6	Material contracts, irrevocable commitments and letters of intent	500

RULE 26.	DOCUMENTS TO BE ON DISPLAY	501
	Note on Rule 26	
	Copies of documents	502

RULE 27.	DOCUMENTS SUBSEQUENTLY SENT TO SHAREHOLDERS	503
27.1	Material changes	503
27.2	Continuing validity of profit forecasts	503

SECTION K. PROFIT FORECASTS

RULE 28.		505
28.1	Standards of care	505
	Note on Rule 28.1	
	Existing forecasts	505
28.2	The assumptions	505
	Notes on Rule 28.2	
	1. *Requirement to state the assumptions*	505
	2. *General rules*	506
28.3	Reports required in connection with profit forecasts	507
28.4	Publication of reports and consent letters	508
28.5	Subsequent documents — continuing validity of forecast	508
28.6	Statements which will be treated as profit forecasts	508
28.7	Taxation, extraordinary items and minority interests	510
28.8	When a forecast relates to a period which has commenced	510

Contents

SECTION L. ASSET VALUATIONS

RULE 29.   511
   29.1 Valuations to be reported on if given in connection with an offer   511
   29.2 Basis of valuation   512
          Note on Rule 29.2
          Provision of adjusted net asset value information   513
   29.3 Potential tax liability   513
   29.4 Current valuation   514
   29.5 Opinion and consent letters   514
   29.6 Waiver in certain circumstances   514

SECTION M. TIMING AND REVISION

RULE 30. MAKING THE OFFER DOCUMENT AND THE OFFEREE BOARD CIRCULAR AVAILABLE   515
   30.1 The offer document   515
   30.2 The offeree board circular   515
   30.3 Making documents and information available to shareholders, employee representatives and employees   515
          Note on Rule 30.3
          Shareholders, employee representatives and employees outside the EEA   516

RULE 31. TIMING OF THE OFFER   517
   31.1 First closing date   517
   31.2 Further closing dates to be specified   517
   31.3 No obligation to extend   517
   31.4 Offer to remain open for 14 days after unconditional as to acceptances   517
   31.5 No extension statements   517
          Notes on Rule 31.5
          1. *Firm statements*   518
          2. *Reservation of right to set statements aside*   518
          3. *Competitive situations*   518
          4. *Recommendations*   519
          5. *Rule 31.9 announcements*   519

31.6		Final day rule (fulfilment of acceptance condition, timing and announcement)	519
		Notes on Rule 31.6	
	1.	Extension of offer under Rule 31.6(a)	520
	2.	Rule 31.6(c) announcement	520
	3.	The Competition Commission and the European Commission	520
	4.	Competitive situations	521
31.7		Time for fulfilment of all other conditions	521
		Note on Rule 31.7	
		The effect of lapsing	521
31.8		Settlement of consideration	521
31.9		Offeree company announcements after day 39	521
31.10		Return of documents of title	522

RULE 32.		REVISION	523
32.1		Offer open for 14 days after posting of revised offer document	523
		Notes on Rule 32.1	
	1.	Announcements which may increase the value of an offer	523
	2.	When revision is required	523
	3.	When revision is not permissible	523
	4.	Triggering Rule 9	524
32.2		No increase statements	524
		Notes on Rule 32.2	
	1.	Firm statements	524
	2.	Reservation of right to set statements aside	524
	3.	Competitive situations	525
	4.	Recommendations	525
	5.	Rule 31.9 announcements	525
32.3		Entitlement to revised consideration	526
32.4		New conditions for increased or improved offers	526
32.5		Competitive situations	526
		Notes on Rule 32.5	
	1.	Dispensation from obligation to post	526
	2.	Guillotine	526
32.6		The offeree board's opinion	526
32.7		Informing employees	527

RULE 33.	**ALTERNATIVE OFFERS**	528
33.1	Timing and revision	528
	Notes on Rule 33.1	
	1. Elections	528
	2. Shutting off	528
33.2	Shutting off cash underwritten alternatives	528
	Notes on Rule 33.2	
	1. Further notices	529
	2. Rule 9 offers	529
33.3	Reintroduction of alternative offers	529
RULE 34.	**RIGHT OF WITHDRAWAL**	529

SECTION N. RESTRICTIONS FOLLOWING OFFERS AND POSSIBLE OFFERS

RULE 35.		531
35.1	Delay of 12 months	531
35.2	Partial offers	531
	Note on Rules 35.1 and 35.2	
	When dispensations may be granted	532
35.3	Delay of 6 months before acquisitions above the offer value	533
35.4	Restrictions on dealings by a competing offeror whose offer has lapsed	533
	Note on Rules 35.3 and 35.4	
	Determination of price	533

SECTION O. PARTIAL OFFERS

RULE 36.		535
36.1	Panel's consent required	535
36.2	Acquisitions before the offer	535
36.3	Acquisitions during and after the offer	535
	Notes on Rule 36.3	
	1. Discretionary fund managers and principal traders	535
	2. Partial offer resulting in less than 30%	535
36.4	Offer for between 30% and 50%	536
36.5	Offer for 30% or more requires 50% approval	536
36.6	Warning about control position	536
36.7	Scaling down	536

36.8	Comparable offer		537
	Notes on Rule 36		
	1.	*Allotted but unissued shares*	537
	2.	*Dual consideration offers for 100%*	537
	3.	*Use of tender offers*	537

SECTION P. REDEMPTION OR PURCHASE BY A COMPANY OF ITS OWN SECURITIES

RULE 37.			539
37.1	Possible requirement to make a mandatory offer		539
	Notes on Rule 37.1		
	1.	*Persons who will not be required to make a mandatory offer*	539
	2.	*Acquisitions of interests in shares preceding a redemption or purchase*	539
	3.	*Situations where a mandatory obligation may arise*	539
	4.	*Prior consultation*	540
	5.	*Disqualifying transactions*	540
	6.	*Renewals*	540
	7.	*Responsibility for making an offer*	541
	8.	*Inadvertent mistake*	541
37.2	Limitation on subsequent acquisitions		541
	Note on Rule 37.2		
	Calculation of percentage thresholds		541
37.3	Redemption or purchase of securities by the offeree company		541
37.4	Redemption or purchase of securities by the offeror company		542

SECTION Q. DEALINGS BY CONNECTED EXEMPT PRINCIPAL TRADERS

RULE 38.		543
38.1	Prohibited dealings	543
	Note on Rule 38.1	
	Suspension of exempt status	543
38.2	Dealings between offerors and connected exempt principal traders	543
	Note on Rule 38.2	
	Competition reference periods	543

38.3		Assenting securities and dealings in assented securities	543
		Note on Rule 38.3	
		Withdrawal rights under Rule 13.5	543
38.4		Voting	544
38.5		Disclosure of dealings	544
		Notes on Rule 38.5	
	1.	Dealings and relevant securities	544
	2.	Method of disclosure	545
	3.	Exception	545
	4.	Recognised intermediaries dealing in proprietary capacity	545

APPENDIX 1. WHITEWASH GUIDANCE NOTE

1.	Introduction	547
2.	Specific grant of waiver required	547
	Notes on Section 2	
	1. Early consultation	548
	2. Other legal or regulatory requirements	548
3.	Disqualifying transactions	548
4.	Circular to shareholders	548
5.	Underwriting and placing	550
6.	Announcements following shareholders' approval	550
	Note on Section 6	
	Copies of announcements	550
7.	Subsequent acquisitions by potential controllers	551

APPENDIX 2. FORMULA OFFERS GUIDANCE NOTE

1.	Introduction	553
2.	Specification of the formula	553
3.	Date on which the formula crystallizes	553
4.	Estimate of the formula offer value	553
5.	Maximum and minimum prices	554
6.	Rule 6	554
7.	Rules 9 and 11	554
8.	"Floor and ceiling" conditions	554
9.	Offeree board obligations	555

APPENDIX 3. DIRECTORS' RESPONSIBILITIES AND CONFLICTS OF INTEREST GUIDANCE NOTE

1.	Directors' responsibilities	557
2.	Financial advisers and conflicts of interest	558

APPENDIX 4. RECEIVING AGENTS' CODE OF PRACTICE

1.	Introduction	559
2.	Qualifications for acting as a receiving agent	560
3.	The provision of the offeree company's register	560
4.	Counting of acceptances	562
5.	Counting of purchases	562
6.	Offers becoming or being declared unconditional as to acceptances before the final closing date	562
7.	Disclaimers in receiving agents' certificates	562

APPENDIX 5. TENDER OFFERS

1.	Panel's consent required	565
	Notes on Section 1	
	1. Calculation of percentage of shares in which a person is interested	565
	2. Tender offers in competition with other types of offer under the Code	565
2.	Procedure and clearance	566
3.	Details of tender offer advertisements	566
	Notes on Section 3	
	1. Future offers	568
	2. Limit on contents of tender advertisements and circulars	568
4.	Circulars from the board of the offeree company	568
5.	Announcement of the result of a tender offer	568
6.	Prohibition of further transactions during a tender offer	568

APPENDIX 6. BID DOCUMENTATION RULES FOR THE PURPOSES OF REGULATION 10 OF THE TAKEOVERS DIRECTIVE (INTERIM IMPLEMENTATION) REGULATIONS 2006

DOCUMENT CHARGES

1.	Scale of document charges	571
2.	Valuation of offer for document charges	571
3.	"Whitewash" documents	571
4.	Mergers	572
5.	Tender offers	572
6.	Payment of document charges	572
7.	VAT and other tax	572

Index 573

Chapter 1

The Takeover Panel

Mark Warham
Director General
The Takeover Panel

1.1 Introduction

The Takeover Panel (the "Panel") is an independent body, established in 1968, whose main functions are to issue and administer the Takeover Code (the "Code") and to supervise and regulate takeovers and other matters to which the Code applies in accordance with the General Principles and Rules set out in the Code. The Code is designed principally to ensure that shareholders are treated fairly and are not denied the opportunity to decide on the merits of a takeover and that shareholders of the same class are afforded equivalent treatment by an offeror. The Code also provides an orderly framework within which takeovers are conducted. In addition, it is designed to promote, in conjunction with other regulatory regimes, the integrity of the financial markets.

The commercial merits of takeovers are not the responsibility of the Panel; these are matters for the companies concerned and their shareholders. Wider questions of public interest are the concern of the governmental authorities in the UK and, in some circumstances, the European Community, through the Office of Fair Trading, the Competition Commission or the European Commission.

Since its establishment, the composition and powers of the Panel have evolved as circumstances have changed and the marketplace has developed. Most recently, on 20 May 2006, the European Directive on Takeovers Bids (the "Directive") was implemented in the UK as a consequence of which the Panel received certain statutory powers for the first time.

The essential characteristics of the Panel's system of takeover regulation are flexibility, certainty and speed founded upon a principles-based approach to regulation, enabling the parties to an offer to know where they stand under the Code in a timely fashion. These characteristics are important to the financial community in order to avoid over-rigidity of the Rules and the risk of takeovers becoming delayed by litigation of a tactical nature, which may frustrate the ability of shareholders to decide the outcome of an offer. The Panel Executive believes that while the status of the Panel and the status of the Code is different following implementation of the Directive, the practical day-to-day impact of the legislative changes will be small and the Panel's relationship with its regulated community will be largely unaffected. The Panel will continue to regulate takeover activity in the UK with a flexible approach, offering speed and certainty in decision-making and seeking to ensure compliance with the Code through consensus with the parties involved.

The Code comprises six General Principles and 38 Rules. The six General Principles (which are taken directly from the Directive) replace the ten General Principles which appeared in the Code immediately prior to implementation of the Directive but they are broadly consistent with them. They apply to takeovers and other matters to which the Code applies. They are expressed in broad general terms and the Code does not define the precise extent of, or limitations on, their application. They are applied in accordance with their spirit in order to achieve their underlying purpose. The General Principles are as follows:

(i) all holders of the securities of an offeree company of the same class must be afforded equivalent treatment; moreover, if a person acquires control of a company, the other holders of securities must be protected;

(ii) the holders of securities of an offeree company must have sufficient time and information to enable them to reach a properly informed decision on the bid; where it advises the holders of securities, the board of the offeree company must give its views on the effects of implementation of the bid on employment, conditions of employment and the locations of the company's places of business;

(iii) the board of an offeree company must act in the interests of the company as a whole and must not deny the holders of securities the opportunity to decide on the merits of a bid;

(iv) false markets must not be created in the securities of the offeree company or of any other company concerned by the bid in such a way that the rise or fall of the prices of the securities becomes artificial and the normal functioning of the markets is distorted;
(v) an offeror must announce a bid only after ensuring that he/she can fulfil in full any cash consideration, if such consideration is offered, and after taking all reasonable measures to secure the implementation of any other type of consideration; and
(vi) an offeree company must not be hindered in the conduct of its affairs for longer than is reasonable by a bid for its securities.

These General Principles encapsulate the essential spirit of the Code. They underlie the Rules of the Code and the accompanying Notes.

1.2 Implementation of the Directive

The Directive was adopted by the European Parliament and the Council of the European Union on 21 April 2004 after almost 20 years of discussion. On 18 November 2005 the Panel and the Code Committee of the Panel (the "Code Committee") published a public consultation paper (PCP 2005/5) entitled "The Implementation of the Takeovers Directive". PCP 2005/5 contained amendments to the Code to reflect both the requirements of the Directive and of the implementing legislation contained in Chapter 1 of Part 22 of the Company Law Reform Bill (the "Bill") which was introduced into the House of Lords on 1 November 2005.

Early in March 2006, the Department of Trade and Industry (the "DTI") announced that because it was unlikely that the Bill would have completed the Parliamentary process by 20 May 2006 (i.e. the date by which the Directive was required to be implemented into national law) it had decided that regulations would be made under powers in the European Communities Act 1972 to make the changes required to implement the Directive on an interim basis. The Takeovers Directive (Interim Implementation) Regulations 2006 (the "Regulations") came into force on 20 May 2006 to meet the implementation deadline for the Directive. They will cease to have effect as soon as the relevant provisions of the Bill come into force.

The Regulations will apply to transactions that are covered by the Directive; for the most part, in the UK, that will mean bids for UK registered companies that are traded on a regulated market in the UK. Until the relevant provisions of the Bill come into force, therefore, the Code will have statutory effect only in relation to a transaction and rule subject to the requirements of the Directive. The Panel will continue to regulate all other transactions covered by the Code as it does now. Once the relevant provisions of the Bill come into force, the Panel's statutory powers will extend to all transactions to which the Code applies.

Further details of the Directive and the amendments made to the Code to reflect the requirements of the Directive are set out in paragraph 1.4.4.

1.3 Flexibility of the Code: application according to underlying purpose

A crucial characteristic of the Code is its flexibility. Notwithstanding that the status of the Code will be different following the implementation of the Directive, the Panel will continue to regulate takeover activity in the UK with a flexible approach. Central to the approach is the concept that it is the spirit of the Code which must be observed and not just the letter.

Situations frequently arise in takeovers which could not reasonably have been envisaged by the authors of any rule book. The Panel Executive is able to respond to such situations by interpreting the Rules to achieve the result that it believes most fairly reflects the underlying purpose of the Code in the particular circumstances. In the world of takeovers, populated by inventive people, well able to find a way round rigid rules, it is important for the Panel Executive to have this flexibility and to be able to go back to the General Principles and the spirit underlying them in deciding how the Code should be interpreted. The Panel is able to derogate or grant a waiver to a person from the application of a Rule, provided that, in the case of a transaction subject to the Directive, the General Principles are respected.

1.4 Code amendment and recent Rule changes

In addition to this flexibility of interpretation, the Panel, through the Code Committee, also has the power to make amendments to the

Code. Matters leading to possible amendment to the Code might arise from a number of sources, including specific cases which the Panel has considered, market developments or particular concerns of those operating within the markets.

In the ordinary course of events, once it has been agreed that a particular matter is to be pursued, the Code Committee will prepare and publish a Public Consultation Paper ("PCP") seeking the views of interested parties on the proposals and setting out the background to, reasons for and (where applicable) full text of the proposed amendment. Consultation periods in relation to PCPs vary depending on the complexity of the subject but will usually be between one and two months. It is the Code Committee's policy to make copies of all non-confidential responses it receives to a PCP available on request. Following the end of the consultation period, the Code Committee will publish its conclusions on the proposed amendment, taking account of the responses received, together with the final Code amendments, in a Response Statement ("RS").

In certain exceptional cases, the Code Committee might consider it necessary to amend the Code on an expedited basis, for example because a particular market development appears to the Code Committee to require that the proposed amendment be made more quickly than the usual public consultation process would permit. In such cases, the Code Committee will publish the amendment with immediate effect and without prior formal consultation, followed in due course by a PCP seeking views on the amendment, which might be later modified, or removed altogether, depending on the Code Committee's conclusions following the consultation process.

Where, in the opinion of the Code Committee, any proposed amendment to the Code either does not materially alter the effect of the provision in question or is a consequence of changes to relevant legislation or regulatory requirements, the Code Committee may publish the text of the amendment without any formal consultation process.

Recent Rule changes

By the end of May 2006, the Code Committee had made a number of amendments to the Code through the issue of a total of 23 RSs following on from the publication of the relevant PCPs. Five of those RSs were published in the 12-month period leading up to the end of May 2006. Brief details of the amendments made pursuant to those five RSs are summarised below.

1.4.1 Dealings in derivatives and options: disclosure issues

Dealings in derivative products and the extent to which such dealings should be disclosed has been a matter of concern to the Panel for over 10 years. In recent years there have been significant increases in the volume of trading in derivatives and options during offer periods. In response to this, the Code Committee issued PCP 2005/1 which set out outline proposals relating to dealings in derivatives and options such as that they should be treated as if they were dealings in shares. These proposals were, in the main, welcomed and in May 2005 the Code Committee published PCP 2005/2 which proposed specific amendments to the Code in relation to disclosure. In August 2005 RS 2005/2 was published and the amendments it introduced took effect in November 2005.

The most significant change that resulted from these amendments was the extension of the application of Rule 8.3 (which sets a 1 per cent threshold for the disclosure of dealings) from securities "owned or controlled" to "interests" in securities. By virtue of the newly introduced definition of "interests in securities" a person who has long economic exposure, whether absolute or conditional, to changes in the price of securities will be treated as interested in those securities.

In summary, a person will be treated as having an interest in securities if, inter alia, he: (i) owns them; (ii) controls the voting rights in respect of them; (iii) has a call option or written put option in respect of them; or (iv) has a long derivative (such as a contract for differences) referenced to them. Note 1 on the definition provides that the number of securities in which a person is treated as having an interest is the aggregate gross number. However, if each of the following conditions is met, the Panel will normally allow offsetting positions to be netted off against each other: (a) the offsetting positions are in respect of the same class of relevant security; (b) the offsetting positions are in respect of the same investment product; (c) save for the number of securities in question, the terms of the offsetting positions are the same; and (d) the counterparty to the offsetting positions is the same in each case.

RS 2005/2 also introduced new definitions of the terms "relevant securities" and "dealings". The latter provided that a dealing includes any action which results in an increase or decrease in the number of securities in which a person is interested or in respect of which he has a short position, including: (i) acquiring or disposing or securities; (ii) taking, granting, acquiring, disposing of, entering into, closing out, terminating, exercising or varying an option in respect of securities; (iii) subscribing or agreeing to subscribe for securities; (iv) exercising or converting any securities carrying conversion or subscription rights; (v) acquiring, disposing of, entering into, closing out, exercising any rights under or varying a derivative referenced to securities; and (vi) entering into, terminating or varying the terms of any agreement to purchase or sell securities.

As regards timing, a new Note 7 on Rule 8 provides that a disclosure of dealings is not required under Rule 8.3 unless the person is interested in 1 per cent or more of any class of relevant securities at midnight (London time) on the date of the dealing or was so interested at midnight on the previous business day. Note 7 also includes an anti-avoidance provision in relation to "bed and breakfasting" arrangements. RS 2005/2 also extended the previous 12 noon deadline for disclosures under Rule 8.3. Note 3 on Rule 8 now provides that public disclosure required by Rule 8.3 must be made no later than 3.30 pm (London time) on the business day following the date of the transaction.

1.4.2 Dealings in Derivatives and Options: control issues

PCP 2005/3, published in November 2005, set out proposals to amend the Code in connection with issues relating to the control of Code companies as a result of dealings in derivatives and options. RS 2005/3 was issued in April 2006 and the relevant amendments to the Code took effect on 20 May 2006.

RS 2005/3 introduced amendments as a result of which interests by virtue of long derivatives referenced to, and options in respect of, shares in Code companies will now be taken into account for the purposes of the provisions of the Code relating to control. Most significantly in this regard, RS 2005/3 amended the circumstances in which a mandatory offer obligation is triggered pursuant to Rule 9.1, which had previously been determined by reference to holdings of shares carrying voting rights, so as to take into account other "interests" in shares carrying voting rights (i.e. by reference to the definition of "interests in securities" introduced by RS 2005/2). Amendments were similarly introduced to the restrictions on acquisitions imposed by Rule 5.1, which had previously been determined by reference to holdings of shares and rights over shares carrying voting rights, so as to take into account "interests" in such shares by virtue of long derivative positions.

RS 2005/3 also amended the offer price setting provisions of Rules 6, 9.5 and 11 so as to set out the basis on which the price paid for the acquisition of an interest in shares is to be determined.

The Code Committee concluded in RS 2005/3 that, whilst Rule 9.1 should be amended so as to be triggered as a result of acquiring interests in shares by virtue of derivatives and options, Rules 9.3(a) and 10 should remain unchanged, so that interests in shares arising by virtue of derivatives and options would not count towards satisfaction of an offeror's acceptance condition. However, the Code Committee also concluded that, in certain specific circumstances, an offeror should be required to make a further offer following the lapsing of its mandatory offer and amended Note 2 on Rule 9.3 accordingly.

RS 2005/3 further introduced a new status, "recognised intermediary" status, which, inter alia, grants certain disclosure exemptions to trading desks whose primary function is client-serving business, and not proprietary business. Recognised intermediary status is described in greater detail in paragraph 1.5 below.

1.4.3 Abolition of the SARs

PCP 2005/4 proposed that The Rules Governing Substantial Acquisitions of Shares ("the SARs") should be abolished. The SARs were introduced in 1980 following a number of market raids for the shares of listed companies. The purpose of the SARs was to restrict the speed with which a person could increase his holding of shares and rights over shares to an aggregate of between 15 per cent and 29.9 per cent of the voting rights of a company. In particular, SAR 1 provided that, subject to the limited exceptions set out in SAR 2, a person could not, in any period of seven days, acquire shares carrying voting rights in a company or rights over shares representing 10 per cent or more of the voting rights if that would take his aggregate holding of shares and rights over shares to between 15 per cent and 29.9 per cent. In addition, under SAR 3, a person was required to disclose any acquisition of shares carrying voting rights or rights over such shares (i) if that would take his aggregate holding of shares and rights over shares through 15 per cent, or (ii) if his aggregate holding of shares and rights over shares was between 15 per cent and 29.9 per cent and would increase to or beyond any whole percentage figure as a result of the acquisition.

The principal rationale for abolishing SARs 1 and 2 was that the Panel's general approach to share dealings is permissive rather than restrictive, focusing on the consequences of particular dealings rather than seeking to prohibit them. As a result, the Code only restricts share dealings in very specific circumstances where it is appropriate to do so on account of some overriding policy concern. In the opinion of the Code Committee, no such policy concern existed in relation to acquisitions below the 30 per cent level – i.e. in circumstances where control (as defined in the Code) of a company was not being acquired or being consolidated. Therefore, the Code Committee believed that it was no longer appropriate for the Panel to restrict the speed at which a person could acquire shares (or interests in shares), and thereby the ability of shareholders to sell their shares, below the 30 per cent level. Furthermore, in view of the fact that a major reason for the disclosure requirements of SAR 3 was to underpin compliance with the restriction in SAR 1, and given the proposed abolition of SAR 1, the Code Committee did not consider it appropriate of the Panel to retain SAR 3. RS 2005/4 adopted these proposals and the SARs were abolished with effect from 20 May 2006. However, as was also proposed in PCP 2005/4, the rules relating to the conduct of tender offers formerly set out in SAR 4 were retained and included in Appendix 5 to the Code.

1.4.4 *The Implementation of the Directive*

As mentioned in paragraph 1.2, PCP 2005/5 contained proposals from the Panel and the Code Committee for amendments to the Code in order to reflect both the requirements of the Directive and the implementing legislation contained in Chapter 1 of Part 22 of the Bill. These amendments affected the Panel, its constitution and powers, and the Rules of the Code and came into force on 20 May 2006.

The main changes for the Panel arising from the implementation of the Directive related to: (i) the scope of its jurisdiction, its constitution and the functions of its constituent committees; (ii) new powers to obtain information and enforce the Code; (iii) sanctions that the Panel will be able to impose; and (iv) confidentiality of information and cooperation between the Panel and regulatory authorities in the UK and overseas. In conjunction with this, the Panel took the opportunity to review its own internal procedures and operations (including its judicial procedures). All of these changes were incorporated into a new Introduction to the Code.

The changes proposed to the jurisdiction of the Code included the following:

(i) the residency test which applied to companies registered in the UK and traded on a regulated market in the UK would no longer apply (AIM and OFEX are not regulated markets in the UK);
(ii) the Code would continue to apply to offers for other listed and unlisted public companies and certain private companies essentially in the same way as it did before implementation of the Directive and accordingly the residency test would continue to apply to these companies; and
(iii) as required under Article 4.2 of the Directive, the Panel would have shared jurisdiction with regulators in other Member States of the European Economic Area in certain circumstances (for example, where the offeree company is registered in the UK and has its securities admitted to trading only on a regulated market in a Member State other than the UK). Except in these so-called "shared jurisdiction" cases, the Code would continue to apply to takeover and merger transactions, however effected. This would include partial offers, offers for minorities, schemes of arrangement and dual holding company transactions.

The Panel's new Committee structure arising from PCP 2005/5 is outlined in paragraph 1.7 below. In addition to the Hearings Committee and the Code Committee, Nomination and Remuneration Committees were also established. The Panel's new powers to require information and documents, to enforce the Code through the courts and to require the payment of compensation in certain restricted circumstances, all of which were introduced by the implementing legislation, are outlined in paragraph 1.11. In addition, the Directive placed the Panel under a specific duty of confidentiality and a duty to cooperate as appropriate with takeover supervisory, financial services and other relevant regulators in all Member States. These new duties are outlined in paragraph 1.13.

The changes to the Code affected the General Principles, the Definitions and the Rules. Article 3 of the Directive contains a set of six general principles, the overall substance and content of which are very similar to the original Code General Principles. The Code Committee decided, following an analysis of the two sets of general principles, that the existing Code General Principles should be replaced in their entirety with the Directive General Principles.

The Directive provides that any derogations or waivers from Rules made to implement the Directive have to respect the general principles set out in the Directive. Further, Article 4.5 of the Directive provides that a derogation may be granted or a waiver given only if it is specifically provided for in the relevant Rule or in other circumstances specified in the Directive, in which case a reasoned decision must be given. The implementing legislation has provided the Panel with a statutory power to grant derogations and waivers consistent with Article 4.5 and this was included in a Rule in the new Introduction. The Code Committee also proposed adding a few derogations of a specific nature into the Rules.

The most significant change to the definitions affected the definition of "persons acting in concert". The Directive definition differed from the Code definition in three key respects: (i) it did not require active cooperation between parties; (ii) it was not limited to parties cooperating through the acquisition of shares by any of them; and (iii) it included persons who cooperated with the offeree company with a view to frustrating the successful outcome of a bid. The Code Committee believed that a change to the Code definition of "acting in concert" to bring it into line with the Directive would, at least in relation to the first two key aspects, bring the definition more into line with the Panel's existing practice. The third change relating to frustrating action was new but would only have significance when shares were acquired.

The Code Committee also identified that some changes were required to the mandatory bid provisions in Rule 9. These included an adjustment in the period over which the price payable (the "equitable price") was calculated and the circumstances in which that price might be adjusted. Some amendments were also required to some of the dispensations from Rule 9 to ensure that, in accordance with Article 3(1)(a) (new General Principle 1), when a person acquires control of a company, "the other holders of securities are protected".

Rule 21.1, dealing with frustrating action, had to be amended to bring it into line with the slightly wider definition of frustrating action in Article 9 of the Directive. Furthermore, certain provisions relating to offers including consideration in cash had to be amended to ensure compliance with Article 3(1)(e) (new General Principle 5), which requires that an offeror must announce a bid only after ensuring that he/she can fulfil any cash consideration.

The Directive introduced only a few completely new requirements into the Code. These were principally concerned with the offeror and offeree companies providing information about a bid to their respective employee representatives or employees and, in the case of the offeree company, giving employee representatives the opportunity to comment on the effects of the bid on employment. There were also some additions to the content requirements of an offer document and the offeree board's views on the offer, which required some amendments to Rules 24 and 25 respectively. The Code Committee also proposed a new Rule relating to the provision of offer documentation into jurisdictions outside the European Economic Area.

1.4.5 Miscellaneous Code amendments

RS 2006/1 was issued in April following consultation on the various miscellaneous amendments proposed in PCP 2006/1. Whilst the amendments affected a large number of the Rules, in most cases they did not affect the substance of the Rules. A large number of the changes related simply to changes in terminology used in other regulations to which the Code refers.

Two of the amendments proposed in PCP 2006/1 were of a more substantive nature. First, a change to the definition of "dealings" means that both the acquisition and the disposal of voting or general control over securities constitute dealings, even where the transfer of voting control is conditional. However, where a transfer of voting control relates purely to the administrative exercise of voting rights, the Panel will normally be prepared to grant a dispensation from the requirement to disclose the transfer. Second, a new Rule 25.2 was introduced which requires an offeree company either to make its own statement or, in certain circumstances, to confirm the statement made by the offeror in relation to any known material changes in the offeree company's financial or trading position since the date of its last published audited accounts.

1.5 Exempt status and recognised intermediary status

On occasion there have been concerns that the introduction or application of certain provisions of the Code would operate so that trading activities for certain persons or groups would effectively have to be curtailed, for example because of the risk of their trading activities having untoward consequences for their group's corporate finance clients. Accordingly, in order to avoid fettering the market unnecessarily and because the risks of so doing could be minimised to an acceptable level, for example by appropriate checks and undertakings, "exempt" status and "registered intermediary" status were introduced in 1986 and 2006 respectively.

1.5.1 Exempt principal trader status

Exempt principal trader status was originally introduced as exempt market maker status following the formation of integrated investment banks at the time of Big Bang and was designed to cater for the Code consequences of investment banks owning market makers. If, because they belonged to the same group, such market makers had been held to be acting in concert with an offeror client of the corporate finance department, serious consequences would have followed. For example, if purchases of shares took the aggregate holdings of the bank through 30 per cent, each party would have incurred a mandatory bid obligation under Rule 9. The Panel therefore developed the concept of exempt market maker status which was redefined as exempt principal trader status by RS 2004/3. This category covers persons who are registered as market makers with the London Stock Exchange (or are accepted by the Panel as market makers) and Stock Exchange member firms which deal as principal in "order book securities" (e.g. securities traded on the SETS and SETSmm systems). If exemption is granted, the actions of the principal trader do not have Code consequences for the client of the related corporate finance department.

1.5.2 Recognised intermediary status

As mentioned in paragraph 1.4.2 above, in May 2006 the concept of recognised intermediary status was introduced by RS 2005/3. A recognised intermediary is that part of the trading operations of a bank or securities house which is accepted by the Panel as a recognised intermediary for the purposes of the Code.

Recognised intermediary status was introduced for two reasons. First, it was considered inappropriate for a mandatory offer to be triggered by a derivative or option position acquired by a client-serving desk in a client-serving capacity. Second, as a means of determining the desks which could benefit from the disclosure exemption in Rule 8.3(d).

If a desk is granted recognised intermediary status then the following dispensations will apply:

(i) to the extent that the desk has interests in shares in a client-serving capacity (but not proprietary interests) by virtue of positions in derivatives or options, those interests will not be taken into account in establishing whether it (or the organisation of which it forms part) is interested, for the purposes of Rule 9.1, in 30 per cent or more of a company's shares carrying voting rights; and

(ii) to the extent that the desk deals in relevant securities in a client-serving capacity, it will be exempted from disclosing those dealings (but not proprietary dealings) in relevant securities under Rule 8.3(d).

If any part of the trading operations of a bank or securities house wishes to be accepted by the Panel as a recognised intermediary, it must apply to the Panel to be granted such status and it will have to comply with any requirements imposed by the Panel as a condition of its granting such status. The Panel may grant recognised intermediary status to trading desks if they trade as principal primarily in a client-serving capacity, i.e. in order to fulfil orders received from clients, to respond to a client's requests to trade, or to hedge positions arising out of these activities. The criteria which must be satisfied in order for a desk to be granted recognised intermediary status by the Panel were set out in RS 2005/3 and are available on the Panel's website.

As regards the exemption from disclosing client-serving dealings in relevant securities, the Code Committee stated in RS 2005/3 its belief that the disclosure rules should strike an appropriate balance between, on the one hand, giving market makers and other intermediaries sufficient freedom to execute client orders and, on the other, ensuring that shareholders are provided with information about dealings which may be significant to them. The Code Committee stated that it will review the rationale for recognised intermediary status and in particular it will consider whether recognised intermediary status strikes such an appropriate balance. The review of the operation of the new status is planned for June 2007 at which time the Code Committee will also carry out a broader review of the operation of the changes introduced in relation to derivatives and options referred to in paragraphs 1.4.1 and 1.4.2.

1.6 Some key Rules

In addition to the General Principles, the Code contains a series of Rules. Like the General Principles, they too are to be interpreted to achieve their underlying purpose. Therefore, their spirit must be observed as well as their letter. Most of the individual Rules are also accompanied by Notes setting out interpretations and practices which have become established by actual cases brought before the Panel or the Panel Executive. This illustrates the way in which practice has developed the Code.

In this Chapter, it is appropriate to highlight briefly some particular Rules underpinning the General Principles; later Chapters deal with some of the Rules in more detail.

1.6.1 Equality of treatment and protection of non-controlling shareholders

Perhaps the best known Rule of the Code is Rule 9, which prescribes the circumstances in which a mandatory offer must be made, the terms on which it must be made and the person who is primarily responsible for making it. It is a classic application of the requirement for equal treatment of all shareholders. Control of a company cannot be bought by paying a premium price to the controlling shareholder(s) and leaving the remainder behind with a new controller. For the purpose of the Code, acquiring interests in shares carrying 30 per cent or more of the voting rights of a company is regarded as conferring effective control.

The mandatory offer requirement of Rule 9.1 will be triggered whenever: (i) a person acquires (whether by a series of transactions over a period of time or not) an *interest* in shares which, taken together with shares in which persons acting in concert with him are interested, carry 30 per cent or more of the voting rights of a company; or (ii) a person, together with persons acting in concert with him, is *interested* in shares which in aggregate carry not less than 30 per cent of the voting rights of a company, but does not hold more than 50 per cent of such voting rights and that person, or any person acting in concert with him, acquires an *interest* in any other shares which increases the percentage of shares carrying voting rights in which he is *interested*.

Rule 11 is also based on the principle that shareholders should be afforded equal treatment. Rule 11 requires an offer to be in cash or accompanied by a cash alternative whenever an offeror or any person acting in concert with him acquires, for cash, any interest in shares of any class under offer in the offeree company during the offer period. Further, it provides that where the shares of any class under offer in the offeree company, in which interests are acquired for cash by an offeror or any person acting in concert with him during the offer period or the 12 months prior to its commencement, carry 10 per cent or more of the voting rights exercisable at meetings of that class, the offer must be in cash or accompanied by a cash alternative at not less than the highest price paid by the offeror (or any person acting in concert with him) during those periods. Rule 11 also requires a full share offer where an offeror has acquired, for shares, interests in shares of any class of the offeree company carrying 10 per cent or more of the voting rights of the class in the three months prior to the commencement of the offer period.

Rule 6 provides that where an offeror or any person acting in concert with the offeror acquires an interest in shares in the offeree company in the three month period prior to the commencement of the offer period (or even before that) or during the offer period, the offer to shareholders must be on no less favourable terms.

The Takeover Panel

Under Rule 16, favourable deals for particular shareholders are prohibited.

1.6.2 Sufficiency of time, information and advice

Rule 31.1 requires an offer to be open for at least 21 days following the date on which the offer document is posted. Rule 32.1 requires that if an offer is revised, the offer must be kept open for at least 14 days following the date on which the revised offer document is posted.

Rule 23 requires shareholders to be given sufficient information and advice to enable them to arrive, in good time, at properly informed decisions regarding the offer. The Rule 23 obligation, which attaches to all information provided to shareholders, whether emanating from the offeror or offeree, is reinforced by the requirements of Rule 3.

Under Rule 3, the offeree company must appoint a competent independent adviser, whose views on the offer must be made known to all shareholders. As a result, they have the benefit of that adviser's views, as well as the opinion of the directors.

1.6.3 Shareholders to be given an opportunity to decide on the merits of a bid

Rule 21.1 provides that during the course of an offer, or even before the date of the offer if the board of the offeree company has reason to believe that a bona fide offer might be imminent, the board must not, without the approval of shareholders in general meeting, take any action which may result in any offer or bona fide possible offer being frustrated or in shareholders being denied the opportunity to decide the bid on its merits. Shareholder approval may not be required where it is felt that (i) the proposed action is in pursuance of a contract entered into earlier or another pre-existing obligation; or (ii) a decision to take the proposed action had been taken before the beginning of the period referred to above which was partly or fully implemented before the beginning of that period or, if not, was in the ordinary course of business.

1.6.4 Preservation of fair markets

Disclosure is the principal way in which the Panel seeks to preserve a fair market in the shares of companies subject to bids. Rule 8, together with other disclosure rules, require prompt disclosure of dealings in relevant securities (which include the entering into of options and derivatives) by all relevant parties. Rule 8.3, as amended with effect from 7 November 2005, requires daily disclosure of dealings in relevant securities by any person who is interested (directly or indirectly) in 1 per cent or more of any class of relevant securities of the offeror or the offeree company.

Rule 4.1 prohibits dealings in securities of the offeree company by any person (other than the offeror) who is privy to confidential price-sensitive information concerning an offer or contemplated offer before the announcement of the approach or offer, or termination of the discussions.

Rule 20.1 requires information about companies involved in an offer to be made equally available to all offeree company shareholders as nearly as possible at the same time and in the same manner.

Rule 19.3 requires parties to an offer or potential offer to take care not to issue statements which, while not factually inaccurate, may mislead shareholders and the market or create uncertainty.

1.6.5 Fulfilling consideration obligations

Rule 2.5 provides that an offeror should only announce a firm intention to make an offer when that offeror has every reason to believe that it can and will continue to be able to implement the offer.

Rule 2.5 also requires that when the offer is for cash or includes an element of cash, the announcement must include confirmation by an appropriate third party (e.g. the offeror's bank or financial adviser) that resources are available to the offeror sufficient to satisfy full acceptance of the offer. Rule 24.7 contains a similar requirement in relation to cash confirmation in respect of the offer document itself.

1.6.6 Offeree company not to be hindered in its affairs for longer than is reasonable

The Code contains detailed rules relating to the timetable within which an offer must be implemented. One of the reasons for this is to avoid the offeree company from being the subject of siege as a result of a bid for longer than is reasonable.

Rule 2.4(b) sets out the so-called "put up or shut up" rule which is also designed to prevent offeree companies from being the subject of siege for longer than is reasonable. At any time following the announcement of a possible offer (provided the potential offeror has been publicly named) the offeree company may request that the Panel impose a time limit for the potential offeror to clarify its intentions with regard to the offeree company. If a time limit is imposed, the potential offeror will be required either to make an offer for the offeree company or to announce that it does not intend to make an offer for the offeree company, in which case the potential offeror will be subject to certain timing restrictions in relation to making another offer.

1.7 The Panel and its Committees

Following implementation of the Directive, a number of changes have been made to the structure of the Panel and its Committees. In particular, these changes have required that the rule-making and judicial functions of the Panel are completely separate. A brief description of the membership, functions, responsibilities and general activities of the Panel and certain of its Committees is set out below.

1.7.1 The Panel

The Panel assumes overall responsibility for the policy, financing and administration of the Panel's functions and for the functioning and operation of the Code. The Panel operates through a number of Committees and is directly responsible for those matters which are not dealt with through one of its Committees.

The Panel comprises up to 34 members:

(i)   the Chairman, who is appointed by the Panel;
(ii) up to two Deputy Chairmen, who are appointed by the Panel;
(iii) up to 20 other members, who are appointed by the Panel; and
(iv) individuals appointed by each of the following bodies:

- The Association of British Insurers
- The Association of Investment Trust Companies
- The Association of Private Client Investment Managers and Stockbrokers

- The British Bankers' Association
- The Confederation of British Industry
- The Institute of Chartered Accountants in England and Wales
- Investment Management Association
- The London Investment Banking Association (with separate representation also for its Corporate Finance Committee and Securities Trading Committee)
- The National Association of Pension Funds.

The Chairman and the Deputy Chairmen are designated as members of the Hearings Committee. Each other Panel member appointed by the Panel under paragraphs (i) to (iii) above is designated upon appointment to act as a member of either the Panel's Code Committee or its Hearings Committee. The Panel members appointed by the bodies under paragraph (iv) above become members of the Hearings Committee without further designation by the Panel. In performing their functions on the Hearings Committee and the Panel, such members act independently of the body which has appointed them and not as that body's agent or delegate, and exercise their own judgment as to how to perform their functions and how to vote.

No member of the Code Committee may simultaneously or subsequently be a member of the Hearings Committee.

1.7.2 The Code Committee

The Code Committee represents a spread of shareholder, corporate, practitioner and other interests within the Panel's regulated community. Up to 12 members of the Panel are designated by the Panel as members of the Code Committee.

The Code Committee carries out the rule-making functions of the Panel and is solely responsible for keeping the Code (other than certain matters set out in the Introduction, which are the responsibility of the Panel itself) under review and for proposing, consulting on, making and issuing amendments to the Code.

1.7.3 The Hearings Committee

The Hearings Committee of the Panel comprises the Chairman, up to two Deputy Chairmen, up to eight other members designated by the

Panel and the individuals appointed by the bodies listed at paragraph 1.7.1(iv) above.

The principal function of the Hearings Committee is to review rulings of the Executive. The Hearings Committee also hears disciplinary proceedings instituted by the Executive when the Executive considers that there has been a breach of the Code. The Hearings Committee may also be convened for hearings in certain other circumstances.

The Terms of Reference and Rules of Procedure of the Hearings Committee can be found on the Panel's website (www.thetakeoverpanel.org.uk).

Rulings of the Hearings Committee are binding on the parties to the proceedings and on those invited to participate in those proceedings unless and until overturned by the Takeover Appeal Board (see paragraph 1.9).

1.8 The Panel Executive

The day-to-day work of takeover supervision and regulation is carried out by the Executive. In carrying out these functions, the Executive operates independently of the Panel. This includes, either on its own initiative or at the instigation of third parties, the conduct of investigations, the monitoring of relevant dealings in connection with the Code and the giving of rulings on the interpretation, application or effect of the Code. The Executive is available both for consultation and also the giving of rulings on the interpretation, application or effect of the Code before, during and, where appropriate, after takeovers or other relevant transactions.

The Executive is staffed by a mixture of employees and secondees from law firms, accountancy firms, investment banks and other organisations. It is headed by the Director General, usually an investment banker on secondment, who is an officer of the Panel. The Director General is assisted by Deputy and Assistant Directors General (who are permanent), one or two Secretaries (usually lawyers on secondment from prominent law firms) and various other members of the Executive's permanent and seconded staff (including a number of secondee Assistant Secretaries). In performing their functions, the secondees act independently of the bodies which have seconded them.

The Assistant Secretaries are primarily responsible for dealing with the daily volume of telephone enquiries. They have the main responsibility for communicating with practitioners and parties to bids. They receive the initial enquiries and they disseminate the Executive's responses and rulings.

The nature of the Executive's rulings will depend on whether or not the Executive is able to hear the views of the other parties involved. If the Executive is not able to hear the views of other parties involved, it may give a conditional ruling (on an ex parte basis) which may be varied or set aside when any views of the other parties have been heard; if the Executive is able to hear the views of other parties involved, it may give an unconditional ruling. An unconditional ruling is binding on those who are made aware of it unless and until overturned by the Hearings Committee or the Takeover Appeal Board. In addition, such persons must comply with any conditional ruling given by the Executive for the purpose of preserving the status quo pending the unconditional ruling.

The Executive contains a specialist market surveillance team which monitors market dealings in shares of companies which are either in an offer period or which the Executive has been informed may go into an offer period. This has proved crucial in enforcing compliance with the disclosure requirements of the Code (in particular, Rule 8), in monitoring for abuses of the "exempt" status of the market making, principal trading and fund management divisions of financial institutions, and generally in checking for breaches of the Code through stock market dealings by parties to a takeover. The market surveillance team also plays an important role in monitoring the activities of institutions awarded "recognised intermediary" status under the amendments to the Code introduced on 20 May 2006. Securities firms and market operators regularly receive enquiries from the market surveillance team as to why transactions have not been disclosed and, occasionally, requests for a more detailed account of the reasons for a particular transaction. The team plays a vital role in identifying transactions which might require an announcement under Rule 2 of the Code where there is evidence of speculation or informed dealing in

The Takeover Panel

the market but where no announcement has been made of an offer or possible offer.

The function of the Executive and its relationship with the Panel has not been significantly affected by the implementation of the Directive.

1.9 Takeover Appeal Board

The Takeover Appeal Board (the "Board") is an independent body which hears appeals against rulings of the Hearings Committee. It replaces the former Appeal Committee. The Chairman and Deputy Chairman of the Board will usually have held high judicial office, and are appointed by the Master of the Rolls. Other members, who will usually have relevant knowledge and experience of takeovers and the Code, are appointed by the Chairman (or, failing that, the Deputy Chairman) of the Board. The names of the members of the Board are available on the Board's website (www.thetakeoverappealboard.org.uk).

Any party to a hearing before the Hearings Committee (or any person denied permission to be a party to a hearing before the Hearings Committee) may appeal to the Takeover Appeal Board against any ruling of the Hearings Committee or the chairman of the hearing (including in respect of procedural directions).

Proceedings before the Board are generally conducted in a similar way to those before the Hearings Committee, using the procedure set out in the Board's Rules which are available on its website. The Board may confirm, vary, set aside, annul or replace the contested ruling of the Hearings Committee.

1.10 Relationship between the Panel and the Courts

The proceedings of the Panel are, as with other public bodies, open to judicial review by the courts. There have been very few instances in which leave to apply for judicial review has been sought. One example was the Datafin case, which related to rival bids for

McCorquodale in December 1986. The Master of the Rolls, Lord Donaldson, held that:

> "in the light of the special nature of the Panel, its functions, the market in which it is operating, the timescales which are of interest in that market and the need to safeguard the position of third parties, who may be numbered in thousands, all of whom are entitled to continue to trade upon an assumption of the validity of the Panel's rules and decisions, unless and until they are quashed by the court, I should expect the relationship between the Panel and the court to be historic rather than contemporaneous. I should expect the court to allow contemporary decisions to take their course, considering the complaint and intervening, if at all, later and in retrospect by declaratory orders which would enable the Panel not to repeat any error and would relieve individuals of the disciplinary consequences of any erroneous finding of breach of the rules."

The Guinness case was the subject of a Court of Appeal judgment in July 1988. In this case the courts also indicated their reluctance to interfere in the Panel's decisions. Lord Diplock held that there was a public interest in the Panel acting to enforce the Code and, since no injustice had been done by the Panel's refusal to adjourn its case against Guinness, there was no case for judicial review.

The Court of Appeal's approach was confirmed in late 1988, when Grand Metropolitan sought judicial review of the Panel's decision not to require any remedy for breaches of the Code that the Panel held had been committed by Irish Distillers and Pernod Ricard, when the latter was gathering irrevocable undertakings to support its successful offer. The High Court refused to grant Grand Metropolitan an expedited order for the judicial review hearing on the grounds that the Court of Appeal had made it plain that such proceedings were not intended to reverse Panel decisions taken in the course of takeovers. As a result, the proceedings were discontinued. Judgments like these demonstrate the courts' support for the Panel and thereby lend authority to its decisions.

The Court of Appeal's decision in the Datafin case underlies the approach taken in relation to the implementation of the Directive. For example, following implementation, rulings of the Panel have binding effect, parties to a takeover are not able to sue each other for breach of a rule-based requirement and a transaction, once completed, may not be unpicked.

1.11 Enforcement of the Code

The Panel seeks to ensure compliance with the Code through a consensual approach with the parties engaged in takeover activity. It is the practice of the Panel, in discharging its functions under the Code, to focus on the specific consequences of breaches of the Code with the aim of providing appropriate remedial or compensatory action in a timely manner. In certain circumstances the Panel may issue compliance rulings to restrain a person from acting in breach of rules or from following a particular course of action pending a Panel ruling on whether that action would be in breach of the Code. Furthermore, in respect of certain breaches of the Code, disciplinary action may be appropriate (see paragraph 1.12). Following implementation of the Directive the Panel has certain new statutory enforcement powers, further details of which are set out below.

1.11.1 Compliance rulings

If the Panel is satisfied that:

(i) there is a reasonable likelihood that a person will contravene a requirement imposed by or under rules; or
(ii) a person has contravened a requirement imposed by or under rules,

the Panel may give any direction that appears to it to be necessary in order:

(A) to restrain a person from acting (or continuing to act) in breach of rules;
(B) to restrain a person from doing (or continuing to do) a particular thing, pending determination of whether that or any other conduct of his is or would be a breach of rules; or
(C) otherwise to secure compliance with rules.

1.11.2 Compensation rulings

Where a person has breached any of the Rules of the Code requiring the payment of money, for example, Rules 6, 9 and 11, the Panel may make a ruling requiring the person concerned to pay, within such period as it specifies, to the holders, or former holders, of securities of the offeree company, such amount as it thinks just and reasonable so as to ensure that such holders receive what they would have been entitled to receive if the relevant Rule had been complied with.

1.11.3 Enforcement by the Courts

The implementing legislation provides the Panel with a new power in certain circumstances to seek enforcement by the courts. If the court is satisfied that:

(i) there is a reasonable likelihood that a person will contravene a requirement imposed by or under the Code; or
(ii) a person has contravened a requirement imposed by or under rules or a requirement imposed under Regulation 6 of the implementing legislation,

the court may make any order it thinks fit to secure compliance with the requirement. Any failure to comply with a resulting court order may be a contempt of court.

1.11.4 Power to require information and documents

The Panel expects any person dealing with it to do so in an open and cooperative way. It also expects prompt cooperation and assistance from persons dealing with it and those to whom enquiries and other requests are directed. Following implementation of the Directive, the Panel has a new power to require documents and information where they are reasonably required in connection with the exercise of its functions. A note describing how the Executive intends to exercise this power on behalf of the Panel is available on the Panel's website.

1.12 Disciplinary Powers

The Panel's approach to disciplinary action and the main sanctions available to it will not change significantly following the implementation of the Directive. The disciplinary rules of the Panel in connection with breaches and alleged breaches of the Code are as follows:

1.12.1 Disciplinary action

The Executive may itself deal with a disciplinary matter where the person who is to be subject to the disciplinary action agrees the facts and the action proposed by the Executive. In any other case, where it considers that there has been a breach of the Code, the Executive may commence disciplinary proceedings before the Hearings Committee. A note setting out the factors that the Executive will take into account when deciding whether to initiate disciplinary action and in proposing the appropriate sanction to the Hearings Committee is available on the Panel's website.

1.12.2 Sanctions or other remedies for breach of the Code

If the Hearings Committee finds a breach of the Code or of a ruling of the Panel, it may:

(i) issue a private statement of censure;
(ii) issue a public statement of censure;
(iii) suspend or withdraw any exemption, approval or other special status which the Panel has granted to a person, or impose conditions on the continuing enjoyment of such exemption, approval or special status, in respect of all or part of the activities to which such exemption, approval or special status relates;
(iv) report the offender's conduct to a United Kingdom or overseas regulatory authority or professional body (most notably the FSA) so that that authority or body can consider whether to take disciplinary or enforcement action (for example, the FSA has power to take certain actions against an authorised person or an approved person who fails to observe proper standards of market conduct, including the power to fine); or
(v) publish a Panel Statement indicating that the offender is someone who, in the Hearings Committee's opinion, is not likely to

comply with the Code. The cold-shouldering rules of the FSA and certain professional bodies would then apply in terms of which members of the FSA and those professional bodies would be obliged, in certain circumstances, not to act for the person in question in a transaction subject to the Code, including any dealing in relevant securities requiring disclosure under Rule 8.

The Panel has, in practice, experienced very little difficulty in enforcing its rules in the large number of cases that it has dealt with over 38 years.

1.13 Confidentiality, information sharing and cooperation

The Panel has always been scrupulous about ensuring that confidential information provided to it in the course of applying the Code is kept confidential. On implementation of the Directive, the Panel was placed under a specific duty of confidentiality so that information received by the Panel in connection with the exercise of its statutory functions may not be disclosed without the consent of the individual or business to which it relates, except as permitted by the implementing legislation.

The Panel and the FSA are under a duty to take such steps as they consider appropriate to cooperate with each other and with other supervisory authorities designated for the purposes of the Directive and with regulators outside the UK having functions similar to the FSA or to the Panel including by the sharing of information which the Panel and the FSA are permitted to disclose.

The Panel and the FSA have established close cooperation arrangements since the entry into force of the Financial Services and Markets Act 2000. The Panel does not envisage that its change of status following implementation of the Directive and the new powers it has been given will alter the nature of the relationship between the FSA and the Panel. The Panel will continue to be able to report breaches of the Code by authorised financial advisers in relation to takeover bids to the FSA, as at present, and any such breaches will continue to be taken into account by the FSA in assessing whether such persons are fit and proper to be authorised for business of that sort.

Chapter 2

The Approach, Announcements and Independent Advice

Simon Marchant
Partner
Freshfields Bruckhaus Deringer

2.1 General considerations

This Chapter identifies the companies and transactions to which the Code applies. These rules are set out in Section 3 of the Introduction to the Code which has been substantially revised to reflect the implementation of the EU Directive on Takeover Bids (the "Directive"). One of the main changes to the Introduction is to the scope of the Takeover Panel's jurisdiction. The Panel is required by the Directive to take jurisdiction over a number of companies not previously covered by the Code.

This Chapter also deals with Section D of the Code: Rules 1 to 3. These rules are concerned with the crucial "pre-bid" period. The importance of this period cannot be over-emphasised. The commercial and tactical aspects – including the fundamental decision whether or not to proceed with the bid – can assume paramount importance. The success or failure of the bid may hang on decisions taken at this stage. The pressures on all those involved can be enormous. Speed is critical and the whole enterprise can take on a rather awesome momentum of its own. Once the formal press announcement is released the die is irretrievably cast. The Panel reiterated in its 2003 Annual Report that notwithstanding the time pressure on decisions taken in the "pre-bid" period, it is essential that the Executive is consulted under Section 6(b) of the Introduction to the Code where there is any doubt whatsoever as to whether a proposed course of action is in accordance with the General Principles or the Rules of the Code.

The Panel has placed increasing emphasis on the special duty which advisers have to ensure that their clients are aware of their responsibilities under the Code. It is often the advisers who will be criticised by the Panel when things go wrong (for example, the criticism of Nabarro Wells & Co Limited ("Nabarro Wells") in the Panel's ruling on Transcomm plc in March 2004, referred to in Section 2.6.1 below). The Introduction to the Code now states that financial advisers have a particular responsibility to comply with the Code and to ensure, so far as they are reasonably able, that their client and its directors are aware of their responsibilities under the Code and will comply with them (Section 3(f)).

The Panel is determined to ensure that all members of a board of directors – not just those entrusted with the day-to-day conduct of a bid – share responsibility for compliance with the Code. Appendix 3 to the Code spells out in detail the obligation to keep all directors fully informed and the responsibility of all directors to monitor the conduct of a bid.

The Code is made up of 6 General Principles (these are the 6 General Principles set out in the Directive which replaced the original 10 General Principles) and 38 detailed Rules. The General Principles are relevant to interpreting the Rules – they are "applied in accordance with their spirit in order to achieve their underlying purpose" (*see* Section 2(b) of the Introduction). The following are particularly relevant to Section D:

General Principle 1:

> "All holders of the securities of an offeree company of the same class must be afforded equivalent treatment; moreover, if a person acquires control of a company, the other holders of securities must be protected."

General Principle 5:

> "An offeror must announce a bid only after ensuring that he/she can fulfil in full any cash consideration, if such is offered, and after taking all reasonable measures to secure the implementation of any other type of consideration."

General Principle 6:

"An offeree company must not be hindered in the conduct of its affairs for longer than is reasonable by a bid for its securities."

One more "General Principle" should be added: for all intents and purposes, a press announcement is every bit as important as the offer document itself.

This Chapter will consider a variety of press announcements ranging from the (increasing) "talks are in progress" or "we are considering making an offer" kind to the formal announcement of the takeover. Whatever the type, all press announcements in the takeover context are designed to achieve the same purpose: to provide information which the market is entitled to rely upon and, where appropriate, to provide information needed to avoid the creation of a false market. In either case, press announcements must be prepared to the highest standards of care and accuracy. Once statements are made in a press announcement, the Panel will invariably expect the parties to adhere to them. In effect, there is little to distinguish the press announcement from the formal offer or defence documents which follow.

2.2 Companies and transactions to which the Code applies

Section 3 of the Introduction to the Code identifies the companies and transactions to which the Code applies. As explained above, it was substantially amended in May 2006 to reflect the implementation of the Takeover Directive. The Directive determines the scope of the jurisdiction of the competent authority in any EU Member State by reference to the location of the registered office of the offeree and the regulated market on which its securities are traded.

2.2.1 *UK, Channel Islands and Isle of Man registered and traded companies*

The Code applies to offers for companies as well as Societas Europaea which have their registered office in the UK, the Channel Islands or the Isle of Man, and have any of their securities admitted to trading on a regulated market (which includes the London Stock Exchange's main market but not AIM) in the UK or on a stock exchange in the Channel Islands or the Isle of Man (other than those companies which are covered by shared jurisdiction arrangements, *see* Section 2.2.3 below). These companies already fell within the Code prior to the implementation of the Directive, but only if they satisfied the Panel's residency test. This would be the case if the Panel considered that they had their place of central management and control in the UK, the Channel Islands or the Isle of Man. The test no longer applies in respect of any of these companies. Therefore, for example, the current position is that if a company is registered in the UK and has its shares admitted to trading on the London Stock Exchange, it is covered by the Code even if its place of central management is overseas (this reverses the position of Xstrata as discussed below).

2.2.2 Other companies

The Code also applies to all offers (not falling within Section 2.2.1 or Section 2.2.3) for public and certain private companies and Societas Europaea which have their registered offices in the UK, the Channel Islands or the Isle of Man and which are considered by the Panel to have their place of central management and control in these territories. When considering where a company is resident, the Panel will look at the structure of the Board, the functions of the directors and where they are resident. Sometimes the Panel may also look at other relevant major influences on the management of the company, for example, in the case of an investment trust, the identity and location of the investment manager.

Even if the directors of a target company not meeting the residence test volunteer to the Panel to subject themselves to the Code or incorporate a reference to the Code in the company's articles of association, the Panel will normally refuse to accept jurisdiction.

In March 2002 the Panel reinforced this position when it dismissed an appeal by Xstrata against a ruling of the Executive that Xstrata, a new UK holding company whose place of central management would be in Switzerland, should not be subject to the jurisdiction of the Panel. The Panel expressed its reluctance to depart from the normal test and that the discretion to do so should be exercised very rarely. The Panel

The Approach, Announcements and Independent Advice

stated that it has long regarded the place of central management as a critical test of jurisdiction since it is the Panel's view that those companies whose place of central management is not in the UK may feel less able readily to respond to the authority and requirements of the Panel. Note that the Code would now apply to any offer for Xstrata (or similar non-resident companies) as it is an English incorporated company and has its shares admitted to trading on the London Stock Exchange. However, the Panel's approach to the residency test still applies to offers for the companies which are traded on AIM, for example, as this is not a regulated market.

Offers for private companies satisfying the residency test are only subject to the Code if any of their securities have been admitted to the Official List within the past 10 years, or if dealings and/or bid offer prices for their securities have been regularly published for at least six months within the past 10 years, whether via a newspaper, electronic price quotation system (such as OFEX) or otherwise, or if any of their securities have been subject to a marketing arrangement within the past 10 years, or if they have filed a prospectus for the issue of securities within the past 10 years. The Introduction acknowledges that the provisions of the Code may not be appropriate to all such private companies and the Panel may therefore apply the Code with a degree of flexibility in suitable cases.

In its 2002 Annual Report, the Panel commented on the practice of re-registering a public company as a private company, with the result that the Code does not then apply to any offer for that company provided it does not fall within one of the categories described in the previous paragraph. The Panel advised that it would expect the circular convening the general meeting to effect the conversion to explain that one of the consequences of re-registration would be to take the company outside the ambit of the Code. The Panel should be consulted in advance in order to ensure that the circular contains an explanation of the Code and the implications for shareholders of re-registration. Under a requirement inserted into the Introduction to the Code in December 2003, a public company should consult the Executive if it has more than one beneficial owner and proposes to re-register as a private company to which the Code will not apply. This is reflected in Section 3(e) of the Introduction to the Code, under which early consultation with the Panel is advised before re-registration if the relevant company has more than one shareholder so guidance can be given by the Panel on the appropriate disclosure to be made regarding the loss of Code protection.

2.2.3 Shared jurisdiction

Section 3 of the Introduction to the Code deals with matters necessary to implement Article 4.2(b), (c) and (e) of the Directive relating to shared jurisdiction in cases involving UK and other EEA registered and traded companies.

The Panel will share the regulation of an offer with a relevant competent authority in another member state of the European Economic Area (a "Member State") when the offeree company is: (a) a UK registered company whose securities are not admitted to trading on a UK regulated market but are admitted to trading on a regulated market in one or more Member States; (b) a company registered in another Member State whose securities are admitted to trading only on a UK regulated market; or (c) a company registered in another Member State whose securities are admitted to trading on regulated markets in more than one Member State including the UK if: (i) the company's securities were first admitted to trading on a UK regulated market; (ii) the company's securities were admitted to trading simultaneously on more than one regulated market on or after 20 May 2006 (but not on a regulated market in the Member State in which it has its registered office) and the company notifies the Panel and the relevant regulatory authorities on the first day of trading that it has chosen the Panel to regulate it; or (iii) the company had its securities admitted to trading on more than one regulated market before 20 May 2006 and were admitted simultaneously, and either the competent authorities of the relevant Member States agree before 19 June 2006 that the Panel should be the regulator or, failing that, the company chooses on 19 June 2006 to be regulated by the Panel. In any case falling within *(c)(ii)* or *(c)(iii)*, the company will have to notify a Regulatory Information Service of the selection of the Panel as the relevant regulator without delay.

On the basis set out in Article 4.2(e) of the Directive, the Panel will be responsible under *(b)* and *(c)* above for regulating matters relating to the consideration offered, in particular the price, and matters relating

The Approach, Announcements and Independent Advice

to the "bid procedure" (e.g. announcements of offers and the contents of the offer document) and under *(a)* for matters relating to the information to be provided to employees of the offeree company and matters relating to "company law" (e.g. fixing the control threshold for a mandatory offer, any derogation from the obligation to launch an offer and provisions relating to frustrating action). In each case, a supervisory authority in another Member State will be responsible for those matters not regulated by the Panel.

Section 3(d) of the Introduction to the Code states that early consultation with the Panel is advised in shared jurisdiction cases so that guidance can be given on how any conflicts between the relevant rules may be resolved and, where relevant, which provisions of the Code apply pursuant to Article 4.2(e) of the Directive.

2.2.4 *Transactions*

The Code has always applied to a wider range of transactions than those covered by the Directive – the Directive applies only to public, control-seeking offers. Following implementation of the Directive, except in relation to cases covered by the shared jurisdiction arrangements (*see* Section 2.2.3 above), the Code continues to apply to takeover bids and mergers however effected (including by means of statutory merger or Court approved scheme of arrangement) and also to other transactions which are used to obtain or consolidate control of a relevant company. This includes, for example, the acquisition of control pursuant to the exercise of "drag along" rights contained in a company's articles of association (*see* the Panel's 2001 Annual Report). The transaction in question need not involve the acquisition of a controlling interest: the Code will also apply to partial offers, offers by a parent for the minority in its subsidiary, and other transactions where control of a company is to be obtained or consolidated. The shared jurisdiction arrangements apply only to offers that fall within the narrow, Directive-based definition of an offer (coming from Article 2.1(a) of the Directive), which covers only public, control seeking offers (whether mandatory or voluntary). This would not capture, for example, a scheme of arrangement under Section 425 of the Companies Act 1985. However, it is important to note that if a company covered by the shared jurisdiction arrangements also falls under one of the other limbs of the Panel's jurisdiction as discussed in Sections 2.2.1 and 2.2.2 (for example, if it is UK registered company, only traded overseas, but centrally managed in the UK) then a transaction falling within the wider Code definition of an offer referred to in the preceding paragraphs will be relevant for Code purposes.

For the avoidance of doubt, it has now been made clear that the Code applies to all relevant transactions at any stage of their implementation, including, for example, when an offer is in contemplation but has not been announced.

2.2.5 Dual listed companies and newco structures

Since August 2002 the Code has applied to the establishment of a dual holding company structure involving a UK-resident plc. These are corporate groups with dual holding companies, typically listed on different exchanges but having identical boards which operate the group as a single economic enterprise. With the May 2006 changes, the Code will apply to a dual holding company transaction involving a UK company with shares admitted to trading on a regulated market in the UK and any other UK company, which the Panel considers to be resident in the UK, Channel Islands or the Isle of Man. The shared jurisdiction provisions referred to in Section 2.2.3 will not apply as these only apply to transactions falling within the narrow, Directive-based definition of an offer.

Where the Code applies the Code company will usually be treated as the offeree and the offer is regarded as a securities exchange offer. Whilst the normal Code rules would then apply, the Panel indicated in the consultation paper on dual listed company transactions issued in April 2002 (PCP 11) that certain Rules, principally those relating to the offer timetable and acceptances, would be applied flexibly having regard to the particular circumstances. Nevertheless, there may be cases where there is no doubt that the substance of a dual holding company transaction is the acquisition by a Code company of a non-Code company. In such circumstances, the Panel may be willing to agree that the Code should not apply. The public consultation paper referred to above also contains guidance on how the Code will be applied to newco structures (where a new holding company acquires both parties).

2.2.6 Dual jurisdiction

A company which is subject to the Code may also be subject to the jurisdiction of other foreign regulators. In such circumstances, the Panel recommends early consultation so that guidance can be given on how any conflicts between the relevant requirements may be resolved.

It is increasingly common for offers to be structured to comply with both the rules of the Code and the "tender offer" rules of the US Securities and Exchange Act of 1934. Areas of particular conflict between the US and UK rules may include market purchases, the timing of the first closing date, withdrawal rights and disclosure requirements, depending upon whether the target is listed in the US, share (or other security) consideration is offered or the relevant US exemptions (*see* below) are available. The extent of relief provided by the exemptions referred to above depends on the size of a non-US offeree's US shareholder base. If US-resident beneficial shareholders hold 10 per cent or less of the shares of a non-US offeree (as calculated in accordance with the relevant rules), the bid qualifies for the "Tier I" exemption and the bidder is able to conduct its bid in accordance with "home country" rules (i.e. the City Code in the case of a bid for a UK-resident company) and certain additional (largely procedural) requirements stipulated in the exemption. If US-resident beneficial shareholders hold more than 10 per cent but not more than 40 per cent of the shares of a non-US offeree, the bid qualifies for the "Tier II" exemption, which provides more limited exemptive relief. The cross-border exemptions do not exempt bidders from US securities law liability for misleading statements and omissions and fraudulent or manipulative acts in connection with such transactions.

Where the target company has a significant number of shareholders in any foreign jurisdiction, appropriate advice should be taken at an early stage as documentation is now required to be circulated to all shareholders unless a dispensation is available.

2.3 The approach

Rule 1 deals with the "approach".

2.3.1 Notifying the offeree

Rule 1(a) requires that an offer must be put forward, in the first instance, to the offeree board or to its advisers. The degree of contact will, in practice, vary according to the nature of the bid. Where the bid is unilateral or "hostile", pre-announcement contact is likely to be minimal. In some cases, it may take the form of a telephone call to the chairman to say that a press announcement will be released in five minutes. Many hours can be spent planning how to get hold of the chairman to receive such a call.

2.3.2 Identity

The importance of the identity of the offeror is emphasised by Rule 1(b): where the approach is not made by the ultimate or potential offeror, his identity must be disclosed at the outset. This applies even in the case of a cash bid, where it might be assumed that identity is not important. The provision is repeated in Rule 2.5(b), which requires the offeror to be identified in the formal press announcement.

Occasionally, it may not be clear who is to be regarded as the "offeror" – for example, where the offer is made by a subsidiary or a special bid vehicle, or where the bidding company is controlled by a consortium. In such circumstances, the Panel should be consulted and may be expected, in appropriate cases, to apply a "look-through" principle to the parent or "quasi" parent requiring the identity of that "parent" or controller to be disclosed.

The Panel may also need to be consulted as to who should take responsibility for documents and announcements under Rule 19.2, for example whether the board of the bid vehicle is of sufficient substance or whether the board of an appropriate parent would also be required to take responsibility (see Note 5 to Rule 19.2). The Panel is likely to require some or all of the parent board to take responsibility if control over the bid vehicle is effectively exercised at the parent company level.

Rule 1(c) provides that the board of directors on the receiving end of an approach is entitled to be satisfied that the offeror is, or will be, in a position to implement the offer in full.

2.4 Announcing the offer

The Code places a very strict obligation on offerors and their financial advisers to exercise due care before announcing an offer. This is on the basis that a firm offer will inevitably have a profound effect on the offeree company and the market price of its shares. While investors in a company which is the subject of an offer appreciate that it may fail due to lack of acceptances or other regulatory problems, they expect that the offer will only be withdrawn for other reasons in a small minority of cases.

There are two particularly important Code provisions to note in this respect:

General Principle 5:

> "An offeror must announce a bid only after ensuring that he/she can fulfil in full any cash consideration, if such is offered, and after taking all reasonable measures to secure the implementation of any other type of consideration."

Rule 2.5(a):

> "An offeror should only announce a firm intention to make an offer after the most careful and responsible consideration. Such an announcement should be made only when an offeror has every reason to believe that it can and will continue to be able to implement the offer. Responsibility in this connection also rests on the financial adviser to the offeror."

General Principle 5 (which replaced a similar general principle – General Principle 3) relates to the steps a bidder should take to ensure the offer consideration will be available before announcing the offer. The announcement of an offer that includes cash must now include confirmation by the financial adviser that resources are available to the offeror sufficient to satisfy full acceptance of the offer. This was previously only the case on mandatory offer announcements – for voluntary offers the cash confirmation would be given in the offer document. Rule 24.7 continues to require a similar confirmation to be given in the offer document.

Although Rule 2.5(a) makes it clear that a financial adviser shares responsibility for ensuring the offeror will be able to implement the offer, under Rule 2.5(c) and Rule 24.7 it is clear that the adviser giving the confirmation will not be expected to produce the cash itself provided "it acted responsibly and took all reasonable steps to assure itself that the cash was available".

An example of the application of these responsibilities was the proposed offer by Luirc for Merlin Properties. The offeror was a newly incorporated British Virgin Island company with a nominal capital. When the bid was announced the offeror had received a comfort letter that funds were available, but no formal loan agreement had been negotiated. The Panel ruled that no announcement of the bid should have been made before the offeror had received an irrevocable commitment to provide the funds. The Panel's ruling stated that:

> "Compliance with [this General Principle (what was then General Principle 3, now General Principle 5 and Rule 2.5(a))] is of great importance. The announcement of an offer is always highly significant for the offeree company and will usually affect its share price. If the offer is subsequently withdrawn, at the very least a false market in the shares in the offeree company is likely to have been created.
>
> The Executive's view is that, when a financial adviser is acting for a newly created offeror, such as an off-the-shelf overseas company, the standard of care required under General Principle 3 [now General Principle 5] clearly has an additional dimension. In short, the only way in which such an offeror and its financial adviser can be sure that funds will be available is to have an irrevocable commitment from a party upon whom reliance can reasonably be placed, for example a bank, at the time of the announcement of the offer."

In some circumstances the financial adviser giving the cash confirmation may be required to come up with the cash itself. The following extract from the Panel's 1991 Annual Report is a salutary lesson:

> "In a cash offer Rule 24.7 requires the offer document to contain confirmation, normally by the offeror's bank or financial adviser,

that there are resources available to the offeror sufficient to satisfy full acceptance of the offer. If accepting shareholders are not paid and the Panel considers that the party giving the cash confirmation did not act responsibly and did not take all reasonable steps to assure itself that the cash was available, the Panel may look to the party giving the confirmation to produce the cash itself.

It is a matter of judgement in each case for the party giving the cash confirmation to satisfy itself that there will be funds available to meet the offer. In making that judgement, the party giving the cash confirmation will be influenced by a variety of matters such as the standing of the offeror, the extent and nature of its relationship with the offeror and the size of the offer. In the rare event of cash not subsequently being made available to accepting shareholders, the Executive will investigate what steps were taken by the party giving the cash confirmation.

In a recent case an offeror failed to pay certain of the accepting shareholders and the Executive found that the adviser that gave the cash confirmation in the offer document had not exercised adequate care in ensuring that cash would be available to the offeror. The Executive ruled that the adviser concerned should pay the consideration that was due under the offer and the outstanding payments were duly made."

In April 2005, the Executive issued Practice Statement no. 10 relating to cash offers financed by the issue of offeror securities. The Executive noted that:

"If an offer, which was to be financed by the issue of offeror securities, lapses or is withdrawn owing to a failure to fulfil a condition relating to the issue, the Executive will wish to be satisfied that [General Principle 3 (as it was) and Rule 2.5(a) (as it was)] were complied with (so that, on announcement, the offeror and its financial adviser had had every reason to believe that the offer could and would be implemented)."

The Executive also thought that:

> "In order to satisfy [General Principle 3 (as it was), Rule 2.5(a) (as it was)] and Rule 24.7, it was the responsibility of the party giving the cash confirmation and the offeror (and, if it is not the cash confirmer, the offeror's financial adviser) to take all reasonable steps, before the announcement of the offer, to satisfy themselves that the issue of new securities will be successful, and that the offeror will have the necessary cash available to finance the full acceptance of the offer."

Rule 2.5(a) requires the offeror's pre-annoucement due diligence exercise to cover all aspects of implementing the offer, not just ensuring the availability of consideration.

The Panel's statement in August 1989 dealing with Wm Low's lapsed bid for Budgens is therefore still required reading in this area. Following the announcement of its bid, Wm Low discovered details about Budgens' working capital and borrowings which led it to conclude that the offer no longer made financial sense. Since the bid was conditional on Wm Low's shareholders' approval, the Panel agreed to its being withdrawn on the basis that, with the Directors of Wm Low changing their earlier recommendation to vote in favour, shareholders would inevitably withhold their consent. But, in the inquest that followed, the Panel had some strong words of criticism to say about Wm Low's financial advisers and about what was then General Principle 3 [(now part of Rule 2.5(a))], including the following:

> "Compliance with this principle is of great importance. The announcement of an offer inevitably has a profound effect upon the market. The share price of the offeree company will be affected and, in consequence, if the offer is subsequently withdrawn – for whatever reason – many people may have dealt on the basis of expectations which are not fulfilled. Against this background, General Principle 3 attempts to reduce to a minimum the number of offers which are withdrawn by placing upon potential offerors and their advisers an obligation to exercise due care before making an offer. This Code duty is of a standard similar to that which the law imposes upon professional people or indeed anyone who purports to possess some special skill. It is a duty to display that standard of skill and

care which would ordinarily be expected of someone exercising or professing to exercise the particular skill in question. The Panel stresses that General Principle 3 is designed to protect shareholders of the offeree company and those who might deal or consider dealing in the shares of the offeree company. Accordingly, to the extent that it is practically possible to exercise care, the Code duty arising under General Principle 3 cannot be limited simply to setting out conditions to which a particular offer is subject.

The practical content of the Code duty to exercise appropriate care will inevitably depend upon all the circumstances of the case. Where there is a unilateral offer, it may be very difficult for the offeror to obtain reliable detailed information concerning the business of the offeree company. The issue of what is reasonable in each case turns in part upon the likely reaction of the offeror to unanticipated developments or revelations following the announcement of an offer. If, for example, a very large company were proposing to take over a small company just to obtain a particular product, it might be perfectly reasonable for it not to investigate the profitability or borrowings of the target, because subsequent revelations relating to those aspects of the target's business would not be relevant to the offeror. But, on the other hand, in the case of a proposed merger of companies of similar size, the offeror is likely to be much more sensitive to the precise financial position of the offeree. In such a situation, which existed in the present case, it is necessary for the offeror, where it has the opportunity to do so, to take greater care to investigate that position in advance."

In April 2005, the Executive issued Practice Statement no. 11 relating to working capital requirements in cash and securities exchange offers and it stated that the Executive's practice in this area was that in the event of an offer lapsing as a result of working capital concerns, the Executive would wish to be satisfied that the offeror and its financial adviser had, at the time of announcement of the offer, complied with, what was at the time of the Practice Statement, General Principle 3 and Rule 2.5(a).

In its 1997 Annual Report, the Panel commented as follows:

> "Subject to the need to maintain secrecy, parties and their advisers should . . . seek to address all potential concerns in relation to the offeree company before issuing an announcement of a firm intention to make an offer. To the extent that this is possible, these concerns should be identified in advance by undertaking appropriate due diligence. However, the scope for doing so will depend upon, in particular, whether or not the offeror has the cooperation of the offeree board."

2.5 Secrecy

2.5.1 The basic obligation

Rule 2.1 sets out the fundamental obligation that secrecy should be maintained at all times. This is closely linked with the requirement in Rule 2.2(e) that where more than a very small number of people (essentially those who need to know in the companies concerned and their immediate advisers) are included in pre-bid discussions, the Panel should be consulted and an announcement must be made.

2.5.2 Advisers' obligations

Note 1 to Rule 2.1 places advisers under a specific obligation to warn clients about the requirement for secrecy and, indeed, about their responsibilities under the Code in general.

2.5.3 Proof printing

Note 2 to Rule 2.1 draws specific attention to a particular aspect of the need for secrecy – that of proof printing. Little can be added to the Code's own warning – except that often the imagination may be less fertile than one thinks, and many codes are surprisingly easy to break.

2.5.4 Employee consultation

In its 1997 Annual Report, the Panel noted that:

> "It has always been a Code principle that the interests of employees should be considered in addition to those of shareholders.

The Approach, Announcements and Independent Advice

However, concerns have recently been raised with the Executive that, contrary to statutory or other obligations, proposed significant redundancies are sometimes announced in relation to a takeover or merger before there has been any process of employee consultation."

The Panel will normally permit consultation with a very restricted number of employee representatives before an offer is publicly announced if there is to be significant restructuring or rationalisation. The Panel's consent will be subject to the information only being disclosed to specific individuals and on a confidential basis. If there is a leak, an immediate public announcement must be made.

However, after a bid announcement has been made meetings with employees, in their capacity as such, can normally be held without any of the Code restrictions which would apply to meetings with shareholders and analysts. Accordingly, employee consultation can take place following an initial bid announcement but before any final decision on the consequences for employment is taken or published.

The Directive sets out specific requirements for offeror and offeree companies to communicate with their employees in the context of a takeover. In accordance with Article 14, these are additional requirements to those employee consultation rules that already exist in Member States (the relevant legislation in the UK being the Employee Information and Consultation Regulations that applied from April 2005). Under Article 6.1, as soon as a bid is made public the boards of the offeree company and of the offeror must inform their respective employee representatives or, where there are no such representatives, the employees themselves. Rule 2.6 of the Code has been amended in order to reflect the requirements of Article 6.1 (along with Article 8.2, which requires information to be made readily and promptly available) (*see* Section 2.7.4 below). Under Article 6.2, when an offer document is made public the boards of the offeree company and of the offeror must communicate it to their respective employee representatives, or where there are no such representatives, the employees themselves. The requirement of this Article (along with those of Article 8.2) have been implemented by the introduction of a new sub-paragraph in Rule 30.1.

2.6 Pre-bid announcements

2.6.1 When an announcement is required

Rules 2.2 to 2.4 deal with the difficult issue of pre-formal offer announcements. The Panel's paramount concern is to avoid the creation of a false market: see General Principle 4. The difficulty is to strike the balance between achieving this objective and protecting the legitimate commercial interests of potential offerors (who on the whole would not want to reveal their hands until they had dotted the "i's" and crossed the "t's").

An excellent explanation of the background to this perennial of topical issues is to be found in the Panel's 1988 Annual Report. In it, the Panel dealt firmly with the reluctant offeror as follows:

> "Announcements
>
> An area that has caused the Executive some concern over the last year relates to the timing and quality of information released relating to an offer. It is amongst the more important tasks of the Panel to ensure that information is made available equally to all shareholders, and also that the parties to an offer use every endeavour to prevent the creation of a false market in the securities of the companies concerned throughout the offer. Accordingly, although this is not a new problem and was the subject of a Panel Statement last September, its importance is such that it is worth repeating here.
>
> There has on several occasions been a considerable amount of speculation concerning a possible offer; in some cases it has been well founded but in others it has not. But, whenever there is such speculation, the companies and their advisers must consider whether an announcement is required under Rule 2.2 of the Code.
>
> In particular, Rule 2.2(d) imposes an obligation on the potential offeror to make an announcement when, before an approach has been made, the offeree company is the subject of rumour and speculation, or there is an untoward movement in its share price,

The Approach, Announcements and Independent Advice

and there are reasonable grounds for concluding that it is the potential offeror's actions which have led to the situation.

The rule can sometimes pose difficulties for an offeror, particularly when he is in the process of finalising his plans. So there may be a reluctance to make an announcement, leading the offeror to accept, perhaps too readily, alternative explanations as to why there is speculation or an untoward price movement, rather than the most likely one, which is that his security is inadequate. But the Code requires that where there is speculation or an untoward price movement, but the offeror and his advisers do not propose to make an immediate announcement, the Panel should be consulted."

The Panel further emphasised its position in its 1996 Annual Report where, having stressed the need for secrecy pre-announcement and the necessity of "prior and full consultation with [the Executive] in respect of the announcement obligations under Rule 2", the Panel went on to state:

"The Executive also wishes to emphasise that a requirement on a potential offeror to make an announcement of its interest under Rule 2.2(d) can, and often does, arise prior to any decision being made to proceed with such an offer, or prior to the funding needed for such an offer being finalised. The Executive takes the view that if there is rumour and speculation relating to a particular offeree company or there is an untoward movement in its share price and there are reasonable grounds for concluding that this is as a result of the potential offeror's actions, then, even if the potential offeror has not yet decided to proceed with an offer, an announcement of its possible interest is required."

The Panel made it clear that the Executive considers that potential offeror and offeree companies and their respective advisers should not only keep a close watch on the offeree company's share price, but should also monitor the media for any evidence of rumour and speculation.

Rules 2.2(a) and (b) are straightforward, requiring an announcement when a firm intention to bid is notified to the offeree board or when the offeror triggers a Rule 9 obligation.

Rules 2.2(c), (d) and (f)(i) all apply when there is rumour and speculation concerning the offeree, or an "untoward" movement in its share price. Paragraph (c) covers the position after an approach to the offeree has been made. Paragraph (d) applies before an approach if there are reasonable grounds for concluding that the rumour and speculation or movement in the share price resulted from some action of the offeror – inadequate security or otherwise. Paragraph (f)(i) applies when a purchaser is being sought for a holding, or aggregate holdings, of shares carrying 30 per cent or more of the voting rights of a company, or when the board of a company is seeking potential offerors.

Note 1 of Rule 2.2 makes it clear that whether or not a movement is "untoward" is for the Panel to determine, on the following basis:

> "The question will be considered in the light of all relevant facts and not solely by reference to the absolute percentage movement in the price. Facts which may be considered to be relevant in determining whether a price movement is untoward for the purposes of Rules 2.2(c), (d) and (f)(i) include general market and sector movements, publicly available information relating to the company, trading activity in the company's securities and the time period over which the price movement has occurred. This list is purely illustrative and the Panel will take account of such other factors as it considers appropriate."

After an approach to the offeree company (in the case of Rule 2.2(c)), or after an offer is first actively considered (in the case of Rule 2.2(d)), or after the board starts to seek one or more potential offerors (in the case of Rule 2.2(f)(i)), there is an obligation to consult the Panel at the latest when the offeree company becomes the subject of any rumour and speculation or where there is a price movement of 10 per cent or more above the lowest share price since the time of the approach etc. An abrupt price rise of a smaller percentage (e.g. a rise of five per cent in the course of a single day) could also be regarded as untoward and accordingly the Panel should be consulted in such circumstances.

Practice Statement no. 6 of 2004 outlines how the Executive interprets Rule 2 in the context of a company announcing a strategic review of its business. Often in these circumstances an offer is one of a number

The Approach, Announcements and Independent Advice

of options under review and it is not always clear whether a strategic review announcement will trigger the commencement of an offer period. If the announcement does refer to an offer as being an option under consideration this will automatically start an offer period (this mirrors the definition of "offer period" as covering a "proposed or possible offer"). If the review concludes that the offer will not be pursued then the company must make a public announcement in order for the offer period to end.

If the announcement does not refer to an offer, the Executive will make direct enquiries of the board. If an offer is one option actively under consideration and there is either rumour about the offer or an untoward movement in the company's share price, the Executive will require the company to make an announcement. At this point the offer period will commence. If the review subsequently concludes not to pursue the offer, a further public announcement is required to end the offer period.

Companies are strongly encouraged to consult with the Executive prior to making any strategic review announcements in order to avoid any misunderstanding. The Panel's Annual Report for 2003 states that notwithstanding the requirement to consult the Panel "the parties should not delay an announcement in order to consult the Panel if it is clear that an announcement is required."

An announcement may also be required when more than a very restricted number of people are approached in various capacities, for example in order to arrange financing for the offer (including to pre-market an underwriting), to seek irrevocable undertakings or to organise a consortium to make the offer (Rule 2.2(e) and (f)(ii)). Before making any such approach, the Panel should be consulted.

Neither the Rule nor the notes indicate what is meant by more than a "restricted" number of people in this context. However, the Panel in its Annual Report for 2003 stated that in practice the Panel must always be consulted prior to more than six external parties being approached. Like any other person privy to price-sensitive information concerning an offer, the external parties approached must, as required by Rule 2.1, keep the offer discussions secret and must not themselves approach additional third parties without consulting the

Panel. There is, however, experience of more than six external parties being accepted with the Panel's approval.

Rule 2.3 establishes a clear demarcation of responsibility for making pre-bid announcements. Before the offeree board has been approached, the obligation is that of the offeror and its advisers. The Panel in its Annual Report for 2003 advised that whilst the obligation is on the offeror, the offeror should keep a close watch on the offeree company's share price and monitor the press, newswires and internet bulletin boards for any rumour and speculation. Once an approach has been made to the board of the offeree company, the primary responsibility will normally rest with the offeree and steps must be taken to keep a close watch on its share price. Rule 2.3 also includes a reminder that the offeror should not resort to any "strong arm tactics" to prevent the offeree from making an announcement or seeking a suspension of dealings from the Exchange. The Panel also advised in its Annual Report for 2003 that if the offeror's approach is rejected by the offeree, the announcement obligation will normally revert to the offeror as only the offeror will then know whether it intends to proceed with the offer. In cases of doubt as to where the announcement obligation lies, the Panel should be consulted. Where the offer is to be recommended, Rule 2.3 suggests that a possible alternative to an immediate announcement may be to obtain a suspension (if permitted) followed shortly by an announcement.

In February 1992 the Panel ruled that Rule 2.2(c), (d) and (e) had been breached prior to the Petrocon bid for James Wilkes. On this occasion, the share price of Wilkes had increased by some 26 per cent before an announcement was made. Apart from share purchases, the bidder's advisers approached institutional shareholders in confidence to establish the likely reaction to a bid without the consent of the Panel. On both counts, the advisers were criticised. The responsibility then passed to James Wilkes and its advisers when the approach was made over the weekend, and they were criticised for failing to insist on an announcement.

In February 1996, in connection with Rentokil's unilateral offer for BET, the Panel concluded that Rentokil's financial advisers should have been more alert to the need to consult the Panel under Rule 2 of the Code. In that case, there was market speculation and the Panel

The Approach, Announcements and Independent Advice

took the view that, given the market rumour and the fact that Rentokil was at an advanced stage of preparation for a possible offer, the Panel should have been consulted immediately upon such rumours commencing. The Panel also emphasised that, as part of such consultation, there is an obligation on the financial adviser to provide the Panel with background information in order for the Panel to make a full assessment of the situation, and went on to underline the importance of prior and full consultation with the Panel in respect of the announcement obligation under Rule 2 of the Code, particularly in the context of a possible unilateral offer. The Executive similarly criticised in March 2004 Nabarro Wells, financial adviser to Transcomm plc, for its failure to consult the Executive as required by Note 1 on Rule 2.2. Transcomm had been in discussions with British Telecommunications plc for a number of months before making an announcement that it was in talks that might lead to an offer for the company. During the period prior to the announcement, although the share price moved from 11p per share to 14.5p per share, Nabarro Wells determined, without consulting the Executive, that no announcement was required. In its statement the Executive emphasised the importance which the Panel attaches to Rule 2.2 and to the making of timely announcements.

It is worth noting that since the introduction of the market abuse regime in the Financial Services and Markets Act 2000, failure to make an announcement where there is a regulatory obligation to do so can amount to market abuse. The Financial Services Authority's Disclosure Rules also contain announcement obligations for companies on the London Stock Exchange's main market.

2.6.2 Possible offer announcements

Rule 2.4(a) confirms that (except in the case of a Rule 9 bid) a brief announcement that talks are taking place or that a potential offeror is considering making an offer will be sufficient when an announcement obligation is triggered by Rule 2.2. In the last few years, there has been a significant increase in the number of possible offer announcements both by bidders and targets. In its 2005 Annual Report, the Panel noted:

> "... the trend towards offers being announced at a preliminary stage has continued. There has been much comment about the

increased incidence of so-called "virtual bids". Early announcements of possible offers are made for a variety of reasons, but a leak, or fear of leaks, is often a factor. Leaks are a source of great concern to the Panel and the Executive cooperates with the Financial Services Authority to facilitate its investigation of possible insider dealing and other market abuse. Parties may also have other reasons for an early announcement, for example to allow due diligence to take place or to allow other issues (such as obtaining clearances or authorisations) to be resolved. In future, the need for parties to negotiate with pension fund trustees and to fulfil their obligations under the Information and Consultation Directive will further add to the likelihood of early announcements. The Code has developed to cater for the rise in possible offer announcements, both through the introduction of the "put up or shut up" provision and through the regulation of statements made by potential offerors and the regime applicable to pre-conditions."

As noted in the extract above, Rule 2.4 was amended in 2004 to deal with statements made in possible offer announcements. Rule 2.4 now also gives the Panel the express power, at a target's request, to order a bidder to make an offer or to announce it will not be making an offer: the "put up or shut up" regime (*see* Section 2.6.3 below for more details).

The regime for the proposed terms of a possible offer announcement as set out in Rule 2.4(c) requires that the Panel be consulted in advance of any statement relating to the proposed terms of a possible offer. Where a potential offeror makes an unqualified statement about the terms of a possible offer, for example if it specifies a price, it will be bound by those terms. As this applies equally to formal and informal statements there will consequently need to be strict public relations controls in place. Proposed terms can, within limits, be qualified so long as any qualification is capable of objective determination. For example a bidder may specify a possible offer price but reserve the right to bid at a lower price in certain circumstances. A subsequent bid at a lower price will then be permitted where the specific circumstances of the particular qualification have arisen. Qualifications that will always be permitted are a target board's recommendation and a firm offer by a third party (the satisfactory outcome of a due diligence exercise will never be permitted). Where the terms refer to an anticipated price range, an approximate price, or a relative price, prior consultation with the Panel will be required. From a tactical point of view, an offeror must be careful to include those qualifications that it wishes to make use of while still trying to avoid disclosing the terms on which it is considering making a firm bid.

With the consent of the Panel, a possible offer announcement can include pre-conditions and these can be subjective in nature (*see* Section 2.7.2 below for further details). The announcement must make it clear whether these pre-conditions are waivable and must also emphasise that there is no certainty an offer will be made.

A party which announces a possible offer is not subject to any specific timetable unless the target requests the Panel to intervene (i.e. requests a "put up or shut up" ruling). In its 2001 Annual Report, the Panel clarified its general approach in this regard:

> "Following such an announcement [a possible offer announcement] there is no fixed deadline in the Code by which a potential offeror must clarify his intentions. The timing of any subsequent announcements will depend, *inter alia*, on the reaction of the offeree board to the potential offeror and the state of preparedness of the potential offeror.
>
> Where the offeree board is prepared to enter into a dialogue with the potential offeror, many months may pass before an offer is finally made. Provided the target company is content for the uncertainty to continue, the Executive would not normally seek to intervene in the process. However, in certain circumstances, usually where the potential offeror is unwelcome, the target company may request the Executive to intervene by imposing a deadline by which the potential offeror must clarify his intentions, i.e. "put up or shut up".
>
> In this regard, "put up" is communicated by way of a Rule 2.5 firm offer announcement and "shut up" by way of a no intention to bid statement.
>
> Requests by the target company for the offeror to be required to "put up or shut up" are generally made at the early stages of an

offer period. In such cases, the Executive endeavours to balance the interests of shareholders in not being deprived of the opportunity to consider the possibility of an offer against potential damage to the target company's business arising from the uncertainty surrounding the company and the distraction for management. In this regard, the Executive's normal approach is to seek clarification by the potential offeror within six to eight weeks from the original announcement of the possible offer. If a request is made at a later stage, the Executive will consider the circumstances at that time.

If the potential offeror clarifies his intentions by way of a no intention to bid statement, this statement will be governed by Rule 2.8 and the potential offeror will normally be prevented from making an offer for the company for a period of six months (unless there is a material change of circumstances and subject to any specific reservations set out in the statement). However, if the Executive considers that the offeree company has suffered excessive siege as a result of the potential offeror's actions, it may impose the restrictions contained within Rule 35.1(b) and prevent the potential offeror from making an offer for a period of 12 months."

The Panel did consult in 2001 on whether it should introduce into the Code an express obligation to issue "refresher" announcements every six weeks once an announcement has been made under Rule 2.4(a). It decided against this but emphasised that the onus remains on parties to possible bids and their advisers to comply with existing legal and regulatory disclosure requirements. In this context, the following requirements are relevant: General Principles 2 and 4 and Rule 23 of the Code, the UK Listing Authority's Listing and Disclosure Rules and Section 397 Financial Services and Markets Act 2000. The Panel also indicated that it would continue to exercise its general power to require an announcement to be made as and when, in its view, circumstances so demand.

2.6.3 "Put up or shut up" and "no intention to bid" statements

The "put up or shut up" regime is aimed at preventing an offeree from suffering from a protracted period of speculation before an offer

The Approach, Announcements and Independent Advice

is announced or a potential offeror issues a "no intention to bid" statement. At the offeree's request, the Panel can require a bidder by a specified date either to announce an offer under Rule 2.5 or to announce that it will not proceed with an offer. This concept was incorporated into the Code for the first time as new Rule 2.4(b) in 2004 reflecting a number of years of Panel practice. Two examples since the Rule was incorporated into the Code are the Panel rulings in 2005 on approaches by the Glazer family for Manchester United plc and the Macquarie Group for the London Stock Exchange (note that there are numerous previous rulings). It is only the offeree that can request a ruling under this provision. There is no need for the offeree to wait until negotiations with a potential offeror have completely broken down before asking for a deadline, however this may result in making the offeror more hostile and should therefore be carefully considered. The benchmark deadline likely to be set by the Panel is six to eight weeks from the initial approach where the request has been made at the start of the offer period. There is some flexibility in cases where the request is made later in order to take account of the time already passed.

Where the offeror "shuts up", it will then be prevented from making an offer for six months under Rule 2.8. It can make an earlier offer if circumstances arise and it has specifically reserved the right to make an offer in those circumstances. In the context of a Rule 2.8 announcement following a "put up or shut up" ruling, the offeror is restricted in the reservations that will give it the right to make an earlier offer. These are: (i) where the target board recommends its offer; (ii) where another person makes a firm bid (not just a possible offer announcement); and (iii) if the target announces a whitewash or reverse. If the offeror reserves the right to bid again with the target board's recommendation, it must first get the Panel's consent to approach the target for that recommendation. If no such recommendation is received, no further approach is permitted within the six month lock-out period.

A bidder may also voluntarily issue a Rule 2.8 announcement where it decides not to make an offer. The Panel should be consulted before issuing such a statement particularly if it is intended to include specific reservations to set aside the statement (Note 1 on Rule 2.8). The restrictions on reservations set out above do not apply to "voluntary" Rule 2.8 announcements. A bidder will then be restricted from making an offer for the target for six months unless an event occurs which the bidder has specifically reserved as giving it the right to announce an earlier offer.

Note that the Panel applies this rule not only to formal public statements but also to informal or private comments, which are subsequently publicly reported. It also takes the view that a simple denial of speculation as to the person's intention to make a bid, even though falling short of an explicit statement that the person does not intend to make a bid, will still be caught. So Rule 2.8 contains traps for the unwary.

2.6.4 Statement of interest by potential competing bidder

The Code also deals with holding statements by potential rival offerors. During the battle for control of National Westminster Bank plc ("NatWest") the Executive (and, on appeal, the Panel) refused to impose a "put up or shut up" timetable on the Royal Bank of Scotland ("RBS") in the early stages of the offer period. The Bank of Scotland ("BOS") had announced a firm intention to bid for NatWest and RBS had announced, following press speculation, that it had been considering and would continue to consider its position. BOS requested that the Panel impose a deadline on RBS to clarify its position as the announcement had, in BOS's view, created market uncertainty and had allowed RBS to obtain an unfair advantage over BOS. RBS submitted that it had done nothing to create or increase market uncertainty. The Panel refused to set a firm deadline for RBS to clarify its intentions but indicated that Day 50 appeared to the Panel to be the latest day for clarification of RBS's position – although the Panel reserved the right to specify an earlier or later date depending upon developments.

Note 1 on Rule 19.3 was amended after the RBS/BOS/NatWest offers and now provides that it is not acceptable for a holding statement by a potential rival bidder to remain unclarified for more than a limited time in the later stages of an offer period. On the MSREF offer for Canary Wharf, Brascan (a potential rival offeror) was required to clarify its intention 10 days before a target shareholder meeting to approve the transaction (equivalent to Day 50 of a conventional offer timetable) and a potential rival bidder for Ask Central was given until Day 53 to clarify its intention. The Panel's concern is that target shareholders have sufficient time to accept the first offer if the rival bidder decides not to bid. The most recent example was on the Ferrovial/BAA offer where a rival Goldman Sachs-led consortium was given a deadline of Day 50 of the Ferrovial offer to clarify its intentions.

2.7 Bid announcements

2.7.1 *Announcement of a firm intention to make an offer*

The provisions of Rule 2.5(a) require that a firm intention to make a bid should only be announced when the offeror has every reason to believe that it can and will be able to implement the offer.

The required contents of an announcement of a firm intention to make an offer (as opposed to a "talks announcement") are specified in Rule 2.5(b). In particular, the announcement must:

(a) set out the terms of the offer – detailed terms will be included, although a number of "further terms" are postponed until the offer document (*see* Rule 24.6);
(b) identify the offeror – the questions mentioned above about who is the offeror (*see* Section 2.3.2) will again need to be considered;
(c) give details of any relevant securities of the offeree company in which the offeror or any person acting in concert with it has an interest or in respect of which he has a right to subscribe, in each case specifying the nature of the interests of rights concerned. Similar details of any short positions (whether conditional or absolute and whether in the money or otherwise), including any short position under a derivative, any agreement to sell or any delivery obligation or right to require another person to purchase or take delivery, must also be stated;
(d) include details of any relevant securities of the offeree in respect of which the offeror or any of its associates has procured an irrevocable commitment or a letter of intent;
(e) give details of any relevant securities of the offeree which the offeror or any person acting in concert with it has borrowed or lent, save for any borrowed shares which have been either on-lent or sold;

(f) include all conditions (including normal conditions relating to acceptances, listing, and increase of capital) to which the offer or the posting of it is subject;
(g) give details of any agreements or arrangements to which the offeror is a party which relate to the circumstances in which it may or may not invoke or seek to invoke a pre-condition or a condition to its offer and the consequences of its doing so, including details of any break fees payable as a result (*see* Rule 2.5(b)(vii));
(h) give details of any arrangements in relation to relevant securities within Note 6(b) to Rule 8 (*see* Chapter 3); and
(i) include a summary of the provisions of Rule 8 (the rule requiring disclosure of dealings during an offer period).

As explained in Section 2.4, the offer announcement must now include confirmation from the financial adviser that resources are available to the offeror sufficient to satisfy full acceptance of the offer where it is a cash offer.

Two points on the notes to Rule 2.5 are worth mentioning:

(a) a reminder is given that the language used in the announcement should clearly and concisely reflect the position being described. This reflects the general requirement that press announcements be prepared with a standard of care and accuracy effectively equivalent to that imposed on the formal offer document; and
(b) there is a warning that the Panel should be consulted before any condition is included which is not entirely objective, which is effectively a cross-reference to Rule 13.

2.7.2 *Pre-conditional offer announcements*

In the last few years, there was an increasing number of pre-conditional offers i.e. an offer that will only be made if certain pre-conditions are satisfied. The most common pre-conditions relate to regulatory clearances where these are unlikely to be obtained in the usual Code timetable. Some examples include General Electric's share exchange offer for Amersham, Carnival Corporation's initially hostile offer for P&O Princess Cruises, the proposed merger between Granada and Carlton, Southern Electric's offer for Scottish Hydro, the merger creating GlaxoSmithKline, which was subject to a regulatory clearance pre-condition, E.ON's bid for Powergen, which was subject to nine regulatory pre-conditions, and Lloyds TSB's hostile offer for Abbey National which was conditional on the OFT indicating, in terms satisfactory to Lloyds TSB, that the transaction would not be referred to the Competition Commission and on the Abbey National board recommending the bid. Lloyds TSB reserved the right to waive the pre-conditions. Carnival Corporation's first offer for P&O Princess Cruises was also subject to a financing pre-condition in respect of the cash element of the offer (later reformulated as a pre-condition to a partial cash alternative). Lafarge's hostile offer for Blue Circle likewise included a financing pre-condition (that funding for the offer was arranged on terms satisfactory to it).

In light of the increasing use of pre-conditions, the Code Committee issued Consultation Paper 2004/4 ("PCP 2004/4") and Response Statement 2004/4 ("RS 2004/4") in which it reviewed its previous approach to pre-conditions. Changes were made to the Code in April 2005. The Code Committee considered it necessary to look separately at pre-conditional possible offer announcements made under Rule 2.4 and pre-conditional firm offer announcements made under Rule 2.5. The Panel takes a much stricter approach to permitted pre-conditions in firm offer announcements on the basis that the announcement of a pre-conditional offer under Rule 2.5 is intended and required to provide a high level of certainty. The inclusion of pre-conditions in either type of announcement requires prior consultation with the Panel.

The standard for including pre-conditions in a Rule 2.5 announcement is now the same as that which is applied by Rule 13 to conventional offer conditions. Rule 13.3 sets out the pre-conditions that will be acceptable to the Panel in a Rule 2.5 announcement. Except with the consent of the Panel, an offer must not be announced subject to a pre-condition unless the pre-condition concerned:

(a) relates to OFT/Competition Commission or European Commission clearance; or
(b) involves a material official authorisation or regulatory clearance relating to the offer and either the offer is publicly recommended by the offeree or the Panel is satisfied that it is likely to prove

impossible to obtain the authorisation or clearance within the Code timetable.

The Code Committee decided against allowing greater flexibility and the test set out in Rule 13.4(a) now applies to the invocation of pre-conditions included in a Rule 2.5 annoucement. Although many different types of pre-conditions have been used in the past, from April 2005, an offeror is only allowed to include the pre-conditions described above and the Panel will no longer allow wide and/or subjective pre-conditions in Rule 2.5 announcements. According to the Code Committee in RS 2004/4, the circumstances in which the Panel should be prepared to consider exercising its discretion to allow pre-conditions outside the permitted categories are likely to be very limited, for example if it relates to a matter concerning the offeree that is likely to be incapable of resolution within the normal offer timetable and is a matter without which it would be unreasonable to expect the offeror to make the offer at all.

Pre-conditional Rule 2.5 announcements have sometimes contained a pre-condition in relation to financing (i.e. that the offeror will have the facilities in place to finance the cash element of a bid) or in relation to the adequacy of working capital for the enlarged group. In PCP 2004/4 and in RS 2004/4, the Code Committee proposed that the same prohibition on financing conditions on offers should now normally also apply to financing pre-conditions. These will only be allowed in exceptional circumstances.

However, as set out in the Note on Rule 13.1 and Rule 13.3, in exceptional circumstances, the Panel may be prepared to accept a pre-condition related to financing either in addition to another pre-condition permitted by Rule 13.3 or otherwise; for example where due to the likely period required to obtain any necessary material official authorisation or regulatory clearance, it is not reasonable for the offeror to maintain committed financing throughout the offer period, in which case:

(a) the financing pre-condition must be satisfied (or waived), or the offer must be withdrawn, within 21 days after the satisfaction (or waiver) of any other pre-condition(s) permitted by Rule 13.3; and

(b) the offeror and its financial adviser must confirm in writing to the Panel before annnoucement of the offer that they are not aware of any reason why the offeror would be unable to satisfy the financing pre-condition within that 21 day period.

The Panel exercised its discretion to allow the pre-conditional offer by Boots for Unichem in October 2005 to include a pre-condition that the two companies be reasonably satisfied for the purposes of the requirements of the FSA and the UKLA that the necessary financing facilities would be available on reasonable market terms following completion of their merger to provide for the working capital requirements of the group.

It is clear from PCP 2004/4 and RS 2004/4 that the Panel has adopted the same approach to working capital conditions and a bidder is not able to include a working capital pre-condition on a standalone basis.

As regards possible offer announcements made under Rule 2.4, subjective pre-conditions can be included and do not have to be confined to anti-trust clearances etc. This is on the basis that, since the making of the offer still remains within the discretion of the potential offeror even where the pre-conditions are satisfied, neither shareholders nor the market can gain any more certainty from a requirement that only objective pre-conditions will be permissible. Therefore, a possible offer can be pre-conditional on, for example, offeree board recommendation, satisfactory due diligence or arranging financing. However, in order to avoid false market concerns, it must be clear from the wording of any possible offer announcement whether or not the pre-conditions must be satisfied before an offer can be made or whether they are waivable (*see* the Note on Rule 2.4). If a pre-condition is not stated to be waivable, the potential offeror would not normally be permitted to make an offer unless the pre-condition was clearly satisfied.

In order to ensure that shareholders and the market are not confused as to whether a potential offeror is committed to proceed if the pre-conditions are satisified, a pre-conditional Rule 2.4 offer announcement should include a prominent warning to the effect that the announcement does not amount to a firm intention to make an offer and that, accordingly, there can be no certainty that any offer will be made even if the pre-conditions are satisfied or waived.

2.7.3 Disclosure in the offer announcement of side agreements relating to pre-conditions and conditions

In December 2001, the Code was amended to impose an obligation to disclose side agreements (whether formal or informal) relating to offer pre-conditions and conditions. When a firm intention to make an offer is announced, that announcement must include details of any agreements or arrangements to which the offeror is party which relate to the circumstances in which it may or may not invoke or seek to invoke a pre-condition or a condition to its offer and the consequences of its doing so, including details of any break fees payable as a result. This requirement has been incorporated as Rule 2.5(b)(vii), in addition to the existing requirements.

It should be noted that this obligation extends to agreements in relation to the acceptance condition, for example if a bidder undertakes to a lending bank that it will not declare the offer unconditional as to acceptances unless at least 75 per cent acceptances are achieved.

This obligation should not generally extend to a disclosure letter entered into between an offeror and an offeree where one or more of the conditions to the offer contains an explicit carve out for information disclosed in writing by the offeree to the offeror – although this should be confirmed with the Panel on a case-by-case basis.

The Panel stated that, in exceptional circumstances, it would be able to grant dispensation from this obligation in respect of documents which are commercially sensitive and/or do not have a bearing on the offer. Furthermore, in the context of regulatory side agreements, the Panel will have the ability to grant dispensation from the obligation of disclosure where the offeree and its advisers confirm in writing that disclosure would be likely to prejudice negotiations with the relevant regulatory authority to an extent which is material in the context of the offer.

Under the normal principles of the Code, parties are required to behave in a manner which is consistent with what has been publicly

The Approach, Announcements and Independent Advice

disclosed. However, the Panel has acknowledged that where parties had good commercial reasons to amend the terms of side agreements once they had been publicly disclosed, the Panel could grant them dispensation to do so.

2.7.4 Circulation of announcement

When an offer period commences, the offeree is required to circulate the relevant announcement to its shareholders. It also has to circulate the firm Rule 2.5 offer announcement. Also, both the offeror and the offeree have to make the Rule 2.5 announcement readily available to their employee representatives or, where there are no such representatives, to the employees themselves. This Rule also imposes a requirement on the offeror and offeree, where necessary, to explain the implications of the announcement. Following RS 2004/3, there is an additional requirement to include a summary of the provisions of Rule 8.

When the bid is hostile, this obligation on the offeree is often rather grudgingly discharged: a repudiatory letter from the offeree board dismissing the bid is accompanied by an Appendix with the detailed terms and conditions of the offer set out in tiny type designed to discourage all but the most persistent readers!

2.7.5 Consequences of announcement

Following an announcement of a firm intention to make an offer, the offeror must normally proceed with the offer unless, in accordance with the provisions of Rule 13, the offeror is permitted to invoke a pre-condition to the posting of the offer or would be permitted to invoke a condition to the offer if the offer were made. An exception to Rule 2.7 is that an offeror is released from the obligation to proceed if a competitor has already posted a higher offer or, with the consent of the Panel, if the offeree is about to embark on a transaction which would amount to a frustrating action within Rule 21 (*see* Chapter 7).

2.7.6 Announcement of numbers of relevant securities in issue

In July 2003 new Rule 2.10 was introduced which requires the offeree company, when an offer period begins, to announce, as soon as possible and in any case by 9.00am on the next business day, details of all classes of relevant securities issued by the offeree company, together with the numbers of such securities in issue. An offeror or potential offeror must also announce the same details relating to its relevant securities by 9.00am on the business day following any announcement identifying it as an offeror or potential offeror, unless it has stated that its offer is likely to be solely in cash. The announcement should include, where relevant, the International Securities Identification Number for each relevant security. If the information included in an announcement made under Rule 2.10 changes during the offer period, a revised announcement must be made as soon as possible. Note 1 on Rule 2.10 (introduced by Response Statement 2005/2) states that, for the purposes of that Rule, options to subscribe for new securities in the offeree company or an offeror are not to be treated as a class of relevant securities. Note 2 to Rule 2.10 makes it clear that only relevant securities which are held and in issue outside treasury should be included in the announcement.

The Panel explained in PCP 14 issued in April 2003 that there had been cases where a party had failed to comply with the dealing disclosure obligations in Rule 8 because it had been unaware either of the exact number of relevant securities in issue or that holdings or dealings in certain lines of stock were disclosable. The sources on which firms often rely for the relevant information were not always up to date or accurate and a company's issued share capital can alter frequently. Therefore the Panel considered it would be in the interests of the market generally for every company whose securities are subject to the dealing disclosure regime in Rule 8 to announce the exact number of the relevant securities in issue and keep the market updated of any subsequent changes.

2.8 Independent advice

2.8.1 *Offeree company*

Once the offeree board has been approached, it must obtain competent independent advice. The Panel has been at pains to stress the importance of the adviser's role in assisting the board in presenting its views, and in ensuring that full information, and the board's

The Approach, Announcements and Independent Advice

reasoned arguments, are circulated to shareholders. In its 2002 Annual Report, in reference to Rule 3.1 the Panel stated:

> "Financial advisers within groups which have an advisory relationship with an offeror are not normally regarded as appropriate persons to give advice to the offeree board on an offer. In this context, broking relationships with an offeror are considered in the same light as other types of advisory relationship. Whilst it is accepted that the strength and nature of broking relationships, and the services provided under them, vary widely, such relationships generally create a potential conflict of interest.
>
> In one or two recent cases, groups have assumed that a potential conflict of interest arising from an offeror broking relationship can be addressed satisfactorily by the broker standing down from its role for the duration of the offer. The Executive's view is that this action will not normally be sufficient to resolve concerns as to independence. Therefore, in cases where an offeree adviser's group has an offeror broking relationship, the Executive should be consulted at an early stage."

The notes to Rule 3.1 amplify the basic rule, and cover:

(a) management buyouts and offers by controlling shareholders (stressing the importance of the independence of the advice obtained in these circumstances);
(b) the situation where there is uncertainty about the financial information in the offeree's most recently published financial results – important factors must be highlighted by the board and the independent adviser; and
(c) the situation where either the board or the adviser is unable to form a view on, or to recommend, an offer. In these circumstances, the arguments in favour and against should be clearly set out.

Where there is a disagreement between the board and its advisers, shareholders should be informed, and the Panel consulted.

2.8.2 Offeror company

The offeror board is under a similar obligation to seek independent advice where the offer is a reverse takeover (i.e. where the offeror may need to increase its existing issued voting equity share capital by more than 100 per cent) or where the directors have a conflict of interest. Examples of a conflict of interest given in the notes to Rule 3.2 include significant cross-shareholdings between offeror and offeree, a common substantial shareholder or the existence of a number of common directors.

Advice obtained under Rule 3.2 should be obtained by the offeror board before the offer is made and should address the question of whether the offer is in the shareholders' interests. The offeror shareholders must be given sufficient time to consider this advice before any meeting is held at which a vote is to be taken on the offer.

2.8.3 The financial adviser

Rule 3.3 (and Appendix 3) reinforces the requirement that financial advice must be independent and, indeed, must be seen to be independent. If one part of a multi-service organisation acts for the offeror, another part of it will not usually be permitted to act for the offeree. In addition, those with a significant interest in, or financial connection with, either the offeror or offeree will normally be disqualified. For example, if the investment management arm of a bank advises an investment trust, the corporate finance arm will not normally be able to act for that trust in a bid as an independent Rule 3 adviser.

In its 1995 Annual Report, the Panel emphasised the importance of independent advice. In the Report, the Panel stated:

> "The Panel has always regarded it as of paramount importance that the adviser should be sufficiently independent so that its advice should be objective beyond question.
>
> A prospective adviser to an offeree company might not be considered sufficiently independent, for example, if it has had a recent advisory role with the offeror or has a very close advisory relationship with a large shareholder in the offeree company. The precise circumstances of every case will be different, links may be economic or advisory and sometimes quite a fine judgement will have to be made. The views of the offeree company's

The Approach, Announcements and Independent Advice

board will always be an important factor. The Panel strongly recommends early consultation with the Executive in any case where the independence of an adviser could be in doubt."

This is echoed in Note 1 to Rule 3.3. An example of the application of this Note 1 was the role of Dresdner Kleinwort Benson in relation to the offer by Abbey National for Cater Allen (as reflected in Panel Statement 1997/9). In that case, the Panel upheld a ruling by the Executive that Dresdner Kleinwort Benson would not be an appropriate person under Note 1 on Rule 3.3 to give independent advice to Cater Allen in relation to the recommended offer by Abbey National. This was due to Kleinwort Benson's "close, recent and continuing" advisory relationship with Abbey National; Kleinworts had been one of Abbey's advisers since flotation. The Panel emphasised the importance of the adviser not only being, but being viewed objectively as being, independent. Cater Allen therefore had to appoint another adviser to give advice under Rule 3.1.

A further example of the importance the Panel ascribes to the independence of Rule 3 financial advisers is given in Panel Statements 2002/18 and 2002/20 on the role of Corporate Synergy in a circular issued by Alexanders Holdings (now renamed Quays Group, "Alexanders") to its shareholders seeking, among other matters, approval for the waiver by the Panel of the obligation under Rule 9 of the Code that would have otherwise have arisen for Orb Estates to make a general offer for Alexanders. Following investigation into a complaint made by a shareholder in Alexanders, the Executive concluded that Alexanders' financial adviser, Corporate Synergy, was not sufficiently independent from Orb Estates to provide independent advice to the Alexanders board and must therefore step down as the Rule 3 adviser to Alexanders for the purposes of the transaction. Corporate Synergy had recently acted as adviser to Orb Estates in connection with another transaction. The Executive further advised that if the transaction was to proceed, a new independent adviser must be appointed and a further circular sent to Alexanders' shareholders. The Panel also criticised Corporate Synergy for failing to adequately consult the Executive in relation to the issue of its own independence.

Appendix 3 also deals with the problem of conflicts of interest and "material confidential information", particularly where the financial adviser has previously advised one of the other parties to the bid. This arose specifically out of the difficulties which ensued on the TKM bid for Molins, which were dealt with in the Panel Statement of 30 June 1987. The conclusion is that conflicts of interest cannot necessarily be resolved by the creation of internal Chinese walls.

The Panel has also considered whether the nature of a financial adviser's fee arrangements may give rise to a conflict of interest that would prevent it from acting as a Rule 3 adviser. On 16 July 1999 the Panel stated:

> "Arrangements which reward an adviser to the offeree dependent on failure of a hostile offer, irrespective of the offer price, give rise to, or create the perception of, an actual or potential conflict of interest. In these circumstances, the adviser will normally be disqualified from acting as independent Rule 3 adviser. Similar considerations will apply to any fee payable on failure of an offer below an unrealistically high price. The Executive should be consulted in any case of doubt. The Panel may in appropriate cases require disclosure in the offer documentation to enable the arrangements to be subjected to public scrutiny."

This followed the takeover by the Great Universal Stores of Argos. A new Note 3 on Rule 3.3 was introduced into the Code in July 2000 implementing this statement and requiring consultation with the Panel where fee arrangements might be such as to create a conflict of interest. The note does not explicitly require a success fee to be disclosed, as was envisaged in the statement.

A frequent question is whether a bank which has a loan relationship with a bidder can also act as Rule 3 adviser to the target. This would have to be cleared with the Panel who should allow it, provided the bank is not providing the finance for the offer itself.

Chapter 3

Share Dealings – Restrictions and Disclosure Requirements

Andy Ryde and Roland Turnill
Partners
Slaughter and May

3.1 Introduction

This Chapter is principally concerned with the Rules of the City Code on Takeovers and Mergers (the "Code") which restrict, or which require the disclosure of, dealings in shares before and during a takeover bid. However, other relevant regulations will also be considered such as the Companies Act 1985 (as amended) (the "Companies Act"), the Criminal Justice Act 1993 (the "CJA 1993") and the Financial Services and Markets Act 2000 ("FSMA").

It will be apparent from the above list of regulations that one of the principal concerns in the takeovers field is to ensure that all the different sets of rules which apply to the transaction in hand have been identified and, where they overlap, to ensure that due consideration is given to each. Steps taken with one set of regulations in mind may have adverse consequences under another and a balance may have to be struck. Furthermore, not all rules are absolute in their application; in particular, the rules set out in the Code are not strictly construed and, even where their meaning appears clear, may be relaxed or perhaps even extended in particular circumstances. How such rules may be applied is often a matter of judgement based on experience but discussions with the Panel on Takeovers and Mergers (the "Panel") on points of difficulty will be a regular feature of major transactions.

Three sets of regulations not addressed in detail in this Chapter (although there are references where appropriate) are the Listing Rules, Disclosure Rules and Prospectus Rules (collectively, the

"Listing Regime") of the Financial Services Authority (the "FSA"). This is on the basis that the Listing Regime is not normally directly relevant to dealings in shares during a takeover bid. However, it should be borne in mind that it may be relevant in certain circumstances (particularly those rules relating to the announcement of, or the obtaining of shareholder consent for, significant transactions and limiting the scope of indemnities which a listed company can give to third parties buying shares on its behalf).

An added complication are the recent amendments made to the Code. In 2004 and 2005 the Code Committee of the Panel (the "Code Committee") issued a number of consultation papers proposing changes to the Code to reflect the increasing amount of dealing in derivatives and options and the introduction of the European Directive on Takeover Bids (Directive 2004/25/EC) (the "Takeover Directive"). These consultations resulted in a number of changes being made to the Code in November 2005 and May 2006 and this Chapter seeks to explain those changes and their effect in practice (so far as they are relevant to dealings in shares). One area of the Code Committee's consultation process that has resulted in significant changes being made is in respect of the Rules Governing Substantial Acquisitions of Shares (the "SARs"). As will be explained, the Code Committee has abolished the SARs, with the exception of SAR 4 relating to tender offers.

3.1.1 The Takeover Directive

Following many years of debate, the Takeover Directive was published on 21 April 2004 and entered into force on 20 May 2004. It was implemented in the UK on 20 May 2006 (the deadline set out in the Directive) by the Takeovers Directive (Interim Implementation) Regulations 2006 (the "Takeover Regulations"). As their name implies, the Takeover Regulations are an interim measure designed to ensure the timely implementation of the Takeover Directive in the UK. They will be superseded by Part 22 of the Company Law Reform Bill ("CLR Bill") (probably in early 2007). The Takeover Regulations implement those provisions of the Takeover Directive that must be implemented by Member States, whereas the CLR Bill contains not only those provisions but also further provisions to be implemented following the Company Law Review consultation process.

Implementation of the Takeover Directive was preceded by a lengthy DTI and Panel public consultation process designed to ensure that the Code complies with the terms of the Takeover Directive.

To a large extent, the Panel's modus operandi and its day-to-day relationship with the regulated community has been largely unaffected by implementation of the Takeover Regulations. While there has been little practical change, changes have been made to the statutory framework within which the Panel operates, to the Panel structure, to its powers and sanctions and to the Code's General Principles. The amendments, and amendments made to the Companies Act as a result of the Takeover Directive, as far as they are relevant to share dealings and disclosure requirements, are outlined below.

3.2 Applicability of the rules

The first question to be addressed in this area is: in what circumstances do the particular regulations apply, if at all? We are not only concerned here with the type of transaction to which each set of regulations can apply but also with the level of stake in the target company at which a particular set of rules becomes significant. These levels are described in the following paragraphs.

3.2.1 The Code

Broadly speaking, the Code applies to offers for all companies (and Societas Europaea) which have their registered offices in the UK, the Channel Islands or the Isle of Man and have securities which are (or, in certain cases, have been) traded on a regulated market in the UK. It also applies to public companies (such as AIM-listed companies) which do not have securities traded on a regulated market but which are considered by the Panel to be resident in the UK, the Channel Islands or the Isle of Man.

As will already be apparent, one of the main functions of the Code is to regulate changes of "control" in the companies to which it applies: thus, the Code is not generally applicable to offers relating only to non-voting or non-equity capital (except offers under Rule 15), but it does cover transactions, not amounting to full takeover offers, in which "control" is obtained or consolidated. "Control" for Code purposes is deemed to be exercised by those with an interest in 30 per cent or more of the voting rights (*see* "Definitions" Section of the Code) in the target either alone or as part of a "concert party" (*see* Section 3.3.3 below). The concept of having an "interest" in securities has been broadened to include options and derivatives in which the relevant party has a long position. It should be noted that all percentages of voting rights, share capital and "relevant securities" in the Code should be calculated by reference to the relevant percentage held and in issue outside of treasury (*see* the definition of "treasury shares" in the "Definitions" Section of the Code).

The Rules of the Code of most relevance to dealings in shares which might result in "control" being obtained or consolidated are Rules 5 and 9. Rule 5 has the effect of prohibiting the acquisition by a person and its concert parties of interests in shares carrying 30 per cent or more of the voting rights of a company or, where a person and its concert parties are already interested in shares carrying between 30 per cent and 50 per cent of the voting rights, the acquisition of an interest in any other shares carrying such voting rights.

There are certain exemptions to the prohibition in Rule 5. If an acquisition of shares is made under one of the exemptions, it will almost always be necessary for the acquiror to make a general offer to acquire all remaining shares in the company, for cash or with a cash alternative, at the highest price paid by it or its concert parties during the 12 months prior to the announcement of the offer (Rule 9). This has the effect both of allowing shareholders the chance of an exit from a company in which "control" has changed and of ensuring that all shareholders are able to benefit from any control premium paid by the acquiror in reaching the 30 per cent threshold.

Even where the acquiror does not trigger the 30 per cent threshold but voluntarily launches a takeover offer, it will be required by the Code to make its offer on no less favourable terms than the highest price paid by it for target shares during the previous three months. This, again, aims to ensure equality of treatment for shareholders by allowing them to participate in any premium paid in acquiring the initial stake.

Share Dealings – Restrictions and Disclosure Requirements

The Code also contains detailed rules concerning the disclosure of dealings during the offer period. These rules are not restricted to dealings by the parties to the offer. For example, if a person is directly or indirectly interested in one per cent or more of any class of relevant securities of the target or offeror, he must generally disclose his dealings during the offer period (Rule 8.3(a)).

3.2.2 SARs

The Code Committee's response paper RS 2005/4 'Abolition of the SARs' makes it clear that the Code Committee believes that it is no longer appropriate for the Panel to restrict the speed at which a person may acquire shares (or interests in shares), and thereby the ability of shareholders to sell their shares, in circumstances where control of a company is not being acquired or consolidated.

The SARs were originally designed to counter a rash of "dawn raids" and their primary purpose was to control the build-up of substantial stakes in a target company by slowing down the rate at which stakes were acquired, thereby allowing small shareholders the chance to participate in any premium which was payable in connection with the establishment of a large holding. They also allowed the management of the target company to consider the position in the interests of shareholders and take appropriate action.

However, the Code Committee believes that such a prohibition does not continue to serve a useful function and, with one exception, has abolished the SARs. The exception is that SAR 4 relating to tender offers has been retained in a new Appendix 5 to the Code.

It will be interesting to see whether the abolition of the SARs heralds the return of the "dawn raid" as a stakebuilding tactic.

3.2.3 Companies Act

The Companies Act will be relevant in a variety of circumstances. The acquisition of any shares in a UK-incorporated public company may lead to an obligation to disclose, at the request of that company, whether the acquiror is, or has within the previous three years been, interested in its shares, along with certain other details (Sections

212(1) and (2)). Where the holding of a person, or a group of persons acting in concert, reaches 3 per cent in nominal value of the voting shares in a public company, then a duty to notify the company of this fact generally arises (Sections 198–210). Certain subsequent dealings in voting shares will also be subject to disclosure.

The Companies Act contains powers compulsorily to purchase minority shareholdings once an offer for shares in the target has been accepted by holders of 90 per cent of the shares of the relevant class to which the offer relates, excluding any shares in the company held as treasury shares. Hence, any shareholder with a holding of more than one-tenth of the shares to which an offer relates is able to thwart the operation of this mechanism and remain an unwanted minority holder. Note that, for offers made on or after 20 May 2006, Schedule 2 of the Takeover Regulations has replaced the Companies Act provisions in relation to squeeze-out – the relevant provisions of the Takeover Regulations are discussed in 3.4.3 below.

Finally, as became apparent in the aftermath of the takeover by Guinness of the Distillers Company, the provisions of the Companies Act (Section 151 *et seq.*) restricting the giving by a company of financial assistance in connection with the purchase of its own shares may be in point, not only in connection with any purchase of shares in a target, but also in relation to indemnities given by offerors in connection with various aspects of share-for-share offers.

3.2.4 CJA 1993 and FSMA

Part V CJA 1993 applies to dealings in shares on regulated markets, including the London Stock Exchange, regardless of the place of incorporation or residence of the company whose shares are being transferred. Its primary purpose is to prohibit certain dealings by, and activities of, persons who have inside information. In particular, when in possession of inside information, it is an offence not only to deal or to "encourage" others – such as corporate employees or clients – to deal, but also to disclose the information other than in proper performance of the functions of an employment, office or profession.

FSMA, which, so far as relevant, came into force on 1 December 2001, controls the manner in which securities may be offered and admitted to listing on the Official List (in addition to regulating "investment business" in the UK). It also contains provisions relevant to all takeovers, such as restrictions on financial promotions (Section 21) and provision for an offence relating to misleading statements or courses of conduct (Section 397).

In addition, FSMA introduced a statutory regime for the control of market abuse. This regime was amended on 1 July 2005 by the implementation of the Market Abuse Directive.

These provisions result in a considerable potential overlap between the jurisdiction of the FSA and the Panel. In light of this, the FSA and the Panel have agreed a set of operating guidelines which are intended, *inter alia*, to assist in determining how each of them should exercise its functions in cases of jurisdictional overlap. The operating guidelines provide that where, during a takeover bid, matters arise which may amount to market misconduct, the FSA will not exercise its powers during the bid save in exceptional circumstances (*see* Section 3.4.2.5 below). As explained further in Section 3.4.2.5 below, it is expected that the Operating Guidelines may be amended in light of the implementation of the Takeover Directive, though this has not happened yet.

Finally, it will always be necessary to consider whether law and regulation in other jurisdictions is relevant to share dealings in a takeover. Particular care will need to be taken where securities are listed on more than one market to ensure that the requirements of each stock exchange (which may conflict) are complied with.

3.3 Fundamental concepts

Before turning to a detailed examination of the applicable law and regulation, we should perhaps clarify the meanings of certain fundamental concepts.

3.3.1 *Interests in securities*

When considering interests in shares or relevant securities under the Code, the focus has historically been on direct holdings of shares or relevant securities and restrictions have been applied to persons "purchasing securities". However, in recent years much market activity has moved from the cash to the derivative market and developments in market practice mean that persons with long derivative or option positions may exercise significant de facto control over the underlying securities.

In the case of a long contract for differences ("CFD"), the counterparty with whom the CFD holder takes out the contract will typically hedge its exposure by acquiring the shares which underly the CFD. The counterparty will also often agree (sometimes informally) to exercise the voting rights attaching to these shares in accordance with the wishes of the CFD holder. Therefore, while the holder of a CFD will not appear on the register of shareholders of the company in question, it may be able to control the exercise of votes in respect of a significant proportion of its shares. Furthermore, the terms of the CFD may enable the CFD holder to receive the underlying shares acquired by the counterparty in settlement of the CFD.

For example, in the case of BAE Systems' offer for Alvis during 2004, BAE Systems obtained irrevocable commitments from a number of funds which had entered into CFDs referenced to shares representing approximately 16 per cent of the issued share capital of Alvis. Some of these funds entered into commitments with BAE Systems to "request physical settlement of the CFDs in accordance with market practice . . . and then to assent to the offer all shares received by them as a result of this physical settlement process". Other CFD holders who did not give such a commitment to BAE Systems expressly consented to the counterparty with whom they had entered into a CFD giving BAE Systems a standard irrevocable commitment to accept the offer in respect of the Alvis shares held by it as a hedge against its position under the relevant CFD.

Similarly, in the same year a number of funds entered into long CFDs referenced to shares in Marks and Spencer during the period of Revival Acquisitions' interest in the company. These funds sought to put pressure on the board of Marks and Spencer to grant Revival Acquisitions access to carry out due diligence. The funds were aware that their statements of support would be made public and their intention was to influence the debate on whether due diligence access should be granted.

As a result of these developments, the Code Committee issued two Consultation Papers on dealings in derivatives and options and, on 5 August 2005, Response Statement RS 2005/2 was issued. This consultation process led to a number of changes to the Code to ensure that it covers all relevant interests and not just traditional holdings of shares or other securities.

The changes to the Code are not just applicable to CFDs but also to other types of derivatives, such as spread bets. Similarly, they are also applicable to dealings in options because, despite the differences between options and derivatives, counterparties to options may also hedge their exposure by acquiring the shares underlying the option and persons holding call options may obtain a measure of de facto control over shares in a similar way to holders of long CFDs.

To implement these changes, the Code Committee created a new definition of "interests in securities" to include the holders of certain options and derivatives as well as the holders of legal title to the shares. A person will be treated as having an "interest in securities" where he owns them; has the right (whether conditional or absolute) to exercise or direct the exercise of voting rights attaching to them (or has general control of them); where, pursuant to an agreement to purchase, option or derivative, he is obliged to take delivery of them or has the right or option to acquire them or call for their delivery (whether such right, option or obligation is conditional or absolute); or where he is party to a derivative whose value is determined by their price and which results, or may result, in his having a long position in them. Consequently, the Rules of the Code now refer to "the acquisition of interests in securities", rather than the old formulation of "purchasing securities".

It should be noted that a person with a short position in securities will not be treated as interested in them and will therefore not be subject to a disclosure obligation, although the Code Committee has stated that it will keep this point under review.

In summary, the changes mean that derivatives and options are treated in much the same way as holdings of shares. Therefore, persons with a long position in derivatives referenced to, or options in respect of, one per cent or more of the shares of a target company (or, if appropriate, an offeror company) are required to disclose all dealings in relevant securities of the company concerned (regardless of whether any underlying shares are held). Similarly, dealings in derivatives and options by parties to an offer and persons whose interests in the shares of a company fall into the 30 per cent to 50 per cent band should be treated under the Code in the same way as dealings in the underlying shares. When used in this Chapter in the context of the Code, "interests in securities" has the meaning given in the "Definitions" section of the Code.

3.3.2 Dealings

The November 2005 amendments to the Code also included a new definition of "dealings" to ensure that the provisions of the Code which require disclosure of dealings pick up all relevant transactions (including those involving derivatives and options). The definition of "dealings" under the Code now covers any action which results in an increase or decrease in the number of securities in which a person is interested or in respect of which he has a short position. When used in this Chapter in the context of the Code, "dealings" has the meaning given in the "Definitions" section of the Code.

3.3.3 Concert parties

The term "concert parties", which used to describe gatherings at the end of the pier in seaside resorts, was adopted by the Panel in the early days of the Code to describe associated parties acting together. For most purposes under the Code and for disclosure purposes under the Companies Act, the holdings or acquisitions of shares in a target company by parties "acting in concert" are aggregated. The concert party concept is defined and expressed in different ways in the Code and the Companies Act – but in each case concert parties are capable of being constituted even where there is no formal concert party agreement.

For Code purposes, a concert party is a combination of persons who cooperate to achieve or consolidate "control" of the target or to frustrate the successful outcome of a bid (*see* "Definitions" Section of the Code). The Code definition of a concert party has been amended in light of the requirements of the Takeover Directive. It no longer

Share Dealings – Restrictions and Disclosure Requirements

requires active cooperation between the parties, it is not limited to parties cooperating through the acquisition of shares by any of them and it includes persons who cooperate with the target company with a view to frustrating the successful outcome of a bid. It is the Panel's view (see Panel Statement 2005/10) that the first two of these changes brings the definition into line with the Panel's existing practice under which it could rule that parties were acting in concert despite the fact that, at the relevant time, they were not actively engaged in the acquisition of shares. The consequences of these changes will only bite under Rules 6, 9 and 11 when any of the relevant parties do acquire shares.

Furthermore (and also as a consequence of the implementation of the Takeover Directive), a person and each of its "affiliated persons" will be deemed to be acting in concert with each other. An "affiliated person" is defined as any undertaking in respect of which any person (a) has a majority of the shareholders' or members' voting rights; (b) is a shareholder or member and has the right to appoint or remove a majority of its board; (c) is a shareholder or member and alone controls a majority of the shareholders' or members' voting rights pursuant to an agreement with other shareholders or members; or (d) has the power to exercise, or actually exercises, dominant influence or control.

The Code also provides that certain persons, including holding companies, sister subsidiaries, 20 per cent-owned associated companies, directors, connected advisers, pension funds and the pension funds of associated companies are presumed to be acting in concert with a company unless the contrary is established. Likewise, investors in a bidding consortium are presumed to be acting in concert with the offeror and, if they are part of a larger organisation, the Panel should be consulted to establish which other parts of the organisation will also be regarded as acting in concert.

The notes to the definition of "acting in concert" give additional guidance as to how the term is understood by the Panel. In relation to other parts of a financial services organisation of which a consortium investor is part, for example, the Panel will consider waiving the presumption if the investment in the consortium amounts to less than

50 per cent of the share capital of the offeror. The Panel will normally waive the presumption in relation to other parts of the organisation if the investment in the consortium is 10 per cent or less (Note 6 on the definition of "acting in concert"). Similarly, the Panel will normally regard the presumption of concertedness between a company and its pension fund as having been rebutted if an independent third party has absolute discretion regarding dealing, voting and offer acceptance conditions relating to the fund (Note 7 on the definition of "acting in concert").

The presumption that advisers will act in concert with their clients (presumption 5 of the definition of "acting in concert") was considered in the case of Songbird Acquisition Limited's bid for Canary Wharf Group plc (*see* Panel Statement 2004/12). In its statement of 23 April 2004, the Panel made it clear that the presumption does not only apply to advisers who have been engaged to act on the offer or on a transaction related to the offer; other advisers which have a relationship with the offeror or target company (or a concert party thereof) will also be presumed to be acting in concert with that party. The presumption can, however, be rebutted (as it in fact was in the Canary Wharf case). The question of whether or not the presumption should be rebutted is determined by the Panel, taking into account all relevant factors including whether the adviser is named in the company's annual report and accounts, and whether the adviser has stood down or offered to do so, and if so why.

A new note has also been added to the definition of acting in concert, as part of the amendments referred to above, to clarify the position regarding persons giving irrevocable undertakings. It confirms that a person will not normally be treated as acting in concert with an offeror or target company by reason only of giving an irrevocable commitment, but states that the Panel will consider the position of such a person in order to determine whether he is acting in concert if either: (a) the terms of the irrevocable commitment give the offeror or target company either the right (whether conditional or absolute) to exercise or direct the exercise of the voting rights attaching to the shares or general control of them; or (b) the person acquires an interest in more shares. It therefore provides that the Panel should be consulted before the acquisition of any further interest in shares in such circumstances.

In addition to the definition and the notes which follow it, there are a number of other provisions of the Code which are relevant to understanding the concept of "acting in concert". These provisions include, notably, the Notes on Rule 9.1 (*see* further Section 3.4.4.4 below).

Note 2 on Rule 9.1 provides that the Panel will normally presume that shareholders who make or threaten to make a "board control-seeking proposal" at any general meeting of a company are acting in concert with each other and with the proposed directors. Parties will be presumed to be acting in concert from the time that an agreement or understanding between them is reached so any purchase of the company's shares by any of them thereafter could give rise to a mandatory offer obligation.

Similarly, Note 5 on Rule 9.1 provides that the Panel must be consulted before the acquisition of an interest in shares where:

(a) the aggregate number of shares in which the directors, any other persons acting, or presumed to be acting, in concert with the directors and the trustees of an employee benefit trust ("EBT") are interested will carry 30 per cent or more of the voting rights (or, if already carrying 30 per cent or more, will increase further) as a result of the acquisition; or

(b) a person or group of persons acting, or presumed to be acting, in concert is interested in shares carrying 30 per cent or more (but does not hold shares carrying more than 50 per cent) of the voting rights and it is proposed that an EBT acquires an interest in any other shares.

The Note states that the Panel will consider "all relevant factors" in concluding whether the trustees of an EBT are acting in concert with the directors and/or a controller or group of persons acting, or presumed to be acting, in concert. The Note contains a non-exhaustive list of factors which will be taken into account.

For the purposes of Rule 9.1, the Panel has traditionally treated a group of persons acting in concert as a single person. Usually, therefore, the person responsible for making the mandatory offer (the person whose acquisition triggered the mandatory bid) will extend it to shareholders outside the concert party but not to members of the concert party itself. Following the Panel's Annual Report for 2002/3, however, the person responsible for making the offer may extend it to other concert party members if it wishes, although he is under no obligation to do so.

Similarly, the Companies Act treats persons as acting together in a less formal manner than the normal, strict legal meaning of contractual agreement; for instance, Section 204 treats two or more persons as one (for some purposes) where there exists any "agreement or arrangement" between them for the acquisition of shares; it makes it clear that these words include a non-legally binding agreement or arrangement, provided that there is mutuality of undertakings, expectations or understandings and provided the agreement or arrangement contains obligations as to the retention, use or disposal of the relevant shares.

3.3.4 Associates

Another recurrent concept is that of "associates". Holdings of "associates" are of particular relevance to the disclosure requirements of the Code – dealings by associates in relevant securities must generally be disclosed in the same way as those of the offeror and target (Rule 8.1). The term "associates" includes anyone who may have an interest or potential interest (whether commercial, financial or personal) in the outcome of an offer and who directly or indirectly is interested or deals in relevant securities of the offeror or target (*see* "Definitions" Section of the Code). Normally, companies in the same group, associated companies, companies' pension funds, connected advisers, persons controlling, controlled by or under the same control as connected advisers, directors, employee benefit trusts and persons with material trading arrangements with the parties to a bid are all regarded as "associates", whether or not they are or are deemed to be acting in concert with either party.

Under the compulsory acquisition provisions in Schedule 2 of the Takeover Regulations, shares held by the offeror and its associates prior to the offer being made do not count towards achieving the 90 per cent acceptance threshold: they are excluded from both the numerator and denominator of the fraction. In this context "associate" is more tightly defined than under the Code (Schedule 2, paragraph

8(5)); it includes companies in the same group (*see* Section 736), companies controlled de facto by the offeror (the term used in paragraph 8(5)(c) is "substantially interested", but for the meaning of this *see* paragraph 8(7)(a) and (b)) as well as Companies Act Section 204 concert parties of the offeror.

3.4 Restrictions on the freedom to deal

Turning to detailed rules, we will first deal with the rules which apply in the context of a takeover to prohibit or restrict share dealings.

3.4.1 *Statutory prohibitions or restrictions on dealings*

3.4.1.1 CJA 1993
Part V CJA 1993 came into force on 1 March 1994 and was designed to bring English law into line with the EC Insider Dealing Directive (89/592/EEC). The Act renders it an offence for an individual to:

(a) deal in price-affected securities if he has inside information relating thereto which he holds as an "insider" (i.e. by virtue of his directorship, employment, shareholding, office or profession or which he has obtained from an inside source) (Section 52(1));
(b) encourage any other person (which would include a company) to deal in securities which he himself is prohibited from dealing in (Section 52(2)(a)); or
(c) disclose the inside information to another person other than in the proper performance of the functions of his employment, office or profession (Section 52(2)(b)).

It should be noted that, as referred to above, these offences can only be committed by *individuals* (and not by companies). However, the scope of the offence provided for in Section 52(1) extends to catch individuals who procure dealings by other persons, including companies (Section 55).

3.4.1.2 *Relationship with FSMA*
There are certain aspects of the insider dealing prohibition provided for in CJA 1993 which are similar in application and scope to the FSMA market abuse regime. Market abuse is addressed further in Section 3.4.2.2 below.

3.4.1.3 Contravention

A contravention of Part V CJA 1993 results in exposure to the risk of a fine or imprisonment under Section 61(1). However, Section 63(2) makes it clear that no contract is void or unenforceable merely because it is made in contravention of the Act.

3.4.1.4 Consequences for takeovers

The insider dealing legislation will normally have the effect of preventing share dealing in price-affected securities by a potential offeror who, as part of pre-bid due diligence, has been given price-sensitive information by the target. This is because the *individuals* in receipt of the price-sensitive information are likely to be taken to have procured or encouraged any such dealings in contravention of Section 52(1) or Section 52(2)(a). Similarly, such individuals, the directors of the offeror and others in the know will be prohibited from dealing in price-affected securities on their own account and, even in the absence of receipt of confidential information, they will be prevented from dealing on their own account by their knowledge that a bid is in contemplation.

However, most of the prohibitions in the Act do not apply where the only relevant inside information is that the acquiring party is contemplating a takeover offer and the dealings are made to facilitate the offer – the "market information" defence (Section 53(4), paragraph 3, Schedule 1, Part V CJA 1993). It is, therefore, not an offence for directors or employees of a potential offeror to procure purchases of the shares of a target by the offeror or others in the knowledge that a full scale bid is in contemplation, if the dealing is to facilitate the completion or carrying out of the bid, provided they have no other relevant inside information.

It is important to consider the implications of undertaking due diligence prior to the announcement of an offer, as this may affect the availability of the market information defence. Even where pre-bid due diligence is proposed, it may be possible to avoid insider dealing concerns by setting up a Chinese wall arrangement within the financial adviser to the offeror. Under such an arrangement, information provided by the target would be vetted for price-sensitivity by employees of the offeror's financial adviser who were not engaged in providing advice to the offeror. Only information which was not price-sensitive would be passed to the offeror and the offeror's advisory team. It is worth noting that, for CJA 1993 purposes, there is no reason why the Chinese wall arrangement should not be set up within the offeror rather than within its financial adviser. However, this would give rise to market abuse concerns under FSMA (as a result of the fact that both companies and individuals can commit market abuse) (*see* further Section 3.4.2.2 below).

In general, CJA 1993 should not normally inhibit purchases of target shares following an announcement of a bid. This is because, if the bid is hostile, then the offeror is unlikely to have received confidential information and, if recommended, it is unlikely that any information will remain price-sensitive following announcement of the bid, since the target will have taken all information into account in recommending the offer. This point is not, however, beyond doubt and the offeror will need to be satisfied that there is no expectation of profit attributable to the price-sensitive information, because the information is reflected in the offer price.

3.4.1.5 *Appointment of investigating inspectors*
Section 168 FSMA confers power on the Secretary of State and the FSA to appoint inspectors to investigate whether any offence under Part V CJA 1993 has been committed. Section 177 then lays down penalties for refusal to comply with these investigations. Although a refusal to answer any questions put by the inspectors will entitle the inspectors to bring the case before the court, the court may only punish a reluctant interviewee if it is satisfied that he has acted without reasonable excuse in refusing to reply.

3.4.1.6 *Contracts for differences – no longer a loophole*
It is no longer possible to offset the expenses of a bid by the use of cash-settled derivatives contracts (including CFDs) linked to the share price of the target or the share prices of companies in the same business sector as the target. Such contracts were controversially used in the bid by Trafalgar House for Northern Electric. Trafalgar House effectively bet that the share price of a number of electricity distribution companies (including Northern Electric) would rise as a result of its offer by striking a series of CFDs with its investment bank, Swiss Bank Corporation. After consultation with the Panel (which had initially concluded that Trafalgar House's strategy was legitimate),

the Securities and Investment Board (now the FSA) effectively prohibited the use of derivative contracts for the purpose of offsetting the expenses of a bid by issuing a guidance document in December 1996 (under Section 206 Financial Services Act 1986) which stated that such contracts should not be entered into on the basis of inside information (including information that a bid may be made) where they would provide only a cash benefit and would not constitute a step towards the accomplishment of the takeover. The guidance reflected legal advice received by the Securities and Investment Board to the effect that cash-settled derivatives do not facilitate the accomplishment of takeovers and that the parties to them cannot therefore rely on the CJA 1993 "market information" defence. Although the Securities and Investment Board guidance no longer has any statutory underpinning (the Financial Services Act 1986 having been repealed in its entirety by FSMA) it is nevertheless still considered to reflect best practice and to be an accurate statement of the law. The Code of Market Conduct (made under Section 119(1) FSMA) reinforces the position by stating that an example of market abuse would be "an offeror or potential offeror entering into a transaction in a qualifying investment, on the basis of inside information concerning the proposed bid, that provides merely an economic exposure to movements in the price of the target company's shares (for example, a spread bet on the target company's share price)" (MAR 1.3.2(2)(E)).

It should be noted, however, that neither CJA 1993 nor the Securities and Investment Board's guidance (nor, indeed, the FSMA market abuse regime) has the effect of completely prohibiting the use of derivative contracts in the context of takeovers (particularly where such contracts are capable of physical settlement). Indeed, there have been a number of recent examples of their use or attempted use as part of pre-bid stake-building efforts. As will be evident, however, the legal and regulatory consequences of their use are not wholly straightforward.

3.4.2 FSMA

3.4.2.1 Section 397 – Misleading statements and practices
Section 397(3) FSMA may be particularly significant in the context of takeovers. It makes it an offence to do any act or engage in a course of conduct which creates a false or misleading impression as to the

market value of any investments if this is done for the purpose of creating that impression and of thereby inducing a person to deal, or refrain from dealing, in those investments. It is a defence under Section 397(5) to show that a person reasonably believed his act or conduct would not create a false or misleading impression.

If associates of a target purchase shares as a defensive tactic against a dawn raid, the clear aim is to create a misleading impression as to the value of the target's shares. However, it seems (at least, it is the DTI's view) that if all relevant facts are disclosed, no such impression will be created. Hence, if the associate puts his motives on the screen at the time of his bid for the stock, it seems that no offence would be committed. Of course, this suggested course is unlikely to arouse much enthusiasm among the broking community and, if he immediately discloses his dealing under Rule 8 of the Code (*see* Section 3.5.2.1 below), probably there is little risk of prosecution. The position would be similar in respect of agreements with the target to sell its shares.

Liability may also be incurred by the offeror and its associates. Purchases of the offeror's shares by associates in takeovers where the consideration includes shares in the offeror could amount to a breach of Section 397(3). Much will depend upon the purpose of such acquisition: if it is genuinely for a long-term investment, it is hard to see how the section is contravened; but if the main purpose is merely to inflate the value of the offeror's share price, there may be a breach. A share support operation, of the type carried out on the Guinness bid for Distillers, would therefore be a criminal offence under Section 397(3) (at the time of these events the relevant statutory provision was Section 13(1)(a)(i) of the Prevention of Fraud (Investments) Act 1958).

Further criminal liability may be incurred if purchases of offeror shares are carried out by an associate with the benefit of an indemnity from the offeror as this may also involve unlawful financial assistance by the offeror for the purpose of the acquisition of its own shares, which is an offence under Section 151 of the Companies Act. In this area it should be noted that, if a false market in any listed securities arises, then the relevant listed company must consider whether it is required by the Disclosure Rules and/or the Listing Rules to release information to the public. Where a company is under such an obligation, a failure to comply with it can, arguably, amount to a course of conduct for Section 397 purposes.

3.4.2.2 The Market Abuse Regime

The general impact of Directive 2003/6/EC of 28 January 2003 on insider dealing and market manipulation (and certain secondary legislation adopted under it) is outside the scope of this Chapter. However, the Financial Services and Markets Act 2000 (Market Abuse) Regulations 2005 (the "Regulations"), which implement certain provisions of the Directive and came into force on 1 July 2005, made considerable changes to the statutory market abuse regime put in place under FSMA.

3.4.2.2.1 Categories of abusive behaviour

The Regulations replaced the old Section 118 FSMA with a new Section 118. Instead of the three categories of abusive behaviour which used to exist (misuse of information, misleading conduct and market distortion) there are now seven categories, which cover similar ground but which set out more precise descriptions of the behaviour that is prohibited. These categories are:

(a) an insider deals or attempts to deal in a qualifying investment or related investment on the basis of inside information relating to the investment in question;

(b) an insider discloses inside information to another person otherwise than in the proper course of the exercise of his employment, profession or duties;

(c) behaviour (not falling within (a) or (b) above) which:

  (i) is based on information which is not generally available to those using the market, but which, if available to a regular user of the market would be or would be likely to be regarded by him as relevant when deciding the terms on which transactions in qualifying investments should be effected; and

  (ii) is likely to be regarded by a regular user of the market as a failure on the part of the person concerned to observe the standard of behaviour reasonably expected of a person in his position in relation to the market;

(d) the behaviour consists of effecting transactions or orders to trade (other than for legitimate reasons and in accordance with accepted market practices) which:

    (i) give or are likely to give a false or misleading impression as to the supply of or demand for, or as to the price of, one or more qualifying investments; or

    (ii) secure the price of one or more such investments at an abnormal or artificial level;

(e) the behaviour consists of effecting transactions or orders to trade which employ fictitious devices or any other form of deception or contrivance;

(f) the behaviour consists of the dissemination of information by any means which gives or is likely to give a false or misleading impression as to a qualifying investment by a person who knew or could reasonably be expected to have known that the information was false or misleading; and

(g) the behaviour (not falling within (d), (e) or (f) above):

    (i) is likely to give a regular user of the market a false impression as to the supply of, demand for or price or value of qualifying investments; or

    (ii) would be or would be likely to be regarded by a regular user of the market as behaviour that would distort or would be likely to distort the market in such an investment

and the behaviour is likely to be regarded by a regular user of the market as a failure on the part of the person concerned to observe the standard of behaviour reasonably expected of a person in his position in relation to the market.

The regular user test in the old Section 118 does not appear in the Directive and is therefore retained only for those categories of abusive behaviour which are not drawn from the Directive. These provisions will expire after a period of three years, prior to which the Treasury intends to review them and decide whether or not they should be renewed.

The behaviour described in paragraphs (a) to (g) above, whether by one person alone or by two or more persons acting jointly or in concert, must occur in relation to (i) qualifying investments admitted to trading on a prescribed market, (ii) qualifying investments in respect of which a request for admission to trading on such a market has been made, or (iii) in the case of behaviour under (a) or (b) above, investments which are related investments in relation to such qualifying investments.

3.4.2.2.2 Prescribed markets and qualifying investments

The Regulations extend the scope of the UK's market abuse regime. Prescribed markets include all EEA regulated markets, except in relation to the "regular user" categories of abuse, which are not drawn from the Directive. Any financial instrument admitted to trading on a regulated market is covered. This means that behaviour is now covered if it happens:

(a) in the UK in relation to financial instruments traded on prescribed markets which are based in the EEA; or
(b) in the UK or abroad in relation to financial instruments traded on prescribed markets which are based in the UK.

3.4.2.2.3 Insiders

An "insider" is defined in Section 118B as any person who has inside information:

(a) as a result of his membership of an administrative, management or supervisory body of an issuer of qualifying investments;
(b) as a result of his holding in the capital of an issuer of qualifying investments;
(c) as a result of his having access to the information through the exercise of his employment, profession or duties;
(d) as a result of his criminal activities; or
(e) which he has obtained by other means and which he knows, or could reasonably be expected to know, is inside information.

3.4.2.2.4 Inside information

Section 118C defines "inside information". The definition varies slightly, depending upon the type of investment to which the information relates and the nature of the "insider" in question. The common features are that the information:

(a) must be of a precise nature;
(b) must not be generally available; and

Share Dealings – Restrictions and Disclosure Requirements

(c) (except in relation to commodity derivatives) would, if generally available, be likely to have a significant effect on the price of the qualifying investments.

3.4.2.3 Consequences of market abuse

The FSA has wide-ranging powers of penalty under FSMA. The FSA is able to impose an unlimited fine (Section 123(1) refers to "a penalty of such amount as it considers appropriate"). The FSA also has the option of electing not to impose a fine but to publish a public censure of the offender instead (Section 123(3)).

The largest fine levied by the FSA to date was imposed on Shell Transport and Trading Company, Royal Dutch Petroleum Company and the Royal Dutch/Shell Group of Companies ("Shell"), who were fined £17 million for market abuse and breach of the Listing Rules without admitting or denying culpability. The market abuse occurred in relation to the misstatement of its proved reserves, which led to Shell being investigated for the old "misleading conduct" limb of market abuse. Individuals have also received large fines: on 21 December 2004, Robert Bonnier, a managing partner of Indigo Capital LLC, was fined £290,000 for issuing "materially inaccurate statements which created a false or misleading impression amounting to market abuse" (*see* FSA press notice 110/2004).

As referred to above (*see* Section 3.4.1.2), much of the behaviour prohibited by the Regulations bears some resemblance to the offence of insider dealing provided for in CJA 1993 and many of the cases brought by the FSA since the market abuse regime came into force on 1 December 2001 have been for the misuse of information. On 21 December 2005, for example, Jonathan Malins, finance director of Cambrian Mining, was fined £25,000 for dealing ahead of an announcement of a new share placing and again prior to the announcement of the company's interim results. Similarly, in April 2005, Arif Mohammed, a former PricewaterhouseCoopers audit manager, was fined £10,000 for dealing based on knowledge he had received about an audit client for whom he was working. After a somewhat indifferent start (the first prosecution for market abuse was not brought until February 2004), there is some evidence that the market abuse regime is now being utilised more frequently by the FSA.

3.4.2.4 Defences

Under the new Section 118A(5), behaviour does not amount to market abuse if:

(a) it conforms with a rule which includes a provision to the effect that behaviour conforming with the rule does not amount to market abuse;
(b) it conforms with Commission Regulation (EC) No 2273/2003 of 22 December 2003 regarding exemptions for buy-back programmes and stabilisation of financial instruments; or
(c) it is done by a person acting on behalf of a public authority in pursuit of monetary policies with respect to exchange rates or the management of public debt or foreign exchange reserves.

Furthermore, the FSA is not able to impose a penalty where there are reasonable grounds for it to be satisfied that the relevant person believed, on reasonable grounds, that his behaviour did not amount to market abuse and took all reasonable precautions and exercised all due diligence to avoid engaging in market abuse (Section 123(2)). This is a defence only against a penalty and not against a finding of market abuse. In order to utilise this defence, the grounds on which the person believed that he was not committing market abuse must be objectively reasonable.

The FSA has produced a Code of Market Conduct (under Section 119(1)) which, *inter alia*, outlines behaviour that will not amount to market abuse. Most notably in the context of takeovers, the Code of Market Conduct includes provisions which are similar in effect to the market information defence provided for in CJA 1993 (*see* Section 3.4.1.4 above).

Compliance with the Code of Market Conduct and reliance on legal advice may discharge the burden of proof for the purposes of Section 123(2).

3.4.2.5 *The effect of FSMA on the Panel*

As a result of the market abuse regime, there is a significant potential overlap between the jurisdiction of the Panel and that of the FSA in relation to takeovers. There was some initial concern that this overlap might result in hostile participants dragging the FSA into contested bids as a tactic. In order to allay these fears, the Government introduced a provision into FSMA to enable the FSA (with Treasury approval) to establish a safe harbour for behaviour which complies with the Code (Section 120). The FSA has done this at MAR 1.10.3G to 1.10.6C of the Code of Market Conduct. Here it states that compliance with, among other rules, Rule 8 of the Code (disclosure of dealings during the offer period) will not constitute a breach of the market abuse regime.

The 2000/2001 Annual Report of the Panel stated that the FSA was keen to minimise the situations in which it may be required to interpret the Code. It was partly due to this concern that the FSA, when drafting the safe harbour provisions, avoided giving a blanket safe harbour for the entire Code.

In addition (and as discussed in 3.2.4 above), the Panel and the FSA have agreed a set of operating guidelines (the "Operating Guidelines") which are intended, *inter alia*, to assist in determining how each of them should exercise its functions in cases of jurisdictional overlap. The Operating Guidelines provide that where, during a takeover bid, matters arise which may amount to market misconduct, the FSA will not exercise its powers during the bid save in exceptional circumstances. The exceptional circumstances referred to in the Operating Guidelines are:

(a) where the Panel asks the FSA to use its power to impose penalties or its powers to seek injunctive or restitutionary relief from the courts;
(b) where the Panel is unable to investigate properly due to a lack of cooperation by the relevant person;
(c) where the suspected misconduct falls within the misuse of information prohibition under the market abuse regime (Section 118(2)(a) FSMA) or Part V CJA 1993 (insider dealing);
(d) where a person has deliberately or recklessly failed to comply with a Panel ruling;
(e) where the suspected misconduct extends to securities or a class of securities which may be outside the Panel's jurisdiction; or
(f) where the suspected misconduct threatens or has threatened the stability of the financial system.

In any event, the FSA will consult with the Panel before taking any action which may affect the timetable or outcome of a takeover bid. The Operating Guidelines also contain similar principles relevant to situations where there is jurisdictional overlap between the Panel and the FSA but no takeover bid is actually in progress.

While a January 2005 explanatory paper issued by the Panel suggested that the Panel and the FSA would be reviewing the Operating Guidelines in light of the implementation of the Takeover Directive, there have not been any subsequent changes to the guidelines as yet even though (as in paragraph (c) above) in places they refer to provisions which have been subsequently amended.

3.4.3 Companies Act

Although the Companies Act does not expressly prohibit or restrict dealings in shares during a takeover, there are certain aspects of the compulsory acquisition procedure (which is now set out in Schedule 2 to the Takeover Regulations) which may impact on the desirability of such dealings by an offeror or its associates.

In order to exercise the right to purchase compulsorily outstanding minority shareholdings following a bid, an offeror must have acquired or unconditionally contracted to acquire "by virtue of acceptances of the offer" (i) not less than 90 per cent in value of the shares of the class "to which the offer relates" and (ii) 90 per cent of the voting rights attaching to those shares (paragraph 2 of Schedule 2). The definition of "shares" for these purposes excludes treasury shares.

In considering these tests, shares in the target purchased by an offeror after the offer has been made (i.e. after the posting of the offer document) may also be treated as acquired by virtue of an acceptance of the offer (paragraph 2(14) and (15) of Schedule 2) if:

(a) the value of the consideration for which they are acquired or contracted to be acquired (the "acquisition consideration") does not at that time exceed the value of the consideration specified in the terms of the offer; or

(b) those terms are subsequently revised so that, when the revision is announced, the value of the acquisition consideration (calculated at the time of the acquisition) no longer exceeds the value of the consideration specified in those terms.

Shares in the target purchased after the offer has been made by those who are "associates" of the offeror for the purposes of these provisions (i.e. group companies, companies in which the offeror is substantially interested, nominees and concert parties (paragraph 8(5)) may be "shares to which the offer relates" if their purchase fulfils condition (a) or (b) above (paragraph 8(3)). If the purchasing associates then assent such shares to the offer, they may thus be counted towards the 90 per cent threshold for the exercise of compulsory purchase rights. However, any shares owned by associates before the offer is made by the posting of the offer document are ignored in calculating whether the 90 per cent level has been attained (paragraph 8(1)).

Purchases of target company shares by an offeror or its associates after the making of an offer (i.e. after the posting of the formal offer document) should, therefore, have no adverse effect on the offeror's ability to reach a position where it can exercise compulsory acquisition rights over minority shareholdings. However, where shares are purchased either by the offeror or an associate before the offer is formally made, the level of acceptances required for the exercise of compulsory purchase rights will be 90 per cent of a correspondingly smaller proportion of the target's total share capital (and, therefore, potentially more difficult to achieve).

Another point to note relates to the drafting of irrevocable commitments to accept an offer. A "takeover offer" is defined in paragraph 1(1) of Schedule 2 as "an offer to acquire all the shares . . . (other than shares which at the date of the offer are already held by the offeror) being an offer on terms which are the same in relation to all the shares to which the offer relates".

Paragraph 1(10) provides that:

> "The reference in subparagraph (1) to shares already held by the offeror includes a reference to shares which he has contracted to acquire . . . but that shall not be construed as including shares which are the subject of a contract . . . entered into by the holder

either for no consideration and under seal or for no consideration other than a promise by the offeror to make the offer."

It follows from this that irrevocable commitments should either:

(a) be drafted so as to be for no consideration and executed as a deed; or
(b) contain as their sole consideration a promise by the offeror to make the offer.

Otherwise, the shares which are the subject of irrevocable commitments are excluded for compulsory acquisition purposes (in the same way that a market purchase of shares made before the offer would be excluded) counting neither towards the numerator nor the denominator in determining whether the 90 per cent threshold has been reached and thus making it more difficult to apply the compulsory acquisition procedure.

3.4.4 Prohibitions or restrictions imposed by the Code

3.4.4.1 Dealings by offerors and their associates
Before turning to the detailed rules of the Code, it is worth recording that there was, during 1997, speculation that the Panel might change the Code to restrict the ability of a bidder and its advisers to buy shares in the market during an offer period. This was largely prompted by the takeover in December 1996 of Northern Electric by CalEnergy, the US utility. Some commentators have said that Northern Electric was acquired too cheaply because CalEnergy had an unfair advantage as it was able to buy 30 per cent of Northern Electric's shares while the price was depressed owing to the possibility of a referral to the former Monopolies and Mergers Commission. The price recovered when the bid was cleared and the offer received only 20 per cent acceptances. But with 30 per cent already in hand, CalEnergy gained control by the narrowest of margins. Some have, therefore, called on the Panel to adopt the US practice where a bidder is barred from market purchases once an offer has been made. Others, including Northern Electric's chairman, have asked for the 30 per cent threshold up to which a bidder can buy to be cut to 15 per cent, or for purchases to be prohibited at a time when there is regulatory uncertainty. However, many others take the view that there is no

good public policy reason for restricting market activity during a bid. If shareholders are willing to sell out early at or below the offer price in return for certainty, then that is their prerogative (and, of course, the bidder will be barred by the insider dealing legislation from buying if it has price-sensitive information about a likely regulatory outcome that the market does not). It appears that the Panel has no current plans to amend the Code in this regard, which is in keeping with its preferred approach of a permissive approach to dealings, focusing on consequences and disclosure.

3.4.4.2 Rule 4 – dealings prior to and during the offer period

Between the time when there is reason to suppose an offer or approach is contemplated and the announcement of that offer or approach, Rule 4.1 prohibits all dealings in the securities of the target or (on a share-for-share offer) the offeror by any person who is privy to price-sensitive information concerning the offer or possible offer, apart from dealings in target securities by the offeror itself.

One difficulty which sometimes arises in this context, normally in connection with joint or consortium offers, is the identification of the offeror (i.e. the party which *is* permitted to deal in target securities notwithstanding its being in possession of confidential price-sensitive information). Note 2 on Rule 4.1 provides that the Panel must be consulted before any acquisitions of interests in target company securities are made by members or potential members of a consortium and that it will not normally be appropriate for members of a consortium to acquire interests in such securities unless, for example, there are arrangements to ensure that such acquisitions are made proportionate to members' interests in the consortium company or under arrangements which give no profit to the party making the acquisition. These restrictions will not, of course, apply to a party which can properly be characterised as an offeror (including a joint offeror).

Note 3 provides a limited exception to the Rule 4.1 prohibition allowing a party acting in concert with the offeror to deal provided that it is done on the basis that the offeror carries the economic risk and is entitled to the rewards of the transaction. Careful consideration of the insider dealing legislation and Listing Rules provisions on indemnity arrangements *(see* paragraph 10.2.4 of the Listing Rules) will, however, be required before any such transaction is implemented.

Note 4 amplifies Rule 4.1 and prohibits dealings, until the position is publicly clarified, where an announcement has been made that an offer is contemplated and discussions are then terminated or the offeror decides not to proceed with the offer; this prohibition extends to all persons (including the offeror) privy to price-sensitive information. Note 5 further prohibits directors and financial advisers from dealing contrary to advice given by them in relation to an offer.

Once an offer has been announced, Rule 4.2 prohibits the offeror and its concert parties from selling any securities in the target except with the prior consent of the Panel and following 24 hours' public notice that such sales might be made; the Panel's consent will not be given where the offer is a mandatory offer under Rule 9, and no sales at a price below the value of the offer will, in any event, be permitted. Once notice of a possible sale has been given under this Rule, neither the offeror nor its concert parties may acquire an interest in any target securities and any revision to the terms of the offer will be permitted only in exceptional circumstances. The Panel should also be consulted whenever the offeror or its concert parties proposes to enter into or close out any type of transaction which may result in target securities being sold during the offer period (either by that party or by the counterparty to the transaction). The Rule is designed to prevent offerors and persons acting in concert with them from misleading or manipulating the market and is also therefore a reflection of General Principle 4 of the Code which addresses false markets.

The Panel will give dispensation in exceptional circumstances from the usual consequences of a sale under Rule 4.2. It did so in March 2003 in connection with the hostile offer by Capital Management and Investment PLC ("CMI") for Six Continents plc. The offer involved the issue of a very large number of CMI shares as consideration relative to the number already in issue. In order to avoid potential concerns under Rule 6 (*see* Section 3.4.4.5 below) about whether the offer could be valued at a price at or above the prices paid by CMI as part of its pre-offer stake-building, the Panel Executive agreed with CMI's proposal that it would sell those shares which had been acquired and donate the profit to charity. The Panel Executive ruled (Panel Statement 2003/7) that the disposal by CMI of its shares in Six Continents was not intended to mislead or manipulate the market but rather was a pragmatic solution to any potential concerns arising under Rule 6. The Panel Executive therefore gave its consent under Rule 4.2 to the sale by CMI of its shares in Six Continents and ruled that the usual consequences of a sale under Rule 4.2 should not apply in this case.

Panel Statement 2003/5 addressed Rule 4.2 in light of the behaviour of Indigo Capital LLC ("Indigo") in relation to Regus PLC. In this case, Indigo had entered into CFDs referenced to shares in Regus. The Panel Executive considered that the closing out of such a CFD by Indigo during the offer period should be treated as equivalent to the sale of the underlying shares represented by the CFD, and as such subject to Rule 4.2. This was on the basis, discussed above, that it will most often be the case that a party with whom a CFD is entered into will hedge its exposure by acquiring an equivalent number of shares in the target company in the market. Similarly, when such a CFD is closed out, the party with whom the CFD was entered into can reasonably be expected to sell the shares it had acquired to hedge its exposure.

In addition, as mentioned above, Rule 4.2 requires that when a sale of relevant securities is permitted by the Panel Executive, no such sale can be made at below the prevailing offer price and thereafter neither the offeror nor any person acting in concert with it may acquire an interest in any securities of the target company. The Executive said that in a case such as the Indigo case where the offeror had not announced the price of its offer, it would normally treat the requirement of Rule 4.2 that sales cannot be made at below the offer price as setting a ceiling on the price at which the potential offeror would subsequently be allowed to make its formal offer, that ceiling being the price at which the relevant securities were sold.

In the Indigo case itself, however, in view of the fact that the closing out of the CFD was not disclosed to the market at the time (as it should have been) such that, in fact, there was no misleading impression that could have been created and also that to set a ceiling on the price would have the undesirable effect of possibly depriving Regus shareholders of any offer being made by Indigo at above the price at which they closed out the CFD, the Panel Executive ruled (on an ex parte basis) that the closing out of the CFD should not set a ceiling on the price of any future offer for Regus by Indigo. The Executive also considered it relevant in making this ruling that further CFDs in respect of the same aggregate number of underlying shares were entered into by Indigo on the same date as the closing out of the CFD and that the number of underlying shares concerned was small.

The Panel Executive, however, ruled that the restriction on future purchases of shares set out in Rule 4.2 should apply as a consequence of the closing out of the CFD, such that during the offer period neither Indigo, nor any person acting in concert with it, would be permitted to acquire any further Regus shares or to enter into any further derivatives referenced to Regus shares. Indigo accepted the ruling.

In July 1998, the Panel introduced Rule 4.4 which prohibited financial advisers and stockbrokers (and their related entities except for exempt principal traders and exempt fund managers) to a target company (or any associated companies) from dealing in interests in target company securities during an offer period. Following recent amendments to the Code, the prohibition now prevents financial advisers and stockbrokers during an offer period from:

(a) either for their own account or on behalf of discretionary clients, acquiring interests in target company shares; or
(b) making any loan to a person to assist them in acquiring any such interests (save for lending in the ordinary course of business to established customers); or
(c) entering into any indemnity or option or other arrangements which may be an inducement for a person to retain, deal or refrain from dealing in relevant securities of the target company.

The introduction of this Rule followed controversial examples of purchases by a target's advisers. A Note on Rule 4.4 now makes it clear that restriction (c) above does not prevent an adviser to a target company from procuring irrevocable commitments or letters of intent not to accept an offer.

The Panel has also encountered some instances of offerors, target companies and persons associated with them borrowing or lending securities or seeking to unwind such transactions during an offer period. The Panel expressed concern that the purpose underlying the borrowing or lending may have been to secure a tactical advantage or to manipulate the price or location of securities (*see* PCP 2004/3). On 25 April 2005, a new Rule 4.6 was introduced to address these concerns. Rule 4.6 prohibits the following persons from entering into or taking action to unwind a securities borrowing or lending transaction without first obtaining the consent of the Panel:

(a) the offeror;
(b) the target;
(c) any company associated with the offeror or target;
(d) a connected adviser or persons controlling, controlled by or under the same control as such an adviser;
(e) a pension fund of the offeror or the target or of an associated company of either of them (unless the fund is managed by an independent third party); and
(f) any other person acting in concert with the offeror or with the target.

If the Panel gives consent, it will normally require the transaction to be disclosed in accordance with Rule 8 as if it were a dealing in securities (Note 3 on Rule 4.6 and *see* Note 5(a) on Rule 8).

In addition, the Panel has added a new Note 17 on Rule 9.1, which codifies the Panel's practice that persons who have borrowed or lent shares will be treated for the purposes of Rule 9 as if they hold the voting rights in respect of the shares which have been borrowed or lent.

3.4.4.3 *Rule 5 – timing restrictions on acquisitions*
Subject to certain exceptions, Rule 5.1 prohibits the acquisition by any person of interests in shares if the result of such acquisition would be (i) to increase the number of shares in which that person is interested (when aggregated with the holdings of that person's concert parties) to a number of shares carrying 30 per cent or more of the target's voting rights or (ii) to increase (by any amount) a similarly aggregated interest in 30 per cent or more of the target's voting rights. The Rule ceases to apply once a person acquires interests in shares carrying more than 50 per cent of a company's voting rights.

The position in respect of irrevocable commitments and Rule 5 has also been recently amended. The old Rule 5.1 made reference to "rights over shares", which included "any rights acquired by a person by virtue of "an . . . irrevocable commitment to accept an offer to be made by him". This meant that Rule 5.1 did not apply to irrevocable commitments *not* to accept an offer. However, the amended Rule 5 no longer uses this definition. Instead, the preamble to Rule 5 specifies that, for the purposes of Rule 5 only, "the number of shares in which a person will be treated as having an interest includes any shares in respect of which he has received an irrevocable commitment". Since "irrevocable commitment" as defined in the Code includes both commitments to accept and commitments not to accept an offer, it appears that the obtaining of such irrevocable commitments will now fall within the scope of Rule 5 and thus count towards the relevant threshold.

As will be seen below, one of the exceptions to Rule 5.1 is that the relevant acquisition immediately precedes the announcement of a recommended offer. Accordingly, although the restrictions in Rule 5 are capable of applying to irrevocable commitments, they can be avoided if the irrevocable commitments are executed immediately before the announcement of a firm intention to make an offer, provided the offer is to be recommended. This is another reason why it is often appropriate for irrevocable commitments to be executed on the evening prior to any announcement of an offer.

It should be noted that Rule 5 differs from the mandatory offer provisions in Rule 9 (*see* Section 3.4.4.4 below) in that receipt of an irrevocable commitment only constitutes an "interest in securities" for the purposes of Rule 5 and not Rule 9. This means that a bidder can obtain irrevocable commitments over 30 per cent or more of the target's voting shares where permitted by Rule 5 (most significantly where the offer is recommended) without triggering the mandatory offer provisions in Rule 9. However, Rule 5 would preclude a bidder from obtaining irrevocable commitments over 30 per cent or more of the target's voting shares in the context of a hostile bid (unless it fell within the "single shareholder" exemption in Rule 5.2(a)). It should further be noted that, even if the offeror does not mind incurring a Rule 9 obligation, he may be prevented from doing so by Rule 5.

The main exceptions to Rule 5.1 (set out in Rule 5.2) are acquisitions of interests in shares carrying voting rights:

(a) from a single shareholder where it is the only acquisition within a period of seven days (although this exception is not available in respect of an acquisition made after the announcement of a firm intention to make an offer where posting of the offer document is not subject to a pre-condition, nor where the acquisition is from a principal trader or a fund manager managing investment accounts on behalf of more than one underlying client, regardless of whether or not on a discretionary basis);

(b) which immediately precede and are conditional upon the announcement of a recommended offer (or, if the offer is not recommended, the acquisition is made with the consent of the board of the target);

(c) made after the announcement of a firm (unconditional) intention to make an offer;

   (i) with the agreement of the target's board;
   (ii) where either that or any competing offer is or has been recommended;
   (iii) where the first closing date of that or any competing offer has passed and it has been established that there will be no referral of the relevant offer to the Competition Commission or further action under the EC Merger Regulation; or
   (iv) where the offer has become unconditional in all respects; or

(d) by way of acceptance of an offer.

In addition, there are a number of Notes to Rule 5.1 which clarify its scope. For example, Note 5 states that Rule 5.1 does not apply to acquisitions of interests in shares which do not increase the percentage of shares carrying voting rights in which that person is interested (e.g. if a shareholder takes up his entitlement under a fully underwritten rights issue or if a person acquires shares on exercise of a call option). Similarly, Note 2 provides that the Rule does not cover acquisitions of new shares, securities convertible into new shares, rights to subscribe for new shares (other than pursuant to a rights issue) or new or existing shares under a share option scheme (albeit that the acquisition of new shares as a result of the exercise of conversion or subscription rights or options must be treated as an acquisition from a single shareholder falling within exception (a) above).

Prior to August 1998 there was a further important exception which allowed persons holding (together with their concert parties) shares carrying between 30 and 50 per cent of the voting rights in a company to acquire, during any 12-month period, additional shares carrying up to one per cent of the voting rights. Following a review, however, the Panel decided that the interests of shareholders generally would best be served by removing this exception which allowed an acquiror to "creep" to control.

Acquisitions of interests in shares under exception (a) above must be notified by noon the following business day to the target, a regulatory information services ("RIS") and the Panel under Rule 5.4. Rule 5.3 states that any such acquisition of interests in shares will preclude the possibility of making further acquisitions under that exception unless the acquiror makes an offer for all the shares in the target and that offer subsequently lapses.

One interesting feature of the interaction between Rule 5.3 and the exceptions set out in Rule 5.2 is that a bidder will not be able to use the exceptions to facilitate the making of market purchases in furtherance of a hostile offer:

(a) which is subject to the jurisdiction of the Office of Fair Trading;
(b) in relation to which the offeror has elected not to make a submission to the Office of Fair Trading (such that no clearance decision will be forthcoming from the Office of Trading); and
(c) where there is no competing offer.

In these circumstances the offeror will be prevented from making any market purchases (subject to the thresholds set out in Rule 5.1), which may have an adverse effect on its chances of success.

It should be noted, however, that any acquisition made under one of the exceptions to Rule 5 will almost inevitably bind the acquiror to make an offer under Rule 9, as referred to below.

3.4.4.4 Rule 9 – the mandatory offer
Rule 9 has been amended in light of the requirements of the Takeover Directive and to reflect the broader concept of "interests in securities" which now permeates the Code. The Rule now states that, where a

person acquires an interest in target shares which (taken together with shares in which persons acting in concert with him are interested) carry 30 per cent or more of the voting rights in the target, the acquiror and (depending on the circumstances) its concert parties are required (except with the consent of the Panel) to make a cash offer for the outstanding shares in the target (although the offer need not extend to shares held in treasury) at a price not less than the highest price paid for target shares by the acquiror or its concert parties during the 12 months prior to the announcement of that offer. This requirement is also triggered by any acquisition of an interest in shares by a person who, together with his concert parties, is interested in shares carrying not less than 30 per cent of the voting rights in the target if such person does not hold shares carrying more than 50 per cent of such voting rights and if the effect of such acquisition is to increase the percentage of the shares carrying voting rights in which that person is interested.

The changes made to the Code in light of the Takeover Directive make it explicit that the highest price paid for target shares must also be offered where the offeror or its concert parties acquire any interest in target shares after the announcement of an offer under Rule 9 and before the offer closes for acceptance and make it clear that an offer will not be required where control of the target company is acquired as a result of a voluntary offer. In addition, in determining the level of consideration which must be offered under a Rule 9 mandatory offer the Code previously looked back over the 12 month period prior to the commencement of the offer period. Following the implementation of the Takeover Directive, the Code now looks at the period beginning not more than 12 months before the announcement of the mandatory offer (Rule 9.5(a)). As the "offer period" might have been triggered by an event occurring prior to the announcement of the mandatory offer, the amended rule might result in a shorter period of time being considered in some cases.

A mandatory offer made pursuant to Rule 9 may not be subject to any conditions other than an acceptance condition which will be satisfied upon the offeror having received acceptances in respect of shares which, together with shares acquired or agreed to be acquired before or during the offer, will result in the offeror and concert parties holding shares carrying more than 50 per cent of the voting rights of the target (Rule 9.3(a)). Rule 9.3(a) is reinforced by Rule 9.3(b) which provides that no acquisition of any interest in shares which would trigger a mandatory offer obligation may be made if the making or implementation of such offer would or might be dependent on the passing of a resolution at any meeting of shareholders of the offeror or upon any other conditions, consents or arrangements.

In addition, any offer made under Rule 9 must (if the relevant jurisdictional criteria are met) contain a term that it will lapse if, before the first closing date of the offer or the date when the offer becomes unconditional (whichever is the later), it is referred to the Competition Commission or the European Commission initiates Phase II proceedings under the EC Merger Regulation (Rules 9.4, 12.1(a) and 12.1(b)).

Most of the difficult issues which arise in the context of Rule 9 concern whether or not particular persons are "acting in concert". Such issues are the subject of Section 3.3.3 above and Chapter 4. Issues do also arise, however, in relation to whether or not particular acquisitions of interests in shares or securities should have the effect of triggering the mandatory offer obligation.

In this connection, Note 11 on Rule 9.1 previously stated that normally, where shareholdings in a company are reduced by sales or diluted as a result of an issue of new shares, the provisions of Rule 9 will apply to the reduced or diluted holding. As a result, controlling shareholders were not able to restore their holdings to original levels by the acquisition of shares without incurring an obligation to make a general offer. In July 1999 the Panel considered the position of controlling shareholders and concluded that it was appropriate to permit controlling shareholders some ability to purchase further shares, notwithstanding that they (or the concert party of which they formed part) held 30 per cent or more of the voting rights in a company. Accordingly (and after further amendment in May 2006), Note 11 now provides that if a person or group of persons acting in concert reduces its interest in shares, but without reducing its interest to less than 30 per cent, such person or persons may subsequently acquire an interest in further shares without incurring an obligation to make a Rule 9 offer, provided that (i) the total number of shares in which interests are acquired on this basis in any period of 12 months does not exceed one per cent of the voting share capital for the time being and (ii) the percentage of shares in which the relevant person or persons acting in concert are interested following any such acquisition does not exceed the highest percentage of shares in which such person or persons were interested in the previous 12 months. Parties with a controlling interest will not, as a result, be permitted to increase the percentage of shares in which they are interested progressively from one year to the next. A reduction of the percentage of shares in which a person or concert party is interested by dilution will be treated in the same way as a sale for these purposes.

Similarly, Rule 37.1 provides that when a company redeems or purchases its own voting shares, any resulting increase in the percentage of shares carrying voting rights in which a person is, or a group of persons acting in concert are, interested will be treated as an acquisition for the purposes of Rule 9. Note 1 on Rule 37.1, however, provides that a person so interested who comes to exceed the limits in Rule 9.1 as a result of a company's redemption or purchase of its own shares will not normally incur an obligation to make a mandatory offer unless that person is a director, or the relationship of the person with any one or more of the directors is such that the person is, or is presumed to be, acting in concert with any of the directors. For this purpose, a person who has appointed a representative to the board of the company is treated as a director. Note 1 goes on to provide that there is no presumption that any or all of the directors are acting in concert solely by reason of a proposed redemption or repurchase or by reason of a decision to seek shareholder authority for a redemption or repurchase.

It is worth noting that the exception provided for in Note 1 on Rule 37.1 will not apply if a person (or any relevant member of a group of persons acting in concert) who is interested in shares has acquired an interest at a time when he had reason to believe that a redemption or purchase by the company of its own shares would take place (Note 2). In any event, the Panel must be consulted in advance in any case where Rule 9 might be relevant (Note 4). This will include any case where a person or group of persons acting in concert is interested in shares carrying 30 per cent or more of the voting rights of a company, but does not hold shares carrying more than 50 per cent of such voting rights, or where such person(s) may become interested in shares carrying 30 per cent or more of such voting rights on full implementation of the proposed redemption or purchase of own shares. Further, the Panel must be consulted if the aggregate interests of the directors and any other persons acting in concert, or presumed to be acting in concert, with any of the directors amount to 30 per cent or more of such shares, or may be increased to 30 per cent or more on full implementation of the proposed redemption or purchase of own shares.

Notwithstanding the foregoing, there are certain circumstances in which the Panel will be prepared to waive an obligation which would otherwise arise under Rule 9. Note 1 of the "Notes on Dispensations From Rule 9" provides, *inter alia*, as follows:

> "When the issue of new securities as consideration for an acquisition or a cash subscription would otherwise result in an obligation to make a general offer under this Rule, the Panel will normally waive the obligation if there is an independent vote at a shareholders' meeting. The requirement for a general offer will also be waived, provided there has been a vote of independent shareholders, in cases involving the underwriting of an issue of shares."

Rule 37.1 (*see* above) contains a similar provision regarding the waiver of a mandatory offer obligation which would otherwise arise following the redemption or purchase by a company of its own shares. Detailed rules concerning the obtaining of a waiver are set out in Appendix 1 to the Code (the Whitewash Guidance Note).

It should be noted, however, that the Panel will not (as specified in Note 1) normally grant a waiver if the person to whom the new securities are to be issued or any persons acting in concert with him have purchased shares in the company in the 12 months prior to posting of the shareholder circular relating to the proposals but subsequent to negotiations, discussions or the reaching of understandings or agreements with the directors of the company in relation to the proposals. Similarly, any waiver will be invalidated if there are any such purchases between the posting of the circular and the holding of the meeting of independent shareholders.

On 16 August 2002 (in Panel Statement 2002/17), the Panel announced that it had dismissed an appeal against the decision of the Panel Executive to grant a waiver from the obligation that would otherwise have arisen under Rule 9.1 in connection with a proposed issue of shares in Alexanders Holdings PLC ("Alexanders") to Orb Estates PLC ("Orb Estates") as consideration for the acquisition by Alexanders of certain subsidiaries of Orb Estates. The shares proposed to be issued to Orb Estates amounted to approximately 75.1 per cent of Alexanders' enlarged share capital. On 19 August 2002 (in Panel Statement 2002/18), the Panel gave the reasons for its decision. The decision of the Panel considered, *inter alia*, disqualifying transactions, put options and equality of treatment. The Panel Executive confirmed that the provision regarding disqualifying transactions (referred to above) was introduced to ensure equality of treatment for all shareholders and to prevent some shareholders being allowed a cash exit from the company while the remaining body of shareholders was not afforded that option. Accordingly, this safeguard should not apply when an acquisition of shares is made at a time when a proposed transaction which will give rise to a change in control is not in contemplation. It is only where the transaction and the purchase of target company shares can be regarded in some way as part of the same overall transaction that there can be equality concerns.

Similarly, the Panel held that the relevant date for determining whether the constituent elements of a disqualifying transaction are present in relation to the entry into of a put option is the date on which the put option agreement is executed. This is when the acquiror incurs the potential obligation to acquire the shares and, therefore, when equal treatment of all holders of target company securities under General Principle 1 should be considered.

It should be noted that, in the course of making the amendments discussed above, the Code Committee also amended the "Notes on Dispensations From Rule 9" concerning enforcement of security for a loan, rescue operations, inadvertent mistake and gifts to codify some of the circumstances in which the provisions of Rule 9 will not apply and to therefore reduce the number of specific dispensations it is required to give.

3.4.4.5 Rule 6 – minimum level of consideration
Under Rule 6.1, an offer may not be made on less favourable terms (but need not necessarily be in cash, even if the acquisitions were for cash) than the highest price paid by the offeror or its concert parties for interests in target shares during the three months prior to the commencement of the offer period or during the period between commencement of the offer period and formal announcement of the offer. This obligation may also arise in respect of acquisitions made prior to the three-month period if the Panel considers there are circumstances which render this necessary to give effect to the general principle that all holders of securities be treated equally. The Panel will not normally exercise this discretion unless the sellers, or other parties to the transactions giving rise to the interests, are directors of, or other persons closely connected with, the offeror or target (Note 2).

Note 4 on Rule 6 explains how to calculate the highest price paid. The price paid for purchases of shares is simply the price agreed between the purchaser and the vendor. In the case of an unexercised call option, the price paid will normally be treated as the middle market price of the relevant shares at the time the option is entered into. In the case of a call option which has been exercised, the price paid will normally be treated as the amount paid on exercise of the option together with any amount paid by the option-holder on entering into the option. In the case of a written put option (whether exercised or not), the price paid will normally be treated as the amount paid or payable on exercise of the option less any amount paid by the option-holder on entering into the option. In the case of a derivative, the price paid will normally be treated as the initial reference price of the underlying derivative together with any fee paid on entering into the derivative. However, if any of the option exercise prices or derivative reference prices is calculated by reference to the average price of a number of acquisitions by the counterparty of interests in underlying securities, the price paid will normally be determined to be the highest price at which such acquisitions are actually made.

Note 1 on Rule 6 provides that the Panel will, "in exceptional circumstances", permit offers at a price which does not match one paid less than three months earlier. The factors which the Panel will take into account in determining whether to exercise this discretion include whether the relevant acquisition was made on terms then prevailing in the market, changes in the market price of the shares since the relevant acquisition and whether interests in shares have been acquired at high prices from directors or other persons closely connected with the offeror or target.

If, following the formal announcement of an offer, any interest in target shares is acquired at a price exceeding the offer price, the offer must be revised immediately to reflect the terms of such purchase (Rule 6.2).

Both Rules 6.1 and 6.2 acknowledge that acquisitions of interests in shares giving rise to obligations under those rules may also give rise to obligations under Rule 11 (*see* Section 3.4.4.6 below). Compliance with Rule 11 will normally be regarded as satisfying Rule 6.

Note 3 on Rule 6 applies where interests in shares in a target have been acquired at a relevant time and the offer includes securities as consideration. The Note makes clear that the securities offered as consideration must, at the date of announcement of the firm intention to make the offer, have a value at least equal to the highest relevant price paid. The Note goes on to say that if there is a restricted market in the securities of the offeror, or if the amount of securities to be issued is large in relation to the amount already issued, the Panel may require justification of prices used to determine the value of the offer. Note 3 was discussed in Panel Statement 2003/7 published in March 2003 in connection with the hostile offer by Capital Management and Investment PLC ("CMI") for Six Continents plc. CMI was an AIM-listed cash shell with a net asset value of about £41 million. Six Continents was a FTSE 100 company. Prior to announcement of its offer, CMI acquired shares representing about 0.3 per cent of Six Continents' issued share capital. CMI's basic offer was on a share-for-share basis with a partial cash alternative. The Panel Executive stated that, given the very great number of new CMI shares that were being offered as consideration, Note 3 was applicable in establishing whether the value of the offer was at least equal to the highest price paid by CMI in buying Six Continents shares in the market. The Executive said that Note 3 recognised that, in cases where the amount of listed securities to be issued was large in relation to the amount already issued, the market price of the offeror's shares at the time of announcement of the offer might not be capable of providing an accurate yardstick against which to determine whether the offeror had satisfied its Rule 6 obligation. The Executive went on to explain that it had accepted CMI's proposal that it should sell the Six Continents shares it had acquired and donate the profits to charity in order to solve any potential concerns under Rule 6. This ruling by the Executive makes it clear that a listed bid vehicle which is proposing a reverse takeover containing a share-for-share element and which has recently acquired target shares in the market may find it very difficult to justify to the Panel its valuation of the offer for Rule 6 purposes. The Executive also ruled that the sale by CMI of the shares it had acquired in Six Continents would not give rise to any consequences under Rule 4.2 (*see* Section 3.4.4.2 above).

3.4.4.6 *Rule 11 – mandatory cash offers and mandatory securities offers*
Under Rule 11.1, acquisitions for cash by an offeror or its concert parties:

(a) during the offer period, and within 12 months prior to its commencement, of any interests in shares of any class under offer carrying 10 per cent or more of the voting rights exercisable at a class meeting of that class; or
(b) during the offer period, of any interests in shares of any class under offer,

will require the offeror to make its offer for that class in cash, or to make a cash alternative available, at not less than the highest price paid for the relevant interest in shares during those 12 months or during the offer period, as appropriate. Note 1 on Rule 11.1 explains how to calculate the highest price paid for different types of interest in shares in these circumstances. The process is exactly the same as that set out in Note 4 on Rule 6 (*see* 3.4.4.5 above).

Interests acquired in exchange for securities will normally be deemed to be acquired for cash unless the seller, or other party to the transaction giving rise to the interest, is required to hold the securities received or receivable in exchange until either the offer has lapsed or the offer consideration has been posted to accepting shareholders (Note 5 on Rule 11.1). This Rule was amended in July 1998 to include the requirement to make a cash alternative available where *any* target shares of the class under offer are purchased by the offeror or its concert parties during the offer period. This amendment followed criticism of offerors using the 10 per cent threshold as a loophole to allow them to make cash purchases during the offer period favouring a minority of shareholders. The rule was subsequently further amended to reflect the broader concept of "interests in securities" discussed above.

On 21 February 2002, the Code Committee inserted a new rule (Rule 11.2) which requires the making of a securities offer in similar circumstances to those in which a cash offer is required by Rule 11.1. The effect of Rule 11.2 is to require a securities exchange offer if, during or within three months prior to the commencement of the offer period, the offeror and persons acting in concert with it have acquired, in exchange for securities, interests in shares of the class under offer carrying 10 per cent or more of the voting rights exercisable at a class meeting of that class. There are a number of important Notes on Rule 11.2:

(a) Note 1 provides that the securities offered pursuant to Rule 11.2 must be offered on the basis of the number of consideration securities received or receivable by the relevant sellers, or other parties to the transactions giving rise to the interests, for each target company share rather than on the basis of securities equivalent to the value of the securities received or receivable by the sellers or other parties at the time of the relevant purchases. The Panel clarified in Response Statement 6 that it currently takes into account corporate action (such as a rights issue or a share split) if as a result shareholders would not be treated equally and also requires any special features, such as contingent value rights, attached to securities offered to a seller to be attached to securities to be made available under any offer.

(b) Note 2 provides a discretion to the Panel to require a securities offer even where the 10 per cent threshold has not been reached, or where the relevant purchase took place more than three months prior to the commencement of the offer period: exercise of the discretion will normally be limited to situations where the sellers of the relevant shares or other parties to the transactions giving rise to the interests are directors of, or other persons closely connected with, the offeror or target company.

(c) Note 3 makes clear that where an offeror acquires target shares in exchange for securities and the offeror has arranged for these securities to be immediately placed for cash on the seller's behalf (a vendor placing), then there should be no obligation to provide a securities offer to all shareholders.

The Panel clarified in July 2000, by the addition of a new Note 12 on Rule 11.1, that where a new offer is announced in accordance with Note (a)(iii) on Rule 35.1 (i.e. following anti-trust clearance from the Competition Commission or the European Commission), acquisitions of interests in target company shares made for cash during the competition reference period will be deemed to be acquisitions during the new offer period for the purposes of Rule 11.1(b). Note 7 on Rule 11.2 makes clear that acquisitions during the competition reference period will also be deemed to be acquisitions during the new offer period for the purposes of Rule 11.2 (and so may trigger an obligation to make a securities exchange offer available to all shareholders).

3.4.4.7 Rule 16 – special deals with favourable conditions

When an offer is in progress or is reasonably in contemplation, Rule 16 prohibits the offeror or its concert parties from dealing in target shares or entering into arrangements which involve acceptance of the offer, if there are favourable conditions attached which are not available to all target shareholders. Irrevocable undertakings to accept an offer should not, therefore, confer any valuable benefit on the person giving the undertaking – a point also of importance in ensuring that the shares which are the subject of such an undertaking count for the purposes of the squeeze-out provisions of the Takeover Regulations.

In addition, an arrangement made with a person who, while not a shareholder, is interested in shares carrying voting rights in a target (such as options or derivatives holders), is also prohibited under Rule 16 if favourable conditions are attached which have not been extended to the shareholders. However, there is no requirement to extend any offer, or any "special deal" falling within Rule 16, to persons who are interested in shares but are not shareholders.

Note 1 on Rule 16 specifies that arrangements where there is a promise to make good to a seller of shares any difference between the sale price and the price of any subsequent successful offer are arrangements to which Rule 16 applies. Similarly, an irrevocable undertaking, combined with an option to put if the offer fails, will be prohibited by Rule 16.

The Panel has over time developed a flexible approach to interpreting Rule 16 where one or more shareholders in the target company participate in a vehicle making the offer. Otherwise, management buy-outs would effectively be prohibited, to the potential detriment of existing target shareholders, as well as offers by one or more such shareholders. The Panel has therefore usually ruled that when two or more persons form a consortium whereby each can properly be considered to be a joint offeror, Rule 16 is not contravened if one or more of them is already a shareholder in the target company. Subject to that, joint offerors may make arrangements between themselves concerning the future membership, control and management of the business being acquired.

In the context of what constitutes a joint offeror, the Panel issued Panel Statement 2003/25 on 21 November 2003 concerning Brascan Corporation's appeal against an earlier Panel ruling that arrangements between the members of a consortium, formed with a view to the potential acquisition of Canary Wharf Group plc, did not contravene Rule 16. The Panel stated that the criteria for assessing whether or not a person was a joint offeror were as follows:

(a) What proportion of the equity share capital of the bid vehicle will the person own after completion of the acquisition?
(b) Will the person be able to exert a significant influence over the future management and direction of the bid vehicle?
(c) What contribution is the person making to the consortium?
(d) Will the person be able to influence significantly the conduct of the bid?
(e) Are there arrangements in place to enable the person to exit from his investment in the bid vehicle within a short time or at a time when other equity investors cannot?

In dismissing the appeal, the Panel stressed that each case must be decided upon its own facts and that earlier decisions on different facts are of little precedent value.

3.4.4.8 Competitive bid processes

The Panel raised concerns in a consultation paper issued in October 2001 about the ability of the then framework of the Code to resolve competitive situations in an orderly fashion and create as little uncertainty for the shareholders of the target as possible.

With these concerns in mind the Panel adopted a number of changes to the Code which, it is hoped, will limit the times when the Code fails to resolve a competitive situation in an orderly and timely manner. In terms of the subject matter of this Chapter, the following amendment is particularly relevant. The Panel has inserted Rule 35.4 which states that, except with the consent of the Panel, where an offer has been one of two or more competing offers and has lapsed, neither that offeror, nor any concert party of that offeror, may acquire any interest in shares in the target company on more favourable terms than those made available under its lapsed offer until each of the competing offers has either been declared unconditional in all respects or has itself lapsed. This amendment has closed the loophole which previously allowed lapsed competitive bidders the possibility of frustrating the other offeror's bid.

3.5 Disclosure of share dealings

Next, we will address the subject of disclosure of share dealings. Although disclosure should be no more than a mechanical exercise, it may be important in the early, planning stages of a transaction and is easy to overlook once a bid is under way, when information may be difficult to collect in the time required. Further, the disclosure requirements of the Code have been considerably extended in recent years and there are difficulties in interpreting certain parts of the Companies Act provisions, particularly in relation to concert parties.

3.5.1 Companies Act

Statutory provisions concerning the disclosure of information relating to particular shareholdings in public companies are contained in Part VI Companies Act. These provisions are of application whether or not a takeover bid is imminent or in progress and even if an acquiring person has no intention at any stage of making a bid for the "target" company.

3.5.1.1 Interests subject to the Companies Act

3.5.1.1.1 Relevant share capital

The duty of disclosure operates only in respect of shares comprised in a company's "relevant share capital". This is defined in Section 198(2) as meaning issued share capital carrying the right to vote in all circumstances at general meetings of the company (excluding any shares in the company held as treasury shares). Section 210A allows the Secretary of State to make regulations amending this definition.

Sections 198–203 (as amended) require any person who acquires (whether in a single transaction or a series of transactions) a "notifiable interest" in the target's relevant share capital to give notice in writing of such fact to the target within two business days of his achieving that level.

3.5.1.1.2 Notifiable interests

A notifiable interest arises for most purposes at a three per cent holding of the relevant share capital of the target. However, certain holdings, including shares held by fund managers, are not disclosable until a 10 per cent level is reached (Section 199(2)). In the vast majority of cases connected with a bid, it will be the three per cent level which is relevant. Once the relevant percentage level is attained, further notice has to be given each time the interest increases or decreases to an extent which takes the holder through a percentage point level (after rounding down) (*see* Section 199(5)(b) and Section 200); for example, an acquisition which increases the stake from three per cent or more of the target to four per cent or more, or a disposal which reduces the stake from 12 per cent or more to less than 12 per cent. Moreover, under Section 198(3) a person who has interests in shares must notify if he becomes aware of any change of circumstances or any facts which entail him reaching the notifiable percentage (e.g. a condition is met conferring full voting rights on his shares and taking him over the three per cent level). Notice must also be given of a disposal which reduces the interest to less than three per cent of the target's capital (Section 199(5)(a)). By virtue of Section 211, the target company is required to keep a register of interests notified to it pursuant to these provisions which may be inspected by its members. If listed, the target is also required by the Listing Regime to disclose in any prospectus issued by it details of interests of three per cent or more and to disseminate publicly any notifications received without delay (*see* Prospectus Rules, paragraph 2.3 and Listing Rules 9.6.7).

Interests acquired as a result of acceptance of a conditional takeover offer prior to such offer having become or been declared unconditional as to acceptances are exempt (Section 209(1)(e)). For the purposes of this exemption, "takeover offer" has the meaning given in Section 428(1) (in the context of the compulsory acquisition procedure). However, there is a view that, where a potential bidder acquires a notifiable interest in shares when it takes irrevocable commitments from shareholders, that interest is not covered by the takeover exemption. This view produces the rather illogical result that at the point when the takeover offer is made and accepted in accordance with the terms of the undertaking, the bidder's interest (if it was notifiable) then becomes exempt, thus obliging the bidder to notify the target that it has ceased to have a notifiable interest in its shares. This is one of the reasons why irrevocable commitments are generally not entered into until the evening prior to the announcement of an offer.

3.5.1.1.3 An "interest" for the purposes of the Companies Act

An "interest" includes any interest in shares, including interests arising under an unfulfilled or conditional contract or by virtue of an option (Section 208). It is a difficult question as to whether a person who acquires nil-paid rights thereby obtains an "interest" in a company's shares, but it would seem that only when the shares to which the rights relate are registered (or should have been registered) does the disclosure obligation arise, although this is at odds with the better view of the position under Section 212. A nominee's interest is, however, disregarded; where shares are registered in the name of a nominee, the disclosure obligation falls on the beneficial owner, not the nominee (Sections 208(3) and 209(1)(a)). A person is also deemed to be "interested" in shares (under Section 203(2)) if a body corporate is interested in them and the directors of that body corporate are accustomed to act on the first person's instructions, or the first person is entitled to exercise or control the exercise of one-third of the voting rights of the body corporate in general meeting. Similarly, shares of spouses and their infant children are aggregated for the purposes of these provisions under Section 203(1). A recognised market maker does not have an interest in shares owned by him in that capacity for the purposes of these provisions (*see* Section 209). However, the market makers' exemption cannot be manipulated to avoid the requirements of Section 198. In any event, market makers are required to disclose interests of, or in excess of, three per cent or any higher percentage point to an RIS. It should be noted that the Stock Exchange Electronic Trading Service ("SETS") was introduced in October 1997, bringing automated order-driven trading to FTSE 100 stocks. There are accordingly no longer any recognised market makers in FTSE 100 securities and so the market makers' exemption in Section 209 has ceased to be available to dealers in such securities; as a result, dealers which had previously benefited from the exemption are now subject to the full disclosure requirements of the Companies Act.

3.5.1.1.4 Concert parties
Sections 204–206 require disclosure of interests arising under concert party arrangements. An interest in shares bears the same meaning in the context of these provisions as in Sections 198–203. Concert party arrangements are defined to include a non-legally binding arrangement where the parties have mutuality of undertakings, expectations or understandings, but exclude underwriting and sub-underwriting agreements (Section 204). The concept of an "arrangement" would probably catch circumstances where parties merely communicate in some way without necessarily any express oral or written statement – and thereby create expectations in each other of how each will behave in the future. Hence, potentially, the ambit of these provisions is very wide. However, the concert party agreements and arrangements concerned are only those which include provision for the acquisition by one or more of the parties of interests in the shares of a target company and which impose obligations with respect to "their use, retention or disposal" (Section 204(2)(a)). The disclosure obligations in relation to a concert party agreement or arrangement arise only when interests in shares have in fact been acquired under the agreement or arrangement (Section 204(2)(b)).

The consequence of such an agreement or arrangement is that, under Section 205(1), each of the parties to it is deemed to be interested in all the shares in which each of the other parties is interested. (There are obligations contained in Section 206 on each party to keep the others informed of details relating to its interests.) It is, therefore, not possible secretly to build a significant stake in a target company by means of splitting holdings between numerous concert parties. In discharging notification obligations under these provisions, concert parties are required to specify in which shares they have interests by virtue of them being deemed to have interests in shares in which other parties are interested (Section 205(4)(c)); in addition, they must state the names and (so far as known to them) addresses of the other concert parties.

3.5.1.1.5 *Section 212 notices*

Pursuant to Section 212 a public company may require any person whom the company "knows or has reasonable cause to believe" to be, or to have been at any time during the three immediately preceding years, interested in any of its shares (whether or not the number of shares exceeds the three per cent level):

(a) to confirm or deny that fact;
(b) to give particulars of any interests he has or has had during the previous three years;
(c) if any other person has been interested in the same shares, to give "so far as lies within his knowledge" particulars with respect to that other interest; and
(d) if he is no longer interested in shares in the target, to give "so far as lies within his knowledge" particulars of the identity of the person who acquired his interest.

It is worth noting that, at least on one view (*see* Section 3.5.1.1.2 above), a potential offeror will have an interest in the relevant share capital of the target company if it obtains an irrevocable commitment from a shareholder to accept the offer when made. Accordingly, a target company would, on this basis, be entitled to serve a Section 212 notice on a potential offeror to ascertain details of any irrevocable commitments received. There is, therefore, a clear advantage for the offeror in irrevocable commitments not normally being entered into until the evening prior to the announcement of an offer or possible offer.

A reply to any notice given by a company under Section 212 must be given within any "reasonable time as may be specified in the notice"

(Section 212(4)). In cases of urgency (for example during the closing stages of a contested bid) a "reasonable time" would not generally be more than two days (*see Lonrho v Edelman* (1989) BCC 68) and may be 24 hours, or even less. Here, too, a person is deemed to be interested in shares if he is a party to a concert party arrangement (Section 212(5)).

It would seem that a person is, for the purposes of Section 212, "interested in shares" comprised in a company's relevant share capital merely by virtue of him holding nil-paid rights. This follows from Section 212(6) which provides that Section 212 applies to persons who have, or previously had, rights to subscribe for shares and that references to interests in shares should be read accordingly. However, the position is not entirely clear. Certainly, such a view has somewhat anomalous consequences: it would seem odd that rights are not disclosable under Section 198 (*see* Section 3.5.1.1.3 above) and also cease to be disclosable under Section 212 once fully paid (until the resulting shares become entered on the register of members), because they are not then "a right to subscribe for shares".

For the purposes of Section 212, the nominee exclusion under the provisions previously discussed does not apply and a person is deemed to be interested in shares even if he is interested only as a nominee (*see* Section 209, which applies only to Sections 198–202). Thus a nominee can be required to give details, so far as known to him, of the true owner of the shares; clearly this is the most sensible approach since the Sections aim at ensuring the fullest information possible is available to a company. Where, however, the true owner is not required by Sections 198–203 himself to give notice of his interest (by virtue of that interest not being a notifiable interest), it may be possible to extend the period during which a target company is unable to ascertain the true owner of some of its shares by the device of giving instructions for the acquisition of shares through a chain of nominees each of whom is unaware of the identity of any others in the chain apart from those immediately next to him. The target company would then be obliged to send out a series of notices before identifying the person at the end of the chain.

It is worth noting that Swiss banks, for example, regard themselves as bound by secrecy laws which prevent them from answering

Section 212 notices; there are, however, doubts, both (it appears) under Swiss law and (certainly) in relation to the obligations under the Companies Act as to whether reliance on such grounds for refusing to answer a Section 212 notice may be regarded as excusing the recipient from the consequences of such refusal (*see Re Geers Gross* [1987] 1 WLR 1649).

3.5.1.1.6 Consequences of contravention of the Companies Act
Failure to give notice as required by Sections 198–203 (and the concert party provisions in Sections 204–206) or to respond to a notice under Section 212 is an offence, which may be punished by imprisonment or a fine (Section 210(3) and Section 216(3)). In addition, the shares in question may be disenfranchised; disenfranchisement may be effected by the target under powers in its articles of association, by the Secretary of State under Section 210(5) (in the case of failure to observe the provisions of Sections 198–206) or by the court at the instigation of the target company under Section 216(1) (in the case of failure to answer a Section 212 notice). The basic approach of the courts in this area is that the company has an unqualified right to know who owns its shares (*see Re Geers Gross* [1987] 1 WLR 1649). However, problems may arise in an interlocutory application in deciding whether there has genuinely been an untruthful answer to the notice.

Companies are required to maintain registers of interests notified under Sections 198–206 (Section 211) and of notices given and replies received under Section 212 (Section 213). Obviously, these registers may contain information useful to any person contemplating a bid for the company concerned and the registers are required to be made available for inspection. But although Section 212 gives a company extensive powers in relation to its shareholders, it is perhaps worth mentioning that many companies continue to be ignorant of the identity of their shareholders because they do not exercise their Section 212 rights. In many instances, therefore, there is no register from which information may be gleaned. Even where companies do have such registers, attempts have been made to avoid publicising the information which a Section 212 notice may reveal by sending out notices which appear to be given under that Section, but which (arguably) are not; replies are then not registered. The effectiveness of such ploys must be open to doubt.

3.5.2 The Code

The provisions of the Code relating to disclosure of dealings normally only apply during an offer period (i.e. after the time when an announcement has been made of a proposed or possible offer) (*see* "Definitions" Section of the Code).

3.5.2.1 Rule 8 – disclosure of dealings during the offer period

During an offer period, Rule 8 requires parties to a takeover, and their "associates", to disclose publicly, by 12 noon on the business day following the transaction, all dealings in "relevant securities" whether for the parties' own account or for the account of discretionary investment clients; such disclosure is made to an RIS and the Panel (Rule 8, Notes 3, 4 and 5). By virtue of Note 12, the Rule 8.1 obligation extends to cover a potential offeror (and persons acting in concert with it) which has been the subject of an announcement that talks are taking place (whether or not the potential offeror has been named) or which has announced that it is considering making an offer. Such a potential offeror and its concert parties must also disclose the procuring of irrevocable commitments or letters of intent in accordance with Rule 8.4. Any disclosures made pursuant to Note 12 must include the identity of the potential offeror as required by Note 5.

The definition of "relevant securities" includes securities of the target which are being offered for or which carry voting rights and securities of the offeror which carry substantially the same rights as any to be issued as consideration for the offer. However, disclosure of dealings in relevant securities of an offeror is not required where it has been announced that an offer or possible offer is, or is likely to be, solely in cash (Note 2).

During an offer period, Rule 8.3 requires any person, whether or not associated with the offeror or target, who is interested (directly or indirectly) in one per cent or more of any class of relevant securities publicly to disclose dealings by that person in such securities to an RIS and the Panel.

The Panel has stated that it attaches great importance to compliance with this Rule on the basis that "disclosure underpins market transparency which, in turn, constitutes a fundamental protection for shareholders and others who deal in the UK securities markets" (Panel Statement 2003/16). Where people act pursuant to any sort of understanding to acquire an interest in relevant securities, they will be deemed to be a single person for the purposes of this Rule (Rule 8.3(b)); and where relevant securities are managed on a discretionary basis by an investment management group then (unless the Panel agrees) all funds under management will be treated as the investments of a single person (Rule 8.3(c)). This Rule applies equally to exempt fund managers (whether or not connected with the offeror or target) as to any other one per cent holder. It does not, however, apply to a recognised intermediary acting in a client-serving capacity unless, of course, the recognised intermediary is an exempt principal trader connected with the offeror or target (in which case disclosure under Rule 38.5 is required (Rule 8, Note 9) (*see* Section 3.6.1 below), or is an associate of the offeror or target (in which case disclosure under Rule 8.1 is required). See Section 3.6.2 below for further information about recognised intermediary status.

Rule 8.3 was considered by the Panel in response to BC Capital Partners' proposed offer for Mitchell's & Butler plc ("M&B") (Panel Statement 2003/9). M&B was to become one of two successor companies to Six Continents plc following the latter's demerger. This prompted the question of how to determine a one per cent holder in relation to M&B, prior to the time of the demerger becoming effective and dealings in shares in M&B commencing. The Panel Executive ruled that a relevant person's percentage holding in the When Issued shares of M&B should be aggregated with that person's percentage holding in Six Continents' shares since a holding in Six Continents' shares would, at the time the demerger became effective, translate into an equivalent holding in M&B shares. Therefore, a person that held 0.5 per cent of Six Continents' shares and acquired 0.8 per cent of the When Issued shares of M&B was treated as being a one per cent holder in relation to M&B (although not Six Continents, *see* below), notwithstanding that he did not hold one per cent in either stock individually.

Six Continents itself was already in an offer period following an announcement made by Sun Capital Partners Limited. However, as a holding of When Issued shares in M&B would not translate into an effective holding in Six Continents, there was no need to aggregate shareholdings in M&B and Six Continents when calculating percentage interests in Six Continents.

Rule 8 was substantially modified in the wake of the Guinness affair. In particular, Note 10 now states that stockbrokers and other financial intermediaries are expected to cooperate with the Panel in its enquiries, including by identifying clients. The requirement for cooperation with the Panel is now reinforced by provisions set out in the Market Conduct volume of the FSA Handbook. These state, in broad terms, that a firm which acts for any person in connection with a transaction to which the Code applies must cease to act for that person if it has reasonable grounds for believing that the person in question, or his principal, is not complying or is not likely to comply with the Code; and provide such information and assistance as the Panel may reasonably require to perform its functions.

In Panel Statement 2003/5 issued in January 2003 the Panel Executive publicly criticised Indigo Capital LLC ("Indigo") and one of its managing partners for dealing in relevant securities of Regus PLC and not disclosing this information in accordance with Rule 8. At the time, Note 2 on Rule 8 defined "relevant securities" as including the shares of the target company in question and also any derivatives (such as CFDs referenced to such shares). Note 2 went on to make clear that each of the entering into and closing out or variation of a derivative was regarded as a "dealing" in the derivative concerned and, therefore, subject to the disclosure requirements of Rule 8. In this case Indigo had dealt in a number of shares and CFDs after the offer period had begun and had not disclosed these dealings as required by Rule 8 by 12 noon on the business day following the relevant dealings.

Rule 8 was modified in April 2005, following the Code Committee's consultation on market-related issues, to include a specific provision requiring the obtaining or giving of irrevocable commitments or letters of intent to be disclosed publicly. It had been the Panel's practice for some time to require such disclosure, under Note 6 on Rule 8, regarding "indemnity and other arrangements". However, the Code now contains Rule 8.4(a), which requires those procuring either irrevocable commitments or letters of intent to publicly disclose the details. Note 14 to Rule 8 lists the details to be disclosed, which include details of the terms of the letter or commitment. In addition, Rule 8.4(b) requires a person who has given an irrevocable commitment or a letter of intent and no longer intends to comply with its terms to either announce an update of the position or to notify the company and the Panel, so that the company can make the necessary announcement. It should be noted that no separate disclosure is required under Rule 8.4(a) if the information is included in a Rule 2.5 announcement which is released no later than 12 noon on the business day following the date on which the irrevocable commitment or letter of intent is procured. This is a further reason to execute these documents on the evening before the announcement of a firm intention to make an offer.

Disclosures under Rule 8 and Rule 38.5 should contain the information detailed in the Panel's specimen forms. Notes 4(a) and (b) on Rule 8 allow disclosure of dealings by e-mail to the Panel. Following the consultation on market-related issues, the details to be included in public disclosures (Note 5(a) to Rule 8) have been expanded. In addition, the Panel was concerned that certain persons proposing to deal in interests in shares of a party to an offer during an offer period might not be familiar with their Code disclosure obligations. The Panel has therefore included a summary of the Rule 8 requirements on its website, and amended Rules 2.4 and 2.5 to require this summary to be included in announcements.

3.5.2.2 Other disclosure obligations under the Code
Rule 7.1 requires an immediate public announcement to be made whenever there is an acquisition of an interest in shares which triggers an obligation to increase an offer under Rule 6, to make a mandatory offer under Rule 9 or to make a mandatory cash or securities offer under Rule 11. Such an announcement should, whenever practicable, state the nature of the interest, the number of shares concerned and the price paid.

Following an acquisition of an interest in shares from a single shareholder permitted by Rule 5.2(a), a public announcement is required not later than 12 noon on the following business day (Rule 5.4); normally, however, such an announcement will be preceded by the announcement of a Rule 9 offer.

Share Dealings – Restrictions and Disclosure Requirements

Disclosures of shareholding interests and of dealings are also required when an announcement is issued on a bid closing date, or on an offer being declared unconditional as to acceptances, or on an offer being revised (Rule 17), and must be included in offer and defence documents (Rules 24.3 and 25.3). Rules 17, 24.3 and 25.3 have been amended as of 7 November 2005 to take into account the effect of the revised disclosure obligations in relation to dealings in options and derivatives. Although these rules required amendment to bring them into line with the new definitions of "interests in securities" and "dealings", the overriding principle behind these changes has been to ensure that the content requirements of a Rule 17 announcement, offer and defence documents are consistent with the disclosure required under paragraph (b) of Note 5(a) on Rule 8, following a Rule 8.1 dealing.

Specifically, the Rule 17 announcement, offer and defence documents are required to include the full extent of the relevant securities of the target in which the offeror (or persons acting in concert) is interested or in which it has a short position. In addition, a Rule 17 announcement requires details of acceptances, including the extent to which acceptances have been received from persons acting in concert with the offeror or in respect of shares which were the subject of an irrevocable commitment or letter of intent; and details of any relevant securities of the target in respect of which the offeror (or any of its associates) has an outstanding irrevocable commitment or letter of intent. In addition, the Rule 17 announcement, offer and defence documents must detail securities borrowed or lent by the offeror (or persons acting in concert) in order to facilitate a full understanding of the extent to which the voting rights attached to the relevant securities of the parties to the offer are currently controlled by such persons. This is another example of how the Code Committee is trying to achieve greater disclosure of complex trading transactions.

The Panel amended Note 42 on Rule 24.3 on 21 February 2002 with the effect of relaxing the restrictions on disclosing dealings in shares before or during the offer period on an aggregated basis (subject to the requirement that no significant dealings are thereby concealed). The Code Committee of the Panel was of the opinion that there are occasions when there is little benefit in listing a large number of transactions during or shortly before the offer period. It therefore decided that all purchases and sales during the offer period can be aggregated. Furthermore, the Code Committee decided:

(a) to extend to three months the period prior to the offer period during which dealings may be aggregated on a monthly basis; and
(b) to permit dealings in the nine months prior to that period to be aggregated on a quarterly basis.

The Note requires that acquisitions and disposals should not be netted off, that the highest and lowest prices should be stated and that disclosure should distinguish between different categories of interest in relevant securities and short positions. It is also worth noting that the entirety of the provisions in Note 42 on Rule 24.3 are now subject to a full list of all dealings (together with a draft of the proposed aggregate disclosure) being sent to the Panel for approval prior to the posting of the offer documentation, and being available for inspection.

3.6 Miscellaneous

We will now deal briefly with some miscellaneous topics concerning share dealings of which advisers on a takeover will need to have some understanding.

3.6.1 Dealings by principal traders and fund managers

There was a good deal of confusion about how the Code treated dealings by connected principal traders and fund managers. On 25 April 2005, following the consultation on market-related issues, the Code was amended, mainly to clarify and codify elements of the Panel's practice which had developed over time. It is, perhaps, simplest to address the provisions which apply to both principal traders and fund managers before looking at the Code provisions which are specific to one or the other.

The term "market maker" was previously used in the Code, but was replaced with the term "principal trader" on 25 April 2005, as the Panel had adopted this term following the introduction of SETS (*see* Section 3.5.1.1.3 above), after which there were no recognised market makers in SETS-traded securities. It also reflects the policy which has been adopted by the Panel for some time that all principal trading activities (not just market making activities) should be eligible for exempt status (*see* below).

The Panel has also introduced a new defined term, that of "connected adviser". Connected advisers normally include only:

(a) in relation to the offeror or target – an organisation which is advising that party in relation to the offer and a corporate broker to that party;
(b) in relation to a person who is acting in concert with the offeror or the target – an organisation which is advising that person either in relation to the offer or in relation to the matter which is the reason for that person being a member of the relevant concert party; and
(c) in relation to a person who is an associate of the offeror or of the target by virtue of being a member of its group – an organisation which is advising that person in relation to the offer.

The Code definition of "acting in concert" contains a presumption (presumption 5) that a connected adviser acts in concert with its client and, if its client is acting in concert with the offeror or the target, the connected adviser is also presumed to act in concert with the offeror or target, in respect of the interests in shares of that adviser and the persons controlling, controlled by or under the same control as, that adviser. Hence, when the adviser is part of a larger financial services organisation, the presumption of concertedness extends to all entities within that group.

However, principal traders and fund managers who can demonstrate to the Panel's satisfaction their independence from corporate advisory and corporate broking operations in their group are granted exempt status. Exempt status is obtained by application to the Panel. The Panel will consider all relevant factors in deciding any applications including group structure, separate physical location, the history of the organisation as a whole (including past records of cooperative or independent action), the extent of the use of common services, common directorship, financial interests of the relevant executives in the group as a whole and the existence of an effective compliance department. The effect of exempt status is to remove the principal trader or fund manager from the presumption of concertedness that would otherwise apply. However, the principal trader or fund manager will still be regarded as connected with the offeror or target company, as appropriate (*see* Note 3 on the definitions of "exempt fund manager" and "exempt principal trader").

It should be noted that exempt status is not relevant unless the sole reason for the connection is that the principal trader or fund manager is controlled by, controls or is under the same control as a connected adviser to the offeror, target, or person acting in concert with the offeror or target (Note 2 on the Code definitions of "exempt fund manager" and "exempt principal trader"). If a fund manager or principal trader's exempt status is not relevant, or if they do not have exempt status, Rule 7.2 applies. Connected fund managers and principal traders will not normally be presumed to be acting in concert with an offeror or potential offeror until that party's identity as an offeror or potential offeror is publicly announced, or (if earlier) the time at which the fund manager or principal trader had actual knowledge of the possibility of an offer being made by a person with whom it is connected (Rule 7.2(a)). When this is the case, Rules 4.2, 4.6, 5, 6, 9, 11 and 36 will be relevant. Similarly, under Rule 7.2(b), connected fund managers and principal traders will not normally be presumed to be acting in concert with the target until the commencement of the offer period, or (if earlier) the time at which the fund manager or principal trader had actual knowledge of the possibility of an offer being made. Rules 4.4, 4.6, 5 and 9 may then be relevant.

The Code has also been amended to reflect the Panel's practice of permitting a connected non-exempt principal trader or fund manager, after it is presumed to be acting in concert, to acquire or sell interests in target shares so as to flatten its book position within a short period (usually 24–48 hours) of being presumed to be acting in concert. The Panel will then not apply the usual Code consequences to dealings undertaken with its consent in this way (*see* Notes 3 and 4 to Rule 7.2).

3.6.2 Recognised intermediary status

As part of the amendments made to the Code in relation to dealings in derivatives and options, the Code Committee reviewed the status

Share Dealings – Restrictions and Disclosure Requirements

of investment institutions under the Code. The product of this review was the creation of a new "recognised intermediary status" for trading desks which trade as a principal for client-serving purposes. This status allows the interests of the recognised intermediary in shares as a result of positions in derivatives and options not to be taken into account in establishing whether the trading desk (or the organisation of which it forms part) is interested in 30 per cent or more of a company's shares carrying voting rights for the purposes of Rule 9.

The rationale behind the introduction of recognised intermediary status is that certain investment institutions, especially client-serving desks of investment banks, are likely to have substantial derivatives and options positions in the ordinary course of their business and this should not require them to make mandatory offers under Rule 9.1.

To obtain recognised intermediary status, the desk must apply to the Panel and satisfy a number of suitability conditions regarding the nature of its activities and the organisation of which it forms part.

It should be noted that recognised intermediary status is an entirely separate regime from the exempt status regime. Hence, where a recognised intermediary is (or is part of) an exempt principal trader connected with an offeror or target company, the position under the Code remains unchanged. For example, where a client-serving desk enjoys the benefits of being a recognised intermediary, its interests and dealings in relevant securities are not treated as interests of or dealings by a person acting in concert with the corporate advisory client with which it is connected.

3.6.3 Fund managers

3.6.3.1 Restrictions on dealings
Although Rules 38.1 to 38.4 (*see* Section 3.6.4.1 below) do not specifically apply to exempt fund managers, the Panel has stated that it "would not expect such a fund manager to take any action with the intention of assisting the group's corporate finance clients because this would undermine the basis on which exempt status was granted to it".

3.6.3.2 Disclosure – Rule 8
An exempt fund manager who is connected with the offeror or target (and so falls within the definition of "associate"), and who deals in

relevant securities for the account of discretionary investment clients, is required to make private disclosure of such dealings to the Panel (Rule 8.1(b)(ii)). If, however, a connected exempt fund manager holds a greater than one per cent interest in the relevant securities, then it will have to make the usual public disclosure under Rule 8.3 (in which case, private disclosure will not normally be required in addition (Rule 8.1(b)). The latter is also true, of course, of non-connected fund managers holding a one per cent (or greater) interest, but non-connected principal traders are under no such obligation.

Connected fund managers which do not enjoy exempt status must make public disclosure of their dealings in the normal way (Rule 8.1(b)(i)).

3.6.4 Principal traders

3.6.4.1 Restrictions on dealings
Granting exempt status to many principal traders left a risk of concerted actions, which was considered by the Panel to be more acute in respect of market making, involving the use of the organisation's own capital, than in respect of discretionary fund management, where managers owe fiduciary duties to their investment clients and are therefore less likely to take action to assist the organisation's corporate finance clients. Accordingly, Rule 38.1 prohibits an exempt connected principal trader from dealing with the purpose of assisting the offeror or target; Rule 38.2 also prohibits the offeror and its concert parties from dealing as principal, during the offer period, with an exempt principal trader connected with the offeror in shares of the target; Rule 38.3 states that such a principal trader may not assent its shares to the offer or purchase such shares in assented form until after the offer is unconditional as to acceptances; and Rule 38.4 prohibits shares owned by an exempt connected principal trader from being voted in the context of an offer. In order to ensure compliance with Rules 38.1 and 38.2, the Code now states that during an offer period, an offeror and persons acting in concert with it must not acquire an interest in any securities of the target company through any anonymous order book system, or through any other means, unless it can be established that the seller (or other party to the transaction in question) is not an exempt principal trader connected with the offeror (Rule 4.2(b)).

Dealings by exempt principal traders are also relevant for the purposes of Rule 9. The Panel Executive has adopted a standard approach to aggregation which requires compliance officers of multi-service financial organisations to monitor closely the aggregate holdings of the group so as to ensure that Rule 9 is not breached. This is now reflected in Note 16 on Rule 9.1, which states that Rule 9 will be relevant if the aggregate number of shares in which all persons under the same control (including any exempt fund manager or exempt principal trader) are interested carry 30 per cent or more of the voting rights of the relevant company. However, if recognised intermediary status has not fallen away under Note 3 of the definition of recognised intermediary, a recognised intermediary acting in a client-serving capacity will not be treated as interested in any securities, unless they are held in a proprietary capacity and fall within paragraph 3 or 4 of the definition of "interests in securities".

Note 16 also provides that if such a group of persons includes a principal trader and the aggregate number of shares in a company in which the group is interested approaches or exceeds 30 per cent of the voting rights, the Panel may consent to the principal trader continuing to acquire shares in the company without consequence under Rule 9.1, provided that the company is not in an offer period and the number of shares which the principal trader holds does not at any relevant time exceed three per cent of the voting rights of the company.

3.6.4.2 *Disclosure*

Before the Code Committee amended the Code to take into account dealings in derivatives and options, an unconnected principal trader who dealt in that capacity did not have to make disclosure under Rule 8.3 when his holding rose above one per cent (in contrast to the position for an unconnected fund manager and all other shareholders). As part of its review of the status of investment institutions under the Code, the Code Committee has developed further the Code's long-standing disclosure exception for recognised market makers and other intermediaries. Under the amended regime, the exception from disclosure under Rule 8.3(d) applies to all investment desks enjoying recognised intermediary status. In practice, this exception is more widely available than previously, when only available to unconnected principal traders. For example, a trading desk not registered as a market maker with the LSE or an LSE-registered member firm dealing as principal in order book securities could both potentially apply for recognised intermediary status but would not constitute a principal trader. Some commentators assume that connected principal traders have a similar immunity from disclosure so that market making arms of investment banks are able secretly to build up stakes in the target while another part of the organisation is advising the bidder. In fact, this is not the case. Exempt connected principal traders (i.e. within the same group as the financial adviser or broker) are already required to disclose all dealings (although in aggregated form) under Rule 38.5 (*see* Note 9 on Rule 8) via an RIS by 12 noon on the business day following the dealing, while connected principal traders which are not exempt will have disclosure obligations under Rule 8.1.

Chapter 4
Mandatory and Voluntary Offers and their Terms

Christopher Pearson and Nick Adams
Partners
Norton Rose

4.1 Introduction

Rules 9 to 13 restrict the freedom which a party has at common law in his decision whether or not to bid for control of a company to which the Code applies and, where he does make a bid, to choose the consideration he offers and the conditions which he attaches to his bid.

They do this in a number of ways:

(a) Rule 9 obliges a person (or persons acting in concert) to make a bid in certain circumstances, specifies the minimum consideration to be offered and limits the conditions which can be attached to the bid;
(b) Rule 10 requires a voluntary bid to contain a minimum acceptance condition;
(c) Rule 11 requires a voluntary bidder in certain situations to offer a minimum cash price, a cash alternative or to make a securities offer;
(d) Rule 12 requires a particular term to be included in an offer which could trigger a reference to the UK or EC competition authorities; and
(e) Rule 13 prohibits certain types of condition.

(Different principles apply to partial offers, which are governed by Rule 36 and are covered in Chapter 5.)

Most of the rules referred to in this Chapter are qualified by wording "except with the consent of the Panel". It is therefore important to understand the philosophy of the Panel in these matters.

4.2 The mandatory offer and its terms

Rule 9 provides that where

(a) a person (which can be an individual as well as a company)
(b) acquires an interest in shares in a company
(c) which in itself, or when aggregated with shares in which the person and persons acting in concert with it are already interested
(d) carries 30 per cent or more of the voting rights of the company

then such person must make an offer

(a) to acquire all other equity shares in the company (whether voting or non-voting, but excluding any shares held in treasury) and
(b) to acquire any other class of transferable securities in the company carrying voting rights (again, excluding any shares held in treasury)

on the terms and conditions required by Rule 9, and on no other conditions.

The Rule also requires such a bid where a person who (together with any persons acting in concert with it) is already interested in shares carrying 30 per cent or more of the voting rights of a company, but does not hold shares carrying more than 50 per cent of such rights, acquires an interest in other shares carrying voting rights. The provisions permitting such a person to acquire up to one per cent of the voting rights in any period of 12 months were abolished in August 1998. However, the Panel has considered the position of persons (and members of concert parties) interested in shares carrying more than 30 per cent of the voting rights of companies where such interests are reduced by sales or diluted as a result of the issue of new shares but remain in excess of 30 per cent. The Panel has concluded that it is appropriate to permit such persons some ability to acquire an interest in further shares in these circumstances, notwithstanding that they (or the concert party of which they form part) already hold an interest in shares carrying 30 per cent or more of the voting rights of the company. This is dealt with in more detail in 4.2.4.6 below.

Mandatory and Voluntary Offers and their Terms

A person will be treated as having an "interest in shares" if: (1) he owns the shares; (2) he has the right (whether conditional or absolute) to exercise or direct the exercise of the voting rights attaching to them or has general control of them; (3) by virtue of any agreement, he has the right or option to acquire them or call for their delivery or is under an obligation to take delivery of them; or (4) he is party to a long derivative under which he will benefit from a rise in price of the relevant shares. Consequently, the thresholds for the triggering of a mandatory offer obligation pursuant to Rule 9.1 are not limited by reference to holdings of shares carrying voting rights but will also take into account other interests in shares acquired by virtue of long derivatives, call options and written put options. A person will not normally be treated as having acquired an interest in further shares just because the nature of his interest has changed (for example, where a person acquires shares upon the exercise of a call option over existing shares). In these cases, the aggregate number of shares in which the person would be interested will usually remain the same (Note 18 to Rule 9.1).

Rule 9 is based on General Principle 1, which provides that where a person acquires control of a company, the other holders of securities must be protected.

"Control" is defined in the Definitions section of the Code as an interest, or interests, in shares carrying in aggregate 30 per cent or more of the voting rights of a company.

From time to time there have been suggestions that the 30 per cent figure should be reduced – indeed it is lower in certain other financial capitals whose takeover codes are based on the City Code. Article 5 of the Takeover Directive requires Member States to introduce rules relating to mandatory bids but does not specify the threshold at which a mandatory bid has to be made: this is left to individual Member States to determine. In the UK, the 30 per cent threshold is thought to strike an appropriate balance between protecting minority shareholders and not unduly restricting takeover activity.

The 1991 Annual Report of the Panel contained the following helpful explanation of the philosophy underlying Rule 9:

"The philosophy underlying this Rule is that, if effective control of a company is obtained by the acquisition of shares, the principle of equality of treatment for shareholders requires that all shareholders should have the opportunity to obtain the price per share paid for that control (it will usually be a premium price) and that they should have the opportunity to get out of the company if they do not like what has happened."

An important bolstering of this principle is contained in Rule 9.6, which requires directors (and their related interests) who sell shares to a person (or enter into options, derivatives or other transactions with a person) which would trigger a Rule 9 obligation to make it a condition of the sale (or other relevant transaction) that the person will make a Rule 9 bid, and for the time being to remain on their board so as to ensure proper conduct of the bid. This important provision should not be overlooked; it imposes an obligation on the seller of the shares and its significance is indicated by the fact that an equivalent of Rule 9.6 appeared in the Code before the remainder of Rule 9.

4.2.1 The terms and conditions of mandatory bids

4.2.1.1 Price

Rule 9.5(a) requires that a mandatory offer must be in cash (or be accompanied by a cash alternative) at not less than the highest price paid by the offeror or any person in concert with it for any interest in shares of the relevant class during the 12 months prior to the announcement of that offer. Rule 9.5(b) also states that if after a Rule 9 offer has been made for a class of shares, but before it closes for acceptance, the offeror or anyone acting in concert with it acquires a further interest in shares of that class at above the offer price, it must increase its offer price for that class of shares to not less than the highest price paid for the interest so acquired.

Note 1 to Rule 9.5 explains that sometimes, where a significant number of acquisitions which have to be taken into account for the purposes of this Rule have been securities exchange transactions, the principle of equality of treatment may make it undesirable that the offer be a cash only offer, and that the same securities, but with a cash offer or alternative, be offered.

Mandatory and Voluntary Offers and their Terms

Rule 9.5(c) grants the Panel a discretion to adjust the highest price calculated under Rules 9.5(a) and 9.5(b). Note 3 identifies some of the considerations which the Panel will take into account in deciding whether to make such an adjustment; one situation might be where the acquisitions were made before financial problems in the target company became publicly known and the mandatory bid is being made as part of a rescue operation. The price payable in any of the situations set out in Note 3 will be the price that is fair and reasonable taking into account all the factors that are relevant to the circumstances. In any case where the highest price is adjusted, the Panel will publish its decision.

The other notes to Rule 9.5 give further guidance on the price to be offered, including where dealings in options and derivatives are relevant.

4.2.1.2 *Competition references*
Rule 9.4 requires any mandatory bid to which Rule 12 applies (*see* 4.4 below) to contain the term required by Rule 12.1 providing that the offer will lapse in the event of a reference being made to either the UK or EC competition authorities for an in-depth competition investigation. If clearance is then obtained, the offer must be re-made as soon as practicable, although Note 1 to Rule 9.4 envisages situations where intervening action taken with the consent of the Panel may make this unnecessary. However, it cannot be a condition of a mandatory bid that there is a clearance from the competition authorities.

4.2.1.3 *Acceptance condition*
Rule 9.3 requires that, except with the consent of the Panel, a mandatory bid must be conditional only upon acceptances being received which result in the offeror and its concert party holding shares carrying more than 50 per cent of the voting rights. Note 1 to Rule 9.3 recognises that there will be no such condition where 50 per cent of the voting rights are already held before the offer is made.

4.2.1.4 *Other conditions*
Rule 9.3 prohibits other conditions being attached to mandatory bids. As a consequence it is not possible to include in mandatory offers the detailed protective conditions customarily included in voluntary offers (*see* 4.3.3 below) regarding material adverse change, or consents of shareholders, or clearances by third parties.

As far as material adverse changes are concerned, this is treated as entirely the risk of the person whose acquisition has triggered the obligation to make a mandatory bid.

As far as consents are concerned, again this is treated as something the offeror should have thought about before triggering the bid, although Note 3 to Rule 9.3 indicates that the Panel will consider a request for dispensation, which will be heavily qualified, in exceptional circumstances such as where a cash alternative can only be made available out of the proceeds of a placing of securities for which listing is a pre-condition.

As far as regulatory clearances are concerned, the difficulties to which this would give rise are such that Rule 9.3(b) proscribes the making of an acquisition which would trigger a mandatory bid if the mandatory bid's implementation would be dependent upon such a clearance, although Note 3(b) to Rule 9.3 envisages situations in which a dispensation from this may be granted.

4.2.2 Who are deemed to be "persons acting in concert"?

This question is a crucial one, since the aggregation of the interests in shares of people who are deemed to be acting in concert may result in an obligation to make a bid. The opening sentence in the Notes to Rule 9.1 states: "The majority of questions which arise in the context of Rule 9 relate to persons acting in concert".

Concert parties for the purposes of the Code are not necessarily the same as "persons acting together" for the purposes of the statutory obligation to report interests in shares of concert parties contained in the Companies Act 1985. The Definitions section of the Code defines the term as follows:

> "Persons acting in concert comprise persons who, pursuant to an agreement or understanding (whether formal or informal), cooperate to obtain or consolidate control . . . of a company or to frustrate the successful outcome of an offer for a company."

There is a deeming provision in the definition which states that a person and each of its "affiliated persons" will be acting in concert all

Mandatory and Voluntary Offers and their Terms

with each other. Affiliated persons include undertakings in respect of which any person has a majority of, or controls a majority of, the shareholders' voting rights, has the right to appoint or remove a majority of the board of directors or has the power to exercise, or actually exercises, dominant influence or control.

The definition then continues with a series of presumptions as to those persons who are in concert. These fall into six self-contained categories; someone in one of these categories is presumed to be in concert only with those in the same category and not with those in another category. However, the presumptions are rebuttable, and they are not meant to be exhaustive. They are followed by a series of Notes discussed in other contexts in this Guide. This Chapter will concentrate on the guidance given in those Notes and in the Notes to Rule 9.1 which is of particular relevance to Rule 9.

4.2.2.1 *Persons coming together to act in concert or shareholders voting together*

If persons already interested in shares carrying 30 per cent or more of the voting rights in a company but not previously acting in concert merely decide to cooperate to obtain or consolidate control of a company, this will not normally trigger a bid. However, once they have come together, the acquisition of an interest in any further shares by one of them could trigger a mandatory offer (Note 1 to Rule 9.1).

The Panel does not normally regard the action of shareholders voting together on particular resolutions as indicative of a group acting in concert. However, it might in certain circumstances decide differently, with the result that subsequent acquisitions of interests in shares could trigger a mandatory offer.

An exception to this general principle is contained in Note 2 to Rule 9.1, introduced in 2002. The Panel will normally presume shareholders who requisition or threaten to requisition the consideration of a "board control-seeking proposal" at a shareholders' meeting, together with their supporters, to be acting in concert with each other and with the proposed directors. In determining if a proposal is board control-seeking, the Panel will have regard to a number of factors, including the specific factors listed in Note 2.

4.2.2.2 Break-up of concert parties

Note 1 to the Definitions indicates that the Panel needs clear evidence before it will accept that parties, once held to be in concert, are no longer in concert. This will be particularly relevant where the original objective of the concert party having been achieved and cooperation having ceased, one of its members wishes to make a further acquisition without triggering a mandatory offer.

The composition of concert parties can also change. The sale of its interest in shares by an outgoing member of the concert party to a continuing member may, in certain circumstances, trigger an obligation on the part of the purchaser to make a mandatory bid. Note 4 to Rule 9.1 describes these circumstances.

4.2.2.3 Acquisition of part only of an interest in shares

Difficult questions arise when a shareholder who holds more than 30 per cent sells less than 30 per cent to a single purchaser or two or more purchasers who are acting in concert. One often sees a sale of 29.99 per cent in these circumstances, obviously designed to save the purchaser from Rule 9. In such circumstances the Panel are rightly curious as to whether seller and purchaser are effectively acting in concert in respect of all their shares so that a mandatory offer should be made.

The Panel will take account of such factors as whether the seller is an "insider", whether the price paid effectively contained a control premium, and whether there are any arrangements (however informal) between seller and purchaser regarding the seller's shares. Obviously fine judgements will be involved and the fact that the seller retains a substantial number of shares over which it intends to act independently will be helpful in rebutting any presumption of concerted behaviour. Similar considerations will arise where the seller remains interested in shares but without itself owning any of such shares, or where the acquisition is not of the shares themselves but of another type of interest in shares. Note 6 to Rule 9.1 provides guidance on the point, but each case is inevitably different and the Panel should always be consulted.

4.2.2.4 Employee benefit trusts

Note 5 to Rule 9.1, introduced in 2002, concerns trustees of employee benefit trusts ("EBTs") as potential concert parties. The Panel must be

Mandatory and Voluntary Offers and their Terms

consulted when an acquisition is proposed and the aggregate number of shares in which the directors, those persons acting in concert with them and the trustees of an EBT are interested would as a result carry 30 per cent or more of the voting rights or, if already carrying 30 per cent or more, would increase further. Similarly, the Panel must be consulted where a person or a group of persons acting in concert is interested in shares carrying 30 per cent or more (but does not hold shares carrying more than 50 per cent) of the voting rights of a company, and it is proposed that an EBT acquires an interest in shares. The mere establishment and operation of an EBT will not by itself give rise to a presumption that the trustees are acting in concert with the directors and/or a controller (or group of persons acting in concert). However, the Panel will consider all relevant factors in making their determination, including the non-exhaustive list contained in Note 5.

4.2.3 Dispensations from Rule 9

The Code acknowledges that in certain circumstances it would be inequitable, and therefore unnecessary in order to satisfy the equality of treatment principle, to require a mandatory bid to be made.

There is a specific dispensation at the end of Rule 9.1 for control achieved through a voluntary bid. In addition, there are a series of notes (Dispensation Notes) at the end of Rule 9 which list six situations in which the Panel may, or will, dispense with the need to make an offer. These are as follows.

4.2.3.1 The "Whitewash" procedure
The Whitewash dispensation is available on the issue of new securities, either as consideration for an acquisition or on a cash subscription. Where such an issue is of such a size that it would otherwise trigger a Rule 9 bid, the Panel will normally waive the obligation to make the bid if the requirements of Dispensation Note 1 and of Appendix 1 to the Code are complied with. Particular features of these requirements (which are additional to those of the UK Listing Authority (the "UKLA")) are:

(a) the issue must be approved at a shareholders' meeting of the company issuing the securities, the vote must be conducted by

poll rather than a show of hands, and only independent shareholders may vote;
(b) the circular to shareholders convening the meeting must give full details of the transaction, comply with the detailed requirements of paragraph 4 of Appendix 1 as to its contents; it must contain a number of warnings, and include competent independent advice on the proposals; it is noteworthy that a Whitewash circular is one of the few documents that the Panel insists it must approve before it is sent to shareholders; and
(c) the Whitewash dispensation is not available if there have been "disqualifying" acquisitions of interests in shares of the company during the preceding 12 months by the person or persons to whom the new securities are to be issued (or persons acting in concert with it or them) and those dealings occurred after discussions on the transaction to be approved by the Whitewash had begun (*see* paragraph 3 of Appendix 1).

The philosophy behind this dispensation is that the vote gives independent shareholders the opportunity to veto the change of control before it takes place. Further, if there is a premium for control involved it accrues to the company, and therefore to all shareholders, rather than to a selling shareholder.

Consistent with this philosophy, the persons to whom the new shares are to be issued may not otherwise acquire any interest in shares in the company during the period between posting of the circular and the time shareholders' approval is obtained. Once approval has been obtained, there is no restriction (apart from those restrictions applying generally by virtue of Rules 5 and 9) on such persons acquiring any interest in other shares in the company.

4.2.3.2 Foreclosure on security for a loan

Where shares or other securities are pledged as security for a loan and the lender forecloses as a result of the borrower's default, the lender may find itself (either alone or with persons with whom it is in concert) holding an interest in shares carrying more than 30 per cent of the voting rights. Where the threshold is crossed purely as a result of such a foreclosure, the Panel will not normally require the lender to make a mandatory offer provided that a sufficient number of the shares over which it has an interest are sold within a limited period to persons unconnected with the lender. In order to prevent the lender exercising control, it must consult with the Panel as to the ability to exercise its voting rights prior to such a sale.

The Panel will apply similar principles to the appointment of a receiver, an administrator or a liquidator. That person will not normally be required to make a mandatory offer, but a purchaser from him will be subject to Rule 9.

4.2.3.3 Rescue operations

Where a company is insolvent or prospectively insolvent because it is undercapitalised, the directors will obviously wish to restore it to solvency, either by issuing new shares in exchange for new cash, or by arranging with certain of its loan creditors to exchange their debt for shares. Usually its financial difficulties will be such that its existing equity shares are worth little, so that meaningful new capital is likely to represent more than 30 per cent of the voting share capital after the rescue.

However, sometimes the financial crisis may be such that there is no time to go through the Whitewash procedure before the directors would have to call in the receiver. Dispensation Note 3 indicates that in such circumstances the Panel may, out of financial necessity, waive the need for a mandatory bid without the need for a Whitewash resolution provided that shareholder approval is given for the rescue operation after it has happened or the Panel is satisfied that some other provision is made for the protection of independent shareholders. If neither of these solutions is available, the rescuer will be required to make a mandatory offer, although the Panel may consider an adjustment to the highest price required by Rule 9.5(a).

4.2.3.4 Inadvertent mistake

Dispensation Note 4 acknowledges that sometimes there may be a crossing of the 30 per cent threshold as a result of an innocent mistake. In that event the Panel will not normally require a mandatory offer if the holding is within a short period reduced to below 30 per cent by sales to persons unconnected with the purchaser (or the percentage of shares carrying voting rights in which the person, together with persons acting in concert with him, is interested is otherwise reduced to below 30 per cent in a manner satisfactory to the Panel). In order to prevent any such person exercising control in the meantime, the Panel must be consulted as to the ability to exercise voting rights prior to such sales.

It should be noted that a dispensation is not necessarily available if a purchaser knowingly acquires an interest in shares carrying more than 30 per cent of the voting rights on the basis that it will place out a sufficient percentage of this interest to reduce its holding to below 30 per cent. Note 7 to Rule 9.1 envisages situations in which dispensation may be given in such circumstances, but if the Panel regards it as a situation in which a premium has been paid for control it will require a mandatory offer to be made.

4.2.3.5 Where 50 per cent will not accept
Dispensation Note 5 acknowledges that there is no point in making a mandatory offer if persons holding shares carrying 50 per cent or more of the voting rights state in writing that they will not accept it. This is because it is pointless to make the offer if the acceptance condition will not be satisfied. However, the Panel must be consulted so that it can be assured of the factual background.

4.2.3.6 Enfranchisement of non-voting shares
If a person crosses a Rule 9 threshold as a result of non-voting shares in which it is already interested being enfranchised, Dispensation Note 6 provides that it will not be required to make a mandatory offer unless it had reason to believe at the time of becoming interested in the non-voting shares that enfranchisement would take place. This dispensation reflects the fact that the person has not crossed the threshold by a voluntary act.

4.2.3.7 Redemption or purchase by a company of its own shares
The position where a person's interest in shares is caused to cross the threshold by reason of a reduction or redemption of share capital, or a purchase of its own shares, by the company itself is covered by Rule 37.1 rather than a Dispensation Note to Rule 9. The removal in August 1998 of the one per cent "creeper" provisions (*see* 4.2 above)

Mandatory and Voluntary Offers and their Terms

resulted in a number of perceived difficulties in the application of Rule 37.1, particularly as regards directors. Following a detailed review, the Panel's policy is now set out in Panel Statement 1999/17.

4.2.4 Other points in relation to Rule 9

4.2.4.1 Who must make the offer
The person whose acquisition causes the 30 per cent threshold to be crossed or who acquires an interest in further shares triggering a Rule 9 obligation has primary responsibility to make the bid (Rule 9.1). However, Rule 9.2 provides that where there is a concert party the principal members of the party may also be obliged to make the offer depending on the circumstances of the case. The Note to Rule 9.2 provides some guidance, but consultation with the Panel as to who should make the bid where there is a concert party is highly desirable. The person required to make a mandatory offer may extend the offer to other concert parties, but will not normally be required to do so.

4.2.4.2 The chain principle
If a person or group of persons acquires statutory control of any company which is interested, either directly or through intermediate companies, in shares of a second company, the Panel may require a mandatory bid if such a bid would have been triggered if that person or group of persons had directly acquired the interest in the shares of the second company owned by the first company. Generally speaking, however, the Panel will not apply this principle (which is set out in Note 8 to Rule 9.1) unless either the interest in shares which the first company has in the second company is significant in relation to the first company, or unless one of the main purposes of acquiring control of the first company was to secure control of the second company. The Panel should be consulted in any relevant case.

4.2.4.3 Triggering Rule 9 during the course of a voluntary offer
Rule 5.2 may permit a voluntary offeror to take its interest in shares in the offeree above the 30 per cent threshold during an offer period (although Note 4 to Rule 32.1 may preclude its doing so unless the existing offer can remain open for acceptance for at least 14 further days). The obvious situation in which a bidder might want to trigger a Rule 9 bid would be one where it felt obliged to pick up a parcel of

shares overhanging the market. If it does so, it must immediately waive all conditions other than those permitted by Rule 9. If a voluntary offeror wishes to make such an acquisition, Note 9 to Rule 9.1 requires the Panel to be consulted in advance.

4.2.4.4 Restrictions on exercise of control by an offeror

Rule 9.7 provides that until the mandatory offer document is posted neither the offeror nor any of its concert parties may exercise, or procure the exercise of, votes attaching to any shares in the offeree, and no nominee of the offeror or any of its concert parties may be appointed to the offeree board.

4.2.4.5 Convertible securities, warrants and options

Generally speaking, the acquisition of securities convertible into, warrants in respect of, or options or other rights to subscribe for, *new* shares does not give rise to an obligation to make a general offer under Rule 9, although the subsequent exercise of the conversion or subscription rights or options will be treated as an acquisition of an interest in the shares for the purposes of the Rule. Even then the exercise of those conversion or subscription rights will not usually be regarded as triggering a general offer if the issue of the convertible securities or subscription rights was approved by a Whitewash procedure, unless there have been intervening acquisitions of interests in further voting shares.

Any holder of conversion or subscription rights who intends to exercise such rights and will, as a result, become interested in shares carrying 30 per cent or more of the voting rights of a company must consult the Panel before doing so to determine whether a mandatory offer obligation would arise under Rule 9 and if so at what price.

4.2.4.6 The yo-yo principle

A person's interest in shares can be reduced by a number of events, such as a sale by it or an issue of further shares by the company itself or a transfer by the company of shares out of treasury. If the effect of this event is to reduce its interest in shares to below 30 per cent of the voting rights, it will still have to make a mandatory offer if it subsequently makes a further acquisition and as a result the number of shares in which it is interested would, once again, carry more than 30 per cent of the voting rights (unless it qualifies for one of the

Mandatory and Voluntary Offers and their Terms

dispensations). It is treated for all purposes as starting from the base of its reduced percentage and subsequently crossing the 30 per cent threshold by voluntary action. These principles, which are set out in Note 11 to Rule 9.1, can give rise to practical difficulties and again consultation with the Panel will usually be required.

Note 11 to Rule 9.1 permits, in limited circumstances, acquisitions by persons (or groups of persons acting in concert) who are interested in shares carrying more than 30 per cent of the voting rights of a company. If such a person or group of persons reduces its interest but not to less than 30 per cent, then they may subsequently acquire an interest in further shares, subject to the following restrictions, without incurring an obligation to make a general offer:

(a) the total number of shares in which interests may be acquired under this Note in any period of 12 months must not exceed one per cent of the voting share capital for the time being; and
(b) the percentage of shares in which the relevant person or group of persons acting in concert is interested following any acquisition must not exceed the highest percentage of shares in which such person or group of persons was interested in the previous 12 months.

The Panel will regard a reduction of the percentage of shares in which the person or group is interested as a result of dilution following the new issue of shares as also being relevant for these purposes.

4.2.4.7 Insincere Rule 9 bids

A mandatory offer may also be triggered during the course of, for example, a management buy-in by an entrepreneur who needs a listed vehicle and who has to buy more than 30 per cent of a listed company, but where acceptances are placed out in order to secure a sufficient spread of shareholdings to maintain a quotation; these bids are generally known as insincere Rule 9 bids. Notwithstanding the fact that it is announced that acceptances are being placed out in order to maintain the shareholder spread necessary for a continued listing, the Panel takes the view that the public shareholders should be put into a position whereby they can accept the same terms as the seller or his concert party, in case they do not like the new management.

4.2.5 Practical effects of Rule 9

Rule 9 has three important effects in practice:

(a) it discourages a holding of interests in shares which carry more than 29.99 per cent of the voting rights of a company;
(b) it discourages a voluntary bidder from making a market purchase permitted by Rule 5.2 if it wants to maintain a full set of conditions to its offer; and
(c) it encourages persons who might be in concert and who are close to (or over) the 30 per cent threshold to consult the Panel.

For the above reasons Rule 9 bids are not frequent.

4.3 The voluntary offer and its terms

In accordance with Rule 2.5(b)(vi) an offeror is required to announce all the conditions of an offer at the time that a firm intention to make a bid is announced. Generally speaking, the conditions attaching to an offer to purchase the share capital of a target company are a matter for the offeror. However, the Code does impose certain restrictions so as to ensure that its General Principles are honoured.

4.3.1 When a particular form of consideration is required

Rule 11.1 requires an offer to be in cash, or have a cash alternative, if:

(a) the offeror and its concert parties have acquired interests in voting shares during the offer period or within the preceding 12 months, and the interests so acquired carry 10 per cent or more of the voting rights currently exercisable at a class meeting of that class (in which case the cash price offered must be not less than the highest price paid during such a period);
(b) any interest in shares of any class under offer in the offeree company is acquired for cash by an offeror or any person acting in concert with it during the offer period (in which case the cash price offered must be not less than the highest price paid during such a period); or

(c) in the view of the Panel there are circumstances which render such a course necessary in order to give effect to General Principle 1.

This requirement is additional to the minimum value requirement contained in Rule 6 (*see* Chapter 3).

The Notes to the Rule contain guidance on how the price paid for any acquisition of an interest in shares (either through the direct purchase of shares or through entering into an option or derivative) will be determined. There is also particular guidance in relation to the conversion or exercise of securities convertible into, warrants in respect of, or options or other rights to subscribe for, new shares.

There are a number of other important points contained in the Notes to Rule 11.1. Note 2 provides that the Panel will not normally allow sales to be netted off against acquisitions in calculating the 10 per cent limit. Note 5 indicates that acquisitions of interests in shares in exchange for securities will normally be deemed to be acquisitions for cash on the basis of the value of the securities at the time of the acquisition (unless the recipient is required to hold the securities received or receivable until either the offer has lapsed or consideration has been posted to accepting shareholders). Note 8 provides guidance as to how the percentages are calculated if there is a rights issue in progress.

It is important to note that Rule 11.1 can be triggered after the offer period commences (although the Notes to Rule 32.1 contain restrictions on this in the 14 days before the last date on which the offer can become unconditional as to acceptances). If an acquisition of an interest in shares is made which triggers it at a time when there is a cash alternative which is not lower than the acquisition price, there is no problem. If there is no cash alternative, Note 6 requires an immediate announcement of the necessary revision of the offer to include a cash alternative at not less than the transaction price. Similarly there must be a revision and an immediate announcement if the transaction price exceeds the present offer price. Difficulties can arise if it is a person deemed to be in concert with the offeror, rather than the offeror itself, which makes an acquisition which triggers the Rule; in the Guinness/Distillers bid a purchase of shares in

Distillers at above the bid price was made by a party which the Panel ruled, after completion of the bid, to have been in concert with Guinness; the Panel ruled (Panel Statement 1989/13) that Guinness should top up, by payments to Distillers' former shareholders, its purchase price to the level to which it would have been required to revise its offer by Rule 11.1.

The Rule is effectively an (albeit limited) exemption from General Principle 1, in that it enables an offeror to acquire an interest in shares for cash without making a cash alternative available to other shareholders provided that the aggregate interest acquired represents less than 10 per cent and no interest in shares is acquired for cash during the offer period. It is for this reason that Rule 11.1(c) envisages that there may be circumstances in which General Principle 1 requires there to be a cash alternative even if the 10 per cent threshold is not crossed. Note 4 indicates that this discretion will not normally be exercised unless the vendors or the parties to the transaction giving rise to the interests are directors of, or otherwise closely connected with, the bidder or the target company.

Rule 11.2 requires that, where interests in shares of any class of the offeree company carrying 10 per cent or more of the voting rights currently exercisable at a class meeting of that class have been acquired by an offeror and any person acting in concert with it in exchange for securities in the three months prior to the commencement of and during the offer period, such securities will normally be required to be offered to all other holders of shares of that class. Note 1 to Rule 11.2 provides that any securities required to be offered must be offered on the basis of the same number of consideration shares received or receivable by the vendor or other party to the transaction for each offeree company share rather than on the basis of securities equivalent to the value of the securities received or receivable at the time of the relevant acquisition.

Rule 11.3 enables a bidder to seek dispensation from the obligation to pay the highest price given during the relevant period and the Note to that Rule sets out the factors which the Panel might take into account when considering such an application. These factors are not expressed to be exhaustive; the Panel might well take into account a substantial collapse in the target company's share price after the acquisitions were made as a result of new information about its business becoming publicly available.

4.3.2 The acceptance condition

Rule 10 requires there to be an unwaivable condition in any offer for voting equity share capital or for other transferable securities carrying voting rights that the offer will not become or be declared unconditional as to acceptances unless the bidder has acquired or agreed to acquire (either under the offer or by other contract) shares carrying over 50 per cent of the voting rights.

The rationale for the 50 per cent threshold is that the bidder will control the board of the target, and thus have management control, even if transactions between the bidder and the target will be restricted under the Related Party Transaction Rules set out in Chapter 11 of the UKLA's Listing Rules. The Panel normally regards 50.01 per cent control as determinative. In the Minorco/Consgold bid, the Panel required Consgold to withdraw a US anti-trust action once Minorco held over 50 per cent, even though the directors of Consgold had received Counsel's opinion that having decided that the action was in the interests of Consgold they were not free as a matter of law to change their position without there being a relevant change in the interests of the company (which did not mean the interests of the majority shareholder).

Note 1 envisages that there can be certain exceptional circumstances where Rule 10 can be waived, but it would be important to consult the Panel at the earliest stage in such a situation. If an offeror wished to acquire less than 50 per cent it might consider the alternative of making a partial offer under Rule 36 (*see* Chapter 5).

In the 1995 Granada/Forte bid, such dispensation was granted by the Panel. The Council of Forte, although holding less than 0.1 per cent of Forte's shares, held a majority of the voting rights in Forte. Rule 10 requires that a bidder acquires 50 per cent of voting rights before a bid can be declared unconditional. However, when Granada made the initial offer it was unclear whether the Council would be legally able to accept the offer. The Panel agreed that Granada could make its offer conditional on acceptance by a majority of ordinary shareholders.

Note 2 to the Rule requires the offeror to take account in his acceptance condition of all shares carrying voting rights which are unconditionally allotted or issued before the offer becomes or is declared unconditional as to acceptances. By implication it does not allow the condition to take into account shares which can be issued as a result of conversion rights or options being exercised after the offer closes. It is a common feature of conversion rights and share option schemes that they can be exercised in connection with a takeover and normally these rights will persist for a period after the offer closes.

The difficulties which this can cause were illustrated in the Boots offer for Ward White in 1989. Ward White had a class of convertible preference shares which, if fully converted, would have increased the ordinary share capital of Ward White by more than 40 per cent. Boots made offers, each subject to a separate acceptance condition, for both the convertible preference shares and the ordinary shares. The last date for lodging conversion notices was the day before the last day on which Boots could (by virtue of Rule 31.6) declare its offers unconditional as to acceptances (failing which declaration its bids would have to lapse). The question arose as to whether ordinary shares which would in due course be allotted on conversion, but which could not yet be allotted, should or should not be taken into account in deciding whether the acceptance condition in the offer for the ordinary shares was satisfied. A decision either way could have produced a bizarre result, depending upon patterns of exercise of the conversion rights which could not be known when the Panel had to make its decision. The difficulties inherent in deciding which approach was preferable were indicated by the fact that the Panel Executive's ruling was reversed by the full Panel on appeal, who decided that the literal interpretation of Note 2 should be followed and that only ordinary shares actually allotted could be taken into account.

This ruling (Panel Statement 1989/15) makes it important that offerors carefully consider all potential subscription and conversion rights when framing and deciding upon the timing of their offers. In order to ensure that an offeror has sufficient information for this purpose, Note 3 to Rule 10 requires the offeree company to provide all such information to an offeror on request.

Mandatory and Voluntary Offers and their Terms

Given the number of respects in which a 50 per cent level of acceptances triggers actions under the Code, and also the psychological effect of a bidder announcing that it has achieved 50 per cent acceptances, the Panel attaches considerable importance to the verification of acceptances. In 1988, Blue Circle declared its bid for Birmid Qualcast unconditional as to acceptances when it thought it had attained that level, but in fact had not done so because of a mistaken double counting. In the aftermath of that bid the Panel introduced a number of detailed provisions relating to the verification of acceptances, which are set out in Notes 4 to 7 to Rule 10 and in the Receiving Agents' Code of Practice set out in Appendix 4 to the Code.

One feature of these provisions is that an offeror's receiving agent can only treat an acceptance as valid if it is accompanied by the relative share certificate, or in the absence of such a certificate, specified confirmatory documentation. This Rule reflects the basic equitable principle that a vendor's inability to produce his share certificate puts his purchaser on notice that there might be inconsistent proprietary rights. In the case of shares held through CREST, proof of ownership of shares in dematerialised form is provided electronically to the offeror's receiving agent.

Notwithstanding that Rule 10 only requires a 50 per cent acceptance condition, it is usual for offer documents to specify a 90 per cent level in the acceptance condition. This level is chosen because it is the threshold at which the compulsory purchase provisions of Section 429 Companies Act 1985 can apply. Attainment of that level also facilitates the conversion of the target company to a private company, able to take advantage of the more liberal regime in the Companies Act 1985 for private companies, following completion of the takeover. However, such conditions retain to the offeror the right to waive that condition down to a lower level, subject to the Rule 10 minimum of 50 per cent. Usually a bidder will declare the offer unconditional as to acceptances once the 50 per cent level has been obtained so as to accelerate further acceptances, although this is very much a tactical consideration. For example, financiers of a bid (particularly where the bid is highly leveraged, such as in most MBOs) may require a guarantee and supporting charges from the target company; this can only be given after the target has become a private company, at which stage it is possible to go through the various procedures under

Section 155 and following of the Companies Act 1985. Generally speaking, it is necessary to be certain that the compulsory purchase provisions can be activated to achieve this, and in such cases it may not be possible to waive the 90 per cent level (this is because the holders of five per cent or more of the target company could in theory apply to the court for cancellation of any special resolution passed to convert the target into a private company). Another possibility might be where the offeree is in financial or other difficulty and unfettered control is considered necessary.

Where an offer includes shares held by the target in treasury, the target is not permitted to accept the offer until after it has become unconditional as to acceptances (Rule 4.5), so treasury shares cannot be used to meet the 50 per cent acceptance condition.

Rule 10 does not apply to offers effected by schemes of arrangement under the Companies Act 1985, for which shareholder approval is given by a majority in number of those voting, representing at least 75 per cent in nominal value of those shares voted, approving the transaction at a shareholders' meeting at which only independent shareholders may vote.

4.3.3 *Other conditions*

Offer documents in voluntary bids usually contain very detailed conditions. They need to be identified at the earliest stage, since Rule 2.5(b)(vi) requires all conditions to be identified when a firm intention to make an offer is announced.

These conditions generally fall into three categories, namely those:

(a) requiring specific action in order to enable the offer to proceed;
(b) concerning possible governmental action or regulatory action which might be triggered by the offer; and
(c) giving the offeror the opportunity to withdraw if there is material adverse change in relation to the target company.

4.3.3.1 Conditions requiring specific action
If the takeover is a Class 1 transaction for the bidder, or if its unissued share capital or its directors' share issuing powers are insufficient to

Mandatory and Voluntary Offers and their Terms

implement the offer, the bidder will have to make its offer conditional upon the necessary resolutions of its own shareholders.

It is standard practice for offeror shareholder resolutions to approve not only the offer but also any increased or revised offer approved by the offeror's board. This is both to give the offeror flexibility and because the Code timetable might render it impracticable to convene another EGM to seek further shareholder approval. However, the UKLA will need to be consulted where a listed offeror proposes to increase an offer without obtaining a further shareholder authority. Unusually, in the 1995 North West Water/NORWEB bid, North West Water undertook to seek shareholder approval for a revised offer announced less than seven days before the North West Water EGM or after the EGM, by means of a postal ballot. It was stated that the directors considered this mechanism to be desirable to consider any increase in the offer.

Where offeror shares are to be issued by way of consideration, a listing for them will have to be a condition. Where a cash bid is being financed by the issue of offeror securities, the bid may only be conditional on matters that are necessary, as a matter of law or regulatory requirement, to issue those securities. Generally the only permissible conditions will therefore be the passing of any necessary shareholder resolution and listing of the securities.

If the target company has already put proposals to its own shareholders for some transaction or other, it is permissible to make it a condition of the bid that the proposals are approved, or alternatively voted down. For example, in 2003 Capital Management & Investment, the bid vehicle of Hugh Osmond, made its bid for Six Continents conditional on Six Continents' shareholders not approving the proposed demerger of Six Continents' pub and hotel businesses (and its bid lapsed when the demerger proposals were approved). If such a transaction is proposed by the offeree's board to its shareholders after the bid is announced, this situation will normally be covered by one of the conditions referred to in Section 4.3.3.3 below.

If the target company's Articles of Association contain restrictions on the ownership of shares, these will need to be amended before the bid can be completed.

4.3.3.2 Regulatory matters

Where some form of licence is fundamental to the offeree company's business, the confirmation of the relevant regulatory authority's approval to the change of control is usually made a specific condition.

Bids will usually contain a condition about clearance from the UK competition authorities (a condition which supplements the Rule 12 provision referred to later in this Chapter) and those involving an important US dimension will refer to the expiry of all US anti-trust waiting periods.

Such specific provisions are usually backed up by more general provisions referring to all necessary official authorisations being obtained and no adverse regulatory action being taken. Such regulatory action, particularly when taken overseas, is in many ways analogous to the situation which can arise in relation to a UK or EC competition reference for an in-depth competition investigation. There is, however, an important difference between what happens to a bid if there is a reference to competition authorities of the kind envisaged in Rule 12 and what happens if there is a reference to a regulatory authority only covered by the more general condition. This is because, if a bid lapses because of a "Rule 12 reference", the offeror may re-bid as soon as regulatory clearance is obtained from the UK or EC competition authorities, whereas if a bidder lapses its offer because of another type of regulatory reference it is precluded by Rule 35.1 from re-bidding within 12 months unless the Panel gives it dispensation.

This distinction did not make any difference in the 1989 Hoylake bid for BAT. BAT had an insurance subsidiary in the US and various US regulatory reviews were instituted, as a result of which Hoylake had to lapse its bid. The regulatory procedures having been completed, Hoylake requested Rule 35.1 dispensation in order to re-bid. This was given (Panel Statements 1989/20 and 1989/21) on the basis that the new bid would have to follow exactly the same shortened timetable as applies when a bid which has lapsed under Rule 12 is re-made. The analogy with the Rule 12 situation was clear in this bid, but may not always be so; Note (b) to Rules 35.1 and 35.2 encourages reference to the Panel as soon as possible where delays in regulatory reviews become apparent.

4.3.3.3 *Material change in circumstances conditions*

Such conditions perform a very important function, at least in theory, because (if the offeror cannot lapse its bid under the acceptance condition or Rule 12) they give the offeror its only opportunity to walk away from the bid if it finds something seriously amiss with the target company's business in the course of the takeover. It has no opportunity to exact warranties, and where the bid is not recommended will have had no opportunity to conduct a due diligence exercise. Further, an offeree company is likely to publish more information during the course of a takeover bid than it would normally do – indeed it is obliged by General Principle 2 and Rule 23 to give shareholders sufficient information to enable them to reach a properly informed decision on the bid and not to withhold relevant information from them. Apart from this, target companies tend to become subjected to heavy press scrutiny. Much about the offeree's business will therefore become public knowledge during the course of the bid, and if the information is bad news the offeror will need the opportunity to withdraw.

Material change conditions will usually cover a number of situations, including transactions outside the ordinary course of business, litigation, the discovery of provisions of loan documents or contractual obligations which would restrict completion of the bid or affect the offeree's business and compliance with environmental laws.

The words "material" and "adverse" appear with some regularity in these conditions, as they do in certain regulatory conditions. This, and indeed the general approach to regulatory and material change conditions, is governed by two requirements of Rule 13. The first of these requirements is that an offer must not normally be subject to conditions which depend solely on subjective judgements by the directors of the offeror. It is acknowledged in the Rule that elements of subjectivity are unavoidable in certain circumstances, but it is clear that the Panel will expect to be consulted unless such conditions follow the usual form. The second requirement is covered in 4.3.4 below.

4.3.4 *Invoking conditions*

Rule 13.4 provides that an offeror should not invoke a condition (other than an acceptance condition or a condition included pursuant to Rule 12) so as to cause its offer to lapse unless the circumstances which give rise to a right to invoke the condition are of material significance to the offeror in the context of the offer. Practitioners were reminded that the Panel may restrict the circumstances in which a condition may be invoked in the *Corporate Services Group ("CSG")* case (Panel Statement 1999/7) where an offeror made an offer conditional on there being no changes to the board of CSG, and later sought to invoke the condition following certain board changes. The Panel Executive ruled that the condition could not be invoked because the changes could not be regarded as sufficiently material.

The issue was looked at again by the Panel in connection with the offer by WPP for Tempus (Panel Statement 2001/15). The Panel met on 31 October 2001 to hear an appeal by WPP against the Panel Executive's refusal to allow WPP to invoke the material adverse change condition in relation to its offer for Tempus. WPP was of the view that there had been a material adverse change in the prospects of Tempus after the announcement of WPP's offer and, in particular, following the events in the US on 11 September.

It was agreed between the parties that the issue for the Panel was whether WPP had established that there had been a material adverse change in the prospects of Tempus which was of material significance to WPP in the context of its offer for Tempus. There was disagreement, however, about the definition of "material" for these purposes.

The Panel received submissions in relation to the various commercial issues, including in relation to the prospects of Tempus and its profitability. The Panel also had regard to the rationale for the acquisition as expressed in the WPP offering documentation.

As regards "materiality" the Panel took the view that meeting the test specified in the Code requires an adverse change of very considerable significance striking at the heart of the purpose of the transaction in question, analogous to something that would justify frustration of a legal contract. The Panel took the view that to accept a lower test would allow an offeror to use a material adverse change condition to defeat the object of the Code Rules and previously expressed Panel policy. The Panel, accordingly, did not accept the test proposed by WPP that it is sufficient if there has been "a change which undermines, from the offeror's perspective, the rationale for having made the offer at the price and on the terms specified".

The Panel did consider that a change in general economic circumstances may legitimately be relied upon when seeking to invoke the relevant condition, but only if and to the extent that in doing so meets the requirements mentioned above.

The Panel's conclusion is worth noting:

> "For an offeror to invoke a material adverse change condition and so withdraw its offer requires, in the opinion of the Panel, the offeror to demonstrate to the Panel that exceptional circumstances have arisen affecting the offeree company which could not have reasonably been foreseen at the time of the announcement of the offer. The effect of the circumstances in point must be sufficiently adverse to meet the high test of materiality [mentioned above] and judged, at least in the present type of case, not in terms of short-term profitability but on their effect on the longer-term prospects of the offeree company. Indeed, as WPP made clear it was the longer-term prospects of Tempus which had provided the strategic rationale for the offer and this seemed to the Panel to be central to the value which WPP placed on Tempus at that time.
>
> The Panel considered the submissions of the parties and the arguments they made at the time of the hearing, including but not limited to the basis of the attempts to predict the future profits of Tempus, the longer term effects of the events of 11 September on Tempus, the general economic decline affecting the advertising industry before and after the posting of the offer and the strategic reasons for WPP's offer for Tempus. The Panel came to the conclusion, on the evidence before it, that WPP had failed to demonstrate that ... there was a material adverse change in the context of the bid such as to entitle them to invoke the material adverse change condition, and had so failed by a considerable margin. The appeal, therefore, failed."

WPP's arguments would not have been assisted by the market purchases of Tempus shares which it made on 17 September. However, the Panel's ruling is not based on those purchases.

The Panel Executive issued Practice Statement No. 5 in April 2004 which clarified the statement it had made that the test of "material significance" required an adverse change that was "analogous ... to something that would justify frustration of a legal contract". Some practitioners had interpreted this to mean that a bidder would need to demonstrate legal frustration in order to be able to invoke a condition to an offer. The Panel Executive confirmed that although the standard required is high, it does not require the offeror to demonstrate frustration in the legal sense.

In August 2004 the Code Committee issued Panel Consultation Paper 2004/4 which contained a number of proposed changes to the Code relating to conditions. In this paper the Code Committee considered whether the strict test for invoking conditions contained in Note 2 to Rule 13 should apply to bespoke conditions, which may have been heavily negotiated between the offeror and the offeree. Although the Code Committee concluded that Note 2 on Rule 13 should apply in all cases, a new Note to Rule 13 was proposed which would make it clear that in determining whether a condition can be invoked the Panel should be able to take account of whether or not the condition was the subject of negotiation, whether the condition was expressly drawn to the offeree company shareholders' attention in the offer document and its consequences clearly explained and whether the condition was included to take account of the particular nature of the business of the offeree company. This proposal was, however, withdrawn by the Code Committee following consultation, largely on the basis that inclusion of a list of specific factors to be taken into account might result in undue weight being given to those factors. Nevertheless, the Committee reiterated that the factors listed above remain of general relevance.

An amendment to the Code made in April 2005 imposes an obligation on an offeror to use all reasonable efforts to ensure the timely satisfaction of the conditions to its offer (Rule 13.4(b)). This is to prevent an offeror seeking to cause a condition which is not subject to a materiality threshold (such as a condition included pursuant to Rule 12) not to be satisfied in order to lapse a bid where the offeror would be unable to rely on a material adverse change condition or other protective condition to do so.

In some circumstances an offer will include conditions relating to the bidder which benefit the target (known as "offeree protection conditions"), as well as standard conditions which benefit the bidder. Offeree protection conditions are generally only found in securities exchange offers, particularly where the bidder and target are of a similar size. Rule 13.5, introduced in April 2005, provides that an offeree company should not invoke such a condition unless the circumstances which give rise to the right to invoke the condition are of material significance to the shareholders of the offeree company in the context of that offer. Note 1 to that rule makes it clear, however, that the circumstances in which the Panel may permit an offeree company to invoke a condition are not necessarily the same as those in which an offeror would be permitted to invoke a condition. The Panel retains flexibility to consider each case on its merits, taking into account the circumstances giving rise to the right to invoke the condition, for example, the size of the offeree company relative to the offeror and the recommendation of the Board of the offeree company. Rather than simply having to decide whether an offer should lapse or not, Note 2 provides that the Panel should also have the flexibility to require, as an alternative, the introduction of withdrawal rights, so that shareholders who had accepted the relevant offer would be given a period of time to withdraw their acceptance.

Rule 35.1 reinforces Rule 13, in that a bidder which lapses its offer will, subject to certain exceptions set out in the notes to Rule 35, have to wait a year before bidding again.

An interesting insight into the Panel's attitude to such situations arose in the Severn Trent bid for Caird in 1990. Early in 1990 Caird had issued a profit forecast for the year. When Severn Trent announced its offer for Caird later in the year it made it a condition that the board of Caird would re-confirm the profit forecast. It did not, reducing the forecast downwards by some 15 per cent. Severn Trent decided to lapse its bid and applied to the Panel for dispensation under Rule 35.1 to re-bid at a lower price. In the meantime it had acquired more than 10 per cent of Caird's ordinary share capital in the market at its original offer price, so that the Panel would also have had to give dispensation under Rule 11.1. The Panel declined dispensation purely by reference to Rule 35.1. In its ruling (Panel Statement 1990/20) it noted that Severn Trent must have been somewhat sceptical as to the likelihood of the profit forecast being reaffirmed when it made that reaffirmation a condition of the bid; it did so aware of the provisions of Rule 35.1 and therefore must live with the consequences.

The question was looked at again in 1995 when the Panel was asked to permit Trafalgar House to make a new bid for Northern Electric following its decision to lapse its offer following a substantial fall in the market value of the Regional Electricity Companies as a result of a statement by Professor Littlechild, the Director General of the Office of Electricity Regulation. At the time it decided to lapse Trafalgar House held 76 per cent acceptances.

Trafalgar House submitted that the circumstances were so exceptional as to justify the Panel permitting a new offer. It contended that shareholder interests would best be served by a new offer. There was substantial shareholder support for a new offer. The Northern Electric Board stated it would not agree to a new offer until the regulatory uncertainty was removed. The Panel refused to consent to Trafalgar launching a new bid. Although unusual, the circumstances did not justify the granting of a dispensation under Rule 35.

4.4 Competition law issues

Bidders also have to consider the possible application of competition laws – in particular, UK merger control under the Enterprise Act 2002 and EC merger control under the EC Merger Regulation. The application of merger control rules will at the very least have an impact on the timetable, especially if an in-depth competition investigation is opened – that is, if in the UK a reference is made to the Competition Commission ("CC") or at EC level the European Commission initiates Phase 2 proceedings.

There are specific tests for determining whether these merger control rules apply. The UK test is based on the UK turnover of the target or the parties' market share. The EC test is based on the parties' turnovers worldwide, within the EU and within EU Member States. A transaction may fall under either or both sets of rules. If the latter, the European Commission is granted exclusive jurisdiction subject broadly to two exceptions, one of which allows the merger to be referred back to the UK authorities and the other of which enables them to take parallel jurisdiction over certain aspects of the transaction. Also, in limited circumstances, the European Commission may be requested to review a transaction over which it does not otherwise have jurisdiction, instead of the national authorities. Rule 12 requires every offer to which either of these competition regimes might be relevant to contain a term whereby it will lapse if, before the first closing date or the date when the offer becomes or is declared unconditional as to acceptances,

(a)   the merger is referred to the CC; or
(b)   the European Commission initiates Phase 2 proceedings (an in-depth EC competition investigation equivalent to a CC reference) under the EC Merger Regulation, or refers the merger back to the UK and it is then referred to the CC.

Both the UK and the EC competition authorities are subject to timetables within which decisions on whether a competition reference is to be made must be taken, which timetables do not necessarily tie in with the first closing date. Both authorities are well aware of the timetabling constraints of the Code and endeavour to meet them, but cannot always do so. If there is a delay the Panel will usually "freeze" the bid timetable at the request of either the bidder or the target. If the competition authority concerned subsequently decides not to refer or not to initiate proceedings, the bid timetable will start again.

If there is a CC reference or initiation of EC Phase 2 proceedings, the offer must lapse, and there will usually be a lengthy period whilst the competition determination is being made. In 2000 the Panel amended the approach to these reference periods and added a definition of a competition reference period to the Definitions section of the Code. The underlying aim is to acknowledge that a referred offeror is in a similar position to a "potential offeror", to prevent a continuation of an offer campaign during this period and to ensure equality of information amongst competing offerors. During this period Rule 21 continues to apply, with limited exceptions. The requirements of the Code relating to the release of information by either the offeror or the offeree do not continue to apply, but Rule 19.8 provides that any statements made during such a period must be substantiated or withdrawn if the merger is subsequently cleared and a further offer is made. The Note to Rule 12.2 sets out the other provisions of the Code which remain relevant, in most cases with some specific modifications.

If the merger is cleared at the end of the in-depth competition investigation, the offeror may make a new offer provided that it does so within 21 days after the announcement of the clearance or decision; this dispensation from the usual 12-month no-bid requirement is contained in Note (a)(iii) to Rules 35.1 and 35.2.

Chapter 5

Provisions Applicable to all Offers, Partial Offers and Redemption or Purchase by a Company of its own Securities

Mark Gearing
Partner
Allen & Overy

5.1 Introduction

This Chapter deals with three sections of the Takeover Code:

(a) provisions applicable to all offers (Section H);
(b) partial offers (Section O); and
(c) redemption or purchase by a company of its own securities (Section P).

The rules of the Code, like the General Principles, are applied by the Panel in accordance with their spirit to achieve their underlying purpose. In order to understand the practical application of the rules, it is therefore important to appreciate the spirit or philosophy underlying the particular rules, and not just the precise wording used. A common purpose of the three sections covered by this Chapter is to ensure that shareholders are treated fairly and that shareholders of the same class are afforded equivalent treatment. This reflects General Principle 1 and is one of the principal purposes of the Code as stated in its introduction.

5.2 Provisions applicable to all offers

Section H of the Code falls into two parts:

(a) a substantive part, comprising rules to ensure equivalent treatment (Rules 14 to 16); and
(b) an administrative part, comprising rules on the timing and content of announcements of acceptance levels and provisions relating to proxy forms (Rules 17 and 18).

5.2.1 Equivalent treatment

Rule 14 contains requirements for comparable offers where there is more than one class of equity share capital and Rule 15 contains requirements for appropriate offers for convertible securities (including warrants and options). Rule 16 prohibits special deals being made with certain shareholders (or other persons interested in shares carrying voting rights) offering them favourable conditions.

5.2.1.1 *Rule 14 – comparable offers for different classes of equity*
Rule 14.1 provides that, where an offeree company has more than one class of equity share capital, the offeror must make a comparable offer for each class, whether such class carries voting rights or not. If, however, an offer is made for non-voting shares only, it is not necessary to make an offer also for the voting class. This reflects the fact that the Code is principally concerned with the acquisition of voting control. The Panel requires prior consultation in all Rule 14 cases.

If shares have uncapped rights to either dividends or capital, they will be equity share capital for the purposes of Section 744 of the Companies Act 1985. The Code acknowledges, however, that the requirement to make a comparable offer need not apply to shares which are equity only on technical grounds. For instance, some shares which are designed to be equity share capital under the Companies Act may have extremely limited or remote equity rights. Unless a company is in financial difficulties, and there is a real possibility of a winding up, the existence or otherwise of uncapped rights to dividends (as opposed to capital) is likely to be the most relevant factor. If, for example, these rights are subject to the company first having to make an unrealistic level of profits, the Panel will not usually regard the shares as equity for the purposes of Rule 14.1.

In order to save holders of non-voting (or limited voting) equity shares from being "stranded" because of low acceptances for that

Provisions Applicable to all Offers

class, Rule 14.1 states that an offer for such shares should not be conditional upon any particular level of acceptances unless the offer for the voting equity is also conditional on the success of the offer for the non-voting (or limited voting) equity. In practice, such a condition in the offer for the voting equity cannot be waived unless the acceptance condition in the other offer is waived or deemed to be satisfied. An alternative is to include the acceptance condition for the non-voting equity in the conditions of the offer for the voting equity. The Code does not expressly prevent the offer for the non-voting equity share capital from being made subject to other conditions which are different and independent from those in the voting equity offer. Rule 14.2 provides that separate offers must be made for each class of shares.

In what circumstances can a public company have more than one class of equity shares? In the case of certain companies, there is one class of voting equity shares and another class of non-voting equity shares, or only limited voting, or even weighted voting, equity shares. Other companies (principally investment trusts) divide their equity capital into income shares and capital shares with rights deferred to another class of equity.

There are a number of companies whose shares are admitted to the Official List or traded on the Alternative Investment Market ("AIM") which have two or more classes of publicly quoted equity shares. However, the Code is not limited to companies which have securities admitted to trading on a regulated market. The Code also applies, *inter alia*, to all public companies (and certain private companies) which have their registered offices in the UK, the Channel Islands or the Isle of Man and which have their place of central management and control in one of those jurisdictions. The Code therefore covers all public companies, even those without securities admitted to trading, as well as certain private companies where there has been some public involvement in the previous 10 years.

In the last few years, there have been a number of offers for companies with two or more classes of equity shares. Recent examples include the offers by Fuller, Smith & Turner for George Gale and Company (ordinary shares and "A" ordinary shares) and the offers by James Reed & Partners for Reed Health Group (ordinary shares and "B" ordinary shares), both dated November 2005.

If an offeree company has more than one class of equity shares, it will be necessary to determine what is a "comparable" offer for the purposes of Rule 14.1. A number of questions will arise. For instance, where there are differing voting rights, should the offeror give a premium for voting control and, if so, how much? Can it offer a different type of consideration, such as shares or other paper for one class and cash for the other?

The Code sets down a method of assessing the comparability of offers involving two or more classes of equity share capital which are admitted to the Official List or traded on AIM. It states that the ratio of the values of the offers for the two classes should normally equal the average of the ratios of the middle market quotations of the two classes over the six months before the offer period (which, for securities traded through the Stock Exchange Electronic Trading Service, will be the average of the mid-prices of the quotations for the relevant days as they appear in the Stock Exchange Daily Official List). The Panel will not normally allow any other ratio to be used unless the advisers to the offeror and the offeree company are jointly able to justify it. Thus, in practice, an alternative ratio can usually only be used in the case of a recommended bid.

The six-month average ratio was used, for example, in the two offers by Clayform Properties for Stead and Simpson in 1988 and 1989. But the use of that ratio can produce some odd results. What happens if the difference between the prices of the two classes of share has been affected by rumours of a takeover bid or by the offeror's purchases of offeree company shares? The offeror, if it is seeking to gain control, is almost inevitably going to be purchasing voting shares in preference to limited voting or non-voting shares. Even if it does not make purchases, the possibility of a bid is likely to drive up the price of the voting shares compared with the other shares.

For instance, the first offer by Clayform for Stead and Simpson put values on the two classes of share, one voting and one non-voting, of £14.50 and £1.51 (a ratio of 9.6:1). By the time of the second bid a year later, however, the market price of the voting shares had increased significantly and the ratio of the prices under the second bid was 14.2 to one.

The Code only provides a method of valuation where both classes of share are admitted to the Official List or to trading on AIM. If one or more of the classes is not admitted to the Official List or to trading on AIM, no specific guidance is given – the Code merely requires that the ratio of the offer values must be justified to the Panel in advance. This is what happened, for example, in the recommended offers by American Express for Sharepeople Group (an unlisted company), made in December 2000, where the offeror was able to justify to the Panel the ratio of the offer values as between the offeree company's ordinary shares and two classes of preference shares, which were both treated as equity. It is no doubt easier to justify a ratio to the Panel where the offers are recommended by the offeree company's directors, and supported by its independent financial adviser, than where they are hostile.

The Code also does not provide any guidance on the question of comparability in the type of consideration under offer. In practice, however, an offeror may find it difficult to persuade the Panel that one type of consideration (e.g. cash) can be offered to one class of equity and another type of consideration (e.g. securities) be offered to another class. It is possible, however, to offer different types of securities to different classes.

Finally, it should be noted that, although Rule 14 does not require comparable offers to be made for non-voting, non-equity share capital, offers for non-equity securities may be required under Rule 15 (*see* 5.2.1.2 below) if, for example, they are convertible into equity shares.

5.2.1.2 Rule 15 – *appropriate offers for convertibles etc.*
If an offer is made for voting equity share capital or for other transferable securities carrying voting rights and the offeree company also has in issue securities conferring rights to convert into equity or warrants (or other rights) to subscribe for equity, Rule 15 requires an appropriate offer (or proposal) to be made for such convertibles, warrants or other rights. Equality of treatment is required.

The Code requires that, wherever practicable, the offer or proposal for the convertibles or warrants should be despatched at the same time as the main offer. If this is not practicable (and often it is not, particularly in hostile offers), the Panel must be consulted. Rule 15 provides that the offeree company's board must obtain independent advice on the offer or proposal. The substance of this advice must be made known to the holders of the securities in question, together with the board's view. It is particularly important to note this requirement in the case of a hostile offer as it will usually be necessary for at least some of the offeree's directors to remain in office, and to retain advisers, for at least a short period after the main offer is declared unconditional, so as to advise on any Rule 15 offer or proposal.

All relevant documents issued to offeree shareholders in connection with an offer for the shares in the offeree company must also, where practicable, be issued at the same time (for information) to the holders of convertibles and warrants. It may not, however, be practicable to do this in a hostile offer, as the offeror may not have the names and addresses of all the warrant holders – there is no requirement on companies to keep a register of warrant (i.e. option) holders which is available to outsiders and the Panel has not traditionally required the offeree company to disclose such information.

If the terms of the convertibles or warrants enable the holders to exercise their rights during the course of the offer and to accept the offer following any such exercise, that fact must be made clear in the documents. Again, whether it is practicable for the offeror to do this in a hostile offer situation (i.e. whether the offeror will have sufficient details of when the rights are exercisable) is another question.

If the terms of the convertibles or warrants do, in fact, provide that the conversion or subscription rights become exercisable during the course of a general offer for the company or shortly after the offer becomes unconditional, it may be worth enquiring of the Panel whether it is necessary to put forward a further offer or proposal to the holders of such rights as the existence of the main offer itself may (depending on its terms) be sufficient to ensure that they can sell out if they wish. If, however, an alternative offer closes before the convertibles or warrants become exercisable, simply leaving holders to exercise their rights and accept the main offer may not be sufficient. In the share for share offer by Goshawk Insurance Holdings for Matheson Lloyd's Investment Trust in June 1997, for example, warrant holders could not exercise their warrants in time to benefit from a partial cash alternative and they therefore received a separate cash offer.

Consideration should be given to the tax consequences, especially for option holders, of exercising their rights and accepting the offer as compared with other forms of proposal, for example cash payments for releasing their rights or the grant of equivalent rights in the offeror. If the rights do not lapse (but will be exercisable again in the future), it may be in the interests of the offeror, just as much as the holders of the rights, for proposals to be made to get rid of those rights.

To protect individual holders of such rights from being "stranded" against their will, the Code provides that the offer or proposal to them should not normally be made conditional on any particular level of acceptances. It is permissible, however, to make the main offer for the equity share capital also conditional on a particular level of acceptances under the Rule 15 offer (e.g. 90 per cent – convertibles and warrants may be subject to the compulsory acquisition provisions of Part 13A of the Companies Act 1985 or, where relevant, Schedule 2 to the Takeover Directive (Interim Implementation) Regulations 2006, but not employee share options). Depending on the terms of the rights in question, it may also be possible to put the Rule 15 proposal forward by way of a scheme to be considered at a meeting of the relevant holders – where the resolution to approve the scheme will require a majority of votes in favour (normally a 75 per cent majority) and, frequently, a substantial number of holders present (in person or by proxy) to form a quorum. Normally such a proposal, once approved, is binding on all the holders of the rights in question.

What is an "appropriate" offer or proposal? The Code does not give any guidance but, in practice, it is normally sufficient for Rule 15 purposes to offer the "see-through" price – that is the price which would be payable under the main offer for any ordinary shares arising from the exercise of the conversion or subscription rights, less a deduction for any price payable on the exercise of the subscription rights. There may be difficulties in arriving at a see-through price where the main offer consists of or includes shares in the offeror so that its value fluctuates in accordance with market conditions. Furthermore, if the calculation would leave a negative figure (i.e. the rights are "out of the money") there may be an argument for saying no offer or proposal is appropriate and offering nothing.

In the case of Agip Investments' recommended cash offer for Lasmo in December 2000, for example, the Panel agreed that the redemption of Lasmo's convertible bonds in accordance with their terms was sufficient and that no separate Rule 15 offer or proposal was necessary. This was on the basis that the conversion terms were significantly less attractive to holders than redeeming the bonds at par. Agip also stated in the offer document that it would procure redemption of the bonds within a certain timeframe.

In other cases, even if the rights are "out of the money", the offeror may in any event want to offer something to encourage holders of the securities to sell out, particularly if the conversion or subscription rights do not lapse following the offer. As noted above, if a takeover offer is made for convertibles or warrants, as a separate class, non-assented securities may be subject to compulsory acquisition if sufficient acceptances are received.

Another way of making an appropriate offer could be to offer an equivalent convertible or option in the offeror company. The offer by Hiscox for Hiscox Select Insurance Fund in December 1997, for example, included an offer of a substantially equivalent convertible loan stock in Hiscox for the convertible loan stock in Hiscox Select Insurance Fund.

The offer of an equivalent option can be of particular interest to employees with share options in the target where their option scheme is appropriately worded. The offer of an equivalent option could enable them to take advantage of the roll-over relief provisions in Schedule 3 (for employee "Save As You Earn" share option schemes) or Schedule 4 (for discretionary "Executive" share option schemes) to the Income Tax (Earnings and Pensions) Act 2003, where the share option scheme is tax approved. Care should be taken to ensure that, by granting options over its shares to the offeree company's employees, the offeror does not breach any limit as to the total number of its shares under option and that the subscription price payable under the new options (which should reflect the price payable under the original options granted by the target) is not below par unless there are arrangements enabling the shortfall to be paid up out of reserves.

Provisions Applicable to all Offers

The principle of equality of treatment applies to option holders in the same scheme, but different treatment between option holders in different schemes should be acceptable (unless it is being done as a way of giving particular shareholders a special deal which would contravene Rule 16).

It is possible for a particular type of share to be both equity (at least in the technical sense) and also convertible. In these circumstances, the question arises whether there should be a "comparable" offer under Rule 14 or an "appropriate" offer under Rule 15. As noted above, this can lead to a significant difference in the required offer value. In a hostile situation, where any Panel Executive ruling prior to the offer announcement is likely to be "ex parte" only, an offeror may wish to make its offer conditional on Panel confirmation that the shares in question will be treated under, say, Rule 15 and not Rule 14. An example of this was in TI's offer for Dowty in April 1992.

If an offer for convertible securities is required by Rule 9 or Rule 14, compliance with the relevant rule will be regarded as satisfying the obligation to make an appropriate offer or proposal under Rule 15.

5.2.1.3 Rule 16 – special deals with favourable conditions

Rule 16 prohibits an offeror (or persons acting in concert with it) from making arrangements with shareholders or dealing in shares in the offeree company if there are favourable conditions attached which are not extended to all offeree company shareholders. The prohibition applies both during an offer and when one is reasonably in contemplation. It also extends to entering into arrangements to deal in shares or arrangements which involve acceptance of an offer. It also applies in the six months following a successful offer, during which period Rule 35.3 prohibits a successful offeror from acquiring shares in the offeree company at a price higher than that available under the offer.

Following the amendments made to the Code which came into effect on 7 November 2005, which flowed from Public Consultation Papers 2005/1 and 2005/2 and Response Statement 2005/2, Rule 16 also now prohibits any arrangement with a person who is interested in shares carrying voting rights in the offeree company (e.g. a person with a long derivative or option position, who is not necessarily a shareholder) if favourable conditions are attached which are not being extended to all shareholders. The amended rule makes clear, however, that there is no requirement for an offeror to extend any offer, or any "special deal" falling within Rule 16, to persons who are not shareholders of the offeree company but who have another interest in offeree company shares.

Rule 16 is an expansion of General Principle 1 of the Code which provides that all holders of securities of the same class in an offeree company must be afforded equivalent treatment.

The prohibition on special deals imposed by Rule 16 frequently raises difficult issues for both practitioners and the Panel. The Code gives specific guidance regarding four circumstances which have commonly required consideration under this rule.

5.2.1.3.1 Top-ups
One sort of special deal which is expressly prohibited is where the offeror buys the shares outright but the seller says that he wants a top-up if the offeror subsequently pays more under a general offer for the target. Top-ups of this nature were quite common at one time, but now they are prohibited. To enable certain shareholders to be able to hedge their bets (i.e. to get their money whether or not the offer succeeds and to get the maximum paid under the offer) would not be treating all shareholders equally. Similarly, the rule also prohibits shareholders entering into an irrevocable commitment to accept an offer if it is combined with a put option exercisable if the offer fails. But what about an irrevocable commitment combined with a put option exercisable if the offer is not made? Also, what about a top-up in the event of a third party offer at a higher price? Arguably, such arrangements may not fall foul of Rule 16 but the Panel would need to be consulted. An offeror may obtain an irrevocable commitment combined with a call option over the shares in question, as the shareholder is not then given a definite exit.

Arrangements made by an offeror with a person acting in concert with it, whereby that person acquires an interest in offeree company shares, are not prohibited provided that the offeror bears all the risks and receives all the benefits and the concert party receives no other benefit (or potential benefit), for example a fee for undertaking the acquisition, beyond normal expenses and carrying costs. In cases of doubt, the Panel should be consulted. Rule 4 will also be relevant in these circumstances (*see* Note 3 to Rules 4.1 and 4.2).

5.2.1.3.2   *Disposal of assets*
Another way of giving a special deal to a person interested in shares in the offeree company would be to enter into a transaction to dispose of some of the offeree company's assets to him at a favourable price. To guard against this, the Panel has said that, if the disposal is agreed before the offer is unconditional, then it will normally require that:

(a) the independent adviser to the offeree publicly states that the terms of the transaction are fair and reasonable; and
(b) the offeree company's shareholders give their approval at a general meeting (with only independent shareholders voting and the votes being given on a poll).

Accordingly, a disposal of assets in these circumstances is normally only possible in a recommended offer situation. If the assets in question are not material in the context of the offer (e.g. they represent, say, less than one per cent of the value of the offer), the Panel may be satisfied with a "fair and reasonable" statement from the offeree company's independent adviser without also requiring independent shareholder approval; the Panel would need to be consulted where this might be a possibility.

The arrangements between Guinness and LVMH, in the context of the Guinness/GrandMet merger in November 1997, potentially fell within this category. LVMH was a substantial holder of GrandMet shares and its arrangements with Guinness included an extension of the brands distributed through their joint distribution network, to include certain GrandMet brands, as well as payment of a significant sum to LVMH. The GrandMet directors were required to state in the merger document that, having been so advised by their independent financial adviser, the arrangements were fair and reasonable so far as the other GrandMet shareholders were concerned. In addition, LVMH did not vote at the meeting of independent GrandMet shareholders required to approve the merger, which was effected by means of a scheme of arrangement of GrandMet.

A more recent example is provided by the offer by NTL for Virgin Mobile in April 2006. Virgin Enterprises, a member of the Virgin Group which held approximately 71 per cent of the existing issued share capital of Virgin Mobile, entered into a brand licence which allowed the NTL Group to make use of the Virgin brand. Since members of the Virgin Group were both a party to the brand licence and shareholders in Virgin Mobile, the Panel required the licence to be approved by a simple majority of independent shareholders voting at a general meeting of Virgin Mobile. In addition, the independent Virgin Mobile directors stated in the offer document that the terms of the brand licence represented "an arm's length, commercially negotiated agreement and, therefore, [were] fair and reasonable". A similar statement was made by Virgin Mobile's independent financial adviser.

If a disposal is agreed after an offer has become unconditional, the Panel will want to be satisfied that there was in fact no pre-arrangement. The Panel will be similarly concerned if, for example, more favourable trading arrangements are entered into with shareholders after an offer has become unconditional.

A disposal of certain of the offeror's assets to an offeree shareholder would also need to be considered in terms of Rule 16.

5.2.1.3.3 Finders' fees
If a person interested in shares in the offeree company is paid a finder's fee for the part he has played in promoting an offer this may be a special deal. The Panel will, however, normally permit it if the finder's interest in the shares is not substantial (less than one per cent, say) and the amount of the finder's fee is normal – that is, it is not more than would have been paid to the finder if he was not interested in the offeree company's shares. Finders' fees are now rarely encountered in practice.

5.2.1.3.4 Management retaining an interest
To keep the management of the offeree company financially involved in the business, the offeror may wish the management to retain an equity interest. Often this is achieved by allowing the management to exchange their shares in the offeree company for shares in the offeror, whereas non-management shareholders are not given the same

Provisions Applicable to all Offers

opportunity. This issue is likely to arise, in particular, with management buy-outs ("MBOs") or similar types of transaction, as the Panel's Annual Report for 1997–1998 highlighted.

In these types of cases, the difference in treatment between management and other shareholders is permitted provided that certain criteria are met. In particular, the risks as well as the rewards associated with a shareholding must apply to the management's retained interest. Accordingly, an option to put shares on the offeror in the future at the price paid under the general offer will not normally be permitted, as the management would not run the risks of loss as well as the rewards. On the other hand, putting a reasonable floor on the level of loss, with a corresponding cap on the possible upside for the management's retained interest, may be permissible.

As a result of the implementation of the Takeover Directive, and in particular the requirement that any derogation from the rules must "respect" the General Principles, the Panel has tightened up its requirements under Note 4 to Rule 16 for giving its consent to arrangements of this nature (*see* paragraph 8.3 of Section C of PCP 2005/5, Articles 3(1)(a) and 4 (5) of the Takeover Directive and Note 4 to Rule 16 in the latest edition of the Code which came into effect on 20 May 2006). As previously, the Panel will invariably require that the independent adviser to the offeree company publicly states that in his opinion the terms of the transaction are fair and reasonable. More particularly, however, the Panel will also now invariably require, as a further condition of its consent, that the arrangement is approved at a general meeting of the target's shareholders, with votes being given on a poll and the management shareholders and any other interested party being disenfranchised. Previously, the Panel had a discretion not to require independent shareholder approval which, in recent years, it could usually be expected to exercise if the offeror and the management of the offeree company together held less than five per cent (or the management held less than, say, one per cent) of the equity share capital of the offeree company. Removing any discretion whatsoever will inevitably lead to a requirement for independent shareholder approval in a greater number of cases than in the past.

Where the offeree company's management can properly be characterised as acting as joint offeror rather than as a concert party of the offeror (*see* 5.2.1.3.5 below), Rule 16 will not be relevant and the management will be free to enter into its own arrangements without the need for those arrangements to be the subject of separate independent advice to target shareholders or independent shareholder approval. By way of example, when BL Davidson (a 50/50 joint venture company owned by the Davidson family and the British Land Company) made a cash offer for Asda Property Holdings in August 2001, the Davidson family and British Land were treated as joint offerors with the result that Rule 16 did not apply to the arrangements whereby the Davidson family exchanged its 29 per cent stake in Asda for shares in the bidding vehicle. This may be contrasted with the offer by Dundonald Holdings for Grantchester Holdings in August 2002, where it could not be said that the management team, who agreed to subscribe for a proportion of the shares in the bidding vehicle (and to roll over certain of their options in the offeree company for options over preference shares in the bidding vehicle), were acting as joint offerors and therefore the arrangements needed independent shareholder approval under Note 4 on Rule 16.

In referring to "management" in Note 4 on Rule 16, the Panel usually interprets this to mean those directors involved in executive management. The Panel may also be prepared to allow the holdings of those directors' immediate families to be included in the management's arrangements, if otherwise permitted. In addition, the Panel may be prepared to allow management below offeree company director level to participate in the arrangements, provided they are sufficiently key (e.g. they are directors of a principal operating subsidiary). See, for example, the recommended proposals for the acquisition of the Peacock Group by Henson No. 1 Limited in November 2005, where the holdings of the spouse of one of the executive directors and of two members of management below board level were included in the share exchange proposals.

It may not always be appropriate to give management a continuing equity participation, but an offeror may still wish to retain and incentivise members of the offeree company's management who may also be shareholders. One way of doing this may be to enter into enhanced employment arrangements, such as new or improved service contracts or bonus arrangements. As a result of the implementation of the Takeover Directive, for the reasons stated above, the Panel will now invariably require, as a condition of giving its consent to such arrangements, that the independent financial adviser to the offeree company publicly states that in its opinion such arrangements are fair and reasonable (*see* Note 4 on Rule 16).

Another approach to avoiding a Rule 16 issue, where it is intended that only certain offeree shareholders roll over their stakes in the offeree company in to shares in the bidding vehicle, may be to structure the arrangements so that all offeree shareholders are at least offered the same opportunity even if it will not be attractive to all of them. This proved possible, for example, in the offer for Delancey Estates in April 2001: all shareholders were offered cash for their Delancey shares and two types of loan note, one guaranteed and the other unguaranteed but convertible in to the unlisted equity of the ultimate parent company of the bidding vehicle. A mechanism was thereby found to enable relevant offeree shareholders (which included both management and non-management shareholders) to have a continuing equity participation post completion whilst affording all other shareholders the same opportunity in compliance with General Principle 1 and Rule 16. A similar situation appears to have arisen in the offer by Metroyard for MBA Bailey Associates in December 2002, where the offeree company directors (and certain connected parties) elected to receive an unlisted share alternative which was also made available to all shareholders but not recommended by the offeree company's independent adviser.

5.2.1.3.5 *Joint offerors*
In the same way that Rule 16 does not apply to a genuine offeror who already holds shares in the offeree company, in respect of any arrangements it may make regarding its own shares in the offeree company or otherwise, the Panel acknowledges that Rule 16 is not relevant where two or more persons come together to form a consortium on such terms and in such circumstances that each of them can properly be considered to be a joint offeror. The distinction between receiving a special deal as offeree company shareholder (which is subject to the prohibitions and restrictions in General Principle 1 and Rule 16) and acting as joint offeror (where it is not) can be a fine one. A genuine offeror is seen as a person who, alone or with others, seeks to obtain control of an offeree company and who, following the acquisition of

control, can expect to exert a significant influence over the offeree company, to participate in distributions of profits and surplus capital and to benefit from any increase in the value of the offeree company, while at the same time bearing the risk of a fall in its value resulting from the poor performance of the company's business or adverse market conditions.

In determining whether a person can properly be considered to be an offeror (or joint offeror), rather than simply acting in concert with the offeror, the Panel Executive will consider the following factors:

(a) What proportion of the equity share capital of the bid vehicle will the person own after completion of the acquisition?
(b) Will the person be able to exert a significant influence over the future management and direction of the bid vehicle?
(c) What contribution is the person making to the consortium?
(d) Will the person be able to influence significantly the conduct of the bid?
(e) Are there arrangements in place to enable the person to exit from his investment in the bid vehicle within a short time or at a time when other equity investors cannot?

The appropriateness of these factors was endorsed by the Panel in the case concerning Canary Wharf Group (see Panel Statement 2003/25). The Panel did, however, stress that the above factors should not be regarded as exhaustive, and that it is also necessary to ensure that, even if the criteria seem to be satisfied to a degree sufficient to justify treating the person in question as an offeror, the arrangements looked at as a whole are consistent with General Principle 1 and Rule 16. The Panel also said that no single factor should be regarded as determinative, nor is it necessary that a person satisfies each factor.

In the Canary Wharf case, the Panel was satisfied that a particular offeree company shareholder should be treated as a joint offeror and that, accordingly, the terms of the consortium arrangements in which he was involved did not infringe General Principle 1 or Rule 16. It was found, in that case, that the shareholder concerned would have in excess of 30 per cent of the equity in the bid vehicle, making him the largest single shareholder, and that the consortium arrangements gave him significant influence over the direction of the bid vehicle and the future management of the business. It was also found that the shareholder was making a substantial contribution to the consortium, both in financial and managerial terms, and that he was exposed to substantial risks and had no arrangements for a short term exit. The Panel did, however, also stress that each case must be decided upon its own facts and that therefore previous decisions arrived at on different facts are likely to be of little help in determining the acceptability of consortium arrangements in other cases.

The offer by Copthorn for Countryside Properties in November 2004 provided another example of an instance where the Panel agreed to treat certain offeree company shareholders as joint offerors. Copthorn was the bid vehicle for a consortium comprising Uberior Ventures and members of the Cherry family, who together held approximately 17 per cent of Countryside Properties. It was proposed that, after the offer was declared wholly unconditional, the Cherry family and Uberior would each acquire 50 per cent of the shares in Copthorn's indirect parent, Copthorn Holdings, and the Panel agreed to treat both the Cherry family and Uberior as joint offerors for the purpose of Rule 16.

A more recent example of a bid by joint offerors is provided by the offer for *eircom* Group plc in May 2006 by BCM Ireland Holdings Limited, a bid vehicle formed for the purpose of making the offer by Babcock & Brown Capital Limited and the *eircom* Employee Share Ownership Trust. These two shareholders held approximately 28.8 per cent and 21.4 per cent respectively of *eircom's* issued ordinary share capital and, following completion of the offer, they would hold 65 per cent and 35 per cent respectively of the issued ordinary share capital of the bid vehicle. Both shareholders provided equity financing for the offer and it is understood that both would be able to exert significant influence over the business of *eircom* following completion of the transaction.

It follows that, where an offeree company shareholder cannot be characterised as a joint offeror, and is not involved in the management of the offeree company, a special deal involving a roll-over into shares in the bidding vehicle (when all other shareholders would not be given the same opportunity) is not generally capable of being approved by independent shareholder vote, with the benefit of a "fair and reasonable" statement from the offeree company's independent financial adviser, and will be prohibited by the overriding requirement for shareholders of the same class to be afforded equivalent treatment, as set out in General Principle 1.

Rule 16 is concerned with special deals for particular shareholders which are (or may be) on favourable terms. It also follows, therefore, that Rule 16 (and General Principle 1) will not be relevant where a particular shareholder voluntarily accepts a less favourable deal than other shareholders (as happened, for example, in the offer by Britannia Living for The Range Cooker Company in November 2002, where one of the offeree company directors agreed to waive his entitlement to part of the cash consideration payable under the terms of the offer).

Full particulars of any special arrangements between the offeror or any person acting in concert with it and any of the directors, shareholders or recent shareholders of the offeree company, having any connection with or dependence upon the offer, will need to be disclosed in the offer document under Rule 24.5.

In all cases of possible special deals, the Panel should be consulted. The prohibition on special deals imposed by Rule 16 is subject to the Panel agreeing otherwise.

5.2.2 Administrative provisions

Rules 17 and 18 contain certain administrative provisions relating to all offers. Rule 17 deals with announcements of acceptance levels and Rule 18 with certain provisions in forms of acceptance.

5.2.2.1 Rule 17 – announcements of acceptance levels
Rule 17.1 requires an announcement of the level of acceptances to be made after the occurrence of certain events, namely:

(a) any expiry date – that is, any date on which the offeror could allow the bid to lapse if insufficient acceptances have been received. This will obviously include the first closing date of an offer, usually 21 days after the despatch of the offer document; it will also include any subsequent closing date if the offer is

extended; the Code states that a date on which any alternative form of consideration available under the offer expires is also to be treated as an expiry date, even if the offer itself is not due to expire at that time;
(b) when the offer becomes or is declared unconditional as to acceptances – that may of course also be an expiry date, though not necessarily, and it could be before or after the first closing date;
(c) whenever the offer is revised – if a revision is required as a result of a purchase of offeree company shares, that will also require an immediate announcement under Rule 17.1; and
(d) whenever the offer is extended – that may also be an expiry date, though not necessarily.

The deadline for announcements required by Rule 17.1 is 8.00 a.m. on the first business day following the relevant event. However, on the final day of the offer (i.e. the day beyond which the offer cannot be extended if not unconditional as to acceptances – normally the 60th day after posting), the announcement must normally be made by 5.00 p.m. on that day – not 8.00 a.m. on the following business day. If an offer is likely to reach the final day, the offeror and its advisers should consider Rule 31.6 closely in advance as it has a number of detailed requirements about timing.

Rule 17.1 also specifies what must be included in the announcement. Following the amendments made to the Code, which came into effect on 7 November 2005 and flowed from Public Consultation Paper 2005/2 and Response Statement 2005/2, a Rule 17 announcement must now state:

(a) the number of shares for which acceptances of the offer have been received, specifying the extent to which acceptances have been received from persons acting in concert with the offeror or in respect of shares which were subject to an irrevocable commitment or a letter of intent procured by the offeror or any of its associates;
(b) details of any relevant securities of the offeree company in which the offeror or any person acting in concert with it has an interest or in respect of which he has a right to subscribe, in each case specifying the nature of the interests or rights concerned (similar details of any short positions, whether conditional or

absolute and whether in the money or otherwise, including any short position under a derivative, any agreement to sell or any delivery obligation or right to require another person to purchase or take delivery, must also be stated);
(c) details of any relevant securities of the offeree company in respect of which the offeror or any of its associates has an outstanding irrevocable commitment or letter of intent; and
(d) details of any relevant securities of the offeree company which the offeror or any person acting in concert with it has borrowed or lent, save for any borrowed shares which have been either on-lent or sold,

and the announcement must specify the percentages of each class of relevant securities represented by these figures.

A Rule 17 announcement must include a prominent statement of the total number of shares which can be counted towards satisfaction of the acceptance condition and must specify the percentages of each class of relevant securities represented by these figures. The Code has strict rules for determining what acceptances and share purchases may be counted towards fulfilling an acceptance condition (*see* Rule 10 including, in particular, Notes 4 and 5). Accordingly, an acceptance of the offer may only be counted for this purpose if (in cases where the acceptance is effected by means of CREST without an acceptance form) the transfer to the relevant member's escrow account has settled in respect of the relevant number of shares on or before the last time for acceptance or (where the acceptance is effected by means of an acceptance form) the acceptance is received by the offeror's receiving agent on or before such time and the form is completed to a suitable standard and:

(a) the form is accompanied by the relevant share certificates and, where necessary, other documents to show title; or
(b) in the case of a holding in CREST, it is covered by a transfer to the relevant member's escrow account, details of which are provided in the form; or
(c) the acceptor is registered in the register of members as the holder of the shares in question as at the final time for acceptance and those shares are not included as acceptances in any other respect; or
(d) the acceptance form is certified by the target's registrar.

Provisions Applicable to all Offers

Similarly, share purchases may only be counted if:

(a) the offeror (or its nominee or, in a Rule 9 offer, a person acting in concert with it) is the registered holder of the shares; or
(b) a duly executed transfer in favour of the offeror (or its nominee or, in a Rule 9 offer, concert party) has been received and is accompanied by the relevant share certificates or is certified by the target's registrar.

The Panel should be consulted if the offeror wishes to make any other statement about acceptance levels in a Rule 17 announcement. In practice, if it is wished to refer to other acceptances and share purchases which do not meet the above standards, this is usually permissible, subject to prior Panel approval, provided they are referred to separately and their status is made clear.

If an offer is to become or be declared unconditional as to acceptances before the final closing date, the criteria for determining which acceptances and purchases can be counted towards fulfilling the acceptance condition (although not necessarily for the purposes of a Rule 17 announcement) are more strict in one particular respect (*see* Rule 10, Note 6). In these circumstances, it is not possible to take account of acceptances solely on the grounds that they are from a registered holder, unless they are also accompanied by share certificates or (in the case of a holding in CREST) covered by a transfer to the relevant member's escrow account or (in any case) certified by the target's registrar.

In addition, before the offer becomes or is declared unconditional as to acceptances, the offeror's receiving agent must have issued a certificate which states the number of acceptances and purchases which comply with the above requirements. A copy of that certificate must be sent to the Panel and the offeree company's financial adviser as soon as possible.

The above requirements were introduced in to the Code following the situation which arose in the Blue Circle offer for Birmid in 1988. In that case there was an announcement that there were sufficient acceptances and purchases for the bid to become unconditional. It was, however, subsequently found that some incomplete purchases had been included and a further announcement had to be made that the bid had in fact lapsed.

Rule 24.6 of the Code requires an offer document to state that the offeror will make announcements on the required occasions and what will be included within those announcements.

An announcement under Rule 17 must be published in accordance with the requirements of Rule 2.9. However, in the case of companies whose securities are not admitted to listing or trading, it would normally be permissible to write to all shareholders instead of making an announcement.

5.2.2.2 Failure to announce
If the offeror, having announced the offer to be unconditional as to acceptances, fails to announce the details required by Rule 17.1 by 3.30 p.m. on the following business day, then automatically every acceptor has the right to withdraw his acceptance. Subject to Rule 31.6, that right to withdraw cannot be stopped for at least eight days and then it can only be stopped by the offeror reconfirming that the bid is unconditional, assuming of course that by the end of that eight days it is still unconditional. If too many people have withdrawn, the bid may no longer be unconditional as to acceptances.

On the final day, however, when Rule 31.6 applies, an offer must either become or be declared unconditional as to acceptances or lapse. If it becomes or is declared unconditional as to acceptances, it is generally not then capable of becoming conditional as to acceptances again. The words "Subject to Rule 31.6" in Rule 17.2(b) seem to infer that the right of withdrawal cannot be terminated beyond the 60-day limit. What is less clear, but is presumably the case, is that the withdrawal rights themselves cease to be exercisable beyond the final time for lodging acceptances which can be taken into account for the purposes of Rule 31.6. This would be consistent with when the general right of withdrawal ceases to be exercisable under Rule 34.

Rule 17.2 also used to provide, as an alternative sanction for failure to announce within the requisite time limits, for the temporary suspension of listing of the offeree company's shares (if admitted to the Official List) and, if appropriate, the offeror's shares. Suspension was not, of course, a particularly good sanction in that the persons most affected by any suspension would normally be the investing shareholders rather than (or in addition to) the recalcitrant management of the company. Not surprisingly, therefore, this sanction has finally been deleted in the new edition of the Code which came into effect on 20 May 2006 (as proposed in PCP 2006/1 issued on 10 February 2006) on the basis that it was unlikely to have been imposed in practice in any event.

5.2.2.3 General statements about acceptances and withdrawals

During an offer, particularly in a competitive situation, an offeror or its advisers may be tempted to make general statements about the level of acceptances received, or the number, or percentage of shareholders who have accepted the offer. In these circumstances, the Panel will require an immediate announcement to be made in conformity with Rule 17. As noted above, a formal Rule 17 announcement will need to make clear which acceptances can be counted towards fulfilling the acceptance condition.

Conversely, an offeree company may wish to draw attention to withdrawals of acceptances. In this case, the Panel requires prior consultation before any announcement is made. The Panel is usually concerned to ensure, in particular, that the market is not misled by conflicting announcements of withdrawals and acceptances. Rule 19.3 will also be relevant: an offeree company should not make statements about levels of support from its shareholders unless their up-to-date intentions have been clearly stated to the company or its advisers and satisfactory verification (which usually means written) can be provided to the Panel.

5.2.2.4 Rule 18 – proxies etc. in acceptances

Rule 18 relates to the appointment of proxies to exercise voting rights and other sorts of rights. The offeror will frequently include, as part of the terms of acceptance, a provision by which an accepting shareholder appoints the offeror, or someone nominated by him, as the acceptor's proxy and authorises that person to exercise rights on his behalf. The purpose of this is normally to enable the offeror to exercise the rights attached to the acceptor's shares in the offeree company between the time when the offer goes wholly unconditional and the time when the offeror gets itself registered on the register of members. In the absence of any other arrangement, until the offeror becomes the registered holder of the shares, the rights attached to them would continue to be exercisable by the accepting shareholder.

Rule 18 states that the appointment as proxy should be expressed in terms that it will become effective only if the offer has become wholly unconditional or (in the case of voting by the proxy) if the resolution in question concerns the last remaining condition of the offer (other than any admission to listing or admission to trading condition) and the offer would either become wholly unconditional (save for satisfaction of any such condition) or lapse depending upon the outcome of the resolution in question. This exception is to enable votes to be cast at an EGM of the offeree company if one is needed for the purposes of the offer. In order for an offeror to benefit from the appointment, it may be necessary for it to waive any outstanding, waivable conditions save for the admission to listing or admission to trading condition which, if applicable, will always be the last condition to be satisfied.

One other circumstance in which the Panel is likely, in practice, to permit the offeror to use proxies acquired as a result of the acceptance process, before the offer has become wholly unconditional, is where the offeree company proposes to dispose of certain assets for which shareholder approval is required and the offer is conditional on the proposed sale not being approved at the offeree company's EGM.

The Code goes on to say that the offeror can only use the votes to satisfy the conditions of the offer. In other words, it would not be possible for the offeror (e.g. if it had cold feet about the offer) to exercise voting rights over shares in the offeree company to defeat the conditions of its offer. In these circumstances, however, an offeror may be able to lapse its offer on an expiry date if it has failed to satisfy the 90 per cent acceptance condition which is usually inserted for compulsory acquisition purposes.

The proxy form must also make it clear that the appointment ceases to be valid if the acceptor withdraws his acceptance.

Finally, it has to be made clear that the appointment relates only to the shares which are the subject of the acceptance. In other words, if (say) Barclays Bank has several million shares in the offeree company registered in its name, all as nominee, and it is instructed by one person to accept the offer, an appointment of the offeror as a proxy in relation to those shares may not be taken as an appointment in relation to all the other shares in the offeree company held by Barclays.

Rule 18 does not restrict the terms on which a proxy may be obtained, or other shareholder rights acquired, otherwise than as a term of acceptance.

5.3 Partial offers

The provisions of the Code on partial offers (Section O, Rule 36) are also concerned with the application of the General Principle of equivalent treatment.

Partial offers are relatively uncommon and there are usually no more than a handful in a typical year. Recent examples include the offer by Zoo Hotels to acquire up to 29 per cent of the Groucho Club London in April 2001, the offer by Carnival Corporation to acquire up to 20 per cent of P&O Princess Cruises in March 2003 (in connection with the proposed combination of Carnival and P&O Princess under a dual listed company structure), the hostile offer by GPG Group to acquire an additional 25 per cent of De Vere in March 2004 and the offer by Amor Holdings to acquire approximately 51 per cent of Partridge Fine Arts in December 2005.

Panel consent is always required for a partial offer. This consent is normally granted if it would not result in the offeror and its concert parties being interested in shares carrying 30 per cent or more of the votes. A person can, of course, buy shares to give himself up to 29.9 per cent without incurring a mandatory bid obligation under Rule 9 of the Takeover Code and, following the abolition of the Rules Governing Substantial Acquisitions of Shares (the "SARs" as they used to be known), there is no longer any restriction on the speed with which a person may acquire shares (or interests in shares) below the 30 per cent level.

There are three ways in which a person is able to acquire shares (or interests in shares) of up to 29 per cent of a company: (a) through purchases of shares (or acquisitions of other interests in shares); (b) by means of a tender offer (the rules for which are now contained in Appendix 5 of the Code); and (c) by means of a partial offer. Shares purchases may, for example, be made from particular shareholders or as part of a market operation conducted by the purchaser's broker. However, if the purchaser wishes to make an offer to all shareholders, he will need to do a tender or partial offer. A tender offer is made by means of a simple advertisement which must be published in two national newspapers (although a circular in the same form as the advertisement may also be posted) and it need only be open for a minimum period of seven days. A tender offer provides a more straightforward procedure than a partial offer, which is subject to the Code in the normal way and is therefore a lengthier and more costly process. A tender offer is also particularly relevant in the context of companies whose shares are not admitted to trading (where a person is not therefore able to acquire shares in the market).

A tender offer must, however, be for cash only and cannot be subject to any conditions, other than receipt of acceptances amounting to at least one per cent. Thus, where the offer consideration includes securities or conditions are to be attached to the acquisition of shares (e.g. the approval of the purchaser's own shareholders), a purchaser will have to resort to a partial offer regulated under the Code. The amount of information which can be imparted during a tender offer is also strictly limited; in particular, no form of argument or persuasion is allowed, whereas a partial offer under the Code is not so restricted. Zoo Hotels had to proceed by way of partial offer rather than tender offer, in its attempt to acquire up to 29 per cent of the Groucho Club, both because its offer consideration comprised Zoo shares and because its offer was unsolicited and competitive with another, general offer requiring it to be able to argue the relative merits of its offer. Zoo Hotels' partial offer was not, however, subject to any conditions: partial offers which cannot result in the offeror holding 30 per cent or more need not be subject to any acceptance condition.

A tender offer would also not be an option for an offeror who wants to acquire shares carrying 30 per cent or more of the votes, unless the offeror already controls the majority of the votes and the Panel believes the circumstances justify the use of a tender offer. Where a partial offer is made which could result in the offeror and its concert

Provisions Applicable to all Offers

parties being interested in shares carrying 30 per cent or more of the voting rights, the Panel will normally grant its consent, but only on the following conditions:

(a) the holders of over 50 per cent of the voting rights in the offeree company (excluding those held by the offeror and its concert parties) must approve the offer, even though they do not necessarily accept the offer; the way in which such approval would normally be sought is that, in the acceptance form sent out with the partial offer document, or possibly in a separate form, there will be a box for shareholders to tick to indicate their approval to the partial offer (this is what was required, for example, in the partial offer by GPG Group to acquire an additional 25 per cent of De Vere, given that GPG Group already held a 10 per cent stake); and

(b) where the offer could not result in the offeror holding more than 50 per cent of the voting rights of the offeree company, the offer must not be declared unconditional as to acceptances unless acceptances are received for not less than the number of shares offered for – that number must be stated precisely in the offer document (see, again, the partial offer by GPG Group for De Vere).

The purpose of the first condition is to ensure that "over 50 per cent" approve the making of a partial offer which, if successful, will result in the offeror and its concert parties acquiring "control" of the offeree company without all shareholders being given the opportunity to exit for 100 per cent of their shareholdings. Rule 36.5 also now makes clear that the "over 50 per cent" approval requirement applies to over 50 per cent of the voting rights held by shareholders who are "independent" of the offeror and persons acting in concert with it, rather than over 50 per cent of the voting rights not held by the offeror concert party.

The purpose of the second condition above is to prevent an offeror acquiring what is effective control without paying the full price – that is the offer must be fully successful. Normally, an offeror under a partial offer will permit shareholders to accept an offer for as many shares as they like, guaranteeing that their acceptances will be accepted only to the extent of their proportionate holdings. Thus, if a significant number of shareholders accept for amounts substantially in excess of their proportionate holdings, the offeror may well receive acceptances for more than the total number of shares it has offered for. In view of this, it is not normally difficult to satisfy the second condition if the price is attractive enough.

Partial offers which could result in the offeror and its concert parties being interested in shares carrying 30 per cent or more but holding less than 100 per cent of the voting rights of a company will not normally be permitted if there have been selective or significant acquisitions by the offeror or its concert parties in the last 12 months or if interests in shares were acquired by any of them after the offer was reasonably in contemplation. The reason for this is, again, so as not to favour certain shareholders (i.e. those who were able to sell out in full as a result of one of the offeror's acquisitions) over shareholders generally.

For the same reason, the Code (Rule 36.3) prohibits the acquisition of any interest in shares being made either:

(a) during the partial offer (and this applies even for offers for less than 30 per cent); or
(b) in the 12 months after the end of the offer period if the offer was successful, unless the Panel consents.

These rules apply to concert parties (including non-exempt discretionary fund managers) just as much as they do to the offeror. The Panel is likely to grant its consent only if:

(a) the offer results in less than 30 per cent being owned by the offeror and its concert parties (subject, of course, to Rules 5 and 9); or
(b) there are circumstances in which, under Rule 35, an offeror would be allowed to renew a full offer within 12 months of its lapsing (e.g. if the offeree company's board recommends it or if there is a rival offer).

In the case of a partial offer which could result in the offeror holding shares carrying over 50 per cent of the voting rights of the offeree company, Rule 36.6 requires the offer document to contain specific and prominent reference to this and to the fact that, if the offer succeeds, the offeror and its concert parties will be free (subject to Rule 36.3 and, where relevant, Note 4 on Rule 9.1) to acquire further shares without incurring any obligation under Rule 9 to make a general offer (i.e. it will have what is known as "buying freedom"; Note 4 on Rule 9.1 will be relevant where, as a result of the partial offer, the offeror does not itself hold shares carrying over 50 per cent of the voting rights). Such a disclosure was required, for example, in the partial offer by Amor Holdings to acquire approximately 51 per cent of Partridge Fine Arts. It is also noteworthy in that case that the offeror undertook to offer to purchase the remaining shares not acquired by it pursuant to the partial offer, but not any earlier than 12 months after the partial offer became unconditional.

Rule 36.7 specifies how scaling down of acceptances is to be effected. All shareholders' acceptances up to the relevant percentage of their holdings offered for must be accepted in full. Where shares in excess of that percentage have been tendered by shareholders, the same proportion of such excess shares must be accepted from each shareholder.

Rule 36.8 states that, if a partial offer is made for a company with more than one class of equity share capital which could result in the offeror and its concert parties being interested in shares carrying 30 per cent or more of the voting rights, comparable offers must be made for each class (*see* Rule 14). Although the Code is silent on the point, the question also arises whether an appropriate offer or proposal needs to be made for any convertible securities (*see* Rule 15) and, if so, whether for all such securities or only on a partial basis.

In July 1992 Jack Chia-MPH made an offer for all the shares in Boustead. The offer was structured so that the first three out of every five Boustead shares were offered one cash sum, with a lesser cash sum being offered for all or any part of the balance of shares held. Following this offer, the Panel inserted a new note to Rule 36 stating that its consent must be sought if any such dual consideration offer is contemplated, where a lower consideration is offered for the balance of shareholders' holdings, and that it may treat such an offer as a form of partial offer. The two-tier offer by Panther Securities for Elys (Wimbledon) in March 1996, in which Panther offered a higher price for the first one out of every three Elys shares held, was accordingly treated as a partial offer.

In July 2003 a shareholder in Monsoon made an offer to sell put options over shares representing 20 per cent of Monsoon's issued share capital. The shareholder and its concert parties already owned 72.5 per cent and therefore the offer meant that this combined shareholding would increase to 92.5 per cent on the offer becoming unconditional and the put options being exercised. The offer was not, however, treated as a partial offer (or tender offer) regulated by the Code. It appears that the principal reason for the Panel taking this view was that it was an offer to sell put options, as opposed to an offer to buy shares directly. As a general principle, however, the Panel was concerned to see that all shareholders were treated equally.

Generally speaking, the other provisions of the Code (e.g. as to disclosure) apply to a partial offer regulated by the Code, in the same way as they do to a general offer, except to the extent the context otherwise requires.

5.4 Redemption or purchase of own securities

Section P (Rule 37) of the Code deals with the redemption or purchase by a company of its own securities. Such purchases can, of course, effectively be a back-door method of obtaining control. If a director or a person acting in concert with him was to hold a substantial block of voting shares, any purchase of other voting shares would increase the percentage which the existing block represents. It would, therefore, give that person greater control.

To protect the minority and to preserve the principle that a person may not obtain or consolidate effective control of a Code company without making an offer to all shareholders, Rule 37.1 provides that a mandatory offer obligation (under Rule 9) will arise in certain circumstances if the percentage of shares carrying voting rights in which a person or group of persons acting in concert is interested increases beyond the limits provided for in Rule 9 as a result of the redemption or purchase by a company of its own shares.

Provisions Applicable to all Offers

Following implementation of the Companies (Acquisition of Own Shares) (Treasury Shares) Regulations 2003 (SI 2003 No. 1116), which came into force on 1 December 2003, a company that purchases its own shares can choose whether to cancel them immediately or to hold up to 10 per cent (of its issued share capital) in treasury. Treasury shares can be held on to by the company concerned, used for its employee share plans, resold for cash or cancelled at some future date. Shares held in treasury continue to form part of the company's issued share capital but, for so long as they are held in treasury, the voting rights in respect of them are suspended. Accordingly, for the purposes of the Code (including, for example, the calculation of percentages for Rule 9 and Rule 37 purposes), it is only shares in issue *outside* treasury which are relevant (*see* Panel Statement 2003/26).

There have been a number of changes to Rule 37.1 in recent years. Prior to Panel Statement 1999/17, published in October 1999, there was a presumption that all the directors of a company, including any shareholders represented on the board, were acting in concert simply by reason of the company seeking shareholders' authority (and being authorised) to redeem or purchase any of its own securities. Where a company annually renewed its authority to buy-in its own shares, which is often the case in practice, this had the effect of all the directors being perpetually presumed to be acting in concert with each other for this purpose. This meant, in turn, that the ability of any director to buy further shares was severely inhibited where all the directors had a combined holding of between 30 per cent and 50 per cent, particularly following the abolition in August 1998 of the "creeper" provision (which had allowed a person holding between 30 per cent and 50 per cent to buy further shares carrying up to one per cent of the voting rights of a company in any 12-month period without triggering a mandatory offer). After a brief experiment at allowing directors some limited purchasing freedom to mitigate the effect of abolishing the "creeper" provision, the Panel then abolished the presumption that the directors as a whole are acting in concert solely by reason of a proposed redemption or purchase by a company of its own shares or the decision to seek shareholders' authority for any such redemption or purchase (*see* Panel Statement 1999/17 and Rule 37.1 in the latest edition of the Code).

Accordingly, Rule 37.1 is now applied on the following basis:

(a) a director or a person acting in concert with him will normally incur an obligation to make a mandatory offer under Rule 9 (unless a whitewash is obtained as referred to in paragraph (d) below) if, as a result of a redemption or purchase by a company of its own shares, that director and any concert party comes to be interested in 30 per cent or more of the voting rights of the company in question or, if already interested between 30 per cent and 50 per cent, his percentage interest is increased (but the directors as a whole are no longer presumed to be acting in concert with each other solely by reason of the proposed redemption or purchase);

(b) a person who has appointed a representative to the board of the company, and managers of investment trusts, will be treated on the same basis as directors and may incur a mandatory offer obligation under Rule 9 in the circumstances described in (a) above;

(c) any other person (i.e. one who is not a director, nor acting in concert with any director, nor represented on the board, nor a manager of an investment trust) will not normally incur an obligation to make a mandatory offer under Rule 9 provided that he has not purchased any shares in the company at a time when he had reason to believe that a redemption or purchase for which requisite shareholder authority existed was being, or was likely to be, implemented in whole or in part (a company cannot therefore impose a mandatory offer obligation on an unwelcome shareholder by buying in its own shares); and

(d) the Panel will usually waive any mandatory offer obligation resulting from a redemption or purchase by a company of its own shares provided there have been no disqualifying transactions and there is a vote of independent shareholders and the other procedures set out in Appendix 1 to the Code are followed before the implementation of any redemption or purchase (any such waiver, or "whitewash", must be renewed at the same time as the shareholders' authority for the purchase of shares is renewed under Sections 164 to 166 Companies Act 1985. There are numerous examples of such waivers being sought in the last year, including those by Mithras Investment Trust, Shore Capital Group, Real Estate Opportunities, Tower, Caledonia Investments, JJB Sports, Tottenham Hotspur, Marylebone Warwick Balfour and Public Recruitment Group).

Provisions Applicable to all Offers

Each individual director is required to draw the attention of the board to any interest in relevant securities of that director and any person acting in concert with him at the time any redemption or purchase of the company's own shares is proposed, and whenever shareholders' authority for any such redemption or purchase is to be sought. The Panel requires prior consultation in any case where Rule 9 might be relevant. In appropriate cases, the Panel may require inclusion in the circular to shareholders of confirmation by the directors that they are not aware of any agreements or understandings between directors or persons acting in concert with them.

When is Rule 37 likely to be relevant? It is likely that the maximum number of shares which a company admitted to the Official List will propose to buy-back will normally be less than 15 per cent of its equity, in view of the additional requirements imposed by the UK Listing Authority (the "UKLA") where 15 per cent or more is to be bought back (*see* paragraph 12.4 of the Listing Rules). If, for example, there is a buy-back of 15 per cent, an interest in 25.5 per cent before the buy-back will become an interest in 30 per cent afterwards. In other words, any director and persons acting in concert with him would have to be interested in at least 25.5 per cent of the voting rights before a whitewash is needed. Thus, if a director and his concert parties are interested in 25.5 per cent or more of the voting rights, they should stop all purchases of voting shares as soon as the board starts contemplating proposals for the company to buy-back its own shares. Even if they are interested in less than 25.5 per cent of the voting rights, they may be prohibited from purchasing shares for other reasons (e.g. because of the Model Code (*see* Annex 1 to Chapter 9 of the Listing Rules), Rule 4 of the Code or the insider dealing or market abuse legislation). If they are already interested in between 30 per cent and 50 per cent, they should of course not make any further purchases in any event if, absent some other dispensation, they wish to avoid a mandatory offer obligation.

The share buy-back authority sought by Mallett in April 2002 provided an example of where a director was deemed by the Panel to be acting in concert with a family trust, in which the director was also a beneficiary, as a result of which a whitewash was needed to waive the obligation that would otherwise have arisen to make a general offer to all shareholders following implementation of the proposed share buy-back.

There are certain cases when a buy-back may not be permitted at all, even if a whitewash had previously been obtained, without a further, specific shareholders' approval. Normally a buy-back will not be allowed (without such further approval) during an offer or if the target company's board has reason to believe that an offer might be "imminent" (Rule 37.3). The notice of the shareholders' meeting called to approve a buy-back in such circumstances must contain information about the offer or anticipated offer. The Panel may, however, consent to the buy-back without a further shareholders' approval if it is in pursuance of a contract entered into earlier or another pre-existing obligation (see also Article 9 of the Takeover Directive). If it is felt that these circumstances exist, the Panel must be consulted and its consent to proceed without a shareholders' meeting obtained.

An interesting question arises where a company already has a buy-back programme in place which is managed by an independent third party (e.g. its broker) and the board subsequently has reason to believe that an offer for the company might be imminent: would the company need to obtain a further, specific shareholders' approval to continue with the buy-back programme in these circumstances? Listing Rule 12.2.1(2) allows purchases of a listed company's own shares to continue to take place in a prohibited period, provided that the company's broker makes its trading decisions in relation to the company's shares independently of, and uninfluenced by, the company concerned. It is suggested that, in these circumstances, it should be possible for such a buy-back programme to continue provided that the original instruction to the company's broker was given before Rule 37.3 came into play, it is irrevocable and the broker does not know of any approach to the company concerned. The Panel should be consulted in cases where this might be an issue.

In practice, a company seeking to defend itself against an unwelcome bidder is unlikely to want to buy-back its own shares during the course of the offer as that would increase the percentage of shares in issue (outside of treasury, where relevant) which any unwelcome bidder may be interested in. Where a buy-back forms part of an offeree company's defence strategy, it will therefore usually propose the buy-back subject to the hostile offer lapsing. This is what Blue Circle did, for example, as part of its successful defence against an

Provisions Applicable to all Offers

offer from Lafarge in the first half of 2000. This case also provides an example of the rule, referred to above, that a mandatory offer obligation will not be imposed on an unwelcome shareholder in such circumstances. During the course of its offer, Lafarge had purchased 19.99 per cent, and its financial adviser had purchased 9.61 per cent, of Blue Circle. As part of its defence, Blue Circle promised to return capital to its shareholders, in part through a purchase of its own shares, if Lafarge's offer did not succeed. Blue Circle duly followed up with a share buy-back in May 2000, after the lapse of Lafarge's offer. On the basis that Lafarge was not represented on the board of Blue Circle and that both Lafarge and its financial adviser agreed not to vote on the shareholder resolution to authorise the share buy-back, the Panel agreed that any increase in their combined holding to 30 per cent or more, as a result of the buy-back, would not give rise to a mandatory bid obligation under Rule 9.

If, unusually, a buy-back is effected by the offeree company during an offer, there will be an obligation to disclose it as a dealing under Rule 8 and in the offeree company's circular to its shareholders under Rule 37.3(c). The circular will in any event have to contain details of all shares bought back during the 12 months before the offer. Similarly, if the offeror purchases its own shares during the course of a share exchange offer, that counts as a dealing in relevant securities which will have to be disclosed under Rule 8 and in the offer document under Rule 37.4(b). Rules 37.3(c) and 37.4(b) also require the offeree company and the offeror, respectively, to disclose in the documents sent to offeree company shareholders the extent to which shares repurchased in the offer period (and, in the case of the offeree company only, during the 12 months prior to its commencement) were cancelled or held in treasury.

The redemption or purchase of non-voting shares (e.g. most preference shares) will not be relevant to Rule 37 which (like Rule 9) is concerned with voting rights.

Before a company starts a buy-back programme, it is always worth considering if there are any Code implications, in addition to the usual tax, financial and corporate law considerations.

Chapter 6

Documents from the Offeror and the Offeree

Carlton Evans
Partner
Linklaters

6.1 Introduction

Takeover documentation, particularly in contested offers, may often appear at first sight to be subject to few guiding principles. However, in respect of general approach and detailed contents, the content of takeover documentation is closely controlled, principally by the Code and, to a lesser extent, by a number of other sources of regulation, such as the Listing Rules (the "Listing Rules"), the Prospectus Rules (the "Prospectus Rules") and the Disclosure Rules (the "Disclosure Rules") of the UK Financial Services Authority (the "FSA") and the Financial Services and Markets Act 2000 (the "FSMA").

Over the years there has been an increase in the detailed information required by the Code in offer documentation and in the precision with which the more technical elements are drafted. This is partly due to the fact that the Code has become a document drafted in increasingly legal terms which require close study in order that all of its provisions can be properly reflected in offer documents. In addition, the offer document is a legal document (it constitutes an offer which, on acceptance, sets up a contractual relationship), and it and other documents may have other legal consequences (if, for example, they contain misrepresentations or defamatory statements) and their drafting has to reflect this.

On 20 May 2006, a number of substantive changes were made to the Code relating to the content of takeover documentation pursuant to the provisions of the European Directive on Takeover Bids (2004/25/EC) (the "Directive") which was implemented into UK law by way of the Takeovers Directive (Interim Implementation) Regulations 2006 (the "Interim Regulations").

As their name implies, these regulations are an interim measure in order to ensure implementation of the Directive by no later than 20 May 2006 and will cease to have effect as soon as the relevant provisions of the Company Law Reform Bill ("CLRB") come into force (which is anticipated to occur in Spring 2007). Generally, the Interim Regulations only apply to transactions to which the Directive applies – i.e. takeovers of companies admitted to a regulated market, which would include the London Stock Exchange but not AIM.

From 20 May 2006, the Panel and the Code were placed on a statutory footing in relation to takeover offers to which the Interim Regulations apply. This has led to a two track regime which will continue until the enactment of the CLRB. Where the particular transaction is outside the scope of the Interim Regulations, for example a takeover offer for a company whose shares are admitted to AIM or a takeover effected by way of scheme of arrangement, the Code General Principles and Rules (including in respect of the content of offeror and offeree documents) will continue to operate for such transactions on the same non-statutory basis as they did prior to 20 May 2006.

A number of additional "updating" amendments to the Code were also brought into force on 20 May 2006: these also impact on the contents of offeror and offeree documents.

6.2 General obligations in respect of documents

6.2.1 The spirit of the Code

The Introduction to the Code identifies the difference between its General Principles and the Rules. The General Principles, expressed in broad terms, are "essentially statements of good standards of commercial behaviour". The Rules fall into two categories; some of them are expansions of the General Principles and others are provisions governing specific aspects of takeover procedure. Neither the General Principles nor the Rules are framed in technical language and both are to be interpreted so as to achieve their underlying purpose.

Documents from the Offeror and the Offeree

Thus, the Code is to be interpreted in accordance with its spirit rather than its letter, although its letter, in giving detailed guidance as to procedure, must not be ignored.

This approach applies as much to documentation as to any other aspect of a takeover. The documents issued by a company to its shareholders, or to the shareholders of another company, have to be drafted in a way which, whilst complying with the detailed requirements of the Code, enables those shareholders to consider and evaluate fairly the arguments put forward in the course of a takeover.

6.2.2 General responsibilities in respect of offer documentation

In the context of documentation, the General Principle of the Code that is particularly relevant is General Principle 2 which requires that:

> "2 The holders of the securities of an offeree must have sufficient time and information to enable them to reach a properly informed decision on the bid; where it advises the holders of securities, the board of the offeree must give its view on the effects of implementation of the bid on employment, conditions of employment and the locations of the company's places of business."

This Principle is, to a large extent, repeated in Rule 19.1 and is supplemented by Rule 23. These Rules state:

> "19.1 Standards of care
> Each document or advertisement issued, or statement made, during the course of an offer must be prepared with the highest standards of care and accuracy and the information given must be adequately and fairly presented. This applies whether it is issued by the company direct or by an adviser on its behalf."

> "23 The general obligation as to information
> Shareholders must be given sufficient information and advice to enable them to reach a properly informed decision as to the merits or demerits of an offer. Such information must be available to shareholders early enough to enable them to make a decision in good time. No relevant information should be withheld

from them. The obligation of the offeror in these respects towards the shareholders of the offeree is no less than an offeror's obligation towards its own shareholders."

Whatever the detailed information, comment or advice contained in offer documentation, the correct approach is that of common sense and commerciality – namely, do the documents say what they are intended to say, do they give appropriate information and are they likely to be understood by the persons who are to receive them, not all of whom will have the same level of commercial knowledge and sophistication?

6.2.3 Specific standards of care – the notes on Rule 19.1

Rule 19.1 contains a number of notes intended to emphasise and enlarge upon the obligations of that Rule. Accordingly, the language used in documents should be unambiguous so as to reflect "clearly and concisely" the position being described. The source for any fact that is material to an argument must be disclosed, together with sufficient detail to enable the significance of the fact to be assessed. Quotations must not be taken out of context, details of their origin must be given, and the board of the company using the quotation must be prepared to substantiate or corroborate comments quoted. Pictorial representations and diagrams must be presented without distortion, and charts, graphs and other similar diagrams must be to scale. The parties to a takeover will often want to use performance figures in a way which bolsters their respective arguments – this is not forbidden, but graphs and charts used must give a fair view and the basis for them should be justifiable. The Panel must be consulted in advance if television, videos, audio tapes, etc. are to be used.

In addition, Note 7 on Rule 19.1 refers to potential liabilities for misleading the market imposed by Section 397 FSMA (*see* paragraph 6.12.3 below).

Finally, it is important to note that, as Note 1 on Rule 19.1 makes clear, the Panel regards financial advisers as being responsible for guiding their clients and any relevant public relations advisers with regard to information released during the course of an offer.

6.2.4 Directors' responsibility statements – Rule 19.2

The above provisions are buttressed by the requirement in Rule 19.2 that the directors of the relevant company should expressly accept responsibility for the information contained in each document or advertisement issued or published in connection with an offer and confirm that, to the best of their knowledge and belief (having taken all reasonable care to ensure that such is the case), the information contained in the document or advertisement is in accordance with the facts and, where appropriate, that it does not omit anything likely to affect the import of such information. This public assumption of responsibility may result in the directors taking on a potential liability in tort to persons who act in reliance on statements contained in the document under the principle established in *Hedley Byrne* v *Heller* (1964) AC 465.

In effect, this states that, if a misstatement has been made negligently to a person who is sufficiently proximate in circumstances where it is foreseeable that that person may suffer economic loss, the person making the statement will be liable in damages to a person who suffered loss by relying on the statement. In many cases, it would be reasonable to assume that a shareholder to whom a document or advertisement is addressed may be able to show reliance on the information presented to him in considering what action he should take with regard to a takeover.

A more immediate remedy, used particularly in hostile or competing bids is for parties to bids (or occasionally shareholders) to complain to the Panel about the accuracy of statements made by others involved in a particular bid with a view to seeking a public retraction or clarification. In hostile or competing bids, such complaints can occur on an almost daily basis.

A modified form of responsibility statement is permitted when information about another company contained in a document has been compiled from published sources (such as its report and accounts), in which case, responsibility need only be taken for "the correctness and fairness of its reproduction and presentation". Thus, on a hostile bid, the factual information set out in the offer document relating to the target will be covered by the qualified form of responsibility statement but, on a recommended bid, the board of the offeree will be required to take full responsibility for information relating to the offeree. Furthermore, certain types of advertising (such as product or corporate advertising not bearing on an offer) do not need to carry a responsibility statement (*see* paragraph 6.9.3 below).

On a securities exchange offer, where an offer document constitutes, or is accompanied by, a prospectus (or a document containing information which is regarded by the FSA as being equivalent to that of a prospectus), under the Prospectus Rules, the offeror directors are required to take responsibility for the whole of the prospectus or equivalent document.

In exceptional circumstances, the Panel may be willing to consent to the exclusion of a director from the responsibility statement but, in such cases, the omission and the reasons for it must be stated in the document or advertisement.

6.2.5 *Appointment of board committees and verification*

Since many boards of directors are too large to be a viable body for preparing documentation (and most executive directors will continue to spend the majority of their time running the business), it is common practice for a board of directors to delegate day-to-day conduct of the offer including the detailed consideration of documentation to a committee. The directors must believe that the members of the committee are competent to do the work and must disclose all relevant facts relating to themselves or otherwise relating to the documentation. Notwithstanding any delegation, however, all the directors retain ultimate responsibility, as is made clear by Section 1 of Appendix 3 to the Code. This requires the circulation of papers and information to the board (including all non-routine agreements and other obligations entered into by a company in the context of the offer) and the holding of board meetings, as necessary, throughout the offer period. By this means, no director should be able to claim that he is relieved from his responsibility for the contents of documentation.

The requirement to prepare documents to prospectus standards and the assumption of responsibility by all the directors means that the

Documents from the Offeror and the Offeree

directors and their advisers usually undertake a full and detailed verification exercise to check the facts and the bases and assumptions for any statements of opinion or belief contained in documentation.

6.2.6 Holding statements

Rule 19.3 requires that parties to an offer or potential offer (and their advisers) must take care not to issue statements which, whilst not factually inaccurate, may mislead shareholders and the market or may create uncertainty. This general provision is supplemented by one specific example of an unacceptable statement, being a statement by an offeror "to the effect that it may improve its offer without committing itself to doing so and specifying the improvement". This Rule is a reflection of General Principle 4 (which requires parties to endeavour to avoid the creation of a false market) and is designed to prevent an offeror indicating that it might increase (or otherwise alter the terms of) its offer before it is able to commit itself to doing so. Practice Statement 7 makes clear that Rule 19.3 is not limited to statements about increases in the financial value of an offer – the Rule extends to any statement which may mislead shareholders or the market or which may create uncertainty (whether or not such statement is factually accurate).

Note 1 on Rule 19.3 emphasises that holding statements (such as an offeror stating that it may need to consider its position in light of new developments or a potential competing offeror stating that it is considering making an offer) made in the later stages of an offer period should be clarified within a limited time. Before any such statements are made, the Panel must be consulted about the period within which clarification must be given.

In its ruling on the holding statement issued by the Royal Bank of Scotland Group plc ("RBS") in relation to its contemplated bid in 1999 for National Westminster Bank plc, during the Bank of Scotland's offer for National Westminster Bank, the Panel stated that it would be inappropriate to require RBS to clarify its statement earlier than Day 39 and that it was fair to make Day 50 the latest appropriate day for clarification (although the Panel reserved the right to specify an earlier or later date depending upon developments). However, in the later case of a potential competing offer for Ask Central plc in 2004, the Panel deemed that, for the purposes of Rule 19.3, one week before Day 60 was sufficient for the potential competing offeror to make a firm offer.

Practice Statement 8 states that, if the Panel grants an offeror an extension to Day 60, it will normally grant a corresponding extension to any date by which a statement by a potential competing offeror must be clarified in accordance with Note 1 on Rule 19.3. In relation to schemes of arrangement, Practice Statement 14 states that the Panel will normally set the latest date for clarification under Note 1 on Rule 19.3 on or around 10 calendar days prior to the date of the shareholders' meetings but will consider each case on its facts and may set a date which falls after the date of the shareholders' meeting but prior to the court hearing.

6.2.7 Release of documents to other parties

Rule 19.7 requires that, before the offer document is made public, a copy must be lodged with the Panel. Copies of all other documents and announcements bearing on an offer and of advertisements and any material released to the media must, at the time of release, be lodged with the Panel and the advisers to all other parties to the offer. It is no longer permitted to release documents or announcements to the media under an embargo, the intention being to prevent the selective leaking of information or "front running" the contents of offer documentation through the press. Further requirements in relation to the publication and circulation of announcements and offer documents by both the offeror and the offeree are given at paragraphs 6.6, 6.7 and 6.9 below.

6.3 Offer document contents

The following analysis of the documentation to be issued by the respective parties to a takeover assumes that an offer is not recommended. In general, however, the rules apply equally to a recommended offer, governing whatever the offeror and offeree companies publish jointly.

6.3.1 Commercial issues, terms and conditions

First and foremost, the offer document will deal with the main commercial terms and arguments for the offer – the price, the commercial logic and general "puff" for the offeror, its management and its expertise. It will also set out in full all the terms and conditions attached to the offer. These terms will include: –

(a) information about the consideration (e.g. the type of consideration, any alternative consideration, whether consideration shares carry the right to the next dividend, and the rights attached to consideration preference shares or loan stock);
(b) detailed information on the circumstances in which an offer can be revised;
(c) the timetable for announcements and when rights of withdrawal arise;
(d) detailed information about acceptances; and
(e) the warranties, undertakings and authorities given by an accepting shareholder by reason of his execution of a form of acceptance.

All terms and conditions of an offer must be set out in full, without merely cross-referencing to Rules of the Code (although this requirement has been mitigated in one respect *see* paragraph 6.3.5 below). The requirement that all the conditions be comprehensive is illustrated by Rules 31.5 and 32.2 which prohibit extensions to, or increases in, the offer in cases where the offeror has indicated that the offer will not be extended or, as the case may be, increased unless the right to do so has been specifically reserved, with precise details of the circumstances which would trigger an extension or increase.

6.3.2 Specific content requirements – Rule 24

The specific Code requirements for an offeror to satisfy concerning the contents of an offer document are to be found in Rule 24. These requirements may also extend to documents that are not technically offer documents, such as circulars sent to shareholders by a potential offeror which has announced an offer but subject to a pre-condition relating to action by offeree shareholders (such as the rejection of a proposed acquisition or disposal).

Rule 24.1 states that an offeror will be required to cover the following points in the offer document:

(a) its intentions with regard to the future business of the offeree;
(b) its strategic plans for the offeree and their likely repercussions on employment and the locations of the offeree's places of business;
(c) its intentions regarding any redeployment of the fixed assets of the offeree;
(d) its long-term commercial justification for the offer; and
(e) its intentions with regard to the continued employment of the employees and management of the offeree and of its subsidiaries including any material change in the conditions of employment.

In relation to sub-paragraph (e), prior to 20 May 2006 the offeror was merely required to describes its intentions with regard to the continued employment of the employees and the practice evolved that this requirement would be met with the rather anodyne statement that the employment and other rights of employees would be "safeguarded". It remains to be seen whether this disclosure will now need to be "upgraded" in order to comply with the more onerous requirements of Rule 24.1.

In addition, under the regime effective from 20 May 2006, where the offeror is a company, and insofar as it is affected by the offer, the offeror must also disclose information for (a), (b) and (c) with regard to itself.

6.3.3 Financial and other information – Rule 24.2

Rule 24.2 requires financial and other information on the offeror and offeree to be included. It contains different requirements depending on the nature of the offeror and whether the offer is for cash or includes offeror securities.

6.3.3.1 UK Listed Offerors – cash offers
Where the offeror is a company incorporated under the Companies Act 1985 (or its predecessors) which is listed on the official list maintained by the FSA (the "Official List") or traded on the Alternative Investment Market ("AIM"), and the consideration for the offer is cash only, Rule 24.2 only requires, in respect of the offeror, two years' profit and loss account information, a net assets statement as at the date of the latest published accounts, the names of the offeror's

directors, and a description of the offeror's business and its financial and trading prospects (Rule 24.2(b)). This reduced scope of information does not apply to partial offers (even if they are solely cash).

6.3.3.2 UK Listed Offerors – securities exchange offers

Where the offeror is incorporated under the Companies Act 1985 (or its predecessors) and its shares are listed or quoted on the Official List or admitted to trading on AIM, and the consideration includes securities, or unless the Panel has otherwise agreed, Rule 24.2(a) requires that the offer document must show the following information in respect of the offeror:

(a) profit and loss account information for the last three financial years for which that information has been published;
(b) the latest published audited balance sheet;
(c) a cash flow statement if provided in the last published audited accounts;
(d) all known material changes in the financial and trading position since the publication of the last published audited accounts (or a negative statement);
(e) details of any interim or preliminary announcement made since the last published audited accounts;
(f) inflation-adjusted information (if it has been published previously);
(g) significant accounting policies and any points from the notes to the accounts which are of major relevance to an appreciation of the figures;
(h) details of any effects of changes in accounting policies which result in figures not being comparable to a material extent;
(i) the names of the offeror's directors;
(j) the nature of the offeror's business and its financial and trading prospects; and
(k) a summary of the principal contents of each material contract (not being a contract entered into in the ordinary course of business) entered into by the offeror or any subsidiary in the two years before the commencement of the offer period.

6.3.3.3 Non UK Listed Offerors

Where the offeror is not a Companies Act company or its shares are not listed on the Official List or admitted to trading on AIM (and whether the consideration is securities or cash), it should disclose so much of the information set out in Rule 24.2(a) as is appropriate and such further information as the Panel may require (Rule 24.2(c)(i)).

The Code also requires additional information about persons who are participating in an offeror whose shares are not listed on the Official List or admitted to trading on AIM (e.g. shareholders in a consortium company formed for the offer). The identity of such persons and details of their interests must be disclosed as well as such other information as the Panel may require. The ability of the Panel to require information means that in appropriate cases the Panel should be consulted in advance, so that the offer document can be properly prepared. Where an offeror whose shares are not listed on the Official List or admitted to trading on AIM is the subsidiary of another company, the Panel will normally look through the offeror and require information on the ultimate holding company in the form of group accounts (Note 1 to Rule 24.2), though sometimes an intermediate group company, if sufficiently large compared with the offeree, will suffice.

Most of the information required under Rule 24.2(a) also has to be given in respect of the offeree.

6.3.3.4 Other information – Rule 24.2(d)

Rule 24.2(d) sets out further contents requirements for the offer document. These include:

(a) the date when the document is despatched;
(b) the name and address of the offeror (including, where the offeror is a company, the type of company and the address of its registered office) and, if appropriate, the person making the offer on behalf of the offeror;
(c) the identity of any person acting in concert with the offeror and, to the extent that it is known, the offeree including, in the case of a company, its type, registered office and relationship with the offeror and, where possible, the offeree;
(d) details of each class of security for which the offer is made (including whether those securities will be transferred "cum" or "ex" any dividend and the maximum and minimum percentages of those securities which the offeror undertakes to acquire);

(e) the terms of the offer, including the consideration offered for each class of security, the total consideration offered and the particulars of the way in which the consideration is to be paid in accordance with Rule 31.8;
(f) all conditions (including normal conditions relating to acceptances, admission to listing, admission to trading and increase of capital) to which the offer is subject;
(g) the particulars of all documents required;
(h) procedures to be followed for acceptance of the offer;
(i) market prices for the securities to be acquired;
(j) details of any agreements or arrangements to which the offeror is a party which relate to the circumstances in which it may or may not invoke or seek to invoke a condition to its offer and the consequences of doing so, including details of any break fees payable as a result;
(k) in a securities exchange offer, full particulars of the terms of the securities being offered including the rights attaching to them;
(l) the national law that will govern contracts concluded between the offeror and the holders of the offeree's securities as a result of the offer and the competent courts;
(m) the compensation (if any) offered for the removal of "breakthrough" rights pursuant to Article 11 of the Directive together with particulars of the way in which the compensation is to be paid and the method employed in determining it; and
(n) details of any arrangement of the payment of an inducement fee or similar arrangement as referred to in Rule 21.2 (see further below at paragraph 6.8.3).

All offer documents must also contain a description of how the offer is financed and the source of the finance; exceptions may be made, but only with the consent of the Panel (Rule 24.2(f)).

6.3.4 Shareholdings and dealings – Rule 24.3

Rule 24.3 contains a list of information required concerning shareholdings and dealings of the offeror (and its directors) in the shares of the offeree (which can vary depending on whether the offer is a securities exchange offer or not). The Rule was amended on 7 November 2005 to reflect the changes made to Rule 8 in relation to the widening of the disclosure of interests in shares to encompass options and derivatives referenced to offeror or offeree shares. Under Rule 24.3, the offer document must contain details of any shares of the offeree in which the offeror has an interest or right to subscribe. "Interest" is defined as "a long economic exposure whether absolute or conditional to changes in the price of securities" and a person is treated as having an interest in shares if, inter alia, he owns them, has the right to direct voting rights, has the right or obligation to take delivery of the shares or if he is a party to any derivative whose value is determined by reference to the price of the underlying shares. Rule 24.3 also requires short positions in relation to shares and derivatives referenced to those shares to be disclosed.

Under Rule 24.3 (c), dealings by any person whose interests have to be disclosed under Rule 24.3(a) for the period beginning 12 months prior to the commencement of the offer period (which is when the announcement of a proposed or possible offer is first made) and ending with the latest practicable date before printing of the offer document are required to be disclosed. "Dealings" is construed widely and again extends to financial products referenced to offeree shares.

In the case of a securities exchange offer, equivalent information has to be given by the persons required to disclose their interests and dealings in offeree shares in relation to any interests and dealings they might have in offeror shares.

Note 2 on Rule 24.3 states that, provided that *inter alia* no significant dealings are thereby concealed, disclosure of:

(a) dealings during the offer period can be aggregated;
(b) dealings in the three months prior to that period can be aggregated on a monthly basis; and
(c) dealings in the nine months prior to that period can be aggregated on a quarterly basis.

6.3.5 *General information required by Rule 24*

Other information required by Rule 24 includes:

(a) in the case of a securities exchange offer, whether and in what manner the emoluments of the directors of the offeror will be

Documents from the Offeror and the Offeree

affected by the acquisition of the offeree or any associated transaction, or an appropriate negative statement (Rule 24.4);
(b) details of any agreement, arrangement or understanding (including any compensation arrangement) between the offeror or any concert party and any of the directors, recent directors, shareholders or recent shareholders of the offeree having any connection with or dependence upon the offer (Rule 24.5);
(c) confirmation from the offeror's bank or financial adviser of the existence of financial resources to satisfy any cash payable under an offer (although this confirmation does not operate as a guarantee that funds will be available) (Rule 24.7). A conditional confirmation is not permitted. Prior to 20 May 2006, a conditional confirmation was acceptable in "exceptional circumstances" with the consent of the Panel, although this rarely arose. Practice Statement 10 made it clear that, where an offeror proposed to finance a cash offer (or a cash alternative to a securities exchange offer) by an issue of new securities, the Panel did not regard this as "exceptional circumstances" and, accordingly, would not allow the cash confirmation given to be conditional upon the success of the issue of the new offeror securities;
(d) a statement as to the ultimate ownership of any securities acquired in pursuance of the offer (Rule 24.8);
(e) a statement that, where securities offered as consideration are to be listed on the Official List or admitted to trading on AIM, the relevant listing or admitting to trading condition will only be satisfied when the announcement of admission has been made. Where securities are offered as consideration and it is intended that they should be admitted to listing or to trading on any other investment exchange, the Panel should be consulted (Rule 24.9);
(f) an estimate by an appropriate adviser of the value of a class of securities which is not admitted to trading proposed to be issued as consideration (Rule 24.10). If the adviser is not able to provide an estimate, a statement to that effect must be included in the offer document. In these circumstances, however, it will not normally be possible for the offeror to satisfy the Panel that the value of its offer exceeds the price of any purchases of offeree shares that might have been made to which Rule 6 applies and offerors should ensure that no such purchases are made unless a Rule 24.10 valuation can be published or a full cash alternative provided; and

(g) a clear statement as to the procedure for shutting off any cash-underwritten alternative (Rule 24.13).

The amount of information required will vary depending on whether or not the offer is a securities exchange offer, and the complete and detailed list must be read from the Code itself, but there is one further and very important requirement which must be noted. According to Rule 24.6, the offer document must state the time allowed for acceptance of the offer and any alternative offer and reflect appropriately the full terms relating to acceptance levels, time of announcements, rights of withdrawal, etc., which are contained in those parts of Rules 13.4(a), 13.5 (if applicable) 17 and 31 to 34 of the Code (*see* Chapter 7). It must also reflect the terms of Notes 4 to 8 on Rule 10 relating to acceptances and purchases and confirmation of good title to shares. However, the amount of small print which would be required if all details were to be set out in full has been substantially reduced by the Code permitting a cross-reference to Notes 4 to 6 and Note 8 on Rule 10, since they deal with what are regarded as largely technical matters.

Rule 26 sets out the documents which must be made available for inspection by the offeror and requires that the offer document must specify them and where they can be inspected. From 20 May 2006, the offer document itself must also be made available for inspection.

The offer document must normally be sent to shareholders of the offeree within 28 days of the announcement of a firm intention to make the offer (Rule 30.1).

6.4 Offeree Circular contents – Rule 25

Within 14 days of the despatch of the offer document, the board of the offeree must normally send a circular to its shareholders. The circular is subject to various general requirements set out in Rule 23 and must contain the opinion of the board of the offeree on the offer and the substance of the advice given to it by its independent financial advisers (Rule 25.1). The opinion of the offeree board must include its views on:

(a) the effects of implementation of the offer on all the company's interests, including, specifically, employment; and
(b) the offeror's strategic plans for the offeree and their likely repercussions on employment and the locations of the offeree's place of business as set out in the offer document pursuant to Rule 24.1.

If the offeree board is divided on the merits, the minority should also publish its views, pursuant to Note 2 on Rule 25.1 and the Panel will normally require that such views be circulated by the offeree.

In a recommended offer, these opinions will be contained in the offer document itself. In a hostile offer, they will be contained in the "defence document" which will seek to refute the arguments and the commercial logic put forward by the offeror.

Rule 25 sets out specific content requirements for the first major circular from the offeree board. To a large extent, Rule 25 reflects the information requirements imposed on the offeror by Rule 24.

Prior to 20 May 2006, there was no requirement under the Code for the offeree to include in its first major circular any details relating to the latest financial or trading position of the offeree. Following the changes made to the Code on that date, under Rule 25.2, the first major circular from the offeree board advising shareholders on an offer (whether recommending acceptance or rejection of the offer) must contain all known material changes in the financial or trading position of the offeree subsequent to the last published audited accounts or a statement that there are no known material changes. This gives the shareholders the benefit of knowing that such statements had been considered by those best placed to understand the offeree's affairs (i.e. the offeree's directors). Under Rule 24.1(e) of the Code, the offeror is already required to include this information in its offer document in relation to an offeree. In a combined document (i.e. if the offer is recommended) this information will now be the responsibility of the offeree board. Additional information that needs to be contained in the first major circular from the offeree includes:

(a) interests and dealings in the offeror's and the offeree's shares (Rule 25.3);

(b) information about directors' service contracts (including particulars of former contracts, if such contracts have been replaced or amended within six months of the date of the document) (Rule 25.4). This Rule is designed to ensure that any compensation payments to outgoing directors ("golden parachutes") which are arranged at, or shortly before, the making of the offer, are fully disclosed to the public. Aggregation of the remuneration payable under service contracts is no longer permitted and full details of each director's remuneration package must be given;

(c) any arrangement in relation to securities of the offeree, such as indemnities or options, must also be disclosed or, if there are none, there should be an appropriate negative statement (Rule 25.5);

(d) the first major circular from the offeree board advising shareholders on the offer must also contain a summary of the principal contents of any material contract (not being a contract entered into in the ordinary course of business) entered into by the offeree or any subsidiary in the two years before the commencement of the offer period (Rule 25.6).

In order to comply with Article 9.5 of the Directive, with effect from 20 May 2006, Rule 30.2(b) requires an offeree to append to its document an opinion from the representative of its employees on the effect of the offer on employment, provided that such opinion is received "in good time" before publication. Respondents to the Panel's consultation on the changes to the Code required by the Directive expressed concern that the effect of this Rule was to require the offeree to consult with its employees prior to the offer being announced. This issue is of particular concern on a recommended offer where the Rule 2.5 announcement and the combined offer document (containing information both on the offeror and the offeree) could be published on the same day – this would not be possible if the offeree was required to obtain the opinion of employee representatives. As a result, the Panel clarified that, in their opinion, both the Directive and the Code required information to be provided to employees but that consultation was not required and that there was no intention to change the existing practice of publishing a combined document in the case of a recommended offer. The Panel also confirmed that where the employee opinion is not available at the time of the publication of the offeree document, there would be no requirement on the offeree to circulate the opinion of its employee representatives subsequently.

It will be interesting to see how market practice develops in relation to this Rule and, notwithstanding the technical position, whether or not offerees decide to consult with employee representatives and/or circulate their views after publication of the offeree circular.

6.5 Criminal Liability for non-compliant documents

From 20 May 2006, all parties involved in a takeover offer subject to the Interim Regulations (i.e. within the scope of the Directive) need to consider the new criminal offence for non-compliance with the contents requirements for offeror and offeree documents set out in Rules 24 to 27 of the Code. The offence is set out in Regulation 10 of the Interim Regulations. The DTI's view is that the offence is necessary to implement the Directive's requirement that EEA States should have in place sanctions which are "effective, proportionate and dissuasive".

The purpose of the offence is to ensure a high standard of care in the drafting of bid documentation, with a sanction for failure to meet those standards. However, the imposition of criminal liability has surprised market participants, particularly as there is no requirement for non-compliance with the disclosure requirements to cause loss to any person. The offence is punishable by a fine and catches not only wilful non-compliance, but also non-compliance due to recklessness and failure to take "all reasonable steps" to ensure compliance.

With regard to the offer document, the offence is committed by "the person making the bid" and also by any of such person's directors, officers or members who caused the document to be published. It seems logical that directors, as persons responsible for the offer document under Rule 19, should be caught by this new offence but the term "officer" extends to both the company secretary and a "manager" (a term of somewhat imprecise scope in an English context). Directors and officers of the offeree are also at risk of prosecution for the new offence, so far as offeree documents are concerned.

"Members" (i.e. shareholders) of the offeror are also at risk where they cause the offer document to be published – and the scope of the offence is such that directors and officers of that member, if it is a body corporate, may also be criminally liable. This will be of particular concern in the case of "take private" bids where a new bid vehicle is traditionally used, and in the case of takeover offers by wholly-owned subsidiaries.

Although the drafting of the offence may be revisited by the DTI when the CLRB takes effect, the offence as drafted in the Interim Regulations is also of relevance to the offeror's financial adviser as potentially "the person making the bid". Historically, it has been common practice for the financial adviser to make the offer to offeree shareholders on the offeror's behalf. Whilst it is arguable that it is the offeror, and not the financial adviser (as the offeror's agent), who should be regarded as "the person making the bid", the legislation's lack of clarity in this regard may well encourage a cautious approach from financial advisers.

6.6 Publication of Documents

The Directive requires that an offer document must be "made public". An offeror is therefore required to include its offer document in the documents made available for display pursuant to Rule 26. It must also make an announcement in accordance with Rule 2.9 (i.e. notification to a Regulatory Information Service ("RIS")) that the offer document has been posted, with details of where it can be inspected.

Under Rule 19.7, an offeror is required to lodge a copy of the offer document with the Panel before it is made public. The Panel has confirmed that it will be acceptable to continue with the existing market practice of despatching documents to the Panel under the direction of the financial adviser at the same time as they are being posted to shareholders.

The offeror will also be required to make the offer document (as is the case for a Rule 2.5 announcement) "readily available" to the offeror's (but not the offeree's) employee representatives or employees. Although not expressly permitted, it is likely that website publication will be sufficient to discharge this obligation.

Documents from the Offeror and the Offeree

Offerees must put their documents on display, with details of posting and availability for inspection announced in accordance with Rule 2.9 (i.e. notification to a RIS). They must also make all offer documents and offeree documents "readily available" to the offeree's employee representatives or employees. As explained above, website publication is likely to be sufficient. In the context of a recommended offer, information required to be included in the offeree document will normally be incorporated into the offer document and so the offeree's publication requirements described above will apply to the offer document.

6.7 Circulation of Documents

From 20 May 2006, Rule 30.3 provides that the requirement to make information and documents available to shareholders and employees or their representatives applies wherever those shareholders or employees are located, unless there is "sufficient objective justification" for their not applying. This is contrary to market practice prior to 20 May 2006 where, generally speaking, offer documents were not sent to shareholders in countries where there were expensive registration requirements or a greater risk of liability in relation to the offer document.

The Note on Rule 30.3 provides a derogation setting out the circumstances in which there would be "sufficient objective justification" for not applying the Rule. Those circumstances include where the laws of a non-EEA State may result in a significant risk of civil, regulatory or criminal exposure for the offeror of offeree if the information or document is sent into that jurisdiction without amendment and either (i) less than three per cent of the shares of the offeree are held by registered shareholders located there or (ii) circumstances are such that it would be proportionate for the Panel to grant a dispensation (having regard to factors such as the cost involved, number of shares involved and any delay to the timetable). Automatic exemption under (i) will be available in many cases where there are limited numbers of shareholders in the relevant jurisdictions but specific derogations may be required for other countries and this may need to be factored into the offer timetable.

6.8 Specific issues

6.8.1 Profit forecasts and asset valuations (Rules 28 and 29)

It is not uncommon, particularly in contested offers, for the offeror or offeree, in support of their respective positions, to make a profit forecast, although this may not always be made in the first document from either side. This may, however, be unavoidable if, whether deliberately or not, a profit forecast has been made in some previous public pronouncement. If this is the case, then it will have to be made again and reported upon, unless the Panel agrees to the contrary. The full requirements for profit forecasts are dealt with in Chapter 8. In the context of the documentation, therefore, it should be noted that the Code lays considerable emphasis on the standards of care which are required and the document in which the forecast appears must also contain a statement of the assumptions on which the forecast has been made. The accounting policies and calculations must be examined and reported on by the auditors or consultant accountants, and any financial adviser mentioned in the document must also report on the forecast. Their reports are published in the appropriate document.

Asset valuations, which occur less frequently, tend to be made in the case of companies with a large and potentially undervalued asset base (e.g. property companies or retail store chains (*see* Chapter 8)). The relevant document containing the valuation will have to contain the valuation report of an independent valuer and the basis of valuation must be clearly stated.

6.8.2 Merger benefits statements – Note 8 on Rule 19.1

Note 8 on Rule 19.1 imposes additional requirements when merger benefits statements are made. Merger benefits statements are quantified statements made about the expected financial benefits of a proposed takeover or merger (e.g. statements quantifying synergy benefits or indicating an earnings enhancement). These additional requirements include the publication of the bases of the belief supporting any such statement together with reports by financial advisers and accountants that the statement has been made with due care and consideration. There will also have to be an explanation of the constituent elements sufficient to enable shareholders to understand the relative importance of those elements.

In any case in which a party to a takeover wishes to make a merger benefits statement, it should consult the Panel in advance. However, substantiation of merger benefits statements will only be required in the case of securities exchange offers and will not normally apply in the case of a recommended securities exchange offer unless a competing offer is made and the merger benefits statement is subsequently repeated by the party which made it or the statement otherwise becomes a material issue.

6.8.3 Inducement fees – Rule 21.2

Details of any inducement fee payable by an offeree to an offeror if its offer fails for some reason must be fully disclosed in the press release announcing the offer and in the offer document (Rule 21.2). Inducement fees must be *de minimis* (normally no more than one per cent of the value of the offeree calculated by reference to the offer price) and the offeree board and its financial adviser must confirm to the Panel in writing that they each believe the fee to be in the best interests of shareholders. Subsequently, the relevant documents must be put on display when the offer document is posted.

Practice Statement 4 sets out, *inter alia*, further parameters for determining the maximum amount permitted for an inducement fee. The one per cent limit may be calculated on the basis of the fully diluted equity share capital of the offeree, and where necessary, should take into account VAT payable on the fee. For the purposes of determining the offeree's fully diluted equity share capital, only options and warrants that are "in the money" may be included in the calculation and such instruments must be valued on a "see-through" basis taking into account the offer price and any exercise price. Further, where the fee is agreed prior to the announcement of a firm offer, the value of the offeree should be determined by reference to the expected value of the offer at the time the fee is agreed. On a securities exchange offer, the value of the offeree should be fixed by reference to the value of the offer at the time of announcement of the offer.

Practice Statement 4 also sets out the matters which should normally be addressed in the written confirmations to the Panel which the offeree board and its financial adviser must provide under Rule 21.2, namely:

(a) confirmation that the inducement fee arrangements were agreed as a result of normal commercial negotiations;
(b) an explanation of the circumstances in which the fee becomes payable and the basis on which such circumstances were considered appropriate;
(c) any relevant information concerning possible competing offerors, for example, the status of any discussions, the possible offer terms, any pre-conditions to the making of an offer, the timing of any such offer etc;
(d) confirmation that there are no other side agreements or understandings in relation to the relevant arrangements that are not fully disclosed; and
(e) confirmation that, in the opinion of the offeree board and its financial adviser, the agreement to pay the inducement fee is in the best interests of offeree shareholders.

Finally, Practice Statement 4 states that an offeree may agree inducement fees with two or more offerors or potential offerors, each up to the relevant one per cent limit, notwithstanding that, in certain circumstances, the aggregate amount payable by the offeree might consequently exceed one per cent of the value of the offeree.

Inducement fees may also be entered into between offerees and third parties as part of a defence strategy (in relation to, for example, the acquisition of an asset or business). Though not technically covered by Rule 21.2, such agreements are caught by Rule 21.1(b)(v) (whereby an offeree is prevented from entering into a contract otherwise than in the ordinary course of business during the course of an offer unless it has obtained prior shareholder approval). In these circumstances, provided the proposed inducement fee is *de minimis* and the other safeguards set out in Rule 21.2 are observed (including in relation to disclosure), the Panel will normally permit such an arrangement.

Practice Statement 14 further refined the interpretation of Rule 21.2 in light of market developments. Where an implementation or exclusivity agreement is entered into by the offeror and the offeree, any payment made by the offeree for breach of such an agreement where the breach has not caused the offer to fail will fall outside Rule 21.2 (and the Panel requires a statement to that effect to be contained in the relevant agreement).

The Panel must be consulted at the earliest opportunity in all cases where an inducement fee or any similar arrangement is proposed. This includes break fees, penalties, put or call options or other provisions having similar effects, regardless of whether such arrangements are considered to be in the ordinary course of business. (Note also that inducement fees may be constrained for other reasons, e.g. the Companies Act 1985 (especially regarding financial assistance under Section 151), the Listing Rules (e.g. under paragraph LR 10.2.7) and the common law (e.g. directors' fiduciary duties)).

6.9 Other documents

6.9.1 Circulation of the offer announcements

In the course of a bid, a number of other documents are issued by or on behalf of the parties, the first of which will be a either a "talks announcement" under Rule 2.4(a) or a Rule 2.5 announcement of a firm intention to make an offer. Prior to 20 May 2006, an offeree was required to circulate to its shareholders and lodge with the Panel the first of these two announcements. However, where a "talks announcement" had been made and an offer period triggered, there was no obligation to circulate to shareholders a subsequent "firm intention" announcement under Rule 2.5. From 20 May 2006, an offeree is required to circulate a "firm intention" Rule 2.5 announcement even where an offer period has been triggered by an earlier "talks announcement".

Under Rule 2.6(a), a talks announcement must be sent by the offeree to its shareholders and to the Panel. Under Rule 2.6(b)(i), a Rule 2.5 "firm intention" announcement or a circular summarising the terms and conditions of the offer, together where necessary with an explanation of the implications of the announcement, must be sent by the offeree to its shareholders and to the Panel. This document is often accompanied by the offeree board's preliminary views, for example advising shareholders to take no action pending further consideration by the board, or outright rejection.

Under Rule 2.6(b)(ii), both offerors and offerees must also make a Rule 2.5 announcement, or a circular summarising its terms, "readily available" to their respective employee representatives or, where there are no such representatives, to the employees themselves. The Panel takes the view that this obligation may be satisfied by posting the text of the announcement on the offeror or offeree's respective websites, and reflects this in a Note on Rule 2.6.

6.9.2 Subsequent documents – Rule 27

After the initial offer and defence documents have been issued, there is likely to be a succession of documents issued by the offeror and offeree containing further arguments and information. These documents must comply with the provisions of Rule 27 and contain details of any material changes in information previously published by or on behalf of the relevant party during the offer period and, if there have been no material changes, this fact must be stated. However, there must be updated information on such matters as interests in shares and dealings, offeror directors' emoluments, changes to offeree directors' service contracts, etc. Where a profit forecast has been made, any subsequent document must also contain a statement by the directors that the forecast remains valid for the purpose of the offer and that the financial advisers and accountants who reported on the forecast have indicated that they have no objection to their reports continuing to apply (*see* Rules 27.2 and 28.5).

There is, however, a limit to the time in which information in offer documents can be released to shareholders. Rule 31.6 basically requires that, subject to various exceptions, the acceptance condition must be satisfied by acceptances and purchases made by 1.00 p.m. on the sixtieth day after posting the offer document. Consequently the last document from the offeror which can contain a revision of the offer must be issued on Day 46 (in the absence of any competing offer or other exceptional circumstance). This is because Rule 32, dealing with revised offers, requires any revised offer to be kept open for at least 14 days after posting. In order to give the offeror seven days to

Documents from the Offeror and the Offeree

consider the final arguments of the offeree, the offeree is, therefore, restricted by Rule 31.9, except with the consent of the Panel, from issuing new material information after Day 39.

During the bid by The Great Universal Stores plc ("GUS") for Argos plc in 1999, the Panel allowed Argos to release certain trading information after Day 39. GUS was allowed, as a consequence, to decide whether or not it wished, in the light of this information, to increase or extend its offer. GUS chose to do neither and its offer succeeded. Rule 31.9 has since been amended to insert these consequences expressly into the Code.

6.9.3 Advertisements – Rule 19.4

The provisions of the Code which apply to advertisements should also be noted. Rule 19.4 prohibits advertisements unless they fall within certain prescribed categories. This Rule was introduced after a series of high-profile advertising campaigns which were generally not considered appropriate to the proper conduct of takeovers. Accordingly, advertisements relating to an offer are, in effect, limited to statements of fact (e.g. reminders as to closing times, announcements which have to be made or advertisements of preliminary or interim results) and, in most cases, will have to include the directors' responsibility statement and be cleared by the Panel in advance.

6.10 Offers to holders of convertible securities and options – Rule 15

Rule 15 requires that, when an offer is made for voting equity share capital or for other transferable securities carrying voting rights and the offeree has convertible securities outstanding, the offeror must make an appropriate offer or proposal to the holders of those securities to ensure that their interests are safeguarded. "Appropriate" is often fixed by reference to the see-through price of the underlying securities but, in appropriate circumstances, may be more.

Whenever practicable, the offer or proposal should be sent out at the same time as the main offer but, if this cannot be done, it should be sent out as soon as practicable thereafter. It should contain the advice of a competent independent financial adviser and the board's views on the offer or proposal.

Many offerees will have share option schemes outstanding and the provisions of Rule 15 apply to those schemes. In most cases it will not be practicable to send out proposals to option holders until after the offer document has been published; indeed, in most cases, proposals will only be put to option holders after the offer has gone unconditional. Proposals on option schemes may take a number of forms, such as providing for cash payments or rollover into an option scheme of the offeror.

Regardless of when an appropriate offer or proposal is made, all relevant documents issued to shareholders of the offeree should, if practicable, be issued simultaneously to holders of convertible securities and options (Note on Rule 15).

6.11 The Listing Rules

In some cases, information will have to be given to the shareholders of a listed offeror. An announcement will have to be made if the takeover offer is a Class 2 transaction, which will generally be the case in a transaction in which the value of any factors such as the gross assets being acquired or the profits before tax of the offeree or the aggregate value of the consideration being given exceeds five per cent (but is less than 25 per cent) of the gross assets, profits before tax, or market value of the ordinary shares (as the case may be) of the offeror (as determined by the tests set out in Chapter 10 of the Listing Rules).

If the tests in Chapter 10 show that the value or amount of any of the factors applicable to the offeree is 25 per cent or more of the appropriate measure for the offeror, the proposed takeover will qualify as a Class 1 transaction and the shareholders of the offeror will usually have to approve the takeover at a general meeting. In this case, a circular will be sent to them containing information about the proposed transaction (the detailed requirements are set out in Chapter 13 of the Listing Rules) as well as any necessary resolutions to approve the acquisition. These may include, for example, resolutions to increase the share capital of the offeror and to increase the directors' authority to allot shares under Section 80 of the Companies Act 1985.

A listed offeror may also have to prepare and publish a prospectus (or a document containing information which is regarded by the FSA as being equivalent to that of a prospectus – see further below) if it is offering its own securities, either as consideration or to its own shareholders to provide funds for a cash offer. This will generally be required where:

(a) a new class of securities, which are to be listed, is offered by way of consideration;
(b) shares of an existing listed class are to be issued; and
(c) debt securities, which are to be listed, of any amount are to be issued.

The information to be contained in the prospectus (or equivalent document) is set out in the Prospectus Rules. The prospectus should be incorporated in or sent out with the offer document. If a prospectus becomes necessary as a result of a revision to an offer, it should be sent out with the revised offer document, but it may be permitted to be sent out later. It should in any event be sent out before an offer goes unconditional in order to avoid having to adjust the information to take account of the offeree having become a member of the offeror's group.

The Prospectus Rules provide that there is no requirement for a prospectus to be published in relation to takeovers and mergers involving a securities exchange offer if an "equivalent document" is produced. However, the FSA applies a full vetting process to these documents to determine "equivalence" so the scope for circumventing the disclosure requirements of the Prospectus Rules is limited. One of the advantages of preparing an equivalent document is that there is no requirement to produce a supplementary prospectus with the effect that withdrawal rights under Section 87Q(4) of FSMA do not apply. On the other hand, the main advantage of preparing a prospectus is that "passport rights" are available enabling the document to be sent to the offeree's shareholders throughout the EU (subject to any translation requirements).

6.12 Financial Services and Markets Act 2000

6.12.1 Financial promotion

Offer documents will be, but defence documents will often not be, financial promotions pursuant to Section 21 FSMA – that is, communications of "an invitation or inducement to engage in investment activity". These documents can only be communicated by, or with the approval of, an authorised person unless they fall within the exemptions contained in the FSMA (Financial Promotion) Order 2005 (the "Order").

Article 62 of the Order exempts from Section 21 FSMA any communication in connection with the sale of a body corporate. Offer documents appear, on their face, to fall within this exemption and this interpretation seems to have been approved by the FSA. Although the exemption was envisaged to deal with more limited transactions and HM Treasury has indicated that it may restrict the scope of the exemption, the latest set of regulations (which came into effect on 1 July 2005) have not addressed this issue. However, great care needs to be taken before proceeding in reliance on this exemption. If this exemption is not available, offer documents do not fall within any of the exemptions contained in the Order and would, therefore, need to be communicated and/or approved by an authorised person. Approval may even be needed for offer documents previously communicated by authorised persons to permit later separate communications of such documents by unauthorised persons (such as the offeror itself which may, for example, wish to publish the offer document on its website).

The making and/or approval by authorised persons of financial promotions is governed by Chapter 3 of the FSA's Conduct of Business Rules. It contains various provisions limiting its application in respect of takeovers.

Defence documents will not, in many circumstances, fall within the definition of financial promotion (by virtue of their encouraging the offeree shareholders not to accept the offer) but, even if they do, if sent only to shareholders of the offeree, they will often be exempt by virtue of Article 43 of the Order.

Documents from the Offeror and the Offeree

6.12.2 Market abuse

Sections 118 to 131 FSMA provide for a civil law offence of market abuse.

This is considered further in Chapter 9. However, for the purposes of the market abuse regime, in publishing documentation, all parties must ensure that they take reasonable care to ensure that information contained in announcements which are disseminated through an RIS (such as an offer announcement or the offer document) is not false or misleading. This would be done by ensuring that all such statements had been properly verified.

6.12.3 Misleading statements

In addition to potential tortious liabilities for misrepresentation and/or defamation (*see* paragraph 6.2.4 above), all parties must also bear in mind the provisions of Section 397(1) FSMA which makes it an offence knowingly or recklessly to make a statement, promise or forecast which is misleading, false or deceptive or dishonestly to conceal any material facts, if the statement, promise, forecast or concealment is made for the purpose of inducing another person to enter or offer to enter into, or to refrain from entering or offering to enter into, an investment agreement or to exercise, or refrain from exercising, any rights conferred by an investment. Thus, if misleading statements are made or material facts are concealed by either side in a takeover bid which induce a shareholder to accept or reject an offer or to vote a particular way on a resolution and if the statement is made deliberately or recklessly or if the concealment is made dishonestly, criminal sanctions may follow.

6.13 Companies Act 1985

Only two provisions of the Companies Act 1985 directly impact on the content requirements for offeror and offeree documents.

6.13.1 Section 314

Section 314 provides that, in connection with any transfer of shares in a company resulting from an offer, the offer document should contain details of any payment to be made to a director of the company by way of compensation for loss of office or in connection with his retirement from office. The CLRB contains draft proposals to amend Section 314 of the Companies Act 1985. The directors' duty of disclosure on a takeover would be removed and the duty to send a written memorandum to the shareholders would rest on the offeree (clause 199(3) of the CLRB).

6.13.2   Part XIIIA – Sections 428 to 430F

These sections provide for the compulsory acquisition of outstanding shareholdings if the appropriate conditions as to acceptances of the offer are met. Assuming that an offeror is successful in declaring his offer wholly unconditional and those conditions are met, the final documents to be sent out by the offeror will be the prescribed forms of notice to the non-assenting minority shareholders of the offeree under Section 429.

Changes were required to Part XIIIA to ensure consistency with the Directive and to implement the recommendations of the Company Law Review in its Final Report in July 2001 (except to the extent that they are not consistent with the Directive). These proposed changes are set out in the CLRB. Until the CLRB comes into force, however, Schedule 2 of the Interim Regulations sets out the compulsory acquisition procedures for takeovers within the scope of the Directive, replacing Part XIIIA for such transactions.

6.14   The use of websites in takeovers

Increasingly, companies involved in takeovers are keen to put offer-related documentation on their websites. Additionally, and as noted in paragraph 6.6 above, following the changes made to the Code on 20 May 2006, offerors and offerees are likely to use websites to make information in relation to the offer available to their respective employees.

The use of websites is likely to give rise to the following issues:

(a)   Inclusion of offer-related information in a section of the website may well be regarded as financial promotion, giving rise to the issues discussed above.

(b) The need to restrict access to offer-related information posted on a website from certain overseas shareholders (similarly to restrictions on where offer documentation may be posted).
(c) As the Panel indicated in its 1999/2000 Annual Report, use of the internet and websites does not cause particular concern provided that the Code's principles of care, responsibility and availability of documentation apply. Accordingly:
   (i) Rules 19.1 (Standards of Care) and 19.3 (Unacceptable Statements) apply;
   (ii) directors will be required to take responsibility for such information in the same way as if it were posted (Rule 19.2);
   (iii) CD-ROMs and copies of all relevant website pages must be lodged with the Panel and advisers to the other parties at the time of release (Rule 19.7);
   (iv) the posting of information on a website will not satisfy the obligation under Rule 20.1 to notify all offeree shareholders of material new information or significant new opinions. Accordingly, a financial adviser to the offeror or offeree must, by noon on the business day following posting of information on a website, provide the Panel with a letter confirming that no material information or significant new opinions have been placed on such websites.

Generally, access to offer-related information on the website is likely, in practice, to be the subject of a disclaimer designed to address each of the above issues.

Chapter 7

Conduct During the Offer; Timing and Revision; and Restrictions Following Offers

David Pudge
Partner
Clifford Chance LLP

7.1 Introduction

The most significant reform of the Takeover Code for many years came into effect on 20 May 2006 simultaneously with the coming into force of the legislation which implements the EU Takeovers Directive. The extent of the changes to the text of the Takeover Code is unprecedented with nearly every page being affected.

Despite the extent of the technical changes, the Takeover Panel system is broadly preserved and the Panel's stated approach is "business as usual". As a result, although there will inevitably be some changes in detail and in practice, the general approach to the conduct of takeover offers is likely to remain largely unchanged.

As in previous years, the most recent Annual Report of the Takeover Panel reiterated that the Takeover Code is designed to ensure good business standards and fairness to shareholders. Maintaining fair and orderly markets is crucial to this task. The three essentially distinct (although reasonably adjacent) areas of the Takeover Code which are the subject of this Chapter play an important role in achieving these goals and involve the balancing of the often conflicting interests of the offeror, target shareholders, the target company itself and potential competing offerors.

The EU Takeovers Directive will ultimately be implemented in the UK through the Company Law Reform Bill but as that piece of legislation was not going to be in force by the 20 May 2006 deadline for implementation of the Directive, the Government introduced some interim regulations (the Takeovers Directive (Interim Implementation) Regulations 2006 (the "Regulations")) to give effect to the Directive. These Regulations will be superseded, in due course, by the relevant provisions of the Company Law Reform Bill. The Regulations only amend the legal and regulatory framework for UK takeover offers to the extent necessary to reflect the requirements of the Directive. As a result, there are some differences between the regulation of takeover offers for companies which have their securities listed on the Official List as these are subject to the Directive and the regulation of schemes of arrangement generally and of offers for companies with securities admitted to trading on AIM or Ofex, as these are not subject to the Directive.

The identity of which regulatory authority is the ultimate arbiter for any enforcement action taken in connection with a breach of the Takeover Code depends on whether or not the relevant offer is subject to the Directive. Where the offer is subject to the Directive, it will be the Panel (and no longer the Financial Services Authority (the "FSA")) which will be the ultimate arbiter. The reason for this is that the Regulations now give the Panel a range of statutory enforcement powers enabling it to enforce the Takeover Code in relation to any transaction which is within the ambit of the Directive.

The range of new sanctions and powers available to the Panel include the power to require disclosure to it of documents and information, the ability to require compensation to be paid to target shareholders and the power to seek enforcement orders from the Courts. The Panel has, however, indicated that it does not expect to need to exercise these powers, pointing to the near 100 per cent compliance record with its rulings under the previous non-statutory regime.

To the extent that any enforcement action in connection with a breach of the Takeover Code is required in respect of a transaction which is not subject to the Directive, then it will still be the FSA which will have the ultimate enforcement powers.

The FSA also remains responsible for taking enforcement action in all cases of market abuse. Whilst compliance with the Takeover Code

Conduct During the Offer; Timing and Revision; and Restrictions Following Offers

will not always ensure immunity from allegations of market abuse, the FSA has declared that behaviour conforming with certain specific rules of the Takeover Code will be a safe harbour from being considered market abuse.

One notable change to the Takeover Code (resulting from implementation of the Directive) is the replacement of the long established General Principles of the Code with the principles set out in the Directive. This has a number of implications, particularly in the context of regulating equality of information (*see* 7.2.5 below) and frustrating action (*see* 7.2.8 below). In practice, the impact of these changes is likely to be limited as there are few substantive differences. The Panel will, however, only be able to grant waivers of and exemptions from Code rules to the extent this is consistent with the General Principles.

7.2 Conduct during the offer

The first area covered in this chapter, "Conduct during the offer" (Section I of the Takeover Code – Rules 19 to 22), is principally concerned with the rules governing the release of information during the course of a takeover and the rules which control the taking of frustrating action by the board of a target company faced with a hostile takeover bid.

The cornerstone is Rule 19 (which is also addressed in Chapter 6). This Rule deals with both responsibility for information released during the course of an offer and the manner of its release.

The Panel has made it clear that a breach of the rules relating to the release of information during a bid will be treated as "a grave matter". There was in the past a perception that if the principals or financial advisers wanted to leak something then the public relations advisers could be left to talk freely to the press. As is made clear in the Introduction to the Takeover Code, however, the Panel regards the Takeover Code as applying not only to financial advisers and their clients but also any other advisers to or representatives of any entity to which the Takeover Code applies. In 1997 the Panel was heavily critical of Triplex Lloyd and its PR advisers, Citigate, over the leak by

Citigate of confidential information obtained by Triplex Lloyd under Rule 20.2 (equality of information to competing offerors) in the course of the competing bids for William Cook. The Panel described this behaviour as being "reprehensible".

A combination of the Panel seeking to crack down on leaks to the press and the application of the market abuse regime and rules regulating the dissemination of price sensitive information has resulted in the so-called "Friday night drop", whereby a story is deliberately placed in the Sunday press ahead of a Monday announcement, ceasing to be a feature of takeover bids.

7.2.1 Rule 19.1

Rule 19.1 sets out the standard of care which must be adopted not only in the preparation of formal offer documents or advertisements, but also in the making of statements to the media. Each document, advertisement, or statement must be produced to the highest standards of accuracy and the information given must be adequately and fairly presented.

This last point was highlighted in the Enterprise Oil bid for LASMO in 1994 when LASMO was criticised by the Panel for making excessive claims in its defence document.

The Notes on Rule 19.1 deal with the following areas which are of particular concern to the Panel based on its past experience of over-imaginative offer participants:

(a) language should be "unambiguous". For example, the word "agreement" must be used with care. The document or announcement should not convey the impression that there is a legally binding agreement on a particular matter when this is not the case;

(b) comments on future profits and prospects, asset values and the likelihood of the revision of an offer should be avoided. These may give rise to obligations to report formally on future profits or the benefits of the proposed transaction;

(c) quotations should not be used out of context and must be capable of being substantiated. Copyright issues can also arise,

Conduct During the Offer; Timing and Revision; and Restrictions Following Offers

      especially if a whole article or a page from a newspaper is being reproduced;
(d) diagrams should not be distorted and, when relevant, should be to scale; and
(e) sources for material facts and origins for quotations must be included. (This is vigorously enforced by the Panel. For example, in the Arco bid for Aran Energy in 1995, the Panel obliged Arco to issue a statement clarifying certain sources.)

The Notes on Rule 19.1 include specific requirements in relation to statements about the expected benefits of a proposed takeover (particularly synergy benefit statements). These additional requirements are only relevant in cases where the expected benefits are quantified and the relevant statement is made in the context of a securities exchange offer which is not recommended or when a recommended offer becomes competitive and the statement is repeated or becomes a material issue.

Where the requirements contained in the relevant Note (Note 8 on Rule 19.1) do apply, the basis on which the merger benefits statement is being made must be clearly stated, reports must be obtained from the financial advisers and the accountants that the statement has been made with due care and consideration and a sufficient explanation provided of the constituent elements of the expected benefits to enable shareholders to understand their relative importance. Similar requirements apply to statements that the transaction will enhance earnings per share where this depends on material benefits arising from the takeover.

As the need to report on a "merger benefits" statement only arises in the context of a contested share exchange offer, this is still pretty much uncharted territory. One example of a merger benefits statement being reported on under Rule 19.1 arose in 1998 in the course of Wolverhampton & Dudley's hostile bid for Marston, Thompson & Evershed plc.

7.2.2 *Responsibility for information*

Rule 19.2 provides that each document issued to shareholders or each advertisement published in connection with an offer must state that the directors of the offeror and/or, where appropriate, the target company, accept responsibility for the information contained in it. This involves the inclusion of a statement that, to the best of the relevant directors' knowledge and belief (having taken all reasonable care to ensure that such is the case), the information contained in the document or advertisement is in accordance with the facts and, where appropriate, that it does not omit anything likely to affect the import of such information. The implications of such an express acceptance of responsibility have been discussed in Chapter 6.

In addition, Rule 19.3 prohibits the issue of statements which, while not factually inaccurate, may mislead shareholders and the market or may create uncertainty. In particular, an offeror should not make a statement to the effect that it may improve its offer without committing itself to doing so and specifying the improvements. In January 2006, Honeywell International Inc was publicly criticised by the Panel Executive for failing to comply with this Rule after it made an announcement that it was considering whether to raise its offer for First Technology plc at a time when there was no certainty that it would in fact make an increased offer.

In Practice Statement 7, the Panel Executive has emphasised that Rule 19.3 is not limited to statements about increases in the financial value of an offer. The Executive interprets the reference to "may improve its offer" as also encompassing statements about offer amendments of a non-financial nature, for example, possible changes to the structure or non-financial terms of the offer.

The Notes on Rule 19.3 also highlight that neither the offeror nor the board of a target company may make statements about the level of support it has from shareholders or other persons (for example, holders of derivatives such as contracts for differences or persons with de facto control over the shares in question) unless the Panel is satisfied that the statement reflects the up to date intentions of the relevant persons and has been verified to the Panel's satisfaction. This means that a relatively simple statement about the level of shareholder opposition to a bid (such as that issued by Thistle Hotels plc in 2003 in the context of its defence against a hostile bid from its main shareholder, BIL International Limited), can involve considerable discussion with the Panel concerning precisely what evidence is required. The evidence will normally take the form of a written confirmation from the person concerned. As a result of the amendments made to the Code in April 2005, these letters confirming the relevant shareholder's support will then need to be publicly disclosed in accordance with Rule 8.4, details will need to be included in any relevant offer or defence document and a copy of the letters put on display.

In 1999 the Panel Executive was required to consider whether statements made by the directors of Argos plc regarding the trading of its Dutch shops in the course of the successful hostile offer from Great Universal Stores in April 1998 were misleading under Rule 19.3. In its defence document, Argos had stated that these shops were trading well ahead of expectations, but shortly afterwards internal Argos documents apparently indicated the contrary. Having considered the issues, the Panel Executive concluded that there had been no breach of the Code. The statement was true at the time it was made and therefore was not misleading within the meaning of Rule 19.3. Even though the position changed shortly afterwards, this did not need to be reported on as a material change under Rules 23 or 27.1 as the turnover of the five Dutch shops represented less than one per cent of Argos's turnover.

The inclusion of an express responsibility statement by the directors, the requirement for documentation to be prepared to the highest standards of accuracy and the provisions of Rule 19.3 plus the risk of civil or criminal liability for knowingly or recklessly making misleading statements have combined to make it essential to conduct a proper verification exercise. This normally involves the preparation of detailed verification notes. It is generally regarded as insufficient simply to refer to the directors' responsibilities in the board minutes which approve the relevant document. The Regulations have also introduced a new criminal offence for non-compliance with certain of the contents requirements for offer and defence documentation which is likely only to increase the focus on ensuring that an appropriately thorough and considered verification exercise is undertaken in order to mitigate the risk of committing the offence (*see* Regulation 10 of the Regulations).

7.2.3 Release of information

The following are some of the different ways in which information can be released during an offer.

7.2.3.1 Advertisements

Takeover advertisements are relatively rare – largely as a result of the Panel introducing rules controlling their use following some of the more heated battles in the mid-1980s.

Rule 19.4 provides that the publication of advertisements connected with an offer or potential offer is prohibited unless the advertisement falls within one of the specific exempt categories listed in the Code. Advertisements include not only press advertisements but also advertisements in other media such as television, radio, video, audio tape and poster.

Three of the key exemptions are:

(a) product advertisements not bearing on an offer or potential offer (these do not have to receive prior clearance from the Panel although if in doubt the Panel must be consulted);
(b) corporate image advertisements not bearing on the offer or potential offer, but these must be cleared by the Panel in advance. This is presumably because there is a fine line between genuine corporate image advertisements and those which, although they do not refer to the existence of an offer, are nevertheless geared to affect the market's perception of an offer; and
(c) advertisements confined to non-controversial information about an offer (e.g. reminders as to closing time or the value of an offer). During Banco Santander's offer for Abbey in 2004, advertisements were placed in national newspapers to remind Abbey's 1.8 million retail shareholders of approaching deadlines and of the existence of a shareholder telephone helpline.

The Panel normally requires 24 hours' prior notice of a request to clear an advertisement and the proofs submitted to them must have been approved by the financial adviser. The Panel will not verify the accuracy of statements submitted for clearance but may comment on proposed wording.

Conduct During the Offer; Timing and Revision; and Restrictions Following Offers

Each advertisement connected with an offer or potential offer must clearly and prominently identify the party on whose behalf it is being published. Given the limited circumstances in which advertisements are permitted, it is difficult to envisage that this would not be clear in any event.

7.2.3.2   Telephone campaigns

Telephone campaigns designed to sway wavering shareholders or other persons interested in shares are not all that common and the rules relating to them are complex. The key requirement is contained in Rule 19.5 which provides that, except with the consent of the Panel, telephone campaigns may be conducted only by staff of the financial adviser who are fully conversant with the requirements of, and their responsibilities under, the Code. Where this is impractical (e.g. because of the large number of shareholders concerned), other persons can be employed with the consent of the Panel but only in accordance with the strict procedures laid down in the Code, including supervision by the financial advisers. The Panel will also want to vet the written script for any such campaign and its principal concern will be to ensure that the information being given is fair and not misleading. The Panel also undertakes the regulation of cold-calling in takeovers. Note 3 on Rule 19.5 provides that the Panel must be consulted before a telephone campaign is conducted with a view to gathering irrevocable commitments in connection with an offer.

7.2.3.3   Interviews and debates

As regards television and radio interviews, the rules which apply here probably explain why most interviews of parties involved in takeover bids are particularly dull (except where the chairman or finance director has not been properly briefed!). Parties should in general avoid the release of any new material and any public confrontation between representatives of the offeror and target, or between competing offerors. In the Panel's own words the parties should also avoid "anything ... which leads to any kind of gladiatorial combat". Rule 19.6 which applies here does not say much for the level of confidence in the integrity of our media:

> "Parties involved in offers should, if interviewed on radio or television, seek to ensure that the sequence of the interview is

not broken by the insertion of comments or observations by others not made in the course of the interview."

In other words, it is important for the parties to lay down the ground rules before agreeing to be interviewed so as to avoid a distorted message being broadcast.

7.2.4 Distribution and availability of documents and announcements

Rule 19.7 imposes certain practical obligations in relation to the distribution of offer documents and announcements. Before the offer document is made public, a copy must be lodged with the Panel. Copies of all other documents and announcements relating to a takeover and of advertisements and any material released to the press must at the time of release be lodged with both the Panel and also with the advisers to all other parties to the offer. Accordingly, it would not only be unprofessional but also contrary to the Code for the financial advisers to fail to organise for copies of offer documents, press announcements, etc., to be delivered to the target's financial advisers at the time of issue.

Where the release of documents occurs outside normal business hours, the advisers to the other parties must be informed of the release immediately, if necessary by telephone. Special arrangements may also need to be made to ensure that the material is delivered directly to them and to the Panel.

The principle behind this Rule is that no party to an offer should be put at a disadvantage owing to a delay in receiving new information.

7.2.5 Equality of information to shareholders

Rule 20.1 seeks to ensure that all shareholders are kept properly informed by requiring that information about companies involved in a takeover bid should be made available to all target company shareholders as nearly as possible at the same time and in the same manner. Not only does this preserve equal treatment for shareholders but it helps to avoid the creation of a false market and reduces the potential for insider dealing. The Panel stressed the importance which it attaches to this principle in 1995 with regard to the Kværner/Amec bid, where the Panel Executive investigated the source of speculation about the level of Amec's profits for 1996. In that case the Panel concluded that the PR advisers had failed to take sufficient care in their discussions with analysts when making comments about Amec's likely profits in 1996.

The Notes on Rule 20.1 contain two important exceptions to the equality of information principle. The most important of these relates to the provision of information in confidence by a target company to a bona fide potential offeror or vice versa. The reason for this exemption is to allow a target company to provide a prospective offeror with certain confidential information to enable it to decide whether to proceed with an offer; without this the target company's shareholders might well be deprived of the benefit of an offer which would otherwise have been made for their shares (this is a theme that runs through the Code).

Following the implementation of the EU Takeovers Directive, information and offer documentation must be made readily and promptly available to the holders of target company securities at least in those Member States on whose regulated markets the target's securities are admitted to trading and to the representatives of the employees of the target company and the offeror or, where there are no such representatives, to the employees themselves. This requirement coupled with the new General Principle 1 (all holders of target securities must be afforded equivalent treatment) means that the relevant information must be provided to all shareholders and employees/employee representatives wherever they may be (including, potentially, those resident in jurisdictions into which such materials have often not been distributed in the past, such as the USA, Canada, Australia and Japan). The Code contains a very limited derogation from the requirement to provide offer documentation to target company shareholders and employees resident outside the EEA, principally, where to do so would cause disproportionate problems under local securities and other laws. It is important to note that the Panel has indicated that this derogation will not normally apply in respect of such persons resident within any EEA member state (*see* the note on Rule 30.3).

As regards employees/employee representatives (as opposed to shareholders), the Code does not require that a copy of the relevant information or document be sent to all employees/employee representatives; it must simply be made available to them. Accordingly, it would seem that this obligation could be satisfied by placing the information on an appropriate part of the company's website. The Code Committee has indicated this requirement to provide information does, however, apply in respect of all full-time and part-time employees on a group-wide basis wherever they may be located subject only to a very limited derogation equivalent to the one referred to above.

There is a concern that the changes to the Code in this area will impose significant additional cost and timing burdens on the parties to a takeover due to the need to check and ensure compliance with applicable local securities laws and regulations in all relevant jurisdictions.

7.2.6 Meetings

Meetings are dealt with in Note 3 on Rule 20.1. Although meetings are not altogether prohibited, the Rules reflect the fact that the overriding objective is to prevent material new information being disclosed selectively. The offeror or target may, for example, hold meetings with selected shareholders or other persons interested in the securities of the bidder or target, or with analysts or brokers, provided that:

(a) no material new information is released;
(b) no significant new opinions are expressed; and
(c) except with the consent of the Panel, an appropriate representative of the financial adviser or corporate broker to the party convening the meeting is present. That representative must then confirm in writing to the Panel, not later than 12 p.m. on the business day following the date of the meeting, that no material new information was released and that no significant new opinions were expressed at the meeting. The Panel polices this requirement strictly.

If material new information or a significant new opinion does emerge, a circular giving details of the new matter must be sent to all shareholders as soon as possible thereafter and must include the normal directors' responsibility statement. In the final stages of an offer, a newspaper advertisement may also be required. If the new information or opinion cannot be properly substantiated, the circular or advertisement should make this clear and include a formal retraction.

The question of what constitutes "material" new information has to be judged on a case-by-case basis. Guidance on what can amount to "new" information for these purposes has been provided by the Panel Executive in Practice Statement 9 (issued in March 2004).

The requirements of the Code relating to meetings can also extend to meetings which take place before a formal offer period has, technically, commenced for Code purposes. In those circumstances, the requirement is that no material information should be released, nor any significant opinions expressed, which will not be included in the formal announcement of the offer, if and when made.

7.2.7 Equality of information to competing offerors

As noted above, one exception to the rule on equality of information to all shareholders is the provision of information in confidence by a target company to a bona fide potential offeror or vice versa. Rule 20.2 provides that any such information must, however, be given on request equally and promptly to another offeror or bona fide potential offeror even if that other offeror is less welcome. This requirement will usually only apply when there has been a public announcement of the existence of the offeror or potential offeror to which information has been given. However, this obligation can also be triggered where one potential offeror is informed authoritatively (normally by the target or its advisers) of the existence of another potential offeror even if there has been no public statement made to this effect. Equally it will be triggered if there is a public announcement of an approach or talks concerning a possible offer even if the potential offeror involved is not named in that announcement.

There is a practical limitation to this Rule as the Code provides that the less-welcome offeror must specify the questions to which it requires answers. It cannot simply make a general request to receive all information provided to its competitor. This tends to lead to extremely lengthy and detailed questionnaires being sent to the target's advisers by the offeror's advisers in an attempt to catch any and all information which might conceivably be of interest.

It is important, therefore, that the flow of information from a target company to its preferred bidder is carefully controlled not only to avoid the prospect of having to give valuable commercial information to an unwelcome bidder but also to ensure that there is an accurate record of what information has been provided to any particular potential bidder.

It has always been clear that Rule 20.2 applies not just to information which is provided in written form but also to information which is provided orally. However, Practice Statement 2 (issued by the Panel Executive in 2004) clarified that Rule 20.2 also extends to site visits and meetings with the management of the target company. As a result, if one bidder (or potential bidder) has been granted access to conduct a site visit or to talk to management then equal access must be granted to any other bidder (or potential bidder) that requests it. In light of this, target companies will need to give particular thought to whether to allow a bidder, such as a potential white knight, to talk to management in light of the prospect of having to allow a hostile bidder similar access.

Rule 20.2 was in issue in the battle for Midland Bank in 1992. HSBC Holdings (a Hong Kong & Shanghai Bank subsidiary) announced a recommended offer for Midland and some weeks later Lloyds Bank announced that it was considering making an offer for Midland. One pre-condition of Lloyds making an offer was that it received all the information which HSBC had received from Midland and such information being satisfactory to it. Midland was concerned that passing confidential commercially sensitive information to a competitor could ultimately cause damage to its shareholders. The Panel had to decide whether it should modify or relax Rule 20.2 since it was not disputed that Lloyds was other than a "bona fide potential offeror" for the purposes of the Rule. In the circumstances the Panel decided not to modify or relax the Rule and Midland was obliged to hand over to Lloyds the information which had previously been passed to HSBC. In the Panel's view the likelihood of damage being done to Midland shareholders was greater if the relevant information was withheld than if it were given to Lloyds.

Conduct During the Offer; Timing and Revision; and Restrictions Following Offers

It should also be noted that where the information was originally released by the target under a confidentiality agreement then the "unfriendly" competing offeror will also be required to enter into a confidentiality agreement with the target.

The only restrictions which may be placed on information which is provided under Rule 20.2 relate to:

(a) maintaining the confidentiality of the information;
(b) preventing the use of the information to solicit customers or employees; and/or
(c) restricting the use of the information solely in connection with an offer or potential offer.

Any conditions imposed in this way should be no more onerous than those imposed on any other offeror or potential offeror to whom information is provided. Clearly, the target cannot insist on being provided with any equivalent "standstill" protections.

The Panel has also clarified that if a target company wishes, with the consent of the relevant third party, to release to a preferred offeror information that is otherwise subject to a confidentiality agreement, the target company must ensure that it also has authority to pass that information to any other offeror or bona fide potential offeror in compliance with Rule 20.2.

There are specific provisions of the Code (*see* the notes on Rule 20.2 and Rule 20.3) which deal with the equality of information where one of the competing offerors is a management buyout ("MBO") team. An MBO offeror must, on request, promptly furnish the independent directors of the offeree or its advisers with all the information which it has furnished to its equity or debt financiers (Rule 20.3). This then forms the basis of the information which has to be furnished to competing offerors but only in so far as it is information generated by the target company. The Panel expects the directors of the target company who are involved in making the MBO offer to cooperate with the independent directors of the target company and its advisers in assembling such information.

7.2.8 Restrictions on frustrating action (Rule 21)

Although in the year to 31 March 2005 only 11 out of some 114 takeovers in the UK were hostile, the provisions of the Code which restrict the ability of the target company to take action which might frustrate an offer are extremely important in practice.

7.2.8.1 Impact of the Takeovers Directive

The implementation of the EU Takeovers Directive has attempted to create a more level playing field for takeover offers and takeover defences across Europe, but appears to have largely failed. The Directive lacks real teeth as Member States are permitted to opt out of a number of key provisions including Article 9, which requires the board of a target company to obtain shareholder approval before taking *any* action (other than seeking alternative bids) which may result in the frustration of the bid. The UK Government has decided to opt into Article 9 of the Directive. Under Article 9, the prohibition on taking frustrating action without first obtaining shareholder consent applies from the time the target company is informed of a bid until the bid lapses. Member States may, however, stipulate that this restriction applies from an earlier stage, such as from the time the target board first becomes aware that a bid is imminent (which is how the prohibition is framed in Rule 21.1 of the Code). However, as Member States have the right under the Directive to "opt out" of implementing the provisions regulating the use of defensive measures (albeit with scope for individual companies to opt back in), the Directive fails to create the level playing field desired by its architects.

7.2.8.2 Shareholder approval

The restrictions on frustrating action are contained in Rule 21 of the Takeover Code and are reinforced by the General Principle 3. Rule 21 prohibits the target board from taking any action which may result in any offer or bona fide offer being frustrated unless the board has obtained shareholder approval. As mentioned above, this applies whether during the course of an offer or even before the date of the offer, if they have reason to believe that a bona fide offer might be imminent. If the proposed action is in pursuance of a contract entered into earlier or another pre-existing obligation or decision of the target company's board, the Panel must be consulted and its consent to proceed without a shareholders' meeting obtained. It should,

Conduct During the Offer; Timing and Revision; and Restrictions Following Offers

however, be noted that the board of a company is, subject to directors' fiduciary duties, free to put in place defence planning initiatives (e.g. poison pills) at any time when an offer is not in contemplation (although these are very rarely employed in the UK).

Rule 21 specifically applies to any decision by the target company directors to:

(a) issue any further shares in the target company;
(b) grant any options over any unissued shares in the target company;
(c) create or issue any convertible securities (e.g. convertible loan stock) or securities carrying the right to subscribe for company shares (e.g. warrants);
(d) make any disposal or acquisition of assets of a "material amount" (the Panel will normally consider relative values of 10 per cent or more as being of material amount and 10 per cent becomes 15 per cent in the event that the disposal or acquisition takes place during a reference to the Competition Commission or where the European Commission has initiated proceedings or made a referral); or
(e) enter into any contracts other than in the ordinary course of business.

Generally, it should be appreciated that this is a non-exhaustive list of prohibited acts. As a result, it is important that the Panel is consulted in advance if there is any doubt as to whether any proposed actions would fall within Rule 21.

General Principle 3 and Rule 21 are based on the premise that it is for the shareholders of the target company (not its directors or management) to determine the outcome of the offer. Thus it is open to the target company directors to put proposals to shareholders which would have the effect of defeating the bid, so long as those proposals can only be implemented with the consent of shareholders. An example of this was the proposal by BPB, as part of its ultimately unsuccessful defence to the hostile bid by Saint-Gobain in the Autumn of 2005, to return cash to shareholders subject to obtaining the necessary shareholder approvals. The London Stock Exchange made a similar proposal earlier this year as part of its defence against the unwelcome bid from Macquarie Bank. The vote on a proposal which might potentially frustrate an offer is, of course, open to all shareholders and therefore if the potential offeror has managed to establish a significant shareholding in the target company then it would be free to vote against the proposed course of action.

In deciding how best to defend the company against an unwelcome bid, the directors of the target must, of course, have regard to their general duties as directors and in the exercise of their powers be satisfied, after taking advice, that such powers are being exercised for a proper purpose and in the interests of the company.

It may be tempting for the board of directors of a target company to consider extending service contracts or amending them to increase directors' remuneration as a protective reaction to a bid. The Panel will regard this as entering into a contract other than in the ordinary course of business and therefore as outlawed if the new or amended contract or terms contribute "an abnormal increase" in the directors' entitlements or a "significant improvement" in the directors' terms of service.

The target company may well have an existing executive share option scheme and the question may arise of granting further options to executives over shares in the target company. As already mentioned, the grant of options over unissued shares in the offeree company is prohibited unless approved by shareholders in general meeting. However, the Panel will normally permit the grant of options under an existing established share option scheme where the timing and level of the grants are in accordance with the company's normal practice (e.g. as regards timing, during a "window" period after announcement of year-end or interim results).

Other things to watch for include interim dividends otherwise than in the normal course or making changes to the pension scheme arrangements: in such circumstances the Panel should always be consulted in advance.

Further, it is important for a target board to bear in mind the aggregation principle. Separate matters may be aggregated and treated as covered by the Rule notwithstanding that individually they might not be regarded as sufficiently material.

Conduct During the Offer; Timing and Revision; and Restrictions Following Offers

7.2.8.3 Inducement fees

Rule 21.2 regulates inducement fees (often called "break fees"), which are payable by a target in the event that an offer does not succeed and other similar arrangements. The fee must be *de minimis* (normally no more than one per cent, inclusive of VAT, of the offer value), fully disclosed (both in the formal offer announcement and in the offer document itself) and confirmed to the Panel by the target board and its financial advisers as being in their view in the best interests of shareholders. In Practice Statement 15 (issued in November 2005), the Panel Executive confirmed that either each of the board and its financial adviser must separately give the confirmation or a single letter must be signed by both. A letter from the adviser on behalf of the board is not acceptable. In Practice Statement 4, the Executive confirmed that, from a Code perspective, multiple break fee arrangements, entered into with different offerors and each up to the one per cent offer value limit, are permissible even if consequently the target company could face paying more than one of them. Target companies will still, however, need to consider the other legal and regulatory constraints (including financial assistance issues and the provisions of the Listing Rules) on agreeing to pay a break fee or multiple break fees. The way in which such fees can be structured and the ability to agree appropriate break fees with competing bidders came sharply into focus in relation to the competing bids from Permira and CVC/TPG for Debenhams.

Practice Statement 15 also clarified that any agreements imposing restrictions on a target company, which trigger a payment on breach and which have the effect of preventing the offer from proceeding or causing it to fail (because, for example, the target board successfully solicits a higher bid) are considered by the Panel Executive as falling within Rule 21.2. Therefore, the maximum total payments to the offeror for such breaches (including any inducement fee) should be one per cent of the value of the target company, as set out in that Rule. The Executive does, however, recognise that payments by the target for breaches which have not either prevented the offer from succeeding or caused the offer to fail will fall outside Rule 21.2.

7.2.9 Activities by associates

Until the Code was amended in July 1998, the target's advisers could deal in target company shares as principal during the offer period with the intent of thwarting a bid (this issue was considered by the Panel in the Cal Energy/Northern Electric bid in December 1996). This type of activity by associates of the offeree is now prohibited. This change reflects the view of the Panel that it is for the target company's shareholders and not its financial advisers or other associates to determine the outcome of a bid. There is, however, a carve-out for the activities of exempt principal traders and fund managers connected with the relevant financial adviser or broker.

Changes made to the Code in April 2005 also impose restrictions on securities borrowing and lending transactions without the Panel's consent by offerors, the target company and certain other persons connected with them, including their associates (Rule 4.6).

7.3 Timing and revision

The second main area covered in this Chapter, "Timing and Revision" (Section M of the Code – Rules 30 to 34), is very much the "nuts and bolts" of takeover practice in that it covers the detailed and somewhat technical rules governing the timing of the various steps in a takeover bid, the rules relating to the introduction of different forms of bid consideration and those relating to increased offers.

The two most important basic principles underlying the rules relating to the timing and revision of offers are as follows:

(a) the duration of a bid should be limited. This is in recognition of the disruption caused by a hostile bid to the target company and its board in taking their attention away from the day-to-day management of the target's business; and

(b) the shareholders of the target company should, however, have sufficient time to be able to consider any offer for their shares and any competing offer for their shares on their merits.

As a result, certain events have to happen by certain times, whilst other events cannot happen before certain periods of time have expired.

7.3.1 *Offer timetable*

The key times or dates in a bid timetable are as follows.

7.3.1.1 Posting date (Day 0)

The offer document should normally be posted within 28 days of the announcement of a firm intention to make an offer (Rule 30.1). References to days are generally to calendar days – weekends and public holidays are treated like any other day.

In practice, the offer document is often posted as quickly as possible to increase the pressure on the target in the case of a hostile bid or to seek to reduce the risk of there being a competing bid in the case of a recommended offer.

Clearly the speed with which the offer document is posted following the formal announcement of the offer may well impact on the ability of the employee representatives to prepare a statement of their views of the offer in time for that statement to be included in the relevant target company document. It will therefore be interesting to see whether the requirements in relation to communications to and from employee representatives will result in an increase in the number of instances where, on a recommended transaction, the offer is announced and the offer document posted simultaneously.

7.3.1.2 Day 14 (counting forwards from the posting date and excluding the posting date)

This is the last day for the target board to advise shareholders of its views on the offer. In any event, it must publish a circular containing its opinion of the offer as soon as practicable after publication of the offer document (Rule 30.2). The board of the target company must post the circular to its shareholders and make it readily and promptly available to its employee representatives or, where there are no such representatives, the employees themselves. As with the posting of an offer document, the circular must be put on display in accordance with Rule 26 and its posting announced in accordance with Rule 2.9. Further, the target board is required to append to the circular any opinion from the representatives of its employees on the effects of the offer on employment, provided such opinion is received in good time before publication of the circular.

7.3.1.3 Day 21

An offer must initially be open for at least 21 days after its posting (Rule 31.1). Therefore, the first closing date of an offer will normally be 21 days from the date of posting of the offer document, although it can be later than Day 21. This does not, however, prevent the offer from becoming unconditional at an earlier date.

7.3.1.4 Day 35

This is the first day on which an offer may close (i.e. no longer be available for acceptance), assuming it has been declared unconditional as to acceptances on the first closing date (assuming that is Day 21). This is because Rule 31.4 provides that after an offer has become or is declared unconditional as to acceptances, the offer must remain open for acceptance for not less than 14 days after the date on which it would otherwise have expired.

This Rule allows a shareholder who has been unable to make up his mind, or who perhaps wanted to see whether control would pass without his support, a period of 14 days beyond the date when the offer would otherwise have expired to accept the offer. When, however, an offer is unconditional as to acceptances from the outset, it is not necessary to keep the offer open for a further 14 days provided the position has been made clear in the offer document.

If the offer became wholly unconditional on Day 21, then Day 35 will also be the last date for payment of the consideration under the offer to shareholders who accepted the offer. The reason for this is that Rule 31.8 requires the consideration to be posted within 14 days of the later of:

(a) the first closing date of the offer;
(b) the date on which the offer became or was declared wholly unconditional; and
(c) the date of receipt of a valid acceptance complete in all respects.

As a result, where an offer becomes or is declared unconditional as to acceptances on Day 60 but does not become unconditional in all respects (i.e. all other conditions satisfied or waived) until Day 81, the consideration will not have to be posted until Day 95.

7.3.1.5 Day 39

Except where the Panel has otherwise consented (having been consulted "in good time"), this is the last day of the offer period for the target board to announce "any material new information" (Rule 31.9). This Rule covers announcements relating to trading results, profit or dividend forecasts, asset valuations, proposals for dividend payments and material acquisitions or disposals. This is a non-exhaustive list and these matters are referred to in the Rule as illustrative examples of the types of new information which could be considered material.

Rule 31.9 provides that, where a matter which might result in a Rule 31.9 announcement being made after Day 39 is known to the target company, every effort should be made to bring forward the date of the announcement. If it is not practicable to make the announcement before Day 39 or the matter arises after Day 39, then the Panel will normally extend the offer period and, in particular, move Day 46 (the last day for posting a revision of the offer) and/or Day 60 (the final date for declaring the offer unconditional as to acceptances: *see* 7.3.1.8), as appropriate, to a later date. This is precisely what happened in April 2003, in the context of the competing bids for Oxford Glycosciences plc by Celltech Group plc and Cambridge Antibody Technology plc. The Panel Executive extended Day 39 for up to 20 days to allow Oxford Glycosciences to announce its trading results. The offer timetable was subsequently re-set, with Day 46 deemed to fall 7 days after the announcement of the trading results.

In cases where an offer is subject to a competition condition and the Office of Fair Trading or the European Commission (as the case may be) has not yet announced whether or not a second stage investigation will be initiated, the Panel will normally extend Day 39 to the second day following the announcement of the relevant decision with consequent changes to Day 46 and Day 60 (*see* Note 3 on Rule 31.6).

During last year's hostile bid by Saint-Gobain for BPB, Saint-Gobain sought an extension of Day 39 in circumstances where it had been delayed in making the requisite competition filing with the European Commission with the inevitable consequence that the relevant decision would be delayed beyond Day 39. Although the Panel was prepared to grant the timetable extension in these unprecedented circumstances, Saint-Gobain was required to undertake that neither it nor any of its concert parties would acquire any interest in or rights over any BPB shares (other than in very limited circumstances) until such time as the European Commission published its decision as to whether or not to initiate a second stage investigation into the competition issues affecting the proposed transaction.

7.3.1.6 Day 42

This is the last date for fulfilment of all other conditions of the bid, assuming the offer became or was declared unconditional as to acceptances on the first closing date and the first closing date was Day 21.

Rule 31.7 provides that, except with the consent of the Panel, all conditions must be fulfilled or the offer must lapse within 21 days of the first closing date or the date the offer becomes or is declared unconditional as to acceptances, whichever is the later. The Panel will normally only grant consent if the outstanding conditions involve a material official authorisation or regulatory clearance in relation to the offer and it has not been possible to obtain an extension under Rule 31.6 (see 7.3.1.5 above). Thus if an offer is not declared unconditional as to acceptances until Day 60 (which is common where there are competing offers), all other conditions must normally be satisfied by Day 81 (i.e. Day 60 plus 21). (Timetable extensions are discussed in 7.3.2 below.)

Day 42 is perhaps best known because of Rule 34 which provides that the offer must confer upon an accepting shareholder a right of withdrawal of his acceptance after the expiry of 21 days from the first closing date of the initial offer (which, as indicated above, is normally Day 21) unless the offer has become unconditional as to acceptances. This is of considerable importance in a competitive bid situation since this enables an accepting shareholder to change his mind at the last minute; it is not possible for an offeror to provide in the offer document that acceptances of the offer should be irrevocable (i.e. not capable of being withdrawn) after Day 42. Equally, it is important that an offeror clearly sets out this withdrawal right in its offer document. Confusion over the timing of withdrawal rights in the Thistle/BIL bid in 2003 resulted in BIL having to allow Thistle shareholders withdrawal rights from an earlier date than the Code would otherwise have strictly required.

Competing offerors and target companies in hostile bids commonly try to take advantage of the existence of withdrawal rights by sending withdrawal forms to the target company's shareholders pointing out that they have the right to withdraw any acceptance of the relevant offer document. (This does not, however, prevent the offer from being declared unconditional at an earlier date).

The right of withdrawal conferred by Rule 34 may, however, be varied by individual agreement and an offeror will normally attempt to extract a waiver of this right from a target shareholder, who has agreed to give an irrevocable undertaking to accept the offer.

A right of withdrawal can also be imposed by the Panel as an alternative to allowing a target company to invoke, or cause an offeror to invoke, a so-called "offeree protection condition" (*see* Rule 34 and Note 2 on Rule 13.5).

7.3.1.7 Day 46
This is the last day for posting a revision of the offer since an offer must be kept open for at least 14 days from the date of posting the revised offer document to shareholders (Rule 32.1) (thus giving them time to consider the revised offer on its merits) and the last day on which the offer is able to become unconditional as to acceptances is Day 60.

Day 46 will also normally be the last day for the offeror to make an announcement as to trading results, profits, dividends etc. where the offer involves an element of share exchange (i.e. the offeror is offering its shares). This is because such an announcement may have the effect of increasing the value of the offeror's shares and thus amount to a revision of its bid.

The Code contains specific rules which address what happens if there are still two (or more) competing bidders at Day 46 (*see* 7.3.1.12 below).

7.3.1.8 Day 60
As indicated above, this is the final day for an offer to become or be declared unconditional as to acceptances (Rule 31.6). In other words, if the offeror has not achieved the minimum level of acceptances on which its bid is conditional by Day 60, its offer will lapse.

Day 60 can be extended with the consent of the Panel but Rule 31.6 makes it clear that the Panel will normally only consent to such an extension if:

(a) a competing offer has been announced;
(b) the target board agrees;
(c) there is an announcement of the target company's results after Day 39 (as already mentioned above);
(d) the offeror's receiving agent requests an extension for the purpose of issuing to the offeror or its financial advisers a certificate stating the number of acceptances and shares otherwise acquired, such certificate being required before an offer may be declared unconditional as to acceptances (Note 4 on Rule 10); or
(e) withdrawal rights are introduced by the Panel under Rule 13.5 as a result of an "offeree protection condition" being triggered.

In circumstances where a competing offer has been announced, both offerors will normally be bound by the timetable established by the posting of the competing offer document. As a result the normal bid timetable can be extended considerably in the event of competing bids (especially where complex competition issues are involved) and become somewhat of a marathon. This explains why bid battles can go on for some months in spite of the normal 60-day rule.

Examples of situations where a target company has found itself beseiged for a very extended period include Watmoughs in the face of competing bids from Quebecor and Webinvest in 1998; and National Westminster Bank in the face of bids from Bank of Scotland and Royal Bank of Scotland in 2000. More recent examples include Safeway in the face of the bid from Morrisons, the expressions of interests from other supermarket groups and the related Competition Commission inquiry and Canary Wharf in the face of bids from two private equity-backed consortia (Silvestor and CWG).

One of the more notable cases of Day 60 being extended was in December 1996 when Northern Electric was defeated by CalEnergy following the Panel's decision to extend Day 60 following disclosure of a general success fee payable to one of Northern Electric's advisers which had been purchasing Northern shares as principal with a view to frustrating the bid. This fee had not previously been disclosed when the Panel had given its approval for the share-buying activity and CalEnergy had not had an opportunity to address this issue in its submission to the Panel. The Panel exercised its discretion under Rule 31.6 to extend the closing date for the offer from 20 December 1996 (at which date CalEnergy had 49.7 per cent acceptances) to 1 p.m. on 24 December 1996 (at which date CalEnergy had 50.3 per cent). As a result of the amendments made to the Code in July 1998, share buying by the associates of the offeree during the offer period is now prohibited (*see* 7.2.9 above), but this decision still serves as an example of the discretion which the Panel is capable of exercising in order to ensure "fair play".

An unusual situation arose in the Wolverhampton & Dudley Breweries offer for Marston, Thompson and Evershed plc at the end of 1998. This involved the use for the first time in the UK of the so-called "pac man" defence whereby the target of an unwelcome offer makes a counter offer for the offeror. Following the posting by Wolverhampton of its offer document to Marston shareholders, Marston announced its counter offer for Wolverhampton on Day 39 to the offer timetable.

This raised a number of issues, including, in particular, whether the Wolverhampton timetable should be rebased so that it would run parallel with the Marston's timetable. This would have set the same finishing date for both bids with the potential risk of both offers becoming unconditional as to acceptances, thereby giving rise to a situation which could not legally be performed, that is, each could not take over the other.

Various "tie break" proposals were discussed, but in the end the Panel rejected arguments that the two offers should run on the same timetable and decided to freeze Day 39 on Wolverhampton's timetable until the posting of Marston's offer, instead of rebasing the timetables, thereby preserving for Wolverhampton the opportunity to complete its offer before the first closing date of the Marston offer. In addition, the Panel insisted that the Marston bid was subject to a non-waivable condition that the Wolverhampton bid must have lapsed. History shows that Wolverhampton's offer was declared wholly unconditional on Day 60 with over 70 per cent acceptances.

It is also worth noting that the Panel will not normally grant consent to an offer being declared unconditional as to acceptances after Day 60 of the relevant timetable in the case of competing bids unless the Panel's consent is sought before Day 46. This amendment to Rule 31.6 was introduced in February 2002 and is linked to Rule 32.5 which is aimed at addressing the position where competing bids continue to subsist on Day 46 (see 7.5 below).

In Practice Statement 8, the Panel Executive considered the application of Rule 31.6 and Rule 32.1 (see 7.3.1.7 above) to a situation where a potential competing offeror, which may or may not have previously announced its interest, is considering announcing a rival offer **after** Day 46 of the existing offeror's offer. This Practice Statement confirmed that, in such a case, the Executive would usually grant an extension to Day 60 (with a corresponding extension to Day 46) of the existing offeror's timetable, provided that the target board consented to such an extension.

7.3.1.9 Day 81
As referred to above, this will be the last day for fulfilment of all other conditions if the offer is declared unconditional as to acceptances on Day 60. This is another example (Day 42 was the first) of the application of Rule 31.7.

7.3.1.10 Day 95
As already indicated above, the consideration must be settled no later than 14 days after the offer becomes or is declared wholly unconditional (Rule 31.8). Therefore, this is the latest theoretical date for such settlement (assuming that the offer is declared unconditional as to acceptances on Day 60 and Day 60 is not extended).

7.3.1.11 *Trigger date for compulsory acquisition of the minority*
In order to implement the compulsory acquisition of minority shareholders pursuant to the provisions of the Companies Act 1985, the offeror must have achieved the requisite 90 per cent threshold within a prescribed period. This is prescribed by statute and is not, therefore, affected by an extension to the Code takeover timetable.

The Regulations which have implemented the EU Takeovers Directive have also amended the statutory rules which govern the right of the offeror to acquire compulsorily (or "squeeze-out") a recalcitrant minority in the context of an offer which is subject to the Directive. Where the offer is subject to the Directive (i.e. offers for companies listed on a regulated market but not those traded on AIM or Ofex), the squeeze-out rights must be exercised within the period of three months from the end of the time allowed for acceptance of the bid. This potentially provides the offeror with greater flexibility than has previously been the case.

In all other cases, the deadline for achieving the requisite 90 per cent threshold will, for the time being, remain at four months after the posting of the offer document. This is, however, due to change as and when the Company Law Reform Bill is finally enacted.

7.3.1.12 Competing bids on Day 46
Rules were introduced in 2002 to deal with the relatively unusual situation of there being two outstanding offers for a target on Day 46 (the last day for the posting of a revised offer). The purpose of the rules was to introduce a more certain process aimed at delivering maximum value to shareholders (*see* Rule 32.5).

The previous rules had been tested on a couple of occasions – the competing bids for Energy Group by Texas Utilities and Pacificorp and the competing bids for Hyder from WPD and Nomura. In each of those cases, the Panel had, following discussions with the competing bidders and the relevant target company, determined that the rival bidders should file sealed formula bids with the Panel. The Panel would then notify the "winning" bidder of the level at which it must announce its final offer. However, in each case, only one bidder ultimately complied with these procedures. Following much debate over the failings of the old regime, the Code rules were revised.

The revised rules have introduced an "open" auction process, the terms of which are to be determined on each occasion by the Panel. The idea is that there should be a short period of time during which the auction takes place. During this auction, a rival bidder would be given a set period within which to respond to any revised offer announced by its competitor but with the Panel having the power to impose a final "guillotine" on the time period during which the auction takes place.

The Panel has, on a number of occasions, issued formal statements setting out the process to be followed under these new rules where there are competing bids on Day 46. The first was in relation to the competing bids for Debenhams although, in that case, the open auction process was not actually invoked as the CVC/TPG consortium initiated a pre-emptive (and successful) increase of its offer after the Panel had confirmed the terms of the open auction process but prior to Day 46 (the day when the "open" auction process was to apply). An even more high profile occasion was in relation to the competing bids for Canary Wharf in 2004. More recently, the Panel issued a statement on the auction procedure which applied in relation to the competing bids for QXL Ricardo plc in March 2005.

As an alternative to an auction process, the Panel will consider any other procedure (including potentially a "sealed bid" process) which is agreed between the competing offerors and the board of the target company. In determining the detail of any procedure which is to be followed, the Panel is likely to give considerable weight to the views of the target company in order to seek to maximise the value which can be generated for target shareholders.

7.3.2 Timetable extensions

As already mentioned, regulatory issues can impact on the offer timetable. Whilst the Panel attaches importance to the strict offer timetable, it is prepared to be flexible (particularly, in the case of recommended offers) in accommodating delays or extensions which arise from regulatory issues.

So what are the available options if the required regulatory clearances are unlikely to be obtained within the normal offer timetable?

There are, principally, three options:

(a) make the offer subject to a pre-condition that regulatory approval is obtained – this approach was adopted in relation to the Boots/Alliance Unichem merger; GE's offer for Amersham plc; the Carnival/P&O Princess merger; and E.ON AG's bid for Powergen. The Panel must be consulted in advance if such a pre-conditional bid is to be announced;

(b) seek an extension of Rule 31.6 (the requirement that the acceptance condition must be satisfied by midnight on Day 60). This has the effect of also extending what would otherwise be the last date for satisfying or waiving all other offer conditions; or

(c) seek an extension of Rule 31.7 (the requirement that all other conditions must be satisfied within 21 days of the offer becoming or being declared unconditional as to acceptances) in order to be able to close off withdrawal rights by declaring the offer unconditional as to acceptances whilst allowing more time to satisfy the other conditions.

An example of an extension of Rule 31.7 (Day 81) arose on the Federal Mogul/T&N bid. The bid was announced on 13 November 1997 and was declared unconditional as to acceptances in December 1997 before withdrawal rights arose. The Panel granted an extension of Rule 31.7 in order to allow more time in which to obtain the necessary regulatory clearances. However, the timetable became greatly extended as delays in obtaining these regulatory clearances were encountered and the offer only became unconditional in all respects in the middle of March 1998. During this period the T&N shareholders who had accepted the offer could not receive their consideration and were not free to withdraw acceptances and sell their shares in the market. There was press criticism of the Panel and the parties to the bid and questions were raised as to whether Federal Mogul should have been required to pay interest to those accepting shareholders or, alternatively, the Panel should have reintroduced withdrawal rights.

The Panel is now reluctant to accede to requests to extend Rule 31.7 and instead prefers to grant extensions to Rule 31.6 to avoid shareholders being locked in – this means that the offeror has an extended timetable in which to complete the offer but cannot declare its offer unconditional as to acceptances (thereby ending withdrawal rights) until it is satisfied that all other conditions to the offer can be fulfilled (or waived) within the next 21 days. The offeror must always bear in mind that the time period in which it must reach the requisite compulsory acquisition threshold begins to run from the posting of the offer document and does not take account of timetable extensions under the Code (*see* 7.3.1.11 above).

As a practical point, it should also be noted that, in circumstances where the documentation made available to shareholders included a predicted date for the satisfaction of all conditions or the posting of the offer consideration to shareholders, the consent of the Executive to a timetable extension will normally be subject to a requirement that notice of the extension be posted to shareholders (*see* Practice Statement 13). An announcement of the extension will not suffice, and posting will normally be required by the Executive even where the previous documentation has included a warning that the predicted timetable is only indicative and may change.

7.4 Extensions of the offer

In what circumstances will an extension of the offer be important?

(a) If an offeror has failed to achieve control by a specified closing date, it may well wish to extend its offer to give itself more time to persuade shareholders by its arguments to accept it. It has been mentioned above that an offer may not be extended beyond Day 60 unless the offer has become or been declared unconditional as to acceptances by such date. Subject to this, if an offeror wishes to extend its offer, it has two options. It can either announce an extension specifying the next closing date or, if the offer is unconditional as to acceptances, it may state that the offer will remain open until further notice.

(b) Once an offeror has gained control it will normally leave its offer open in order to allow dissentients to accept and to allow it to gather in further acceptances to the extent necessary to be able to utilise the compulsory acquisitions provisions under the Companies Act 1985 to "squeeze-out" the outstanding minority (*see* 7.3.1.11 above).

An offeror is not, however, obliged to extend its offer (Rule 31.3). If, for example, its acceptance condition has not been satisfied by a specified closing date then, as was the case in Macquarie Bank's bid for the London Stock Exchange earlier this year, the offeror is free to lapse its offer.

Rule 31.5 (and the notes to that Rule) deal in some detail with what are known as "no extension statements". The basic idea is that shareholders should not be misled into thinking that they must accept an offer by a certain date only to find later that the offeror has granted a further extension. If an offeror wants to extend its offer it must specifically reserve the right to do so and this must be prominently displayed in the offer document and not lost in the small print of the appendices.

If, however, a competitive situation arises after an offeror has made a no extension statement, the whole picture changes and the offeror can choose not to be bound by its statement provided shareholders are informed promptly and certain other requirements are satisfied.

In 2003, a new Note 5 on Rule 31.5 was introduced permitting an offeror not to be bound by a previously made no extension statement in the light of any material new information announced by the target company after Day 39 of the offer timetable. With the Panel's permission the offer may be extended, provided that notice to that effect is given as soon as possible, and in any event within four business days after the target company's announcement, with shareholders being informed in writing of this extension at the earliest opportunity.

7.5 Revisions and increases

The timing requirements relating to revisions are referred to above, for example no revision after Day 46 (*see* 7.3.1.7 above). Revisions will be obligatory in certain circumstances such as an acquisition of any interest in shares above the offer price (Rule 6.2) or in the event of an obligation to introduce a cash offer under Rule 11.1. Rule 32.3 provides that if an offer is revised, all shareholders who accepted the original offer must be entitled to the revised consideration.

As regards increased offers (as distinct simply from offers which are revised, although it is rare for a revision not to represent an increase), Rule 32.2 contains substantially equivalent restrictions on no increase statements as those outlined in relation to no extension statements and dealt with in Rule 31.5.

The reasons for these restrictions were explained in the 1999 Panel ruling in the context of the competing bids for CALA plc. An MBO vehicle, Dotterel Limited, and Miller 1999 plc had each announced bids for CALA plc. Miller announced the revised offer of 200 pence per CALA share and stated that this increased offer was final and would not be increased further except that Miller reserved the right to increase its offer up to a maximum of 210 pence per share in the event of a bid being made for CALA at a higher value than its increased offer of 200 pence in cash.

Dotterel indicated its intention to announce a matching offer of 200 pence per share – basically relying on the shares held by management and the support of institutional shareholders for existing management to win the day. Miller sought consent from the Panel to increase its offer if a matching offer was made. The Panel ruled that as Miller had not reserved the specific right to increase its offer in the event of a matching (as opposed to higher) bid, then Miller was prohibited from doing so.

The Panel ruling went on to explain that:

> "This Rule seeks to set a balance between the potential disadvantages to shareholders from this consequence and the undesirable consequences for shareholders and the markets if they cannot rely on the accuracy of statements made by an offeror. As a matter of policy, and in the absence of 'wholly exceptional circumstances', it is more important that the principle of certainty and orderly conduct should be upheld rather than to risk compromising this principle to accommodate the apparent disadvantages which may result from the application of the Rule in a particular case."

This ruling was, however, the subject of a certain amount of press criticism on the basis that this apparently inflexible application of Rule 32.2 potentially deprived the CALA shareholders of a further higher bid from Miller.

By way of contrast, Service Corporation International's offer for Great Southern Group in 1994 provided an interesting example of the Panel exercising its discretion to grant a dispensation to allow SCI to increase its bid after a "no increase statement" had been made in a press release, but, as a result of an oversight it was not accompanied by a specific reservation of the right to increase its bid should a competitive situation arise. The Panel accepted that, because this was a genuine mistake, the circumstances of the case were "wholly exceptional" and granted a dispensation. It is clear that the Panel were heavily influenced in reaching this decision by the fact that arrangements were made to compensate shareholders who sold in the market as a result of being misled by the press release.

Care should also be taken to ensure that statements made by the offeror company, or its controlling shareholder, cannot be construed under Rule 32.2 as a no increase statement. It is relatively easy to be inadvertently tripped up by this Rule. In November 2002 Hugh Osmond, a controlling shareholder in Twigway which had made an indicative offer of 320–350 pence per share for the Pizza Express restaurant group, was quoted in the press as saying that the offeror company would "not reconsider the price under any circumstances unless there's some bloody good reason, and right now I can't think of one". The Panel immediately required a statement from Twigway clarifying that Mr Osmond's comments did not represent a "no increase" statement under Rule 32.2. Equally, Aviva had to publish a statement clarifying that comments made in a press interview following its approach to the Prudential concerning a possible merger earlier this year did not amount to a "no increase" statement.

Whilst on the subject of increased offers, it is worth noting that Rule 32.4 recognises that the offeror may need to introduce new conditions into its bid in the event of an increase. For example, if it introduces a securities element to the consideration it will need a condition that the new securities be admitted to listing and/or trading. Panel consent is, however, required for inclusion of any such condition. This will only be permitted to the extent necessary to implement the increased offer.

7.6 Alternative offers

Generally the rules outlined above apply equally to alternative offers. Rule 33.1 specifies that these will include cash alternative offers.

Difficult questions arise, however, with regard to alternative offers, in particular in relation to closing or shutting them off.

First, with regard to "mix and match" offers – that is, where shareholders may elect to vary the proportion in which they are to receive different forms of consideration subject to other shareholders making contrary elections (because there are limits on the different forms of consideration available) – these are not regarded as alternative offers and the availability to "mix and match" may be closed without notice on any closing date provided this has been clearly stated in the offer document.

Secondly, with regard to the shutting off of alternative offers, the general rule, as indicated, is that once an offer has become or is declared unconditional as to acceptances, all alternative offers (in the same way as the principal offer itself) must remain open for a minimum of 14 days.

Thus, waverers must also be given the benefit of jumping on the bandwagon with regard to alternative offers.

Also, as with the principal offer under Rule 31.3, if on a closing day an offer is not unconditional as to acceptances, an alternative offer may be closed without prior notice – that is, there is no obligation to extend it.

Rule 33.2 deals with shutting off cash underwritten alternatives. Cash underwritten alternatives involve large underwriting fees and offerors are naturally keen to stop commitment commissions running as soon as control of the target has been won. The effect of this Rule is to allow an offeror to shut off a cash alternative earlier than other forms of consideration provided:

(a) the value of the cash underwritten alternative (which must be provided by third parties) is, at the time of announcement, more than half the maximum value of the offer; and
(b) it has specifically given notice that it reserves the right to close the cash alternative on a stated date, being not less than 14 days later than the date of the notice, or to extend it.

Rule 33.2 will not apply to a cash alternative provided to satisfy the requirements of Rule 9. In other words, an offeror required to make a cash bid under Rule 9 will not be able to shut it off on the date its offer

Conduct During the Offer; Timing and Revision; and Restrictions Following Offers

becomes or is declared unconditional as to acceptances but must keep it open for a further minimum period of 14 days.

Rule 33.3 deals with the reintroduction of alternative forms of consideration. Generally, unless a statement has been made that a form of consideration will not be reintroduced, it may be reintroduced at a later date, having lapsed or closed for acceptance in the interim. Reintroduction is treated as a revision and therefore must be open for 14 days and cannot be effected later than Day 46.

7.7 Restrictions following offers and possible offers

The final area covered by this Chapter deals principally with Rule 35.1 of the Code which contains the rule restricting a new offer from being launched within 12 months of the lapsing or withdrawal of a previous offer.

7.7.1 *Circumstances when an offer must lapse*

An offer must lapse if:

(a) an offeror does not obtain sufficient acceptances to be able to declare its offer unconditional as to acceptances by Day 60 (examples of this have included the Wickes/Focus Do It All and the Lafarge/Blue Circle bids);
(b) any detailed investigation by the relevant competition authority takes place (an example of this is the lapse of the original bid announced by Wm Morrison Supermarkets plc for Safeway plc in January 2003); or
(c) having declared the offer unconditional as to acceptances, the other conditions to the offer are not satisfied within 21 days then the offer must lapse.

When an offer lapses any tendered acceptances also lapse. The offeror is therefore left with only the shares it has acquired through purchases. Its stake will usually be less than 30 per cent of the target. However, if as a result of acquisitions, it was forced to make a Rule 9 offer which failed, an offeror could be left with a stake of 30 per cent or more.

7.7.2 Freedom to sell target shares

Once the offer has lapsed, the offeror is no longer subject to the Code restriction on disposing of target shares (Rule 4.2) and can therefore sell them. If it decides to retain all or some of the shares, the degree of influence it can exert over the target will depend on the size of its stake.

There is generally no restriction on an offeror making market purchases after its offer has lapsed. However the Code was amended in 2002 to provide that, where there have been competing offers, a lapsed offeror cannot acquire an interest in shares in the target company on more favourable terms than those made available under its lapsed offer until such time as the competing offer has either lapsed or become wholly unconditional. This is intended to prevent an offeror which has lapsed its offer from making market purchases with a view to frustrating a competing offer which is still continuing. It does not, however, prevent an unsuccessful offeror from acquiring an interest in target company shares once the "successful" offer has become wholly unconditional, which could potentially still frustrate the ability of the successful offeror to obtain 100 per cent control of the target.

7.7.3 Rule 35 – delay of 12 months

Whatever the size of the offeror's stake in the target, its continued presence on the shareholder register is likely to be a source of both concern and possible irritation to the target. The target will not know what the offeror's intentions are.

The Code provides some protection against the "siege" being renewed immediately, the offeror cannot launch a new offer (or partial offer) within 12 months of its original offer lapsing unless the new offer is recommended or a competing offer has been made or the new offer follows the giving of clearance by the relevant competition authority (Rule 35.1). Accordingly, Wm Morrison was able to announce a renewed recommended offer for Safeway in December 2003 following the completion of the detailed review of the supermarket industry undertaken by the UK's Competition Commission as a result of Morrison's initial offer for Safeway in January 2003.

The Panel may also grant consent for a new offer to be made in circumstances where it is likely to prove, or has proved, impossible to obtain material regulatory clearances relating to the offer within the Code timetable.

The Panel's general approach to Rule 35.1 was explained in its statement of 17 March 1995 relating to the appeal by Trafalgar House against a Panel Executive decision that Trafalgar House should not be permitted to make an immediate new offer for Northern Electric.

> "Rule 35.1 is designed to create a reasonable balance between giving shareholders an opportunity to consider offers for their shares and enabling the business of the company in which they have invested to be carried on without continuous uncertainty and dislocation. Inevitably the effect of this Rule may be to prevent for a period of time a new offer by a failed offeror, at whatever price, being made to shareholders in the offeree company."

On that occasion the Panel made it clear that Rule 35 is regarded as one of the more important rules of the Code and that only on rare occasions would it be prepared to grant a dispensation. Trafalgar House allowed its offer to lapse on Day 60 (with acceptances of 76.5 per cent) three days after a pricing review of all electricity companies which led to a substantial fall in the market value of shares in electricity companies generally. The Panel ruled that those circumstances did not warrant the granting of a dispensation to enable Trafalgar House immediately to make a new offer at a lower price to take account of the pricing review without having first obtained the consent of the board of Northern Electric.

Rule 35.2 makes it clear that Rule 35.1 also applies following partial offers whether or not that offer has become or been declared wholly unconditional. This is to cover the possibility of successive partial offers for less than 30 per cent of a company. When such an offer has become or been declared wholly unconditional, the 12 month period runs from that date. In addition, Rule 35.1 applies following a partial offer for more than 50 per cent of the voting rights of the target which has not become or been declared wholly unconditional (*see* Rule 35.2(b)).

In the 12 months following an offer lapsing, neither the offeror nor its concert parties can (i) announce an offer or possible offer; (ii) acquire any interest in shares if this would give rise to an obligation to make a mandatory bid under Rule 9; (iii) acquire any interest in, or procure an irrevocable commitment in respect of, shares in the offeree if the shares in which such person, together with persons acting in concert with him, would be interested and the shares in respect of which he, or they, had acquired irrevocable commitments would in aggregate carry 30 per cent or more of the voting rights of the offeree; (iv) make any statement which raises or confirms the possibility that an offer might be made for the offeree; or (v) take any steps in connection with a possible offer for the offeree where knowledge of the possible offer might be extended outside those people within the offeror and its immediate advisers who need to know about it. However, (iv) and (v) above will not normally apply where the offer lapsed as a result of a detailed competition review being initiated or as a result of some other material regulatory approval not being obtained within the normal offer timetable and the offeror is continuing to seek the relevant approval with a view subsequently to making a new offer with the consent of the Panel. Once the 12 months have elapsed, an offeror is free to acquire further shares or make another offer. Rule 9 continues to apply and the offeror will be forced to make an offer if it (together with its concert parties) takes its stake from below 30 per cent to 30 per cent or more, or if it acquires any interest in further shares in the company where it already has between 30 per cent and 50 per cent.

As mentioned in 7.7.2 above, acquisitions by or on behalf of an offeror which was one of two (or more) competing offerors and whose offer has lapsed are subject to a further restriction. Any such acquisitions cannot be made on more favourable terms than those of the lapsed offer without the consent of the Panel until such time as the other competing offer has become or been declared unconditional or has lapsed.

It should also be noted that a potential offeror (and its concert parties) may be prevented from taking certain steps in relation to a target company (including making an offer for, or acquiring shares in, the target) for 6 months if the potential offeror makes a statement that it does not intend to make an offer for that company (*see* Rule 2.8). This

Rule can only be circumvented with the consent of the Panel, unless there is a material change of circumstances or an event has occurred which the potential offeror specified in its statement as an event which would enable the no intention to bid statement to be set aside. By way of example, when Aviva withdrew its proposal for a merger with Prudential earlier this year, it reserved the right, for the purposes of Rule 2.8, to make an offer for the Prudential in the event that either a third party announced a firm intention to make an offer for the Prudential or the Prudential board agreed to recommend the offer.

Finally, it should be noted that if an offer is declared unconditional in all respects but a minority remains outstanding then a six-month delay is likely to be required by the Panel before the offeror or any person acting in concert with him can make a second offer, or acquire any interest in shares, on more favourable terms than those which were available under the previous offer (Rule 35.3). Again this is to ensure fair treatment for shareholders in the target company and to seek to establish a level playing field as between competing offerors or potential offerors.

Chapter 8

Profit Forecasts and Asset Valuations

Ursula Newton
Partner
PricewaterhouseCoopers LLP

8.1 Profit forecasts

8.1.1 Introduction

Profit forecasts are an extremely important feature of public takeovers in the UK, and particularly those that are contested. A forecast of the current year's profits underpins the value of any target company's shares and, where a bidder is offering paper, a forecast by the bidder can be crucial in supporting its own share price and thus supporting the value of its offer.

All the Code Rules exist for a reason and Rule 28, on profit forecasts, is no exception. Prior to the Code's introduction in the late 1960s, there were a number of scandals where takeovers were effected in circumstances where profit forecasts had been made which subsequently proved to have been exceedingly optimistic. Rule 28 is designed to ensure that shareholders are protected from being misled by inaccurate forecasts, whether too high or too low.

8.1.2 What is a profit forecast?

A profit forecast can be defined as any published expectation of financial results for the last accounting period (if it has not yet been audited), the current period or for a future period. Where the period has already finished, the term employed is a profit estimate, but all the same rules apply whether it is a profit estimate or a forecast. It is worth noting at the outset that a profit forecast should be a best assessment made by the directors of the likely outturn for the period – it should not be a hoped for target.

This definition may appear straightforward but a company and its advisers have to take great care to ensure that the company does not inadvertently make a profit forecast. This was demonstrated in the bid by Kvaerner for AMEC several years ago, when a director of Financial Dynamics, the public relations adviser to AMEC, gave "an impression of a level of AMEC's future profits that was not being made public, and had not been prepared and reported on in accordance with the Code". AMEC had subsequently to disassociate itself from the information, and Financial Dynamics was criticised by the Panel for failing to take sufficient care in its discussions with analysts which resulted in what were described as "serious breaches of the Code".

Any public statement that can be construed as putting a floor or ceiling on anticipated results would be regarded as a profit forecast, as would a statement of any data from which a calculation of future profits may be made. The Code makes it clear that it is not necessary for the statement to mention a particular figure or even the word profit. For example, a chairman might respond to questions at an AGM regarding the current year performance by commenting that the current year's results will be better than the previous year's. Such a statement would be regarded as a forecast. Another example might be where an investment trust forecasts its next year's dividend which, given that at least 85 per cent of such a trust's profits must be paid out in dividends, sets both a floor and a ceiling on the annual profits.

Profit "projections", however, are something different and are not allowed under the Code. Projections are where a company calculates the possible future profits which could arise under certain circumstances but, because the projections look too far ahead and are thus highly uncertain, they are not capable of being reported on as required by Rule 28. It has been argued that, in certain circumstances (such as management buyouts of public companies), it would be appropriate to inform shareholders of projected profits that management believes it will be able to achieve over the next few years. Nevertheless, the high degree of uncertainty surrounding such projections and the consequent hazards of misleading shareholders has meant that disclosure of such information is not permitted.

8.1.3 The Code

In common with the UK Listing Authority Listing Rules (the "UKLA Rules") and the recently enacted Prospectus Directive, there is no requirement under the Code to issue a profit forecast except that, if there is already a profit forecast on the public record before a bid is made, this will normally have to be repeated and reported on or, with the agreement of the Panel, a revised forecast may be substituted. The Code requires that, at the outset, an adviser should invariably check whether or not its client has a forecast on the record.

Rule 28 starts in a suitably cautionary manner. It says there are obvious hazards attached to the forecasting of profits and emphasises the need for the highest standards of accuracy and fair presentation. It is very easy to get a forecast wrong and thus the Code requires that a forecast is prepared with scrupulous care and objectivity by the directors, who have sole responsibility for it.

8.1.4 The forecast

The principal assumptions on which the forecast is based must be stated and the forecast must, in most circumstances, be reviewed and reported on by both the auditors or consultant accountants and the financial advisers. These reports need to be included in the offer or defence document and also in any announcement if that is made earlier.

Once a forecast has been made, its continuing validity must usually be confirmed in each subsequent document that is issued, so as to make sure that any significant changes are notified to shareholders.

The degree of risk of getting a forecast wrong increases with the length of time that is forecast ahead. For this reason, it is relatively unusual for a forecast to extend beyond the current financial year, particularly if the current year is not well advanced.

Whether a forecast can actually be reported on at all can depend upon the nature of the business. It is much easier to forecast the results of a business such as an aircraft manufacturer (with its long order books) than it is for a high street retailer where a week of seasonal trading can result in a significant range of possible financial results. In the financial services industry, the results of a life assurance company are so highly dependent upon its annual actuarial evaluation carried out at the end of the financial year that any forecast issued prior to that exercise carries a very significant degree of uncertainty.

In contrast, the electricity industry has tended to be a very stable and predictable business which can be forecast some way ahead. In September 1995 Manweb forecast not only its profits to March 1996 but its profits to March 1997.

It is not uncommon for a profit forecast to be revised upwards during the offer period. This is perfectly permissible and in theory would seem logical, because as time passes, the company would become increasingly certain about its actual profitability, and there is less need to provide a contingency for unexpected developments. In practice, however, whilst such a revision sets a higher future earnings figure, it leaves the company open to the potential criticism of manipulating its financial reporting.

8.1.5 Merger benefits statements

During the Granada takeover of Forte in 1996, Granada published a circular which included a statement that the ongoing profit of Forte could be improved by over £100 million under Granada's ownership. At the time, no specific rule in the Code governed such a statement although it was subject to the general standards of care. The Code was amended in 1997 by Rule 19.1 to cover "merger benefits" and "earnings enhancement statements" published during the course of a takeover. Such statements are now regularly seen in supporting the rationale for merger-style transactions.

Rule 19.1 was introduced in order to ensure that there is a high standard of rigour underlying any statements that offeror companies make about the expected future savings they will achieve following the takeover, and to enable defending companies to identify weaknesses in the proposed level of benefits being put in front of shareholders. This rule requires disclosure of the bases of belief underlying the directors' statement, an analysis of the constituent elements of the estimate, and a base figure for comparison. Accountants and financial

Profit Forecasts and Asset Valuations

advisers are required to report independently whether such a statement has been made with "due care and consideration". The Rule has been clarified to confirm that these two requirements only apply if the statement is made in connection with a hostile offer and the expected merger benefits are quantified. The work involved in order for the directors to be satisfied that it is appropriate to make such a statement should not be underestimated. The bid for Abbey National by Lloyds Bank involved highly detailed assumptions regarding their statement being published by Lloyds, all of which would have needed careful consideration by the directors.

Parties wishing to make such statements which are not intended to be interpreted as profit forecasts must include an explicit and prominent disclaimer to the effect that such statements should not be interpreted to mean that earnings per share will necessarily be greater than the preceding year. If, based on such a statement, a reader is able to calculate or infer the prospective profits of the enlarged group or at least determine a floor or ceiling for such profits, the statement will be subject to the rules governing profit forecasts. Parties to a takeover who are in doubt as to the interpretation of such a statement are encouraged to consult the Panel in advance.

8.1.6 Exceptions

There are certain exceptions to the requirement for a profit forecast to be reported on, most of which relate to unaudited preliminary statements of annual results and interim results published during the offer period.

Preliminary results, as long as they are prepared to the standard required by the UKLA Rules, will never have to be reported on because it is assumed that subsequently they will be audited.

In relation to interim announcements:

(a) an offeror's interims need not be reported on if the offeror is offering cash or is offering shares which will not represent more than 10 per cent of the enlarged group's share capital; and
(b) an offeree's interims have to be reported on if the bid is hostile but not if it is agreed. Such a situation occurred with the interim

information issued by the LSE during the period of the hostile bid by Macquarie in January 2006. Prior to the announcement of any bid interims may be released without the need to be reported on. However, in the event that the offer, when made, was not recommended by the Board, the interims would at this later stage need to be reported on.

The other major exception, in addition to those relating to interim and preliminary results, is that a forecast made by an offeror offering solely cash need not be reported on.

8.1.7 Format of the forecast

There are no rules concerning the format in which the profit forecast must be made. Indeed the forecast need not even mention a number. A statement that profits will be higher than last year or that the result will be breakeven, are both fully acceptable ways of making a forecast.

Whilst the directors and their advisers would often feel that to give a range of profits might be the most realistic approach, in practice a single figure is usually given, qualified by the words "not less than", "of the order of", or "approximately". These phrases have tended to be interpreted in subtly differing ways, with "not less than" meaning that one might actually expect to exceed the stated number by a small amount, perhaps a few percentage points. "Of the order of" might imply that one would expect the result to be a few percentage points either side of the stated figure. However, this form of disclosure is a lot less attractive than "not less than" as it implies much less certainty in the minds of the directors about the robustness of its forecast.

It is worth noting that the more precise or comprehensive the forecast, the greater the amount of work required by the company and its advisers. The directors may find that they have to balance their preference for more detailed information, for example profit by division or country, against the downside risk of any published element of the forecast not being achieved. In such circumstances, it would be expected that each published element of the forecast would require the same degree of rigorous analysis (and prudence) which would be applied to a total number.

Profit Forecasts and Asset Valuations

If there is anything out of the ordinary which means it is not possible simply to tax effect the pre-tax figure to arrive at earnings, the abnormal items, such as unusual tax charges or major extraordinary items, must also be given.

One major caveat to a profit forecast is allowed and that is that the directors are entitled to qualify it as being made "in the absence of unforeseen circumstances".

8.1.8 *The assumptions underlying the forecast*

It is a protection for shareholders that the principal assumptions upon which the forecast is based have to be published, but in practice it is unusual for many of the assumptions to be particularly interesting or informative in relation to the specific circumstances of the company. For example, they will almost invariably refer to there being no change in exchange rates or in the current rate of inflation.

Assumptions must identify clearly those factors that are within the directors' control and those that are not. Thus, an assumption that a new product will be launched would not be in the directors' control if the launch was subject to approval by a regulatory authority, but its introduction would be within the directors' control if there were no authorisations still awaited. In addition, the assumptions should only cover items that have a material effect on the forecast.

The directors have sole responsibility for the assumptions in the forecast, although in practice they often need substantial advice and guidance from their accountants and financial advisers in formulating and wording the assumptions. The directors of a substantial, multi-location group would typically need more assistance, given the range and complexity of factors potentially affecting such a group's results.

In order to arrive at the directors' best estimate of the likely results, assumptions must clearly be realistic, and the directors cannot cover themselves by making an assumption on something which may well be wrong – for example, assuming that the company will not suffer a strike when in fact one is threatened would not be allowable.

There are certain assumptions that are not acceptable under the Code. For example, an assumption which in effect says nothing more than "we assume the forecast will be achieved" is not permitted. An example of this would be the assumption that "sales will be in accordance with budget". This is meaningless for the shareholders who do not know how demanding the budget is, and therefore are none the wiser regarding the preparation of the forecast. An assumption that is allowed would be, for example, "market demand will continue in line with recent trends and seasonal patterns". In this example, market demand is an uncertainty beyond the company's control.

That latter assumption is an example of what assumptions are supposed to be, that is useful to shareholders in helping them to form a view as to the reasonableness and reliability of the forecast.

Published assumptions tend to be quite standard, but there are often one or two that are specific to a particular industry. One memorable example was stated by Devenish in its defence against Boddington in 1991 in assuming that there would be no abnormal weather conditions – this being relevant because the level of beer sales is so highly dependent upon the weather. Predictably, Boddington referred to it as more a weather forecast than a profit forecast! The forecast of Manweb referred to earlier assumed that weather conditions would be in line with the experience of the last 30 years.

There is a second level of assumptions which are always in existence but are not published and these could be described as the detailed working assumptions. These will be reviewed by the accountants and financial advisers and discussed with the company in the same way as the published assumptions. It is important that such assumptions are identified because some could be critical to the achievement of the forecast and hence require careful consideration.

8.1.9 Responsibility

The Code is quite clear about who is responsible for making a profit forecast. Sole responsibility for a forecast lies with the directors. The reason for this is entirely logical. The people in the best position to determine the likely profits, and to take account of all relevant factors, and to know about current problems which could affect profits, are the directors. Having sole responsibility focuses the directors' minds and is designed to ensure that the directors do not either merely rely on their staff to produce the numbers without reviewing the outcome or wholly rely on their professional advisers. It is, after all, the forecast made by the directors.

This does not mean that the financial advisers and accountants have no responsibilities. They are expected to carry out their duties with appropriate care and skill so as to express an opinion on the forecast. Indeed, failure to do so could involve legal liability.

One principal way in which the directors are able to demonstrate that they have taken due care in compiling the forecast is to commission a commentary "long-form" report from auditors or consulting accountants, which will then be discussed with the directors. Such a report is of particular use to non-executive directors or directors who are executives of particular divisions or subsidiaries but who nevertheless have to take responsibility for the forecast as a whole. It is also an important benefit to the financial advisers in meeting its own responsibilities in relation to the forecasts.

Having discussed the long-form report with the accountants and the financial advisers, the directors often refine or amend their forecast in the light of the matters which have been raised. Such a revision sometimes involves either taking a different view on a particular item in the forecast or, more typically, including a contingency element which the directors decide is necessary to take account of the various uncertainties which inevitably exist in a forecast. One thing that experience suggests is that if anything is not going to go as expected in a forecast, it is far more likely to have an adverse effect on profits than a positive one.

Forecasts are often put together and reviewed in a very short period of time to meet the requirements of the Code timetable. A company may not have adequate resources to do all the work necessary and so it is sometimes the case that auditors provide assistance in elements of the preparation of a profit forecast. However, such work must be appropriate and clearly distinguished from the reporting work; an auditor's independence would be impaired if it both prepared a forecast and then had to report on it in public. Moreover, only the directors and staff of the company have sufficient detailed knowledge of the company's affairs to prepare a forecast of the required quality.

8.1.10 Preparation of a long-form report

There are a number of key matters that would typically be investigated by the accountants and reported in the long-form report in order to satisfy themselves on a forecast. Normally a review would address the following:

(a) how much of the forecast profit has already been achieved according to the company's management accounts;
(b) how reliable those management accounts have been in the past, or if certain items typically needed adjusting, for example, the stock figure which was always found to be incorrect when the stock was actually counted;
(c) whether the same accounting policies had been followed as in the past – it would be inappropriate for the forecast to assume plant and machinery was written off over 20 years when in last year's audited accounts it was written off over 15;
(d) how realistic and complete the assumptions to be published were and commentary thereon;
(e) an explanation of how the forecast had been prepared. The reliability of the forecast, and thus the extent to which there should be a contingency provision, will depend upon whether such a forecast had been done in exactly the same way many times before or whether it was a rushed, one-off exercise using short-cut methods;
(f) the accuracy of previous forecasts, as a prudent contingency would be required where there is evidence of major errors in forecasting in the past;
(g) a comparison of the figures included in the forecast with those of equivalent periods in previous years with explanations for the changes;
(h) the analysis of the sensitivity of profits to changes in the assumptions. Such an analysis is key, for example, if sales are two per cent less than budget, how much might this affect profits?

The forecast will have been based upon information available at the time it was prepared. After the main review work has been completed

Profit Forecasts and Asset Valuations

and immediately prior to issue of the forecast, further information may become available, and this should be compared with that used in the preparation of the forecast to ensure it is consistent.

The same updating exercise will be required when any subsequent documents are issued to shareholders by the company since the validity of the forecast has to be reconfirmed by the directors, and in addition, the accountants and financial advisers have to confirm that they have no objection to their published reports continuing to apply.

Although the directors have sole responsibility for the forecast, under the Code the financial adviser is required to discuss the assumptions with the company and report that it has satisfied itself that the forecast is being made by the directors with due care and consideration. In accordance with the Standard (SIR 3000) issued by the Auditing Practices Board, the accountant will report that "the forecast has been properly compiled on the basis of the assumptions made by the Directors".

The way in which the financial adviser satisfies its obligation to comment on whether the forecast has been prepared with due care and consideration will differ depending upon the investment bank. As a minimum a bank will read and rely to a great extent on the long-form report produced by the accountants; at the other end of the spectrum the bank may question the accountants and the company in great detail based, *inter alia*, on the facts included in the long-form report. The extent of the bank's work will depend upon the approach of the bank involved, the firm of auditors involved, the difficulty of the industry in terms of forecasting, and the extent to which the bank knows the client.

The auditors or reporting accountants have their explicit responsibility under the Code to examine the accounting policies and calculations and to report on them in the relevant documents issued by the company.

At first sight such a report might appear to be very limited in scope. After all, if the forecast adds up and there is no distortion arising because different accounting policies have been used, then the job might appear to be done. However, whilst there is no overt statement about the assumptions, the Code requires that accountants should not allow an assumption to be published which appears to be unrealistic and there is a general expectation that, if a firm of accountants reports on a profit forecast, it implies a reliability which goes beyond this restricted form of wording. The accountants effectively have to satisfy themselves that the profit forecast on which they are reporting has been made by the directors with proper care and consideration, taking into account all relevant factors, and that the forecast is credible.

It is perhaps of interest to note that the UK is very different from the US environment as regards profit forecasts. In the UK, it is recognised that forecasts depend upon subjective judgements and are subject to inherent uncertainties. Consequently although accountants are not able to verify profit forecasts (a misconception, at times, of the press and others), they are nevertheless able to express an opinion thereon. In the US, no doubt influenced by the litigious environment, profit forecasts are not part of takeover defences and, despite "safe harbour" rules in certain circumstances, auditors or consulting accountants do not issue reports on them in the same way.

8.1.11 Conclusion

A forecast of profits is an extremely important piece of information for an investor during a takeover. Forecasts often result in an increased offer being made by the bidder. They sometimes persuade shareholders not to accept an offer. Where forecasts prove to be wrong, particularly when the actual result is less than the forecast, this can cause loss to investors and is clearly a serious matter. Whilst the Code is designed to minimise the risk of a forecast not being met, this can and does on occasion happen, either because of circumstances which could not reasonably have been envisaged when the forecast was drawn up, or because a forecast was not drawn up with requisite care and the review process was inadequate.

The Panel does investigate situations where forecasts have not been met to see whether there has been a breach of the Code. Whilst there have not been any completed legal cases in the UK, some legal actions have been mounted against financial advisers and auditors which have reached court before ending up in a compromise settlement. However, until a case is actually completed in court, there will remain

Profit Forecasts and Asset Valuations

some doubt regarding the precise responsibilities of directors, financial advisers and accountants in this area.

It is, of course, open to question whether the increasingly litigious environment in the UK, combined with a legal system that can still make accountants liable for 100 per cent of a claim (irrespective of what proportion they were actually responsible for), will lead us down the US route and result in profit forecasts not being made and much less information on the future being provided to shareholders during takeovers.

8.2 Asset valuations

Asset valuations are very similar to profit forecasts as far as the Code is concerned. Valuations are used, principally by a target company, to defend against an offer or to argue for a higher price, based on furnishing information to shareholders about the asset value of the company. The Code, through Rule 29, ensures that such information is given only where it is properly supported by a report from an independent valuer unconnected with the parties to the transaction.

During the Granada bid for Forte, Forte used a number of defences including a valuation of their hotels – this resulted in a revalued net assets per share of 334p, which can be compared to Granada's initial lower offer of 323p, and their final offer of 373p per share.

8.2.1 Valuations and offers

Valuations given in connection with an offer typically apply to companies whose share prices tend to be influenced by asset values as opposed to profits, and good examples of this are oil exploration companies and property companies. But any kind of asset valuation is covered by the Code. For example, there have been a number of cases in recent years where valuations of pension fund surpluses have been given.

The Code requires a valuation to be supported by an opinion from an appropriately qualified valuer, which in the UK is likely to be a member of the Royal Institution of Chartered Surveyors ("RICS"), the Institute of Revenues Rating and Valuation ("IRRV") or the

Incorporated Society of Valuers and Auctioneers ("ISVA"). In addition, the valuer must have sufficient current knowledge of the asset being valued, together with the skills and understanding necessary to make the valuation.

A requirement was introduced in 1998 dealing with valuations of the other parties' assets. The bidder or target can only publish a valuation of the other parties' assets if a valuation is unqualified and up to appropriate standards. In exceptional cases, it is permitted for one party to comment on the others' valuation. The interpretation of this part of the rule by the Panel leads to an interesting consequence: until one party has issued a formal valuation during the offer, the Panel does not allow the other party to refer to an old valuation. Accordingly, a bidder is unlikely to be able to comment on the trend in net assets per share shown by a target's financial statements until an up-to-date valuation has been issued by the target. The Panel needs to be consulted on this area in advance.

Whereas if a profit forecast is "on the record" it has to be reported on, an asset valuation has to be reported on only if it is made in connection with an offer. So, for example, the directors' estimates of asset values, which are frequently included in audited accounts, can be reproduced in offer or defence documents when setting out statements of assets, and need not be supported by an independent valuer, provided the asset values are not a particularly significant factor and are not given undue prominence.

8.2.2 Basis of valuation

Clearly, a valuation is of little use to shareholders or any other party unless the basis of that valuation is set out clearly.

The appropriate basis of a valuation depends on the type of asset, for example properties in use by a company should be valued at open market value for existing use, whereas investment properties should be valued at open market value. The detailed requirements are set out in the Code.

Furthermore, the valuation of land, buildings and plant must be made in accordance with the Appraisal and Valuation Manual issued by RICS. A point of detail came up in the Bilton defence in 1998 concerning whether or not the valuation should be gross or net of purchasers' costs. Normal practice is for it to be net of purchasers' costs, although Rule 29 is not explicit on this point.

The Panel may, in certain circumstances, permit the provision of information additional to the basic valuation. For example, in the hostile offer for Wolverhampton & Dudley Breweries, a valuation report was also prepared based upon the value of the pubs if sold as one block rather than individually. In addition, in the hostile offer for Blue Circle a "calculation of worth" valuation was presented to illustrate the potential development value of certain properties which would not be reflected in the open market values. However, the Panel should be consulted in advance in such circumstances and may require additional disclosures if an alternative valuation is to be used.

Where there is a material tax liability which would arise on sale of the asset, this should be disclosed. There are also detailed disclosures required for land with development potential including the costs of development and an estimated value once development has been completed.

8.2.3 Exceptions

There is one exception to the rule that a valuation must be fully supported by a report. Where the target company has a large number of properties – perhaps a retailer with hundreds of high street shops, or a house builder with many half-built houses – the Panel is sometimes prepared to allow a valuation of a representative sample by the professional valuer which is then extrapolated by the directors to give a value for the portfolio as a whole. This is not because the costs of a full valuation would be prohibitive, but rather that the time required to carry out a valuation is not available.

Any valuation must state the effective date at which the assets were valued, which is particularly relevant in times of rapidly changing property prices. It is possible to use a valuation that is not current but, since the valuer must state that he is satisfied that a valuation at the current date would not be materially different, it must effectively be up-to-date before it can be published.

Chapter 9
Application of the Market Abuse Regime to Takeovers

Annabel Sykes
Partner

Umesh Kumar
Senior Associate
Freshfields Bruckhaus Deringer

9.1 Introduction

The market abuse regime, which is a very significant part of the Financial Services and Markets Act 2000 ("FSMA"), is a civil regime under which the Financial Services Authority (the "FSA") can take disciplinary or enforcement action against a person who commits market abuse or who requires or encourages another to engage in behaviour which, if engaged in by the first person, would have amounted to market abuse. The FSA's extensive powers are described further in 9.5 below.

The market abuse regime sits alongside the criminal offences relating to insider dealing and market manipulation. It also applies in addition to relevant regulatory requirements of the FSA, the specified markets and the City Code. There are some important areas of overlap between the jurisdiction of the FSA and that of the Takeover Panel in the context of transactions governed by the City Code. Accordingly, the purpose of this Chapter is to:

(a) explain the main controversies surrounding the market abuse regime;
(b) set out some background to the regime;
(c) give the definition of market abuse;
(d) describe the FSA's powers; and
(e) explain how the regime impacts on takeovers.

Important revisions to the market abuse regime to implement the Directive on Insider Dealing and Market Manipulation (Market Abuse) (2003/6/EC) (the "Directive") took effect on 1 July 2005 and are reflected in this chapter. The manner of implementation chosen by the Treasury has increased the complexities of advising in what was already a highly regulated area. Broadly, in so far as they were not encompassed in the provisions implementing the Directive, prohibitions in the previous market abuse regime have been preserved, subject to a "sunset" clause, which means that the relevant provisions will cease to have effect on 30 June 2008.

9.2 Controversial aspects of market abuse

The market abuse regime was announced by the Government in 1998. It was then (and continues to be) described as a civil regime, notwithstanding the wide ranging definition (which is discussed in more detail in 9.4 below) and the fact that it applies to everyone, whether individual or incorporated and whether authorised or not. An important consequence of its classification as civil was that early drafts of the Financial Services and Markets Bill did not include the additional protections required by the European Convention on Human Rights ("ECHR") which apply when a matter is in substance criminal (however it is classified under the applicable domestic law). After widespread lobbying, the Government conceded that the regime was at least arguably criminal for ECHR purposes. As a result, the FSMA includes a provision which prevents the use of evidence against a person under the market abuse regime where that evidence has been obtained from him under compulsion and a legal assistance scheme in relation to market abuse.

Another important aspect of the regime is also controversial. The FSA is required by the FSMA to publish the Code of Market Conduct ("COMC") to give guidance on whether behaviour amounts to market abuse. Where the COMC provides that something is not market abuse, that is conclusive of the matter. Where it indicates that something may be market abuse, that is evidential only. Given this, in market abuse matters the FSA is to some extent legislator, whilst also being investigator, prosecutor and judge. Again, this raises issues of basic fairness and ECHR concerns.

Additionally, with limited exceptions in certain of the new provisions, there is no explicit requirement in the definition of market abuse that a person must be of a particular state of mind before he commits market abuse.

Finally, retention of the pre-existing market abuse provisions, to the extent that they are super-equivalent to the requirements of the Directive, is also controversial.

9.3 Background to the market abuse regime

The Government's stated purpose in introducing the regime was so "the FSA will be able to impose a fine on any person or firm, *whether regulated or not*, who engages in [market] abuse" (emphasis added).

Unfortunately, in crafting the regime the Government appears to have overlooked the fact that General Principle 6 of the City Code provides:

> "All parties to an offer must use every endeavour to prevent the creation of a false market in the securities of an offeror or the offeree company. Parties involved in offers must take care that statements are not made which may mislead shareholders or the market",

and that the Takeover Panel has over many years dealt successfully with market abuse in the context of takeovers.

The Takeover Panel has always sought to preserve its exclusive jurisdiction over matters relating to takeovers because it is only too well aware of the tactical opportunities which overlapping regulatory jurisdiction can provide. Accordingly, it wanted the Government to include in the Financial Services and Markets Bill two amendments relating to market abuse in the context of takeovers. The first of these – the "safe harbour" amendment – was designed to ensure that where a person, in the opinion of the Takeover Panel, complied with relevant provisions of the City Code that person did not commit market abuse. The second – the "gatekeeper" amendment – was designed to ensure that no disciplinary or enforcement action could be taken in respect of market abuse committed during the course of a takeover except at the request of the Panel. Both were supported by the Opposition and the safe harbour amendment was briefly included in a late version of the Bill when the Government was defeated on the point in the House of Lords.

The Treasury offered a rival, and from the point of view of takeover regulation, a less satisfactory version of the safe harbour amendment in the form of what is now Section 120 FSMA. This provides:

"(1) The [FSA] may include in [the COMC] provision to the effect that in its opinion behaviour conforming with the City Code –

(a) does not amount to market abuse;
(b) does not amount to market abuse in specified circumstances; or
(c) does not amount to market abuse if engaged in by a specified description of person."

The effect of Section 120 FSMA is that it is for the FSA (not the Takeover Panel) to determine, in the context of the market abuse regime, whether behaviour complies with the City Code. This raises the possibility of different interpretations by the two different regulators because it is not open to the FSA simply to adopt the Takeover Panel's views. This would amount to an unlawful fettering of the FSA's discretion; something which would open the possibility of a successful judicial review. Further, Section 120 is not as flexible as the Takeover Panel's safe harbour amendment was. Paragraph 3(a) of the Introduction to the City Code provides that the Takeover Panel may modify or relax the application of a City Code provision if it considers that, in the particular circumstances of the case, the provision in question would operate unduly harshly or in an unnecessarily restrictive or burdensome, or otherwise inappropriate, manner. It is common for the Takeover Panel to do this. Where it does so in relation to a rule to which the FSA has given a safe harbour in the COMC (*see* 9.6 below), the person benefiting from the modification or relaxation will not fall within the safe harbour.

The FSA has made statements relevant to both these points in the Enforcement Manual. It has made clear that it will attach considerable

Application of the Market Abuse Regime to Takeovers

weight to the views of the Takeover Panel in interpreting and applying the City Code.

The Government did not include any provisions in the FSMA dealing with the interaction between the City Code and the enforcement by the FSA of the market abuse regime. This was left to the FSA and the Takeover Panel to agree between themselves and consequently, in reaching such agreement, the FSA must avoid fettering its discretion unlawfully because to do so would potentially expose it to a successful judicial review application. Their operating arrangements are summarised in 9.6 below.

9.4 Market abuse explained

Market abuse is defined in Section 118 FSMA. It has three elements, the second of which has three sub-elements. For the purposes of the definition, "behaviour" includes inaction as well as action. References below to investments being admitted to trading should be read to include a situation where an application for such admission has been made in respect of them.

Market abuse is defined as behaviour by any person:

(a) which occurs in relation to qualifying investments admitted to trading on a prescribed market. The Financial Services and Markets Act 2000 (Prescribed Markets and Qualifying Investments) Order 2001 (SI 2001/996) (as amended) prescribes the qualifying investments and relevant markets, for this purpose. Depending on which kind of behaviour is relevant, the legislation has different scope tests.

The retained provisions of the existing market abuse regime cover any investments admitted to trading on any market established under the rules of a UK recognised investment exchange ("RIE"). OFEX is also named as a prescribed market for this purpose. This part of the regime therefore covers investments relevant under the City Code such as shares admitted to trading on the London Stock Exchange or on the Alternative Investment Market. Virt-x Exchange Limited is another RIE on which shares are traded. In the remainder of this chapter, these prescribed markets are referred to as "domestic markets". The legislation also provides that behaviour which occurs in relation to certain investments, such as derivatives (whether or not traded on a specified market) based on appropriately admitted qualifying investments ("relevant products"), is treated as occurring in relation to the qualifying investments themselves.

The other provisions of the market abuse regime cover all investments admitted to trading on a domestic market or a regulated market established or operating in any other EU state. In the remainder of this chapter, these prescribed markets are referred to as "EU markets". In addition, the kinds of behaviour described in (b)(i) and (ii) amount to market abuse where they occur in relation to a "related investment" i.e. an investment whose price or value depends upon an instrument admitted to trading on an EU market; and

(b) which meets any of the following descriptions:

(i) an insider deals or attempts to deal in a qualifying investment or a related investment on the basis of inside information;

(ii) an insider discloses inside information otherwise than in the proper course of his employment, profession or duties;

(iii) the behaviour does not fall in (i) or (ii) and is based on information which is not generally available to those using the market in question but which, if available to a regular user of that market, would be likely to be regarded by him as relevant when deciding the terms on which transactions in investments of the kind in question should be effected ("relevant information"). The behaviour must also be likely to be regarded by a regular user of the market in question as a failure on the part of the person or persons concerned to observe the standard of behaviour reasonably expected of a person in his or their position in relation to the market;

(iv) a person effects transactions or orders to trade (otherwise than for legitimate reasons and in accordance with accepted market practices on the relevant market) which either give or are likely to give a false or misleading

Application of the Market Abuse Regime to Takeovers

(v) impression as to the supply of, or demand for, or as to the price of a qualifying investment or secure its price at an abnormal or artificial level;

(v) a person effects transactions or orders to trade which employ fictitious devices or any other form of deception or contrivance;

(vi) a person disseminates information which gives or is likely to give a false or misleading impression where that person knew or could reasonably be expected to have known this;

(vii) the behaviour does not fall within any of (iv) to (vi) but is nevertheless likely to give a regular user of the market in question a false or misleading impression as to the supply of, or demand for, or as to the price or value of, investments of the kind in question or to be regarded by a regular user of the market in question as behaviour which would, or would be likely to, distort the market in investments of the kind in question. The behaviour must also be likely to be regarded by a regular user of the market in question as a failure on the part of the person or persons concerned to observe the standard of behaviour reasonably expected of a person in his or their position in relation to the market;

(viii) requiring or encouraging behaviour falling within any of (i) to (vii).

The provisions described in (b)(i) to (iii) and, so far as relevant, (viii) are referred to below as the "misuse of information limb" and the remaining provisions as the "market manipulation limb".

In summary, taking (a) and (b) together, the provisions described in (b)(i) to (viii) apply in relation to any investment instrument admitted to trading on a domestic market and in the case of behaviour within:

- (b)(i) and (ii) and, so far as relevant, (viii) to a related investment of such an investment.
- (b)(iii) and (vii) and, so far as relevant, (viii), to a relevant product of such an investment.

The provisions described in (b)(i) and (ii) and (iv) to (vi) and, so far as relevant, (viii), also apply in relation to any investment admitted to trading on an EU market and in the case of behaviour within (b)(i) and (ii) and, so far as relevant, (viii), to a related investment of such an investment.

The territorial scope of the market abuse regime is very wide – it covers not only behaviour which occurs in the UK, but also any behaviour, anywhere in the world, which meets the requirements of (a) above in relation to a domestic market. Therefore any behaviour, wherever it occurs in the world, which relates to offeree securities or derivatives will potentially fall within the regime in cases where those offeree securities fulfil those requirements. The Directive effectively imposes a dual jurisdiction test; behaviour occurring in an EU member state other than the UK but related to investments admitted to trading on a regulated market based in the UK will also amount to market abuse in the jurisdiction in which it occurs.

As regards behaviour within (b)(iii) or (vii), a "regular user" is a reasonable person who regularly deals on the market in question in investments of the kind in question. He acts as a moderator. It is because of his role that, in very broad terms, compliance with existing legal and regulatory requirements, accepted market practice and exchange rules will generally be sufficient to avoid committing market abuse under these provisions. It should be only rarely that the regular user would consider that complying with accepted practice is an unacceptable standard. Behaviour within (b)(iv) is exempted where it is carried out for legitimate reasons and in conformity with accepted market practices. This test is rather different from the regular user test because the relevant competent authority (rather than a hypothetical market user) will have to accept the practices in question.

The misuse of information limb covers similar ground to the criminal insider dealing legislation. However, it covers a much wider range of behaviour because it is not limited to disclosure, requiring and encouraging or dealing. Accordingly, for example, seeking irrevocables will fall within the market abuse regime although it is outside the criminal insider dealing legislation. Behaviour such as underwriting also falls within the misuse of information limb because the regime starts to apply as soon as an application for admission is made.

Application of the Market Abuse Regime to Takeovers

There are significant differences between the misuse of information limb and the criminal insider dealing legislation in other areas. For example, the definition of market abuse does not generally require that a person knew that information was inside information or relevant information. Further, in Consultation Paper 59 (on the COMC) the FSA also indicated that the defences of "no expectation of profit" and "no prejudice through inequality of information" which are available under the criminal insider dealing legislation are not relevant in the context of market abuse. Each of these can play an important role in takeovers.

Instead, the COMC includes (in MAR 1.3.17C) a specific takeover-related defence contemplated in the Directive, which provides that "behaviour, based on inside information relating to another company, in the context of a public takeover bid or merger for the purpose of gaining control of that company or proposing a merger with that company does not of itself [breach the dealing prohibitions]". This covers inside information received, for example, through due diligence. In this respect, it differs from the bid facilitation defence in the criminal insider dealing legislation. The COMC defence also applies, with appropriate modifications, to behaviour within (b)(iii).

The market manipulation limb covers broadly similar ground to Section 397 FSMA (formerly Section 47 FS Act), although it is, in some respects, more extensive.

As mentioned above, the market abuse regime does not require a person to be of a particular state of mind. However, the FSA is not able to exercise most of its powers against a person who can show either that he reasonably believed that he was not either committing market abuse or requiring or encouraging another. Nor can it exercise these powers against a person who took all reasonable precautions and exercised all due diligence to avoid committing market abuse or requiring or encouraging another. These partial defences are likely to make guidance from the FSA and legal advice particularly important precautions in cases which are not straightforward. It will also be relevant whether a person has followed internal consultation and escalation procedures or sought guidance from other relevant regulators (e.g. the Takeover Panel).

9.5 Relevant powers of the Financial Services Authority

The FSA has power to impose an unlimited fine on a person who commits market abuse or censure him publicly. Section 124 FSMA requires the FSA to publish a statement of policy on the imposition of penalties and the amount of those penalties. This statement must also cover the circumstances relevant to a determination of whether a person can avail himself of the reasonable belief or all reasonable precautions defences described above. The Enforcement Manual contains the following non-exhaustive list of factors that the FSA considers relevant:

(a) the nature and seriousness of the behaviour, including whether it was deliberate or reckless, its duration and frequency, its impact on the market and others (including any financial impact) and whether any profit was made or loss avoided;
(b) the behaviour of the person in question, including whether he cooperated with the FSA or the Takeover Panel in any investigations, whether he took any steps to address the market abuse and how promptly and whether he complied with any regulatory rulings;
(c) the sophistication of the market in question;
(d) the ability of another regulator to address the matter – this factor is obviously very important in the context of takeovers;
(e) consistency;
(f) the impact any penalty may have on the interests of the market or any consumers: it is specifically made clear that the FSA recognises that it may not be in the interests of consumers to impose a penalty where this may impact on the timing or outcome of a takeover bid; and
(g) the previous disciplinary record of the person whose behaviour is at issue.

The FSA has indicated that the factors relevant to the form of the penalty (fine or censure) include:

(a) whether the behaviour is serious and the abuser has made money or avoided a loss – all of these factors make a fine more likely;

Application of the Market Abuse Regime to Takeovers

(b) whether the person in question has taken remedial steps (especially if these have been taken at his own initiative) and whether a fine would cause exceptional hardship – either of these factors makes a public censure more likely;
(c) consistency;
(d) any other proceedings taken by the FSA in respect of market abuse – for example, if the FSA chooses to impose or seek restitutionary orders (*see* below) this may make a censure more likely than a penalty.

As regards the likely level of any fine, the FSA has indicated that relevant factors include:

(a) the seriousness of the behaviour in question, including its effect on the relevant market, any financial effect on other market users and its duration and frequency;
(b) whether that behaviour was deliberate or reckless;
(c) whether the person concerned is an individual;
(d) the amount of profit made or loss avoided;
(e) the conduct of the person following behaviour, including whether he cooperated with the FSA or the Takeover Panel in any investigations, whether he took any steps to address the market abuse and how promptly and whether he complied with any regulatory rulings;
(f) his disciplinary record and compliance history;
(g) consistency;
(h) previous action taken by the FSA and any action taken by other regulatory authorities; and
(i) the timing of any agreement reached as to the amount of the penalty (i.e. an early agreement may result in a reduction in the size of the penalty).

The FSA also has power to apply to court to obtain an injunction restraining market abuse or requiring remedial steps to be taken. A court to whom an application of this kind is made may, if so requested by the FSA, impose a penalty of the kind described above. Again, the FSA has given guidance in the Enforcement Manual on factors likely to be relevant to an exercise of its power to seek injunctions. These include:

(a) the nature and seriousness of the misconduct, including its impact on the market and the extent and nature of any financial impact on market users;
(b) whether the conduct has ceased and the interests of consumers are adequately protected;
(c) whether remedial steps are possible;
(d) whether there is a danger of assets being dissipated;
(e) the costs to the FSA compared with the likely resulting benefits;
(f) the disciplinary record and compliance history of the person in question; and
(g) whether another regulator can address the matter.

An example of the sort of remedial step that could be ordered is the correction of a misleading statement. It is unclear whether the injunctive power is wide enough to order the "freezing" of a takeover offer.

The FSA can also apply to court for restitutionary orders or order them on its own initiative where profits have accrued to the person who has committed market abuse or another has suffered loss as a result of it. In contrast to the position regarding injunctions, the reasonable belief and all reasonable precautions defences are available in respect of such orders. The Enforcement Manual includes guidance on the exercise of these powers. Relevant factors include:

(a) whether identifiable persons have suffered quantifiable losses and their number and the extent of any loss;
(b) the costs to the FSA compared with the likely resulting benefits;
(c) the availability of other forms of redress (e.g. through rulings of the Takeover Panel);
(d) whether those who have suffered can bring civil proceedings themselves;
(e) the conduct of those who have suffered loss; and
(f) the context, in particular whether the exercise of such powers might affect the timetable or outcome of any bid.

These disciplinary and restitutionary powers, but not the injunctive powers, are available in relation to a person who requires or encourages another to engage in behaviour which, if engaged in by the first person, would have amounted to market abuse.

Application of the Market Abuse Regime to Takeovers

In some areas (e.g. the ability to impose fines) the FSA's powers extend beyond the Takeover Panel's informal powers. It is also easy to see how the exercise of FSA powers could interfere with a bid timetable or affect the outcome of a bid.

9.6 Impact on takeovers

9.6.1 Overlap

So how much overlap is there between the market abuse regime and the City Code? Less than might be assumed for a number of reasons.

9.6.1.1 The misuse of information limb

Historically, insider dealing in a takeover context was policed by the Takeover Panel. Over the years, responsibility has moved to the London Stock Exchange and the Treasury. The City Code does still include a rule relating to insider dealing (Rule 4.1) which broadly prohibits any dealings in offeree shares or related derivatives before the announcement of a bid except by, or for, the benefit of the bidder. In practice, however, almost all cases within Rule 4.1 also involve insider dealing and are passed on by the Takeover Panel. The FSA will, however, consult the Takeover Panel if it thinks its proposed action in respect of an insider dealing matter may have an impact in relation to the takeover bid.

On a separate point, as mentioned above, the COMC safe harbour which is designed to permit takeover-related activities (MAR 1.3.17C) is different from the equivalent defence under the criminal insider dealing legislation.

9.6.1.2 Market manipulation limb

There is overlap here in two main areas:

(a) the making of disclosures, announcements, communications and releases of information; and
(b) the sale of offeree securities by the offeror or its concert parties, which is permitted by the City Code in very limited circumstances (Rule 4.2).

As regards the first of these, the timing, dissemination or availability, content or standard of care requirements of the City Code (as set out in specified rules) are given a safe harbour in the COMC so that it cannot be argued, for example, that announcements ought to have been made earlier or a different standard of care observed in order to avoid market abuse. Rule 4.2 also has a safe harbour in the COMC. In each case, the safe harbour does not apply to the extent the behaviour in question breaches a General Principle of the City Code relevant to the rule in question.

So a person who complies with the relevant City Code provisions will also have a safe harbour under the market abuse regime. As mentioned above, there is theoretical scope for regulatory disagreement here, which parties to a bid might seek to exploit, in that it is the FSA's view on whether the City Code has been complied with which is relevant for safe harbour purposes. However, it is to be expected that the Takeover Panel and the FSA will manage their relationship so as to minimise the possibility of their reaching different views.

How about City Code provisions which do not benefit from safe harbour status? The previous version of the COMC helpfully stated (by way of guidance, rather than safe harbour):

> "The FSA is satisfied that the remainder of the City Code ... [does] not permit or require behaviour which amounts to market abuse. Much of the City Code is not directed specifically at the types of behaviour prohibited by the [FSMA]; for example, many provisions are directed at ensuring that an offer or stakebuilding is conducted within an orderly framework or that shareholders are treated similarly. Other provisions, such as the rules dealing with the specific content of offeree and offeror documents, are encompassed within the general content standard in Rule 23 of the City Code and have not, therefore, been given a specific safe harbour."

That version of COMC also confirmed (again, by way of guidance) that complying with City Code rules which restrict a person's commercial freedom to acquire shares at the speed he might otherwise choose does not amount to market abuse.

Application of the Market Abuse Regime to Takeovers

These statements are still believed to represent the FSA's views. They are understood to have been omitted from the current version of the COMC following the FSA's commitment to shorten its handbook not because its views have changed.

So a person who complies with the City Code should avoid committing market abuse, either because he has the benefit of a safe harbour or because the City Code is, to a large degree, directed at other matters. But what about a person who breaches the City Code? It seems clear that not every breach of the City Code will amount to market abuse. The FSA is understood to be of the view that shareholder abuse (i.e. failure to treat shareholders equally) with which a significant part of the City Code is concerned is not market abuse. There are also a number of other rules in relation to which it is hard to believe that breach would amount to market abuse – for example Rules 10, 12 and 13 which require the inclusion of certain conditions to an offer and prohibit others. Even a breach of one of the rules of the City Code given a safe harbour may not amount to market abuse, depending on the precise circumstances.

9.6.2 Operating together in practice

Where a City Code breach is potentially also market abuse, the FSA will not necessarily get involved. As Sir Howard Davies, the then Chairman of the FSA, made clear in June 2000:

> "we fully share the objective of ensuring that the FSA is not unhelpfully dragged into takeover battles, with damaging consequences for the way in which takeovers are handled in London ... We believe that outcome can be achieved ... by means of good cooperation between the FSA and the Panel."

The Enforcement Manual and the operating arrangements between the FSA and the Takeover Panel give details on how the two regulators will interact.

First, the FSA will always refer to the Takeover Panel and give due weight to its views. It will also consult the Takeover Panel before exercising its powers if it considers that the exercise may affect the timetable or outcome of a takeover offer. It will expect parties to exhaust procedures for complaint available under the City Code.

Secondly, the FSA will not, save in exceptional circumstances, take action in respect of behaviour to which the City Code is relevant before the conclusion of procedures available under the Code or exercise its powers during the currency of a takeover offer.

The principal circumstances (other than misuse of information cases – see 9.6.1.1 above) in which the FSA is likely to consider exercising its market abuse related powers are stated to be:

(a) where the Takeover Panel is unable properly to investigate due to lack of cooperation by the relevant person;
(b) where a person has deliberately or recklessly failed to comply with a Takeover Panel ruling;
(c) where the Takeover Panel requests the FSA to consider the exercise of its powers;
(d) where the market abuse extends to securities or a class of securities which may be outside the Takeover Panel's jurisdiction;
(e) where the market abuse threatens or threatened the stability of the financial system.

Intervention by the FSA in relation to City Code governed matters is likely to be a rare event and it is likely to be very unusual for this intervention to be contemporaneous. However, as mentioned above, the FSA is unable to fetter its discretion. So, while it is open to the FSA to adopt policy statements of the kind described above, in order to avoid successful judicial review, it will need to consider, in each individual case, whether it is appropriate to follow its policy in the circumstances or whether the case in question is one which merits its intervention. This is where the scope for tactical attempts to involve the FSA lies, although the FSA should be able to minimise the benefits to a person of doing so by being very fast on its feet.

Further, parties to bids may well have observed close liaison between the Panel and the FSA. Where appropriate, they are likely to organise and run simultaneous and cooperative decision-making processes to minimise disruption to the takeover timetable and the possibility of parties to a bid playing them off against one another.

So will we see litigation emerging in takeovers? The jurisdictional overlap does provide some scope for this. However, in practice it has not emerged to date. Further, assuming the Takeover Panel and the FSA continue their close and constructive working relationship the scope appears limited. Indeed the back-up of the wide-ranging powers that the FSA has in respect of market abuse (in particular, the power to fine) provides useful additional support for the Panel. The fact that the FSA clearly attaches importance (in the context of its decision on whether to impose a penalty in respect of market abuse) to cooperation with regulators and to the swift taking of appropriate action should also assist the Panel as it is likely to provide an additional incentive to remedy or compensate for market abuse and to do so quickly.

The operating arrangements also provide guidance on what will happen where an investigation takes place outside the structures of a bid timetable. As a general rule, the FSA and the Takeover Panel will seek to avoid parallel investigations and will decide between them which is the most appropriate investigator, based on the nature of the misconduct, its scale and severity, the need for consistency in the application of powers, the need for expertise and the availability of resources. Where parallel investigations do occur, the arrangements envisage close liaison between the two regulators.

Chapter 10

The Takeover Directive

Julian Francis
Partner
Freshfields Bruckhaus Deringer

10.1 Background

Political agreement on the Takeover Directive was finally reached in December 2003 after 14 years of negotiation. This was only achieved as the result of a controversial compromise which makes the two most important provisions of the Directive optional – Article 9 which prohibits offeree companies from taking defensive action to frustrate bids without shareholder approval and Article 11 which allows offerors to breakthrough certain offeree company restrictions so that they can achieve full control of the offeree company. The European Parliament approved the compromise text on 16 December 2003. The Council gave final approval on 30 March 2004 and the Directive came into force on 20 May 2004. It will now have to be implemented in each Member State (and the three other EEA countries) by 20 May 2006. Only five Member States met the deadline. By the beginning of July the Directive had only been implemented in the United Kingdom, Eire, France, Luxembourg, Germany, Denmark and Hungary.

10.2 The Takeover Directive

Links to the online version of the Takeover Directive can be found at

English: http://europa.eu.int/eur-lex/pri/en/oj/dat/2004/l_142/l_14220040430en00120023.pdf
German: http://europa.eu.int/eur-lex/pri/de/oj/dat/2004/l_142/l_14220040430de00120023.pdf
French: http://europa.eu.int/eur-lex/pri/fr/oj/dat/2004/l_142/l_14220040430fr00120023.pdf

The principal provisions of the agreed text of the Directive are set out below.

10.2.1 Article 1 – scope

The Directive only applies to takeover bids for the securities of a company governed by the law of a Member State if those securities are admitted to trading on a regulated market in one or more Member States. 'Takeover bid' means a public offer (other than by the offeree company itself and whether it is mandatory or voluntary) made to the holders of the securities of a company to acquire all or some of such securities which follows, or has as its objective, the acquisition of control. 'Securities' means transferable securities carrying voting rights in a company (this is thought to mean securities that carry voting rights in all circumstances at general meetings i.e. not preference shares with limited voting rights). So, the scope of the companies and merger transactions covered by the Directive is narrow. However, Member States can choose to regulate a wider range of companies and merger transactions if they want to. The UK will take advantage of this to allow the Takeover Panel to continue to regulate the wider range of companies and merger transactions covered by the Takeover Code. The Directive does not apply to bids for open-ended investment companies. Nor does it apply to bids for central banks.

10.2.2 Article 2 – definitions

Various terms are defined, including 'takeover bid', 'securities', 'persons acting in concert' and 'multiple vote securities'.

10.2.3 Article 3 – general principles

Member States must ensure that the following principles are complied with when implementing the Directive.

- All holders of the securities of an offeree company of the same class must be given equivalent treatment – in particular, if a person acquires control of a company, the other holders of securities must be protected (as 'control' is not defined, it is up to each Member State to decide at what level to apply it).
- Holders of the securities in an offeree company must have sufficient time and information to enable them to reach a properly

informed decision on the bid – the board of the offeree company must give its views on the effects of implementation of the bid on employment, conditions of employment and the company's business locations.
- The board of an offeree company must act in the interests of the company as a whole, and must not deny the holders of securities the opportunity to decide on the merits of the bid.
- False markets must not be created in the securities of the offeree company, the offeror company or any other company concerned by the bid in such a way that the rise or fall in the prices of the securities becomes artificial and the normal functioning of the markets is distorted.
- An offeror may only announce a bid after ensuring that it can fulfil in full any cash consideration it offers and after having taken all reasonable measures to secure the implementation of any other type of consideration.
- Offeree companies must not be hindered in the conduct of their affairs for longer than is reasonable by a bid for their securities.

In order to ensure compliance with these general principles, Member States must ensure that these minimum requirements are observed. In the UK, these general principles will be substituted for the General Principles in the Takeover Code. However, they may also lay down their own additional conditions and more stringent provisions. The UK will take advantage of this to maintain the Takeover Code in very much its current form.

10.2.4 Article 4 – supervisory authority

Each Member State is required to designate an authority to supervise bids, which can be a public or private body. The supervisory authorities are required to exercise their functions impartially and independently from all parties to the bid.

This Article also sets out which supervisory authority will be responsible for supervising a bid. There are two alternatives. The supervisory authority in the Member State in which the offeree company has its registered office will be responsible if the securities of that company are admitted to trading on a regulated market in that Member State (the 'home supervisory authority'). This will usually be the case, as most companies will get a listing in the country where they are incorporated and have their registered office (even if they also get listings elsewhere). However, if the securities of the offeree company are not admitted to trading on a regulated market in the Member State in which the company has its registered office, responsibility will rest with the supervisory authority in the Member State on whose regulated market the securities of the offeree company are admitted to trading (the 'host supervisory authority'), but it will share responsibility with the home supervisory authority.

Separate to the issue of the relevant authority is the question of which takeover rules apply. If there is a single supervisory authority, its takeover rules will apply to the bid. If responsibility for supervision is shared, the Article sets out which takeover rules will apply. Matters relating to the consideration offered in a bid (particularly the price) and to the procedure of the bid (in particular information on the offeror's decision to make an offer, the contents of the offer document and the disclosure of the offer) are to be dealt with in accordance with the takeover rules of the host supervisory authority. Matters relating to information for employees of the offeree company and matters relating to company law (in particular the percentage of voting rights that confers control and any derogation from the obligation to launch a bid, as well as the conditions under which the board of the offeree company may undertake any action that might result in the frustration of the offer) are to be dealt with in accordance with the takeover rules of the home supervisory authority.

Although the examples given are helpful to a certain extent, the terms 'procedure of the bid' and 'company law' are not defined. It is therefore not clear how jurisdiction will be shared and there is no mechanism to resolve any jurisdictional disputes between supervisory authorities. As a result there is likely to be delay and litigation. At present, there are few companies which choose to have their sole listing in a country different from their country of incorporation and registration. However, the number of companies affected may grow as European stock exchanges merge and new electronic markets are developed. It is also not clear how jurisdiction will be shared if one Member State has implemented the Directive and the other Member State has not (and Member States may well implement at different times either before or after the 20 May 2006 deadline).

Supervisory authorities must ensure that information they receive is kept confidential. They are also required to cooperate with each other and other authorities supervising capital markets, supply each other with relevant information and help each other to investigate any breaches of takeover rules made under the Directive.

Supervisory authorities must ensure that the parties to a bid comply with the rules made under the Directive. However, provided the general principles in Article 3 are respected, Member States can, when implementing the Directive, allow derogations from the takeover rules either by including such derogations in the takeover rules (in order to take account of circumstances determined at national level) or by granting the supervisory authorities power to waive the takeover rules to take account of circumstances determined at national level or in other specific circumstances (provided they give a reasoned decision for doing so).

At the insistence of the UK, Article 4(6) was included to make it clear that Member States can choose which body will deal with disputes or irregularities arising under the takeover rules, and whether and under what circumstances parties to a bid are entitled to bring administrative or judicial proceedings. It is also made clear that the Directive does not affect:

- the power that courts may have in a Member State to decline to hear legal proceedings and decide whether or not such proceedings affect the outcome of a bid; or
- the powers of Member States to determine the legal position concerning the liability of supervisory authorities or concerning litigation between the parties to a bid.

The UK has made use of Article 4(6) in its draft implementing legislation to restrict tactical litigation in relation to bids. However, it is unlikely that any other Member States will take advantage of it.

10.2.5 Article 5 – mandatory bid

Member States must ensure that the takeover rules require a mandatory bid for a company if a person (or persons acting in concert with him) acquires securities that, when added to any existing holdings of securities, result in that person having a specified percentage of the voting rights of the company giving him control of it. 'Control' is not defined. The percentage of voting rights that confers control is to be determined by the takeover rules of the Member State where the offeree company has its registered office. Member States are not required to specify the same percentage threshold and there is no maximum threshold (e.g. it could be over 50 per cent of the voting rights of the offeree company).

The mandatory bid must be made at an equitable price. This is defined as the highest price paid by the offeror or its concert parties for the same securities during a period of between six and 12 months prior to the bid (Member States are allowed to fix the period within these parameters). However, provided the general principles in Article 3 are respected, supervisory authorities can be given discretion to adjust this price either upwards or downwards in circumstances and according to criteria which are clearly set out by Member States. Any decision to adjust the equitable price must be substantiated and made public. If before the mandatory bid closes the offeror or any concert party purchases securities at above the offer price, the offeror must increase its offer to not less than that price.

The offeror may offer securities or cash (or a combination of both) as consideration. However, the offeror must offer a cash consideration (at least as an alternative) unless it offers liquid securities admitted to trading on a regulated market in a Member State. In any event, the offeror must offer a cash consideration (at least as an alternative) if the offeror alone or in conjunction with its concert parties has, during a period of between six and 12 months (as determined by the Member State) before the bid was made public and ending on the expiry of the acceptance period, acquired for cash securities carrying 5 per cent or more of the voting rights in the offeree company.

The mandatory bid provision does not apply if the offeror obtains control as part of a general, voluntary offer.

In addition, Member States are allowed to provide for other protections for minority shareholders as long as they do not hinder the normal course of the bid (i.e. they are not allowed to introduce additional protections that would provide defensive measures for offeree companies).

10.2.6 Article 6 – information on the bid

Member States must ensure that rules are in force requiring that the decision to make a bid is made public without delay and that the supervisory authorities are informed of the bid. As soon as the bid has been made public, the boards of the offeror and the offeree company must inform the representatives of their employees (or, where there are no such representatives, the employees themselves).

Member States must also ensure that rules are in force requiring the offeror to draw up and make public in good time an offer document containing certain specific, basic items of information listed in the Directive and, more generally, all the information necessary to enable the holders of securities of the offeree company to reach a properly informed decision on the bid. Before the offer document is made public, the offeror must communicate it to the supervisory authority. It is not necessary for the supervisory authority to approve it, but it can do so if it wants to. When it is made public, the boards of the offeror and the offeree company must communicate it to the representatives of its employees (or, where there are no such representatives, to the employees themselves). Where the offer document is approved by the supervisory authority, it must be accepted for distribution, subject to any translation, in the other Member States on whose markets the securities of the offeree company are admitted to trading without it being necessary to obtain the approval of those supervisory authorities and without their being able to require additional information to be included in the offer document (other than information that is specific to their market in relation to the formalities to be complied with for accepting the bid and for receiving the consideration and the tax to which the consideration will be subject).

Member States must also ensure that rules are in force requiring the parties to a bid to provide the supervisory authority at any time on request with all information in relation to the bid that is necessary for the supervisory authority to discharge its functions.

10.2.7 Article 7 – period for acceptance

Member States must provide that the time allowed for the acceptance of a bid may not be less than two weeks nor more than 10 weeks from the date of publication of the offer document. However, they are allowed to prolong the period on condition that the offeror gives at least two weeks' prior notice of its intention to close the bid. Member States are also allowed to provide for rules modifying the acceptance period in specific cases and to authorise the supervisory authority to grant a derogation in order to allow the offeree company to organise a general meeting to consider the bid.

10.2.8 Article 8 – disclosure of the bid

Member States must ensure that rules are in force that require a bid to be made public so as to ensure market transparency and integrity for the securities of the offeree company, of the offeror or of any other company affected by the bid, and that in particular avoid the publication or dissemination of false or misleading information.

Member States must also make sure that rules are in force that provide for the disclosure of all information or documents required so as to ensure that they are both readily and promptly available to the holders of securities at least in those Member States where the securities of the offeree company are admitted to trading on a regulated market and to the representatives of the employees of the offeree company and the offeror (or, where there are no such representatives, to the employees themselves).

10.2.9 Article 9 – prohibition on taking defensive action to frustrate bids

Member States must ensure that rules are in force requiring that at the latest after the announcement of the bid, and until the result of the bid is made public or the bid lapses, the board of the offeree company should not take any action (other than seeking alternative bids) that may result in the frustration of the offer (and particularly before issuing shares that may result in a lasting impediment to the offeror acquiring control of the offeree company) unless it has the prior authorisation of the general meeting of the shareholders given for this purpose. If the board has a two-tier structure, this restriction applies to both the management and the supervisory board. Any decisions taken prior to this period but not yet partly or completely implemented also require shareholder approval if the decision was outside the normal course of business and its implementation may result in the frustration of the bid. Under Article 12, Member States can decide to opt out of this prohibition. In line with Rule 21 of the Takeover Code, the UK proposes to apply Article 9.

Member States must also ensure that rules are in force requiring that the board of the offeree company draws up and makes public a document setting out its opinion of the bid and the reasons on which it is based, including its views on the effects of implementation on all the interests of the company (including employment) and on the offeror's strategic planning for the offeree company and its likely repercussions on jobs and business locations (as set out in the offer document). The board must append to its document any opinion of the employees' representatives on the effects of implementation of the bid on employment if the board receives it in good time.

10.2.10 Article 10 – disclosure of information (transparency)

Member States must make sure that companies to which the Directive applies publish detailed information on the following:

- the structure of their capital, including securities that are not admitted to trading on a regulated market in a Member State, where appropriate with an indication of the different classes of shares and, for each class of shares, the rights and obligations attaching to it and the percentage of total share capital that it represents;
- any restrictions on the transfer of securities, such as limitations on the holding of securities or the need to obtain the approval of the company or other holders of securities;
- significant direct and indirect shareholdings (including indirect shareholdings through pyramid structures and cross-shareholdings);
- the holders of any securities with special control rights and a description of those rights;
- the system of control of any employee share scheme where the control rights are not exercised directly by the employees;

- any restrictions on voting rights, such as limitations on the right to vote for holders of a given percentage or number of votes, deadlines for exercising the right to vote or systems, whereby, with the company's cooperation, the financial rights attaching to securities are separated from the holding of the securities;
- the agreements between shareholders that are known to the company and that may result in restrictions on the transfer of securities and/or voting rights;
- the rules governing the appointment and replacement of board members and the amendment of the articles of association;
- the powers of board members, and in particular the power to issue or buy-back shares;
- the significant agreements to which the company is a party and that take effect, alter or terminate upon a change of control of the company, and provide detail of their effects except when their nature is such that their disclosure would be seriously prejudicial to the company (unless the company is under another specific legal obligation to disclose them); and
- any agreements between the company and its board members or employees providing for compensation if they resign or are made redundant without valid reason or if their employment ceases because of a takeover bid.

This information must be published in the company's annual report.

Member States must ensure that, in the case of companies whose securities are admitted to trading on a regulated market in a Member State, the board presents an explanatory report to the annual general meeting of the company on these matters.

10.2.11 Article 11 – unenforceability of restrictions on the transfer of securities and certain voting and other rights (breakthrough)

Member States must ensure the following.

- Once a bid has been made public, any restrictions on the transfer of securities in the articles of association of the offeree company (or in contractual agreements between the offeree company and

holders of its securities, or between holders of securities of the offeree company entered into after adoption of the Directive on 30 March 2004) shall not apply *vis-à-vis* the offeror during the time allowed for acceptance of the bid.
- Once a bid has been made public, any restrictions on voting rights provided for in the articles of association of the offeree company (or in contractual agreements between the offeree company and holders of securities, or between holders of securities of the offeree company entered into after adoption of the Directive on 21 April 2004) would cease to have effect when the general meeting of the offeree company is deciding on defensive measures under Article 9 and multiple voting securities would be limited to one vote each at that meeting.
- Following a bid, if the offeror holds 75 per cent of the capital carrying voting rights, no restrictions on the transfer of securities or on voting rights referred to above nor any extraordinary rights of shareholders in relation to the appointment or removal of board members in the articles of association shall apply. Also, at the first general meeting following the bid called by the offeror to amend the articles of association or appoint/remove board members, multiple voting securities would be limited to one vote each – the offeror would have the right to convene a general meeting at short notice.

Under Article 12, Member States can decide to opt out of these provisions. The UK proposes to opt out of Article 11.

The last two provisions do not apply to securities where compensation for the restrictions on voting rights is provided for by specific pecuniary advantages (e.g. preference shares). Where rights are removed as a result of these provisions, equitable compensation must be paid for any loss suffered. The compensation terms must be set by each Member State.

These provisions do not apply where either Member States hold securities in offeree companies that confer special rights on the Member State (e.g. so-called 'golden shares') that are compatible with the Treaty of Rome or to special rights provided for in national law which are compatible with the Treaty or to cooperatives.

10.2.12 Article 12 – opting out of/into Articles 9 and 11

Member States can decide that Articles 9 and/or 11 will not apply to companies with registered offices in their territories. This would allow such companies to take defensive action to frustrate bids and/or mean that the breakthrough provisions in Article 11 would not apply to them. The UK proposes to apply Article 9 but opt out of Article 11. However, such companies can still apply Articles 9 and/or 11 if they want to. If Articles 9 or 11 are applied, Member States can allow such companies to disapply Articles 9 or 11 (and take so-called "reciprocal action") if the offeror (or anyone who controls the offeror) is not subject to the same restrictions (so-called 'reciprocity'). The UK does not intend to allow UK companies to take reciprocal action. However, Article 12 does not appear to allow an offeree company to exercise reciprocity if the offeror is an individual, a company (wherever incorporated) whose securities are not traded on a regulated market in the EU (unless it is a subsidiary of a company incorporated in a Member State all or some of whose securities are traded on a regulated market in the EU) or any company incorporated in a country outside the EU. The last point is particularly surprising as one of the main reasons for introducing Article 12 was to create a level playing field with the US. The drafting of Article 12 does seem to not achieve this, but anyway it was thought that reciprocity would not be allowed against US offerors because it would breach certain international treaties.

This provision is likely to increase protectionism across the EU and kill off any idea of a uniform set of takeover rules throughout the EU. For example, if the UK requires Article 9 to be applied by all UK companies but the Netherlands does not require this for Dutch companies, a UK target company will not be able to take defensive action without prior approval from its shareholders, whereas a Dutch target company will be able to.

Depending on how Member States implement the Directive, the result may well be a tilted playing field between different offerors for the same target company. For example, if France requires Article 9 to be applied by all French companies, France could nevertheless decide that a French target company could disapply Article 9 (and take defensive action without shareholder approval) in relation to a bid by a company incorporated in the EU that did not have restrictions similar to Article 9 (e.g. a Dutch company). However, because Article 9 would apply to any French competing offeror, the French target company would not be allowed to disapply Article 9 in relation to a French competing offeror. So, it would be less easy for the Dutch offeror to take over the French target company than the competing French offeror.

10.2.13   Article 13 – *conduct of the bid*

Member States must ensure that rules are in force that govern the conduct of bids, at least for the following matters:

- the lapsing of bids;
- the revision of bids;
- competing bids;
- the disclosure of the result of bids; and

the irrevocability of bids and the conditions permitted.

10.2.14   Article 14 – *information for and consultation with employees' representatives*

The provisions of the Directive are without prejudice to the rules relating to the provision of information to, and consultation with representatives of the employees of the offeror and the offeree company (and, if provided by the Member State, the rules relating to co-determination with employees) set out in the relevant national laws, and in particular those adopted pursuant to Directives 94/45/EC, 98/59/EC, 2001/86/EC and 2002/14/EC.

10.2.15   Articles 15 and 16 – *squeeze-out and sell-out rights*

Member States must make sure that squeeze-out and sell-out rights are introduced for offerors and offeree company shareholders in line with the provisions in Articles 15 and 16 where there has been a bid made to all the holders of securities of the offeree company for all their securities.

The offeror must be able to require all the holders of the remaining securities to sell it those securities at a fair price in one of the following circumstances (Member States have to choose which one will apply):

- where the offeror holds securities representing not less than 90 per cent of the offeree company's capital carrying voting rights and 90 per cent of the voting rights of the offeree company (Member States can increase both these thresholds up to 95 per cent but not higher); or
- where the offeror has acquired (or firmly contracted to acquire) following acceptance of a bid securities representing not less than 90 per cent of the offeree company's capital carrying voting rights and 90 per cent of the voting rights comprised in the bid.

The offeree company's minority shareholders must be able to require the offeror to buy their remaining securities in one of the same circumstances at a fair price.

Member States must ensure that a fair price is guaranteed. The price must take the same form as the consideration offered in the bid or consist of cash, but Member States may provide that the offeror must offer cash (at least as an alternative). In the case of a voluntary bid, the consideration offered in the bid must be presumed to be fair if the offeror has acquired by acceptance of its offer securities representing not less than 90 per cent of the offeree company's capital carrying voting rights comprised in the bid. In the case of a mandatory bid, the consideration offered in the bid must be presumed to be fair. Member States may provide for these procedures to be applied on a class-by-class basis.

The procedures must be exercised within three months of the end of the time allowed for acceptance of the bid.

10.2.16 Article 17 – sanctions

Each Member State must determine the sanctions to be applied for infringement of takeover rules and take all necessary steps to ensure that they are put into effect. These sanctions must be effective, proportionate and dissuasive.

10.2.17 Article 18 – committee procedure

In relation to Article 6(3) (information to be included in offer documents) the Commission is to be assisted for a four-year period (subject to renewal) by the European Securities Committee in deciding whether or not to adopt further rules about the information to be included in offer documents.

10.2.18 Article 19 – Contact Committee

A Contact Committee is to be appointed to facilitate the harmonised application of the Directive through regular meetings and to advise the Commission, if necessary, on additions or amendments to the Directive.

10.2.19 Article 20 – revision

Because of concerns about the shared supervisory authority regime provision in Articles 4(2) to (4) and the controversy surrounding Articles 9, 10, 11 and 12, there is a specific provision stating that seven years after the Directive comes into force (i.e. after 20 May 2011), the Commission must examine the Directive in the light of the experience acquired in applying it and, if necessary, propose a revision. The examination must also include a survey of the control structures and barriers to bids not covered by the Directive.

10.2.20 Article 21 – timing of implementation

Member States must ensure that the Takeover Directive is implemented into domestic law within two years of it coming into force (i.e. by May 2006).

10.3 Impact of the Directive on EU takeover rules

The full impact of the Directive on takeover rules in the EU cannot currently be assessed because many Member States have not finalised their implementation proposals. The picture will become clearer as Member States implement the Directive. However, some points can be made now.

10.3.1 No uniform set of EU takeover rules

The Directive will not result in a uniform set of takeover rules throughout the EU. Individual countries will continue to have their own takeover rules. This is because:

- it is a minimum standards directive and does not attempt to harmonise EU takeover law except in very limited areas;
- there is very little detail in the Directive;
- the Directive will be implemented differently in each Member State;
- takeover rules in individual Member States will vary because Member States are allowed to impose their own additional and more stringent takeover rules; and
- Articles 9 and 11 will apply differently to target companies depending on how Member States and companies exercise their options.

These points are well illustrated by the mandatory bid requirement in Article 5. The control threshold that triggers the mandatory bid requirement is determined by the rules of the Member State where the offeree company has its registered office – the Directive does not require a uniform control threshold across the EU.

10.3.2 No level playing field for bids in the EU/increased protectionism across the EU

Member States can opt out of Articles 9 and 11. Germany and Luxembourg have opted out of Article 9 and it looks likely that Belgium and the Netherlands will also opt out. All the countries who have already implemented the Directive have opted out of Article 11 and it looks likely that most of the other Member States will also do the same. This will create a tilted playing field for bids in the EU and allow Member States to be protectionist (*see* the analysis of Article 12 above and the examples of what might happen).

10.3.3 Article 11 will have a major impact

If Member States do not opt out of Article 11, this will have a major impact in those countries on companies and structures with share and voting restrictions, multiple voting shares or special voting shares (e.g. dual-listed companies structures which use special voting shares and transfer restrictions to ensure that all shareholders are treated equally and that the two companies operate as a single economic unit).

10.3.4 Shared supervisory jurisdiction will be complicated

There will be complicated issues of shared supervisory jurisdiction (and which Member State's law and takeover rules apply) for companies incorporated in one Member State but whose shares are traded only in another one e.g. a German company whose shares are only traded on the London Stock Exchange (*see* the analysis of Article 4 above).

10.3.5 All listed EU companies will be subject to takeover regulation

All companies incorporated in a Member State with securities admitted to trading on an EU-regulated market will be subject to takeover regulation. There will no longer be 'orphan' companies (for example UK listed plcs that have their place of central management outside the UK, which the Takeover Panel currently refuses to regulate) – at present these have to include certain takeover precautions in their articles of association to reassure investors.

10.3.6 Easier to squeeze-out minority shareholders in Germany, Austria and Spain

Article 15 will make it easier for offerors to squeeze-out minority shareholders in Germany, Austria and Spain.

10.3.7 Mandatory bids will be required in the Netherlands

Article 5 will require the Netherlands to introduce a mandatory bid requirement if an offeror acquires control (although they can fix the control threshold at whatever level they want).

10.4 The future

Following adoption of the Directive, there will remain some significant differences of approach to takeover regulation within Europe. This is acknowledged in Article 20 of the Directive which requires the

Commission to review the Directive in May 2011 and, if necessary, propose changes. The resolution of these differences (e.g. as to the control thresholds which trigger mandatory bids) will potentially have a material effect on the harmonisation of takeover rules. However, while the debate on the Directive has continued over the past 15 years, there have been other influences for change within Europe. In the last six years new takeover rules have been adopted in Germany (2002), Italy (1998) and Austria (1999). This is a response to a number of factors, including the increase in the takeover activity in these countries and the increasing internationalisation of the shareholder profiles of many companies. As companies seek to raise capital internationally, they invite more Anglo-Saxon practices in relation to the conduct of takeovers. So, even if the Directive does not, in itself, help achieve harmonisation in significant areas, there will be other pressures for this to happen over time as the press and other commentators draw attention to the variations in the effect of laws on the interests of shareholders. Nevertheless, there remain significantly different attitudes to stakeholder interests within Europe, and this is likely to perpetuate some differences for some time yet.

THE CITY CODE ON TAKEOVERS AND MERGERS

INTRODUCTION

1 OVERVIEW

The Panel on Takeovers and Mergers (the "Panel") is an independent body, established in 1968, whose main functions are to issue and administer the City Code on Takeovers and Mergers (the "Code") and to supervise and regulate takeovers and other matters to which the Code applies in accordance with the rules set out in the Code. It has been designated as the supervisory authority to carry out certain regulatory functions in relation to takeovers pursuant to the Directive on Takeover Bids (2004/25/EC) (the "Directive"). Its Directive functions are set out in and under The Takeovers Directive (Interim Implementation) Regulations 2006 (the "Regulations"). Rules are set out in the Code (including this Introduction, the General Principles, the Definitions and the Rules (and the related Notes and Appendices)) and the Rules of Procedure of the Hearings Committee.

Further information relating to the Panel and the Code can be found on the Panel's website at www.thetakeoverpanel.org.uk. The Code is also available on the Panel's website.

2 THE CODE

Save for section 2(c) (which sets out a rule), this section gives an overview of the nature and purpose of the Code.

(a) Nature and purpose of the Code

The Code is designed principally to ensure that shareholders are treated fairly and are not denied an opportunity to decide on the merits of a takeover and that shareholders of the same class are afforded equivalent treatment by an offeror. The Code also provides an orderly framework within which takeovers are conducted. In addition, it is designed to promote, in conjunction with other regulatory regimes, the integrity of the financial markets.

The Code is not concerned with the financial or commercial advantages or disadvantages of a takeover. These are matters for the company and its shareholders. Nor is the Code concerned with those issues, such as competition policy, which are the responsibility of government and other bodies.

The Code has been developed since 1968 to reflect the collective opinion of those professionally involved in the field of takeovers as to appropriate business standards and as to how fairness to shareholders and an orderly framework for takeovers can be achieved. Following the implementation of the Directive by means of the Regulations, the rules set out in the Code

A2

INTRODUCTION *CONTINUED*

which are derived from the Directive now have a statutory basis and comply with the relevant requirements of the Directive.

(b) General Principles and Rules

The Code is based upon a number of General Principles, which are essentially statements of standards of commercial behaviour. These General Principles are the same as the general principles set out in Article 3 of the Directive. They apply to takeovers and other matters to which the Code applies. They are expressed in broad general terms and the Code does not define the precise extent of, or the limitations on, their application. They are applied in accordance with their spirit in order to achieve their underlying purpose.

In addition to the General Principles, the Code contains a series of rules. Although most of the rules are expressed in less general terms than the General Principles, they are not framed in technical language and, like the General Principles, are to be interpreted to achieve their underlying purpose. Therefore, their spirit must be observed as well as their letter.

(c) Derogations and Waivers

The Panel may derogate or grant a waiver to a person from the application of a rule (provided, in the case of a transaction and rule subject to the requirements of the Directive, that the General Principles are respected) either:

(i) in the circumstances set out in the rule; or

(ii) in other circumstances where the Panel considers that the particular rule would operate unduly harshly or in an unnecessarily restrictive or burdensome or otherwise inappropriate manner (in which case a reasoned decision will be given).

3 COMPANIES, TRANSACTIONS AND PERSONS SUBJECT TO THE CODE

This section (except for sections 3(d) and (e)) sets out the rules as to the companies, transactions and persons to which the Code applies.

(a) Companies

(i) UK, Channel Islands and Isle of Man registered and traded companies

The Code applies to all offers (not falling within paragraph (iii) below) for companies and Societas Europaea (and, where appropriate, statutory and chartered companies) which have their registered offices in the United Kingdom, the Channel Islands or the Isle of Man if any of their securities are admitted to trading on a regulated market in the United Kingdom or on any stock exchange in the Channel Islands or the Isle of Man.

Takeover Code

A₃

INTRODUCTION *CONTINUED*

(ii) Other companies

The Code also applies to all offers (not falling within paragraph (i) above or paragraph (iii) below) for public and private companies and Societas Europaea (and, where appropriate, statutory and chartered companies) which have their registered offices in the United Kingdom, the Channel Islands or the Isle of Man and which are considered by the Panel to have their place of central management and control in the United Kingdom, the Channel Islands or the Isle of Man, but in relation to private companies only when:—

(A) any of their securities have been admitted to the Official List at any time during the 10 years prior to the relevant date; or

(B) dealings and/or prices at which persons were willing to deal in any of their securities have been published on a regular basis for a continuous period of at least six months in the 10 years prior to the relevant date, whether via a newspaper, electronic price quotation system or otherwise; or

(C) any of their securities have been subject to a marketing arrangement as described in section 163(2)(b) of the Companies Act 1985 at any time during the 10 years prior to the relevant date; or

(D) they were required to file a prospectus for the issue of securities with the registrar of companies or any other relevant authority in the United Kingdom, the Channel Islands or the Isle of Man or to have a prospectus approved by the UKLA at any time during the 10 years prior to the relevant date.

In each case, the relevant date is the date on which an announcement is made of a proposed or possible offer for the company or the date on which some other event occurs in relation to the company which has significance under the Code.

The Panel appreciates that the provisions of the Code may not be appropriate to all statutory and chartered companies referred to in paragraphs (i) and (ii) above or to all private companies falling within the categories listed in paragraph (ii) above and may accordingly apply the Code with a degree of flexibility in suitable cases.

(iii) Shared jurisdiction — UK and other EEA registered and traded companies

The Code also applies (to the extent described below) to offers for the following companies:

(A) a company which has its registered office in the United Kingdom whose securities are admitted to trading on a regulated market in one or more member states of the European Economic Area but not on a regulated market in the United Kingdom;

A4

INTRODUCTION *CONTINUED*

(B) a company which has its registered office in another member state of the European Economic Area whose securities are admitted to trading only on a regulated market in the United Kingdom; and

(C) a company which has its registered office in another member state of the European Economic Area whose securities are admitted to trading on regulated markets in more than one member state of the European Economic Area including the United Kingdom if:

(I) the securities of the company were first admitted to trading only in the United Kingdom; or

(II) the securities of the company are simultaneously admitted to trading on more than one regulated market, but not on a regulated market in the member state of the European Economic Area in which it has its registered office, on or after 20 May 2006, if the company notifies the Panel and the relevant regulatory authorities on the first day of trading that it has chosen the Panel to regulate it; or

(III) the Panel is the supervisory authority pursuant to the second paragraph of Article 4(2)(c) of the Directive.

A company referred to in paragraphs (C)(II) or (III) must notify a Regulatory Information Service of the selection of the Panel to regulate it without delay.

The provisions of the Code which will apply to such offers shall be determined by the Panel on the basis set out in Article 4(2)(e) of the Directive. In summary, this means that:

- in cases falling within paragraph (A) above, the Code will apply in respect of matters relating to the information to be provided to the employees of the offeree company and matters relating to company law (in particular the percentage of voting rights which confers control and any derogation from the obligation to launch an offer, as well as the conditions under which the board of the offeree company may undertake any action which might result in the frustration of an offer) ("employee information and company law matters"); in relation to matters relating to the consideration offered (in particular the price) and matters relating to the offer procedure (in particular the information on the offeror's decision to make an offer, the contents of the offer document and the disclosure of the offer) ("consideration and procedural matters"), the rules of the supervisory authority of the member state determined in accordance with Article 4(2)(b) and (c) of the Directive as the relevant supervisory authority will apply; and

- in cases falling within paragraphs (B) or (C) above, the Code will apply in respect of consideration and procedural matters; in relation to employee information and company law matters, the rules of the supervisory authority in the member state where the offeree company has its registered office will apply.

INTRODUCTION *CONTINUED*

(iv) Open-ended investment companies

The Code does not apply to offers for open-ended investment companies as defined in Article 1(2) of the Directive.

(b) Transactions

In cases falling within paragraphs (a)(i) or (ii) above, the Code is concerned with regulating takeover bids and merger transactions of the relevant companies, however effected, including by means of statutory merger or Court approved scheme of arrangement. The Code is also concerned with regulating other transactions (including offers by a parent company for shares in its subsidiary, dual holding company transactions, new share issues, share capital reorganisations and offers to minority shareholders) which have as their objective or potential effect (directly or indirectly) obtaining or consolidating control of the relevant companies, as well as partial offers (including tender offers pursuant to Appendix 5) to shareholders for securities in the relevant companies. The Code also applies to unitisation proposals which are in competition with another transaction to which the Code applies.

In cases falling within paragraph (a)(iii) above, "offers" means only any public offer (other than by the company itself) made to the holders of the company's securities to acquire those securities (whether mandatory or voluntary) which follows or has as its objective the acquisition of control of the company concerned.

The Code applies to all the above transactions at whatever stage of their implementation, including possible transactions which have not yet been announced.

References in the Code to "takeovers" and "offers" include all transactions subject to the Code as referred to in this section.

The Code does not apply to offers for non-voting, non-equity capital unless they are offers required by Rule 15.

(c) Related matters

In addition to regulating the transactions referred to in section 3(b) above, the Code also contains rules for the regulation of things done in consequence of, or otherwise in relation to, takeovers and about cases where any such takeover is, or has been, contemplated or apprehended or an announcement is made denying that any such takeover is intended.

(d) Dual jurisdiction

Takeovers and other matters to which the Code applies may from time to time be subject to the dual jurisdiction of the Panel and an overseas takeover regulator, including offers for those companies within paragraph (a)(iii) above. In such cases, early consultation with the Panel is advised so that

A6

INTRODUCTION *CONTINUED*

guidance can be given on how any conflicts between the relevant rules may be resolved and, where relevant, which provisions of the Code apply pursuant to Article 4(2)(e) of the Directive.

(e) Re-registration of a public company as a private company

A public company incorporated in the United Kingdom, the Channel Islands or the Isle of Man may decide to re-register as a private company as a result of which, pursuant to section 3(a) above, the Code may no longer apply to it. If the Code would no longer apply in such circumstances and the relevant company has more than one shareholder, early consultation with the Panel is advised before it re-registers as a private company so that guidance can be given by the Panel on the appropriate disclosure to be made to its shareholders about the implications of the loss of Code protection.

(f) Code responsibilities and obligations

The Code applies to a range of persons who participate in, or are connected with, or who in any way seek to influence, intervene in, or benefit from, takeovers or other matters to which the Code applies.

The Code also applies to all advisers to such persons, and all advisers in so far as they advise on takeovers or other matters to which the Code applies. Financial advisers to whom the Code applies have a particular responsibility to comply with the Code and to ensure, so far as they are reasonably able, that their client and its directors are aware of their responsibilities under the Code and will comply with them and that the Panel is consulted whenever appropriate.

The Code also applies to any directors, employees or representatives through whom any body corporate, partnership or other entity to which the Code applies acts. The Panel expects all bodies corporate, partnerships and other entities to which the Code applies to ensure that their relevant directors and employees receive appropriate and timely guidance in respect of the Code and will hold any such entity responsible for its directors' and employees' acts or omissions.

The Code imposes limitations on the manner in which directors can act in connection with takeovers, which may impinge on the duties that the directors of offeror and offeree companies might owe.

The Code applies in respect of the acts and omissions of any person in connection with a takeover or any other matter to which the Code applies, notwithstanding that the offeree company may since have ceased to be subject to the Code.

In this section 3(f), references to "directors" means, in relation to any body corporate, its directors and officers, in relation to any partnership, its partners, and, in relation to any other entity, those persons exercising equivalent functions on behalf of the entity concerned.

Takeover Code

A7

INTRODUCTION *CONTINUED*

In cases of doubt, the Panel must be consulted as to the persons to whom the Code applies.

4 THE PANEL AND ITS COMMITTEES

Save for section 4(d) (which sets out a rule), this section gives an overview of the membership, functions, responsibilities and general activities of the Panel and certain of its Committees.

Details of various other Committees of the Panel are available on the Panel's website.

(a) The Panel

The Panel assumes overall responsibility for the policy, financing and administration of the Panel's functions and for the functioning and operation of the Code. The Panel operates through a number of Committees and is directly responsible for those matters which are not dealt with through one of its Committees.

The Panel comprises up to 34 members:

(i) the Chairman, who is appointed by the Panel;

(ii) up to two Deputy Chairmen, who are appointed by the Panel;

(iii) up to twenty other members, who are appointed by the Panel; and

(iv) individuals appointed by each of the following bodies:—

> The Association of British Insurers
> The Association of Investment Trust Companies
> The Association of Private Client Investment Managers and Stockbrokers
> The British Bankers' Association
> The Confederation of British Industry
> The Institute of Chartered Accountants in England and Wales
> Investment Management Association
> The London Investment Banking Association (with separate representation also for its Corporate Finance Committee and Securities Trading Committee)
> The National Association of Pension Funds.

The Chairman and the Deputy Chairmen are designated as members of the Hearings Committee. Each other Panel member appointed by the Panel under paragraphs (i) to (iii) above is designated upon appointment to act as a member of either the Panel's Code Committee or its Hearings Committee.

Up to twelve Panel members appointed by the Panel under paragraph (iii) above are designated as members of the Code Committee. The Panel may appoint designated alternates for such members of the Code

INTRODUCTION *CONTINUED*

Committee. One designated alternate may act as a member of the Panel (or the Code Committee) in a relevant member's place when he is unavailable.

Up to eight Panel members appointed by the Panel under paragraph (iii) above are designated as members of the Hearings Committee. The Panel may appoint designated alternates for such members of the Hearings Committee. One designated alternate may act as a member of the Panel (or the Hearings Committee) in a relevant member's place when he is unavailable.

The Panel members appointed by the bodies under paragraph (iv) above become members of the Panel's Hearings Committee without further designation by the Panel. Each of these bodies may appoint designated alternates for its appointees. One designated alternate may act as a member of the Panel (or the Hearings Committee) in the relevant member's place when he is unavailable. In performing their functions on the Hearings Committee, these members (and their alternates) act independently of the body which has appointed them (and not as that body's agent or delegate) and exercise their own judgment as to how to perform their functions and how to vote.

Details of the Panel and its Committees, and the names of members of the Panel and the designated alternates, are available on the Panel's website.

(b) The Code Committee

The Code Committee represents a spread of shareholder, corporate, practitioner and other interests within the Panel's regulated community. Up to twelve members of the Panel are designated by the Panel as members of the Code Committee. Its membership from time to time and Terms of Reference are available on the Panel's website.

The Code Committee carries out the rule-making functions of the Panel and is solely responsible for keeping the Code (other than those matters set out in sections 1, 2(a) and (b), 4(a), (b) and (c), 5, 7, 8 and 13 of the Introduction, which are the responsibility of the Panel) under review and for proposing, consulting on, making and issuing amendments to those parts of the Code. The Code Committee's consultation procedures are set out in its Terms of Reference. Amendments to those matters set out in sections 1, 2(a) and (b), 4(a), (b) and (c), 5, 7 and 13 of the Introduction will usually be issued by the Panel. Amendments to those matters set out in section 8 of the Introduction will be agreed by the Takeover Appeal Board and will be issued by the Panel with immediate effect.

Matters leading to possible amendment to the Code might arise from a number of sources, including specific cases which the Panel has considered, market developments or particular concerns of those operating within the markets.

INTRODUCTION *CONTINUED*

Once it has agreed that a particular matter is to be pursued, the Code Committee will prepare and publish a Public Consultation Paper ("PCP") seeking the views of interested parties on the proposals and setting out the background to, reasons for and (where available) full text of the proposed amendment. Consultation periods in relation to PCPs vary depending on the complexity of the subject, but will usually be between one and two months.

Following the end of the consultation period, the Code Committee will publish its conclusions on the proposed amendment, taking account of the responses to the PCP received, together with the final Code amendments in a Response Statement ("RS"). It is the Code Committee's policy to make copies of all non-confidential responses it receives to a PCP available on request.

In certain exceptional cases, the Code Committee might consider it necessary to amend the Code on an expedited basis, for example because a particular market development appears to the Code Committee to require that the proposed amendment be made more quickly than the usual public consultation process would permit. In such cases, the Code Committee will publish the amendment with immediate effect and without prior formal consultation, followed in due course by a PCP seeking views on the amendment, which might be later modified, or removed altogether, depending on the Code Committee's conclusions following the consultation process.

Where, in the opinion of the Code Committee, any proposed amendment to the Code either does not materially alter the effect of the provision in question or is a consequence of changes to relevant legislation or regulatory requirements, the Code Committee may publish the text of the amendment without any formal consultation process.

PCPs and RSs are available on the Panel's website.

(c) The Hearings Committee

The Hearings Committee of the Panel comprises the Chairman, up to two Deputy Chairmen, up to eight other members designated by the Panel and the individuals appointed by the bodies listed at paragraph (a)(iv) above. Its membership from time to time, Terms of Reference and Rules of Procedure are available on the Panel's website.

The principal function of the Hearings Committee is to review rulings of the Executive. The Hearings Committee also hears disciplinary proceedings instituted by the Executive when the Executive considers that there has been a breach of the Code (see section 11 below). The Hearings Committee may also be convened for hearings in certain other circumstances. The operations of the Hearings Committee are described in more detail in section 7 below.

A10

INTRODUCTION *CONTINUED*

The Hearings Committee is assisted in its proceedings by a secretary to the Hearings Committee, usually a partner in a law firm, acting as an officer of the Panel.

(d) Membership and representation restrictions

No person who is or has been a member (or an alternate of a member) of the Code Committee may simultaneously or subsequently be a member (or an alternate of a member) of the Hearings Committee or the Takeover Appeal Board.

When acting in relation to any proceedings before the Hearings Committee or the Takeover Appeal Board, the Panel shall do so only by an officer or member of staff (or a person acting as such).

5 THE EXECUTIVE

This section gives an overview of the functions, responsibilities and general activities of the Executive.

The day-to-day work of takeover supervision and regulation is carried out by the Executive. In carrying out these functions, the Executive operates independently of the Panel. This includes, either on its own initiative or at the instigation of third parties, the conduct of investigations, the monitoring of relevant dealings in connection with the Code and the giving of rulings on the interpretation, application or effect of the Code. The Executive is available both for consultation and also the giving of rulings on the interpretation, application or effect of the Code before, during and, where appropriate, after takeovers or other relevant transactions.

The Executive is staffed by a mixture of employees and secondees from law firms, accountancy firms, corporate brokers, investment banks and other organisations. It is headed by the Director General, usually an investment banker on secondment, who is an officer of the Panel. The Director General is assisted by Deputy Directors General, Assistant Directors General and Secretaries, each of whom is an officer of the Panel, and the various members of the Executive's permanent and seconded staff. In performing their functions, the secondees act independently of the body which has seconded them (and not as that body's agent or delegate). Further information about the membership of the Executive is available on the Panel's website.

6 INTERPRETING THE CODE

This section sets out the rules according to which the Executive issues guidance and rulings on the interpretation, application or effect of the Code.

The Executive gives guidance on the interpretation, application and effect of the Code. In addition, it gives rulings on points of interpretation, application or

INTRODUCTION *CONTINUED*

effect of the Code which are based on the particular facts of a case. References to "rulings" shall include any decision, direction, determination, order or other instruction made by or under rules.

(a) Interpreting the Code — guidance

The Executive may be approached for general guidance on the interpretation or effect of the Code and how it is usually applied in practice. It may also be approached for guidance in relation to a specific issue on a "no names" basis, where the person seeking the guidance does not disclose to the Executive the names of the companies concerned. In either case, the guidance given by the Executive is not binding, and parties or their advisers cannot rely on such guidance as a basis for taking any action without first obtaining a ruling of the Executive on a named basis.

In addition, the Executive may from time to time publish Practice Statements which provide informal guidance as to how the Executive usually interprets and applies particular provisions of the Code in certain circumstances. Practice Statements do not form part of the Code and, accordingly, are not binding and are not a substitute for consulting the Executive to establish how the Code applies in a particular case. Practice Statements are available on the Panel's website.

Panel Statements (see section 7(c) below), statements of the Takeover Appeal Board (see section 8(b) below) and publications of the Code Committee may also contain guidance on the interpretation, application or effect of the Code.

(b) Interpreting the Code — rulings of the Executive and the requirement for consultation

When a person or its advisers are in any doubt whatsoever as to whether a proposed course of conduct is in accordance with the General Principles or the rules, or whenever a waiver or derogation from the application of the provisions of the Code is sought, that person or its advisers must consult the Executive in advance. In this way, they can obtain a conditional ruling (on an ex parte basis) or an unconditional ruling as to the basis on which they can properly proceed and thus minimise the risk of taking action which might, in the event, be a breach of the Code. To take legal or other professional advice on the interpretation, application or effect of the Code is not an appropriate alternative to obtaining a ruling from the Executive.

In addition to giving rulings at the request of a party, the Executive may, on its own initiative, give rulings on the interpretation, application or effect of the Code where it considers it necessary or appropriate to do so.

The nature of the Executive's rulings will depend on whether or not the Executive is able to hear the views of other parties involved. If the Executive

A12

INTRODUCTION *CONTINUED*

is not able to hear the views of other parties involved, it may give a conditional ruling (on an ex parte basis), which may be varied or set aside when any views of the other parties have been heard; if the Executive is able to hear the views of other parties involved, it may give an unconditional ruling. An unconditional ruling is binding on those who are made aware of it unless and until overturned by the Hearings Committee or the Takeover Appeal Board. In addition, such persons must comply with any conditional ruling given by the Executive for the purpose of preserving the status quo pending the unconditional ruling.

Rulings of the Executive, including any grant or refusal to grant a waiver or derogation from the application of any rules, may be referred to the Hearings Committee for review as set out in section 7 below.

7 HEARINGS COMMITTEE

This section gives an overview of the procedural rules which apply to the commencement of proceedings before the Hearings Committee and the procedures followed by the Hearings Committee in connection with hearings before it. The full Rules of Procedure of the Hearings Committee are available on the Panel's website.

(a) Hearings before the Hearings Committee

The Hearings Committee can be convened in the following circumstances:

(i) if a party to a takeover or any other person affected by a ruling of the Executive and with a sufficient interest in the matter, wishes to contest a ruling of the Executive, that party or person is entitled to request that the matter be reviewed by the Hearings Committee; or

(ii) the Executive may refer a matter for review by the Hearings Committee without itself giving a ruling where it considers that there is a particularly unusual, important or difficult point at issue; or

(iii) the Executive may institute disciplinary proceedings before the Hearings Committee when it considers that there has been a breach of the Code or of a ruling of the Executive or the Panel; or

(iv) in other circumstances where the Executive or the Hearings Committee considers it appropriate to do so.

The Hearings Committee can be convened at short notice, where appropriate.

INTRODUCTION *CONTINUED*

(b) Time limits for applications for review by the Hearings Committee; frivolous or vexatious applications

Where a party to a takeover or any other person affected by a ruling of the Executive and with sufficient interest in the matter wishes a matter to be reviewed by the Hearings Committee, the Panel must be notified as soon as possible and, in any event (subject to the following paragraph), within such period as is reasonable in all the circumstances of the case (which shall not be longer than one month from the event giving rise to the application for review).

Where it considers necessary, the Executive may stipulate a reasonable time within which the Panel must be notified. Such time may, depending on the facts of the case, range from a few hours to the one month period referred to above. The Executive may also extend the usual one month period within which the Panel must be notified.

The Chairman (or, failing that, the chairman of the hearing as specified below) may, on behalf of the Hearings Committee, deal with applications for procedural directions or frivolous or vexatious requests that the Hearings Committee be convened without convening the Hearings Committee and without holding a hearing.

(c) Conduct of hearings before the Hearings Committee

The quorum for Hearings Committee proceedings is five. The Chairman or, where he is unavailable, one of the Deputy Chairmen will usually preside as chairman of the proceedings in question ("chairman of the hearing"), although if the Chairman and both Deputy Chairmen are unavailable, another member of the Hearings Committee will be appointed by the Chairman (or, failing that, by the other members of the Hearings Committee) to act as chairman of the hearing.

The Hearings Committee usually conducts its hearings using the procedure set out in its Rules of Procedure, but it (or the chairman of the hearing) may vary such procedure in such manner as it (or he) considers appropriate for the fair and just conduct and determination of the case.

At hearings before the Hearings Committee, the case is usually presented in person by the parties, which include the Executive, or their advisers. Although not usual, parties may, if they so wish, be represented by legal advisers. Usually, the parties are required to set out their case briefly in writing beforehand. The parties are permitted to call such witnesses as they consider necessary, with the consent of the chairman of the hearing.

Proceedings before the Hearings Committee are usually in private, although the chairman of the hearing may, at his discretion, direct otherwise. Parties may request that the hearing be held in public. Any such request is

A14

INTRODUCTION *CONTINUED*

considered and ruled upon by the chairman of the hearing (or, at the discretion of the chairman, by the Hearings Committee itself). In the event of a public hearing, the Hearings Committee or the chairman of the hearing may direct that the Hearings Committee should hear part or parts of the proceedings in private and may impose such other conditions relating to the non-disclosure of information relating to the proceedings as it or he considers necessary and appropriate.

In general, all parties are entitled to be present throughout the hearing and to see all papers submitted to the Hearings Committee. Occasionally, however, a party may wish to present evidence to the Hearings Committee which is of a confidential or commercially sensitive nature. In such exceptional cases, the Hearings Committee or the chairman of the hearing may, if satisfied that such course is justified, direct that the evidence in question be heard in the absence of some, or all, of the other parties involved.

The parties must at the earliest opportunity raise with the chairman of the hearing issues concerning possible conflicts of interest for members of the Hearings Committee and any other objections in relation to the proceedings. Any such issues will be resolved by a ruling of the chairman of the hearing.

Proceedings before the Hearings Committee are informal. There are no rules of evidence. A recording is taken for the Hearings Committee's own administrative purposes, but will not be retained once the proceedings are at an end. In addition, a transcript of the hearing is usually made. A party to the hearing may request a copy of the transcript, which may be provided subject to conditions, including conditions as to its confidentiality and use.

The Hearings Committee provides a copy of its ruling to the parties in writing as soon as practicable following the hearing. As part of the ruling, the Hearings Committee may give directions regarding the effects of the Executive's ruling (if any) and/or its ruling pending the outcome of an appeal (if any).

It is the usual policy of the Hearings Committee to publish its rulings by means of a Panel Statement issued as promptly as possible, having regard to all the circumstances of the case, after the ruling has been provided in writing to the parties. In certain circumstances, the Hearings Committee may issue a Panel Statement of its ruling (without providing supporting reasons) in advance of the publication of its full ruling. The chairman of the hearing may, upon application by any party, redact matters from any Panel Statement in order to protect confidential or commercially sensitive information.

If there is, or may be, an appeal to the Takeover Appeal Board against a ruling of the Hearings Committee (see section 8 below), the Hearings Committee (or the chairman of the hearing) may suspend publication of any Panel Statement, although an interim announcement may be made in these

Takeover Code

A15

INTRODUCTION *CONTINUED*

circumstances where appropriate. If there is an appeal, publication may, at the discretion of the chairman of the hearing, be suspended until after the decision of the Takeover Appeal Board or, in particular if the appeal is upheld, withheld altogether.

Panel Statements are available on the Panel's website.

Rulings of the Hearings Committee are binding on the parties to the proceedings and on those invited to participate in those proceedings, unless and until overturned by the Takeover Appeal Board.

(d) Procedural rulings

The chairman of the hearing may give such procedural rulings as he considers appropriate for the conduct and determination of the case. This includes, for the avoidance of doubt, the ability to extend or shorten any specified time limits.

(e) Right of appeal

Any party to the hearing before the Hearings Committee (or any person denied permission to be a party to the hearing before the Hearings Committee) may appeal to the Takeover Appeal Board against any ruling of the Hearings Committee or the chairman of the hearing (including in respect of procedural directions).

Notice of appeal, including a summary of the grounds of appeal and the remedy requested, must be given within such time as is stipulated by the Hearings Committee or the chairman of the hearing (or, at the discretion of the chairman, by the Hearings Committee itself) or, in the absence of such stipulation, within two business days of the receipt in writing of the ruling of the Hearings Committee or the chairman of the hearing in question.

8 TAKEOVER APPEAL BOARD

This section gives an overview of the Takeover Appeal Board (the "Board") and the procedures followed by the Board in connection with hearings before it. The full procedures of the Board are set out in its Rules, a copy of which is available on the Board's website at www.thetakeoverappealboard.org.uk.

(a) Status, purpose and membership of the Board

The Board is an independent body which hears appeals against rulings of the Hearings Committee. The Board's procedures are described in greater detail below.

The Chairman and Deputy Chairman of the Board will usually have held high judicial office, and are appointed by the Master of the Rolls. Other members, who will usually have relevant knowledge and experience of takeovers and

A16

INTRODUCTION *CONTINUED*

the Code, are appointed by the Chairman (or, failing that, the Deputy Chairman) of the Board. The names of the members of the Board are available on the Board's website.

The Board is assisted in its proceedings by a secretary to the Board (who will not be the person who acted as secretary to the Hearings Committee in the same matter), usually a partner in a law firm.

(b) Conduct of hearings before the Board

The quorum for Board proceedings is three. However, the Board hearing an appeal will usually comprise at least five members. The Chairman or, where he is unavailable, the Deputy Chairman will usually preside as chairman of the proceedings in question ("chairman of the hearing"), although if they are unavailable, another member of the Board will be appointed by the Chairman (or, failing that, by the other members of the Board) to act as chairman of the hearing.

Proceedings before the Board are generally conducted in a similar way to those before the Hearings Committee as set out in section 7(c) above, using the procedure set out in the Board's Rules. In addition, the Board or the chairman of the hearing may give such directions as it or he considers appropriate for the conduct and determination of the case.

The chairman of the hearing may, on behalf of the Board, deal with appeals relating to procedural directions of the Hearings Committee or frivolous or vexatious appeals without convening the Board and without holding an oral hearing.

The Board provides its decision to the parties in writing as soon as practicable. Decisions of the Board are usually published in a public statement, save for matters redacted in order to protect confidential or commercially sensitive information (redaction being allowed following a request by one of the parties to the hearing and at the discretion of the chairman of the hearing). Any public statement of the Board will be issued as promptly as possible, having regard to all the circumstances of the case, after the decision has been provided in writing to the parties. In certain circumstances, the Board may issue a public statement of its decision (without providing reasons at this stage) in advance of the publication of the full decision.

(c) Remedies

The Board may confirm, vary, set aside, annul or replace the contested ruling of the Hearings Committee. On reaching its decision, the Board remits the matter to the Hearings Committee with such directions (if any) as the Board (or the chairman of the hearing) considers appropriate for giving effect to its (or his) decision. The Hearings Committee will give effect to the Board's decision.

INTRODUCTION *CONTINUED*

9 PROVIDING INFORMATION AND ASSISTANCE TO THE PANEL AND THE PANEL'S POWERS TO REQUIRE DOCUMENTS AND INFORMATION

This section sets out the rules according to which persons dealing with the Panel must provide information and assistance to the Panel.

(a) Dealings with and assisting the Panel

The Panel expects any person dealing with it to do so in an open and co-operative way. It also expects prompt co-operation and assistance from persons dealing with it and those to whom enquiries and other requests are directed. In dealing with the Panel, a person must disclose to the Panel any information known to them and relevant to the matter being considered by the Panel (and correct or update that information if it changes). A person dealing with the Panel or to whom enquiries or requests are directed must take all reasonable care not to provide incorrect, incomplete or misleading information to the Panel.

A person is entitled to resist providing information or documents on the grounds of legal professional privilege.

Where a matter has been determined by the Panel and a person becomes aware that information they supplied to the Panel was incorrect, incomplete or misleading, that person must promptly contact the Panel to correct the position. In addition, where a determination of the Panel has continuing effect (such as the grant of exempt status or a concert party ruling), the party or parties to that determination must promptly notify the Panel of any new information unless they reasonably consider that it would not be likely to have been relevant to that determination.

(b) Power to require documents and information

Regulation 6 gives the Panel certain powers to require documents and information in the case of a transaction and rule subject to the requirements of the Directive. It provides that, where documents or information are reasonably required in connection with the exercise of its functions, the Panel may by notice in writing require any person:

(i) to produce any documents that are specified or described in the notice; or

(ii) to provide, in the form and manner specified in the notice, such information as may be specified or described in the notice,

within such reasonable period and at such place as is specified in the notice. It may also require any information or document so provided to be verified or authenticated in such manner as it may reasonably require. Where the Panel

A18

INTRODUCTION CONTINUED

imposes a requirement under Regulation 6, the addressee must comply with that requirement. Failure to comply with any requirement is a breach of the Code.

A person is entitled to resist providing information or documents on the grounds of legal professional privilege.

10 ENFORCING THE CODE

Sections 10(a) to 10(c) set out certain rules pursuant to which the Panel enforces the Code. Section 10(e) sets out the "offer document rules" and the "response document rules" for the purposes of Regulation 10.

It is the practice of the Panel, in discharging its functions under the Code, to focus on the specific consequences of breaches of the Code with the aim of providing appropriate remedial or compensatory action in a timely manner. Furthermore, in respect of certain breaches of the Code, disciplinary action may be appropriate (see section 11 below). For the purposes of Regulation 12(2) in the case of a transaction and rule subject to the requirements of the Directive, no contravention of any requirement imposed by or under rules shall render any transaction void or unenforceable or affect the validity of any other thing.

(a) Requirement of promptness in dealings with the Executive

If a complaint is to be made that the Code has been breached, it must be made promptly, in default of which the Executive may, at its discretion, decide not to consider the complaint. Similarly, where a person who has made a complaint to the Executive fails to comply with a deadline set by the Executive, the Executive may decide to disregard the complaint in question.

(b) Compliance rulings

If the Panel is satisfied that:

(i) there is a reasonable likelihood that a person will contravene a requirement imposed by or under rules; or

(ii) a person has contravened a requirement imposed by or under rules,

the Panel may give any direction that appears to it to be necessary in order:

(A) to restrain a person from acting (or continuing to act) in breach of rules; or

(B) to restrain a person from doing (or continuing to do) a particular thing, pending determination of whether that or any other conduct of his is or would be a breach of rules; or

(C) otherwise to secure compliance with rules.

INTRODUCTION *CONTINUED*

(c) Compensation rulings

Where a person has breached the requirements of any of Rules 6, 9, 11, 14, 15, 16 or 35.3 of the Code, the Panel may make a ruling requiring the person concerned to pay, within such period as is specified, to the holders, or former holders, of securities of the offeree company such amount as it thinks just and reasonable so as to ensure that such holders receive what they would have been entitled to receive if the relevant Rule had been complied with. In addition, the Panel may make a ruling requiring simple or compound interest to be paid at a rate and for a period (including in respect of any period prior to the date of the ruling and until payment) to be determined.

(d) Enforcement by the Courts

Under Regulation 11, in the case of a transaction and rule subject to the requirements of the Directive, the Panel may seek enforcement by the courts. If the court is satisfied that:

(i) there is a reasonable likelihood that a person will contravene a requirement imposed by or under rules; or

(ii) a person has contravened a requirement imposed by or under rules or a requirement imposed under Regulation 6,

the court may make any order it thinks fit to secure compliance with the requirement. Any failure to comply with a resulting court order may be a contempt of court.

(e) Bid documentation rules

For the purposes of Regulation 10, in the case of a transaction and rule subject to the requirements of the Directive, the "offer document rules" and the "response document rules" are those parts of Rules 24 and 25 respectively which are set out in Appendix 6 and, in each case, Rule 27 to the extent that it requires the inclusion of material changes to, or the updating of, the information in those parts of Rules 24 or 25, as the case may be, in relation to the offer documents and offeree board circulars referred to in Rules 30.1 and 30.2 respectively and the revised offer documents and subsequent offeree board circulars referred to in Rules 32.1 and 32.6(a) respectively.

11 DISCIPLINARY POWERS

This section sets out the disciplinary rules of the Panel in connection with breaches and alleged breaches of the Code.

A20

INTRODUCTION *CONTINUED*

(a) Disciplinary action

The Executive may itself deal with a disciplinary matter where the person who is to be subject to the disciplinary action agrees the facts and the action proposed by the Executive. In any other case, where it considers that there has been a breach of the Code, the Executive may commence disciplinary proceedings before the Hearings Committee. The person concerned is informed in writing of the alleged breach and of the matters which the Executive will present to the Hearings Committee. Disciplinary actions are conducted in accordance with the Rules of Procedure of the Hearings Committee, which are available on the Panel's website.

(b) Sanctions or other remedies for breach of the Code

If the Hearings Committee finds a breach of the Code or of a ruling of the Panel, it may:

(i) issue a private statement of censure; or

(ii) issue a public statement of censure; or

(iii) suspend or withdraw any exemption, approval or other special status which the Panel has granted to a person, or impose conditions on the continuing enjoyment of such exemption, approval or special status, in respect of all or part of the activities to which such exemption, approval or special status relates; or

(iv) report the offender's conduct to a United Kingdom or overseas regulatory authority or professional body (most notably the Financial Services Authority ("FSA")) so that that authority or body can consider whether to take disciplinary or enforcement action (for example, the FSA has power to take certain actions against an authorised person or an approved person who fails to observe proper standards of market conduct, including the power to fine); or

(v) publish a Panel Statement indicating that the offender is someone who, in the Hearings Committee's opinion, is not likely to comply with the Code. The rules of the FSA and certain professional bodies oblige their members, in certain circumstances, not to act for the person in question in a transaction subject to the Code, including a dealing in relevant securities requiring disclosure under Rule 8 (so called "cold-shouldering"). For example, the FSA's rules require a person authorised under the Financial Services and Markets Act 2000 ("FSMA") not to act, or continue to act, for any person in connection with a transaction to which the Code applies if the firm has reasonable grounds for believing that the person in question, or his principal, is not complying or is not likely to comply with the Code.

INTRODUCTION *CONTINUED*

12 CO-OPERATION AND INFORMATION SHARING

This section summarises the relevant provisions of the Regulations and sets out the rules as to the basis on which the Panel will effect service of documents under Article 4(4) of the Directive and the professional secrecy obligations applying in relation to information held by the Panel in connection with the exercise of its functions which does not fall within Regulation 7.

The Panel, to the extent it has power to do so, takes such steps as it considers appropriate to co-operate with the FSA, other supervisory authorities designated for the purposes of the Directive and regulators outside the United Kingdom having functions similar to the FSA or to the Panel, including by the sharing of information which the Panel is permitted to disclose (see below). It may also exercise its powers to require documents and information (see section 9(b) above) for this purpose.

Where any supervisory authority designated for the purposes of the Directive by another member state or any authority responsible for the supervision of capital markets in another member state requests the Panel to serve any legal document in pursuance of its obligation of co-operation under Article 4(4) of the Directive, the Panel shall serve that document by first class post to the address specified for service in the request, and shall inform the requesting authority accordingly. No other method of service will be adopted by the Panel, even where the request specifies another method of service. In cases where:

(a) no address for service is specified in the request; or

(b) the request specifies an address for service outside of the United Kingdom; or

(c) service of the document is validly refused by the party upon whom it is to be served; or

(d) the Panel has been unable to serve the document for any other reason,

the Panel shall return the document unserved to the requesting authority, along with a statement of the reasons for non-service.

Under Regulation 7, in the case of a transaction and rule subject to the requirements of the Directive, information received by the Panel in connection with the exercise of its Directive functions may not be disclosed without the consent of the individual (where it concerns a person's private affairs) or business to which it relates except as permitted by the Regulations. Part 2 of Schedule 1 to the Regulations includes gateways to allow the Panel to pass information it receives in the exercise of its Directive functions to United Kingdom and overseas regulatory authorities and other persons in accordance with the conditions laid down in that Schedule. The

A22

INTRODUCTION *CONTINUED*

circumstances in which this may occur include, but are not limited to, the circumstances falling within paragraph 11(b)(iv) above.

Information (in whatever form) relating to the private affairs of an individual or to any particular business not falling within Regulation 7 which is created or held by the Panel in connection with the exercise of its functions, will not be disclosed by the Panel except as permitted in the circumstances set out in Regulations 7(2), (3) and (6). A direct or indirect recipient of such information from the Panel may disclose it in the circumstances set out in Regulations 7(2), (3), (4) and (6).

The Panel works closely with the FSA in relation to insider dealing and market abuse.

13 FEES AND CHARGES

The document charges set out in the Code shall be payable by the persons and in the circumstances set out in the Code.

Third parties shall pay such charges as the Panel may reasonably require for any goods (including copies of the Code) or services (including in relation to the granting, and maintenance, of exempt principal trader or exempt fund manager status as set out in the Definitions section of the Code) it provides. These charges are set out on the Panel's website.

B1

GENERAL PRINCIPLES

1. All holders of the securities of an offeree company of the same class must be afforded equivalent treatment; moreover, if a person acquires control of a company, the other holders of securities must be protected.

2. The holders of the securities of an offeree company must have sufficient time and information to enable them to reach a properly informed decision on the bid; where it advises the holders of securities, the board of the offeree company must give its views on the effects of implementation of the bid on employment, conditions of employment and the locations of the company's places of business.

3. The board of an offeree company must act in the interests of the company as a whole and must not deny the holders of securities the opportunity to decide on the merits of the bid.

4. False markets must not be created in the securities of the offeree company, of the offeror company or of any other company concerned by the bid in such a way that the rise or fall of the prices of the securities becomes artificial and the normal functioning of the markets is distorted.

5. An offeror must announce a bid only after ensuring that he/she can fulfil in full any cash consideration, if such is offered, and after taking all reasonable measures to secure the implementation of any other type of consideration.

6. An offeree company must not be hindered in the conduct of its affairs for longer than is reasonable by a bid for its securities.

DEFINITIONS

Acting in concert

This definition has particular relevance to mandatory offers and further guidance with regard to behaviour which constitutes acting in concert is given in the Notes on Rule 9.1.

Persons acting in concert comprise persons who, pursuant to an agreement or understanding (whether formal or informal), co-operate to obtain or consolidate control (as defined below) of a company or to frustrate the successful outcome of an offer for a company. A person and each of its affiliated persons will be deemed to be acting in concert all with each other (see Note 2 below).

Without prejudice to the general application of this definition, the following persons will be presumed to be persons acting in concert with other persons in the same category unless the contrary is established:—

(1) a company, its parent, subsidiaries and fellow subsidiaries, and their associated companies, and companies of which such companies are associated companies, all with each other (for this purpose ownership or control of 20% or more of the equity share capital of a company is regarded as the test of associated company status);

(2) a company with any of its directors (together with their close relatives and related trusts);

(3) a company with any of its pension funds and the pension funds of any company covered in (1);

(4) a fund manager (including an exempt fund manager) with any investment company, unit trust or other person whose investments such fund manager manages on a discretionary basis, in respect of the relevant investment accounts;

(5) a connected adviser with its client and, if its client is acting in concert with an offeror or with the offeree company, with that offeror or with that offeree company respectively, in each case in respect of the interests in shares of that adviser and persons controlling#, controlled by or under the same control as that adviser (except in the capacity of an exempt fund manager or an exempt principal trader); and

(6) directors of a company which is subject to an offer or where the directors have reason to believe a bona fide offer for their company may be imminent. (See Note 5 on this definition.)

#See Note at end of Definitions Section.

C2

DEFINITIONS *CONTINUED*

NOTES ON ACTING IN CONCERT

1. Break up of concert parties

Where the Panel has ruled that a group of persons is acting in concert, it will be necessary for clear evidence to be presented to the Panel before it can be accepted that the position no longer obtains.

2. Affiliated persons

For the purposes of this definition an "affiliated person" means any undertaking in respect of which any person:

(a) has a majority of the shareholders' or members' voting rights;

(b) is a shareholder or member and at the same time has the right to appoint or remove a majority of the members of its board of directors;

(c) is a shareholder or member and alone controls a majority of the shareholders' or members' voting rights pursuant to an agreement entered into with other shareholders or members; or

(d) has the power to exercise, or actually exercises, dominant influence or control.

For these purposes, a person's rights as regards voting, appointment or removal shall include the rights of any other affiliated person and those of any person or entity acting in his own name but on behalf of that person or of any other affiliated person.

3. Underwriting arrangements

The relationship between an underwriter (or sub-underwriter) of a cash alternative offer and an offeror may be relevant for the purpose of this definition. Underwriting arrangements on arms' length commercial terms would not normally amount to an agreement or understanding within the meaning of acting in concert. The Panel recognises that such underwriting arrangements may involve special terms determined by the circumstances, such as weighting of commissions by reference to the outcome of the offer. However, in some cases, features of underwriting arrangements, for example the proportion of the ultimate total liability assumed by an underwriter, the commission structure or the degree of involvement of the underwriter with the offeror in connection with the offer, may be such as to lead the Panel to conclude that a sufficient level of understanding has been created between the offeror and the underwriter to amount to an agreement or understanding within the meaning of acting in concert. In cases of doubt, the Panel should be consulted.

Takeover Code

DEFINITIONS *CONTINUED*

NOTES ON ACTING IN CONCERT continued

4. Companies Act 1985

This definition applies only in respect of the relevant provisions of the Code. Separate provisions dealing with "persons acting together" are contained in the Companies Act 1985. Any Panel view expressed in relation to "acting in concert" can only relate to the Code and should not be taken as guidance on the interpretation of such statutory provisions.

5. Standstill agreements

Agreements between a company, or the directors of a company, and a person which restrict that person or the directors from either offering for, or accepting an offer for, the shares of the company or from increasing or reducing the number of shares in which he or they are interested, may be relevant for the purpose of this definition. In cases of doubt, the Panel should be consulted.

6. Consortium offers

Investors in a consortium (eg through a vehicle company formed for the purpose of making an offer) will normally be treated as acting in concert with the offeror. Where such an investor is part of a larger organisation, the Panel should be consulted to establish which other parts of the organisation will also be regarded as acting in concert.

Where the investment in the consortium is, or is likely to be, 10% or less of the equity share capital (or other similar securities) of the offeror, the Panel will normally be prepared to waive the acting in concert presumption in relation to other parts of the organisation, including any connected fund manager or principal trader, provided it is satisfied as to the independence of those other parts from the investor. Where the investment is, or is likely to be, more than 10% but less than 50%, the Panel may be prepared to waive the acting in concert presumption in relation to other parts of the organisation depending on the circumstances of the case. (See also Connected fund managers and principal traders in the Definitions Section and Rule 7.2.)

7. Pension funds

The presumption that a company is acting in concert with any of its pension funds will normally be rebutted if it can be demonstrated to the Panel's satisfaction that the assets of the pension fund are managed under an agreement or arrangement with an independent third party which gives such third party absolute discretion regarding dealing, voting and offer acceptance decisions relating to the fund. Where, however, the discretion given is not absolute, the presumption will be capable of being rebutted, provided that the pension fund trustees do not exercise any powers they have retained to intervene in such decisions.

C4

DEFINITIONS *CONTINUED*

NOTES ON ACTING IN CONCERT continued

8. *Sub-contracted fund managers*

Where a fund manager sub-contracts discretionary management of funds to another independent fund manager, the Panel will normally regard those funds as controlled by the latter if the discretion regarding dealing, voting and offer acceptance decisions relating to the funds, originally granted to the fund manager, has been transferred to the sub-contracted fund manager and presumption (4) will apply to the sub-contracted fund manager in respect of those funds. This approach assumes that the sub-contracted fund manager does not take instructions from the beneficial owner or from the originally contracted manager on the dealings in question and that fund management arrangements are not established or used to avoid disclosure.

9. *Irrevocable commitments*

A person will not normally be treated as acting in concert with an offeror or the offeree company by reason only of giving an irrevocable commitment. However, the Panel will consider the position of such a person in relation to the offeror or the offeree company (as the case may be) in order to determine whether he is acting in concert if either:

(a) the terms of the irrevocable commitment give the offeror or the offeree company (as the case may be) either the right (whether conditional or absolute) to exercise or direct the exercise of the voting rights attaching to the shares or general control of them; or

(b) the person acquires an interest in more shares.

The Panel should be consulted before the acquisition of any interest in shares in such circumstances.

Associate

This definition has particular relevance to disclosure of dealings under Rule 8.

It is not practicable to define associate in terms which would cover all the different relationships which may exist in an offer. The term associate is intended to cover all persons (whether or not acting in concert) who directly or indirectly are interested or deal in relevant securities of an offeror or the offeree company in an offer and who have an interest or potential interest, whether commercial, financial or personal, in the outcome of the offer.

Without prejudice to the generality of the foregoing, the term associate will normally include the following:—

(1) an offeror's or the offeree company's parent, subsidiaries and fellow subsidiaries, and their associated companies, and companies of which such

DEFINITIONS *CONTINUED*

companies are associated companies (for this purpose ownership or control of 20% or more of the equity share capital of a company is regarded as the test of associated company status);

(2) connected advisers and persons controlling#, controlled by or under the same control as such connected advisers;

(3) the directors (together with their close relatives and related trusts) of an offeror, the offeree company or any company covered in (1);

(4) the pension funds of an offeror, the offeree company or any company covered in (1);

(5) any investment company, unit trust or other person whose investments an associate manages on a discretionary basis, in respect of the relevant investment accounts;

(6) an employee benefit trust of an offeror, the offeree company or any company covered in (1); and

(7) a company having a material trading arrangement with an offeror or the offeree company.

Cash acquisitions

Acquisitions for cash include contracts or arrangements where the consideration consists of a debt instrument capable of being redeemed in less than 3 years.

Competition reference period

Competition reference period means the period from the time when an announcement is made of the referral of an offer to the Competition Commission or of the initiation of proceedings by the European Commission under Article 6(1)(c) of Council Regulation 139/2004/EC, until the time of an announcement of clearance by the Competition Commission or of the issuance of a decision under Article 8(2) of the said Council Regulation.

Connected adviser

Connected adviser normally includes only the following:

(1) in relation to the offeror or the offeree company:

    (a) an organisation which is advising that party in relation to the offer; and

    (b) a corporate broker to that party;

#See Note at end of Definitions Section.

C6

DEFINITIONS *CONTINUED*

(2) in relation to a person who is acting in concert with the offeror or the offeree company, an organisation which is advising that person either:

(a) in relation to the offer; or

(b) in relation to the matter which is the reason for that person being a member of the relevant concert party; and

(3) in relation to a person who is an associate of the offeror or of the offeree company by virtue of paragraph (1) of the definition of associate, an organisation which is advising that person in relation to the offer.

Such references do not normally include a corporate broker which is unable to act in connection with the offer because of a conflict of interest.

Connected fund managers and principal traders

A fund manager or principal trader will normally be connected with an offeror or the offeree company, as the case may be, if the fund manager or principal trader is controlled# by, controls or is under the same control as:—

(1) an offeror or any person acting in concert with it (for example as a result of being an investor in a consortium (see also Note 6 on the definition of acting in concert));

(2) the offeree company or any person acting in concert with the offeree company; or

(3) any connected adviser to any person covered in (1) or (2).

Control

Control means an interest, or interests, in shares carrying in aggregate 30% or more of the voting rights (as defined below) of a company, irrespective of whether such interest or interests give de facto control.

Date, day and period of time

Unless otherwise stated in the Code:—

(1) a reference to the date of an event is to the time of occurrence of the event on the day in question;

(2) a business day is a day on which the Stock Exchange is open for the transaction of business; and

(3) where a period of time is calculated from a stated event, the day on which that event occurs should be excluded from the calculation of the period (this is not relevant to the definition of an offer period).

#See Note at end of Definitions Section.

Takeover Code

C7

DEFINITIONS *CONTINUED*

Dealings

A dealing includes the following:—

(a) the acquisition or disposal of securities, of the right (whether conditional or absolute) to exercise or direct the exercise of the voting rights attaching to securities, or of general control of securities;

(b) the taking, granting, acquisition, disposal, entering into, closing out, termination, exercise (by either party) or variation of an option (including a traded option contract) in respect of any securities;

(c) subscribing or agreeing to subscribe for securities;

(d) the exercise or conversion, whether in respect of new or existing securities, of any securities carrying conversion or subscription rights;

(e) the acquisition of, disposal of, entering into, closing out, exercise (by either party) of any rights under, or variation of, a derivative referenced, directly or indirectly, to securities;

(f) entering into, terminating or varying the terms of any agreement to purchase or sell securities; and

(g) any other action resulting, or which may result, in an increase or decrease in the number of securities in which a person is interested or in respect of which he has a short position.

Derivative

Derivative includes any financial product whose value in whole or in part is determined directly or indirectly by reference to the price of an underlying security.

NOTE ON DEFINITION OF DERIVATIVE

The term "derivative" is intentionally widely defined to encompass all types of derivative transactions. However, it is not the intention of the Code to restrict transactions in, or require disclosure of, derivatives which are not connected with an offer or potential offer. The Panel will not normally regard a derivative which is referenced to a basket or index of securities, including relevant securities, as connected with an offer or potential offer if at the time of dealing the relevant securities in the basket or index represent less than 1% of the class in issue and, in addition, less than 20% of the value of the securities in the basket or index. In the case of any doubt, the Panel should be consulted.

C8

DEFINITIONS *CONTINUED*

Directors

Directors include persons in accordance with whose instructions the directors or a director are accustomed to act.

Exempt fund manager

An exempt fund manager is a person who manages investment accounts on a discretionary basis and is recognised by the Panel as an exempt fund manager for the purposes of the Code (see Notes under Exempt principal trader).

Exempt principal trader

An exempt principal trader is a principal trader who is recognised by the Panel as an exempt principal trader for the purposes of the Code.

NOTES ON EXEMPT FUND MANAGER AND EXEMPT PRINCIPAL TRADER

1. Persons who manage investment accounts on a discretionary basis and principal traders must apply to the Panel in order to seek the relevant exempt status and will have to comply with any requirements imposed by the Panel as a condition of its granting such status.

2. When a principal trader or fund manager is connected with the offeror or offeree company, exempt status is not relevant unless the sole reason for the connection is that the principal trader or fund manager is controlled# by, controls or is under the same control as a connected adviser to:

(1) the offeror;

(2) the offeree company; or

(3) a person acting in concert with the offeror (for example as a result of being an investor in a consortium) or with the offeree company.

References in the Code to exempt principal traders or exempt fund managers should be construed accordingly. (See also Rule 7.2.)

3. The effect of a principal trader or fund manager having exempt status is that presumption (5) of the definition of acting in concert will not apply. However, the principal trader or fund manager will still be regarded as connected with the offeror or offeree company, as appropriate. Connected exempt principal traders, but not connected exempt fund managers, must comply with Rule 38.

#See Note at end of Definitions Section.

DEFINITIONS *CONTINUED*

NOTES ON EXEMPT FUND MANAGER AND EXEMPT PRINCIPAL TRADER continued

4. In appropriate cases, a fund manager based overseas may be granted special exempt status subject to its satisfying certain conditions. References in the Code to exempt fund managers (with the exception of those in Rule 8.1(b)) include such special exempt fund managers, subject always to the conditions on which such special exempt status is granted in any particular case.

5. In appropriate cases, a trading entity may be granted exempt status on an ad hoc basis subject to the satisfaction of certain conditions. References in the Code to exempt principal traders include persons granted such ad hoc exempt status, for so long as the grant of such exempt status remains valid and subject always to the conditions on which such ad hoc exempt status is granted in any particular case.

Interests in securities

This definition and its Notes apply equally to references to interests in shares and interests in relevant securities.

A person who has long economic exposure, whether absolute or conditional, to changes in the price of securities will be treated as interested in those securities. A person who only has a short position in securities will not be treated as interested in those securities.

In particular, a person will be treated as having an interest in securities if:-

(1) he owns them;

(2) he has the right (whether conditional or absolute) to exercise or direct the exercise of the voting rights attaching to them or has general control of them;

(3) by virtue of any agreement to purchase, option or derivative he:

   (a) has the right or option to acquire them or call for their delivery; or

   (b) is under an obligation to take delivery of them,

whether the right, option or obligation is conditional or absolute and whether it is in the money or otherwise; or

(4) he is party to any derivative:

   (a) whose value is determined by reference to their price; and

   (b) which results, or may result, in his having a long position in them; and

(5) in the case of Rule 5 only, he has received an irrevocable commitment in respect of them.

C10

DEFINITIONS *CONTINUED*

NOTES ON INTERESTS IN SECURITIES

1. Gross interests

The number of securities in which a person is treated as having an interest is normally the gross number, aggregating the number of securities falling under each of paragraphs (1) to (4) (and, for the purposes of Rule 5 only, also paragraph (5)) above. If an interest in securities falls within more than one paragraph, the person shall be treated as interested in the highest number determined under the relevant paragraphs. Short positions should not be deducted.

If each of the following conditions is met, the Panel will normally allow offsetting positions to be netted off against each other:

(a) the offsetting positions are in respect of the same class of relevant security;

(b) the offsetting positions are in respect of the same investment product;

(c) save for the number of securities in question, the terms of the offsetting positions are the same, eg as to strike price and, if appropriate, exercise period; and

(d) the counterparty to the offsetting positions is the same in each case.

2. Interests of two or more persons

As a result of the way in which interests in securities are categorised, two or more persons may be treated as interested in the same securities. For example, where a shareholder grants a call option to another person, the shareholder will be interested in the shares the subject of the option as a result of paragraph (1) of the definition of interests in securities, and the option holder will be interested in those shares as a result of paragraph (3) of the definition.

3. Number of securities concerned

(a) Where the number of securities the subject of an agreement to purchase, option or derivative is not fixed, a person will normally be treated as interested in the maximum possible number of securities.

(b) Where the value of any derivative is determined by reference to the price of a number of securities multiplied by a particular factor, a person will be treated as interested in the number of reference securities multiplied by the relevant factor.

(c) Where a derivative is not referenced to any stated number (or maximum number) of securities, a person will normally be treated as interested in

Takeover Code

C11

DEFINITIONS *CONTINUED*

NOTES ON INTERESTS IN SECURITIES continued

the gross number of securities to changes in the price of which he has, or may have, economic exposure.

4. Securities borrowing and lending

If a person has borrowed or lent securities, he will normally be treated as interested in any securities which he has lent but (except in the circumstances set out in Note 17 on Rule 9.1) will not normally be treated as interested in any securities which he has borrowed. If a person has on-lent securities which he has borrowed, he will not normally be treated as interested in those securities.

5. New shares

Where a person holds securities convertible into, or warrants or options in respect of, new shares, he will be treated as interested in those securities, warrants or options but will not be treated as interested in the new shares which may be issued upon conversion or exercise. However, the acquisition of new shares on conversion or exercise of any convertible securities, warrants or options will be treated as an acquisition of an interest in the new shares which are then issued.

6. Proxies and corporate representatives

A person will not be treated as having an interest in securities by reason only that he has been appointed as a proxy to vote at a specified general or class meeting of the company concerned, or has been authorised by a corporation to act as its representative at any general or class meeting or meetings.

7. Security interests

A bank taking security over shares or other securities in the normal course of its business will not normally be considered to be interested in those shares or securities.

8. Companies Act 1985

This definition applies only in respect of the relevant provisions of the Code. Separate provisions dealing with "interests in shares" are contained in the Companies Act 1985. Any Panel view expressed in relation to interests in securities can only relate to the Code and should not be taken as guidance on the interpretation of such statutory provisions.

9. Acquisitions of interests in securities

(a) References to a person acquiring an interest in securities include any transaction or dealing (including the variation of the terms of an option in

C12

DEFINITIONS *CONTINUED*

NOTES ON INTERESTS IN SECURITIES continued

respect of, or derivative referenced to, securities) which results in an increase in the number of securities (including, where relevant, securities which have been assented to an offer) in which the person is treated as interested.

(b) A person will not be treated as acquiring an interest in securities which are the subject of an irrevocable commitment received by him as a result only of paragraph (3) of the definition of interests in securities.

(c) The Panel should be consulted if an offeror or any person acting in concert with it proposes to enter into a conditional share sale and purchase agreement or option in the context of the offer.

Irrevocable commitments and letters of intent

Irrevocable commitments and letters of intent include irrevocable commitments and letters of intent to accept or not to accept (or to procure that any other person accept or not accept) an offer and also irrevocable commitments and letters of intent to vote (or to procure that any other person vote) in favour of or against a resolution of an offeror or the offeree company in the context of the offer.

OFEX

For the avoidance of doubt in respect of those companies whose securities are traded on the OFEX market ("OFEX"), references to a Regulatory Information Service in Rules relating to public announcements or dealing disclosures should be taken to refer to the Newstrack Service ("Newstrack"). References to OFEX and Newstrack have been included in some Rules for clarity but, in cases of doubt, the Panel should be consulted.

Offer

Any reference to an offer includes any transaction subject to the Code as referred to in section 3(b) of the Introduction.

Offeree company

Any reference to an offeree company includes a potential offeree company.

Offeror

Offeror includes companies wherever incorporated and individuals wherever resident. Any reference to an offeror includes a potential offeror.

Takeover Code

DEFINITIONS *CONTINUED*

Offer period

Offer period means the period from the time when an announcement is made of a proposed or possible offer (with or without terms) until the first closing date or, if this is later, the date when the offer becomes or is declared unconditional as to acceptances or lapses. An announcement that an interest, or interests, in shares carrying in aggregate 30% or more of the voting rights of a company is for sale or that the board of a company is seeking potential offerors will be treated as the announcement of a possible offer. (See also Rule 12.2 regarding competition reference periods.)

Official List

The list maintained by the FSA in accordance with section 74(1) of the FSMA for the purposes of Part VI of the FSMA.

Principal trader

A principal trader is a person who:

(1) is registered as a market-maker with the Stock Exchange, or is accepted by the Panel as a market-maker; or

(2) is a Stock Exchange member firm dealing as principal in order book securities.

Recognised intermediary

A recognised intermediary is that part of the trading operations of a bank or securities house which is accepted by the Panel as a recognised intermediary for the purposes of the Code.

NOTES ON RECOGNISED INTERMEDIARY

1. If any part of the trading operations of a bank or securities house wishes to be accepted by the Panel as a recognised intermediary, it must apply to the Panel to be granted such status and it will have to comply with any requirements imposed by the Panel as a condition of its granting such status.

2. Recognised intermediary status is relevant only for the purposes of Note 16 on Rule 9.1, Note 1(c) on Rule 7.2 and Rule 8.3(d), in each case to the extent only that the recognised intermediary is acting in a client-serving capacity. As a result, subject to Note 3 below, a recognised intermediary will not be treated, for the purposes of Rule 9.1, as interested in (or as having acquired an interest in) any securities by virtue only of paragraph (3) or paragraph (4) of the definition of interests in securities, nor will any dealings by it in relevant securities during an offer period be required to be publicly

C14

DEFINITIONS *CONTINUED*

NOTES ON RECOGNISED INTERMEDIARY continued

disclosed under Rules 8.3(a) to (c), in each case to the extent only that the recognised intermediary is acting in a client-serving capacity.

3. Where a recognised intermediary is, or forms part of, a principal trader connected either with an offeror or potential offeror or with the offeree company, the recognised intermediary will not benefit from the dispensations afforded by Note 16 on Rule 9.1 and Note 1(c) on Rule 7.2 after the time at which the principal trader is presumed to be acting in concert with either the offeror or potential offeror or with the directors of the offeree company (as the case may be) in accordance with Rule 7.2(a) and Rule 7.2(b) respectively. However, in accordance with Rule 7.2(c), where a recognised intermediary is, or forms part of, an exempt principal trader which is connected with either an offeror or potential offeror or with the offeree company for the sole reason that it is controlled# by, controls or is under the same control as a connected adviser to that party, the recognised intermediary will not be presumed to be acting in concert with that party and will therefore continue to benefit from the dispensations afforded by Note 16 on Rule 9.1 and Note 1(c) on Rule 7.2.

Where a recognised intermediary is, or forms part of, an associate of the offeree company, it will not benefit from the exception from disclosure afforded by Rule 8.3(d) after the commencement of the offer period. Where a recognised intermediary is an associate of an offeror or potential offeror, it will not benefit from the exception from disclosure afforded by Rule 8.3(d) after the identity of the offeror or potential offeror of which it is an associate is publicly announced. After such time, dealings should be disclosed under Rule 8.1(a) or, if the recognised intermediary is, or forms part of, an exempt principal trader whose exempt status has not fallen away, Rule 38.5(a) or (b).

For the avoidance of doubt, where a recognised intermediary is, or forms part of, an exempt principal trader, its recognised intermediary status will fall away only if its exempt status falls away.

4. Any dealings by a recognised intermediary which is not acting in a client-serving capacity will not benefit from the dispensations afforded by Note 16 on Rule 9.1, Note 1(c) on Rule 7.2 and Rule 8.3(d) with the result that all such dealings by it will be subject to the provisions of the Code as if those dispensations did not apply.

5. Any dealings carried out by a recognised intermediary for the purpose of avoiding the usual application of the Code to such dealings will constitute a serious breach of the Code. If the Panel determines that a recognised intermediary has carried out such dealings, it will be prepared to rule, inter alia, that recognised intermediary status should be withdrawn for such period of time as the Panel may consider appropriate in the circumstances.

#See Note at end of Definitions Section.

DEFINITIONS *CONTINUED*

Regulated market

A regulated market is a market within the meaning of Article 1(13) of Directive 93/22/EEC (the Investment Services Directive). A list of regulated markets within the EEA is maintained on the website of the EU Commission: europa.eu.int/comm/index_en.htm. UK regulated markets are listed on the Panel's website: www.thetakeoverpanel.org.uk.

Regulatory Information Service

A Regulatory Information Service ("RIS") is any of the services set out in Appendix 3 to the Listing Rules.

Relevant securities

Relevant securities include:—

(a) securities of the offeree company which are being offered for or which carry voting rights;

(b) equity share capital of the offeree company and an offeror;

(c) securities of an offeror which carry substantially the same rights as any to be issued as consideration for the offer; and

(d) securities of the offeree company and an offeror carrying conversion or subscription rights into any of the foregoing.

Securities exchange offer

Securities exchange offer means an offer in which the consideration includes securities of the offeror, other than loan stock or loan notes (unless such stock or notes carry substantially the same rights as any other securities of the offeror in issue or conversion or subscription rights into any such securities or into equity share capital of the offeror).

Shares or securities

(1) Except as set out below or as the context otherwise requires, references to shares, including when used in other expressions such as shareholders (but excluding equity share capital), include securities, and vice versa.

(2) In paragraph 3(a)(iii) and in the second paragraph of section 3(b) of the Introduction, the securities referred to are only transferable securities carrying voting rights.

(3) In paragraphs 3(a)(i) and (ii) and in the first paragraph of section 3(b) of the Introduction, the shares/securities referred to are only those shares/securities comprised in the company's equity share capital (whether voting or non-voting) and other transferable securities carrying voting rights.

C16

DEFINITIONS *CONTINUED*

Stock Exchange

London Stock Exchange plc

Treasury shares

All percentages of voting rights, share capital and relevant securities are to be calculated by reference to the relevant percentage held and in issue outside treasury. A transfer or sale of shares by a company from treasury will normally be treated in the same way as an issue of new shares.

UKLA

The FSA acting in its capacity as the competent authority for the purposes of Part VI of the FSMA

UKLA Rules

UKLA Rules include the Listing Rules, the Disclosure Rules and the Prospectus Rules of the FSA (or any of them as the context may require).

Voting rights

Except for the purpose of Rule 11, voting rights means all the voting rights attributable to the capital of a company which are currently exercisable at a general meeting.

NOTE ON DEFINITIONS

The normal test for whether a person is controlled by, controls or is under the same control as another person will be by reference to the definition of control. There may be other circumstances which the Panel will regard as giving rise to such a relationship (eg where a majority of the equity share capital is owned by another person who does not have a majority of the voting rights); in cases of doubt, the Panel should be consulted.

RULES

SECTION D. THE APPROACH, ANNOUNCEMENTS AND INDEPENDENT ADVICE

RULE 1. THE APPROACH

(a) The offer must be put forward in the first instance to the board of the offeree company or to its advisers.

(b) If the offer, or an approach with a view to an offer being made, is not made by the ultimate offeror or potential offeror, the identity of that person must be disclosed at the outset.

(c) A board so approached is entitled to be satisfied that the offeror is, or will be, in a position to implement the offer in full.

D2

RULE 2. SECRECY BEFORE ANNOUNCEMENTS; THE TIMING AND CONTENTS OF ANNOUNCEMENTS

2.1 SECRECY

The vital importance of absolute secrecy before an announcement must be emphasised. All persons privy to confidential information, and particularly price-sensitive information, concerning an offer or contemplated offer must treat that information as secret and may only pass it to another person if it is necessary to do so and if that person is made aware of the need for secrecy. All such persons must conduct themselves so as to minimise the chances of an accidental leak of information.

NOTES ON RULE 2.1

1. Warning clients

It should be an invariable routine for advisers at the very beginning of discussions to warn clients of the importance of secrecy and security. Attention should be drawn to the Code, in particular to this Rule and to restrictions on dealings.

2. Proof printing

Proof printing documents before a public announcement has been made carries a particular risk of leaks of price-sensitive information; in cases where it is regarded as appropriate to undertake such printing, every possible precaution must be taken to ensure confidentiality.

2.2 WHEN AN ANNOUNCEMENT IS REQUIRED

An announcement is required:—

(a) when a firm intention to make an offer (the making of which is not, or has ceased to be, subject to any pre-condition) is notified to the board of the offeree company from a serious source, irrespective of the attitude of the board to the offer;

(b) immediately upon an acquisition of any interest in shares which gives rise to an obligation to make an offer under Rule 9. The announcement that an obligation has been incurred should not be delayed while full information is being obtained; additional information can be the subject of a later supplementary announcement;

(c) when, following an approach to the offeree company, the offeree company is the subject of rumour and speculation or there is an untoward movement in its share price;

(d) when, before an approach has been made, the offeree company is the subject of rumour and speculation or there is an untoward

Takeover Code

D3

RULE 2 *CONTINUED*

movement in its share price and there are reasonable grounds for concluding that it is the potential offeror's actions (whether through inadequate security or otherwise) which have led to the situation;

(e) when negotiations or discussions are about to be extended to include more than a very restricted number of people (outside those who need to know in the companies concerned and their immediate advisers). An offeror wishing to approach a wider group, for example in order to arrange financing for the offer (whether equity or debt), to seek irrevocable commitments or to organise a consortium to make the offer should consult the Panel; or

(f) when a purchaser is being sought for an interest, or interests, in shares carrying in aggregate 30% or more of the voting rights of a company or when the board of a company is seeking one or more potential offerors, and:

(i) the company is the subject of rumour and speculation or there is an untoward movement in its share price; or

(ii) the number of potential purchasers or offerors approached is about to be increased to include more than a very restricted number of people.

NOTES ON RULE 2.2

1. *Panel to be consulted*

Whether or not a movement in the share price of a potential offeree company is untoward for the purposes of Rule 2.2(c), (d) and (f)(i) is a matter for the Panel to determine. The question will be considered in the light of all relevant facts and not solely by reference to the absolute percentage movement in the price. Facts which may be considered to be relevant in determining whether a price movement is untoward for the purposes of Rule 2.2(c), (d) and (f)(i) include general market and sector movements, publicly available information relating to the company, trading activity in the company's securities and the time period over which the price movement has occurred. This list is purely illustrative and the Panel will take account of such other factors as it considers appropriate. The percentage thresholds specified below in respect of price movements relate solely to the latest point at which consultation with the Panel is required; consultation will not necessarily lead to a requirement to make an announcement.

In the case of Rule 2.2(c), unless an immediate announcement is to be made, the Panel should be consulted at the latest when the offeree company becomes the subject of any rumour and speculation or where there is a price movement of 10% or more above the lowest share price since the time of the approach. An abrupt price rise of a smaller percentage (for example, a rise of

D4

RULE 2 CONTINUED

NOTES ON RULE 2.2 continued

5% in the course of a single day) could also be regarded as untoward and accordingly the Panel should be consulted in such circumstances.

Similarly, in the case of Rules 2.2(d) and (f)(i), the Panel should be consulted when the potential offeree company becomes the subject of any rumour and speculation or where there is a material or abrupt movement in its share price after the time when, in the case of Rule 2.2(d), an offer is first actively considered or, in the case of Rule 2.2(f)(ii), the board starts to seek one or more purchasers or offerors.

2. *Clear statements*

The Panel will not normally require an announcement under Rule 2.2(d) if it is satisfied that the price movement, rumour or speculation results only from a clear and unequivocal public statement, eg (a) a disclosure under the Companies Act 1985; (b) an announcement of a dawn raid or an intention to purchase; or (c) an announcement of a tender offer.

2.3 RESPONSIBILITIES OF OFFERORS AND THE OFFEREE COMPANY

Before the board of the offeree company is approached, the responsibility for making an announcement can lie only with the offeror. The offeror should, therefore, keep a close watch on the offeree company's share price for any signs of untoward movement. The offeror is also responsible for making an announcement once a Rule 9 obligation has been incurred.

Following an approach to the board of the offeree company which may or may not lead to an offer, the primary responsibility for making an announcement will normally rest with the board of the offeree company which must, therefore, keep a close watch on its share price.

A potential offeror must not attempt to prevent the board of an offeree company from making an announcement at any time the board thinks appropriate.

2.4 THE ANNOUNCEMENT OF A POSSIBLE OFFER

(a) Except in the case of a mandatory offer under Rule 9, until a firm intention to make an offer has been notified, a brief announcement that talks are taking place (there is no requirement to name the potential offeror in such an announcement) or that a potential offeror is considering making an offer will normally satisfy the obligations under this Rule. Except with the consent of the Panel, such an announcement should also include a summary of the provisions of Rule 8 (see the Panel's website at www.thetakeoverpanel.org.uk).

RULE 2 CONTINUED

(b) At any time following the announcement of a possible offer (provided the potential offeror has been publicly named), the offeree company may request that the Panel impose a time limit for the potential offeror to clarify its intentions with regard to the offeree company. If a time limit for clarification is imposed by the Panel, the potential offeror must, before the expiry of the time limit, announce either a firm intention to make an offer for the offeree company in accordance with Rule 2.5 or that it does not intend to make an offer for the offeree company, in which case the announcement will be treated as a statement to which Rule 2.8 applies.

(c) (i) Until a firm intention to make an offer has been notified, the Panel must be consulted in advance if any person proposes to make a statement in relation to the terms on which an offer might be made for the offeree company.

(ii) Except with the consent of the Panel, if any such statement is included in an announcement by a potential offeror or is made by or on behalf of a potential offeror, its directors, officials or advisers and not immediately withdrawn if incorrect, the potential offeror will be bound by the statement if an offer for the offeree company is subsequently made, unless it reserved the right not to be so bound at the time the statement was made.

(iii) Where the statement concerned relates to the price of a possible offer (or a particular exchange ratio in the case of a proposed securities exchange offer), except with the consent of the Panel, the potential offeror will not be allowed subsequently to make an offer for the offeree company at a lower value (taking the value of any securities concerned at the date of announcement of the firm intention to make the offer), unless there has occurred an event which the potential offeror specified in the statement as an event which would enable it to be set aside.

(d) Except with the consent of the Panel, the consequences of a statement to which Rule 2.4(c) applies will normally apply also to any person acting in concert with the potential offeror and to any person who is subsequently acting in concert with the potential offeror or such person.

NOTES ON RULE 2.4

1. *Pre-conditions*

The Panel must be consulted in advance if a person proposes to include in an announcement any pre-condition to the making of an offer. Any such pre-conditional possible offer announcement must:

RULE 2 CONTINUED

NOTES ON RULE 2.4 continued

(a) clearly state whether or not the pre-conditions must be satisfied before an offer can be made or whether they are waivable; and

(b) include a prominent warning to the effect that the announcement does not amount to a firm intention to make an offer and that, accordingly, there can be no certainty that any offer will be made even if the pre-conditions are satisfied or waived.

2. *Announcement of a potential competing offer*

The provisions of Rule 2.4(b) will not apply where an offer has already been announced by a third party and the potential offeror makes a statement that it is considering making a competing offer.

See Note 1 on Rule 19.3.

3. *Period for clarification*

The precise time limit imposed in any particular case under Rule 2.4(b) will be determined by reference to all the circumstances of the case and the Panel will endeavour to balance the potential damage to the business of the offeree company arising from the uncertainty caused by the potential offeror's interest against the disadvantage to its shareholders of losing the prospect of an offer.

4. *Extension of time limit*

A time limit for a potential offeror to clarify its intentions imposed under Rule 2.4(b) may be extended only with the consent of the Panel. The Panel's consent will normally be granted if the board of the offeree company consents to the extension.

5. *Reservation of right to set statements aside*

The first announcement in which a statement subject to Rule 2.4(c) is made must also contain prominent reference to any reservation (precise details of which must also be included in the announcement). Any subsequent mention by the offeror of the statement must be accompanied by a reference to the reservation.

6. *Duration of restriction*

The restrictions imposed by Rule 2.4(c) will normally apply throughout the period during which the offeree company is in an offer period and for a further three months thereafter.

7. *Statements by the offeree company*

Any statement made by the offeree company in relation to the terms on which an offer might be made must also make clear whether or not it is being made

RULE 2 *CONTINUED*

NOTES ON RULE 2.4 continued

with the agreement or approval of the potential offeror. Where the statement is made with the agreement or approval of the potential offeror, the statement will be treated as one to which Rule 2.4(c) applies in the same way as if it had been made by the potential offeror itself. Where it is not so made, the statement must also include a prominent warning to the effect that there can be no certainty that an offer will be made nor as to the terms on which any offer might be made.

2.5 THE ANNOUNCEMENT OF A FIRM INTENTION TO MAKE AN OFFER

(a) An offeror should only announce a firm intention to make an offer after the most careful and responsible consideration. Such an announcement should be made only when an offeror has every reason to believe that it can and will continue to be able to implement the offer. Responsibility in this connection also rests on the financial adviser to the offeror.

(b) When a firm intention to make an offer is announced, the announcement must state:—

    (i)   the terms of the offer;

    (ii)   the identity of the offeror;

    (iii) details of any relevant securities of the offeree company in which the offeror or any person acting in concert with it has an interest or in respect of which he has a right to subscribe, in each case specifying the nature of the interests or rights concerned (see Note 2 below and Note 5(a) on Rule 8). Similar details of any short positions (whether conditional or absolute and whether in the money or otherwise), including any short position under a derivative, any agreement to sell or any delivery obligation or right to require another person to purchase or take delivery, must also be stated;

    (iv) details of any relevant securities of the offeree company in respect of which the offeror or any of its associates has procured an irrevocable commitment or a letter of intent (see Note 14 on Rule 8);

    (v)   details of any relevant securities of the offeree company which the offeror or any person acting in concert with it has borrowed or lent, save for any borrowed shares which have been either on-lent or sold;

RULE 2 CONTINUED

(vi) all conditions (including normal conditions relating to acceptances, admission to listing, admission to trading and increase of capital) to which the offer or the posting of it is subject;

(vii) details of any agreements or arrangements to which the offeror is party which relate to the circumstances in which it may or may not invoke or seek to invoke a pre-condition or a condition to its offer and the consequences of its doing so, including details of any break fees payable as a result;

(viii) details of any arrangement of the kind referred to in Note 6(b) on Rule 8;

(ix) a summary of the provisions of Rule 8 (see the Panel's website at www.thetakeoverpanel.org.uk); and

(x) details of any arrangement for the payment of an inducement fee or similar arrangement referred to in Rule 21.2.

(c) Where the offer is for cash, or includes an element of cash, the announcement must include confirmation by the financial adviser or by another appropriate third party that resources are available to the offeror sufficient to satisfy full acceptance of the offer. (The party confirming that resources are available will not be expected to produce the cash itself if, in giving the confirmation, it acted responsibly and took all reasonable steps to assure itself that the cash was available.)

NOTES ON RULE 2.5

1. Unambiguous language

The language used in announcements should clearly and concisely reflect the position being described. In particular, the word "agreement" should be used with the greatest care. Statements should be avoided which may give the impression that persons have committed themselves to certain courses of action (eg accepting in respect of their own shares) when they have not in fact done so.

2. Interests of a group of which an adviser is a member

It is accepted that, for reasons of secrecy, it would not be prudent to make enquiries so as to include in an announcement details of any relevant securities of the offeree company in which other parts of an adviser's group are interested or have short positions or borrowings (see (5) of "acting in concert" in Definitions Section). In such circumstances, details should be obtained as soon as possible after the announcement has been made and the Panel consulted. If the interests, short positions or borrowings are significant, a further announcement may be required.

RULE 2 CONTINUED

NOTES ON RULE 2.5 continued

3. Subjective conditions

Companies and their advisers should consult the Panel prior to the issue of any announcement containing conditions which are not entirely objective (see Rule 13).

4. New conditions for increased or improved offers

See Rule 32.4.

5. Pre-conditions

The Panel must be consulted in advance if a person proposes to include in an announcement any pre-condition to which the posting of the offer will be subject. (See also Rule 13.)

6. Financing conditions and pre-conditions

See the Note on Rules 13.1 and 13.3.

2.6 OBLIGATION ON THE OFFEROR AND THE OFFEREE COMPANY TO CIRCULATE ANNOUNCEMENTS

(a) Promptly after the commencement of an offer period (except where an offer period begins with an announcement under Rule 2.5), a copy of the relevant announcement must be sent by the offeree company to its shareholders and to the Panel.

(b) Promptly after the publication of an announcement made under Rule 2.5:

(i) the offeree company must send a copy of that announcement, or a circular summarising the terms and conditions of the offer, to its shareholders and to the Panel; and

(ii) both the offeror and the offeree company must make that announcement, or a circular summarising the terms and conditions of the offer, readily available to their employee representatives or, where there are no such representatives, to the employees themselves.

Where necessary, the offeror or the offeree company, as the case may be, should explain the implications of the announcement. Any circular published under this Rule should also include a summary of the provisions of Rule 8 (see the Panel's website at www.thetakeoverpanel.org.uk).

RULE 2 *CONTINUED*

NOTES ON RULE 2.6

1. *Full text of announcement under Rule 2.5 to be made available*

Where, following an announcement made under Rule 2.5, a circular summarising the terms and conditions of the offer is sent to shareholders, employee representatives or employees, the full text of the announcement must be made readily and promptly available to them, for example, by placing it on the website of the offeror or the offeree company (as the case may be).

2. *Shareholders, employee representatives and employees outside the EEA*

See the Note on Rule 30.3.

2.7 CONSEQUENCES OF A "FIRM ANNOUNCEMENT"

When there has been an announcement of a firm intention to make an offer, the offeror must normally proceed with the offer unless, in accordance with the provisions of Rule 13, the offeror is permitted to invoke a pre-condition to the posting of the offer or would be permitted to invoke a condition to the offer if the offer were made.

NOTE ON RULE 2.7

When there is no need to post

An announced offeror need not proceed with its offer if a competitor has already posted a higher offer or, with the consent of the Panel, in the circumstances set out in Note 5 on Rule 21.1.

2.8 STATEMENTS OF INTENTION NOT TO MAKE AN OFFER

A person making a statement that he does not intend to make an offer for a company should make the statement as clear and unambiguous as possible. Except with the consent of the Panel, unless there is a material change of circumstances or there has occurred an event which the person specified in his statement as an event which would enable it to be set aside, neither the person making the statement, nor any person who acted in concert with him, nor any person who is subsequently acting in concert with either of them, may within six months from the date of the statement:

(a) announce an offer or possible offer for the offeree company (including a partial offer which would result in the offeror and persons acting in concert with it being interested in shares carrying 30% or more of the voting rights of the offeree company);

RULE 2 *CONTINUED*

(b) acquire any interest in shares of the offeree company if any such person would thereby become obliged under Rule 9 to make an offer;

(c) acquire any interest in, or procure an irrevocable commitment in respect of, shares of the offeree company if the shares in which such person, together with any persons acting in concert with him, would be interested and the shares in respect of which he, or they, had acquired irrevocable commitments would in aggregate carry 30% or more of the voting rights of the offeree company;

(d) make any statement which raises or confirms the possibility that an offer might be made for the offeree company; or

(e) take any steps in connection with a possible offer for the offeree company where knowledge of the possible offer might be extended outside those who need to know in the potential offeror and its immediate advisers.

Failure to comply with this Rule may lead to the period of six months referred to above being extended.

NOTES ON RULE 2.8

1. Prior consultation

Any person considering issuing such a statement should consult the Panel in advance, particularly if it is intended to include specific reservations to set aside the statement.

2. Rule 2.4(b)

Where a statement to which Rule 2.8 applies is made following a time limit being imposed under Rule 2.4(b), the only matters that a person will normally be permitted to specify in the statement as matters which would enable it to be set aside are:

(a) the agreement or recommendation of the board of the offeree company;

(b) the announcement of an offer by a third party for the offeree company; and

(c) the announcement by the offeree company of a "whitewash" proposal (see Note 1 of the Notes on Dispensations from Rule 9) or of a reverse takeover (see Note 2 on Rule 3.2).

3. Concert parties

Where a statement to which Rule 2.8 applies is made otherwise than following a time limit being imposed under Rule 2.4(b), the restrictions imposed by Rule 2.8 will normally apply also to any person acting in concert

RULE 2 CONTINUED

NOTES ON RULE 2.8 continued

with the person making the statement unless it is made clear in the statement, or at the time the statement is made, that any such person acting in concert is continuing to consider making an offer for the offeree company.

4. Media reports

When considering the application of this Rule, the Panel will take into account not only the statement itself but the manner of any subsequent public reporting of it.

Advisers must therefore ensure that directors and officials of companies are warned that they must consider carefully the implications of Rule 2.8, particularly when giving interviews to, or taking part in discussions with, the media. It is very difficult after publication to alter an impression given or remark attributed to a particular person. Control of any possible abuse lies largely with the person being interviewed. In appropriate circumstances, the Panel will require a statement of retraction or clarification.

2.9 PUBLICATION OF AN ANNOUNCEMENT ABOUT AN OFFER OR POSSIBLE OFFER

(a) When an offer or possible offer is announced, the announcement must be published in typed format and sent by fax or electronic delivery either:

(i) to a RIS; or

(ii) if the offeree company is traded on OFEX, to Newstrack.

(b) If the announcement is published outside normal business hours, it must be submitted as required, for release as soon as the relevant service re-opens; it must also be distributed to not less than two national newspapers and two newswire services in the UK.

(c) The requirements under (a) and (b) above are in addition to any other announcement obligation to which the offeror may be subject.

NOTES ON RULE 2.9

1. Distribution and availability of announcements

See Rule 19.7.

2. Rules 6, 7, 9, 11, 17, 30, 31, 32, Appendix 1.6 and Appendix 5

Announcements made under Rules 6.2(b), 7.1, 9.1(Note 9), 11.1(Note 6), 17.1, 30.1(a), 30.2(a), 31.2, 31.6(c), 31.9, 32.1, 32.6(a), Appendix 1.6 and

RULE 2 *CONTINUED*

NOTES ON RULE 2.9 continued

Appendix 5.5 must also be published in accordance with the requirements of this Rule.

2.10 ANNOUNCEMENT OF NUMBERS OF RELEVANT SECURITIES IN ISSUE

When an offer period begins, the offeree company must announce, as soon as possible and in any case by 9.00 am on the next business day, details of all classes of relevant securities issued by the company, together with the numbers of such securities in issue. An offeror or potential named offeror must also announce the same details relating to its relevant securities by 9.00 am on the business day following any announcement identifying it as an offeror or potential offeror, unless it has stated that its offer is likely to be solely in cash.

Any such announcement should include, where relevant, the International Securities Identification Number ("ISIN") for each relevant security.

If the information included in an announcement made under this Rule changes during the offer period, a revised announcement must be made as soon as possible.

NOTES ON RULE 2.10

1. Options to subscribe

For the purposes of this Rule, options to subscribe for new securities in the offeree company or an offeror are not treated as a class of relevant securities.

2. Treasury shares

Only relevant securities which are held and in issue outside treasury should be included in the announcement.

D14

RULE 3. INDEPENDENT ADVICE

3.1 BOARD OF THE OFFEREE COMPANY

The board of the offeree company must obtain competent independent advice on any offer and the substance of such advice must be made known to its shareholders.

NOTES ON RULE 3.1

1. Management buy-outs and offers by controllers

The requirement for competent independent advice is of particular importance in cases where the offer is a management buy-out or similar transaction or is being made by the existing controller or group of controllers. In such cases, it is particularly important that the independence of the adviser is beyond question. Furthermore, the responsibility borne by the adviser is considerable and, for this reason, the board of the offeree company or potential offeree company should appoint an independent adviser as soon as possible after it becomes aware of the possibility that an offer may be made.

2. When there is uncertainty about financial information

When there is a significant area of uncertainty in the most recently published accounts or interim figures of the offeree company (eg a qualified audit report, a material provision or contingent liability or doubt over the real value of a substantial asset, including a subsidiary company), the board and the independent adviser should highlight the factors which they consider important.

3. When no recommendation is given or there is a divergence of views

When it is considered impossible to express a view on the merits of an offer or to give a firm recommendation or when there is a divergence of views amongst board members or between the board and the independent adviser as to either the merits of an offer or the recommendation being made, this must be drawn to shareholders' attention and an explanation given, including the arguments for acceptance or rejection, emphasising the important factors.

The Panel should be consulted in advance about the explanation which is to be given.

3.2 BOARD OF AN OFFEROR COMPANY

The board of an offeror must obtain competent independent advice on any offer when the offer being made is a reverse takeover or when the directors are faced with a conflict of interest. The substance of such advice must be made known to its shareholders.

RULE 3 *CONTINUED*

NOTES ON RULE 3.2

1. General

When the board of an offeror is required to obtain competent independent advice, it should do so before announcing an offer or any revised offer: such advice should be as to whether or not the making of the offer is in the interests of the company's shareholders. Shareholders must have sufficient time to consider advice given to them prior to any general meeting held to implement the proposed offer. Any documents or advertisements issued by the board in such cases must include a responsibility statement by the directors as set out in Rule 19.2.

2. Reverse takeovers

A transaction will be a reverse takeover if an offeror might as a result need to increase its existing issued voting equity share capital by more than 100%.

3. Conflicts of interest

A conflict of interest will exist, for instance, when there are significant cross-shareholdings between an offeror and the offeree company, when there are a number of directors common to both companies or when a person has a substantial interest in both companies.

3.3 DISQUALIFIED ADVISERS

The Panel will not regard as an appropriate person to give independent advice a person who is in the same group as the financial or other professional adviser (including a corporate broker) to an offeror or who has a significant interest in or financial connection with either an offeror or the offeree company of such a kind as to create a conflict of interest (see also Appendix 3).

NOTES ON RULE 3.3

1. Independence of adviser

The Rule requires the offeree company's adviser to have a sufficient degree of independence from the offeror to ensure that the advice given is properly objective. Accordingly, in certain circumstances it may not be appropriate for a person who has had a recent advisory relationship with an offeror to give advice to the offeree company. In such cases the Panel should be consulted. The views of the board of the offeree company will be an important factor.

2. Investment trusts

A person who manages or is part of the same group as the investment manager of an investment trust company will not normally be regarded as an appropriate person to give independent advice in relation to that company.

D16

RULE 3 *CONTINUED*

NOTES ON RULE 3.3 continued

3. Success fees

Certain fee arrangements between an adviser and an offeree company may create a conflict of interest which would disqualify the adviser from being regarded as an appropriate person to give independent advice to the offeree company. For example, a fee which becomes payable to an offeree company adviser only in the event of failure of an offer will normally create such a conflict of interest. In cases of doubt the Panel should be consulted.

SECTION E. RESTRICTIONS ON DEALINGS

RULE 4

NB Notwithstanding the provisions of Rule 4, a person may be precluded from dealing or procuring others to deal by virtue of restrictions contained in the Criminal Justice Act 1993 regarding insider dealing and in the FSMA regarding market abuse. Where the Panel becomes aware of instances to which such restrictions may be relevant, it will inform the FSA.

4.1 PROHIBITED DEALINGS BY PERSONS OTHER THAN THE OFFEROR

(a) No dealings of any kind in securities of the offeree company by any person, not being the offeror, who is privy to confidential price-sensitive information concerning an offer or contemplated offer may take place between the time when there is reason to suppose that an approach or an offer is contemplated and the announcement of the approach or offer or of the termination of the discussions.

(b) No person who is privy to such information may make any recommendation to any other person as to dealing in the relevant securities.

(c) No such dealings may take place in securities of the offeror except where the proposed offer is not price-sensitive in relation to such securities.

4.2 RESTRICTION ON DEALINGS BY THE OFFEROR AND CONCERT PARTIES

(a) During an offer period, the offeror and persons acting in concert with it must not sell any securities in the offeree company except with the prior consent of the Panel and following 24 hours public notice that such sales might be made. The Panel will not give consent for sales where a mandatory offer under Rule 9 is being made. Sales below the value of the offer will not be permitted. After there has been an announcement that sales may be made, neither the offeror nor persons acting in concert with it may acquire an interest in any securities of the offeree company and only in exceptional circumstances will the Panel permit the offer to be revised. The Panel should be consulted whenever the offeror or a person acting in concert with it proposes to enter into or close out any type of transaction which may result in securities in the offeree company being sold during the offer period either by that party or by the counterparty to the transaction.

(b) During an offer period, the offeror and persons acting in concert with it must not acquire an interest in any securities of the offeree company through any anonymous order book system, or through any other means, unless, in either case, it can be established that the seller,

E2

RULE 4 *CONTINUED*

or other party to the transaction in question, is not an exempt principal trader connected with the offeror.

In the case of dealings through an inter-dealer broker or other similar intermediary, "seller" includes the person who has transferred the securities to the intermediary as well as the intermediary itself. (See also Rule 38.2.)

NOTES ON RULES 4.1 and 4.2

1. *Other circumstances in which dealings may not take place*

An offeror or other persons may also be restricted from dealing or procuring others to deal in certain other circumstances, eg before the announcement of an offer, if the offeror has been supplied by the offeree company with confidential price-sensitive information in the course of offer discussions.

2. *Consortium offers and joint offerors*

If an offer is to be made by more than one offeror or by a company formed by a group of persons to make an offer or by any other consortium offer vehicle, the offerors or group involved will normally be considered to be in a consortium for the purpose of this Note.

The Panel must be consulted before any acquisitions of interests in offeree company securities are made by members or potential members of a consortium. If there are existing interests in such securities, it will be necessary to satisfy the Panel that they were acquired before the consortium was formed or contemplated.

It will not normally be acceptable for members of a consortium to acquire interests in offeree company securities unless there are, for example, when a consortium company is to be the offeror, appropriate arrangements to ensure that such acquisitions are made proportionate to members' interests in the consortium company or under arrangements which give no profit to the party making the acquisition. The Panel will also be concerned to ensure that the purposes of the Code are not avoided through characterising persons acting in concert as joint offerors.

3. *No-profit arrangements*

Arrangements made by a potential offeror with a person acting in concert with it, whereby interests in offeree company securities are acquired by the person acting in concert, on the basis that the offeror will bear all the risks and receive all the benefits, are not prohibited by this Rule. Arrangements which contain a benefit or potential benefit to the person acting in concert (beyond normal expenses and carrying costs) are, however, normally prohibited. In cases of doubt, the Panel must be consulted.

RULE 4 *CONTINUED*

NOTES ON RULES 4.1 and 4.2 continued

4. *When an offer will not proceed*

If, after an announcement has been made that offer discussions are taking place or that an approach or offer is contemplated, the discussions are terminated or the offeror decides not to proceed with an offer, no dealings in securities of the offeree company or, where relevant, the offeror, by the offeror or by any person privy to this information may take place prior to an announcement of the position.

5. *No dealing contrary to published advice*

Directors and financial advisers to a company who have interests in securities in that company must not deal in such securities contrary to any advice they have given to shareholders, or to any advice with which it can reasonably be assumed that they were associated, without giving sufficient public notice of their intentions together with an appropriate explanation.

6. *Discretionary fund managers and principal traders*

Dealings in securities of the offeree company by non-exempt discretionary fund managers and principal traders which are connected with the offeror will be treated in accordance with Rule 7.2.

4.3 GATHERING OF IRREVOCABLE COMMITMENTS

Any person proposing to contact a private individual or small corporate shareholder with a view to seeking an irrevocable commitment must consult the Panel in advance.

NOTE ON RULE 4.3

Irrevocable commitments

Where irrevocable commitments are to be sought, the Panel will wish to be satisfied that the proposed arrangements will provide adequate information as to the nature of the commitment sought; and a realistic opportunity to consider whether or not that commitment should be given and to obtain independent advice if required. The financial adviser concerned will be responsible for ensuring compliance with all relevant legislation and other regulatory requirements.

4.4 DEALINGS IN OFFEREE SECURITIES BY CERTAIN OFFEREE COMPANY ASSOCIATES

During the offer period, except for exempt principal traders and exempt fund managers, no financial adviser or corporate broker (or any person controlling, controlled by or under the same control# as any such adviser or corporate broker) to an offeree company (or any of its

#See Note at end of Definitions Section.

E4

RULE 4 *CONTINUED*

parents, subsidiaries or fellow subsidiaries, or their associated companies or companies of which such companies are associated companies) shall, except with the consent of the Panel:—

(i) either for its own account or on behalf of discretionary clients acquire any interest in offeree company shares; or

(ii) make any loan to a person to assist him in acquiring any such interest save for lending in the ordinary course of business and on normal commercial terms to persons with which they have an established customer relationship; or

(iii) enter into any indemnity or option arrangement or any arrangement, agreement or understanding, formal or informal, of whatever nature, which may be an inducement for a person to retain, deal or refrain from dealing in relevant securities of the offeree company.

NOTE ON RULE 4.4

Irrevocable commitments and letters of intent

Rule 4.4(iii) does not prevent an adviser to an offeree company from procuring irrevocable commitments or letters of intent not to accept an offer.

4.5 RESTRICTION ON THE OFFEREE COMPANY ACCEPTING AN OFFER IN RESPECT OF TREASURY SHARES

An offeree company may not accept an offer in respect of treasury shares until after the offer is unconditional as to acceptances.

4.6 RESTRICTION ON SECURITIES BORROWING AND LENDING TRANSACTIONS BY OFFERORS, THE OFFEREE COMPANY AND CERTAIN OTHER PARTIES

During the offer period, none of the following persons may, except with the consent of the Panel, enter into or take action to unwind a securities borrowing or lending transaction in respect of relevant securities:

(a) the offeror;

(b) the offeree company;

(c) a company which is an associate of the offeror or the offeree company by virtue of paragraph (1) of the definition of associate;

RULE 4 *CONTINUED*

(d) a connected adviser and persons controlling#, controlled by or under the same control as any such adviser (except for an exempt principal trader or an exempt fund manager);

(e) a pension fund of the offeror or the offeree company or of a company which is an associate of the offeror or the offeree company by virtue of paragraph (1) of the definition of associate; and

(f) any other person acting in concert with the offeror or with the offeree company.

NOTES ON RULE 4.6

1. *Return of borrowed relevant securities*

The redelivery by a borrower of relevant securities (or equivalent securities) which have been recalled, or the accepting by a lender of the redelivery of relevant securities (or equivalent securities) which have not been recalled, in each case in accordance with an existing securities borrowing or lending agreement, will not normally be treated as taking action to unwind a securities borrowing or lending transaction. However, the Panel will normally require the redelivery or the accepting of the redelivery of such relevant securities to be disclosed.

2. *Pension funds*

Rule 4.6(e) does not apply in respect of any pension funds which are managed under an agreement or arrangement with an independent third party in the terms set out in Note 7 on the definition of acting in concert.

3. *Disclosure or notice where consent is given*

Where the Panel consents to a person to whom Rule 4.6 applies entering into or taking action to unwind a securities borrowing or lending transaction in respect of relevant securities, the Panel will normally require the transaction to be disclosed by that person as if it were a dealing in the relevant securities. Where a person wishes to enter into or take action to unwind more than one lending transaction in respect of relevant securities, the Panel may instead require that person to give public notice that he might do so.

4. *Discretionary fund managers and principal traders*

Securities borrowing or lending transactions by non-exempt discretionary fund managers and principal traders which are subject to Rule 4.6(d) will be treated in accordance with Rule 7.2.

#See Note at end of Definitions Section.

RULE 5. TIMING RESTRICTIONS ON ACQUISITIONS

NB For the purposes of this Rule 5 only, the number of shares in which a person will be treated as having an interest includes any shares in respect of which he has received an irrevocable commitment (see paragraph (5) of the definition of interests in securities).

5.1 RESTRICTIONS

Except as permitted by Rule 5.2:—

(a) when a person (which for the purpose of Rule 5 includes any persons acting in concert with him) is interested in shares which in the aggregate carry less than 30% of the voting rights of a company, he may not acquire an interest in any other shares carrying voting rights in that company which, when aggregated with the shares in which he is already interested, would carry 30% or more of the voting rights; and

(b) when a person is interested in shares which in the aggregate carry 30% or more of the voting rights of a company but does not hold shares which carry more than 50% of the voting rights, he may not acquire an interest in any other shares carrying voting rights in that company. See Note 5.

NOTES ON RULE 5.1

1. When more than 50% is held

This Rule is not relevant to a person who holds shares carrying more than 50% of the voting rights of a company or to a person who obtains such a position by a permitted acquisition.

2. New shares, subscription rights, convertibles and options

Neither the acquisition of new shares, securities convertible into new shares or rights to subscribe for new shares (other than the purchase of rights arising pursuant to a rights issue) nor the acquisition of new or existing shares, or rights in relation to such shares, under a share option scheme is restricted by this Rule. However, the acquisition of new shares as a result of the exercise of conversion or subscription rights or options must be treated for the purpose of this Rule as if it were an acquisition from a single shareholder (see Rule 5.2(a)). The effective date of the acquisition should normally be taken as the date of exercise of conversion or subscription rights or of options.

(See also Note 3 on this Rule.)

3. Allotted but unissued shares

When shares of a company carrying voting rights have been allotted (even if provisionally) but have not yet been issued, for example, under a rights issue when the shares are represented by renounceable letters of allotment, the Panel should be consulted. This Rule may apply to the acquisition of an interest in such shares as it would in the case of an acquisition of an interest in registered shares.

RULE 5 CONTINUED

NOTES ON RULE 5.1 continued

4. "Whitewashes"

This Rule does not prohibit a person from obtaining an interest in shares carrying 30% or more of the voting rights in accordance with Note 1 of the Notes on Dispensations from Rule 9.

5. Maintenance of the percentage of the shares in which a person is interested

The restrictions in this Rule do not apply to an acquisition of an interest in shares which would not increase the percentage of the shares carrying voting rights in which that person is interested, e.g. if a shareholder takes up his entitlement under a fully underwritten rights issue or if a person acquires shares on exercise of a call option.

6. Discretionary fund managers and principal traders

Dealings by non-exempt discretionary fund managers and principal traders which are connected with an offeror will be treated in accordance with Rule 7.2.

7. Gifts

If a person receives a gift of shares or an interest in shares which takes the aggregate number of shares carrying voting rights in which he is interested to 30% or more, he must consult the Panel. (See also Note 3 on Rule 9.5.)

5.2 EXCEPTIONS TO RESTRICTIONS

The restrictions in Rule 5.1 do not apply to an acquisition of an interest in shares carrying voting rights in a company by a person:—

(a) at any time from a single shareholder if it is the only such acquisition within any period of 7 days (see also Rules 5.3 and 5.4). This exception will not apply when the person has announced a firm intention to make an offer and the posting of the offer is not subject to a pre-condition; or

(b) immediately before the person announces a firm intention to make an offer (whether or not the posting of the offer is to be subject to a pre-condition), provided that the offer will be publicly recommended by, or the acquisition is made with the agreement of, the board of the offeree company and the acquisition is conditional upon the announcement of the offer; or

(c) after the person has announced a firm intention to make an offer provided that the posting of the offer is not, at the time of the acquisition, subject to a pre-condition and:

(i) the acquisition is made with the agreement of the board of the offeree company; or

E8

RULE 5 *CONTINUED*

(ii) that offer or any competing offer has been publicly recommended by the board of the offeree company, even if such recommendation is subsequently withdrawn; or

(iii) either:

(1) the first closing date of that offer has passed and it has been announced that such offer is not to be referred to the Competition Commission (or such offer does not come within the statutory provisions for possible reference) and it has been established that no action by the European Commission will any longer be taken in respect of such offer pursuant to Council Regulation 139/2004/EC (or such offer does not come within the scope of such Regulation); or

(2) the first closing date of any competing offer has passed and it has been announced that such competing offer is not to be referred to the Competition Commission (or such competing offer does not come within the statutory provisions for possible reference) and it has been established that no action by the European Commission will any longer be taken in respect of such offer pursuant to Council Regulation 139/2004/EC (or such offer does not come within the scope of such Regulation); or

(iv) that offer is unconditional in all respects; or

(d) if the acquisition is by way of acceptance of the offer; or

(e) if the acquisition is permitted by Note 11 on Rule 9.1 or Note 5 on the Dispensations from Rule 9.

NOTES ON RULE 5.2

1. *Single shareholder*

(a) For the purpose of Rule 5.2(a), a number of shareholders will be regarded as a single shareholder only if they are all members of the same family or of a group of companies which is regarded as one for disclosure purposes under Section 203(2) to (4) of the Companies Act 1985. A principal trader or a fund manager managing investment accounts on behalf of a number of underlying clients (whether or not on a discretionary basis) will not normally be considered to be a single shareholder for the purpose of this Rule. The Panel should be consulted in cases of doubt.

(b) An acquisition of an interest in shares will only be permitted by Rule 5.2(a) if the acquisition relates to a pre-existing holding of shares of the single shareholder concerned.

RULE 5 *CONTINUED*

NOTES ON RULE 5.2 continued

2. Rule 9

An acquisition permitted by Rule 5.2 may result in an obligation to make an offer under Rule 9, in which case an immediate announcement of such an offer must be made.

3. Revision

If an offeror revises its offer, the exceptions allowed by this Rule will apply on the basis of the time periods applicable to the original offer.

4. After an offer lapses

After an offer has lapsed, the restrictions in Rule 5.1 will once again apply to the former offeror.

5.3 ACQUISITIONS FROM A SINGLE SHAREHOLDER — CONSEQUENCES

A person who acquires an interest in shares from a single shareholder permitted by Rule 5.2(a) may not acquire an interest in any other shares carrying voting rights in a company, except in the circumstances set out in Rule 5.2(b), (c), (d) and (e). If that person makes an offer for the company which subsequently lapses, this restriction will cease to apply.

NOTES ON RULE 5.3

1. If a person's interests are reduced

A person who is restricted by this Rule from making further acquisitions will cease to be so restricted if the aggregate number of shares carrying voting rights in which he is interested falls below 30% (in which case he will become subject to Rule 5.1(a)).

2. Rights or scrip issues and "whitewashes"

The restrictions imposed by this Rule do not prevent a person from receiving his entitlement of shares through a rights or scrip issue as long as he does not increase the percentage of shares carrying voting rights in which he is interested. Nor do they prevent a person from acquiring further interests in shares in accordance with the Notes on Dispensations from Rule 9.

5.4 ACQUISITIONS FROM A SINGLE SHAREHOLDER — DISCLOSURE

A person who acquires an interest in shares carrying voting rights in a company from a single shareholder permitted by Rule 5.2(a) must notify

E10

RULE 5 CONTINUED

the company, a RIS and the Panel, not later than 12 noon on the business day following the date of the acquisition, of details of:

(a) that acquisition; and

(b) any shares of the company in which he has an interest or in respect of which he has a right to subscribe, in each case specifying the nature of the interests or rights concerned (see Note 5(a) on Rule 8). Similar details of any short position (whether conditional or absolute and whether in the money or otherwise), including any short position under a derivative, any agreement to sell or any delivery obligation or right to require another person to purchase or take delivery, must also be disclosed.

NOTE ON RULE 5.4

Disclosure of the identity of the person dealing

Any announcement must comply with the requirements of Note 5(a) on Rule 8 regarding the disclosure of the identity of the person dealing and, if different, the owner or controller.

RULE 6. ACQUISITIONS RESULTING IN AN OBLIGATION TO OFFER A MINIMUM LEVEL OF CONSIDERATION

6.1 ACQUISITIONS BEFORE A RULE 2.5 ANNOUNCEMENT

Except with the consent of the Panel in cases falling under (a) or (b), when an offeror or any person acting in concert with it has acquired an interest in shares in the offeree company:—

(a) within the three month period prior to the commencement of the offer period; or

(b) during the period, if any, between the commencement of the offer period and an announcement made by the offeror in accordance with Rule 2.5; or

(c) prior to the three month period referred to in (a), if in the view of the Panel there are circumstances which render such a course necessary in order to give effect to General Principle 1,

the offer to the holders of shares of the same class shall not be on less favourable terms.

If an acquisition of an interest in shares in the offeree company has given rise to an obligation under Rule 11, compliance with that Rule will normally be regarded as satisfying any obligation under this Rule in respect of that acquisition.

6.2 ACQUISITIONS AFTER A RULE 2.5 ANNOUNCEMENT

(a) If, after an announcement made in accordance with Rule 2.5 and before the offer closes for acceptance, an offeror or any person acting in concert with it acquires any interest in shares at above the offer price (being the then current value of the offer), it shall increase its offer to not less than the highest price paid for the interest in shares so acquired.

(b) Immediately after the acquisition, the offeror must announce that a revised offer will be made in accordance with this Rule (see also Rule 32). Whenever practicable, the announcement should also state the number of shares concerned and the price paid.

(c) Acquisitions of interests in shares in the offeree company may also give rise to an obligation under Rule 11. Where an obligation is incurred under Rule 11 by reason of any such acquisition, compliance with that Rule will normally be regarded as satisfying any obligation under this Rule in respect of that acquisition.

RULE 6 *CONTINUED*

NOTES ON RULE 6

1. Adjusted terms

The Panel's discretion to agree adjusted terms pursuant to Rule 6.1(a) or (b) will only be exercised in exceptional circumstances. Factors which the Panel might take into account when considering an application for adjusted terms include:—

(a) whether the relevant acquisition was made on terms then prevailing in the market;

(b) changes in the market price of the shares since the relevant acquisition;

(c) the size and timing of the relevant acquisition;

(d) the attitude of the offeree board;

(e) whether interests in shares have been acquired at high prices from directors or other persons closely connected with the offeror or the offeree company; and

(f) whether a competing offer has been announced for the offeree company.

2. Acquisitions prior to the three month period

The discretion given to the Panel in Rule 6.1(c) will not normally be exercised unless the vendors, or other parties to the transactions giving rise to the interests, are directors of, or other persons closely connected with, the offeror or the offeree company.

3. No less favourable terms

For the purpose of Rule 6.1, except where Rule 9 (mandatory offer) or Rule 11.1 (requirement for cash offer) applies, it will not be necessary to make a cash offer available even if interests in shares have been acquired for cash. However, any securities offered as consideration must, at the date of the announcement of the firm intention to make the offer, have a value at least equal to the highest relevant price paid. If, during the period ending when the market closes on the first business day after the announcement, the value is not maintained, the Panel will be concerned to ensure that the offeror acted with all reasonable care in determining the consideration.

If there is a restricted market in the securities of an offeror, or if the amount of securities to be issued of a class already admitted to trading is large in relation to the amount already issued, the Panel may require justification of prices used to determine the value of the offer.

RULE 6 CONTINUED

NOTES ON RULE 6 continued

4. Highest price paid

For the purpose of this Rule, the price paid for any acquisition of an interest in shares will be determined as follows:

(a) in the case of a purchase of shares, the price paid is the price at which the bargain between the purchaser (or, where applicable, his broker acting in an agency capacity) and the vendor (or principal trader) is struck;

(b) in the case of a call option which remains unexercised, the price paid will normally be treated as the middle market price of the shares which are the subject of the option at the time the option is entered into;

(c) in the case of a call option which has been exercised, the price paid will normally be treated as the amount paid on exercise of the option together with any amount paid by the option-holder on entering into the option;

(d) in the case of a written put option (whether exercised or not), the price paid will normally be treated as the amount paid or payable on exercise of the option less any amount paid by the option-holder on entering into the option; and

(e) in the case of a derivative, the price paid will normally be treated as the initial reference price together with any fee paid on entering into the derivative.

In the case of an option or a derivative, however, if the option exercise price or derivative reference price is calculated by reference to the average price of a number of acquisitions by the counterparty of interests in underlying securities, the price paid will normally be determined to be the highest price at which such acquisitions are actually made.

Any stamp duty and broker's commission payable should be excluded.

The Panel should be consulted in advance if it is proposed to acquire the voting rights attaching to shares, or general control of them.

Where a person acquired an interest in shares more than three months prior to the commencement of the offer period as a result of any option, derivative or agreement to purchase and, within the three month period prior to the commencement of the offer period or after the announcement made in accordance with Rule 2.5 and before the offer closes for acceptance, the person acquires any of the relevant shares, no obligation under this Rule will normally arise as a result of the acquisition of those shares. However, if the terms of the instrument have been varied in any way, or if the shares are acquired other than on the terms of the original instrument, the Panel should be consulted.

RULE 6 *CONTINUED*

NOTES ON RULE 6 continued

5. Cum dividend

When accepting shareholders are entitled under the offer to retain a dividend declared or forecast by the offeree company but not yet paid, purchases in the market or otherwise by an offeror or any person acting in concert with it may be made at prices up to the net cum dividend equivalent of the offer value without necessitating any revision of the offer. Where the offeror or any person acting in concert with it proposes to acquire an interest in shares in reliance on this Note other than by purchasing shares, the Panel should be consulted.

6. Convertible securities, warrants and options

Acquisitions of securities convertible into, warrants in respect of, or options or other rights to subscribe for, new shares will normally only be relevant to this Rule if they are converted or exercised (as applicable). Such acquisitions will then be treated as if they were acquisitions of the underlying shares at a price calculated by reference to the acquisition price and the relevant conversion or exercise terms. In any case of doubt, the Panel should be consulted.

7. Unlisted securities

An offer where the consideration consists of securities for which immediate admission to trading on a regulated market in the United Kingdom is not to be sought will not normally be regarded as satisfying any obligation incurred under this Rule. In such cases the Panel should be consulted.

8. Discretionary fund managers and principal traders

Dealings by non-exempt discretionary fund managers and principal traders which are connected with an offeror will be treated in accordance with Rule 7.2.

9. Offer period

References to the offer period in this Rule are to the time during which the offeree company is in an offer period, irrespective of whether the offeror was contemplating an offer when the offer period commenced.

10. Competition reference period

When, under Rule 12.2, a new offer period begins at the time the competition reference period ends, the three month period referred to in Rule 6.1(a) will be deemed to be the competition reference period.

Takeover Code

E₁₅

RULE 7. CONSEQUENCES OF CERTAIN DEALINGS

7.1 IMMEDIATE ANNOUNCEMENT REQUIRED IF THE OFFER HAS TO BE AMENDED

The acquisition of an interest in offeree company shares by an offeror or any person acting in concert with it may give rise to an obligation under Rule 6 (requirement to increase offer), Rule 9 (mandatory offer) or Rule 11 (nature of consideration to be offered). Immediately after such an acquisition, an appropriate announcement must be made by the offeror. Whenever practicable, the announcement should also state the nature of the interest, the number of shares concerned and the price paid.

NOTE ON RULE 7.1

Potential offerors

The requirement of this Rule to make an immediate announcement applies to any publicly announced potential offeror (whether named or not) either where a public indication of the level of its probable offer has been made and the potential offeror or any person acting in concert with it acquires an interest in shares above that level or where there already exists an offer from a third party and the potential offeror or any person acting in concert with it acquires an interest in shares at above the level of that offer. Disclosure will also be required in accordance with Rule 8.1.

7.2 DEALINGS BY CONNECTED DISCRETIONARY FUND MANAGERS AND PRINCIPAL TRADERS

NB Rule 7.2 and the Notes thereon address the position of connected fund managers and principal traders who either do not have exempt status or whose exempt status is not relevant by virtue of the operation of Note 2 on the definitions of exempt fund manager and exempt principal trader.

(a) Discretionary fund managers and principal traders who, in either case, are connected with an offeror or potential offeror, will not normally be presumed to be acting in concert with that person until its identity as an offeror or potential offeror is publicly announced or, if prior to that, the time at which the connected party had actual knowledge of the possibility of an offer being made by a person with whom it is connected. Rules 5, 6, 9, 11 and 36 will then be relevant to acquisitions of interests in offeree company securities and Rule 4.2 to sales of offeree company securities by such persons. Rule 4.6 will be relevant to securities borrowing and lending transactions.

(b) Similarly, discretionary fund managers and principal traders who, in either case, are connected with the offeree company, will not

401

RULE 7 CONTINUED

normally be presumed to be acting in concert with the offeree company until the commencement of the offer period or, if prior to that, the time at which the connected party had actual knowledge of the possibility of an offer being made for the offeree company and that it was connected with the offeree company. Rules 4.4, 5 and 9 may then be relevant to acquisitions of interests in offeree company securities. Rule 4.6 will be relevant to securities borrowing and lending transactions.

(See also the definition of connected fund managers and principal traders.)

(c) An exempt fund manager or exempt principal trader which is connected for the sole reason that it is controlled# by, controls or is under the same control as a connected adviser will not be presumed to be in concert even after the commencement of the offer period or the identity of the offeror being publicly announced (as the case may be). (See Note 2 on the definitions of exempt fund manager and exempt principal trader.)

NOTES ON RULE 7.2

1. *Dealings prior to a concert party relationship arising*

(a) As a result of Rule 7.2(a) and notwithstanding the usual application of the presumptions of acting in concert, dealings and securities borrowing and lending transactions by discretionary fund managers and principal traders connected with an offeror or potential offeror will not normally be relevant for the purposes of Rules 4.2, 4.6, 5, 6, 9, 11 and 36 before the identity of the offeror or potential offeror has been publicly announced or, if prior to that, the time at which the connected party had actual knowledge of the possibility of an offer being made by a person with whom it is connected.

(b) Similarly, as a result of Rule 7.2(b) and notwithstanding the usual application of the presumptions of acting in concert, dealings and securities borrowing and lending transactions by discretionary fund managers and principal traders connected with the offeree company will not normally be relevant for the purposes of Rules 5 or 9 before the commencement of the offer period or, if prior to that, the time at which the connected party had actual knowledge of the possibility of an offer being made for the offeree company.

(c) Rule 9 will, however, be relevant if the aggregate number of shares in which all persons under the same control# (including any exempt fund manager or exempt principal trader) are interested carry 30% or more of the voting rights of a company. However, provided that recognised intermediary

#See Note at end of Definitions Section.

Takeover Code

E17

RULE 7 CONTINUED

NOTES ON RULE 7.2 continued

status has not fallen away (see Note 3 on the definition of recognised intermediary), a recognised intermediary acting in a client-serving capacity will not be treated as interested in (or as having acquired an interest in) any securities by virtue only of paragraph (3) or paragraph (4) of the definition of interests in securities (other than those held in a proprietary capacity) for these purposes.

If such a group of persons includes a principal trader and the aggregate number of shares in a company in which the group is interested approaches or exceeds 30% of the voting rights, the Panel may consent to the principal trader continuing to acquire interests in shares in the company without consequence under Rule 9.1 provided that the company is not in an offer period and the number of shares which the principal trader holds does not at any relevant time exceed 3% of the voting rights of the company. The Panel should be consulted in such cases.

2. Qualifications

(a) If a connected discretionary fund manager or principal trader is in fact acting in concert with an offeror or with the offeree company, the usual concert party consequences will apply irrespective of whether the offeree company is in an offer period or the identity of the offeror or potential offeror has been publicly announced.

(b) If an offeror or potential offeror, or any company in its group, has funds managed on a discretionary basis by an exempt fund manager, Rule 7.2 may be relevant. If, for example, any securities of the offeree company are managed by such exempt fund manager for the offeror or potential offeror, the exception in Rule 7.2(c) in relation to exempt fund managers may not apply in respect of those securities. The Panel should be consulted in such cases.

3. Dealings by principal traders

After a principal trader is presumed to be acting in concert by virtue of Rules 7.2(a) or (b), it may stand down from its dealing activities. In such circumstances, with the prior consent of the Panel, the principal trader may reduce its interest in offeree company securities or offeror securities, or may acquire interests in such securities with a view to reducing any short position, without such dealings being relevant for the purposes of Rules 4.2, 4.4, 5, 6, 9, 11 and 36, notwithstanding the usual application of the presumptions of acting in concert and Rules 7.2(a) and (b). The Panel will also normally, pursuant to Rule 4.6, consent to connected principal traders taking action to unwind a securities borrowing or lending transaction in such circumstances. The Panel will not normally require such dealings to be disclosed under

RULE 7 CONTINUED

NOTES ON RULE 7.2 continued

Rules 4.6, 8.1(a), 24.3 or 25.3. Any such dealings must take place within a time period agreed in advance by the Panel.

4. Dealings by discretionary fund managers

(a) After a discretionary fund manager is presumed to be acting in concert with an offeror or potential offeror by virtue of Rule 7.2(a), any acquisition by it of any interest in offeree company securities will normally be relevant for Rules 5, 6, 9, 11 and 36. Similarly, any acquisition of any interest in offeree company securities by a discretionary fund manager after it is presumed to be acting in concert by virtue of Rule 7.2(b) will not normally be permitted by virtue of Rule 4.4(i). However, with the prior consent of the Panel, a discretionary fund manager connected with either the offeree company or an offeror or potential offeror will normally be permitted to acquire an interest in offeree company securities, with a view to reducing any short position, without such acquisitions being relevant for the purposes of Rules 4.4(i), 5, 6, 9, 11 and 36, notwithstanding the usual application of the presumptions of acting in concert and Rules 7.2(a) and (b). The Panel will also normally, pursuant to Rule 4.6, consent to connected discretionary fund managers taking action to unwind securities borrowing transactions in such circumstances. Any such acquisitions or unwinding arrangements must take place within a time period agreed in advance by the Panel and should be disclosed pursuant to Rule 8.1(b)(i) or Note 3 on Rule 4.6, as appropriate.

(b) After the commencement of the offer period, with the prior consent of the Panel, a discretionary fund manager connected with an offeror will normally be permitted to sell offeree company securities without such sales being relevant for the purposes of Rule 4.2, notwithstanding the usual application of the presumptions of acting in concert and Rule 7.2(a). Any such sale should be disclosed under Rule 8.1(b)(i).

5. Rule 9

The Panel should be consulted if, once the identity of the offeror or potential offeror is publicly known, it becomes apparent that the number of shares in which the offeror or potential offeror and persons acting in concert with it, including any connected discretionary fund managers and principal traders to which Rule 7.2(a) applies, are interested carry in aggregate 30% or more of the voting rights of the offeree company.

6. Disclosure of dealings in offer documentation

Interests in relevant securities and dealings (whether before or after the presumptions in Rules 7.2(a) and (b) apply) by connected discretionary fund managers and principal traders (unless exempt) must be disclosed in any offer document in accordance with Rule 24.3 and in any offeree board circular in accordance with Rule 25.3, as the case may be. This will not apply

RULE 7 *CONTINUED*

NOTES ON RULE 7.2 continued

in respect of a dealing that has been permitted by Note 3 above and has not been required to be disclosed.

7. Consortium offers

See also Note 6 on the definition of acting in concert where the connected fund manager or principal trader is part of the same organisation as an investor in a consortium.

7.3 PARTIAL OFFERS AND "WHITEWASHES"

The acquisition of an interest in offeree company shares by an offeror or any person acting in concert with it may result in the Panel refusing to exercise its discretion to permit a partial offer or to grant a dispensation under Note 1 of the Notes on Dispensations from Rule 9.

RULE 8. DISCLOSURE OF DEALINGS DURING THE OFFER PERIOD; ALSO INDEMNITY AND OTHER ARRANGEMENTS

8.1 DEALINGS BY PARTIES AND BY ASSOCIATES FOR THEMSELVES OR FOR DISCRETIONARY CLIENTS

(a) Own account

Dealings in relevant securities by an offeror or the offeree company, and by any associates, for their own account during an offer period must be publicly disclosed in accordance with Notes 3, 4 and 5.

(b) For discretionary clients

(i) Dealings in relevant securities by an offeror or the offeree company, and by any associates, for the account of discretionary investment clients during an offer period must be publicly disclosed in accordance with Notes 3, 4 and 5. If, however, the associate is an exempt fund manager connected with an offeror or the offeree company, paragraph (ii) below will apply.

(ii) Except with the consent of the Panel, all dealings in relevant securities made during an offer period for the account of discretionary investment clients by an associate which is an exempt fund manager connected with the offeror or the offeree company must be privately disclosed in accordance with Notes 3, 4 and 5.

If, however, an exempt fund manager is required to disclose publicly under Rule 8.3, such private disclosure will not normally be required in addition.

8.2 DEALINGS BY PARTIES AND BY ASSOCIATES FOR NON-DISCRETIONARY CLIENTS

Except with the consent of the Panel, dealings in relevant securities during an offer period by an offeror or the offeree company, and by any associates, for the account of non-discretionary investment clients (other than an offeror, the offeree company and any associates) must be privately disclosed in accordance with Notes 3, 4 and 5.

8.3 DEALINGS BY PERSONS WITH INTERESTS IN SECURITIES REPRESENTING 1% OR MORE

(a) During an offer period, if a person, whether or not an associate, is interested (directly or indirectly) in 1% or more of any class of relevant securities of an offeror or of the offeree company or as a result of any transaction will be interested in 1% or more, dealings in any relevant securities of that company by such person (or any other person through whom the interest is derived) must be publicly disclosed in accordance with Notes 3, 4 and 5.

RULE 8 CONTINUED

(b) Where two or more persons act pursuant to an agreement or understanding, whether formal or informal, to acquire an interest in relevant securities, they will be deemed to be a single person for the purpose of this Rule.

(c) If a person manages investment accounts on a discretionary basis, he, and not the person on whose behalf the relevant securities (or interests in relevant securities) are managed, will be treated for the purpose of this Rule as interested in the relevant securities concerned. Except with the consent of the Panel, where more than one discretionary investment management operation is conducted in the same group, the interests in relevant securities of all such operations will be treated for the purpose of this Rule as those of a single person and must be aggregated (see Note 8 below).

(d) Rules 8.3(a) to (c) do not apply to recognised intermediaries acting in a client-serving capacity (see Note 9 below).

8.4 IRREVOCABLE COMMITMENTS AND LETTERS OF INTENT

(a) During an offer period, if an offeror or offeree company or any of their respective associates procures an irrevocable commitment or a letter of intent, the offeror or offeree company (as appropriate) must publicly disclose the details in accordance with Notes 3, 4 and 14.

(b) If a person who has given an irrevocable commitment or a letter of intent either becomes aware that he will not be able to comply with the terms of that commitment or letter or no longer intends to do so, that person must:

(i) promptly announce an update of the position together with all relevant details; or

(ii) promptly notify the offeror or offeree company (as appropriate) and the Panel of the up-to-date position. Upon receipt of such a notification, the offeror or offeree company must promptly make an appropriate announcement of the information notified to it together with all relevant details.

NOTES ON RULE 8

1. *Consultation with the Panel*

In any case of doubt as to the application of Rule 8 the Panel should be consulted.

RULE 8 CONTINUED

NOTES ON RULE 8 continued

2. *Dealings in relevant securities of the offeror*

Where it has been announced that an offer or possible offer is, or is likely to be, solely in cash, there is no requirement to disclose dealings in relevant securities of the offeror.

3. *Timing of disclosure*

Both public and private disclosure required by Rules 8.1, 8.2 and 8.4(a) must be made no later than 12 noon on the business day following the date of the transaction.

Public disclosure required by Rule 8.3 must be made no later than 3.30 pm on the business day following the date of the transaction.

4. *Method of disclosure (public or private)*

(a) Public disclosure

Dealings should be disclosed to a RIS or, if the shares are traded on OFEX, to Newstrack, in typed format, by fax or electronic delivery. A copy must also be faxed or e-mailed to the Panel.

If parties to an offer and their associates choose to make press announcements regarding dealings in addition to making formal disclosures, they must ensure that no confusion results.

Public disclosure may be made by the party concerned or by an agent acting on its behalf. Where there is more than one agent (eg an investment bank and a broker), particular care should be taken to ensure that the responsibility for disclosure is agreed between the parties and that it is neither overlooked nor duplicated.

(b) Private disclosure

Private disclosure under Rules 8.1(b)(ii) and 8.2 is to the Panel only. Dealings should be sent by fax or e-mail.

5. *Details to be included in disclosures (public or private)*

(a) Public disclosure (Rules 8.1(a), 8.1(b)(i) and 8.3)

Specimen disclosure forms are available on the Panel's website (www.thetakeoverpanel.org.uk) or may be obtained from the Panel. Public disclosures should follow the format of those forms. Where a disclosure is made pursuant to Rule 8.1(a) or (b)(i), it is not necessary to disclose the same information pursuant to Rule 8.3.

RULE 8 *CONTINUED*

NOTES ON RULE 8 continued

A public disclosure of dealings must include the following information:—

(i) the total of the relevant securities in question of an offeror or of the offeree company in which the dealing took place;

(ii) the prices paid or received (in the case of an average price bargain, each underlying trade should be disclosed);

(iii) the identity of the associate or other person dealing and, if different, the owner or controller of the interest;

(iv) if the dealing is by an associate, an explanation of how that status arises;

(v) details of any relevant securities of the offeree company or an offeror (as the case may be) in which the associate or other person disclosing has an interest or in respect of which he has a right to subscribe, in each case specifying the nature of the interests or rights concerned (see also below and Note 7(b)). Similar details of any short positions (whether conditional or absolute and whether in the money or otherwise), including any short position under a derivative, any agreement to sell or any delivery obligation or right to require another person to purchase or take delivery, must also be disclosed; and

(vi) if relevant, details of any arrangements required by Note 6 below.

For the avoidance of doubt, when a person transacts two or more separate but related dealings executed at or around the same time (for example, the entering into of a derivative referenced to relevant securities and the acquisition of such securities for the purposes of hedging), the disclosure must include the required information in relation to each such dealing so executed.

For the purpose of disclosing identity the owner or controller of the interest must be specified, in addition to the person dealing. The naming of nominees or vehicle companies is insufficient. The Panel may require additional information to be disclosed when it appears to be appropriate, for example to identify other persons who have an interest in the securities in question. However, in the case of disclosure of dealings by fund managers on behalf of discretionary clients, the clients need not be named.

Where an offeror or any person acting in concert with it acquires any interest in offeree company securities on a specially cum or specially ex dividend basis, details of that fact should also be disclosed.

Percentages should be calculated by reference to the numbers of relevant securities given in a company's latest announcement required by Rule 2.10. In the case of a disclosure relating to a right to subscribe, or subscription, for new securities, the Panel should be consulted regarding the appropriate number of relevant securities to be used in calculating the relevant percentage.

E24

RULE 8 CONTINUED

NOTES ON RULE 8 continued

In the case of agreements to purchase or sell, rights to subscribe, options or derivatives, full details should be given so that the nature of the interest, position or dealing can be fully understood. For options this should include a description of the options concerned, the number of securities under option, the exercise period (or in the case of exercise, the exercise date), the exercise price and any option money paid or received. For derivatives this should include, at least, a description of the derivatives concerned, the number of reference securities to which they relate (when relevant), the maturity date (or if applicable the closing out date) and the reference price (and any fee payable on entering into the derivative).

In addition, if there exists any agreement, arrangement or understanding, formal or informal, between the person dealing and any other person relating to the voting rights of any relevant securities under option or relating to the voting rights or future acquisition or disposal of any relevant securities to which a derivative is referenced (as the case may be), full details of such agreement, arrangement or understanding, identifying the relevant securities in question, must be included in the disclosure. If there are no such agreements, arrangements or understandings, this fact should be stated. Where such an agreement, arrangement or understanding is entered into at a later date than the derivative or option to which it relates, it will be regarded as a dealing in relevant securities.

For the purpose of the disclosure of dealings, a futures contract or covered warrant for which exercise includes the possibility of delivery of the underlying securities is treated as an option. A futures contract or covered warrant which does not include the possibility of delivery of the underlying securities is treated as a derivative.

If, following a public disclosure made under Rule 8, interests in relevant securities are transferred into or out of a person's management, a reference to the transfer must be included in the next public disclosure made by that person under Rule 8.

If an associate is an associate for more than one reason, all the reasons must be specified.

A disclosure by an exempt fund manager must specify the name of the offeror or the offeree company with which it is connected and the nature of the connection.

Where a disclosure of a securities borrowing or lending transaction is made pursuant to Note 3 on Rule 4.6, all relevant details should be given.

Where a person to whom Rule 4.6 applies discloses a dealing in relevant securities and has previously borrowed relevant securities from, or lent such

Takeover Code

RULE 8 *CONTINUED*

NOTES ON RULE 8 continued

securities to, another person, the disclosure must be made in a form agreed by the Panel.

(b) Private disclosure (Rules 8.1(b)(ii) and 8.2)

Private disclosure under Rule 8.1(b)(ii) by exempt fund managers connected with an offeror or the offeree company must be in the form required by the Panel. A specimen disclosure form is available on the Panel's website (www.thetakeoverpanel.org.uk) or may be obtained from the Panel.

A disclosure by an exempt fund manager must specify the name of the offeror or the offeree company with which it is connected and the nature of the connection.

A private disclosure under Rule 8.2 must include the identity of the associate dealing, the total of relevant securities in which the dealing took place and the prices paid or received (in the case of an average price bargain, each underlying trade should be disclosed). A specimen disclosure form is available on the Panel's website (www.thetakeoverpanel.org.uk) or may be obtained from the Panel. Rule 8.2 disclosures should follow that format. In the case of dealings in options or derivatives the same information as specified in Note 5(a) is required.

6. Indemnity and other arrangements

(a) For the purpose of this Note, an arrangement includes indemnity or option arrangements, and any agreement or understanding, formal or informal, of whatever nature, relating to relevant securities which may be an inducement to deal or refrain from dealing.

If any person is party to such an arrangement with any offeror or an associate of any offeror, whether in respect of relevant securities of that offeror or the offeree company, not only will that render such person an associate of that offeror but it is also likely to mean that such person is acting in concert with that offeror; in that case Rules 4, 5, 6, 7, 9, 11 and 24 will be relevant. If any person is party to such an arrangement with an offeree company or an associate of an offeree company, not only will that render such person an associate of the offeree company but Note 3 on Rule 9.1 and Rule 25.3 may be relevant.

(b) When an arrangement exists with any offeror, with the offeree company or with an associate of any offeror or of the offeree company in relation to relevant securities, details of such arrangement must be publicly disclosed, whether or not any dealing takes place.

(c) This Note does not apply to irrevocable commitments or letters of intent, which are subject to Rule 8.4 and Note 14.

(d) See also Rule 4.4.

E26

RULE 8 *CONTINUED*

NOTES ON RULE 8 continued

7. Time for calculating a person's interests

(a) Under Rule 8.3, a disclosure of dealings is not required unless the person dealing is interested in 1% or more of any class of relevant securities at midnight on the date of the dealing or was so interested at midnight on the previous business day.

(b) For the purposes of Note 5, the interests and short positions to be disclosed are those existing or outstanding at midnight on the date of the dealing in question.

(c) A person will be treated as interested in relevant securities for the purposes of this Note 7 and Rule 8 if he has disposed of an interest in relevant securities before midnight on the date in question but there exists an agreement, arrangement or understanding, formal or informal, of any nature (but not itself amounting to an interest in the securities) as a result of which he is entitled, or would expect to be able, to acquire an interest in the securities concerned (or equivalent securities) thereafter.

8. Discretionary fund managers

The principle normally applied by the Panel is that where the investment decision is made by a discretionary fund manager, he, and not the person on whose behalf the fund is managed, will be treated as interested in, and having dealt in, the relevant securities concerned. For that reason, Rule 8.3(c) requires a discretionary fund manager to aggregate the investment accounts which he manages for the purpose of determining whether he has an obligation to disclose. The beneficial owner would not normally, therefore, be concerned with disclosure to the extent that his investment is managed on a discretionary basis. However, where any of the funds managed on behalf of a beneficial owner are not managed by the fund manager originally contracted to do so but are managed by a different independent third party who has discretion regarding dealing, voting and offer acceptance decisions, the fund manager to whom the management of the funds has been sub-contracted (and not the originally contracted fund manager) is required to aggregate those funds and to comply with the relevant disclosure obligations accordingly.

This approach assumes that the discretionary fund manager does not take instructions from the beneficial owner (or, in the case of sub-contracted funds, from the originally contracted manager or the beneficial owner) on the dealings in question and that fund management arrangements are not established or used to avoid disclosure.

RULE 8 CONTINUED

NOTES ON RULE 8 continued

9. Recognised intermediaries

The exception in relation to recognised intermediaries must not be used to avoid or delay disclosure of dealings. For example, a dealing in relevant securities by a recognised intermediary, backed by a firm commitment by a person to purchase the relevant securities from the recognised intermediary, will be regarded as a dealing by that person. A commitment may effectively be firm even if not legally binding, for example because of market practice. Such arrangements, therefore, should not be entered into unless appropriate disclosures are to be made. In addition, if such an arrangement is entered into with an offeror or a person acting in concert with the offeror, it might mean that the recognised intermediary is acting in concert with the offeror and normal concert party consequences might follow (such as the application of Rules 4, 5, 6, 7, 9, 11 and 24 and disclosure of dealings by the recognised intermediary under Rule 8.1).

Where a desk with recognised intermediary status deals in relevant securities other than in a client-serving capacity (or re-books a position which was acquired in a client-serving capacity so as to hold it in a proprietary capacity), it should aggregate and, where appropriate, disclose the interests, short positions and rights to subscribe which it holds in a proprietary capacity with those of the rest of the group. However, in making such disclosures, it need not aggregate and disclose details of any interests, short positions and rights to subscribe which it holds in a client-serving capacity.

Exempt principal traders connected with an offeror or the offeree company should, subject to the above, disclose dealings in the manner set out in Rule 38.5. Recognised intermediaries which are associates of the offeror or the offeree company and to which exempt status is not applicable should disclose dealings under Rule 8.1.

10. Responsibilities of intermediaries

Intermediaries are expected to co-operate with the Panel in its dealings enquiries. Therefore, those who deal in relevant securities should appreciate that intermediaries will supply the Panel with relevant information as to those dealings, including identities of clients and full client contact information, as part of that co-operation.

11. Unquoted public companies and relevant private companies

The requirements to disclose dealings apply also to dealings in relevant securities of public companies whose securities are not admitted to trading and of relevant private companies.

RULE 8 CONTINUED

NOTES ON RULE 8 continued

12. Potential offerors

If a potential offeror has been the subject of an announcement that talks are taking place (whether or not the potential offeror has been named) or has announced that it is considering making an offer, the potential offeror and persons acting in concert with it must disclose dealings in accordance with Rule 8.1 and must disclose the procuring of irrevocable commitments, or letters of intent in accordance with Rule 8.4 and such disclosures must include the identity of the potential offeror.

13. Companies Act 1985

In addition to the requirements to disclose under Rule 8, the requirements of Part VI of the Companies Act 1985 as to disclosure of interests may be relevant. It is likely that, where disclosure is necessary under that Act in respect of a notifiable interest in shares and a dealing occurs during an offer period, disclosure will also be necessary under Rule 8.3.

14. Irrevocable commitments and letters of intent

A disclosure of the procuring of an irrevocable commitment or a letter of intent must provide full details of the nature of the commitment or letter including:

(a) the number of relevant securities of each class to which the irrevocable commitment or letter of intent relates;

(b) the identity of the person from whom the irrevocable commitment or letter of intent has been procured. For this purpose, the information which should be disclosed is that which would be required by Note 5(a) on Rule 8 if the person concerned were disclosing a dealing in relevant securities;

(c) in respect of an irrevocable commitment, the circumstances (if any) in which it will cease to be binding; and

(d) in the case of an irrevocable commitment or a letter of intent procured prior to the announcement of a firm intention to make an offer under Rule 2.5, the value (and any other material terms) of the possible offer in respect of which the commitment or letter has been procured. (See Rule 2.4(c).)

No separate disclosure by an offeror is required under Rule 8.4(a) where the relevant information is included in an announcement made under Rule 2.5 which is released no later than 12 noon on the business day following the date on which the irrevocable commitment or letter of intent is procured.

See also Note 9 on the definition of acting in concert.

SECTION F. THE MANDATORY OFFER AND ITS TERMS

RULE 9

9.1 WHEN A MANDATORY OFFER IS REQUIRED AND WHO IS PRIMARILY RESPONSIBLE FOR MAKING IT

Except with the consent of the Panel, when:—

(a) any person acquires, whether by a series of transactions over a period of time or not, an interest in shares which (taken together with shares in which persons acting in concert with him are interested) carry 30% or more of the voting rights of a company; or

(b) any person, together with persons acting in concert with him, is interested in shares which in the aggregate carry not less than 30% of the voting rights of a company but does not hold shares carrying more than 50% of such voting rights and such person, or any person acting in concert with him, acquires an interest in any other shares which increases the percentage of shares carrying voting rights in which he is interested,

such person shall extend offers, on the basis set out in Rules 9.3, 9.4 and 9.5, to the holders of any class of equity share capital whether voting or non-voting and also to the holders of any other class of transferable securities carrying voting rights. Offers for different classes of equity share capital must be comparable; the Panel should be consulted in advance in such cases.

An offer will not be required under this Rule where control of the offeree company is acquired as a result of a voluntary offer made in accordance with the Code to all the holders of voting equity share capital and other transferable securities carrying voting rights.

(See Notes on Dispensations from Rule 9.)

NOTES ON RULE 9.1

PERSONS ACTING IN CONCERT

The majority of questions which arise in the context of Rule 9 relate to persons acting in concert. The definition of "acting in concert" contains a list of persons who are presumed to be acting in concert unless the contrary is established. Without prejudice to the general application of the definition, the following Notes illustrate how the Rule and definition are interpreted by the Panel. Any Panel view expressed in relation to "acting in concert" can relate only to the Code and should not be taken as guidance on the statutory provisions dealing with "persons acting together" contained in the Companies Act 1985.

RULE 9 *CONTINUED*

NOTES ON RULE 9.1 continued

1. Coming together to act in concert

Acting in concert requires the co-operation of two or more parties. When a party has acquired an interest in shares without the knowledge of other persons with whom he subsequently comes together to co-operate as a group to obtain or consolidate control of a company, and the shares in which they are interested at the time of coming together carry 30% or more of the voting rights in that company, the Panel will not normally require a general offer to be made under this Rule. Such parties having once come together, however, the provisions of the Rule will apply so that:—

(a) if the shares in which they are interested together carry less than 30% of the voting rights in that company, an obligation to make an offer will arise if any member of that group acquires an interest in any further shares so that the shares in which they are interested together carry 30% or more of such voting rights; or

(b) if the shares in which they are interested together carry 30% or more of the voting rights in that company and they do not hold shares carrying more than 50% of the voting rights in that company, no member of that group may acquire an interest in any other shares carrying voting rights in that company without incurring a similar obligation.

(See also Note 4 below.)

2. Collective shareholder action

The Panel does not normally regard the action of shareholders voting together on a particular resolution as action which of itself indicates that such parties are acting in concert. However, the Panel will normally presume shareholders who requisition or threaten to requisition the consideration of a board control-seeking proposal either at an annual general meeting or at an extraordinary general meeting, in each case together with their supporters as at the date of the requisition or threat, to be acting in concert with each other and with the proposed directors. Such parties will be presumed to have come into concert once an agreement or understanding is reached between them in respect of a board control-seeking proposal with the result that subsequent acquisitions of interests in shares by any member of the group could give rise to an offer obligation.

In determining whether a proposal is board control-seeking, the Panel will have regard to a number of factors, including the following:

(a) the relationship between any of the proposed directors and any of the shareholders proposing them or their supporters. Relevant factors in this regard will include:

RULE 9 *CONTINUED*

NOTES ON RULE 9.1 continued

(i) whether there is or has been any prior relationship between any of the activist shareholders, or their supporters, and any of the proposed directors;

(ii) whether there are any agreements, arrangements or understandings between any of the activist shareholders, or their supporters, and any of the proposed directors with regard to their proposed appointment; and

(iii) whether any of the proposed directors will be remunerated in any way by any of the activist shareholders, or their supporters, as a result of or following their appointment.

If, on this analysis, there is no relationship between any of the proposed directors and any of the activist shareholders or their supporters, or if any such relationship is insignificant, the proposal will not be considered to be board control-seeking such that the parties will not be presumed to be acting in concert and it will not be necessary for the factors set out at paragraphs (b) to (f) below to be considered. If, however, such a relationship does exist which is not insignificant, the proposal may be considered to be board control-seeking, depending on the application of the factors set out at paragraph (b) below or, if appropriate, paragraphs (b) to (f) below;

(b) the number of directors to be appointed or replaced compared with the total size of the board.

If it is proposed to appoint or replace only one director, the proposal will not normally be considered to be board control-seeking. If it is proposed to replace the entire board, or if the implementation of the proposal would result in the proposed directors representing a majority of the directors on the board, the proposal will normally be considered to be board control-seeking.

If, however, the implementation of the proposal would not result in the proposed directors representing a majority of the directors on the board, the proposal will not normally be considered to be board control-seeking unless an analysis of the factors set out at paragraphs (c) to (f) below would indicate otherwise;

(c) the board positions held by the directors being replaced and to be held by the proposed directors;

(d) the nature of the mandate, if any, for the proposed directors;

(e) whether any of the activist shareholders, or any of their supporters, will benefit, either directly or indirectly, as a result of the implementation of the proposal other than through its interest in shares in the company; and

RULE 9 CONTINUED

NOTES ON RULE 9.1 continued

(f) the relationship between the proposed directors and the existing directors and/or the relationship between the existing directors and the activist shareholders or their supporters.

In respect of a proposal to replace some or all of the directors and the investment manager of an investment trust company, the relationship between the proposed new investment manager and any of the activist shareholders, or their supporters, will also be relevant to the analysis of the factors set out at paragraph (a) above and, if appropriate, paragraphs (c) to (f) above.

In determining whether it is appropriate for such parties to be held no longer to be acting in concert, the Panel will take account of a number of factors, including the following:

(a) whether the parties have been successful in achieving their stated objective;

(b) whether there is any evidence to indicate that the parties should continue to be held to be acting in concert;

(c) whether there is any evidence of an ongoing struggle between the activist shareholders, or their supporters, and the board of the company;

(d) the types of activist shareholder involved and the relationship between them; and

(e) the relationship between the activist shareholders, or their supporters, and the proposed/new directors.

3. Directors of a company

Directors of a company will be presumed to be acting in concert during an offer period or when they have reason to believe that a bona fide offer might be imminent. The normal provisions of this Rule will apply in these circumstances. At other times, directors of a company are not presumed to be acting in concert in relation to control of the company of which they are directors. Subject to the constraints imposed by the Rules, directors are, so far as the Code is concerned, free to deal in the shares of their company. The Panel reserves the right, however, to examine situations closely should the actions of the directors suggest that they may be acting in concert.

If any persons who have indicated their support for the offeree company's directors against an offer thereafter acquire an interest in shares to frustrate the offer, the Panel would consider their position in relation to the directors. The directors of companies defending against an offer, their supporters or

Takeover Code

F₅

RULE 9 *CONTINUED*

NOTES ON RULE 9.1 continued

their advisers, should consult the Panel before acquiring an interest in any shares which might lead to the incurring of an obligation under this Rule.

(See also Note 5 on the definition of acting in concert.)

4. Acquisition of interests in shares by members of a group acting in concert

While the Panel accepts that the concept of persons acting in concert recognises a group as being the equivalent of a single person, the membership of such groups may change at any time. This being the case, there will be circumstances when the acquisition of an interest in shares by one member of a group acting in concert from another member will result in the acquirer of the interest in shares having an obligation to make an offer. Whenever a group acting in concert is interested in shares which together carry 30% or more of the voting rights in a company and as a result of an acquisition of an interest in shares from another member of the group a single member comes to be interested in shares carrying 30% or more or, if already interested in shares carrying over 30%, acquires an interest in any other shares carrying voting rights, the factors which the Panel will take into account in considering whether to waive the obligation to make an offer include:-

(a) whether the leader of the group or the member with the largest individual interest in shares has changed and whether the balance between the interests in the group has changed significantly;

(b) the price paid for the interest in shares acquired; and

(c) the relationship between the persons acting in concert and how long they have been acting in concert.

When the group is interested in shares carrying 30% or more of the voting rights in a company but does not hold shares carrying more than 50% of such voting rights, an offer obligation will arise if an interest in any other shares carrying voting rights is acquired from non-members of the group. When the group holds shares carrying over 50% of the voting rights in a company, no obligations normally arise from acquisitions by any member of the group. However, subject to considerations similar to those set out in the previous paragraph, the Panel may regard as giving rise to an obligation to make an offer the acquisition by a single member of the group of an interest in shares sufficient to increase the shares carrying voting rights in which he is interested to 30% or more or, if he is already interested in 30% or more, which increases the percentage of shares carrying voting rights in which he is interested.

RULE 9 *CONTINUED*

NOTES ON RULE 9.1 continued

For the purpose of calculating the highest price paid in the event of an offer under this Rule, the prices paid for an interest in shares acquired by one member of a group acting in concert from another may be relevant where, for example, all shares or interests in shares held within a group are acquired by that member making the offer or where prices paid between members are materially above the market price.

5. Employee Benefit Trusts

The Panel must be consulted in advance of any proposed acquisition of an interest in shares if the aggregate number of shares in which the directors, any other persons acting, or presumed to be acting, in concert with any of the directors and the trustees of an employee benefit trust ("EBT") are interested will, as a result of the acquisition, carry 30% or more of the voting rights or, if already carrying 30% or more, will increase further. The Panel must also be consulted in any case where a person (or group of persons acting, or presumed to be acting, in concert) is interested in shares carrying 30% or more (but does not hold shares carrying more than 50%) of the voting rights and it is proposed that an EBT acquires an interest in any other shares.

The mere establishment and operation of an EBT will not by itself give rise to a presumption that the trustees are acting in concert with the directors and/or a controller (or group of persons acting, or presumed to be acting in concert). The Panel will, however, consider all relevant factors including: the identities of the trustees; the composition of any remuneration committee; the nature of the funding arrangements; the percentage of the issued share capital in which the EBT is interested; the number of shares held to satisfy awards made to directors; the number of shares in which the EBT is interested in excess of those required to satisfy existing awards; the prices at which, method by which and persons from whom any interests in existing shares have been or are to be acquired; the established policy or practice of the trustees as regards decisions to acquire interests in shares or to exercise, or procure the exercise of, votes in respect of shares in which the EBT is interested; whether or not the directors themselves are presumed to be in concert; and the nature of any relationship existing between a controller (or group of persons acting, or presumed to be acting in concert) and both the directors and the trustees. Its consideration of these factors may lead the Panel to conclude that the trustees are acting in concert with the directors and/or a controller (or group).

No presumption of concertedness will apply in respect of shares held within the EBT but controlled by the beneficiaries.

RULE 9 *CONTINUED*

NOTES ON RULE 9.1 continued

OTHER GENERAL INTERPRETATIONS

6. Vendor of part only of an interest in shares

Shareholders sometimes wish to sell part only of their shareholdings or a purchaser may be prepared to purchase part only of a shareholding. This arises particularly where a purchaser wishes to acquire shares carrying just under 30% of the voting rights in a company, thereby avoiding an obligation under this Rule to make a general offer. The Panel will be concerned to see whether in such circumstances the vendor is acting in concert with the purchaser in such a way as effectively to allow the purchaser to exercise a significant degree of control over the retained shares, in which case a general offer would normally be required. A judgement on whether such significant degree of control exists will obviously depend on the circumstances of each individual case. In reaching its decision, the Panel will have regard, inter alia, to the points set out below.

(a) There might be less likelihood of a significant degree of control over the retained shares if the vendor was not an "insider".

(b) The payment of a very high price for the shares would tend to suggest that control over the entire holding was being secured.

(c) Where the retained shares are in themselves a significant part of the company's capital (or even in certain circumstances represent a significant sum of money in absolute terms), a greater element of independence may be presumed.

(d) It would be natural for a vendor of part of a controlling holding to select a purchaser whose ideas as regards the way the company is to be directed are reasonably compatible with his own. It is also natural that a purchaser of a substantial holding in a company should press for board representation and perhaps make the vendor's support for this a condition of purchase. Accordingly, these factors, divorced from any other evidence of a significant degree of control over the retained shares, would not lead the Panel to conclude that a general offer should be made.

Similar considerations will arise where the vendor remains interested in shares but without itself owning any of such shares, or where the acquisition is not of the shares themselves but of another type of interest in shares.

7. Placings and other arrangements

When a person is to acquire an interest in shares which will result in his being interested in shares carrying 30% or more of the voting rights of a company, the Panel will consider waiving the requirements of this Rule if firm arrangements are made for the number of shares carrying voting rights in

RULE 9 CONTINUED

NOTES ON RULE 9.1 continued

which he is interested to be reduced to below 30% prior to the acquisition (for example, by a placing of shares) or, in certain exceptional circumstances, if an undertaking is given to make such a reduction within a very short period after the acquisition. In all such cases, the Panel must be consulted in advance. The Panel will be concerned to ensure that none of the persons with whom the acquirer enters into transactions in order to reduce his interests is acting in concert with the acquirer; for example, an obligation under this Rule will not be avoided by placing shares with a number of persons having a common link, such as the discretionary clients of a fund manager who would be connected with the acquirer if he were an offeror (unless, in such circumstances, the fund manager would have exempt status).

8. *The chain principle*

Occasionally, a person or group of persons acting in concert acquiring shares resulting in a holding of over 50% of the voting rights of a company (which need not be a company to which the Code applies) will thereby acquire or consolidate control, as defined in the Code, of a second company because the first company itself is interested, either directly or indirectly through intermediate companies, in a controlling block of shares in the second company, or is interested in shares which, when aggregated with those which the person or group is already interested in, secure or consolidate control of the second company. The Panel will not normally require an offer to be made under this Rule in these circumstances unless either:-

(a) the interest in shares which the first company has in the second company is significant in relation to the first company. In assessing this, the Panel will take into account a number of factors including, as appropriate, the assets and profits of the respective companies. Relative values of 50% or more will normally be regarded as significant; or

(b) one of the main purposes of acquiring control of the first company was to secure control of the second company.

The Panel should be consulted in all cases which may come within the scope of this Note to establish whether, in the circumstances, any obligation arises under this Rule.

9. *Triggering Rule 9 during an offer period*

If it is proposed to incur an obligation under this Rule during the course of a non-mandatory offer, the Panel must be consulted in advance. Once such an obligation is incurred, an offer in compliance with this Rule must be announced immediately. If the cash is dependent upon a securities exchange, Note 3 on Rule 9.3 will be relevant.

RULE 9 *CONTINUED*

NOTES ON RULE 9.1 continued

Subject to Note 3 on Rule 9.3, where no change in the consideration is involved it will be sufficient, following the announcement, simply to notify offeree company shareholders in writing of the new number of shares in which the offeror and persons acting in concert with it are interested, of the fact that the acceptance condition (in the form required by Rule 9.3) is the only condition remaining and of the period for which the offer will remain open following posting of the document.

An offer made in compliance with this Rule must remain open for not less than 14 days following the date on which the document is posted to offeree company shareholders and as required by Rules 31.4 and 33.1.

Notes 3 and 4 on Rule 32.1 set out certain restrictions on the incurring of an obligation under this Rule during the offer period.

10. Convertible securities, warrants and options

In general, the acquisition of securities convertible into, warrants in respect of, or options or other rights to subscribe for, new shares does not give rise to an obligation under this Rule to make a general offer but the exercise of any conversion or subscription rights or options will be considered to be an acquisition of an interest in shares for the purpose of the Rule.

The Panel will not normally require an offer to be made following the exercise of conversion or subscription rights provided that the issue of convertible securities, or rights to subscribe for new shares carrying voting rights, to the person exercising the rights is approved by a vote of independent shareholders in general meeting in the manner described in Note 1 of the Notes on Dispensations from Rule 9. However, if the potential controller proposes to acquire any interest in further voting shares following the relevant meeting, the Panel should be consulted to establish the number of shares to which the waiver will be deemed to apply.

Where securities with conversion or subscription rights were issued at a time when no offer obligation on exercise of such rights would arise and no independent shareholders' approval was obtained, the Panel will consider the case on its merits and will have regard, inter alia, to the votes cast on any relevant resolution, the number of shares concerned and the attitude of the board of the company. It is always open to the holder of such rights to dispose of sufficient rights so that, on exercise, the shares in which he would be interested would together carry less than 30% of the voting rights in the company. In circumstances where such rights could not be transferred prior to exercise, the Panel would consider waiving the offer obligation arising upon an exercise of rights provided there was an undertaking to reduce the number of shares carrying voting rights in which he would be interested to below 30% within a reasonable time.

RULE 9 CONTINUED

NOTES ON RULE 9.1 continued

Any holder of conversion or subscription rights who intends to exercise such rights and so to be interested in shares carrying 30% or more of the voting rights of a company should consult the Panel before doing so to determine whether an offer obligation would arise under the Rule and if so at what price (see also Note 2(c) on Rule 9.5).

Where there are conversion or subscription rights currently capable of being exercised, this Rule is invoked at a level of 30% of the existing voting rights. Where they are capable of being exercised during an offer period, Notes 2 and 3 on Rule 10 will be relevant.

(See also Note 14 on Rule 9.1.)

11. *The reduction or dilution of a shareholding*

If a person or a group of persons acting in concert interested in shares carrying more than 30% of the voting rights of a company reduces its interest but not to less than 30%, such person or persons may subsequently acquire an interest in further shares without incurring an obligation to make a general offer subject to both of the following limitations:

(a) the total number of shares in which interests may be acquired under this Note in any period of 12 months must not exceed 1% of the voting share capital for the time being (and, in determining the number of shares in which interests have been acquired in any such 12 month period, any reductions in the number of shares in which the person or group is interested may not be netted off against acquisitions); and

(b) the percentage of shares in which the relevant person or group of persons acting in concert is interested following any acquisition under this Note must not exceed the highest percentage of shares in which such person or group of persons was interested in the previous 12 months.

Both these restrictions apply, and must be tested, at the time of any acquisition proposed under this Note, and by reference to the position which would result immediately upon implementation of the proposed acquisition. On each such occasion, the test must take account of the total issued voting share capital at the relevant time, and total number of shares and highest percentage concerned during the immediately preceding twelve months. As a result, it will not be permitted to increase percentage interests progressively from one year to another.

The Panel will regard a reduction of the percentage of shares in which the person or group is interested as a result of dilution following the issue of new shares as also being relevant for these purposes. Accordingly, dilution of an interest in shares carrying voting rights of more than 30% will give rise to the

RULE 9 *CONTINUED*

NOTES ON RULE 9.1 continued

ability to acquire an interest in further shares on the basis set out in this Note provided that the total percentage of shares carrying voting rights in which the person or group is interested has not been reduced below 30% and subject to the limits stipulated above.

If a shareholding has remained above 50% of the voting rights of a company, or is restored to more than 50% by acquisitions permitted under this Note, further acquisitions are unrestricted by the Rule. Otherwise, a percentage interest in shares carrying voting rights of more than 30% which is reduced or diluted may not be restored to its original level without giving rise to an obligation to make a general offer except as permitted under this Note. However, nothing in this Note affects or restricts subscriptions for new shares approved by independent shareholders in the manner outlined in Note 1 of the Notes on Dispensations from Rule 9. Additionally, in the case of dilution following the issue of new shares, the Panel will also consider waiving the requirements of the Rule if an arrangement can be made whereby shareholders approve, in the manner outlined in Note 1 of the Notes on Dispensations from Rule 9, the restoration of a diluted percentage interest by acquisitions from those to whom new shares are issued.

(See also Rule 37.1.)

12. Gifts

If a person receives a gift of shares or an interest in shares which takes the aggregate number of shares carrying voting rights in which he is interested to 30% or more, he must consult the Panel. (See also Note 3 on Rule 9.5.)

13. Discretionary fund managers and principal traders

Dealings by non-exempt discretionary fund managers and principal traders which are connected with an offeror or the offeree company will be treated in accordance with Rule 7.2.

14. Allotted but unissued shares

When shares of a company carrying voting rights have been allotted (even if provisionally) but have not yet been issued, for example, under a rights issue when the shares are represented by renounceable letters of allotment, the Panel should be consulted. Such shares are likely to be relevant for the purpose of calculating percentages under Rule 9.1.

15. Treasury shares

When an obligation to make an offer is incurred under this Rule, it is not necessary for the offer to extend to shares in the offeree company held in treasury.

RULE 9 CONTINUED

NOTES ON RULE 9.1 continued

16. Aggregation of holdings across a group and recognised intermediaries

Rule 9 will be relevant if the aggregate number of shares in which all persons under the same control# (including any exempt fund manager or exempt principal trader) are interested carry 30% or more of the voting rights of a company. However, provided that recognised intermediary status has not fallen away (see Note 3 on the definition of recognised intermediary), a recognised intermediary acting in a client-serving capacity will not be treated as interested in (or as having acquired an interest in) any securities by virtue only of paragraph (3) or paragraph (4) of the definition of interests in securities (other than those held in a proprietary capacity) for these purposes.

If such a group of persons includes a principal trader and the aggregate number of shares in a company in which the group is interested approaches or exceeds 30% of the voting rights, the Panel may consent to the principal trader continuing to acquire shares in the company without consequence under Rule 9.1 provided that the company is not in an offer period and the number of shares which the principal trader holds does not at any relevant time exceed 3% of the voting rights of the company. The Panel should be consulted in such cases.

17. Borrowed or lent shares

For the purpose of this Rule, if a person has borrowed or lent shares he will be treated as holding the voting rights in respect of such shares save for any borrowed shares which he has either on-lent or sold. A person must consult the Panel before acquiring or borrowing shares which, when taken together with shares in which he or any person acting in concert with him is already interested, and shares already borrowed or lent by him or any person acting in concert with him, would result in this Rule being triggered. In such circumstances, the Panel will then decide, inter alia, how the borrowed or lent shares should be treated for the purpose of the acceptance condition.

18. Changes in the nature of a person's interest

Subject to Note 2 on Rule 9.3, for the purpose of this Rule 9.1, a person will not normally be treated as having acquired an interest in shares as a result only of a transaction under which the number of shares in which he is interested under the different paragraphs of the definition of interests in securities changes but the aggregate number of shares in which he is interested following the transaction remains the same (for example, where the person acquires shares on exercise of a call option).

#See Note at end of Definitions Section.

RULE 9 *CONTINUED*

NOTES ON RULE 9.1 continued

However, a person who was interested in any shares by virtue of paragraph (3) or paragraph (4) of the definition of interests in securities on 20 May 2006 (when such interests first become relevant for the purpose of Rule 9.1) will normally be treated as having acquired an interest in shares if he subsequently becomes interested in such shares by virtue of paragraph (1) or paragraph (2) of the definition of interests in securities.

The Panel should be consulted in all such cases to establish whether, in the circumstances, any obligation arises under this Rule.

9.2 OBLIGATIONS OF OTHER PERSONS

In addition to the person specified in Rule 9.1, each of the principal members of a group of persons acting in concert with him may, according to the circumstances of the case, have the obligation to extend an offer.

NOTE ON RULE 9.2

Prime responsibility

The prime responsibility for making an offer under this Rule normally attaches to the person who makes the acquisition which imposes the obligation to make an offer. If such person is not a principal member of the group acting in concert, the obligation to make an offer may attach to the principal member or members and, in exceptional circumstances, to other members of the group acting in concert. This could include a member of the group who at the time when the obligation arises does not have any interest in shares. In this context, the Panel will not normally regard the underwriter of a mandatory offer, by virtue of his underwriting alone, as being a member of a group acting in concert and, therefore, responsible for making the offer (but see Note 3 on the definition of acting in concert).

An agreement between a person and a bank under which the person borrows money for the acquisition of shares or an interest in shares which gives rise to an obligation under the Rule will not of itself fall within the above.

9.3 CONDITIONS AND CONSENTS

NB This Rule should be read in conjunction with Appendix 4.

Except with the consent of the Panel (see Note 3):—

(a) offers made under this Rule must be conditional only upon the offeror having received acceptances in respect of shares which, together with shares acquired or agreed to be acquired before or during

RULE 9 CONTINUED

the offer, will result in the offeror and any person acting in concert with it holding shares carrying more than 50% of the voting rights; and

(b) no acquisition of any interest in shares which would give rise to a requirement for an offer under this Rule may be made if the making or implementation of such offer would or might be dependent on the passing of a resolution at any meeting of shareholders of the offeror or upon any other conditions, consents or arrangements.

NOTES ON RULE 9.3

1. When more than 50% is held

An offer made under this Rule should normally be unconditional when the offeror and persons acting in concert with it hold shares carrying more than 50% of the voting rights before the offer is made.

2. Acceptance condition

Notes 2-7 on Rule 10 also apply to offers under this Rule.

In the event that an offer under Rule 9 lapses because a purchase may not be counted as a result of Note 5 on Rule 10 and subsequently the purchase is completed, the Panel should be consulted. It will require appropriate action to be taken such as the making of a new offer or the reduction of the percentage of shares in which the offeror and persons acting in concert with it are interested.

In the event that:

(a) an offer under Rule 9 lapsed by virtue of the acceptance condition not having been satisfied in circumstances where the shares which were assented to the offer, together with the shares in which the offeror and persons acting in concert with it were interested at the time the offer lapsed, amounted in aggregate to more than 50% of the shares carrying voting rights; and

(b) subsequently the offeror, or any person acting in concert with it, becomes interested in shares in the offeree company by virtue of paragraph (1) or paragraph (2) of the definition of interests in securities and, when the offer lapsed, the offeror or any person acting in concert with it at that time was interested in such number (or a greater number) of shares in the offeree company by virtue only of paragraph (3) or paragraph (4) of that definition,

then a further offer in accordance with Rule 9 must normally be made if the shares in which the offeror and any persons acting in concert with it are then interested by virtue of paragraph (1) and paragraph (2) of the definition of interests in securities carry 30% or more of the voting rights of the offeree company. The price at which such an offer must be made will normally be the higher of the price at which the lapsed offer was made and the price

RULE 9 *CONTINUED*

NOTES ON RULE 9.3 continued

determined under Note 2(a) on Rule 9.5. The Panel should be consulted in all cases in which this Note may be relevant. (See also Rule 35.1.)

3. When dispensations may be granted

The Panel will not normally consider a request for a dispensation under this Rule other than in exceptional circumstances, such as:—

(a) when the necessary cash is to be provided, wholly or in part, by an issue of new securities. The Panel will normally require that both the announcement of the offer and the offer document include statements that if the acceptance condition is satisfied but the other conditions required by the Note on Rules 13.1 and 13.3 are not within the time required by Rule 31.7, and as a result the offer lapses:

(i) the offeror will immediately make a new cash offer in compliance with this Rule at the price required by Rule 9.5 (or, if greater, at the cash price offered under the lapsed offer); and

(ii) until posting of the offer document in respect of that new offer, the offeror and persons acting in concert with it must consult the Panel as to their ability to exercise, or procure the exercise of, the voting rights of the offeree company attaching to the shares in which they have an interest.

When a dispensation is given, the offeror must endeavour to fulfil the other conditions with all due diligence; or

(b) when any official authorisation or regulatory clearance is required before the offer document is posted. The person who has incurred the obligation under Rule 9 must endeavour to obtain authorisation or clearance with all due diligence. If authorisation or clearance is obtained, the offer document must be posted immediately. If authorisation or clearance is not obtained, the same consequences will follow as if the merger were prohibited following a reference to the Competition Commission or the initiation of proceedings by the European Commission (see Rule 9.4).

9.4 THE COMPETITION COMMISSION AND THE EUROPEAN COMMISSION

Offers under this Rule must, if appropriate, contain the terms required by Rule 12.1(a) and (b).

NOTES ON RULE 9.4

1. *If an offer lapses pursuant to Rule 12.1(a) or (b)*

If an offer under Rule 9 lapses pursuant to Rule 12.1(a) or (b), the obligation under the Rule does not lapse and, accordingly, if thereafter the merger is allowed, the offer must be reinstated on the same terms and at not less than

RULE 9 *CONTINUED*

NOTES ON RULE 9.4 continued

the same price as soon as practicable. If the merger is prohibited, the offer cannot be made and the Panel will consider whether, if there is no order to such effect, to require the offeror to reduce the percentage of shares carrying voting rights in which it and persons acting in concert with it are interested to below 30% or to its original level before the obligation to offer was incurred, if this was 30% or more. The Panel would normally expect an offeror whose offer has lapsed pursuant to Rule 12.1(a) or (b) to proceed with all due diligence before the Competition Commission or the European Commission. However, if, with the consent of the Panel and within a limited period, an offeror reduces the percentage of shares carrying voting rights in which it and persons acting in concert with it are interested to below 30%, or to its original level before the obligation to offer was incurred if that was 30% or more, the Panel will regard the obligation as having lapsed.

2. *Further acquisitions*

While the Competition Commission or the European Commission is considering the case (following a reference or initiation of proceedings) where an obligation to make an offer under this Rule has been incurred, the offeror or persons acting in concert with it may not acquire any interest in further shares in the offeree company.

9.5 CONSIDERATION TO BE OFFERED

(a) An offer made under Rule 9 must, in respect of each class of share capital involved, be in cash or be accompanied by a cash alternative at not less than the highest price paid by the offeror or any person acting in concert with it for any interest in shares of that class during the 12 months prior to the announcement of that offer. The Panel should be consulted where there is more than one class of share capital involved.

(b) If, after an announcement of an offer made under Rule 9 for a class of share capital and before the offer closes for acceptance, the offeror or any person acting in concert with it acquires any interest in shares of that class at above the offer price, it shall increase its offer for that class to not less than the highest price paid for the interest in shares so acquired.

(c) In certain circumstances, the Panel may determine that the highest price calculated under paragraphs (a) and (b) should be adjusted. (See Note 3.)

(d) The cash offer or the cash alternative must remain open after the offer has become or been declared unconditional as to acceptances for not less than 14 days after the date on which it would otherwise have expired (see Rule 31.4).

RULE 9 *CONTINUED*

NOTES ON RULE 9.5

1. Nature of consideration

When an interest in shares has been acquired for a consideration other than cash, the offer must nevertheless be in cash or be accompanied by a cash alternative of at least equal value, which must be determined by an independent valuation.

When there have been significant acquisitions in exchange for securities, General Principle 1 may be relevant and such securities may be required to be offered to all shareholders: a cash offer will also be required. The Panel should be consulted in such cases.

2. Calculation of the price

(a) The price paid for any acquisition of an interest in shares will be determined as follows:

(i) in the case of a purchase of shares, the price paid is the price at which the bargain between the purchaser (or, where applicable, his broker acting in an agency capacity) and the vendor (or principal trader) is struck;

(ii) in the case of a call option which remains unexercised, the price paid will normally be treated as the middle market price of the shares which are the subject of the option at the time the option is entered into;

(iii) in the case of a call option which has been exercised, the price paid will normally be treated as the amount paid on exercise of the option together with any amount paid by the option-holder on entering into the option;

(iv) in the case of a written put option (whether exercised or not), the price paid will normally be treated as the amount paid or payable on exercise of the option less any amount paid by the option-holder on entering into the option; and

(v) in the case of a derivative, the price paid will normally be treated as the initial reference price together with any fee paid on entering into the derivative.

In the case of an option or a derivative, however, if the option exercise price or derivative reference price is calculated by reference to the average price of a number of acquisitions by the counterparty of interests in underlying securities, the price paid will normally be determined to be the highest price at which such acquisitions are actually made.

Any stamp duty and broker's commission payable should be excluded.

RULE 9 CONTINUED

NOTES ON RULE 9.5 continued

Where a person acquired an interest in shares more than 12 months prior to the announcement of the offer made under Rule 9 as a result of any option, derivative or agreement to purchase and, either during the 12 months prior to such announcement or after the announcement and before the offer closes for acceptance, the person acquires any of the relevant shares, no obligation under this Rule will normally arise as a result of the acquisition of those shares. However, if the terms of the instrument have been varied in any way, or if the shares are acquired other than on the terms of the original instrument, the Panel should be consulted.

(b) If any interest in shares has been acquired in exchange for securities which are admitted to trading, the price will normally be established by reference to the middle market price of the securities at the time of the acquisition.

(c) If any interest in shares has been acquired by the conversion or exercise (as applicable) of securities convertible into, warrants in respect of, or options or other rights to subscribe for new shares, the price will normally be established by reference to the middle market price of the shares in question at the close of business on the day on which the relevant notice was submitted. If, however, the convertible securities, warrants, options or other subscription rights were acquired either during the 12 months prior to the announcement of the offer made under Rule 9 or after the announcement and before the offer closes for acceptance, they will be treated as if they were purchases of the underlying shares at a price calculated by reference to the acquisition price and the relevant conversion or exercise terms.

The Panel should be consulted in advance if it is proposed to acquire the voting rights attaching to shares, or general control of them, and in the circumstances described in (b) and (c) above.

3. Adjustment of highest price

Circumstances which the Panel might take into account when considering an adjustment of the highest price include:—

(a) the size and timing of the relevant acquisitions;

(b) the attitude of the board of the offeree company;

(c) whether interests in shares had been acquired at high prices from directors or other persons closely connected with the offeror or the offeree company;

(d) the number of shares in which interests have been acquired in the preceding 12 months;

Takeover Code

F19

RULE 9 *CONTINUED*

NOTES ON RULE 9.5 continued

(e) if an offer is required in order to enable a company in serious financial difficulty to be rescued;

(f) if an offer is required in the circumstances set out in Note 12 on Rule 9.1; and

(g) if an offer is required in the circumstances set out in Rule 37.1.

The price payable in the circumstances set out above will be the price that is fair and reasonable taking into account all the factors that are relevant to the circumstances.

In any case where the highest price is adjusted under Rule 9.5(c), the Panel will publish its decision.

4. Cum dividend

When accepting shareholders are entitled under the offer to retain a dividend declared or forecast by the offeree company but not yet paid, the offeror, in establishing the level of the cash offer, may deduct from the highest price paid the net dividend to which offeree company shareholders are entitled. Where the offeror or any person acting in concert with it has acquired any interest in shares to which this Note may be relevant other than by purchasing shares, the Panel should be consulted.

9.6 OBLIGATIONS OF DIRECTORS

When directors (and their close relatives and related trusts) sell shares to a person (or enter into options, derivatives or other transactions) as a result of which that person is required to make an offer under this Rule, the directors must ensure that as a condition of the sale (or other relevant transaction) the person undertakes to fulfil his obligations under the Rule. In addition, except with the consent of the Panel, such directors should not resign from the board until the first closing date of the offer or the date when the offer becomes or is declared wholly unconditional, whichever is the later.

9.7 RESTRICTIONS ON EXERCISE OF CONTROL BY AN OFFEROR

Except with the consent of the Panel, no nominee of an offeror or persons acting in concert with it may be appointed to the board of the offeree company, nor may an offeror and persons acting in concert with it exercise, or procure the exercise of, the votes attaching to any shares in the offeree company until the offer document has been posted.

RULE 9 CONTINUED

NOTES ON DISPENSATIONS FROM RULE 9

1. Vote of independent shareholders on the issue of new securities ("Whitewash")

(See Appendix 1 for Guidance Note)

When the issue of new securities as consideration for an acquisition or a cash subscription would otherwise result in an obligation to make a general offer under this Rule, the Panel will normally waive the obligation if there is an independent vote at a shareholders' meeting. The requirement for a general offer will also be waived, provided there has been a vote of independent shareholders, in cases involving the underwriting of an issue of shares. If an underwriter incurs an obligation under this Rule unexpectedly, for example as a result of an inability to sub-underwrite all or part of his liability, the Panel should be consulted.

The appropriate provisions of the Code apply to whitewash proposals. Full details of the potential number and percentage of shares in which the person or group of persons acting in concert might become interested (together with details of the different interests concerned) must be disclosed in the document sent to shareholders relating to the issue of the new securities, which must also include competent independent advice on the proposals the shareholders are being asked to approve, together with a statement that the Panel has agreed to waive any consequent obligation under this Rule to make a general offer. The resolution must be made the subject of a poll. The Panel must be consulted and a proof document submitted at an early stage.

When a person or group of persons acting in concert may, as a result of such arrangements, come to hold shares carrying more than 50% of the voting rights of the company, specific and prominent reference to the possibility must be contained in the document and to the fact that the person or group will be able to acquire interests in further shares without incurring any further obligation under Rule 9 to make a general offer.

When a waiver has been granted, as described above, in respect of convertible securities, options or rights to subscribe for shares, details, including the fact of the waiver and the maximum number of securities that may be issued as a result, should be included in the company's annual report and accounts until the securities in respect of which the waiver has been granted have been issued or it is confirmed that no such issue will be made.

Notwithstanding the fact that the issue of new securities is made conditional upon the prior approval of a majority of the shareholders independent of the transaction at a general meeting of the company:—

(a) the Panel will not normally waive an obligation under this Rule if the person to whom the new securities are to be issued or any persons acting in

RULE 9 *CONTINUED*

NOTES ON DISPENSATIONS FROM RULE 9 continued

concert with him have acquired any interest in shares in the company in the 12 months prior to the posting to shareholders of the circular relating to the proposals but subsequent to negotiations, discussions or the reaching of understandings or agreements with the directors of the company in relation to the proposed issue of new securities;

(b) a waiver will be invalidated if any acquisitions of interests in shares are made in the period between the posting of the circular to shareholders and the shareholders' meeting.

In exceptional circumstances, the Panel may consider waiving the requirement for a general offer where the approval of independent shareholders to the transfer of existing shares from one shareholder to another is obtained.

2. Enforcement of security for a loan

Where shares or other securities are charged as security for a loan and, as a result of enforcement, the lender would otherwise incur an obligation to make a general offer under this Rule, the Panel will not normally require an offer if sufficient interests in shares are disposed of within a limited period to persons unconnected with the lender, so that the percentage of shares carrying voting rights in which the lender, together with persons acting in concert with it, is interested is reduced to below 30% in a manner satisfactory to the Panel. The lender must consult the Panel as to its ability to exercise or procure the exercise of the voting rights attaching to the shares in which it is interested at any time before sufficient interests are disposed of, or if the interest in excess of 29.9% is likely to be temporary (for example because the company will be issuing more shares).

In any case where arrangements are to be made involving a transfer of voting rights to the lender, but which do not amount to enforcement of the security, the Panel will wish to be convinced that such arrangements are necessary to preserve the lender's security and that the security was not given at a time when the lender had reason to believe that enforcement was likely.

When, following enforcement, a lender sells all or part of a shareholding, the provisions of this Rule will apply to the purchaser. Although a receiver, liquidator or administrator of a company is not required to make an offer when he acquires an interest in shares carrying 30% or more of the voting rights in another company, the provisions of the Rule apply to a purchaser from such a person.

3. Rescue operations

There are occasions when a company is in such a serious financial position that the only way it can be saved is by an urgent rescue operation which

RULE 9 CONTINUED

NOTES ON DISPENSATIONS FROM RULE 9 continued

involves the issue of new shares without approval by a vote of independent shareholders or the acquisition of existing shares by the rescuer which would otherwise fall within the provisions of this Rule and normally require a general offer. The Panel may, however, waive the requirements of the Rule in such circumstances provided that either:

(a) approval for the rescue operation by a vote of independent shareholders is obtained as soon as possible after the rescue operation is carried out; or

(b) some other protection for independent shareholders is provided which the Panel considers satisfactory in the circumstances.

Where neither the approval of independent shareholders nor any other form of protection can be provided, a general offer under this Rule will be required. In such circumstances, however, the Panel may consider an adjustment of the highest price, pursuant to Note 3 on Rule 9.5.

The requirements of the Rule will not normally be waived in a case where a major shareholder in a company rather than that company itself is in need of rescue. The situation of that shareholder may have little relevance to the position of other shareholders and, therefore, the purchaser from such major shareholder must expect to be obliged to extend an offer under the Rule to all other shareholders.

4. *Inadvertent mistake*

If, due to an inadvertent mistake, a person incurs an obligation to make an offer under this Rule, the Panel will not normally require an offer if sufficient interests in shares are disposed of within a limited period to persons unconnected with him, so that the percentage of shares carrying voting rights in which the person, together with persons acting in concert with him, is interested is reduced to below 30% in a manner satisfactory to the Panel. Any such person must consult the Panel as to his ability to exercise or procure the exercise of the voting rights attaching to the shares in which he is interested at any time before sufficient interests are disposed of, or if the interest in excess of 29.9% is likely to be temporary (for example because the company will be issuing more shares).

5. *Shares carrying 50% or more of the voting rights*

The Panel will consider waiving the requirement for a general offer under this Rule where:—

(a) holders of shares carrying 50% or more of the voting rights state in writing that they would not accept such an offer; or

RULE 9 CONTINUED

NOTES ON DISPENSATIONS FROM RULE 9 continued

(b) shares carrying 50% or more of the voting rights are already held by one other person.

6. Enfranchisement of non-voting shares

There is no requirement to make a general offer under this Rule if a person interested in non-voting shares becomes upon enfranchisement of those shares interested in shares carrying 30% or more of the voting rights of a company, except where shares or interests in shares have been acquired at a time when the person had reason to believe that enfranchisement would take place.

SECTION G. THE VOLUNTARY OFFER AND ITS TERMS

RULE 10. THE ACCEPTANCE CONDITION

NB This Rule should be read in conjunction with Appendix 4.

It must be a condition of any offer for voting equity share capital or for other transferable securities carrying voting rights which, if accepted in full, would result in the offeror holding shares carrying over 50% of the voting rights of the offeree company that the offer will not become or be declared unconditional as to acceptances unless the offeror has acquired or agreed to acquire (either pursuant to the offer or otherwise) shares carrying over 50% of the voting rights.

NOTES ON RULE 10

1. Waiver of 50% condition

In certain exceptional cases, the Panel will consider waiving the requirements of this Rule subject to prior consultation and to appropriate safeguards. This might be appropriate where, for example, following a major change of management policy, it is desired to provide an opportunity for shareholders to dispose of their shares and where the offer is made on behalf of a group of investors who are otherwise wholly unconnected and whose purpose is not to gain control.

2. New shares

For the purpose of the acceptance condition, the offeror must take account of all shares carrying voting rights which are unconditionally allotted or issued before the offer becomes or is declared unconditional as to acceptances, whether pursuant to the exercise of conversion or subscription rights or otherwise. If in any case, for example, as a result of a rights issue, shares have been allotted in renounceable form (even if provisionally), the Panel should be consulted.

3. Information to offeror during offer period and extension of offer to new shares

Following the announcement of a firm intention to make an offer, the offeree company must, on request, provide the offeror as soon as possible with all relevant details of the issued shares (including the extent to which any such shares are held in treasury and details of any agreements to transfer or sell such shares out of treasury) and, to the extent not issued, the allotted shares and details of any conversion or subscription rights or any other rights pursuant to the exercise of which shares may be unconditionally allotted or issued during the offer period. In the case of conditionally allotted shares, the details should include the conditions and the date on which such conditions may be satisfied. In the case of rights, the details should include the number of shares which may be unconditionally allotted or issued during the offer period as a result of the exercise of such rights, identifying separately those

RULE 10 CONTINUED

NOTES ON RULE 10 continued

attributable to rights which commence or expire on different dates, and the various prices at which these rights could be exercised.

The offeree company must immediately notify the offeror of any allotment or issue of shares and of the exercise of any such rights during the offer period and provide the offeror as soon as possible with all relevant details.

The offeror must make appropriate arrangements to ensure that any person to whom shares of a type to which the offer relates are unconditionally allotted or issued during the offer period will have an opportunity of accepting the offer in respect of such shares.

In cases of doubt, the Panel must be consulted.

4. Acceptances

NB 1 Attention is drawn to Note 6 below which will be relevant if an acceptance condition is to be fulfilled before the final closing date.

NB 2 It is a matter for the offeror and its advisers, in particular the receiving agent, to determine whether, for shareholders within CREST, an offer can be accepted (and the acceptance withdrawn) electronically without the need for an acceptance form. If so, the procedure to be adopted must be made clear in the offer document.

An acceptance may not be counted towards fulfilling an acceptance condition unless:—

(a) if it is to be effected by means of CREST without an acceptance form, the transfer to the relevant member's escrow account has settled in respect of the relevant number of shares on or before the last time for acceptance set out in the offeror's relevant document or announcement; or,

if it is to be effected by means of an acceptance form, both:

(b) it is received by the offeror's receiving agent on or before the last time for acceptance set out in the offeror's relevant document or announcement and the offeror's receiving agent has recorded that the acceptance and any relevant documents required by this Note have been so received or relevant escrow transfers identified; and

(c) the acceptance form is completed to a suitable standard (see below) and is:

   (i) accompanied by share certificates in respect of the relevant shares and, if those certificates are not in the name of the acceptor, such other documents (eg a duly stamped transfer of the relevant shares in favour of the acceptor executed by the registered holder and otherwise completed

RULE 10 *CONTINUED*

NOTES ON RULE 10 continued

to a suitable standard) as are required by the practice set out in the then current edition of Company Secretarial Practice — The Manual of the Institute of Chartered Secretaries and Administrators ("the ICSA Manual") in order to establish the right of the acceptor to become the registered holder of the relevant shares; and if an acceptance is accompanied by share certificates in respect of some but not all of the relevant shares then, subject to the other requirements of this sub-paragraph (i) being fulfilled in respect of the shares which are covered by share certificates, the acceptance may be treated as fulfilling the requirements of this sub-paragraph (i) insofar as it relates to those covered shares; or

(ii) in the case of a holding in CREST, covered by a transfer to the relevant member's escrow account, details of which must be provided on the acceptance form; if the acceptance is covered by a transfer to escrow in respect of some but not all of the relevant holding, it may be treated as fulfilling the requirement of this sub-paragraph (ii) in respect of that part of the holding transferred to escrow; or

(iii) from a registered holder or his personal representatives (but only up to the amount of the registered holding as at the final time for acceptance and only to the extent that the acceptance relates to shares which are not taken into account under another sub-paragraph of this paragraph (c)); or

(iv) certified by the offeree company's registrar.

For this purpose an acceptance form is completed to a suitable standard:

(1) where the form constitutes a transfer, if it meets the criteria (other than being duly stamped) for the registration of transfers set out in the ICSA Manual; or

(2) where the form does not constitute a transfer, if it constitutes a valid and irrevocable appointment of the offeror or some person on its behalf as an agent or attorney for the purpose of executing a transfer of the type referred to in (1) above on behalf of the acceptor.

If the acceptance form is executed by a person other than the registered holder, appropriate evidence of authority (eg grant of probate or certified copy of a power of attorney) must be produced as required by the practice set out in the ICSA Manual.

G4

RULE 10 CONTINUED

NOTES ON RULE 10 continued

5. Purchases

NB Attention is drawn to Note 6 below which will be relevant if an acceptance condition is to be fulfilled before the final closing date, and also to Note 8 below which will be relevant if the offeror has borrowed any offeree company shares.

A purchase of shares by an offeror or its nominee (or in the case of a Rule 9 offer, a person acting in concert with the offeror, or its nominee) may be counted towards fulfilling an acceptance condition only if:—

(a) the offeror or its nominee (or in the case of a Rule 9 offer, a person acting in concert with the offeror, or its nominee) is the registered holder of the shares; or

(b) a transfer of the shares in favour of the offeror or its nominee (or in the case of a Rule 9 offer, a person acting in concert with the offeror, or its nominee) executed by or on behalf of the registered holder and otherwise completed to a suitable standard (as specified in paragraph (c) (i) of Note 4 above) and accompanied by the relevant share certificates or certified by the offeree company's registrar is delivered by or on behalf of the offeror to the offeror's receiving agent on or before the last time for acceptance set out in the offeror's relevant document or announcement and the offeror's receiving agent has recorded that the transfer and accompanying documents have been so received.

A person who has agreed to sell shares to the offeror or a person acting in concert with it is not, by virtue only of the agreement, a "nominee" for the purposes of this Note.

The offeror must advise its receiving agent of any parties whose registered holdings or purchases are relevant for the purpose of the acceptance condition. The offeror's receiving agent must then certify the holding of each such party on the basis of the register (or, in relation to holdings in CREST in respect of which CREST maintains the register, the record of securities held in uncertificated form).

6. Offers becoming or being declared unconditional as to acceptances before the final closing date

In determining whether an acceptance condition has been fulfilled before the final closing date, all acceptances and purchases that comply with the requirements of Notes 4 and 5 on Rule 10 may be counted, other than those which fall within paragraph (c)(iii) of Note 4 or Note 8.

7. Offeror's receiving agent's certificate

Before an offer may become or be declared unconditional as to acceptances, the offeror's receiving agent must have issued a certificate to the offeror or its

RULE 10 *CONTINUED*

NOTES ON RULE 10 continued

financial adviser which states the number of acceptances which have been received which comply with Note 4 on Rule 10 and the number of shares otherwise acquired, whether before or during an offer period, which comply with Note 5 on Rule 10 and, in each case, if appropriate, Note 6 on Rule 10, but which do not fall within Note 8 on Rule 10.

Copies of the receiving agent's certificate must be sent to the Panel and the offeree company's financial adviser by the offeror or its financial adviser as soon as possible after it is issued.

8. Borrowed shares

Except with the consent of the Panel, shares which have been borrowed by the offeror may not be counted towards fulfilling an acceptance condition.

RULE 11. NATURE OF CONSIDERATION TO BE OFFERED

11.1 WHEN A CASH OFFER IS REQUIRED

Except with the consent of the Panel in cases falling under (a) or (b), a cash offer is required where:—

(a) the shares of any class under offer in the offeree company in which interests are acquired for cash (but see Note 5) by an offeror and any person acting in concert with it during the offer period and within 12 months prior to its commencement carry 10% or more of the voting rights currently exercisable at a class meeting of that class, in which case the offer for that class shall be in cash or accompanied by a cash alternative at not less than the highest price paid by the offeror or any person acting in concert with it for any interest in shares of that class acquired during the offer period and within 12 months prior to its commencement; or

(b) subject to paragraph (a) above, any interest in shares of any class under offer in the offeree company is acquired for cash (but see Note 5) by an offeror or any person acting in concert with it during the offer period, in which case the offer for that class shall be in cash or accompanied by a cash alternative at not less than the highest price paid by the offeror or any person acting in concert with it for any interest in shares of that class acquired during the offer period; or

(c) in the view of the Panel there are circumstances which render such a course necessary in order to give effect to General Principle 1.

NOTES ON RULE 11.1

1. Price

For the purpose of this Rule, the price paid for any acquisition of an interest in shares will be determined as follows:

(a) in the case of a purchase of shares, the price paid is the price at which the bargain between the purchaser (or, where applicable, his broker acting in an agency capacity) and the vendor (or principal trader) is struck;

(b) in the case of a call option which remains unexercised, the price paid will normally be treated as the middle market price of the shares which are the subject of the option at the time the option is entered into;

(c) in the case of a call option which has been exercised, the price paid will normally be treated as the amount paid on exercise of the option together with any amount paid by the option-holder on entering into the option;

(d) in the case of a written put option (whether exercised or not), the price paid will normally be treated as the amount paid or payable on exercise of the

RULE 11 *CONTINUED*

NOTES ON RULE 11.1 continued

option less any amount paid by the option-holder on entering into the option; and

(e) in the case of a derivative, the price paid will normally be treated as the initial reference price together with any fee paid on entering into the derivative.

In the case of an option or a derivative, however, if the option exercise price or derivative reference price is calculated by reference to the average price of a number of acquisitions by the counterparty of interests in underlying securities, the price paid will normally be determined to be the highest price at which such acquisitions are actually made.

Any stamp duty and broker's commission payable should be excluded.

The Panel should be consulted in advance if it is proposed to acquire the voting rights attaching to shares, or general control of them.

Where a person acquired an interest in shares more than 12 months prior to the commencement of the offer period as a result of any option, derivative or agreement to purchase and, during the offer period or within 12 months prior to its commencement, the person acquires any of the relevant shares, no obligation under this Rule will normally arise as a result of the acquisition of those shares. However, if the terms of the instrument have been varied in any way, or if the shares are acquired other than on the terms of the original instrument, the Panel should be consulted.

2. Gross acquisitions

The Panel would normally regard Rule 11.1(a) as applying to the gross number of shares in which interests are acquired over the relevant period. Shares sold over that period or which are the subject of any short position should not normally be deducted. However, in exceptional circumstances and with the consent of the Panel, shares sold some considerable time before the beginning of the offer period (or shares which are the subject of any short position entered into some considerable time before the beginning of the offer period) may be deducted.

3. When the obligation is satisfied

The obligation to make cash available under this Rule will be considered to have been met if, at the time the acquisition was made, a cash offer or cash alternative at a price per share not less than that required by this Rule was open for acceptance, even if that offer or alternative closes for acceptance immediately thereafter.

RULE 11 *CONTINUED*

NOTES ON RULE 11.1 continued

4. *Equality of treatment*

The discretion given to the Panel in Rule 11.1(c) will not normally be exercised unless the vendors or other parties to the transactions giving rise to the interests are directors of, or other persons closely connected with, the offeror or the offeree company. In such cases, relatively small acquisitions could be relevant.

Rule 11.1(c) may also be relevant when interests in shares carrying 10% or more of the voting rights of a class have been acquired in the previous 12 months for a mixture of securities and cash. The Panel should be consulted in all relevant cases.

5. *Acquisitions for securities*

For the purpose of this Rule, interests in shares acquired by an offeror and any person acting in concert with it in exchange for securities, either during or in the 12 months preceding the commencement of the offer period, will normally be deemed to be acquisitions for cash on the basis of the value of the securities at the time of the purchase. However, if the vendor of the offeree company shares or other party to the transaction giving rise to the interest is required to hold the securities received or receivable in exchange until either the offer has lapsed or the offer consideration has been posted to accepting shareholders, no obligation under Rule 11.1 will be incurred.

See also Note 6 on Rule 11.2.

6. *Revision*

If an obligation under this Rule arises during the course of an offer period and a revision of the offer is necessary, an immediate announcement must be made (but see Rule 32).

7. *Discretionary fund managers and principal traders*

Dealings by non-exempt discretionary fund managers and principal traders which are connected with an offeror will be treated in accordance with Rule 7.2.

8. *Allotted but unissued shares*

When shares of a company carrying voting rights have been allotted (even if provisionally) but have not yet been issued, for example, under a rights issue when the shares are represented by renounceable letters of allotment, the Panel should be consulted. Such shares are likely to be relevant for the purpose of calculating percentages under this Rule.

RULE 11 *CONTINUED*

NOTES ON RULE 11.1 continued

9. Cum dividend

When accepting shareholders are entitled under the offer to retain a dividend declared or forecast by the offeree company but not yet paid, the offeror, in establishing the level of the cash offer, may deduct from the highest price paid the net dividend to which offeree company shareholders are entitled. Where the offeror or any person acting in concert with it has acquired any interest in shares to which this Note may be relevant other than by purchasing shares, the Panel should be consulted.

10. Convertible securities, warrants and options

Acquisitions of securities convertible into, warrants in respect of, or options or other rights to subscribe for, new shares will normally only be relevant to this Rule if they are converted or exercised (as applicable). Such acquisitions will then be treated as if they were acquisitions of the underlying shares at a price calculated by reference to the acquisition price and the relevant conversion or exercise terms. In any case of doubt, the Panel should be consulted.

11. Offer period

References to the offer period in this Rule are to the time during which the offeree company is in an offer period, irrespective of whether the offeror was contemplating an offer when the offer period commenced.

12. Competition reference period

If an offer is announced in accordance with Note (a)(iii) on Rule 35.1, any acquisitions of interests in offeree company shares for cash during the competition reference period will be deemed to be acquisitions during the new offer period for the purposes of Rule 11.1(b).

11.2 WHEN A SECURITIES OFFER IS REQUIRED

Where interests in shares of any class of the offeree company carrying 10% or more of the voting rights currently exercisable at a class meeting of that class have been acquired by an offeror and any person acting in concert with it in exchange for securities in the three months prior to the commencement of and during the offer period, such securities will normally be required to be offered to all other holders of shares of that class.

Unless the vendor or other party to the transaction giving rise to the interest is required to hold the securities received or receivable until either the offer has lapsed or the offer consideration has been posted to accepting shareholders, an obligation to make an offer in cash or to provide a cash alternative will also arise under Rule 11.1.

RULE 11 CONTINUED

NOTES ON RULE 11.2

1. Basis on which securities are to be offered

Any securities required to be offered pursuant to this Rule must be offered on the basis of the same number of consideration securities received or receivable by the vendor or other party to the transaction giving rise to the interest for each offeree company share rather than on the basis of securities equivalent to the value of the securities received or receivable by the vendor or such other party at the time of the relevant purchase. Where there has been more than one relevant acquisition, offeror securities must be offered on the basis of the greater or greatest number of consideration securities received or receivable for each offeree company share.

2. Equality of treatment

The Panel may require securities to be offered on the same basis to all other holders of shares of that class even though the amount purchased is less than 10% or the purchase took place more than three months prior to the commencement of the offer period. However, this discretion will not, normally, be exercised unless the vendors of the relevant shares or other parties to the transactions giving rise to the interests are directors of, or other persons closely connected with, the offeror or the offeree company.

3. Vendor placings

Shares acquired in exchange for securities will normally be deemed to be acquisitions for cash for the purposes of this Rule if an offeror or any of its associates arranges the immediate placing of such consideration securities for cash, in which case no obligation to make a securities offer under this Rule will arise.

4. Management retaining an interest

In a management buyout or similar transaction, if the only offeree shareholders who receive offeror securities are members of the management of the offeree company, the Panel will not, so long as the requirements of Note 4 on Rule 16 are complied with, require all offeree shareholders to be offered offeror securities pursuant to Rule 11.2, even though such members of the management of the offeree propose to sell, in exchange for offeror securities, more than 10% of the offeree's shares.

If, however, offeror securities are made available to any non-management shareholders (regardless of the size of their holding of offeree shares), the Panel will normally require such securities to be made available to all shareholders on the same terms.

RULE 11 *CONTINUED*

NOTES ON RULE 11.2 continued

5. *Acquisitions for a mixture of cash and securities*

The Panel should be consulted where interests in shares carrying 10% or more of the voting rights of a class have been acquired during the offer period and within 12 months prior to its commencement for a mixture of securities and cash.

6. *Acquisitions in exchange for securities to which selling restrictions are attached*

Where an offeror and any person acting in concert with it has acquired interests in shares carrying 10% or more of the voting rights of any class of shares in the offeree company during the offer period and within 12 months prior to its commencement and the consideration received or receivable by the vendor or other party to the transaction giving rise to the interest includes shares to which selling restrictions of the kind set out in the second sentence of Rule 11.2 are attached, the Panel should be consulted.

7. *Applicability of the Notes on Rule 11.1 to Rule 11.2*

See Notes 2, 5, 6, 7, 8, 10 and 11 on Rule 11.1 which may be relevant.

In addition, if an offer is announced in accordance with Note (a)(iii) on Rule 35.1, any acquisitions of interests in offeree company shares for securities during the competition reference period will be deemed to be acquisitions during the new offer period for the purposes of this Rule.

11.3 DISPENSATION FROM HIGHEST PRICE

If the offeror considers that the highest price (for the purpose of Rules 11.1 and 11.2) should not apply in a particular case, the offeror should consult the Panel, which has discretion to agree an adjusted price.

NOTE ON RULE 11.3

Relevant factors

Factors which the Panel might take into account when considering an application for an adjusted price include:—

(a) the size and timing of the relevant acquisitions;

(b) the attitude of the board of the offeree of the company;

(c) whether interests in shares had been acquired at high prices from directors or other persons closely connected with the offeror or the offeree company; and

(d) the number of shares in which interests have been acquired in the preceding 12 months.

RULE 12. THE COMPETITION COMMISSION AND THE EUROPEAN COMMISSION

12.1 REQUIREMENT FOR APPROPRIATE TERM IN OFFER

(a) Where an offer comes within the statutory provisions for possible reference to the Competition Commission, it must be a term of the offer that it will lapse if there is a reference before the first closing date or the date when the offer becomes or is declared unconditional as to acceptances, whichever is the later.

(b) Where an offer would give rise to a concentration with a Community dimension within the scope of Council Regulation 139/2004/EC, it must be a term of the offer that it will lapse if either:—

(i) the European Commission initiates proceedings under Article 6(1)(c); or

(ii) following a referral by the European Commission under Article 9.1 to a competent authority in the United Kingdom, there is a subsequent reference to the Competition Commission,

in either case before the first closing date or the date when the offer becomes or is declared unconditional as to acceptances, whichever is the later.

(c) Except in the case of an offer under Rule 9, the offeror may, in addition, make the offer conditional on a decision being made that there will be no reference, initiation of proceedings or referral. It may state, if desired, that the decision must be on terms satisfactory to it.

NOTE ON RULE 12.1

The effect of lapsing

The offer document must make it clear that the reference to the offer lapsing means not only that the offer will cease to be capable of further acceptance but also that shareholders and the offeror will thereafter cease to be bound by prior acceptances.

RULE 12 *CONTINUED*

12.2 OFFER PERIOD CEASES DURING COMPETITION REFERENCE PERIOD

When an offer or possible offer is referred to the Competition Commission or the European Commission initiates proceedings, the offer period will end. A new offer period will be deemed to begin at the time that the competition reference period ends. If there is no announcement of a new offer in accordance with Note (a)(iii) on Rule 35.1, this offer period will last until either the expiry of the 21 day period provided for in that Note or the announcement by all cleared offerors that they do not intend to make an offer, whichever is the earlier.

NOTE ON RULE 12.2

After a reference or initiation of proceedings

Following the ending of an offer period on a reference or initiation of proceedings, General Principle 3 and Rule 21.1 will normally continue to apply (see also Rule 19.8 and the Notes on Rules 6.1, 11.1, 11.2, 20.1, 20.2, 35.1 and 35.2 and 38.2).

RULE 13. PRE-CONDITIONS IN FIRM OFFER ANNOUNCEMENTS AND OFFER CONDITIONS

13.1 SUBJECTIVITY

An offer must not normally be subject to conditions or pre-conditions which depend solely on subjective judgements by the directors of the offeror or of the offeree company (as the case may be) or the fulfilment of which is in their hands. The Panel may be prepared to accept an element of subjectivity in certain circumstances where it is not practicable to specify all the factors on which satisfaction of a particular condition or pre-condition may depend, especially in cases involving official authorisations or regulatory clearances, the granting of which may be subject to additional material obligations for the offeror or the offeree company (as the case may be).

13.2 THE COMPETITION COMMISSION AND THE EUROPEAN COMMISSION

A condition or pre-condition included pursuant to Rule 12.1(c) is not subject to the provisions of Rules 13.1 or 13.4(a).

13.3 ACCEPTABILITY OF PRE-CONDITIONS

The Panel must be consulted in advance if a person proposes to include in an announcement any pre-condition to which the posting of the offer will be subject.

Except with the consent of the Panel, an offer must not be announced subject to a pre-condition unless the pre-condition:—

(a) is included pursuant to Rule 12.1(c); or

(b) involves a material official authorisation or regulatory clearance relating to the offer and:

(i) the offer is publicly recommended by the board of the offeree company; or

(ii) the Panel is satisfied that it is likely to prove impossible to obtain the authorisation or clearance within the Code timetable.

(See Note 5 on Rule 2.5.)

RULE 13 CONTINUED

NOTE ON RULES 13.1 and 13.3

Financing conditions and pre-conditions

An offer must not normally be made subject to a condition or pre-condition relating to financing. However:

(a) where the offer is for cash, or includes an element of cash, and the offeror proposes to finance the cash consideration by an issue of new securities, the offer must be made subject to any condition required, as a matter of law or regulatory requirement, in order validly to issue such securities or to have them listed or admitted to trading. Conditions which will normally be considered necessary for such purposes include:

(i) the passing of any resolution necessary to create or allot the new securities and/or to allot the new securities on a non-pre-emptive basis (if relevant); and

(ii) where the new securities are to be admitted to listing or to trading on any investment exchange or market, any necessary listing or admission to trading condition (see also Rule 24.9).

Such conditions must not be waivable and the Panel must be consulted in advance; and

(b) in exceptional cases, the Panel may be prepared to accept a pre-condition relating to financing either in addition to another pre-condition permitted by this Rule or otherwise; for example where, due to the likely period required to obtain any necessary material official authorisation or regulatory clearance, it is not reasonable for the offeror to maintain committed financing throughout the offer period, in which case:

(i) the financing pre-condition must be satisfied (or waived), or the offer must be withdrawn, within 21 days after the satisfaction (or waiver) of any other pre-condition or pre-conditions permitted by this Rule; and

(ii) the offeror and its financial adviser must confirm in writing to the Panel before announcement of the offer that they are not aware of any reason why the offeror would be unable to satisfy the financing pre-condition within that 21 day period.

13.4 INVOKING CONDITIONS AND PRE-CONDITIONS

(a) An offeror should not invoke any condition or pre-condition so as to cause the offer not to proceed, to lapse or to be withdrawn unless the circumstances which give rise to the right to invoke the condition or pre-condition are of material significance to the offeror in the context of the offer. The acceptance condition is not subject to this provision.

RULE 13 CONTINUED

(b) Following the announcement of a firm intention to make an offer, an offeror should use all reasonable efforts to ensure the satisfaction of any conditions or pre-conditions to which the offer is subject.

13.5 INVOKING OFFEREE PROTECTION CONDITIONS

An offeree company should not invoke, or cause or permit the offeror to invoke, any condition to an offer unless the circumstances which give rise to the right to invoke the condition are of material significance to the shareholders in the offeree company in the context of the offer.

NOTES ON RULE 13.5

1. When an offeree protection condition may be invoked

The circumstances in which the offeree company will be allowed to invoke, or cause or permit the offeror to invoke, a condition will not necessarily be restricted to those in which the Panel would permit an offeror to invoke a condition. In deciding whether an offeree company may invoke, or cause or permit the offeror to invoke, a condition, the Panel will take into account all relevant factors.

2. Availability of withdrawal rights

If the offeree company is not permitted to invoke, or to cause or permit the offeror to invoke, a condition, the Panel may instead determine in the light of all relevant facts that accepting shareholders should have the right to withdraw their acceptances on such terms as the Panel considers appropriate and, if so, the effect of this on the Code timetable. The ability of the Panel to require the introduction of withdrawal rights in such circumstances and to amend the Code timetable, and also the fact that the offer may cease to be unconditional as to acceptances as a result of such withdrawal rights being introduced, should be incorporated into the terms of the offer.

SECTION H. PROVISIONS APPLICABLE TO ALL OFFERS

RULE 14. WHERE THERE IS MORE THAN ONE CLASS OF SHARE CAPITAL

14.1 COMPARABLE OFFERS

Where a company has more than one class of equity share capital, a comparable offer must be made for each class whether such capital carries voting rights or not; the Panel should be consulted in advance. An offer for non-voting equity share capital should not be made conditional on any particular level of acceptances in respect of that class unless the offer for the voting equity share capital is also conditional on the success of the offer for the non-voting equity share capital. Classes of non-voting, non-equity share capital need not be the subject of an offer, except in the circumstances referred to in Rule 15.

NOTES ON RULE 14.1

1. Comparability

A comparable offer need not necessarily be an identical offer.

In the case of offers involving two or more classes of equity share capital which are admitted to the Official List or to trading on AIM, the ratio of the offer values should normally be equal to the average of the ratios of the middle market quotations taken from the Stock Exchange Daily Official List over the course of the six months preceding the commencement of the offer period. The Panel will not normally permit the use of any other ratio unless the advisers to the offeror and offeree company are jointly able to justify it.

In the case of offers involving two or more classes of equity share capital, one or more of which is not admitted to the Official List or to trading on AIM, the ratio of the offer values must be justified to the Panel in advance.

2. Offer for non-voting shares only

Where an offer for non-voting shares only is being made, comparable offers for voting classes are not required.

3. Treatment of certain classes of share capital

For the purpose of this Rule, the Panel may not regard as equity share capital certain classes of shares which, although equity share capital under the Companies Act 1985, have in practice very limited equity rights. In appropriate cases, the Panel should be consulted.

14.2 SEPARATE OFFERS FOR EACH CLASS

Where an offer is made for more than one class of share, separate offers must be made for each class.

RULE 15. APPROPRIATE OFFER FOR CONVERTIBLES ETC.

(a) When an offer is made for voting equity share capital or for other transferable securities carrying voting rights and the offeree company has convertible securities outstanding, the offeror must make an appropriate offer or proposal to the stockholders to ensure that their interests are safeguarded. Equality of treatment is required.

(b) The board of the offeree company must obtain competent independent advice on the offer or proposal to the stockholders and the substance of such advice must be made known to its stockholders, together with the board's views on the offer or proposal.

(c) Whenever practicable, the offer or proposal should be despatched to stockholders at the same time as the offer document is posted but, if this is not practicable, the Panel should be consulted and the offer or proposal should be despatched as soon as possible thereafter. A copy of the offer or proposal should be lodged with the Panel at the time of issue.

(d) The offer or proposal to stockholders required by this Rule should not normally be made conditional on any particular level of acceptances. It may, however, be put by way of a scheme to be considered at a stockholders' meeting.

(e) If an offeree company has options or subscription rights outstanding, the provisions of this Rule apply mutatis mutandis.

NOTES ON RULE 15

1. When conversion rights etc. are exercisable during an offer

All relevant documents issued to shareholders of the offeree company in connection with an offer must also, where practicable, be issued simultaneously to the holders of securities convertible into, rights to subscribe for and options over shares of the same class as those to which the offer relates. If those holders are able to exercise their rights during the course of the offer and to accept the offer in respect of the resulting shares, their attention should be drawn to this in the documents.

2. Rules 9 and 14

If an offer for any convertible securities is required by Rule 9 or Rule 14, compliance with the relevant Rule will be regarded as satisfying the obligation in Rule 15(a) in respect of those securities.

RULE 16. SPECIAL DEALS WITH FAVOURABLE CONDITIONS

Except with the consent of the Panel, an offeror or persons acting in concert with it may not make any arrangements with shareholders and may not deal or enter into arrangements to deal in shares of the offeree company, or enter into arrangements which involve acceptance of an offer, either during an offer or when one is reasonably in contemplation, if there are favourable conditions attached which are not being extended to all shareholders.

An arrangement made with a person who, while not a shareholder, is interested in shares carrying voting rights in the offeree company will also be prohibited by this Rule if favourable conditions are attached which are not being extended to the shareholders. For the avoidance of doubt, there is no requirement to extend an offer or any arrangement which would otherwise be prohibited by this Rule to any person who is interested in shares, but is not a shareholder.

(See also Rule 35.3.)

NOTES ON RULE 16

1. Top-ups and other arrangements

An arrangement to deal with favourable conditions attached includes any arrangement where there is a promise to make good to a vendor of shares any difference between the sale price and the price of any subsequent successful offer. An irrevocable commitment to accept an offer combined with an option to put the shares should the offer fail will also be regarded as such an arrangement.

Arrangements made by an offeror with a person acting in concert with it, whereby an interest in offeree company shares is acquired by the person acting in concert on the basis that the offeror will bear all the risks and receive all the benefits, are not prohibited by this Rule. Arrangements which contain a benefit or potential benefit to the person acting in concert (beyond normal expenses and carrying costs) are, however, normally prohibited. In cases of doubt, the Panel must be consulted.

2. Offeree company shareholders' approval of certain transactions — eg disposal of offeree company assets

In some cases, certain assets of the offeree company may be of no interest to the offeror. There is a possibility if a person interested in shares in the offeree company seeks to acquire the assets in question that the terms of the transaction will be such as to confer a special benefit on him; in any event, the arrangement is not capable of being extended to all shareholders. The Panel will normally consent to such a transaction, provided that the independent adviser to the offeree company publicly states that in his opinion the terms of the transaction are fair and reasonable and the transaction is

H4

RULE 16 CONTINUED

NOTES ON RULE 16 continued

approved at a general meeting of the offeree company's shareholders. At this meeting the vote must be a vote of independent shareholders and must be taken on a poll. Where a sale of assets takes place after the offer has become unconditional, the Panel will be concerned to see that there was no element of pre-arrangement in the transaction.

The Panel will consider allowing such a procedure in respect of other transactions where the issues are similar, eg a transaction with an offeree company shareholder involving offeror assets.

3. Finders' fees

This Rule also covers cases where a person interested in shares in an offeree company is to be remunerated for the part that he has played in promoting the offer. The Panel will normally consent to such remuneration, provided that the interest in shares is not substantial and it can be demonstrated that a person who had performed the same services, but had not at the same time been interested in offeree company shares, would have been entitled to receive no less remuneration.

4. Management retaining an interest and other management incentivisation

Sometimes an offeror may wish to arrange for the management of the offeree company to remain financially involved in the business. The methods by which this may be achieved vary but the principle which the Panel is concerned to safeguard is that the risks as well as the rewards associated with an equity shareholding should apply to the management's retained interest. For example, the Panel would not normally find acceptable an option arrangement which guaranteed the original offer price as a minimum. The Panel will require, as a condition of its consent, that the independent adviser to the offeree company publicly states that in its opinion the arrangements with the management of the offeree company are fair and reasonable. In addition, the Panel will also require such arrangements to be approved at a general meeting of the offeree company's shareholders. At this meeting the vote must be a vote of independent shareholders and must be taken on a poll. Holdings of convertible securities, options and other subscription rights may also be relevant in determining whether a general meeting is required, particularly where such rights are exercisable during an offer.

Where the offeror wishes to arrange other incentivisation for management to ensure their continued involvement in the business, the Panel will require, as a condition of its consent, that the independent adviser to the offeree company publicly states that in its opinion the arrangements are fair and reasonable.

The Panel must be consulted in all circumstances where this Note may be relevant.

RULE 17. ANNOUNCEMENT OF ACCEPTANCE LEVELS

17.1 TIMING AND CONTENTS

By 8.00 am at the latest on the business day following the day on which an offer is due to expire, or becomes or is declared unconditional as to acceptances, or is revised or extended, an offeror must make an appropriate announcement. The announcement must state:—

(a) the number of shares for which acceptances of the offer have been received, specifying the extent to which acceptances have been received from persons acting in concert with the offeror or in respect of shares which were subject to an irrevocable commitment or a letter of intent procured by the offeror or any of its associates;

(b) details of any relevant securities of the offeree company in which the offeror or any person acting in concert with it has an interest or in respect of which he has a right to subscribe, in each case specifying the nature of the interests or rights concerned (see Note 5(a) on Rule 8). Similar details of any short positions (whether conditional or absolute and whether in the money or otherwise), including any short position under a derivative, any agreement to sell or any delivery obligation or right to require another person to purchase or take delivery, must also be stated;

(c) details of any relevant securities of the offeree company in respect of which the offeror or any of its associates has an outstanding irrevocable commitment or letter of intent (see Note 14 on Rule 8); and

(d) details of any relevant securities of the offeree company which the offeror or any person acting in concert with it has borrowed or lent, save for any borrowed shares which have been either on-lent or sold,

and must specify the percentages of each class of relevant securities represented by these figures. (See also Rule 31.2.)

Any announcement made pursuant to this Rule must include a prominent statement of the total numbers of shares which the offeror may count towards the satisfaction of its acceptance condition and must specify the percentages of each class of relevant securities represented by these figures. The Panel should be consulted if the offeror wishes to make any other statement about acceptance levels in any announcement made pursuant to this Rule.

NOTES ON RULE 17.1

1. Acceptances of cash underwritten alternatives

Acceptances of cash underwritten alternatives do not come within this Rule.

2. General statements about acceptance levels

If, during an offer, any statements, either oral or in writing, are made by an offeror or its advisers about the level of acceptances of the offer or the

RULE 17 *CONTINUED*

NOTES ON RULE 17.1 continued

number or percentage of shareholders who have accepted the offer, an immediate announcement must be made in conformity with this Rule.

3. *Alternative offers*

An announcement under this Rule is also required on the business day following the day on which an alternative offer is due to expire, even if the offer itself is not due to expire at that time.

4. *Publication of announcements*

An announcement under this Rule must be published in accordance with the requirements of Rule 2.9. However, in the case of companies whose securities are not admitted to listing or admitted to trading, it would normally be permissible to write to all shareholders instead of making an announcement.

5. *Statements about withdrawals*

When the offeree company is proposing to draw attention to withdrawals of acceptance, the Panel must be consulted before any announcement is made.

6. *Incomplete acceptances and offeror purchases*

Acceptances not complete in all respects and purchases must only be included in the statement required under this Rule of the total number of shares which the offeror may count towards the satisfaction of its acceptance condition where they could be counted towards fulfilling an acceptance condition under Notes 4, 5 and 6 on Rule 10.

17.2 CONSEQUENCES OF FAILURE TO ANNOUNCE

(a) If an offeror, having announced the offer to be unconditional as to acceptances, fails by 3.30 pm on the relevant day to comply with any of the requirements of Rule 17.1, immediately thereafter any acceptor will be entitled to withdraw his acceptance. Subject to Rule 31.6, this right of withdrawal may be terminated not less than 8 days after the relevant day by the offeror confirming, if such is the case, that the offer is still unconditional as to acceptances and complying with Rule 17.1.

(b) For the purpose of Rule 31.4, the offer must remain open for acceptance for not less than 14 days after the date of such confirmation and compliance.

RULE 18. THE USE OF PROXIES AND OTHER AUTHORITIES IN RELATION TO ACCEPTANCES

An offeror may not require a shareholder as a term of his acceptance of an offer to appoint a proxy to vote in respect of his shares in the offeree company or to exercise any other rights or take any other action in relation to those shares unless the appointment is on the following terms, which must be set out in the offer document:—

(a) the proxy may not vote, the rights may not be exercised and no other action may be taken unless the offer is wholly unconditional or, in the case of voting by the proxy, the resolution in question concerns the last remaining condition of the offer (other than any condition covered by Rule 24.9) and the offer will become wholly unconditional (save, where relevant, for the satisfaction of any condition covered by Rule 24.9) or lapse depending upon the outcome of that resolution;

(b) where relevant, the votes are to be cast as far as possible to satisfy any outstanding condition of the offer;

(c) the appointment ceases to be valid if the acceptance is withdrawn; and

(d) the appointment applies only to shares assented to the offer.

SECTION I. CONDUCT DURING THE OFFER

RULE 19. INFORMATION

19.1 STANDARDS OF CARE

Each document or advertisement issued, or statement made, during the course of an offer must be prepared with the highest standards of care and accuracy and the information given must be adequately and fairly presented. This applies whether it is issued by the company direct or by an adviser on its behalf.

NOTES ON RULE 19.1

1. Financial advisers' responsibility for release of information

The Panel regards financial advisers as being responsible to the Panel for guiding their clients and any relevant public relations advisers with regard to any information released during the course of an offer.

Advisers must ensure at an early stage that directors and officials of companies are warned that they must consider carefully the Code implications of what they say, particularly when giving interviews to, or taking part in discussions with, the media. It is very difficult after publication to alter an impression given or a view or remark attributed to a particular person. Control of any possible abuse lies largely with the person being interviewed. In appropriate circumstances, the Panel will require a statement of retraction. Particular areas of sensitivity on which comment must be avoided include future profits and prospects, asset values and the likelihood of the revision of an offer (see also Note 2 on Rule 20.1).

2. Unambiguous language

The language used in documents, releases or advertisements must clearly and concisely reflect the position being described. In particular, the word "agreement" must be used with the greatest care. Statements must be avoided which may give the impression that persons have committed themselves to certain courses of action (eg accepting in respect of their own shares) when they have not in fact done so.

3. Sources

The source for any fact which is material to an argument must be clearly stated, including sufficient detail to enable the significance of the fact to be assessed; however, if the information has been included in a document previously sent to shareholders, an appropriate cross reference may be made.

RULE 19 CONTINUED

NOTES ON RULE 19.1 continued

4. Quotations

A quotation (eg from a newspaper or a broker's circular) must not be used out of context and details of the origin must be included.

Since quotations will necessarily carry the implication that the comments quoted are endorsed by the board, such comments must not be quoted unless the board is prepared, where appropriate, to corroborate or substantiate them and the directors' responsibility statement is included.

5. Diagrams etc.

Pictorial representations, charts, graphs and diagrams must be presented without distortion and, when relevant, must be to scale.

6. Use of television, videos, audio tapes etc.

If any of these are to be used, even when they do not constitute advertisements (see Rule 19.4), the Panel must be consulted in advance.

7. Financial Services and Markets Act 2000

Persons involved in offers should note that Part VIII (penalties for market abuse) and Section 397 (misleading statements and practices) of the FSMA may be relevant.

8. Merger benefits statements

In order to satisfy the existing standards of information set out in the Code, certain additional requirements may need to be complied with if a party makes quantified statements about the expected financial benefits of a proposed takeover or merger (for example, a statement by an offeror that it would expect the offeree company to contribute an additional £x million of profit post acquisition). These requirements will only need to be complied with in securities exchange offers and will not normally apply in the case of a recommended securities exchange offer unless a competing offer is made and the merger benefits statement is subsequently repeated by the party which made it or the statement otherwise becomes a material issue. These additional requirements include publication of:

(a) the bases of the belief (including sources of information) supporting the statement;

(b) reports by financial advisers and accountants that the statement has been made with due care and consideration;

RULE 19 *CONTINUED*

NOTES ON RULE 19.1 continued

(c) an analysis and explanation of the constituent elements sufficient to enable shareholders to understand the relative importance of these elements; and

(d) a base figure for any comparison drawn.

These requirements may also be applicable to statements to the effect that an acquisition will enhance an offeror's earnings per share where such enhancement depends in whole or in part on material merger benefits.

Parties wishing to make merger benefits statements should consult the Panel in advance. See also Rule 28.6(g).

19.2 RESPONSIBILITY

(a) Each document issued to shareholders or advertisement published in connection with an offer by, or on behalf of, the offeror or the offeree company, must state that the directors of the offeror and/or, where appropriate, the offeree company accept responsibility for the information contained in the document or advertisement and that, to the best of their knowledge and belief (having taken all reasonable care to ensure that such is the case), the information contained in the document or advertisement is in accordance with the facts and, where appropriate, that it does not omit anything likely to affect the import of such information. This Rule does not apply to advertisements falling within paragraphs (i), (ii) or (viii) of Rule 19.4 and advertisements which only contain information already published in a circular which included the statement required by this Rule.

(b) If it is proposed that any director should be excluded from such a statement, the Panel's consent is required. Such consent is given only in exceptional circumstances and in such cases the omission and the reasons for it must be stated in the document or advertisement.

NOTES ON RULE 19.2

1. *Delegation of responsibility*

Offeror and offeree company boards must have regard to section 3(f) of the Introduction and to Section 1 of Appendix 3.

If detailed supervision of any document or advertisement has been delegated to a committee of the board, each of the remaining directors of the company must reasonably believe that the persons to whom supervision has been delegated are competent to carry it out and must have disclosed to the committee all relevant facts directly relating to himself (including his close relatives and related trusts) and all other relevant facts known to him and

RULE 19 CONTINUED

NOTES ON RULE 19.2 continued

relevant opinions held by him which, to the best of his knowledge and belief, either are not known to any member of the committee or, in the absence of his specifically drawing attention thereto, are unlikely to be considered by the committee during the preparation of the document or advertisement. This does not, however, override the requirements of the UKLA Rules relating to the acceptance of responsibility for a prospectus or equivalent document where applicable.

2. Expressions of opinion

The responsibility statement is regarded by the Panel as embracing expressions of opinion in the document or advertisement.

3. Quoting information about another company

Where a company issues a document or advertisement containing information about another company which makes it clear that such information has been compiled from published sources, the directors of the company issuing the document or advertisement need, as regards the information so compiled, only take responsibility for the correctness and fairness of its reproduction or presentation and the responsibility statement may be amended accordingly. Where statements of opinion or conclusions concerning another company or unpublished information originating from another company are included, these must normally be covered by a responsibility statement by the directors of the company issuing the document or advertisement or by the directors of the other company; the qualified form of responsibility statement provided for in this Note is not acceptable in such instances. However, where a responsibility statement relates to a prospectus or an equivalent document, the provisions of the UKLA Rules may affect the form of responsibility statement required.

4. Exclusion of directors

Although the Panel may be willing to consider the exclusion of a director from the responsibility statement in appropriate circumstances, where that statement relates to a prospectus or an equivalent document the provisions of the UKLA Rules may affect the position.

5. When an offeror is controlled

If the offeror is controlled, directly or indirectly, by another person or group, the Panel will normally require that, in addition to the directors of the offeror, other persons (eg directors of an ultimate parent) take responsibility for documents or advertisements issued by or on behalf of the offeror. In such circumstances, the Panel must be consulted.

RULE 19 CONTINUED

19.3 UNACCEPTABLE STATEMENTS

Parties to an offer or potential offer and their advisers must take care not to issue statements which, while not factually inaccurate, may mislead shareholders and the market or may create uncertainty. In particular, an offeror must not make a statement to the effect that it may improve its offer without committing itself to doing so and specifying the improvement.

NOTES ON RULE 19.3

1. *Holding statements*

While an offeror may need to consider its position in the light of new developments, and may make a statement to that effect, and while a potential competing offeror may make a statement that it is considering making an offer, it is not acceptable for such statements to remain unclarified for more than a limited time in the later stages of the offer period. Before any statements of this kind are made, the Panel must be consulted as to the period allowable for clarification. This does not detract in any way from the obligation to make timely announcements under Rule 2.

2. *Statements of support*

An offeror or the offeree company must not make statements about the level of support from shareholders or other persons unless their up-to-date intentions have been clearly stated to the offeror or the offeree company (as appropriate) or to their respective advisers. The Panel will require any such statement to be verified to its satisfaction. This will normally include the shareholder or other person confirming its support in writing to the relevant party to the offer or its adviser and that confirmation being provided to the Panel. Such confirmation will then be treated as a letter of intent. The Panel will not require separate verification by an offeror where the information required by Note 14 on Rule 8 is included in an announcement made under Rule 2.5 which is released no later than 12 noon on the business day following the date on which the letter of intent is procured.

19.4 ADVERTISEMENTS

The publication of advertisements connected with an offer or potential offer is prohibited unless the advertisement falls within one of the categories listed below. In addition, except where the advertisement falls within categories (i) or (viii), it must be cleared with the Panel in advance.

The categories are as follows:—

(i)   product advertisements not bearing on an offer or potential offer (where there could be any doubt, the Panel must be consulted);

RULE 19 CONTINUED

(ii) corporate image advertisements not bearing on an offer or potential offer;

(iii) advertisements confined to non-controversial information about an offer (eg reminders as to closing times or the value of an offer). Such advertisements must avoid argument or invective;

(iv) advertisements comprising preliminary or interim results and their accompanying statement, provided the latter is not used for argument or invective concerning an offer;

(v) advertisements giving information, the publication of which by advertisement is required or specifically permitted by the UKLA Rules;

(vi) advertisements communicating information relevant to holders of bearer securities;

(vii) advertisements comprising a tender offer under Appendix 5;

(viii) advertisements which are notices relating to Court schemes; or

(ix) advertisements published with the specific prior consent of the Panel. (As examples, this might be given if it were necessary to communicate with shareholders during a postal strike or in the circumstances referred to in Note 3 on Rule 20.1.)

NOTES ON RULE 19.4

1. Clearance

When clearance of advertisements is being sought, the Panel should be given at least 24 hours to consider a proof. Such proofs must have been approved by the financial adviser.

2. Verification

The Panel will not verify the accuracy of statements made in advertisements submitted for clearance. If, subsequently, it becomes apparent that any statement was incorrect, the Panel may, at the least, require an immediate correction.

3. Source

Each advertisement connected with an offer or potential offer must clearly and prominently identify the party on whose behalf it is being published.

4. Use of alternative media

For the purpose of this Rule, advertisements include not only press advertisements but also advertisements in other media, such as television, radio, video, audio tape and poster.

RULE 19 CONTINUED

NOTES ON RULE 19.4 continued

5. Forms

Acceptance forms, withdrawal forms, proxy cards or any other forms connected with an offer must not be published in newspapers.

19.5 TELEPHONE CAMPAIGNS

Except with the consent of the Panel, campaigns in which shareholders or other persons interested in shares are contacted by telephone may be conducted only by staff of the financial adviser who are fully conversant with the requirements of, and their responsibilities under, the Code. Only previously published information which remains accurate, and is not misleading at the time it is quoted, may be used in telephone campaigns. Shareholders and other persons interested in shares must not be put under pressure and must be encouraged to consult their professional advisers.

NOTES ON RULE 19.5

1. Consent to use other callers

If it is impossible to use staff of the type mentioned in this Rule, the Panel may consent to the use of other people subject to:—

(a) an appropriate script for callers being approved by the Panel;

(b) the financial adviser carefully briefing the callers prior to the start of the operation and, in particular, stressing:

(i) that callers must not depart from the script;

(ii) that callers must decline to answer questions the answers to which fall outside the information given in the script; and

(iii) the callers' responsibilities under General Principle 1 and Rule 20.1; and

(c) the operation being supervised by the financial adviser.

2. New information

If, in spite of this Rule, new information is given to some shareholders or other persons interested in shares, such information must immediately be made generally available in the manner described in Note 3 on Rule 20.1.

3. Gathering of irrevocable commitments

In accordance with Rule 4.3, the Panel must be consulted before a telephone campaign is conducted with a view to gathering irrevocable commitments in

RULE 19 CONTINUED

NOTES ON RULE 19.5 continued

connection with an offer. Rule 19.5 applies to such campaigns although, in appropriate circumstances, the Panel may permit those called to be informed of details of a proposed offer which has not been publicly announced. Attention is, however, drawn to General Principles 1 and 2.

4. Statutory and other regulatory provisions

Those communicating information falling within this Rule must also take account of the provisions of Section 21 of the FSMA (restrictions on financial promotion) and, where relevant, the provisions of the FSA's conduct of business rules.

Any view expressed by the Panel in relation to the telephoning of shareholders or other persons interested in shares can only relate to the Code and must not be taken to extend to any other regulatory requirement, for example the provisions of the FSMA or the FSA's conduct of business rules.

19.6 INTERVIEWS AND DEBATES

Parties involved in offers should, if interviewed on radio or television, seek to ensure that the sequence of the interview is not broken by the insertion of comments or observations by others not made in the course of the interview. Further, joint interviews or public confrontation between representatives of the offeror and the offeree company, or between competing offerors, should be avoided (see also Note 2 on Rule 20.1).

19.7 DISTRIBUTION AND AVAILABILITY OF DOCUMENTS AND ANNOUNCEMENTS

Before the offer document is made public, a copy must be lodged with the Panel. Copies of all other documents and announcements bearing on an offer and of advertisements and any material released to the media (including any notes to editors) must at the time of release be lodged with the Panel and the advisers to all other parties to the offer and must not be released to the media under an embargo (see also the Note on Rule 26). When the release is outside normal business hours, such advisers must be informed of the release immediately, if necessary by telephone; special arrangements may need to be made to ensure that the material is delivered directly to them and to the Panel. No party to an offer should be put at a disadvantage through delay in the release of new information to it.

RULE 19 *CONTINUED*

19.8 INFORMATION RELEASED FOLLOWING THE ENDING OF AN OFFER PERIOD PURSUANT TO RULE 12.2

The requirements of the Code relating to the release of information do not normally apply once an offer period has ended pursuant to Rule 12.2. However, if thereafter the merger is allowed and, as a result, the offeror announces a further offer, the Panel may require that statements (including valuations of assets) made during the competition reference period be substantiated or, if this is not possible, withdrawn. Consequently, the parties must take care to ensure that any statements made during the competition reference period are capable of substantiation.

RULE 20. EQUALITY OF INFORMATION

20.1 EQUALITY OF INFORMATION TO SHAREHOLDERS

Information about companies involved in an offer must be made equally available to all offeree company shareholders as nearly as possible at the same time and in the same manner.

NOTES ON RULE 20.1

1. *Furnishing of information to offerors*

This Rule does not prevent the furnishing of information in confidence by an offeree company to a bona fide potential offeror or vice versa.

2. *Press, television and radio interviews*

Parties involved in an offer must take particular care not to release new material in interviews or discussions with the media. If, notwithstanding this Note, any new information is made public as a result of such an interview or discussion, a circular must be sent to shareholders and, where appropriate, paid newspaper space taken as required by Note 3 below (see also Note 1 on Rule 19.1).

3. *Meetings*

Meetings of representatives of the offeror or the offeree company or their respective advisers with shareholders of, or other persons interested in the securities of, either the offeror or the offeree company or with analysts, brokers or others engaged in investment management or advice may take place prior to or during the offer period, provided that no material new information is forthcoming, no significant new opinions are expressed and the following provisions are observed. Except with the consent of the Panel, an appropriate representative of the financial adviser or corporate broker to the offeror or the offeree company must be present. That representative will be responsible for confirming in writing to the Panel, not later than 12 noon on the business day following the date of the meeting, that no material new information was forthcoming and no significant new opinions were expressed at the meeting.

If, notwithstanding the above, any material new information or significant new opinion does emerge at the meeting, a circular giving details must be sent to shareholders as soon as possible thereafter: in the final stages of an offer it may be necessary to make use of paid newspaper space as well as a circular. The circular or advertisement must include the directors' responsibility statement. If such new information or opinion is not capable of being substantiated as required by the Code (eg a profit forecast), this must be made clear and it must be formally withdrawn in the circular or advertisement.

RULE 20 *CONTINUED*

NOTES ON RULE 20.1 continued

In the case of any meeting held prior to the offer period, the representative should confirm that no material new information was forthcoming and no significant new opinions were expressed at the meeting which will not be included in the announcement of the offer to be made under Rule 2.5, if and when such announcement is made.

Should there be any dispute as to whether the provisions of this Note have been complied with, the relevant financial adviser or corporate broker will be expected to satisfy the Panel that they have been. Financial advisers or corporate brokers may, therefore, find it useful to record the proceedings of meetings, although this is not a requirement. The financial adviser must ensure that no meetings are arranged without its knowledge.

The above provisions apply to all such meetings held prior to or during an offer period wherever they take place and even if with only one person or firm, unless the meetings take place by chance. Meetings with employees in their capacity as such (rather than in their capacity as shareholders) are not normally covered by this Note, although the Panel should be consulted if any employees are interested in a significant number of shares.

4. Information issued by associates (eg brokers)

Rule 20.1 does not prevent the issue of circulars during the offer period to their own investment clients by brokers or advisers to any party to the transaction provided such issue has previously been approved by the Panel.

In giving to their own clients material on the companies involved in an offer, associates must bear in mind the essential point that new information must not be restricted to a small group. Accordingly, such material must not include any statements of fact or opinion derived from information not generally available. Profit forecasts, asset valuations and estimates of other figures key to the offer should be avoided (unless, and then only to the extent that, the offer documents or circulars themselves contain such forecasts, valuations or estimates).

The associate's status must be clearly disclosed. Clearance before release may in many cases be effected by telephone but where there is doubt a draft must be sent to the Panel as early as possible. In all cases, copies of the final version of circulars must be sent to the Panel at the time of release. Where relevant, the requirements of this Note apply to screen displays.

Attention is drawn to paragraph (2) of the definition of associate, as a result of which, for example, this Note will be relevant to brokers who, although not directly involved with the offer, are associates of an offeror or the offeree company because the broker is in the same group as the financial adviser to an offeror or the offeree company.

RULE 20 CONTINUED

NOTES ON RULE 20.1 continued

When an offer is referred to the Competition Commission or the European Commission initiates proceedings, the offer period ends in accordance with Rule 12.2. Associates must, however, consult the Panel about the issue of circulars as described in this Note during the reference or proceedings. The Panel will normally apply the restrictions in this Note in the period of one month before the relevant authority is expected to make its recommendation or issue its decision as the case may be.

5. Shareholders outside the EEA

See the Note on Rule 30.3.

20.2 EQUALITY OF INFORMATION TO COMPETING OFFERORS

Any information, including particulars of shareholders, given to one offeror or potential offeror, whether named or unnamed, must, on request, be given equally and promptly to another offeror or bona fide potential offeror even if that other offeror is less welcome. This requirement will usually only apply when there has been a public announcement of the existence of the offeror or potential offeror to which information has been given or, if there has been no public announcement, when the offeror or bona fide potential offeror requesting information under this Rule has been informed authoritatively of the existence of another potential offeror.

NOTES ON RULE 20.2

1. General enquiries

The less welcome offeror or potential offeror should specify the questions to which it requires answers. It is not entitled, by asking in general terms, to receive all the information supplied to its competitor.

2. Conditions attached to the passing of information

The passing of information pursuant to this Rule should not be made subject to any conditions other than those relating to: the confidentiality of the information passed; reasonable restrictions forbidding the use of the information passed to solicit customers or employees; and, the use of the information solely in connection with an offer or potential offer. Any such conditions imposed should be no more onerous than those imposed upon any other offeror or potential offeror.

A requirement that a party sign a hold harmless letter in favour of a firm of accountants or other third party will normally be acceptable provided that any

RULE 20 *CONTINUED*

NOTES ON RULE 20.2 continued

other offeror or potential offeror has been required to sign a letter in similar form.

3. Management buy-outs

If the offer or potential offer is a management buy-out or similar transaction, the information which this Rule requires to be given to competing offerors or potential offerors is that information generated by the offeree company (including the management of the offeree company acting in their capacity as such) which is passed to external providers or potential providers of finance (whether equity or debt) to the offeror or potential offeror. The Panel expects the directors of the offeree company who are involved in making the offer to co-operate with the independent directors of the offeree company and its advisers in the assembly of this information.

4. Mergers and reverse takeovers

Where an offer or possible offer might result in an offeror needing to increase its existing issued voting equity share capital by 100% or more, an offeror or potential offeror for either party to such an offer or possible offer will be entitled to receive information which has been given by such party to the other party.

5. The Competition Commission and the European Commission

When an offer is referred to the Competition Commission or the European Commission initiates proceedings, the offer period ends in accordance with Rule 12.2. The Panel will, however, continue to apply Rule 20.2 during the reference or proceedings and, therefore, for the purposes of this Rule alone, will normally deem the referred offeror to be a bona fide potential offeror.

20.3 INFORMATION TO INDEPENDENT DIRECTORS IN MANAGEMENT BUY-OUTS

If the offer or potential offer is a management buy-out or similar transaction, the offeror or potential offeror must, on request, promptly furnish the independent directors of the offeree company or its advisers with all information which has been furnished by the offeror or potential offeror to external providers or potential providers of finance (whether equity or debt) for the buy-out.

RULE 21. RESTRICTIONS ON FRUSTRATING ACTION

21.1 WHEN SHAREHOLDERS' CONSENT IS REQUIRED

During the course of an offer, or even before the date of the offer if the board of the offeree company has reason to believe that a bona fide offer might be imminent, the board must not, without the approval of the shareholders in general meeting:—

(a) take any action which may result in any offer or bona fide possible offer being frustrated or in shareholders being denied the opportunity to decide on its merits; or

(b) (i) issue any authorised but unissued shares or transfer or sell, or agree to transfer or sell, any shares out of treasury;

(ii) issue or grant options in respect of any unissued shares;

(iii) create or issue, or permit the creation or issue of, any securities carrying rights of conversion into or subscription for shares;

(iv) sell, dispose of or acquire, or agree to sell, dispose of or acquire, assets of a material amount; or

(v) enter into contracts otherwise than in the ordinary course of business.

The Panel must be consulted in advance if there is any doubt as to whether any proposed action may fall within this Rule.

The notice convening any relevant meeting of shareholders must include information about the offer or anticipated offer.

Where it is felt that:

(A) the proposed action is in pursuance of a contract entered into earlier or another pre-existing obligation; or

(B) a decision to take the proposed action had been taken before the beginning of the period referred to above which:

(i) has been partly or fully implemented before the beginning of that period; or

(ii) has not been partly or fully implemented before the beginning of that period but is in the ordinary course of business,

the Panel must be consulted and its consent to proceed without a shareholders' meeting obtained.

RULE 21 *CONTINUED*

NOTES ON RULE 21.1

1. Consent by the offeror

Where the Rule would otherwise apply, it will nonetheless normally be waived by the Panel if this is acceptable to the offeror.

2. "Material amount"

For the purpose of determining whether a disposal or acquisition is of "a material amount" the Panel will, in general, have regard to the following:—

(a) the aggregate value of the consideration to be received or given compared with the aggregate market value of all the equity shares of the offeree company; and, where appropriate:

(b) the value of the assets to be disposed of or acquired compared with the assets of the offeree company; and

(c) the operating profit (ie profit before tax and interest and excluding exceptional items) attributable to the assets to be disposed of or acquired compared with that of the offeree company.

For these purposes:

"assets" will normally mean total assets less current liabilities (other than short-term indebtedness); and

"equity" will be interpreted by reference to Note 3 on Rule 14.1.

The figures to be used for these calculations must be:

(a) for market value of the shares of the offeree company, the aggregate market value of all the equity shares of the company at the close of business either:

   (i) on the last day immediately preceding the start of the offer period; or

   (ii) if there is no offer period, on the last day immediately preceding the announcement of the transaction; and

(b) for assets and profits, the figures shown in the latest published audited consolidated accounts or, where appropriate, interim or preliminary statements.

Subject to Note 4, the Panel will normally consider relative values of 10% or more as being of a material amount, although relative values lower than 10% may be considered material if the asset is of particular significance.

If several transactions relevant to this Rule, but not individually material, occur or are intended, the Panel will aggregate such transactions to

RULE 21 CONTINUED

NOTES ON RULE 21.1 continued

determine whether the requirements of this Rule are applicable to any of them.

The Panel should be consulted in advance where there may be any doubt as to the application of the above.

3. Interim dividends

The declaration and payment of an interim dividend by the offeree company, otherwise than in the normal course, during an offer period may in certain circumstances be contrary to General Principle 3 and this Rule in that it could effectively frustrate an offer. Offeree companies and their advisers must, therefore, consult the Panel in advance.

4. The Competition Commission and the European Commission

When an offer is referred to the Competition Commission or the European Commission initiates proceedings, the offer period ends in accordance with Rule 12.2. The Panel will, however, normally consider that General Principle 3 and Rule 21.1 apply during the competition reference period, but on a more flexible basis. For example, issues of shares, which do not increase the equity share capital or the share capital carrying voting rights as at the end of the offer period by, in aggregate, more than 15%, would normally not be restricted; and for the purpose of Note 2, a 15% rather than a 10% test would normally be applied.

5. When there is no need to post

The Panel may allow an offeror not to proceed with its offer if, at any time during the offer period prior to the posting of the offer document:—

(a) the offeree company passes a resolution in general meeting as envisaged by this Rule; or

(b) the Panel has given consent for the offeree company to proceed with an action or transaction to which Rule 21.1 applies without a shareholders' meeting.

6. Service contracts

The Panel will regard amending or entering into a service contract with, or creating or varying the terms of employment of, a director as entering into a contract "otherwise than in the ordinary course of business" for the purpose of this Rule if the new or amended contract or terms constitute an abnormal increase in the emoluments or a significant improvement in the terms of service.

RULE 21 *CONTINUED*

NOTES ON RULE 21.1 continued

This will not prevent any such increase or improvement which results from a genuine promotion or new appointment but the Panel must be consulted in advance in such cases.

7. Established share option schemes

Where the offeree company proposes to grant options over shares, the timing and level of which are in accordance with its normal practice under an established share option scheme, the Panel will normally give its consent. Likewise, the Panel will normally give its consent to the issue of new shares or to the transfer of shares from treasury to satisfy the exercise of options under an established share option scheme.

8. Pension schemes

This Rule may apply to proposals affecting the offeree company's pension scheme arrangements, such as proposals involving the application of a pension fund surplus, a material increase in the financial commitment of the offeree company in respect of its pension scheme or a change to the constitution of the pension scheme. The Panel must be consulted in advance in relation to such proposals.

9. Redemption or purchase by an offeree company of its own securities

See Rule 37.3.

10. Shares carrying more than 50% of the voting rights

The Panel will normally waive the requirement for a general meeting under this Rule where the holders of shares carrying more than 50% of the voting rights state in writing that they approve the action proposed and would vote in favour of any resolution to that effect proposed at a general meeting.

21.2 INDUCEMENT FEES

In all cases where an inducement fee is proposed, certain safeguards must be observed. In particular, an inducement fee must be de minimis (normally no more than 1% of the value of the offeree company calculated by reference to the offer price) and the offeree company board and its financial adviser must confirm to the Panel in writing that, inter alia, they each believe the fee to be in the best interests of shareholders. Any inducement fee arrangement must be fully disclosed in the announcement made under Rule 2.5 and in the offer document. Relevant documents must be put on display in accordance with Rule 26.

The Panel should be consulted at the earliest opportunity in all cases where an inducement fee or any similar arrangement is proposed.

RULE 21 CONTINUED

NOTES ON RULE 21.2

1. Arrangements to which the Rule applies

An inducement fee is an arrangement which may be entered into between an offeror or a potential offeror and the offeree company pursuant to which a cash sum will be payable by the offeree company if certain specified events occur which have the effect of preventing the offer from proceeding or causing it to fail (e.g. the recommendation by the offeree company board of a higher competing offer).

This Rule will also apply to any other favourable arrangements with an offeror or potential offeror which have a similar or comparable financial or economic effect, even if such arrangements do not actually involve any cash payment.

Such arrangements will include, for example, break fees, penalties, put or call options or other provisions having similar effects, regardless of whether such arrangements are considered to be in the ordinary course of business. In cases of doubt, the Panel should be consulted.

2. Statutory provisions

Any view expressed by the Panel in relation to such fees or arrangements can only relate to the Code and must not be taken to extend to any requirements of the Companies Act 1985, e.g. Section 151 or any other relevant law or regulation.

3. "Whitewashes"

This Rule also generally applies to the payment of an inducement fee in the context of a "whitewash" transaction. In this context, the 1% test will normally be calculated by reference to the value of the offeree company immediately prior to the announcement of the proposed "whitewash" transaction.

RULE 22. RESPONSIBILITIES OF THE OFFEREE COMPANY REGARDING REGISTRATION PROCEDURES

The board of the offeree company should take action to ensure that its registrar complies fully with the procedures set out in Appendix 4. The board should also ensure prompt registration of transfers during an offer.

NOTE ON RULE 22

Qualifying periods

Provisions in Articles of Association which lay down a qualifying period after registration during which the registered holder cannot exercise his votes are highly undesirable.

SECTION J. DOCUMENTS FROM THE OFFEROR AND THE OFFEREE BOARD

RULE 23. THE GENERAL OBLIGATION AS TO INFORMATION

Shareholders must be given sufficient information and advice to enable them to reach a properly informed decision as to the merits or demerits of an offer. Such information must be available to shareholders early enough to enable them to make a decision in good time. No relevant information should be withheld from them. The obligation of the offeror in these respects towards the shareholders of the offeree company is no less than an offeror's obligation towards its own shareholders.

NOTES ON RULE 23

1. Material changes

Any document issued to shareholders must include information about any material change in any information previously published by or on behalf of the relevant company during the offer period; if there have been no such changes, this should be stated.

2. Offers conditional on shareholder action

When an offer has been announced which is conditional on action by offeree company shareholders (eg the rejection of a proposed acquisition or disposal), the first major circular sent by the potential offeror to those shareholders must normally include the information which would be required by Rule 24 to be included in that circular if it were an offer document.

3. Shareholders outside the EEA

See the Note on Rule 30.3.

RULE 24. OFFEROR DOCUMENTS

24.1 INTENTIONS REGARDING THE OFFEREE COMPANY, THE OFFEROR COMPANY AND THEIR EMPLOYEES

An offeror will be required to cover the following points in the offer document:—

(a) its intentions regarding the future business of the offeree company;

(b) its strategic plans for the offeree company, and their likely repercussions on employment and the locations of the offeree company's places of business;

(c) its intentions regarding any redeployment of the fixed assets of the offeree company;

(d) the long-term commercial justification for the proposed offer; and

(e) its intentions with regard to the continued employment of the employees and management of the offeree company and of its subsidiaries, including any material change in the conditions of employment.

Where the offeror is a company and insofar as it is affected by the offer, the offeror must also cover (a), (b) and (e) with regard to itself.

24.2 FINANCIAL AND OTHER INFORMATION ON THE OFFEROR, THE OFFEREE COMPANY AND THE OFFER

Except with the consent of the Panel:—

(a) where the consideration includes securities and the offeror is a company incorporated under the Companies Act 1985 (or its predecessors) and its shares are admitted to the Official List or to trading on AIM, the offer document must contain:

(i) for the last 3 financial years for which the information has been published, turnover, net profit or loss before and after taxation, the charge for tax, extraordinary items, minority interests, the amount absorbed by dividends and earnings and dividends per share;

(ii) a statement of the assets and liabilities shown in the last published audited accounts;

(iii) a cash flow statement if provided in the last published audited accounts;

(iv) all known material changes in the financial or trading position of the company subsequent to the last published audited accounts or a statement that there are no known material changes;

RULE 24 *CONTINUED*

(v) details relating to items referred to in (i) above in respect of any interim statement or preliminary announcement made since the last published audited accounts;

(vi) inflation-adjusted information if any of the above has been published in that form;

(vii) significant accounting policies together with any points from the notes to the accounts which are of major relevance to an appreciation of the figures, including those relating to inflation-adjusted information;

(viii) where, because of a change in accounting policy, figures are not comparable to a material extent, this should be disclosed and the approximate amount of the resultant variation should be stated;

(ix) the names of the offeror's directors;

(x) the nature of its business and its financial and trading prospects; and

(xi) a summary of the principal contents of each material contract (not being a contract entered into in the ordinary course of business) entered into by the offeror or any of its subsidiaries during the period beginning two years before the commencement of the offer period, including particulars of dates, parties, terms and conditions and any consideration passing to or from the offeror or any of its subsidiaries;

(b) where the consideration is cash only and the offeror is a company incorporated under the Companies Act 1985 (or its predecessors) and its shares are admitted to the Official List or to trading on AIM, the offer document must contain:

(i) for the last two financial years for which information has been published, turnover and profit or loss before taxation;

(ii) a statement of the net assets of the company shown in the last published audited accounts;

(iii) the names of the company's directors; and

(iv) the nature of the business and its financial and trading prospects;

(c) if the offeror is other than a company referred to in (a) and (b) above, whether the consideration is securities or cash, the offer document must contain:

RULE 24 *CONTINUED*

(i) in respect of the offeror, the information described in (a) above (so far as appropriate) and such further information as the Panel may require in the particular circumstances of the case (see Note 2);

(ii) in respect of any person who has made (or proposes to make or increase) an investment in the offeror for the purposes of the offer such that he has or will have a potential direct or indirect interest in any part of the capital of the offeree company which the Panel regards as equity capital, details of his identity and of his interest in the offeror and such further information as the Panel may require in the particular circumstances of the case (see Note 2); and

(iii) in respect of any person not included in (ii) above whose pre-existing interest in the offeror is such that he has a potential direct or indirect interest of 5% or more in any part of the capital of the offeree company which the Panel regards as equity capital, details of his identity and of his interest in the offeror and such further information as the Panel may require in the particular circumstances of the case (see Note 2);

(d) the offer document (including, where relevant, any revised offer document) must include:

(i) a heading stating "If you are in doubt about this offer you should consult an independent financial adviser authorised under the FSMA";

(ii) the date when the document is despatched, the name and address of the offeror (including, where the offeror is a company, the type of company and the address of its registered office) and, if appropriate, of the person making the offer on behalf of the offeror;

(iii) the identity of any person acting in concert with the offeror and, to the extent that it is known, the offeree company, including, in the case of a company, its type, registered office and relationship with the offeror and, where possible, with the offeree company. (See Note 4);

(iv) details of each class of security for which the offer is made, including whether those securities will be transferred "cum" or "ex" any dividend and the maximum and minimum percentages of those securities which the offeror undertakes to acquire;

(v) the terms of the offer, including the consideration offered for each class of security, the total consideration offered and particulars of the way in which the consideration is to be paid in accordance with Rule 31.8;

RULE 24 *CONTINUED*

(vi) all conditions (including normal conditions relating to acceptances, admission to listing, admission to trading and increase of capital) to which the offer is subject;

(vii) particulars of all documents required, and procedures to be followed, for acceptance of the offer;

(viii) the middle market quotations for the securities to be acquired, and (in the case of a securities exchange offer) securities offered, for the first business day in each of the six months immediately before the date of the offer document, for the last business day before the commencement of the offer period and for the latest available date before the posting of the offer document (quotations stated in respect of securities admitted either to the Official List or to trading on AIM should be taken from the Stock Exchange Daily Official List and, if any of the securities are not so admitted, any information available as to the number and price of transactions which have taken place during the preceding six months should be stated together with the source, or an appropriate negative statement);

(ix) details of any agreements or arrangements to which the offeror is party which relate to the circumstances in which it may or may not invoke or seek to invoke a condition to its offer and the consequences of its doing so, including details of any break fees payable as a result;

(x) details of any irrevocable commitment or letter of intent which the offeror or any of its associates has procured in relation to relevant securities of the offeree company (or, if appropriate, the offeror) (see Note 14 on Rule 8);

(xi) in the case of a securities exchange offer, full particulars of the securities being offered, including the rights attaching to them, the first dividend or interest payment in which the securities will participate and how the securities will rank for dividends or interest, capital and redemption; a statement indicating the effect of acceptance on the capital and income position of the offeree company's shareholders; and details of any applications for admission to listing or admission to trading that have been or will be made in any jurisdiction in respect of the securities;

(xii) in the case of a securities exchange offer, the effect of full acceptance of the offer upon the offeror's assets, profits and business which may be significant for a proper appraisal of the offer;

J6

RULE 24 *CONTINUED*

(xiii) a summary of the provisions of Rule 8 (see the Panel's website at www.thetakeoverpanel.org.uk);

(xiv) the national law which will govern contracts concluded between the offeror and holders of the offeree company's securities as a result of the offer and the competent courts;

(xv) the compensation (if any) offered for the removal of rights pursuant to Article 11 of the Directive together with particulars of the way in which the compensation is to be paid and the method employed in determining it; and

(xvi) details of any arrangement for the payment of an inducement fee or similar arrangement as referred to in Rule 21.2;

(e) the offer document must contain information on the offeree company on the same basis as set out in (a)(i) to (ix) above;

(f) all offer documents must contain a description of how the offer is to be financed and the source of the finance. The principal lenders or arrangers of such finance must be named. Where the offeror intends that the payment of interest on, repayment of or security for any liability (contingent or otherwise) will depend to any significant extent on the business of the offeree company, a description of the arrangements contemplated will be required. Where this is not the case, a negative statement to this effect must be made;

(g) if any document issued by the offeror contains a comparison of the value of the offer with previous prices of the offeree company's shares, a comparison between the current value of the offer and the price of the offeree company's shares on the last business day prior to the commencement of the offer period must be prominently included, no matter what other comparisons are made; and

(h) if any document issued to shareholders of the offeree company in connection with an offer includes a recommendation or an opinion of a financial adviser for or against acceptance of the offer, the document must, unless issued by the financial adviser in question, include a statement that the financial adviser has given and not withdrawn his consent to the issue of the document with the inclusion of his recommendation or opinion in the form and context in which it is included.

Takeover Code

J7

RULE 24 *CONTINUED*

NOTES ON RULE 24.2

1. Where the offeror is a subsidiary company

The Panel will normally look through subsidiaries whose securities are not admitted to trading in interpreting this Rule unless, with the agreement of the Panel, the subsidiary in question is regarded as being of sufficient substance in relation to the group and the offer. Accordingly if the offeror is part of a group, information will normally be required on the ultimate holding company in the form of group accounts.

2. Further information requirements

(a) For the purpose of Rule 24.2(c), the expression "person" will normally include the ultimate owner(s), and persons having control (as defined), of the offeror if not already included under (ii) or (iii). Whilst the precise nature of the further information which may be required to be disclosed under (i), (ii) or (iii) in any particular case will depend on the circumstances of that case, the Panel would normally expect it to include a general description of the business interests of the offeror and/or other person(s) concerned and details of those assets which the Panel considers may be relevant to the business of the offeree company.

(b) The Panel must be consulted in advance in any case to which Rule 24.2(c) applies, or may apply regarding the application of its provisions to that particular case.

3. Partial offers

Where the offer is a partial offer, the offer document must contain the information required under Rule 24.2(a), whether the consideration is securities or cash.

4. Persons acting in concert with the offeror

For the purposes of Rule 24.2(d)(iii), the identity of a person acting in concert with the offeror or the offeree company must be disclosed if the offeree company shareholders need details of that person in order to reach a properly informed decision on the offer. Disclosure will normally include: a person who is interested in shares in the offeree company and (in the case of a securities exchange offer only) the offeror; any person with whom the offeror or the offeree company and any person acting in concert with either of them has any arrangement of the kind referred to in Note 6(b) on Rule 8; any financial adviser which is advising the offeror or the offeree company in relation to the offer; and any corporate broker to either of them. In cases of doubt, the Panel should be consulted.

RULE 24 CONTINUED

NOTES ON RULE 24.2 continued

5. Offers made under Rule 9

When an offer is made under Rule 9, the information required under Rule 24.2(d)(v) must include the method employed under Rule 9.5 in calculating the consideration offered.

24.3 INTERESTS AND DEALINGS

(a) The offer document must state:—

(i) details of any relevant securities of the offeree company in which the offeror has an interest or in respect of which he has a right to subscribe, specifying the nature of the interests or rights concerned (see Note 5(a) on Rule 8). Similar details of any short positions (whether conditional or absolute and whether in the money or otherwise), including any short position under a derivative, any agreement to sell or any delivery obligation or right to require another person to purchase or take delivery, must also be stated;

(ii) the same details as in (i) above in relation to each of:

(a) the directors of the offeror;

(b) any other person acting in concert with the offeror; and

(c) any person with whom the offeror or any person acting in concert with the offeror has any arrangement of the kind referred to in Note 6 on Rule 8;

(iii) in the case of a securities exchange offer, the same details as in (i) above in respect of any relevant securities of the offeror in relation to each of the persons listed in (ii) above; and

(iv) details of any relevant securities of the offeree company and (in the case of a securities exchange offer only) the offeror which the offeror or any person acting in concert with it has borrowed or lent, save for any borrowed shares which have been either on-lent or sold.

(b) If, in the case of any of the persons referred to in Rule 24.3(a), there are no interests or short positions to be disclosed, this fact should be stated. This will not apply to category (a)(ii)*(c)* if there are no such arrangements.

(c) If any person referred to in Rule 24.3(a) has dealt in any relevant securities of the offeree company (or, in the case of a securities

Takeover Code

J9

RULE 24 *CONTINUED*

exchange offer only, of the offeror) during the period beginning 12 months prior to the offer period and ending with the latest practicable date prior to the posting of the offer document, the details, including dates, must be stated (see Note 5(a) on Rule 8). If no such dealings have taken place, this fact should be stated.

(d) See also Rule 37.4(b).

NOTES ON RULE 24.3

1. Directors

In the case of directors, the disclosure should include details of all interests, short positions and borrowings of any other person whose interests in shares the director would be required to disclose pursuant to Parts VI and X of the Companies Act 1985 and related regulations.

2. Aggregation

There may be cases where no useful purpose would be served by listing a large number of transactions. In such cases the Panel will accept in documents some measure of aggregation of each type of dealing by a person provided that no significant dealings are thereby concealed. The following approach is normally acceptable:

(i) for dealings during the offer period, all acquisitions and all disposals can be aggregated;

(ii) for dealings in the three months prior to that period, all acquisitions and all disposals in that period can be aggregated on a monthly basis; and

(iii) for dealings in the nine months prior to that period, acquisitions and disposals can be aggregated on a quarterly basis.

Acquisitions and disposals should not be netted off, the highest and lowest prices should be stated and the disclosure should distinguish between the different categories of interests in relevant securities and short positions. A full list of all dealings, together with a draft of the proposed aggregated disclosure, should be sent to the Panel, for its approval, in advance of the posting of the offer documentation and the full list of dealings should be made available for inspection.

3. Discretionary fund managers and principal traders

Interests in relevant securities and short positions of non-exempt discretionary fund managers and principal traders which are connected with the offeror and their dealings since the date 12 months prior to the offer

RULE 24 CONTINUED

NOTES ON RULE 24.3 continued

period will need to be disclosed under Rules 24.3(a)(ii)(b) and 24.3(c) respectively.

24.4 DIRECTORS' EMOLUMENTS

The offer document must state (in the case of a securities exchange offer only) whether and in what manner the emoluments of the offeror directors will be affected by the acquisition of the offeree company or by any other associated transaction. If there will be no effect, this must be stated.

NOTE ON RULE 24.4

Commissions etc.

Information given under this Rule should include any alterations to fixed amounts receivable or, as far as practicable, the effect of any factor governing commissions or other variable amounts receivable. Grouping or aggregating the effect of the transaction on the emoluments of several or all of the directors will normally be acceptable.

24.5 SPECIAL ARRANGEMENTS

Unless otherwise agreed with the Panel, the offer document must contain a statement as to whether or not any agreement, arrangement or understanding (including any compensation arrangement) exists between the offeror or any person acting in concert with it and any of the directors, recent directors, shareholders or recent shareholders of the offeree company, or any person interested or recently interested in shares of the offeree company, having any connection with or dependence upon the offer, and full particulars of any such agreement, arrangement or understanding.

24.6 INCORPORATION OF OBLIGATIONS AND RIGHTS

The offer document must state the time allowed for acceptance of the offer and any alternative offer and must incorporate language which appropriately reflects Notes 4–8 on Rule 10 and those parts of Rules 13.4(a), 13.5 (if applicable), 17 and 31–34 which impose timing obligations or confer rights or impose restrictions on offerors, offeree companies or shareholders of offeree companies.

RULE 24 *CONTINUED*

NOTES ON RULE 24.6

1. Incorporation by reference

A suitable cross reference to Notes 4–6 and Note 8 on Rule 10 is regarded as being sufficient appropriately to reflect those Notes but cross references to other provisions of the Code are not permitted.

2. Rule 31.6(c)

Rule 24.6 does not apply to the requirement, imposed by Rule 31.6(c), that an announcement as to whether the offer is unconditional as to acceptances or has lapsed should be made by 5.00 pm on the final closing date. Accordingly this requirement should not be reflected in the terms of the offer.

24.7 CASH CONFIRMATION

When the offer is for cash or includes an element of cash, the offer document must include confirmation by an appropriate third party (eg the offeror's bank or financial adviser) that resources are available to the offeror sufficient to satisfy full acceptance of the offer. (The party confirming that resources are available will not be expected to produce the cash itself if, in giving the confirmation, it acted responsibly and took all reasonable steps to assure itself that the cash was available.)

24.8 ULTIMATE OWNER OF SECURITIES ACQUIRED

Unless otherwise agreed with the Panel, the offer document must contain a statement as to whether or not any securities acquired in pursuance of the offer will be transferred to any other persons, together with the names of the parties to any such agreement, arrangement or understanding and particulars of all interests in the securities of the offeree company held by such persons, or a statement that no such interests are held.

24.9 ADMISSION TO LISTING AND ADMISSION TO TRADING CONDITIONS

Where securities are offered as consideration and it is intended that they should be admitted to listing on the Official List or to trading on AIM, the relevant admission to listing or admission to trading condition should, except with the consent of the Panel, be in terms which ensure that it is capable of being satisfied only when the decision to admit the securities to listing or trading has been announced by the UKLA or the Stock Exchange, as applicable. Where securities are offered as consideration and it is intended that they should be admitted to listing or to trading on any other investment exchange or market, the Panel should be consulted.

J₁₂

RULE 24 *CONTINUED*

24.10 ESTIMATED VALUE OF UNQUOTED PAPER CONSIDERATION

When the offer involves the issue of securities of a class which is not admitted to trading, the offer document and any subsequent circular from the offeror must contain an estimate of the value of such securities by an appropriate adviser.

24.11 NO SET-OFF OF CONSIDERATION

The offer document must contain a statement to the effect that, except with the consent of the Panel, settlement of the consideration to which any shareholder is entitled under the offer will be implemented in full in accordance with the terms of the offer without regard to any lien, right of set-off, counterclaim or other analogous right to which the offeror may otherwise be, or claim to be, entitled against such shareholder.

The Panel would only grant consent in exceptional circumstances and where all shareholders were to be treated similarly.

24.12 ARRANGEMENTS IN RELATION TO DEALINGS

The offer document must disclose any arrangements of the kind referred to in Note 6(b) on Rule 8 which exist between the offeror, or any person acting in concert with the offeror, and any other person; if there are no such arrangements, this should be stated. If the directors or their financial advisers are aware of any such arrangements between any other associate of the offeror and any other person, such arrangements must also be disclosed.

24.13 CASH UNDERWRITTEN ALTERNATIVES WHICH MAY BE SHUT OFF

The procedure for acceptance of a cash underwritten alternative which is capable of being shut off must be prominently stated in relevant documents and acceptance forms. In particular, it must be made clear (in the offer document, the acceptance form and any subsequent documents) whether shareholders must lodge their certificates by the closing date of the cash underwritten alternative, in addition to their completed acceptance forms, in order to receive cash.

RULE 25. OFFEREE BOARD CIRCULARS

25.1 VIEWS OF THE BOARD ON THE OFFER, INCLUDING THE OFFEROR'S PLANS FOR THE COMPANY AND ITS EMPLOYEES

(a) The board of the offeree company must circulate to the company's shareholders its opinion on the offer (including any alternative offers). It must, at the same time, make known to its shareholders the substance of the advice given to it by the independent advisers appointed pursuant to Rule 3.1.

(b) The opinion referred to in (a) above must include the views of the board of the offeree company on:

(i) the effects of implementation of the offer on all the company's interests, including, specifically, employment; and

(ii) the offeror's strategic plans for the offeree company and their likely repercussions on employment and the locations of the offeree company's places of business, as set out in the offer document pursuant to Rule 24.1,

and must state the board's reasons for forming its opinion.

(c) If any document issued to shareholders of the offeree company in connection with an offer includes a recommendation or an opinion of a financial adviser for or against acceptance of the offer, the document must, unless issued by the financial adviser in question, include a statement that the financial adviser has given and not withdrawn his consent to the issue of the document with the inclusion of his recommendation or opinion in the form and context in which it is included.

NOTES ON RULE 25.1

1. *When a board has effective control*

A board whose shareholdings confer control over a company which is the subject of an offer must carefully examine the reasons behind the advice it gives to shareholders and must be prepared to explain its decisions publicly. Shareholders in companies which are effectively controlled by the directors must accept that in respect of any offer the attitude of their board will be decisive.

2. *Split boards*

If the board of the offeree company is split in its views on an offer, the directors who are in a minority should also publish their views. The Panel will normally require that they be circulated by the offeree company.

RULE 25 CONTINUED

NOTES ON RULE 25.1 continued

3. *Conflicts of interest*

Where a director has a conflict of interest, he should not normally be joined with the remainder of the board in the expression of its views on the offer and the nature of the conflict should be clearly explained to shareholders. Depending on the circumstances, such a director may have to make the responsibility statement required by Rule 19.2, appropriately amended to make it clear that he does not accept responsibility for the views of the board on the offer. Where the statement relates to a prospectus or an equivalent document, the provisions of the UKLA Rules may affect the position.

4. *Management buy-outs*

If the offer is a management buy-out or similar transaction, a director will normally be regarded as having a conflict of interest where it is intended that he should have any continuing role (whether in an executive or non-executive capacity) in either the offeror or offeree company in the event of the offer being successful.

25.2 FINANCIAL AND OTHER INFORMATION

The first major circular from the offeree board advising shareholders on an offer (whether recommending acceptance or rejection of the offer) must contain all known material changes in the financial or trading position of the offeree company subsequent to the last published audited accounts or a statement that there are no known material changes.

NOTES ON RULE 25.2

1. *Offeree board circular combined with offer document*

Where the first major circular from the offeree board is combined with the offer document, it will be the responsibility of the offeree board to include the information required by this Rule. Accordingly, the offeror will not be required to comply with Rule 24.2(e) insofar as it applies to Rule 24.2(a)(iv).

2. *Offeree board circular posted after offer document*

Where the offeror has included in the offer document information on the offeree company as required by Rule 24.2(e) insofar as it applies to Rules 24.2(a)(iv) and (v), such information does not need to be repeated in the first major circular from the offeree board provided that the statement made in accordance with this Rule makes specific reference to the relevant information disclosed by the offeror in the offer document.

RULE 25 *CONTINUED*

25.3 INTERESTS AND DEALINGS

(a) The first major circular from the offeree board advising shareholders on an offer (whether recommending acceptance or rejection of the offer) must state:—

(i) details of any relevant securities of the offeror in which the offeree company or any of the directors of the offeree company has an interest or in respect of which it or he has a right to subscribe, in each case specifying the nature of the interests or rights concerned (see Note 5(a) on Rule 8). Similar details of any short positions (whether conditional or absolute and whether in the money or otherwise), including any short position under a derivative, any agreement to sell or any delivery obligation or right to require another person to purchase or take delivery, must also be stated;

(ii) the same details as in (i) above in respect of any relevant securities of the offeree company in relation to each of:

(a) the directors of the offeree company;

(b) any company which is an associate of the offeree company by virtue of paragraph (1) of the definition of associate;

(c) any pension fund of the offeree company or of a company which is an associate of the offeree company by virtue of paragraph (1) of the definition of associate;

(d) any employee benefit trust of the offeree company or of a company which is an associate of the offeree company by virtue of paragraph (1) of the definition of associate;

(e) any connected adviser to the offeree company, to a company which is an associate of the offeree company by virtue of paragraph (1) of the definition of associate or to a person acting in concert with the offeree company;

(f) any person controlling#, controlled by or under the same control as any connected adviser falling within *(e)* above (except for an exempt principal trader or an exempt fund manager); and

(g) any person who has an arrangement of the kind referred to in Note 6 on Rule 8 with the offeree company or with any person who is an associate of the offeree company by virtue of paragraphs (1), (2), (3) or (4) of the definition of associate;

#See Note at end of Definitions Section.

RULE 25 *CONTINUED*

(iii) in the case of a securities exchange offer, the same details as in (i) above in respect of any relevant securities of the offeror in relation to each of the persons listed in (ii)*(b)* to *(g)* above;

(iv) details of any relevant securities of the offeree company and (in the case of a securities exchange offer only) the offeror which the offeree company or any person acting in concert with the offeree company has borrowed or lent, save for any borrowed shares which have been either on-lent or sold; and

(v) whether the directors of the offeree company intend, in respect of their own beneficial shareholdings, to accept or reject the offer.

(b) If, in the case of any of the persons referred to in Rule 25.3(a), there are no interests or short positions to be disclosed, this fact should be stated. This will not apply to category (a)(ii)*(g)* if there are no such arrangements.

(c) If any person referred to in Rule 25.3(a)(i) has dealt in any relevant securities of the offeree company or the offeror between the start of the offer period and the latest practicable date prior to the posting of the circular, the details, including dates, must be stated (see Note 5(a) on Rule 8). If any person referred to in Rule 25.3(a)(ii)*(b)* to *(g)* has dealt in relevant securities of the offeree company (or, in the case of a securities exchange offer only, the offeror) during the same period, similar details must be stated. In all cases, if no such dealings have taken place this fact should be stated.

(d) See also Rule 37.3(c).

NOTES ON RULE 25.3

(See also Notes on Rule 24.3 which apply equally to this Rule.)

1. *When directors resign*

When, as part of the transaction leading to an offer being made, some or all of the directors of the offeree company resign, this Rule applies to them in the usual way.

2. *Pension funds*

Rule 25.3(a)(ii)(c) does not apply in respect of any pension funds which are managed under an agreement or arrangement with an independent third party in the terms set out in Note 7 on the definition of acting in concert.

RULE 25 CONTINUED

25.4 DIRECTORS' SERVICE CONTRACTS

(a) The first major circular from the offeree board advising shareholders on an offer (whether recommending acceptance or rejection of the offer) must contain particulars of all service contracts of any director or proposed director of the offeree company with the company or any of its subsidiaries. If there are none, this should be stated.

(b) If any such contracts have been entered into or amended within 6 months of the date of the document, particulars must be given in respect of the earlier contracts (if any) which have been replaced or amended as well as in respect of the current contracts. If there have been none, this should be stated.

NOTES ON RULE 25.4

1. Particulars to be disclosed

Particulars in respect of existing service contracts and, where appropriate under Rule 25.4(b), earlier contracts or an appropriate negative statement must be provided as follows:—

(a) the name of the director under contract;

(b) the date of the contract, the unexpired term and details of any notice periods;

(c) full particulars of the director's remuneration including salary and other benefits;

(d) any commission or profit sharing arrangements;

(e) any provision for compensation payable upon early termination of the contract; and

(f) details of any other arrangements which are necessary to enable investors to estimate the possible liability of the company on early termination of the contract.

It is not acceptable to refer to the latest annual report, indicating that information regarding service contracts may be found there, or to state that the contracts are open for inspection at a specified place.

2. Recent increases in remuneration

The Panel will regard as the amendment of a service contract under this Rule any case where the remuneration of an offeree company director is increased within 6 months of the date of the document. Therefore, any such

RULE 25 CONTINUED

NOTES ON RULE 25.4 continued

increase must be disclosed in the document and the current and previous levels of remuneration stated.

25.5 ARRANGEMENTS IN RELATION TO DEALINGS

The first major circular from the offeree board advising shareholders on an offer, whether recommending acceptance or rejection of the offer, must disclose any arrangements of the kind referred to in Note 6(b) on Rule 8 which exist between the offeree company, or any person who is an associate of the offeree company by virtue of paragraphs (1), (2), (3) or (4) of the definition of associate, and any other person; if there are no such arrangements, this should be stated. If the directors or their financial advisers are aware of any such arrangements between any other associate of the offeree company and any other person, such arrangements must also be disclosed.

25.6 MATERIAL CONTRACTS, IRREVOCABLE COMMITMENTS AND LETTERS OF INTENT

The first major circular from the offeree board advising shareholders on an offer must contain:—

(a) a summary of the principal contents of each material contract (not being a contract entered into in the ordinary course of business) entered into by the offeree company or any of its subsidiaries during the period beginning two years before the commencement of the offer period, including particulars of dates, parties, terms and conditions and any consideration passing to or from the offeree company or any of its subsidiaries; and

(b) details of any irrevocable commitment or letter of intent which the offeree company or any of its associates has procured in relation to relevant securities of the offeree company (or, if appropriate, the offeror) (see Note 14 on Rule 8).

RULE 26. DOCUMENTS TO BE ON DISPLAY

Except with the consent of the Panel, copies of the following documents must be made available for inspection from the time the offer document or offeree board circular, as appropriate, is published until the end of the offer period. The offer document or offeree board circular must state which documents are so available and the place (being a place in the City of London or such other place as the Panel may agree) where inspection can be made:—

(a) memorandum and articles of association of the offeror or the offeree company or equivalent documents;

(b) audited consolidated accounts of the offeror or the offeree company for the last two financial years for which these have been published;

(c) all service contracts of offeree company directors;

(d) any report, letter, valuation or other document any part of which is exhibited or referred to in any document issued by or on behalf of the offeror or the offeree company;

(e) written consents of the financial advisers (Rules 24.2(h) and 25.1(c));

(f) all material contracts (Rules 24.2(a) and (c) and 25.6);

(g) where a profit forecast has been made:

(i) the reports of the auditors or consultant accountants and of the financial advisers (Rule 28.3);

(ii) the letters giving the consent of the auditors or consultant accountants and of the financial advisers to the issue of the relevant document with the report in the form and context in which it is included or, if appropriate, to the continued use of the report in a subsequent document (Rules 28.4 and 28.5);

(h) where an asset valuation has been made:

(i) the valuation certificate and associated report or schedule containing details of the aggregate valuation (Rule 29.5);

(ii) a letter stating that the valuer has given and not withdrawn his consent to the publication of his name in the relevant document (Rule 29.5);

(i) any document evidencing an irrevocable commitment or a letter of intent which has been procured by the offeror or offeree company (as appropriate) or any of their respective associates;

RULE 26 *CONTINUED*

(j) where the Panel has given consent to aggregation of dealings, a full list of all dealings (Note 2 on Rule 24.3);

(k) documents relating to the financing arrangements for the offer where such arrangements are described in the offer document in compliance with the third sentence of Rule 24.2(f);

(l) all derivative contracts which in whole or in part have been disclosed under Rules 24.3(a) and (c) and 25.3(a) and (c) or in accordance with Rule 8.1. Documents in respect of the last mentioned must be made available for inspection from the time the offer document or the offeree board circular is published or from the time of disclosure, whichever is the later;

(m) documents relating to the payment of an inducement fee or similar arrangement (Rule 21.2);

(n) any agreements or arrangements, or, if not reduced to writing, a memorandum of all the terms of such agreements or arrangements, disclosed in the offer document pursuant to Rule 24.2(d)(ix); and

(o) any agreements or arrangements, or, if not reduced to writing, a memorandum of the terms of such agreements or arrangements, of the kind referred to in Note 6 on Rule 8.

NOTE ON RULE 26

Copies of documents

A copy of each document on display must, on request, promptly be made available by an offeror or the offeree company to the other party and to any competing offeror or potential offeror.

RULE 27. DOCUMENTS SUBSEQUENTLY SENT TO SHAREHOLDERS

27.1 MATERIAL CHANGES

Documents subsequently sent to shareholders of the offeree company by either party must contain details of any material changes in information previously published by or on behalf of the relevant party during the offer period; if there have been no such changes, this must be stated. In particular, the following matters must be updated:—

(a) changes or additions to material contracts, irrevocable commitments or letters of intent (Rules 24.2(a), (c) and (d)(x) and 25.6);

(b) interests and dealings (Rules 24.3 and 25.3);

(c) directors' emoluments (Rule 24.4);

(d) special arrangements (Rule 24.5);

(e) ultimate owner of securities acquired under the offer (Rule 24.8);

(f) arrangements in relation to dealings (Rules 24.12 and 25.5); and

(g) changes to directors' service contracts (Rule 25.4).

27.2 CONTINUING VALIDITY OF PROFIT FORECASTS

When a profit forecast has been made, documents subsequently sent to shareholders of the offeree company by the party making the forecast must comply with the requirements of Rule 28.5.

SECTION K. PROFIT FORECASTS

RULE 28

28.1 STANDARDS OF CARE

There are obvious hazards attached to the forecasting of profits; this should in no way detract from the necessity of maintaining the highest standards of accuracy and fair presentation in all communications to shareholders in an offer. A profit forecast must be compiled with due care and consideration by the directors, whose sole responsibility it is; the financial advisers must satisfy themselves that the forecast has been prepared in this manner by the directors.

NOTE ON RULE 28.1

Existing forecasts

At the outset, an adviser should invariably check whether or not his client has a forecast on the record so that the procedures required by Rule 28.3(d) can be set in train with a minimum of delay.

28.2 THE ASSUMPTIONS

(a) When a profit forecast appears in any document addressed to shareholders in connection with an offer, the assumptions, including the commercial assumptions, upon which the directors have based their profit forecast, must be stated in the document.

(b) When a profit forecast is given in a press announcement commencing or made during an offer period, any assumptions on which the forecast is based should be included in the announcement.

NOTES ON RULE 28.2

1. *Requirement to state the assumptions*

(a) It is important that by listing the assumptions on which the forecast is based useful information should be given to shareholders to help them in forming a view as to the reasonableness and reliability of the forecast. This should draw the shareholders' attention to, and where possible quantify, those uncertain factors which could materially disturb the ultimate achievement of the forecast.

(b) There are inevitable limitations on the accuracy of some forecasts and these should be indicated to assist shareholders in their review. A description of the general nature of the business or businesses with an indication of any major hazards in forecasting in these particular businesses should normally be included.

K2

RULE 28 *CONTINUED*

NOTES ON RULE 28.2 continued

(c) The forecast and the assumptions on which it is based are the sole responsibility of the directors. However, a duty is placed on the financial advisers to discuss the assumptions with their client and to satisfy themselves that the forecast has been made with due care and consideration. Auditors or consultant accountants must satisfy themselves that the forecast, so far as the accounting policies and calculations are concerned, has been properly compiled on the basis of the assumptions made.

Although the accountants have no responsibility for the assumptions, they will as a result of their review be in a position to advise the company on what assumptions should be listed in the circular and the way in which they should be described. The financial advisers and accountants obviously have substantial influence on the information about assumptions to be given in a circular; neither should allow an assumption to be published which appears to be unrealistic, or one to be omitted which appears to be important, without commenting appropriately in its report.

2. General rules

(a) The following general rules apply to the selection and drafting of assumptions.

(i) The shareholder should be able to understand their implications and so be helped in forming a judgement as to the reasonableness of the forecast and the main uncertainties attaching to it.

(ii) The assumptions should be specific rather than general, definite rather than vague.

(iii) Assumptions about factors which the directors can influence may be included, provided that they are clearly identified as such. However, assumptions relating to the general accuracy of estimates should be avoided. The following would not be acceptable:—

"Sales and profits for the year will not differ materially from those budgeted for."

"There will be no increases in costs other than those anticipated and provided for."

Every forecast involves estimates of income and of costs and must obviously be dependent on these estimates. Assumptions of the type illustrated above do not help the shareholder in considering the forecast.

RULE 28 CONTINUED

NOTES ON RULE 28.2 continued

(iv) *The assumptions should not relate to the accuracy of the accounting systems. If the systems of accounting and forecasting are such that full reliance cannot be placed on them, this should be the subject of some qualification, in the forecast itself. It is not satisfactory for this type of deficiency to be covered by the assumptions. The following would not be acceptable:—*

"The book record of stock and work-in-progress will be confirmed at the end of the financial year."

(v) *The assumptions should relate only to matters which may have a material bearing on the forecast.*

(b) Even the more specific type of assumption may still leave shareholders in doubt as to its implications, for instance:—

"No abnormal liabilities will arise under guarantees."

"Provisions for outstanding legal claims will prove adequate."

Such phrases might be dismissed on the grounds that the first relates to the unforeseen and the second to the adequacy of the estimating system. In both these examples information would be necessary about the extent or basis of the provision already made and/or about the circumstances in which unprovided for liabilities might arise.

(c) There may be occasions, particularly when the estimate relates to a period already ended, when no assumptions are required.

28.3 REPORTS REQUIRED IN CONNECTION WITH PROFIT FORECASTS

(a) A forecast made by an offeror offering solely cash need not be reported on. With the consent of the Panel, this exemption may be extended to an offeror offering a non-convertible debt instrument.

(b) In all other cases, the accounting policies and calculations for the forecasts must be examined and reported on by the auditors or consultant accountants. Any financial adviser mentioned in the document must also report on the forecasts.

(c) When income from land and buildings is a material element in a forecast, that part of the forecast should normally be examined and reported on by an independent valuer: this requirement does not apply where the income is virtually certain, eg known rents receivable under existing leases.

K4

RULE 28 *CONTINUED*

(d) Except with the consent of the Panel, any profit forecast which has been made before the commencement of the offer period must be examined, repeated and reported on in the document sent to shareholders.

(e) Exceptionally, the Panel may accept that, because of the uncertainties involved, it is not possible for a forecast previously made to be reported on in accordance with the Code nor for a revised forecast to be made. In these circumstances, the Panel would insist on shareholders being given a full explanation as to why the requirements of the Code were not capable of being met.

28.4 PUBLICATION OF REPORTS AND CONSENT LETTERS

Whenever a profit forecast is made during an offer period, the reports must be included in the document addressed to shareholders containing the forecast or, when the forecast is made in a press announcement (including one commencing the offer period), in that announcement. The reports must be accompanied by a statement that those making them have given and not withdrawn their consent to publication. If a company's forecast is published first in a press announcement, it must be repeated in full, together with the reports, in the next document sent to shareholders by that company.

28.5 SUBSEQUENT DOCUMENTS — CONTINUING VALIDITY OF FORECAST

When a company includes a forecast in a document, any document subsequently sent out by that company in connection with that offer must, except with the consent of the Panel, contain a statement by the directors that the forecast remains valid for the purpose of the offer and that the financial advisers and accountants who reported on the forecast have indicated that they have no objection to their reports continuing to apply.

28.6 STATEMENTS WHICH WILL BE TREATED AS PROFIT FORECASTS

(a) When no figure is mentioned

Even when no particular figure is mentioned or even if the word "profit" is not used, certain forms of words may constitute a profit forecast, particularly when considered in context. Examples are "profits will be somewhat higher than last year" and "performance in the second half-year is expected to be similar to our performance and results in the first half-year" (when interim figures have already been published). Whenever a form of words puts a floor under, or a ceiling on, the likely profits of a particular period or contains the data necessary to

RULE 28 CONTINUED

calculate an approximate figure for future profits, it will be treated by the Panel as a profit forecast which must be reported on. In cases of doubt, professional advisers should consult the Panel in advance.

(b) Estimates of profit for a completed period

An estimate of profit for a period which has already expired should be treated as a profit forecast.

(c) Interim and preliminary figures

Except with the consent of the Panel, any unaudited profit figures published during an offer period must be reported on. This provision does not, however, apply to:—

> (i) unaudited statements of annual or interim results which have already been published;
>
> (ii) unaudited statements of annual results which comply with the requirements for preliminary statements of annual results as set out in the UKLA Rules;
>
> (iii) unaudited statements of interim results which comply with the requirements for half-yearly reports as set out in the UKLA Rules in cases where the offer has been publicly recommended by the board of the offeree company; or
>
> (iv) unaudited statements of interim results by offerors which comply with the requirements for half-yearly reports as set out in the UKLA Rules, whether or not the offer has been publicly recommended by the board of the offeree company but provided the offer could not result in the issue of securities which would represent 10% or more of the enlarged voting share capital of the offeror.

The Panel should be consulted in advance if the company is not admitted to the Official List but wishes to take advantage of the exemptions under (ii), (iii) or (iv) above.

(d) Forecasts for a limited period

A profit forecast for a limited period (eg the following quarter) is subject to this Rule.

(e) Dividend forecasts

A dividend forecast is not normally considered to be a profit forecast unless, for example, it is accompanied by an estimate as to dividend cover.

K6

RULE 28 *CONTINUED*

(f) Profit warranties

The Panel must be consulted in advance if a profit warranty is to be published in connection with an offer as it may be regarded as a profit forecast.

(g) Earnings enhancement and merger benefits statements

Parties wishing to make earnings enhancement statements which are not intended to be profit forecasts must include an explicit and prominent disclaimer to the effect that such statements should not be interpreted to mean that earnings per share will necessarily be greater than those for the relevant preceding financial period.

Parties should also be aware that the inclusion of earnings enhancement statements, if combined with merger benefits statements and/or other published financial information, may result in the market being provided with information from which the prospective profits for the offeror or the enlarged offeror group or at least a floor or ceiling for such profits can be inferred. Such statements would then be subject to this Rule. If parties are in any doubt as to the implications of the inclusion of such statements, they should consult the Panel in advance.

See also Note 8 on Rule 19.1.

28.7 TAXATION, EXTRAORDINARY ITEMS AND MINORITY INTERESTS

When a forecast of profit before taxation appears in a document addressed to shareholders, there must be included forecasts of taxation (where the figure is expected to be significantly abnormal), extraordinary items and minority interests (where either of these amounts is expected to be material).

28.8 WHEN A FORECAST RELATES TO A PERIOD WHICH HAS COMMENCED

Whenever a profit forecast is made in relation to a period in which trading has already commenced, any previously published profit figures in respect of any expired part of that trading period, together with comparable figures for the same part of the preceding year, must be stated.

SECTION L. ASSET VALUATIONS
RULE 29

NB All references in the Rule to "The Standards" are to the Royal Institution of Chartered Surveyors' Appraisal and Valuation Standards.

29.1 VALUATIONS TO BE REPORTED ON IF GIVEN IN CONNECTION WITH AN OFFER

When a valuation of assets is given in connection with an offer, it should be supported by the opinion of a named independent valuer. (For the purposes of this Rule, "an independent valuer" means a valuer who meets the requirements of an "external valuer" as defined in the Glossary to the Standards and, in addition, has no connection with other parties to the transaction.)

(a) Type of asset

This Rule applies not only to land, buildings and process plant and machinery but also to other assets, eg stocks, ships, TV rental contracts and individual parts of a business. Where such assets are involved, the Panel should be consulted in advance.

(b) The valuer

In relation to land, buildings and plant and machinery, a valuer should be a corporate member of The Royal Institution of Chartered Surveyors or The Institute of Revenues Rating and Valuation or some other person approved by the Panel. In respect of other types of asset, the valuer should be an appropriately qualified person approved by the Panel. The valuer must be able to demonstrate that he meets any legal or regulatory requirements which apply in the circumstances in which the particular valuation is required and either:

> (i) that he has, in respect of the particular type of property or asset, sufficient current local, national and international (as appropriate) knowledge of the particular market and the skills and understanding necessary to undertake the valuation competently; or
>
> (ii) where he satisfies (i) above, except that he has insufficient current knowledge, that he will be or has been assisted by a person(s) who has/have such knowledge and the skills and understanding necessary to provide the assistance required by the valuer.

(c) In connection with an offer

In certain cases offer documents or defence circulars will include statements of assets reproducing directors' estimates of asset values published with the company's accounts in accordance with Schedule 7 Part I of the Companies Act 1985. The Panel will not regard such

RULE 29 CONTINUED

estimates as "given in connection with an offer" unless asset values are a particularly significant factor in assessing the offer and the estimates are, accordingly, given considerably more prominence in the offer documents or circulars than merely being referred to in a note to a statement of assets in an appendix. In these circumstances, such estimates must be supported, subject to Rule 29.2(e), by an independent valuer in accordance with this Rule.

(d) Another party's assets

A party to a takeover situation will not normally be permitted to issue a valuation, appraisal or calculation of worth of the assets owned by another party unless it is supported by the unqualified opinion of a named independent valuer and that valuer has had access to sufficient information to carry out a property valuation, appraisal or calculation of worth either in accordance with The Standards or, in respect of assets other than land, buildings and machinery, to appropriate standards approved by the Panel. Comments by one party about another party's valuation, appraisal or calculation of worth of its own assets may be permitted in exceptional circumstances. In all cases, the Panel must be consulted in advance.

29.2 BASIS OF VALUATION

(a) The basis of valuation must be clearly stated. Only in exceptional circumstances should it be qualified and in that event the valuer must explain the meaning of the words used. Similarly, special assumptions (see PS 2.3 of The Standards) should not normally be made in a valuation but, if assumptions are permitted by the Panel, they should be fully explained. (See Chapter 5 of The Standards.)

(b) In relation to valuations of land, buildings and plant and machinery, attention is drawn to The Standards.

(c) For non-specialised properties, the basis of valuation will normally be market value as defined in The Standards. Property which is occupied for the purposes of the business will be valued at existing use value. Where a property has been adapted or fitted out to meet the requirements of a particular business, the market value should relate to the property after the works have been completed. Alternatively, the market value may relate to the state of the property before the works had been commenced and the works of adaptation may be valued separately on a depreciated replacement cost basis, subject to adequate potential profitability. Specialised properties occupied by the business should be valued on a depreciated replacement cost basis, subject to adequate potential profitability. Properties held as investments or which are surplus to requirements and are held pending disposal should be valued at market value.

RULE 29 *CONTINUED*

(d) In the case of land currently being developed or with immediate development potential, in addition to giving the market value in the state existing at the date of valuation, the valuation should include:—

    (i) the value after the development has been completed;

    (ii) the value after the development has been completed and let;

    (iii) the estimated total cost, including carrying charges, of completing the development and the anticipated dates of completion and of letting or occupation; and

    (iv) a statement whether planning consent has been obtained and, if so, the date thereof and the nature of any conditions attaching to the consent which affect the value.

(e) In some exceptional cases, it will not be possible for a valuer to complete a full valuation of every property. The Panel may be prepared to regard the requirements of this Rule as met if the valuer carries out a valuation of a representative sample of properties and reports those valuations, with the directors taking sole responsibility for an estimate, based on the sample, to cover the remaining properties. This procedure will be available only where the portfolio as a whole is within the knowledge of the valuer, who must also certify the representative nature of the sample. Where this is done, the document sent to shareholders should distinguish between properties valued professionally and those where the directors have made estimates on the basis of the sample valuation and should also compare such estimates with book values.

NOTE ON RULE 29.2

Provision of adjusted net asset value information

If it is proposed to include adjusted net asset value information, the Panel must be consulted.

29.3 POTENTIAL TAX LIABILITY

When a valuation is given in connection with an offer, there should normally be a statement regarding any potential tax liability which would arise if the assets were to be sold at the amount of the valuation, accompanied by an appropriate comment as to the likelihood of any such liability crystallizing.

RULE 29 *CONTINUED*

29.4 CURRENT VALUATION

A valuation must state the effective date as at which the assets were valued and the professional qualifications and address of the valuer. If a valuation is not current, the valuer must state that a current valuation would not be materially different. If this statement cannot be made, the valuation must be updated.

29.5 OPINION AND CONSENT LETTERS

(a) Publication of opinion

The opinion of value must be contained in the document containing the asset valuation.

(b) Consent

The document must also state that the valuer has given and not withdrawn his consent to the publication of his valuation report.

(c) Valuation certificate to be on display

Where a valuation of assets is given in any document addressed to shareholders, the valuation report must be made available for inspection, in the manner described in Rule 26, together with an associated report or schedule containing details of the aggregate valuation. Where the Panel is satisfied that such disclosure may be commercially disadvantageous to the company concerned, it will allow the report or schedule to appear in a summarised form. In certain cases, the Panel may require any of these documents to be reproduced in full in a document sent to shareholders.

29.6 WAIVER IN CERTAIN CIRCUMSTANCES

In exceptional cases, certain companies, in particular property companies, which are the subject of an unexpected offer may find difficulty in obtaining, within the time available, the opinion of an independent valuer to support an asset valuation, as required by this Rule, before the board's circular has to be sent out. In such cases, the Panel may be prepared exceptionally to waive strict compliance with this requirement. The Panel will only do this where the interests of shareholders seem on balance to be best served by permitting informal valuations to appear coupled with such substantiation as is available. Advisers to offeree companies who wish to make use of this procedure should consult the Panel at the earliest opportunity.

SECTION M. TIMING AND REVISION

RULE 30. MAKING THE OFFER DOCUMENT AND THE OFFEREE BOARD CIRCULAR AVAILABLE

30.1 THE OFFER DOCUMENT

(a) The offer document should normally be posted to shareholders of the offeree company within 28 days of the announcement of a firm intention to make an offer. The Panel must be consulted if the offer document is not to be posted within this period. On the day of posting, the offeror must put the offer document on display in accordance with Rule 26 and announce in accordance with Rule 2.9 that the offer document has been posted and where the document can be inspected.

(b) At the same time, both the offeror and the offeree company must make the offer document readily available to their employee representatives or, where there are no such representatives, to the employees themselves.

30.2 THE OFFEREE BOARD CIRCULAR

(a) The board of the offeree company must publish a circular containing its opinion, as required by Rule 25.1(a), as soon as practicable after publication of the offer document and normally within 14 days and must:

(i) post it to its shareholders; and

(ii) make it readily and promptly available to its employee representatives or, where there are no such representatives, the employees themselves.

On the day of posting, the board of the offeree company must put the circular on display in accordance with Rule 26 and announce in accordance with Rule 2.9 that the circular has been posted and where it can be inspected.

(b) The board of the offeree company must append to the circular containing its opinion a separate opinion from the representatives of its employees on the effects of the offer on employment, provided such opinion is received in good time before publication of that circular.

30.3 MAKING DOCUMENTS AND INFORMATION AVAILABLE TO SHAREHOLDERS, EMPLOYEE REPRESENTATIVES AND EMPLOYEES

The requirements under Rules 2.6, 20.1, 23, 30.1, 30.2, 32.1 and 32.6(a) to provide information or to send or make documents available to shareholders of the offeree company or to employee representatives or

RULE 30 CONTINUED

employees of the offeror or the offeree company apply in respect of all such shareholders, employee representatives or employees, including those who are located outside the EEA, unless there is sufficient objective justification for their not doing so.

NOTE ON RULE 30.3

Shareholders, employee representatives and employees outside the EEA

Where local laws or regulations of a particular non-EEA jurisdiction may result in a significant risk of civil, regulatory or, particularly, criminal exposure for the offeror or the offeree company if the information or documentation is sent or made available to shareholders in that jurisdiction without any amendment, and unless they can avoid such exposure by making minor amendments to the information being provided or documents being sent or made available either:

(a) the offeror or the offeree company need not provide such information or send or make such information or documents available to registered shareholders of the offeree company who are located in that jurisdiction if less than 3% of the shares of the offeree company are held by registered shareholders located there at the date on which the information is to be provided or the information or documents are to be sent or made available (and there is no need to consult the Panel in these circumstances); or

(b) in all other cases, the Panel may grant a dispensation where it would be proportionate in the circumstances to do so having regard, notably, to the cost involved, any resulting delay to the transaction timetable, the number of registered shareholders in the relevant jurisdiction, the number of shares involved and any other factors invoked by the offeror or the offeree company.

Similar dispensations will apply in respect of information or documents which are provided or required to be made available to employee representatives or employees of the offeror or the offeree company.

The Panel will not normally grant any dispensation in relation to shareholders, employee representatives or employees of the offeree company who are located within the EEA.

Takeover Code

M₃

RULE 31. TIMING OF THE OFFER

31.1 FIRST CLOSING DATE

An offer must initially be open for at least 21 days following the date on which the offer document is posted.

31.2 FURTHER CLOSING DATES TO BE SPECIFIED

In any announcement of an extension of an offer, either the next closing date must be stated or, if the offer is unconditional as to acceptances, a statement may be made that the offer will remain open until further notice. In the latter case, or if the offer will remain open for acceptances beyond the 70th day following posting of the offer document, at least 14 days' notice in writing must be given, before the offer is closed, to those shareholders who have not accepted.

31.3 NO OBLIGATION TO EXTEND

There is no obligation to extend an offer the conditions of which are not met by the first or any subsequent closing date.

31.4 OFFER TO REMAIN OPEN FOR 14 DAYS AFTER UNCONDITIONAL AS TO ACCEPTANCES

After an offer has become or is declared unconditional as to acceptances, the offer must remain open for acceptance for not less than 14 days after the date on which it would otherwise have expired (see Rules 33.1 and 33.2). When, however, an offer is unconditional as to acceptances from the outset, a 14 day extension is not required but the position should be set out clearly and prominently in the offer document.

31.5 NO EXTENSION STATEMENTS

If statements in relation to the duration of an offer such as "the offer will not be extended beyond a specified date unless it is unconditional as to acceptances" ("no extension statements") are included in documents sent to offeree company shareholders, or are made by or on behalf of an offeror, its directors, officials or advisers, and not withdrawn immediately if incorrect, only in wholly exceptional circumstances will the offeror be allowed subsequently to extend its offer beyond the stated date except where the right to do so has been specifically reserved. The provisions of Rule 31.4 will apply in any event.

RULE 31 CONTINUED

NOTES ON RULE 31.5

(See also Rule 31.6)

1. Firm statements

In general, an offeror will be bound by any firm statement as to the duration of its offer. Any statement of intention will be regarded for this purpose as a firm statement; the expression "present intention" should not be used as it may be misleading to shareholders.

2. Reservation of right to set statements aside

A no extension statement may be set aside only if the offeror specifically reserved the right at the time the statement was made to set it aside in the circumstances which subsequently arise; this applies whether or not the offer was recommended at the outset. The first document sent to shareholders in which mention is made of the no extension statement must contain prominent reference to this reservation (precise details of which must also be included in the document). Any subsequent mention by the offeror of the no extension statement must be accompanied by a reference to the reservation or, at the least, to the relevant sections in the document containing the details. If the right to set aside the no extension statement has not been specifically reserved as set out above, only in wholly exceptional circumstances will the offeror be allowed to extend its offer (except as required by Rule 31.4), even if a recommendation from the board of the offeree company is forthcoming.

3. Competitive situations

Subject to Note 2 above, if a competitive situation arises after a no extension statement has been made, the offeror can choose not to be bound by it and to be free to extend its offer provided that:—

(a) notice to this effect is given as soon as possible (and in any event within 4 business days after the day of the firm announcement of the competing offer) and shareholders are informed in writing at the earliest opportunity; and

(b) any offeree shareholders who accepted the offer after the date of the no extension statement are given a right of withdrawal for a period of 8 days following the date on which the notice is posted.

(For the purpose of this Note a competitive situation will normally arise following a public announcement of the existence of a new offeror or potential offeror whether named or not. Other circumstances, however, may also constitute a competitive situation.)

RULE 31 *CONTINUED*

NOTES ON RULE 31.5 continued

4. Recommendations

Subject to Note 2 above, the offeror can choose not to be bound by a no extension statement which would otherwise prevent the posting of an increased or improved offer recommended for acceptance by the board of the offeree company.

5. Rule 31.9 announcements

Subject to Note 2 above, if the offeree company makes an announcement of the kind referred to in Rule 31.9 after the 39th day and after a no extension statement has been made, the offeror can choose not to be bound by that statement and to be free to extend its offer if permitted by the Panel under Rule 31.9, provided that notice to this effect is given as soon as possible (and in any event within 4 business days after the date of the offeree company announcement) and shareholders are informed in writing at the earliest opportunity.

31.6 FINAL DAY RULE (FULFILMENT OF ACCEPTANCE CONDITION, TIMING AND ANNOUNCEMENT)

(a) Except with the consent of the Panel, an offer (whether revised or not) may not become or be declared unconditional as to acceptances after midnight on the 60th day after the day the initial offer document was posted. The Panel's consent will normally only be granted:—

(i) in a competitive situation (see Note 4 below); or

(ii) if the board of the offeree company consents to an extension; or

(iii) as provided for in Rule 31.9; or

(iv) if the offeror's receiving agent requests an extension for the purpose of complying with Note 7 on Rule 10; or

(v) when withdrawal rights are introduced under Rule 13.5.

(b) For the purpose of the acceptance condition, the offeror may only take into account acceptances or purchases of shares in respect of which all relevant electronic instructions or documents (as required by Notes 4 and 5 on Rule 10) are received by its receiving agent before the last time for acceptance set out in the offeror's relevant document or announcement. This time must be no later than 1.00 pm on the 60th day (or any other date beyond which the offeror has stated that its offer will not be extended). In the event of an extension with the consent of the Panel in circumstances other than those set out in paragraphs (a) (i) to (iii) above, acceptances or purchases in respect of which relevant

M6

RULE 31 *CONTINUED*

electronic instructions or documents are received after 1.00 pm on the relevant date may only be taken into account with the agreement of the Panel, which will only be given in exceptional circumstances.

(c) Except with the consent of the Panel, on the 60th day (or any other date beyond which the offeror has stated that its offer will not be extended) an announcement should be made by 5.00 pm as to whether the offer is unconditional as to acceptances or has lapsed. Such announcement should include, if possible, the details required by Rule 17.1 but in any event must include a statement as to the current position in the count. (See Note 2.)

NOTES ON RULE 31.6

1. Extension of offer under Rule 31.6(a)

It should be noted that the effect of Rule 31.6(a) is that, unless the offer is unconditional as to acceptances by midnight on the final closing date (or the Panel gives permission for the offer to be extended), the offer will lapse. When, however, there is a Code matter outstanding on the final closing date, it may be inappropriate for the offer to become or be declared unconditional as to acceptances or to lapse at that time. In such a case, the Panel may, in addition to the circumstances set out in Rule 31.6(a), give permission for the offer to be extended, but with no extension of the time by which all relevant electronic instructions or documents in respect of acceptances, withdrawals and purchases must be received for the purpose of the acceptance condition, as referred to in Rule 31.6(b) and Rule 34.

2. Rule 31.6(c) announcement

Under Rule 31.6(c), an announcement as to whether the offer is unconditional as to acceptances or has lapsed should normally be made by 5.00 pm on the final closing date. This requirement should not be reflected in the terms of the offer pursuant to Rule 24.6, but, if there is any question of a delay in the announcement required by Rule 31.6, the Panel should be consulted as soon as practicable. Only in exceptional circumstances will the Panel agree to an offeror's request that this announcement may be made after 5.00 pm.

3. The Competition Commission and the European Commission

If there is a significant delay in the decision on whether or not there is to be a reference or initiation of proceedings, the Panel will normally extend "Day 39" (see Rule 31.9) to the second day following the announcement of such decision with consequent changes to "Day 46" (see Rule 32.1(b)) and "Day 60".

RULE 31 *CONTINUED*

NOTES ON RULE 31.6 continued

4. *Competitive situations*

If a competing offer has been announced, both offerors will normally be bound by the timetable established by the posting of the competing offer document. In addition, the Panel will extend "Day 60" in accordance with any procedure established by the Panel in accordance with Rule 32.5.

The Panel will not normally grant its consent under Rule 31.6(a)(ii) in a competitive situation unless its consent is sought before the 46th day following the posting of the competing offer document.

31.7 TIME FOR FULFILMENT OF ALL OTHER CONDITIONS

Except with the consent of the Panel, all conditions must be fulfilled or the offer must lapse within 21 days of the first closing date or of the date the offer becomes or is declared unconditional as to acceptances, whichever is the later. The Panel's consent will normally only be granted if the outstanding condition involves a material official authorisation or regulatory clearance relating to the offer and it had not been possible to obtain an extension under Rule 31.6.

NOTE ON RULE 31.7

The effect of lapsing

The Note on Rule 12.1 also applies to this Rule.

31.8 SETTLEMENT OF CONSIDERATION

Except with the consent of the Panel, the consideration must be posted within 14 days of the later of: the first closing date of the offer, the date the offer becomes or is declared wholly unconditional or the date of receipt of an acceptance complete in all respects.

31.9 OFFEREE COMPANY ANNOUNCEMENTS AFTER DAY 39

The board of the offeree company should not, except with the consent of the Panel (which should be consulted in good time), announce any material new information (including trading results, profit or dividend forecasts, asset valuations and proposals for dividend payments or for any material acquisition or disposal) after the 39th day following the posting of the initial offer document. Where a matter which might give rise to such an announcement being made after the 39th day is known to the offeree company, every effort should be made to bring forward the date of the announcement, but, where this is not practicable or where the matter arises after that date, the Panel will normally give its consent to a later announcement. If an announcement of the kind

M8

RULE 31 *CONTINUED*

referred to in this Rule is made after the 39th day, the Panel will normally be prepared to grant an extension to "Day 46" (see Rule 32.1(b)) and/or "Day 60" (see Rule 31.6) as appropriate.

(See also Note 3 on Rule 31.6.)

31.10 RETURN OF DOCUMENTS OF TITLE

If an offer lapses, all documents of title and other documents lodged with forms of acceptance must be returned within 14 days of the lapsing of the offer and the receiving agent should immediately give instructions for the release of securities held in escrow.

Takeover Code

M9

RULE 32. REVISION

32.1 OFFER OPEN FOR 14 DAYS AFTER POSTING OF REVISED OFFER DOCUMENT

(a) If an offer is revised, a revised offer document, drawn up in accordance with Rules 24 and 27, must be posted to shareholders of the offeree company. On the day of posting, the offeror must put the revised offer document on display in accordance with Rule 26 and announce in accordance with Rule 2.9 that the document has been posted and where the document can be inspected.

(b) The offer must be kept open for at least 14 days following the date on which the revised offer document is posted. Therefore, no revised offer document may be posted in the 14 days ending on the last day the offer is able to become unconditional as to acceptances.

NOTES ON RULE 32.1

1. Announcements which may increase the value of an offer

Where an offer involves an exchange of equity or potential equity, the announcement by an offeror of any material new information (including trading results, profit or dividend forecasts, asset valuations, merger benefits statements and proposals for dividend payments or for any material acquisition or disposal) may have the effect of increasing the value of the offer. An offeror will not, therefore, normally be permitted to make such announcements after it is precluded from revising its offer. If an announcement of a kind referred to in this Note might fall to be made during the offer period, the Panel must be consulted at the earliest opportunity and an offeror will not be permitted to make a no increase statement as defined in Rule 32.2 prior to the release of the announcement.

2. When revision is required

An offeror will normally be required to revise its offer if it, or any person acting in concert with it, acquires an interest in shares at above the offer price (see Rule 6) or it becomes obliged to make an offer in accordance with Rule 11 or to make a cash offer, or to increase an existing cash offer, under Rule 9.

3. When revision is not permissible

Since an offer must remain open for acceptance for 14 days following the date on which the revised offer document is posted, an offeror will generally not be able to revise its offer, and must not place itself in a position where it would be required to revise its offer, in the 14 days ending on the last day its offer is able to become unconditional as to acceptances. Nor must an offeror place itself in a position where it would be required to revise its offer if it has made a no increase statement as defined in Rule 32.2.

M10

RULE 32 CONTINUED

NOTES ON RULE 32.1 continued

4. Triggering Rule 9

When an offeror, which is making a voluntary offer either in cash or with a cash alternative, acquires an interest in shares which causes it to have to extend a mandatory offer under Rule 9 at no higher price than the existing cash offer, the change in the nature of the offer will not be viewed as a revision (and will thus not be precluded by an earlier no increase statement), even if the offeror is obliged to waive any outstanding condition, but such an acquisition can only be made if the offer can remain open for acceptance for a further 14 days following the date on which the amended offer document is posted.

32.2 NO INCREASE STATEMENTS

If statements in relation to the value or type of consideration such as "the offer will not be further increased" or "our offer remains at xp per share and it will not be raised" ("no increase statements") are included in documents sent to offeree company shareholders, or are made by or on behalf of an offeror, its directors, officials or advisers, and not withdrawn immediately if incorrect, only in wholly exceptional circumstances will the offeror be allowed subsequently to amend the terms of its offer in any way even if the amendment would not result in an increase of the value of the offer (eg the introduction of a lower paper alternative) except where the right to do so has been specifically reserved.

NOTES ON RULE 32.2

1. Firm statements

In general, an offeror will be bound by any firm statement as to the finality of its offer. In this respect, the Panel will treat any indication of finality as absolute, unless the offeror clearly states the circumstances in which the statement will not apply, and will not distinguish between the precise words chosen, ie the offer is "final" or will not be "increased", "amended", "revised", "improved", "changed", and similar expressions will all be treated in the same way. Any statement of intention will be regarded for this purpose as a firm statement; the expression "present intention" should not be used as it may be misleading to shareholders.

2. Reservation of right to set statements aside

A no increase statement may be set aside only if the offeror has specifically reserved the right at the time the statement was made to set it aside in the circumstances which subsequently arise; this applies whether or not the offer was recommended at the outset. The first document sent to shareholders in which mention is made of the no increase statement must contain prominent

RULE 32 *CONTINUED*

NOTES ON RULE 32.2 continued

reference to this reservation (precise details of which must also be included in the document). Any subsequent mention by the offeror of the no increase statement must be accompanied by a reference to the reservation or, at the least, to the relevant sections in the document containing the details. If the right to set aside the no increase statement has not been specifically reserved as set out above, only in wholly exceptional circumstances will the offeror be allowed to increase its offer after a no increase statement, even if a recommendation from the board of the offeree company is forthcoming or if the offer is unconditional in all respects.

3. Competitive situations

Subject to Note 2 above, if a competitive situation arises after a no increase statement has been made, the offeror can choose not to be bound by it and to be free to revise its offer provided that:—

(a) notice to this effect is given as soon as possible (and in any event within 4 business days after the day of the firm announcement of the competing offer) and shareholders are informed in writing at the earliest opportunity; and

(b) any shareholders who accepted the offer after the date of the no increase statement are given a right of withdrawal for a period of 8 days following the date on which the notice is posted.

(For the purpose of this Note a competitive situation will normally arise following a public announcement of the existence of a new offeror or potential offeror whether named or not. Other circumstances, however, may also constitute a competitive situation.)

4. Recommendations

Subject to Note 2 above, the offeror can choose not to be bound by a no increase statement which would otherwise prevent the posting of an increased or improved offer recommended for acceptance by the board of the offeree company.

5. Rule 31.9 announcements

Subject to Note 2 above, if the offeree company makes an announcement of the kind referred to in Rule 31.9 after the 39th day and after a no increase statement has been made, the offeror can choose not to be bound by that statement and to be free to revise its offer if permitted by the Panel under Rule 31.9, provided that notice to this effect is given as soon as possible (and in any event within 4 business days after the date of the offeree company announcement) and shareholders are informed in writing at the earliest opportunity.

RULE 32 CONTINUED

32.3 ENTITLEMENT TO REVISED CONSIDERATION

If an offer is revised, all shareholders who accepted the original offer must be entitled to the revised consideration.

32.4 NEW CONDITIONS FOR INCREASED OR IMPROVED OFFERS

Subject to the prior consent of the Panel, and only to the extent necessary to implement an increased or improved offer, the offeror may introduce new conditions (eg obtaining shareholders' approval or the admission to listing or admission to trading of new securities).

32.5 COMPETITIVE SITUATIONS

If a competitive situation continues to exist in the later stages of the offer period, the Panel will normally require revised offers to be published in accordance with an auction procedure, the terms of which will be determined by the Panel. That procedure will normally require final revisions to competing offers to be announced by the 46th day following the posting of the competing offer document but enable an offeror to revise its offer within a set period in response to any revision announced by a competing offeror on or after the 46th day. The procedure will not normally require any revised offer to be posted before the expiry of a set period after the last revision to either offer is announced. The Panel will consider applying any alternative procedure which is agreed between competing offerors and the board of the offeree company.

NOTES ON RULE 32.5

1. *Dispensation from obligation to post*

The Panel will normally grant dispensation from the obligation to post a revised offer, which is lower than the final revised offer announced by a competing offeror, when the board of the offeree company consents.

2. *Guillotine*

The Panel may impose a final time limit for announcing revisions to competing offers for the purpose of any procedure established in accordance with this Rule taking into account representations by the board of the offeree company, the revisions previously announced and the duration of the procedure.

32.6 THE OFFEREE BOARD'S OPINION

(a) The board of the offeree company must post to the company's shareholders a circular containing its opinion on the revised offer

RULE 32 *CONTINUED*

under Rule 25.1(a), drawn up in accordance with Rules 25 and 27. On the day of posting, the offeree company must put the circular on display in accordance with Rule 26 and announce in accordance with Rule 2.9 that the document has been posted and where the document can be inspected.

(b) The board of the offeree company must append to the circular containing its opinion on a revised offer a separate opinion from the representatives of its employees on the effects of the revised offer on employment, provided such opinion is received in good time before publication of that circular.

32.7 INFORMING EMPLOYEES

(a) When any revised offer document is posted to shareholders of the offeree company, both the offeror and the offeree company must make that document readily and promptly available to the representatives of their employees or, where there are no such representatives, to the employees themselves. On the day of posting, the offeree company must put the circular on display in accordance with Rule 26 and announce in accordance with Rule 2.9 that the document has been posted and where the document can be inspected.

(b) When the board of the offeree company posts to its shareholders a circular containing its opinion under Rule 25.1(a) on a revised offer, it must make that circular readily and promptly available to its employee representatives or, where there are no such representatives, to the employees themselves.

RULE 33. ALTERNATIVE OFFERS

33.1 TIMING AND REVISION

In general, the provisions of Rules 31 and 32 apply equally to alternative offers, including cash alternatives.

NOTES ON RULE 33.1

1. Elections

For the purpose of this Rule, an arrangement under which shareholders elect, subject to the election of other shareholders, to vary the proportion in which they are to receive different forms of consideration is not regarded as an alternative offer and may be closed without notice on any closing date; this must be clearly stated in the offer document.

2. Shutting off

Normally, except as permitted by Rule 33.2, if an offer has become or is declared unconditional as to acceptances, all alternative offers must remain open in accordance with Rule 31.4.

In accordance with Rule 31.3, if on a closing date an offer is not unconditional as to acceptances, an alternative offer (except a cash alternative provided to satisfy the requirements of Rule 9) may be closed without prior notice. However, if, on the first closing date on which an offer is capable of being declared unconditional as to acceptances, the offer is not so declared and is extended, all alternative offers must, except as permitted by Rule 33.2, remain open for 14 days thereafter but may then be closed without prior notice.

33.2 SHUTTING OFF CASH UNDERWRITTEN ALTERNATIVES

Where the value of a cash underwritten alternative provided by third parties is, at the time of announcement, more than half the maximum value of the offer, an offeror will not be obliged to keep that alternative open in accordance with Rules 31.4 or 33.1 if it has given notice to shareholders in writing that it reserves the right to close it on a stated date, being not less than 14 days after the date on which the written notice is posted, or to extend it on that stated date. Notice under this Rule may not be given between the time when a competing offer has been announced and the end of the resulting competitive situation. (See also Rule 24.13.)

RULE 33 *CONTINUED*

NOTES ON RULE 33.2

1. Further notices

Where a notice has been given pursuant to this Rule and the alternative is not closed on the stated date but extended, the offeror must give a further notice in writing to shareholders if it wishes to take advantage of this Rule.

2. Rule 9 offers

This Rule will not apply to a cash alternative provided to satisfy the requirements of Rule 9.

33.3 REINTRODUCTION OF ALTERNATIVE OFFERS

Where a firm statement has been made that an alternative offer will not be extended or reintroduced and that alternative has ceased to be open for acceptance, neither that alternative, nor any substantially similar alternative, may be reintroduced. Where, however, such a statement has not been made and an alternative offer has closed for acceptance, an offeror will not be precluded from reintroducing that alternative at a later date. Reintroduction would constitute a revision of the offer and would, therefore, be subject to the requirements of, and only be permitted as provided in, Rule 32.

RULE 34. RIGHT OF WITHDRAWAL

An acceptor must be entitled to withdraw his acceptance from the date which is 21 days after the first closing date of the initial offer, if the offer has not by such date become or been declared unconditional as to acceptances. This entitlement to withdraw must be exercisable until the earlier of (a) the time that the offer becomes or is declared unconditional as to acceptances and (b) the final time for lodgement of acceptances which can be taken into account in accordance with Rule 31.6. An acceptor must also be entitled to withdraw his acceptance if so determined by the Panel in accordance with Rule 13.5.

SECTION N. RESTRICTIONS FOLLOWING OFFERS AND POSSIBLE OFFERS

RULE 35

35.1 DELAY OF 12 MONTHS

Except with the consent of the Panel, where an offer has been announced or posted but has not become or been declared wholly unconditional and has been withdrawn or has lapsed, neither the offeror, nor any person who acted in concert with the offeror in the course of the original offer, nor any person who is subsequently acting in concert with any of them, may within 12 months from the date on which such offer is withdrawn or lapses either:—

(a) announce an offer or possible offer for the offeree company (including a partial offer which could result in the offeror and persons acting in concert with it being interested in shares carrying 30% or more of the voting rights of the offeree company);

(b) acquire any interest in shares of the offeree company if the offeror or any such person would thereby become obliged under Rule 9 to make an offer;

(c) acquire any interest in, or procure an irrevocable commitment in respect of, shares of the offeree company if the shares in which such person, together with any persons acting in concert with him, would be interested and the shares in respect of which he, or they, had acquired irrevocable commitments would in aggregate carry 30% or more of the voting rights of the offeree company;

(d) make any statement which raises or confirms the possibility that an offer might be made for the offeree company; or

(e) take any steps in connection with a possible offer for the offeree company where knowledge of the possible offer might be extended outside those who need to know in the offeror and its immediate advisers.

35.2 PARTIAL OFFERS

The restrictions in Rule 35.1 will also apply following a partial offer:—

(a) which could result in the offeror and persons acting in concert with it being interested in shares carrying not less than 30% but not holding shares carrying more than 50% of the voting rights of the offeree company whether or not the offer has become or been declared wholly unconditional. When such an offer has become or been declared wholly unconditional, the period of 12 months runs from that date; and

(b) for more than 50% of the voting rights of the offeree company which has not become or been declared wholly unconditional.

N2

RULE 35 *CONTINUED*

The restrictions in Rule 35.1 will not normally apply following a partial offer which could only result in the offeror and persons acting in concert with it being interested in shares carrying less than 30% of the voting rights of the offeree company.

NOTE ON RULES 35.1 and 35.2

When dispensations may be granted

(a) The Panel will normally grant consent under this Rule when:—

(i) the new offer is recommended by the board of the offeree company. Such consent will not normally be granted within 3 months of the lapsing of an earlier offer in circumstances where the offeror either was prevented from revising or extending its previous offer as a result of a no increase statement or a no extension statement or was one of two or more competing offerors whose offers lapsed with combined acceptances of less than 50% of the voting rights of the offeree company; or

(ii) the new offer follows the announcement of an offer by a third party for the offeree company; or

(iii) the previous offer period ended in accordance with Rule 12.2 and the new offer follows the giving of clearance by the Competition Commission or the issuing of a decision by the European Commission under Article 8(2) of Council Regulation 139/2004/EC. Any such offer must normally be announced within 21 days after the announcement of such clearance or decision; or

(iv) the new offer follows the announcement by the offeree company of a "whitewash" proposal (see Note 1 of the Notes on Dispensations from Rule 9) or of a reverse takeover (see Note 2 on Rule 3.2) which has not failed or lapsed or been withdrawn.

(b) The Panel may also grant consent in circumstances in which it is likely to prove, or has proved, impossible to obtain material official authorisations or regulatory clearances relating to an offer within the Code timetable. The Panel should be consulted by an offeror or potential offeror as soon as it has reason to believe that this may become the position.

(c) The restrictions in Rules 35.1(d) and (e) will not normally apply to the extent that the offer lapsed as a result of being referred to the Competition Commission or the European Commission initiating proceedings, or as a result of the offeror failing to obtain another material official authorisation or regulatory clearance relating to the offer within the usual Code timetable, but the offeror is continuing to seek clearance or a decision from the relevant official or regulatory authorities with a view subsequently to making a new

RULE 35 *CONTINUED*

NOTE ON RULES 35.1 and 35.2 continued

offer with the consent of the Panel in accordance with Note (a)(iii) or Note (b) on Rule 35.1.

NB Rule 2.2(e) will continue to apply in these circumstances.

35.3 DELAY OF 6 MONTHS BEFORE ACQUISITIONS ABOVE THE OFFER VALUE

Except with the consent of the Panel, if a person, together with any person acting in concert with him, holds shares carrying more than 50% of the voting rights of a company, neither that person nor any person acting in concert with him may, within 6 months of the closure of any previous offer made by him to the shareholders of that company which became or was declared wholly unconditional, make a second offer to any shareholder in that company, or acquire any interest in shares in that company, on more favourable terms than those made available under the previous offer (see also Rule 6.2(a)). For this purpose the value of a securities exchange offer shall be calculated as at the date the offer closed. In addition, special deals with favourable conditions attached may not be entered into during this 6 months period (see also Rule 16).

35.4 RESTRICTIONS ON DEALINGS BY A COMPETING OFFEROR WHOSE OFFER HAS LAPSED

Except with the consent of the Panel, where an offer has been one of two or more competing offers and has lapsed, neither that offeror, nor any person acting in concert with that offeror, may acquire any interest in shares in the offeree company on more favourable terms than those made available under its lapsed offer until each of the competing offers has either been declared unconditional in all respects or has itself lapsed. For these purposes, the value of the lapsed offer shall be calculated as at the day the offer lapsed.

NOTE ON RULES 35.3 and 35.4

Determination of price

The price paid for any acquisition of an interest in shares will be determined in the manner set out in Note 4 on Rule 6 (other than the final paragraph of that Note).

However, where:

(a) a call option was entered into during any period that was relevant for the purposes of Rule 6 (or Rule 9.5, where relevant) in relation to the previous or lapsed offer; and

N4

RULE 35 CONTINUED

NOTE ON RULES 35.3 and 35.4 continued

(b) that call option is exercised:

(i) during the six month period referred to in Rule 35.3 (in the case of Rule 35.3); or

(ii) before any competing offer has either been declared unconditional in all respects or has itself lapsed (in the case of Rule 35.4),

then the person will be treated as having acquired an interest in shares at the time of such exercise and, for the purposes of Rule 35.3 or Rule 35.4 (as the case may be), the price paid will normally be treated as the amount paid on exercise of the option together with any amount paid by the option-holder on entering into the option.

Where a person acquired an interest in shares before the period referred to in paragraph (a) above as a result of any option, derivative or agreement to purchase and, during the relevant period referred to in paragraph (b) above, the person acquires any of the relevant shares, no obligation under this Rule will normally arise as a result of the acquisition of those shares. However, if the terms of the instrument have been varied in any way, or if the shares are acquired other than on the terms of the original instrument, the Panel should be consulted.

SECTION O. PARTIAL OFFERS

RULE 36

36.1 PANEL'S CONSENT REQUIRED

The Panel's consent is required for any partial offer. In the case of an offer which could not result in the offeror and persons acting in concert with it being interested in shares carrying 30% or more of the voting rights of a company, consent will normally be granted.

36.2 ACQUISITIONS BEFORE THE OFFER

In the case of an offer which could result in the offeror and persons acting in concert with it being interested in shares carrying 30% or more but holding less than 100% of the voting rights of a company, such consent will not normally be granted if the offeror or persons acting in concert with it have acquired, selectively or in significant numbers, interests in shares in the offeree company during the 12 months preceding the application for consent or if interests in shares have been acquired at any time after the partial offer was reasonably in contemplation.

36.3 ACQUISITIONS DURING AND AFTER THE OFFER

The offeror and persons acting in concert with it may not acquire any interest in shares in the offeree company during the offer period. In addition, in the case of a successful partial offer, neither the offeror, nor any person who acted in concert with the offeror in the course of the partial offer, nor any person who is subsequently acting in concert with any of them, may, except with the consent of the Panel, acquire any interest in such shares during a period of 12 months after the end of the offer period.

NOTES ON RULE 36.3

1. Discretionary fund managers and principal traders

Dealings by non-exempt discretionary fund managers and principal traders which are connected with an offeror will be treated in accordance with Rule 7.2.

2. Partial offer resulting in an interest of less than 30%

The consent of the Panel will normally be granted for acquisitions of interests in shares within 12 months of the end of the offer period when a partial offer has resulted in the offeror and persons acting in concert with it being interested in shares carrying less than 30% of the voting rights of a company.

RULE 36 *CONTINUED*

36.4 OFFER FOR BETWEEN 30% AND 50%

When an offer is made which could result in the offeror and persons acting in concert with it being interested in shares carrying not less than 30% but not holding shares carrying more than 50% of the voting rights of a company, the precise number of shares offered for must be stated and the offer may not be declared unconditional as to acceptances unless acceptances are received for not less than that number.

36.5 OFFER FOR 30% OR MORE REQUIRES 50% APPROVAL

Any offer which could result in the offeror and persons acting in concert with it being interested in shares carrying 30% or more of the voting rights of a company must be conditional, not only on the specified number of acceptances being received, but also on approval of the offer, normally signified by means of a separate box on the form of acceptance, being given in respect of over 50% of the voting rights held by shareholders who are independent of the offeror and persons acting in concert with it. This requirement may on occasion be waived if over 50% of the voting rights of the offeree company are held by one shareholder.

36.6 WARNING ABOUT CONTROL POSITION

In the case of a partial offer which could result in the offeror, either alone or with persons acting in concert with it, holding shares carrying over 50% of the voting rights of the offeree company, the offer document must contain specific and prominent reference to this and to the fact that, if the offer succeeds, the offeror or, where appropriate, the offeror and persons acting in concert with it, will be free, subject to Rule 36.3 and, where relevant, to Note 4 on Rule 9.1, to acquire further interests in shares without incurring any obligation under Rule 9 to make a general offer.

36.7 SCALING DOWN

Partial offers must be made to all shareholders of the class and arrangements must be made for those shareholders who wish to do so to accept in full for the relevant percentage of their holdings. Shares tendered in excess of this percentage must be accepted by the offeror from each shareholder in the same proportion to the number tendered to the extent necessary to enable it to obtain the total number of shares for which it has offered.

RULE 36 *CONTINUED*

36.8 COMPARABLE OFFER

When an offer is made for a company with more than one class of equity share capital which could result in the offeror and persons acting in concert with it being interested in shares carrying 30% or more of the voting rights, a comparable offer must be made for each class.

NOTES ON RULE 36

1. Allotted but unissued shares

When shares of a company carrying voting rights have been allotted (even if provisionally) but have not yet been issued, for example, under a rights issue when the shares are represented by renounceable letters of allotment, the Panel should be consulted. It is likely that such shares, and the acquisition of an interest in such shares, will be taken into account for the purpose of this Rule.

2. Dual consideration offers for 100%

If a certain consideration is offered for part of each shareholder's holding and a lower consideration for the balance, such an offer may be treated as a form of partial offer in spite of the fact that the offer is being made for all voting equity share capital not already held. Rule 36.5 may apply and the Panel's consent must be sought if any such offer is contemplated.

3. Use of tender offers

In certain circumstances, with the consent of the Panel, a tender offer may be used instead of a partial offer in which case the Rules set out in Appendix 5 will apply.

SECTION P. REDEMPTION OR PURCHASE BY A COMPANY OF ITS OWN SECURITIES

RULE 37

37.1 POSSIBLE REQUIREMENT TO MAKE A MANDATORY OFFER

When a company redeems or purchases its own voting shares, any resulting increase in the percentage of shares carrying voting rights in which a person or group of persons acting in concert is interested will be treated as an acquisition for the purpose of Rule 9. Subject to prior consultation, the Panel will normally waive any resulting obligation to make a general offer if there is a vote of independent shareholders and a procedure on the lines of that set out in Appendix 1 is followed.

NOTES ON RULE 37.1

1. Persons who will not be required to make a mandatory offer

A person who comes to exceed the limits in Rule 9.1 in consequence of a company's redemption or purchase of its own shares will not normally incur an obligation to make a mandatory offer unless that person is a director, or the relationship of the person with any one or more of the directors is such that the person is, or is presumed to be, acting in concert with any of the directors. A person who has appointed a representative to the board of the company, and investment managers of investment trusts, will be treated for these purposes as a director. However, there is no presumption that all the directors (or any two or more directors) are acting in concert solely by reason of a proposed redemption or purchase by the company of its own shares, or the decision to seek shareholders' authority for any such redemption or purchase.

2. Acquisitions of interests in shares preceding a redemption or purchase

The exception in Note 1 will not apply, and an obligation to make a mandatory offer may therefore be imposed, if a person (or any relevant member of a group of persons acting in concert) has acquired an interest in shares at a time when he had reason to believe that such a redemption or purchase of its own shares by the company would take place. This Note will not normally be relevant unless the relevant person has knowledge that a redemption or purchase for which requisite shareholder authority exists is being, or is likely to be, implemented (whether in whole or in part).

3. Situations where a mandatory obligation may arise

Where the directors are aware that a company's redemption or purchase of its own shares would otherwise give rise to an obligation for a person (or group of persons acting in concert) to make a mandatory offer, the board of

RULE 37 *CONTINUED*

NOTES ON RULE 37.1 continued

directors should ensure that an appropriate resolution to approve a waiver of this obligation is put to independent shareholders prior to implementation of the relevant redemption or purchase and as a pre-condition to its implementation. Additionally, each individual director should draw the attention of the board at the time any redemption or purchase of the company's own shares is proposed, and whenever shareholders' authority for any such redemption or purchase is to be sought, to interests in shares of parties acting in concert, or presumed to be acting in concert, with that director.

4. *Prior consultation*

The Panel must be consulted in advance in any case where Rule 9 might be relevant. This will include any case where a person or group of persons acting in concert is interested in shares carrying 30% or more but does not hold shares carrying more than 50% of the voting rights of a company, or may become interested in 30% or more on full implementation of the proposed redemption or purchase of own shares. In addition, the Panel should always be consulted if the aggregate interests in shares of the directors and any other persons acting in concert, or presumed to be acting in concert, with any of the directors amount to 30% or more, or may be increased to 30% or more on full implementation of the proposed redemption or purchase of own shares.

5. *Disqualifying transactions*

Notwithstanding that the redemption or purchase of voting shares is made conditional upon the prior approval of a majority of the shareholders independent of the transaction at a general meeting of the company:

(a) the Panel will not normally waive an obligation under Rule 9 if the relevant person, or any member of the relevant group of persons acting in concert, has acquired an interest in shares in the knowledge that the company intended to seek permission from its shareholders to redeem or purchase its own shares; and

(b) a waiver will be invalidated if any acquisitions are made by the relevant person, or by any member of the relevant group of persons acting in concert, in the period between the posting of the circular to shareholders and the shareholders' meeting.

6. *Renewals*

Any waiver previously obtained under this Rule will expire at the same time as the relevant shareholders' authority under Sections 164 to 166 of the Companies Act 1985 (whether or not voting shares have in fact been

Takeover Code

RULE 37 *CONTINUED*

NOTES ON RULE 37.1 continued

redeemed or purchased). Accordingly, waivers will normally need to be renewed at the same time as the relevant shareholders' authority is renewed.

7. Responsibility for making an offer

If an obligation arises under this Rule for a general offer to be made and a dispensation is not granted, the prime responsibility for making an offer will normally attach to the person who obtains or consolidates control as a result of the redemption or purchase of its own shares by the company. Where control is obtained or consolidated by a group of persons acting in concert, the prime responsibility will normally attach to the principal member or members of the group acting in concert. In exceptional cases, responsibility for making an offer may attach to one or more directors if, in the view of the Panel, there has been a failure by the board as a whole, or by any one or more individual directors, to address satisfactorily the implications of a redemption or purchase by the company of its own shares in relation to interests in shares of directors or parties acting in concert with one or more of the directors.

8. Inadvertent mistake

Note 4 on the dispensations from Rule 9 may be relevant in appropriate circumstances.

37.2 LIMITATION ON SUBSEQUENT ACQUISITIONS

Subsequent to the redemption or purchase by a company of its own voting shares, all persons will be subject, in acquiring further interests in shares in the company, to the provisions of Rule 9.1.

NOTE ON RULE 37.2

Calculation of percentage thresholds

The percentage thresholds referred to in Rule 9.1 will be calculated by reference to the outstanding voting capital subsequent to the redemption or purchase by the company of its own shares.

37.3 REDEMPTION OR PURCHASE OF SECURITIES BY THE OFFEREE COMPANY

(a) Shareholders' approval

During the course of an offer, or even before the date of the offer if the board of the offeree company has reason to believe that a bona fide offer might be imminent, no redemption or purchase by the offeree company of its own shares may be effected without the approval of the shareholders at a general meeting. The notice convening the meeting must include information about the offer or anticipated offer. Where it is felt that the redemption or purchase is in pursuance of a contract

P4

RULE 37 *CONTINUED*

entered into earlier or another pre-existing obligation, the Panel must be consulted and its consent to proceed without a shareholders' meeting obtained (Notes 1, 5 and 10 on Rule 21.1 may be relevant).

(b) Public disclosure

For the purpose of Rule 8, dealings in relevant securities include the redemption or purchase of, or taking or exercising an option over, any of its own relevant securities by the offeree company.

(c) Disclosure in the offeree board circular

The offeree board circular advising shareholders on an offer must state the amount of relevant securities of the offeree company which the offeree company has redeemed or purchased during the period commencing 12 months prior to the offer period and ending with the latest practicable date prior to the posting of the document, and the details of any such redemptions and purchases, including dates and prices and the extent to which the shares redeemed or purchased were cancelled or held in treasury.

37.4 REDEMPTION OR PURCHASE OF SECURITIES BY THE OFFEROR COMPANY

(a) Public disclosure

For the purpose of Rule 8, dealings in relevant securities include the redemption or purchase of, or taking or exercising an option over, any of its own relevant securities by an offeror.

(b) Disclosure in the offer document

The offer document must state (in the case of a securities exchange offer only) the number of relevant securities of the offeror which the offeror has redeemed or purchased between the start of the offer period and the latest practicable date prior to the posting of the offer document and the details of any such redemptions and purchases, including dates and prices and the extent to which the shares redeemed or purchased were cancelled or held in treasury.

SECTION Q. DEALINGS BY CONNECTED EXEMPT PRINCIPAL TRADERS

RULE 38

38.1 PROHIBITED DEALINGS

An exempt principal trader connected with an offeror or the offeree company must not carry out any dealings with the purpose of assisting the offeror or the offeree company, as the case may be.

NOTE ON RULE 38.1

Suspension of exempt status

Any dealings by an exempt principal trader connected with an offeror or the offeree company with the purpose of assisting an offeror or the offeree company, as the case may be, will constitute a serious breach of the Code. Accordingly, if the Panel determines that a principal trader has carried out such dealings, it will be prepared to rule that the principal trader should cease to enjoy exempt status for such period of time as the Panel may consider appropriate in the circumstances.

38.2 DEALINGS BETWEEN OFFERORS AND CONNECTED EXEMPT PRINCIPAL TRADERS

An offeror and any person acting in concert with it must not deal as principal with an exempt principal trader connected with the offeror in relevant securities of the offeree company during the offer period. It will generally be for the advisers to the offeror to ensure compliance with this Rule rather than the principal trader. (See also Rule 4.2(b).)

NOTE ON RULE 38.2

Competition reference periods

During a competition reference period the restrictions in this Rule will also apply to an offeror subject to the reference and to any person acting in concert with it.

38.3 ASSENTING SECURITIES AND DEALINGS IN ASSENTED SECURITIES

An exempt principal trader connected with the offeror must not assent offeree company securities to the offer or purchase such securities in assented form until the offer is unconditional as to acceptances.

NOTE ON RULE 38.3

Withdrawal rights under Rule 13.5

If withdrawal rights are introduced under Rule 13.5, the acceptances in relation to any securities assented to the offer after it was unconditional as to

RULE 38 CONTINUED

NOTE ON RULE 38.3 continued

acceptances by an exempt principal trader connected with the offeror must be withdrawn and such securities may not be re-assented to the offer unless, following the period agreed by the Panel for withdrawal rights to run, the offer becomes or is declared unconditional as to acceptances.

38.4 VOTING

Securities owned by an exempt principal trader connected with an offeror or the offeree company must not be voted in the context of an offer.

38.5 DISCLOSURE OF DEALINGS

Dealings in relevant securities, during the offer period, by an exempt principal trader connected with an offeror or the offeree company should be aggregated and disclosed to a RIS and the Panel not later than 12 noon on the business day following the date of the transactions, stating the following details:—

(a) if the relevant trading desk has recognised intermediary status and is dealing in a client-serving capacity:

   (i) total acquisitions and disposals; and

   (ii) the highest and lowest prices paid and received; or

(b) if the relevant trading desk does not have recognised intermediary status, or if it does but is not dealing in a client-serving capacity, the details required under Note 5(a) on Rule 8 (see Note 4 on this Rule).

In each case, it should be stated whether the connection is with an offeror or the offeree company. In the case of dealings in options or derivatives, full details should be given so that the nature of the dealings can be fully understood (see Note 5 on Rule 8).

NOTES ON RULE 38.5

1. *Dealings and relevant securities*

See the definitions of dealings and relevant securities in the Definitions Section.

RULE 38 *CONTINUED*

NOTES ON RULE 38.5 continued

2. Method of disclosure

Dealings should be disclosed to a RIS by electronic delivery. A copy must be faxed or e-mailed to the Panel. A specimen disclosure form is available on the Panel's website (www.thetakeoverpanel.org.uk) or may be obtained from the Panel. Disclosures under this Rule should follow that format.

3. Exception

Where it has been announced that an offer or possible offer is, or is likely to be, solely in cash, there is no requirement to disclose dealings in relevant securities of the offeror.

4. Recognised intermediaries dealing in a proprietary capacity

Where an exempt principal trader with recognised intermediary status deals in relevant securities other than in a client-serving capacity (or re-books a position which was acquired in a client-serving capacity so as to hold it in a proprietary capacity), it should aggregate and disclose under Rule 38.5(b) the interests, short positions and rights to subscribe which it holds in a proprietary capacity with those of the group's exempt principal traders which do not have recognised intermediary status. However, in making such disclosures, it need not aggregate and disclose details of any interests, short positions and rights to subscribe which it holds in a client-serving capacity.

APPENDIX 1

WHITEWASH GUIDANCE NOTE

(See Note 1 of Notes on Dispensations from Rule 9.)

1 INTRODUCTION

(a) This note sets out the procedures to be followed if the Panel is to be asked to waive the obligation to make a general offer under Rule 9 which would otherwise arise where, as a result of the issue of new securities as consideration for an acquisition or a cash injection or in fulfilment of obligations under an agreement to underwrite the issue of new securities, a person or group of persons acting in concert acquires an interest, or interests, in shares to an extent which would normally give rise to an obligation to make a general offer.

(b) Where the word "offeror" is used in a particular Rule, it should be taken in the context of a whitewash as a reference to the potential controllers. Similarly, the phrase "offeree company" should be taken as a reference to the company which is to issue the new securities and in which the actual or potential controlling position will arise.

(c) Rules 19 and 20, where relevant, apply equally to information given in connection with a transaction which is the subject of the whitewash procedure.

2 SPECIFIC GRANT OF WAIVER REQUIRED

In each case, specific grant of a waiver from the Rule 9 obligation is required. Such grant will be subject to:—

(a) there having been no disqualifying transactions (as set out in Section 3 below) by the person or group seeking the waiver in the previous 12 months;

(b) prior consultation with the Panel by the parties concerned or their advisers;

(c) approval in advance by the Panel of the circular to shareholders setting out the details of the proposals;

(d) approval of the proposals by an independent vote, on a poll, at a meeting of the holders of any relevant class of securities, whether or not any such meeting needs to be convened to approve the issue of the securities in question; and

(e) disenfranchisement of the person or group seeking the waiver and of any other non-independent party at any such meeting.

App 1.2

APPENDIX 1 *CONTINUED*

NOTES ON SECTION 2

1. *Early consultation*

Consultation with the Panel at an early stage is essential. Late consultation may well result in delays to planned timetables. Experience suggests that the documents sent to shareholders in connection with the whitewash procedure may have to pass through several proofs before they meet the Panel's requirements and no waiver of the Rule 9 obligation will be granted until such time as the documentation has been approved by the Panel.

2. *Other legal or regulatory requirements*

It must be noted that clearance of the circular in accordance with any other legal or regulatory requirement (for example, under the UKLA Rules) does not constitute approval of the circular by the Panel.

3 DISQUALIFYING TRANSACTIONS

Notwithstanding the fact that the issue of new securities is made conditional upon the prior approval of a majority of the shareholders independent of the transaction at a general meeting of the company:—

(a) the Panel will not normally waive an obligation under Rule 9 if the person to whom the new securities are to be issued or any person acting in concert with him has acquired any interest in shares in the company in the 12 months prior to the posting to shareholders of the circular relating to the proposals but subsequent to negotiations, discussions or the reaching of understandings or agreements with the directors of the company in relation to the proposed issue of new securities;

(b) a waiver will be invalidated if any acquisitions of interests in shares are made in the period between the posting of the circular to shareholders and the shareholders' meeting.

4 CIRCULAR TO SHAREHOLDERS

The circular must contain the following information and statements and comply appropriately with the Rules of the Code as set out below:—

(a) competent independent advice to the offeree company regarding the transaction, the controlling position which it will create and the effect which this will have on shareholders generally;

(b) full details of the maximum potential controlling position:

(i) where this is dependent upon the outcome of underwriting arrangements, it should be assumed that the potential controllers will, in addition to any other entitlement, take up their full underwriting participation; and

APPENDIX 1 *CONTINUED*

(ii) where convertible securities, options or securities with subscription rights are to be issued, the potential controller must be indicated on the assumption that only the controllers will convert or exercise the subscription rights, and will do so in full and at the earliest opportunity (the date of which must also be given);

(c) where the maximum potential shareholding resulting from the proposed transaction will exceed 50% of the voting rights of the company, specific and prominent reference to this possibility and to the fact that, subject to Section 7 below, the potential controllers may acquire further interests in shares without incurring any further obligation under Rule 9 to make a general offer;

(d) in cases where the potential controlling position will be held by more than one person, the identity of the potential controllers and their individual potential interests in shares in addition to the information required under (i) below;

(e) a statement that the Panel has agreed, subject to shareholders' approval, to waive any obligations to make a general offer which might result from the transaction;

(f) Rule 19.2 (responsibility statements, etc.);

(g) Rule 21.2 (inducement fees);

(h) Rules 23, 24.1, 24.2 and 25.2 (information to shareholders which must include full details of the assets, if any, being injected);

(i) Rules 24.3 and 25.3 (disclosure of interests and dealings). Dealings in respect of Rule 24.3 should be covered for the 12 months prior to the posting of the circular but dealings in respect of Rule 25.3 need not be disclosed as there is no offer period;

(j) Rules 24.5 and 24.8 (arrangements in connection with the proposal);

(k) Rule 25.4 (service contracts of directors and proposed directors);

(l) Rule 25.6 (material contracts, irrevocable commitments and letters of intent);

(m) Rule 26 (documents to be on display); and

(n) Rules 28 and 29 (profit forecasts and asset valuations relating to the offeree company or relating to assets being acquired by the offeree company).

App 1.4

APPENDIX 1 *CONTINUED*

5 UNDERWRITING AND PLACING

In cases involving the underwriting or placing of offeree company securities, the Panel must be given details of all the proposed underwriters or placees, including any relevant information to establish whether or not there is a group acting in concert, and the maximum percentage which they could come to hold as a result of implementation of the proposals.

6 ANNOUNCEMENTS FOLLOWING SHAREHOLDERS' APPROVAL

(a) Following the meeting at which the proposals are considered by shareholders, an announcement must be made by the offeree company giving the result of the meeting and the number and percentage of offeree company shares in which the potential controllers are, or are entitled to be, interested as a result. The announcement must be published in accordance with the requirements of Rule 2.9.

(b) Where the final controlling position is dependent on the results of underwriting, the offeree company must make an announcement following the issue of the new securities stating the number and percentage of shares in which the controllers are interested at that time.

(c) Where convertible securities, options or securities with subscription rights are to be issued:—

(i) the announcement of the potential controlling position must be made on the basis of the assumptions described in Section 4(b) above;

(ii) following each issue of new securities a further announcement must be made confirming the number and percentage of shares in which the controllers are interested at that time; and

(iii) the information in (i) and (ii) should be included in the company's annual report and accounts until all the securities in respect of which the waiver has been granted have been issued or it is confirmed that no such issue will be made.

NOTE ON SECTION 6

Copies of announcements

Copies of announcements made under this Section should be sent to the Panel.

APPENDIX 1 *CONTINUED*

7 SUBSEQUENT ACQUISITIONS BY POTENTIAL CONTROLLERS

Immediately following approval of the proposals at the shareholders' meeting, the potential controllers will be free to acquire further interests in shares of the offeree company, subject to the provisions of Rules 5 and 9.

Where shareholders approve the issue of convertible securities, or the issue of warrants or the grant of options to subscribe for new shares where no immediate voting rights are obtained, the Panel will view the approval as sanctioning maximum conversion or subscription at the earliest possible moment without the necessity for the making of an offer under Rule 9. However, if the potential controllers propose to acquire further interests in voting shares following the relevant meeting, the Panel should be consulted to establish the number of shares to which the waiver will be deemed to apply.

(See also Note 4 on Rule 9.1 and Rule 37.1.)

APPENDIX 2

FORMULA OFFERS GUIDANCE NOTE

1 INTRODUCTION

When offers are made for the share capital of investment trusts, it is common for the consideration to be calculated by reference to a formula related to the net assets of the offeree company. If offers are made on this basis, there are certain special requirements which must be followed.

2 SPECIFICATION OF THE FORMULA

Since it is common for the result of the formula to differ from net asset value as generally understood, the term "net asset value" should not be used in connection with the consideration to be paid to shareholders. The expression "formula asset value" should be used instead. Where the consideration is expressed by reference to formula asset value, the means by which this figure will be arrived at must be clearly set out in both the offer announcement and the offer document. It will usually be convenient to express this formula algebraically, identifying the significant constituent elements, in a separate appendix.

The Panel does not consider it appropriate to insist on a standard method of calculating net asset values in formula offers. There is, however, a danger of confusion in the minds of shareholders when they are asked to consider the advantages or disadvantages of an offer by reference to net asset values which are calculated by each side on a different basis. Principals and their advisers should, therefore, ensure that wherever reference is to be made to net asset value as an argument for or against an offer, the utmost clarity is used to make plain the basis of calculation. This applies to paid advertisements in the press as well as to documents addressed to shareholders directly.

3 DATE ON WHICH THE FORMULA CRYSTALLIZES

In all circumstances, the consideration payable under the formula should be determined as at the day the offer becomes or is declared unconditional as to acceptances. The formula should then cease to operate, shareholders accepting the offer after that date receiving the consideration thus determined.

4 ESTIMATE OF THE FORMULA OFFER VALUE

The offer announcement must include an estimate of the value of the offer, in pence per share, on the day of the announcement and the offer document must include a similar estimate on the latest practicable date prior to posting.

App 2.2

APPENDIX 2 CONTINUED

5 MAXIMUM AND MINIMUM PRICES

An offeror may include in a formula offer a term that if the formula offer produces a price higher than a specified price (the "maximum price") only that price will be paid and/or a term that if it produces a price lower than a specified price (the "minimum price") then that price will be paid.

6 RULE 6

Since in a formula offer the current value of the offer is only determinable by reference to the value, at any relevant time, of the assets to which the formula is related, an offeror can only be confident that acquisitions of interests in shares during an offer are in conformity with Rule 6 if it is able to calculate the price which would have been payable on the basis of the formula at the time of the acquisitions. Where such calculation is possible and the price paid exceeds the formula price so calculated, it follows that the acquisitions will have been made on the basis of an improved formula and the offeror will, therefore, be required to increase the offer by making the improved formula generally available.

Calculation of the formula price at the time of an acquisition will only be possible if there is co-operation from the board of the offeree company. It is not acceptable for the procedure set out in the previous paragraph to be applied on the basis of estimated net asset values, eg those contained in brokers' circulars. Where there is no co-operation from the board of the offeree company, therefore, the offeror will not be able to use this procedure and any acquisitions which fall to be taken into account for the purposes of Rule 6 will create an obligation to pay at least the same price to all accepting shareholders. Where there are alternative offers, however, the offeror may choose which of the alternatives should be subject to the minimum price.

7 RULES 9 AND 11

Rules 9 and 11 apply equally to formula offers; thus, if appropriate, the cash offer must contain a term guaranteeing a minimum price under the offer at the highest cash price paid in respect of the acquisitions of interests in shares to which the Rules apply.

8 "FLOOR AND CEILING" CONDITIONS

There is no objection to the incorporation of conditions in a formula offer which provide for the offer to lapse in the event that the formula asset value (calculated on the day the offer becomes or is declared unconditional as to acceptances) falls outside specified limits or if movements in certain securities markets' indices exceed specified limits.

Takeover Code

App 2.3

APPENDIX 2 *CONTINUED*

9 OFFEREE BOARD OBLIGATIONS

There is no obligation on the board of the offeree company to provide information relating to the calculation of the formula price until a successful offeror has taken control. Nevertheless, where an offer has a "floor and ceiling" condition related to the formula asset value, the board of the offeree company must announce, within 7 days of the offer becoming or being declared unconditional as to acceptances, whether the formula calculated on the day the offer became or was declared unconditional as to acceptances fell within the specified limits.

Once an offer is wholly unconditional, it is expected that both sides will co-operate in calculating the formula price payable to accepting shareholders. Where agreement is not forthcoming, however, the offeror will not be permitted to determine unilaterally the price payable. Where such circumstances could arise, the offer should provide for an interim payment to be made to accepting shareholders of not less than 85% of the offeror's best estimate of the formula price payable. When the offeror is able to calculate correctly the price payable, the difference should be paid to accepting shareholders as soon as possible; any excess paid to shareholders as a result of an over-estimate of the formula asset value will not be recoverable.

APPENDIX 3

DIRECTORS' RESPONSIBILITIES AND CONFLICTS OF INTEREST GUIDANCE NOTE

1 DIRECTORS' RESPONSIBILITIES

While a board of directors may delegate the day-to-day conduct of an offer to individual directors or a committee of directors, the board as a whole must ensure that proper arrangements are in place to enable it to monitor that conduct in order that each director may fulfil his responsibilities under the Code. These arrangements should ensure that:-

(a) the board is provided promptly with copies of all documents and announcements issued by or on behalf of their company which bear on the offer; the board receives promptly details of all dealings in relevant securities made by their company or its associates and details of any agreements, understandings, guarantees, expenditure (including fees) or other obligations entered into or incurred by or on behalf of their company in the context of the offer which do not relate to routine administrative matters;

(b) those directors with day-to-day responsibility for the offer are in a position to justify to the board all their actions and proposed courses of action; and

(c) the opinions of advisers are available to the board where appropriate.

The above procedures should be followed, and board meetings held, as and when necessary throughout the offer in order to ensure that all directors are kept up-to-date with events and with actions taken.

Any director who has a question concerning the propriety of any action as far as the Code is concerned should ensure that the Panel is consulted.

The Panel expects directors to co-operate with it in connection with its enquiries; this will include the provision, promptly on request, of copies of minutes of board meetings and other information in their possession, or in the possession of an offeror or the offeree company as appropriate, which may be relevant to the enquiry.

App 3.2

APPENDIX 3 CONTINUED

2 FINANCIAL ADVISERS AND CONFLICTS OF INTEREST

Instances where conflicts of interest may arise include those resulting from the possession of material confidential information or where the adviser is part of a multi-service financial organisation, as exemplified below.

(a) Material confidential information

A financial adviser may have the opportunity to act for an offeror or the offeree company in circumstances where the adviser is in possession of material confidential information relating to the other party, for example, because it was a previous client or because of involvement in an earlier transaction. In certain circumstances, this may necessitate the financial adviser declining to act, for example, because the information is such that a conflict of interest is likely to arise. Such a conflict may be incapable of resolution simply by isolating information within the relevant organisation or by assigning different personnel to the transaction; however, when a financial adviser has been actively advising a company which becomes an offeree company, it may be acceptable for it to continue to act.

(b) Segregation of businesses

It is incumbent upon multi-service financial organisations to familiarise themselves with the implications under the Code of conducting other businesses in addition to, for example, corporate finance or stockbroking. If one part of such an organisation is involved in an offer, for example, in giving advice to an offeror or the offeree company, a number of Rules of the Code may be relevant to other parts of that organisation, whose actions may have serious consequences under the Code. Compliance departments of such organisations have an important role in this respect and are encouraged to liaise with the Panel in cases of doubt.

The concepts of "exempt fund managers" and "exempt principal traders" in the Code are in recognition of the fact that fund management and principal trading may be conducted on a day-to-day basis quite separately within the same organisation; but it is necessary for such organisations to satisfy the Panel that this is the case. It is essential, therefore, that such organisations arrange their affairs to ensure not only total segregation of those operations but also that those operations are conducted without regard for the interests of other parts of the same organisation or of their clients. The Code contains a number of Rules which are designed to ensure that the principles on which these concepts are based are upheld.

APPENDIX 4

RECEIVING AGENTS' CODE OF PRACTICE

NB 1 This Appendix should be read in conjunction with Rules 9.3 and 10 and, in particular, Notes 4 — 8 on Rule 10.

NB 2 If an offer relates to securities some or all of which are held in uncertificated form in CREST and in respect of which CREST maintains the register, references in this Appendix to the register shall be deemed to be references to:

(a) the register of securities held in certificated form (if any); and

(b) the record of securities held in uncertificated form maintained by the offeree company's registrar.

1 INTRODUCTION

This Code of Practice has been drawn up by the Panel in consultation with the Confederation of British Industry, the British Bankers' Association and the Registrars Group of the Institute of Chartered Secretaries and Administrators. It is reproduced with the agreement and support of these bodies. In relation to the additions and amendments necessitated by the introduction of CREST, the Panel also consulted CRESTCo Limited.

It is essential when determining the result of an offer under the Code that appropriate measures are adopted such that all parties to the offer may be confident that the result of the offer is arrived at by an objective procedure which, as far as possible, eliminates areas of doubt. This Code of Practice is designed to ensure that those acceptances and purchases which may be counted towards fulfilling the acceptance condition and thus included in the certificate are properly identified to enable the receiving agent to provide the certificate required by Note 7 on Rule 10. Receiving agents are also required to establish appropriate procedures such that acceptances and purchases can be checked against each other and between different categories so that no shareholding will be counted twice.

The principles and procedures outlined in this Code of Practice are, except with the prior consent of the Panel, to be followed in all cases. It must be understood that the Panel expects co-operation between the offeree company's registrar and the offeror's receiving agent to ensure that the procedures can be undertaken in a timely manner. Co-operation is interpreted to include the provision of data in a form convenient for the receiving agent. For example, if the receiving agent so requests, following the announcement of an offer, the registrar should, if practicable, provide the register in computer readable form

App 4.2

APPENDIX 4 *CONTINUED*

(eg by magnetic tape). Whenever possible, if requested to do so, the registrar should provide, in similar form, details of changes to the register rather than a complete new register.

Receiving agents will have direct access to the Panel should they believe that there is insufficient co-operation or that they are being given instructions contrary to this Code of Practice.

2 QUALIFICATIONS FOR ACTING AS A RECEIVING AGENT

A receiving agent to an offer must either:—

(a) be a member of the Registrars' and Receiving Bankers' Committee of the British Bankers' Association; or

(b) be a member of the Registrars Group of the Institute of Chartered Secretaries and Administrators and:

- (i) (1) be responsible for the share register of a listed public company, other than itself, with not less than 20,000 shareholders; or

    (2) be responsible for the share registers of not less than 25 public companies which are admitted to the Official List or to trading on AIM; and

- (ii) (1) have performed the duties of a receiving agent on more than 25 occasions; or

    (2) have been directly involved with keeping share registers of public companies for more than 10 years; or

(c) be an organisation which has satisfied the Panel that it has the experience and resources necessary to act as receiving agent in connection with the relevant offer.

3 THE PROVISION OF THE OFFEREE COMPANY'S REGISTER

(a) When a firm intention to make an offer is announced, the offeree company should instruct its registrar to respond within two business days to a request from the offeror for the provision of the register which should be updated to reflect the position as at the close of business on the date of the request. The registrar should provide details of both participant and account IDs for holdings in CREST.

(b) The offeree company's registrar should also be instructed to keep the register as up-to-date as the register maintenance system will allow. CREST imposes certain obligations on registrars in this respect but for certificated holdings outside CREST the registrar should ensure that

APPENDIX 4 *CONTINUED*

maintenance is such that it can comply with (c) below. The updating procedures should include, in addition to the registration of transfers, the registration of all changes affecting the register (eg grants of representation, marriage certificates, changes of address etc). The receiving agent should also be informed on a daily basis by the offeree company's registrar of any adjustment to holdings in CREST not advised by the CREST operator through register update requests ("RURs").

(c) From the date following the day on which a firm intention to make an offer is announced, the CREST operator will, after the appropriate request, make available to the offeror's receiving agent copies of all RURs generated in relation to the offeree company.

As far as certificated holdings are concerned, the registrar must provide updates, on a daily basis, to the register within two business days after notification of the transfer and, in addition, copies of all documents, including CREST stock deposits, which would lead to a change in the last copy register provided to the offeror must be provided as rapidly. On the final register day* any such information received by the offeree company's registrar but not yet provided to the offeror's receiving agent must be made available for collection by the offeror's receiving agent, at the latest, by noon on the day preceding the final closing date† of the offer.

From the final register day* until the time that the offer becomes or is declared unconditional as to acceptances or lapses, the offeree company's registrar should continue to update the register on a daily basis so that all transfers and other documents which have been received by the offeree company's registrar by 1.00 pm on the final closing date† of the offer are processed by 5.00 pm that day at the latest. In addition, copies of these documents should be relayed immediately to the offeror's receiving agent insofar as not previously notified.

(d) Arrangements should be made to ensure that the offeror's receiving agent has access to the offeree company's registrar at all times, which includes weekends and Bank Holidays, during the period between the final register day* and the time the offer becomes or is declared unconditional as to acceptances or lapses, in order that any queries arising from acceptances and purchases can be investigated and accurate decisions taken.

*† *See definitions at end of Appendix*

APPENDIX 4 *CONTINUED*

4 COUNTING OF ACCEPTANCES

The offeror's receiving agent must ensure that all acceptances counted as valid meet the requirements set out in Note 4 on Rule 10 and, if appropriate, Note 6 on Rule 10.

5 COUNTING OF PURCHASES

The offeror's receiving agent must ensure that all purchases counted as valid meet the requirements (subject to Note 8 on Rule 10) set out in Note 5 on Rule 10 and, if appropriate, Note 6 on Rule 10.

6 OFFERS BECOMING OR BEING DECLARED UNCONDITIONAL AS TO ACCEPTANCES BEFORE THE FINAL CLOSING DATE†

Prior to an offer becoming or being declared unconditional as to acceptances before the final closing date†, the offeror's receiving agent must ensure that the requirements of Note 6 on Rule 10 have been satisfied.

7 DISCLAIMERS IN RECEIVING AGENTS' CERTIFICATES

Certificates issued by the offeror's receiving agent should be unqualified, save for a disclaimer (if necessary) as to limitations on the responsibility of the receiving agent for the errors of third parties which are not evident from the documents available to the receiving agent. A disclaimer in the following form would normally be acceptable; any variation should be specifically agreed by the Panel in advance:-

"In issuing this certificate we have, where necessary, relied on the following matters:

(i) certifications of acceptance forms by the offeree company's registrar;

(ii) certifications by the offeree company's registrar that a transfer of shares has been executed by or on behalf of the registered holder in favour of the offeror company or its nominees;

(iii) confirmation from the offeror of the validity of shares recorded as registered holdings and purchases in the context of Note 8 on Rule 10.

As the offeror company's receiving agent, we have examined with due care and attention the information provided to us, and, as appropriate, made due and careful enquiry of relevant persons, in order that we may

† *See definitions at end of Appendix*

APPENDIX 4 *CONTINUED*

issue this certificate and have no reason to believe that the information contained in it cannot be relied upon but, subject thereto, we accept no responsibility or liability whatsoever in respect of any error of the offeree company's registrar or the offeror company's buying broker for the matters set out above to the extent that we have relied upon them in issuing this certificate."

DEFINITIONS

*final register day — the day two days prior to the final closing date† of an offer.

†final closing date — the 60th day or other date beyond which the offeror has stated that its offer will not be extended.

APPENDIX 5

TENDER OFFERS

1 PANEL'S CONSENT REQUIRED

The Panel's consent is required for any tender offer. The Panel's consent will normally be granted where:

(a) the tender offer could not result in the offeror and persons acting in concert with it being interested in shares carrying 30% or more of the voting rights of the company on the closing date of the tender; or

(b) the tender offer is by a person holding shares carrying more than 50% of the voting rights of a company, is for less than all the shares carrying voting rights held by the minority and the Panel believes the circumstances justify the use of a tender offer.

Where a tender offer to which this Appendix applies is made on the Stock Exchange or on OFEX, this Appendix takes precedence over any requirements of the Stock Exchange and OFEX for the conduct of tender offers. However, the resulting transactions will be subject to the relevant trade and transaction reporting rules and requests for delivery and settlement.

This Appendix does not apply where a tender offer is made solely for the purpose of a company buying in its own shares.

NOTES ON SECTION 1

1. Calculation of percentage of shares in which a person is interested

The percentage of shares in which a person is interested should be calculated by reference to the issued share capital at the time of the announcement of the tender offer after taking into account the latest published information; if, however, it is known at the time of the announcement that by the closing date of the tender offer the issued share capital will have changed, this must also be taken into account.

2. Tender offers in competition with other types of offer under the Code

Where a tender offer is proposed for shares in a company subject to another type of offer under the Code, the following matters will have to be considered:

(a) extension of the offer period in respect of the other offer;

(b) circulation of the tender advertisement to all shareholders; and

(c) disclosure of dealings by the offeror making the tender offer and any associates in the manner set out in Rule 8.

App 5.2

APPENDIX 5 *CONTINUED*

2 PROCEDURE AND CLEARANCE

(a) A person publishing a tender offer for the shares of a company which are admitted to listing on the Official List or to trading on AIM or on OFEX must do so by paid advertisement in two national newspapers and must notify the company concerned of the information specified in Section 3 at least 7 days before the day on which the tender offer closes. The offeror may also circulate copies of the advertisement to shareholders of the company, subject to compliance with the FSMA.

(b) In all other cases, the tender offer must be made by means of a circular to shareholders (containing the same information as for a tender offer advertisement as specified in Section 3) and must be open for acceptance for at least 21 days. A copy of the circular must be provided to the company concerned at the same time as it is posted to shareholders.

(c) Subject to (d) below, the offeror must treat all shareholders on equal terms.

(d) A tender offer must be for cash only but may be at a fixed price or a maximum price; top-up arrangements are not permitted.

(i) Fixed price: if the tenders exceed the number of shares sought, they will be scaled down pro rata.

(ii) Maximum price: if the tender offer is over-subscribed, the striking price will be the lowest price at which the number of shares sought is met and all who tender at or below the striking price will receive that price. If necessary, tenders made at the striking price will be scaled down pro rata or balloted.

If the tender offer is under-subscribed, all who tender will receive the maximum or fixed price, except where fewer shares are tendered than the percentage below which the tender is void.

(e) The text of the advertisement or circular must be cleared by the Panel.

(f) In every case the UKLA, the Stock Exchange or OFEX, as appropriate, and the Panel must be supplied with copies of the final text of the advertisements or circulars at the same time as they are given to the newspapers or are posted to shareholders, as the case may be.

3 DETAILS OF TENDER OFFER ADVERTISEMENTS

(a) The advertisement of a tender offer or circular (as the case may be), which must constitute a firm offer, must include the particulars set out below:—

APPENDIX 5 *CONTINUED*

    (i)   the name of the offeror;

    (ii)   the name of the broker or other agent acting for the offeror;

    (iii) the name of the company whose shares are sought;

    (iv) the maximum number of shares or proportion of voting capital offered for;

    (v)   a statement that, if tenders totalling less than 1% of the voting rights of the company are received, the tender offer will be void. Alternatively, the offeror may indicate a higher percentage below which the tender offer will be void but any figure higher than 5% is not permitted unless approved by the Panel in advance of the announcement of the tender offer;

    (vi) a statement that, subject to (v), a shareholder's tender will be irrevocable;

    (vii) the fixed or maximum price offered;

    (viii) the number and percentage of shares in which the offeror and persons acting in concert with it are interested, specifying the nature of the interests concerned (see Note 5(a) on Rule 8);

    (ix) the closing day and time for the tender; and

    (x)   the arrangements for delivery and settlement (on a basis approved in advance by the Panel).

(b) A tender offer may not be subject to any condition other than (a)(v) above.

(c) If the offeror wishes to make a statement about its future intentions, it must be contained in the advertisement of the tender offer or circular, as the case may be, and should be explicit and unambiguous. The Panel should be consulted in advance with regard to any such statement.

(d) If the offeror wishes, a statement may be made comparing the value of the tender offer with the market value of the shares being offered for.

(e) The advertisement or circular must be restricted to the items above together with any information required under the FSMA, secondary legislation made under that Act or any rule made by the FSA.

App 5.4

APPENDIX 5 CONTINUED

NOTES ON SECTION 3

1. Future offers

If the offeror or a person acting in concert with it makes a statement which implies that the offeror does not intend to make an offer for the company, Rule 2.8 will apply.

2. Limit on contents of tender advertisements and circulars

The limit on the amount of information permissible in tender advertisements and circulars is strictly enforced; no form of argument or persuasion is allowed. Consequently the offeror (or any person acting in concert with it) may not make any statement or otherwise make public any information in connection with the tender offer which is not already contained in the tender offer advertisement or circular itself.

4 CIRCULARS FROM THE BOARD OF THE OFFEREE COMPANY

A copy of any document sent by the board of the offeree company to its shareholders in connection with the tender offer must be lodged with the Panel at the same time as it is posted.

5 ANNOUNCEMENT OF THE RESULT OF A TENDER OFFER

The result of a tender offer must be announced by 8.00 am on the business day following the close of the tender. The announcement must be published in accordance with the requirements of Rule 2.9.

6 PROHIBITION OF FURTHER TRANSACTIONS DURING A TENDER OFFER

The offeror and any person acting in concert with it may not otherwise acquire or dispose of any interest in shares carrying voting rights in the company between the time of the publication of the tender offer and the time when the result of the tender offer is announced.

APPENDIX 6

BID DOCUMENTATION RULES FOR THE PURPOSES OF REGULATION 10 OF THE TAKEOVERS DIRECTIVE (INTERIM IMPLEMENTATION) REGULATIONS 2006

For the purposes of Regulation 10 of the Takeovers Directive (Interim Implementation) Regulations 2006, "offer document rules" and "response document rules" are those giving effect, respectively, to Article 6(3) and the first sentence of Article 9(5) of the Directive (see section 10(e) of the Introduction). The relevant parts of Rules 24 and 25 are set out below. Rule 27 is also relevant to the extent set out in section 10(e) of the Introduction.

"Offer document rules"

Article	Those parts of the Rule set out below which give effect to the Article
Article 6(3)(a)	Rule 24.2(d)(v)
Article 6(3)(b)	Rule 24.2(d)(ii)
Article 6(3)(c)	Rule 24.2(d)(iv)
Article 6(3)(d)	Rule 24.2(d)(v) and Note 5 on Rule 24.2
Article 6(3)(e)	Rule 24.2(d)(xv)
Article 6(3)(f)	Rule 24.2(d)(iv)
Article 6(3)(g)	Rule 24.3(a)(i), (ii)
Article 6(3)(h)	Rule 24.2(d)(vi)
Article 6(3)(i)	Rule 24.1
Article 6(3)(j)	Rule 24.6 (first phrase)
Article 6(3)(k)	Rule 24.2(d)(xi)
Article 6(3)(l)	Rule 24.2(f)
Article 6(3)(m)	Rule 24.2(d)(iii) and Note 4 on Rule 24.2
Article 6(3)(n)	Rule 24.2(d)(xiv)

"Response document rules"

Article	
Article 9(5), first sentence	Rule 25.1(a) and (b)

Doc 1

DOCUMENT CHARGES

Charges are payable on offer documents as set out in this Section.

The document charges are subject to periodic review; until further notice they are payable on all offers valued at £1 million or more. The amount of the charge will depend upon the value of the offer according to the scale set out below.

1 SCALE OF DOCUMENT CHARGES

Value of the offer £ million	Charge £	Charge as a maximum % of the value of the offer %
1 to 5	2,000	0.20
Over 5 to 10	8,500	0.17
Over 10 to 25	14,000	0.14
Over 25 to 50	27,500	0.11
Over 50 to 100	50,000	0.10
Over 100 to 250	75,000	0.08
Over 250 to 500	100,000	0.04
Over 500 to 1,000	125,000	0.03
Over 1,000	175,000	0.02

2 VALUATION OF OFFER FOR DOCUMENT CHARGES

When the charge falls to be calculated on the basis of the value of securities to be issued as consideration, it should be computed by reference to the middle market quotation of the relevant securities at the last practicable date before the publication of the offer document as stated in that document and/or, as the case may be, by reference to the estimate of the value of any unlisted securities consideration given in the document in accordance with Rule 24.10.

When there are alternative offers, the alternative with the highest value will be used to calculate the value of the offer. Offers for all classes of equity share capital and other transferable securities carrying voting rights will be included in the calculation of the value of the offer, but offers for non-voting, non-equity share capital, convertibles, options etc will not.

3 "WHITEWASH" DOCUMENTS

A document charge is payable on all whitewash documents when, if a mandatory offer would be necessary but for the whitewash, its value would be £1 million or more. The Panel should be consulted in cases of whitewashes involving underwriting commitments or the issue of convertible securities.

Doc 2

DOCUMENT CHARGES *CONTINUED*

The scale of charges is set out below:

Value of the offer £ million	Charge £
1 to 5	2,500
Over 5 to 10	5,000
Over 10	10,000

4 MERGERS

When a merger is effected by offers for both companies by a new company created to make the offers, the document charge will be determined by the value of the lower of the two offers.

5 TENDER OFFERS

The document charge does not apply to tender offers under Appendix 5.

6 PAYMENT OF DOCUMENT CHARGES

The financial adviser to the offeror (or, if there is no financial adviser, the offeror) is responsible for the payment of the document charge to the Panel except in the case of a whitewash document when the financial adviser to the offeree company is responsible. Payments should be sent to the Panel when documents are posted.

In all cases, a note setting out the calculation of whether a document charge is payable or not and, if payable, showing the calculations relating to each form of the offer should accompany the offer document (and payment where applicable) sent to the Panel. If the offer is revised, a similar note should be sent to the Panel with the revised offer document and any necessary further payment.

7 VAT AND OTHER TAX

The Customs and Excise authorities have confirmed that, under the arrangements which currently apply, the activities of the Panel are outside the scope of Value Added Tax. Document charges are therefore not liable to VAT and these payments will be treated as disbursements for VAT purposes.

The Panel is advised that the tax treatment of the document charge should follow that of the costs of the offer.

Index

All indexing is to paragraph number

Abbey National
  Banco Santander offer for 7.2.3.1
  Cater Allen, offer for 2.8.3
  Lloyd's TSB hostile offer for 2.7.2, 8.1.5
acceptance condition
  mandatory offers 4.2.1.3
    non-acceptance by 50 per cent 4.2.3.5
  subsequent documentation 6.9.2
  voluntary offers 4.3.2
acceptance period
  Takeover Directive 10.2.7
acceptances
  announcements, levels 5.2.2.1
  general statements regarding 5.2.2.3
  and mandatory offers, non-acceptance by 50 per cent 4.2.3.5
  offer declared unconditional as to 5.2.2.2
  scaling down of, partial offers 5.3
  withdrawals 5.2.2.2
    general statements regarding 5.2.2.3
  see also **acceptance condition; acceptance period; Rule 10 (acceptance condition); Rule 17 (acceptance levels, announcements)**
acquisitions, share dealings
  consideration 3.4.4.5
  part only of interest 4.2.2.3
  partial offers 5.3
  timing restrictions 3.4.4.3
acting in concert
  affiliated persons 3.3.3, 4.2.2
  break-up of concert parties 4.2.2.2
  definitions 3.3.3

  and connected advisers 3.6.1
  persons acting in concert 1.4.4, 4.2.2, 10.2.2
  employee benefit trusts 4.2.2.4
  mandatory offers 3.4.4.4
  persons coming together for purpose of 4.2.2.1
  shares, acquisition of part only 4.2.2.3
  see also **concert parties; share dealings**
administrative provisions (all offers)
  acceptance levels, announcements 5.2.2.1
  failure to announce 5.2.2.2
  general statements regarding acceptances and withdrawals 5.2.2.3
  proxies 5.2.2.4
advertisements
  documentation 6.9.3
  release of information 7.2.3.1
affiliated persons
  and acting in concert 3.3.3, 4.2.2
Agip Investment
  Lasmo, cash offer for 5.2.1.2
AIM (Alternative Investment Market)
  see **Alternative Investment Market (AIM)**
Alexanders Holdings
  Orb Estates, potential offer by 2.8.3, 3.4.4.4
Alliance Unichem
  merger with Boots 7.3.2
Alternative Investment Market (AIM)
  cash offers, offer document contents 6.3.3.1
  equivalent treatment 5.2.1.1
  market abuse regime 9.4

573

securities exchange offers 6.3.3.2
alternative offers 7.6
Alvis
  BAE Systems, offer by 3.3.1
AMEC
  Kvaerner, bid by 8.1.2
  profits (1996), speculation on 7.2.5
American Express
  Sharepeople Group, bid for 5.2.1.1
Amersham
  General Electric's offer for 2.7.2, 7.3.2
Amor Holdings
  Partridge Fine Arts, partial offer for 5.3
announcements
  approach 2.4
    identity of offeror, importance 2.3.2
    offeree, notifying 2.3.1
  bid *see* **bid announcements**
  circulation 2.7.4
  Class 2 transactions, Listing Rules requirement 6.11
  consequences 2.7.5
  distribution and availability 7.2.4
  failure to make
    administrative provisions 5.2.2.2
    pre-bid announcements 2.6.1
  offer *see* **offer announcements**
  pre-bid *see* **pre-bid announcements**
  press
    offeree, notifying 2.3.1
    variety of 2.1
  refresher 2.6.2
  regulatory information service, in accordance with 6.6
  voluntary 2.6.3
Annual Reports, Panel of Takeovers and Mergers *see* **Takeover Panel Annual Reports**
Appeal Board
  function 1.9
applicable companies (City Code) *see* **City Code on Takeovers and Mergers**: companies and transactions applicable to (Introduction, Section 3)

approach
  identify of offeror, importance 2.3.2
  offeree, notifying 2.3.1
  secrecy *see* **secrecy**
Aran Energy
  Arco, bid by 7.2.1
Argos
  Great Universal Stores, takeover by 2.8.3, 6.9.2, 7.2.2
arrangement
  concept of, concert parties 3.5.1.1.4
Articles of Association
  "drag along" rights 2.2.4
  share ownership restrictions 4.3.3
Asda Property Holdings
  BL Davidson, offer by 5.2.1.3.4
Ask Central
  bids for 2.6.4, 6.2.6
asset valuations
  basis of 8.2.2
  "calculation of worth" 8.2.2
  documentation 6.8.1
  exceptions 8.2.3
  and offers 8.2.1
  see also **profit forecasts**
assets, disposal of
  special deals with favourable conditions 5.2.1.3.2
associates
  and conduct during offer 7.2.9
  fund managers, exempt 3.6.3.2
  share dealings 3.3.4
    Code restrictions 3.4.4.1
    Companies Act restrictions 3.4.3
Austria
  minority shareholders in 10.3.6

BAe Systems
  Alvis, offer for 3.3.1
Banco Santander
  Abbey, offer for 7.2.3.1
Bank of Scotland (BOS)
  Nat West, bid for 2.6.4, 6.2.6, 7.3.1.8
banks
  central, Directive not applicable to 10.2.1
  Swiss, and secrecy laws 3.5.1.1.5

Index

BAT
  Hoylake offer 4.3.3.2
BC Capital Partners
  Mitchell's & Butler plc, proposed offer for 3.5.2.1
BCM Ireland Holdings Ltd
  eircom Employee Share Ownership Trust, offer for 5.2.1.3.5
BET
  Rentokil's unilateral offer for 2.6.1
bid announcements
  circulation of 2.7.4
  firm intention to make offer 2.7.1
  pre-conditional offer announcements 2.7.2
  required contents 2.7.1
  side agreements 2.7.3
bid procedure
  definition problems 10.2.4
  and shared jurisdiction 2.2.3
bids
  competitive processes, share dealing restrictions 3.4.4.8
  conduct of, and Directive 10.2.13
  disclosure of, and Directive 10.2.8
  in EU, no level playing field 10.3.2
  information on, and Directive 10.2.6
  insincere 4.2.4.7
  shareholders deciding on merits of 1.6.3
Big Bang
  and exempt principal trader status 1.5.1
BIL International Ltd
  Thistle Hotels, hostile bid for 7.2.2, 7.3.1.6
Birmid Qualcast
  Blue Circle, bid by 4.3.2, 5.2.2.1
BL Davidson
  Asda Property Holdings, offer for 5.2.1.3.4
Blue Circle
  Birmid Qualcast, bid for 4.3.2, 5.2.2.1
  Lafarge's hostile offer for 2.7.2, 5.4, 7.6, 7.7.1, 8.2.2

board committees
  appointment and verification 6.2.5
Boddington
  Devenish defence against 8.1.8
Bonnier, Robert
  fining of 3.4.2.3
Boots
  Alliance Unichem merger 7.3.2
  Unichem, pre-conditional offer for 2.7.2
  Ward White, offer for 4.3.2
Boustead
  Jack Chia-MPH, offer by 5.3
BPB
  Saint-Gobain, unsuccessful defence to hostile bid by 7.2.8.2, 7.3.1.5
Brascan Corporation
  Canary Wharf Group plc, approach to 2.6.4, 3.4.4.7
break fees *see* **inducement fees**
breakthrough rights
  and Directive 10.2.11
Britannia Living
  Range Cooker Company, offer for 5.2.1.3.5
Budgens
  Wm Low, lapsed bid by 2.4
buy-back programmes
  redemption or purchase of own securities 5.4
buying freedom
  and partial offers 5.3

Caird
  Severn Trent, bid by 4.3.4
CALA plc
  bids for 7.5
CalEnergy
  Northern Electric, takeover of 3.4.4.1, 7.2.9, 7.3.1.8
Cambridge Antibody Technology plc
  Oxford Glycosciences, bid for 7.3.1.5
Canary Wharf Group plc
  and General Principle 1 5.2.1.3.5
  offers for 7.3.1.12
    by Brascan Corporation 2.6.4, 3.4.4.7

by MSREF 2.6.4
by Songbird Acquisition Ltd 3.3.3
and Rule 16 5.2.1.3.5
Capital Management and Investment plc
Six Continents plc, hostile offer for 3.4.4.2, 3.4.4.5, 4.3.3.1
Carlton
proposed merger with Granada 2.7.2
Carnival Corporation
P&O Princess Cruises, offer for
hostile 2.7.2
partial 5.3
timetable extensions 7.3.2
cash offers
financial information 6.3.3.1
mandatory *see* **Rule 11**
Cater Allen
Abbey National, offer by 2.8.3
Celltech Group plc
Oxford Glycosciences, bid for 7.3.1.5
CFDs (contracts for differences)
and interests in securities 3.3.1
chain principle
mandatory offers (Rule 9) 4.2.4.2
Chia-MPH, Jack
Boustead, offer for 5.3
Chinese walls
share dealing restrictions 3.4.1.4
Citigate
confidential information, leak of 7.2
City Code amendments
bringing into force 6.1
derivatives and options, dealings in
control issues 1.4.2
disclosure issues 1.4.1
Directive, implementation 1.4.4, 2.1, 2.2, 3.1.1, 3.4.4.4, 7.1
mandatory offers 3.4.4.4
earnings enhancement statements 8.1.5
jurisdiction changes 1.4.4
merger benefits statements 8.1.5
miscellaneous 1.4.5
and Rule changes 1.4
SARs, abolition 1.4.3

share dealings, Takeover Directive 3.1, 3.1.1
City Code on Takeovers and Mergers
advisers 7.2
amendments to *see* **City Code amendments**
asset valuations 8.2.1
breach of
case law 1.10
release of information 7.2
sanctions/remedies 1.12.2
Committee *see* **Code Committee**
companies and transactions
applicable to (Introduction, Section 3)
dual jurisdiction 2.2.6
dual listed companies 2.2.5
public and certain private companies 2.2.2
range of transactions 2.2.4
share dealings 3.2.1
shared jurisdiction arrangements 2.2.3
UK, Channel Islands and Isle of Man registered and traded companies 2.2.1, 3.2.1
control, regulation of changes 3.2.1
enforcement *see* **enforcement of Code**
flexibility 1.3
General Principles and Rules 1.1, 6.2.1
Introduction, Section 3 *see* **City Code on Takeovers and Mergers**, companies and transactions applicable to (Introduction, Section 3)
market abuse regime
operating together 9.6.2
overlap with 9.6.1
see also **market abuse regime**
profit forecasts 8.1.3
Section D (pred-bid period) 2.1
Section H (all offers) 5.2
Section P (redemption or purchase of own securities) 5.4
share dealings, applicability of rules and regulations to 3.2.1

Index

special deals with favourable conditions (Rule 16) *see* **Rule 16: special deals, favourable conditions**
spirit of 6.2.1
status 1.3
structure 1.1
transactions, range of 2.2.4
CJA 1993 *see* **Criminal Justice Act 1993**
Class 1 transactions
  approval of takeover in general meeting 6.11
  and voluntary offers 4.3.3.1
Class 2 transactions
  announcement requirements 6.11
Clayform Properties
  Stead and Simpson, offer for 5.2.1.1
clearances, regulatory
  Competition Commission (CC) 3.4.4.6
  mandatory bids 4.2.1.4
  voluntary bids 4.3.3.2
CLRB (Company Law Reform Bill)
  and Directive 3.1.1, 6.1
CMI *see* **Capital Management and Investment plc**
Code Committee
  City Code amendments 1.4
    derivatives and options dealings 1.4.2
  composition 1.7.2
  functions 1.7.2
  mandatory offers, Rules 3.4.4.6
  Notes on Dispensations From Rule 9, amendment 3.4.4.4
  Public Consultation Papers *see* **PCPs (public consultation papers)**
  and recognised intermediary status 1.5.2, 3.6.2
  on SARs, abolition 1.4.3
Code of Market Conduct
  market abuse regime 9.2, 9.4
  defences 3.4.2.4
Code on Takeovers and Mergers *see* **City Code on Takeovers and Mergers**
COMC *see* **Code of Market Conduct**

Companies (Acquisition of Own Shares) (Treasury Shares) Regulations 2003 5.4
Companies Act
  compulsory purchase provisions, and voluntary offers 4.3.2
  concert parties 3.5.1.1.4
  contravention, consequences 3.5.1.1.6
  convertibles, offers for (Part 13A) 5.2.1.2
  documentation (Section 314) 6.13.1
  equivalent treatment
    comparable offers, different equity classes 5.2.1.1
    convertibles etc, appropriate offers 5.2.1.2
  "interest" for purposes of 3.5.1.1.3
  offer document contents, securities exchange offers 6.3.3.2
  offer timetable, trigger date, compulsory acquisition of minority 7.3.1.11
  Part XIIIA, Sections 428 to 430F 6.13.2
  schemes of arrangement under 4.3.2
  Section 212 notices, share dealing disclosure 3.5.1.1.6, 3.5.1.1.5
  Section 314, documentation 6.13.1
  share dealings
    applicability of rules and regulations 3.2.3
    disclosure *see* **share dealing disclosure**: Companies Act (Part VI)
  misleading statements and practices 3.4.2.1
  redemption or purchase of own securities 5.4
  restrictions 3.4.3
  transactions 2.2.4
  voluntary offers, compulsory purchase provisions 4.3.2
company law
  definition problems 10.2.4
Company Law Reform Bill
  and Companies Act 6.13.1
  Part XIIIA (ss. 428–430F) 6.13.2
  and Directive 3.1.1, 6.1, 7.1

577

and documentation, non-compliant 6.5
Company Law Review
Final Report (2001) 6.13.2
compensation rulings
enforcement of Code 1.11.2
Competition Commission (CC)
anti-trust clearance 3.4.4.6
reference to 4.4
Wm Morrison bid for Safeway 7.7.3
competition law issues
European Commission 3.4.4.6, 4.4
offer timetable 7.3.1.5
competition references
mandatory bids 4.2.1.2
competitive bid processes
Code prohibitions/restrictions 3.4.4.8
compliance rulings
enforcement of Code 1.11.1
concert parties
and affiliated persons 3.3.3
break-up of 4.2.2.2
concepts 3.3.3
disclosure of dealings (Companies Act) 3.5.1.1.4
and employee benefit trusts (EBTs) 3.3.3, 4.2.2.4
see also **acting in concert**
Conduct of Business Rules
financial promotions 6.12.1
conduct during offer
delegation 6.2.5
and Directive 10.2.13
documentation/announcements, distribution and availability 7.2.4
equality of information
to competing offerors 7.2.7
to shareholders 7.2.5
frustrating action, restrictions on *see* **frustrating action**
information
advertisements 7.2.3.1
interviews and debates 7.2.3.3
responsibility for 7.2.2
telephone campaigns 7.2.3.2
meetings 7.2.6

Rule 19.1 7.2.1
timetable *see* **offer timetable**
confidentiality
and Takeover Panel 1.13
conflicts of interest
independent advice 2.8.3
connected adviser
defined 3.6.1
consideration
minimum level, City Code 3.4.4.5
particular form required, voluntary offers 4.3.1
Rules of Code 1.6.5
Consolidated Goldfields
Minorco, bid by 4.3.2
Contact Committee appointment
Takeover Directive 10.2.18
contracts for differences *see* **CFDs (contracts for differences)**
control
and shares *see* **share dealings**: control
convertible securities
appropriate offers for, equivalent treatment 5.2.1.2
documentation 6.10
mandatory offers (Rule 9) 4.2.4.5
Copthorn
Countryside Properties, offer for 5.2.1.3.5
Corporate Synergy
Alexanders Holdings offer 2.8.3
Council of European Union
Takeover Directive, adoption (2004) 1.2
Countryside Properties
Copthorn offer for 5.2.1.3.5
creeper provisions
redemption or purchase of own shares 4.2.3.7, 5.4
CREST
acceptance levels, announcements 5.2.2.1
proof of share ownership provision, voluntary offers 4.3.2
Criminal Justice Act 1993
contravention 3.4.1.3
and FSMA 3.4.1.2

Index

share dealings
  prohibitions/restrictions
    3.4.1.1–3.4.1.6
  rules and regulations 3.2.4
CVC/TPG
  Debenhams, bid for 7.2.8.3, 7.3.1.12

Daily Office List
  London Stock Exchange plc 5.2.1.1
Datafin case
  McCorquodale, rival bids 1.10
Davies, Sir Howard 9.6.2
dawn raids
  and SARs, abolition 3.2.2
de minimis **requirement**
  inducement fees 6.8.3, 7.2.8.3
De Vere
  GPG Group, partial offer by 5.3
"dealings"
  definition 1.4.1
  disclosure obligations 3.5.2.2
debates
  and release of information 7.2.3.3
Debenhams
  bids for 7.2.8.3, 7.3.1.12
defence document
  offeree circular contents (Rule 25) 6.4
defences
  Bilton 8.2.2
  market abuse regime 3.4.2.4
    market information 3.4.1.4, 3.4.1.6
Delancey Estates
  offer for 5.3.1.3.4
demarcation of responsibility requirements
  pre-bid announcements 2.6.1
Department of Trade and Industry
  and documents from offeror, non-compliance 6.5
derivative and option contracts, dealings
  Code, amendments and Rule changes
    control issues 1.4.2
    disclosure issues 1.4.1
  consideration, minimum level 3.4.4.5
  control issues 1.4.2
  disclosure issues 1.4.1
  interests in securities 3.3.1
Devenish
  Boddington, defence against 8.1.8
Directive on Insider Dealing and Market Manipulation (market abuse regime) *see* **market abuse regime**
Directive on Takeovers *see* **Takeover Directive**
directors
  responsibility statements (Rule 19.2) 6.2.4, 7.2.2
disciplinary powers
  action 1.12.1
  sanctions/remedies for breach of Code 1.12.2
disclosure of bid
  pre-bid announcements, FSA Rules 2.6.1
  Takeover Directive 10.2.10
disclosure of information
  derivatives 1.4.1
  fair markets, preservation of 1.6.4
  and recognised intermediary status 1.5.2
disclosure of share dealings *see* **share dealing disclosure**
Distillers Company
  Guinness, bid by 3.2.3, 3.4.2.1, 4.3.1
documentation
  advertisements 6.9.3
  announcements, circulation 6.9.1
  asset valuations 6.8.1
  board committees, appointment and verification 6.2.5
  City Code, spirit of 6.2.1
  contents *see* **offer documents, contents**
  convertible securities and options, offers to holders of 6.10
  defence documents 6.4
  distribution and availability 7.2.4
  general obligations
    board committees 6.2.5
    directors' responsibility statements 6.2.4, 7.2.2

579

general responsibilities 6.2.2
holding statements 6.2.6
other parties, release of documents to 6.2.7
specific standards of care 6.2.3
spirit of Code 6.2.1
holding statements 6.2.6
hostile bids 6.2.4, 6.4
inducement fees 6.8.3
Listing Rules 6.11
merger benefits statements 6.8.2, 7.2.1
non-compliant, criminal liability 6.5
offeree circular contents 6.4
other parties, release to 6.2.7
profit forecasts *see* **profit forecasts**
publication 6.6
quotations 6.2.3
responsibility statements 6.2.4, 7.2.2
standards of care
   general 6.2.2
   specific 6.2.3
subsequent 6.9.2
Takeover Directive 6.1
Dotterel Limited
CALA plc, bid for 7.5
Dowty
TI, offer by 5.2.1.2
"drag along" rights
transactions 2.2.4
Dresdner Kleinwort Benson
Abbey National/Cater Allen offer 2.8.3
dual holding company transactions
dual jurisdiction
application of Code 2.2.6
dual listed companies
application of Code 2.2.5
due diligence
pre-announcement exercise 2.4
Dundonald Holdings
Grantchester Holdings, offer for 5.2.1.3.4

earnings enhancement statements 8.1.5
EBTs (employee benefit trusts)
and concert parties 3.3.3, 4.2.2.4

ECHR (European Convention on Human Rights)
and market abuse regime 9.2
eircom **Employee Share Ownership Trust**
BCM Ireland Holdings Ltd, offer by 5.2.1.3.5
Elys (Wimbledon)
Panther Securities, two-tier offer by 5.3
employee benefit trusts (EBTs)
and concert parties 3.3.3, 4.2.2.4
employee consultation
secrecy obligations 2.5.4
employees
consultation with representatives, and Directive 10.2.14
Energy Group
Texas Utilities/Pacificorp, bid by 7.3.1.12
enforcement of Code
compensation rulings 1.11.2
compliance rulings 1.11.1
courts, by 1.11.3
information requirements 1.11.4
Enforcement Manual (FSA)
market abuse 9.3, 9.5, 9.6.2
Enterprise Act 2002
competition law issues 4.4
Enterprise Oil
LASMO, bid for 7.2.1
E.ON
Powergen, bid for 2.7.2, 7.3.2
equality of information
to competing offerors 7.2.7
to shareholders 7.2.5
equality of treatment
and protection of non-controlling shareholders 1.6.1
equitable price
mandatory bids 10.2.5
equivalent treatment
comparable offers, different equity classes (Rule 14) 5.2.1.1
convertibles, appropriate offers for (Rule 15) 5.2.1.2

Index

special deals with favourable conditions (Rule 16) *see* **Rule 16 (special deals with favourable conditions)**
EU (European Union) *see* **European Union (EU)**
European Commission
   competition law issues 3.4.4.6, 4.4
   offer timetable 7.3.1.5
European Communities Act 1972
   and Takeover Directive 1.2
European Convention on Human Rights
   and market abuse regime 9.2
European Directive on Takeover Bids *see* **Takeover Directive**
European Directive on Takeovers
   Interim Regulations *see* **Takeover Regulations 2006**
European Economic Area
   and shared jurisdiction 2.2.3
European Parliament
   European Directive
      adoption of 1.2
      approval of text 10.1
European Union (EU)
   bids in, no level playing field for 10.3.2
   Council of, adoption of Directive (2004) 1.2
   Directive, impact on takeover rules
      Article 11, impact 10.3.3
      increased protectionism across EU 10.3.2
      no level playing field for bids 10.3.2
      no uniform set of rules 10.3.1
      shared supervisory jurisdiction, complicated nature 10.3.4
      takeover regulation, EU companies subject to 10.3.5
   market abuse regime 9.4
   protectionism, increased 10.3.2
   takeover regulation, companies subject to 10.3.5
Executive
   Assistant Secretaries 1.8
   disciplinary action by 1.12.1
   function 1.8
   and information, responsibility for 7.2.2
   market surveillance team 1.8
   Practice Statements *see* **Practice Statements**
   pre-bid announcements 2.6.1
   rulings 1.8
   staff 1.8
exempt market making status
   and exempt principal trader status 1.5.1
exempt principal trader status
   background 1.5.1
   share dealings 3.6.1
expiry dates
   acceptance levels, announcements 5.2.2.1

fair markets, preservation
   key Rules 1.6.4
false or misleading impression
   FSMA (s.397) 3.4.2.1
Federal Mogul
   T&N plc, bid for 7.3.2
Ferrovial/BAA offer
   and statements of interest by potential competing bidder 2.6.4
50 per cent threshold
   acceptance condition
      mandatory bids 4.2.1.3
      partial offers 5.3
      voluntary offers 4.3.2
   non-acceptance by, mandatory bids 4.2.3.5
   rationale for 4.3.2
financial advisers
   and City Code 7.2
   independent advice requirement 2.8.1
   and multi-service organisations 2.8.3
   responsibilities 2.1
   secrecy 2.5.2
Financial Dynamics
   Kvaerner/AMEC bid 8.1.2

financial information
 cash offers 6.3.3.1
 non-UK listed offerors 6.3.3.3
 securities exchange offers 6.3.3.2
 UK listed offerors 6.3.3.2, 6.3.3.1
financial promotions
 FSMA requirements 6.12.1
Financial Services Authority (FSA) *see* **FSA (Financial Services Authority)**
Financial Services and Markets Act 2000 *see* **FSMA (Financial Services and Markets Act) 2000**
finders' fees
 special deals with favourable conditions 5.2.1.3.3
fines
 market abuse regime 3.4.2.3, 9.5
firm intention to make offer
 bid announcements 2.7.1
 documentation 6.9.1
forecasts, profit *see* **profit forecasts**
foreclosure on security for loan
 Rule 9, dispensations from 4.2.3.2
Forte
 Granada bid 4.3.2, 8.1.5, 8.2
"Friday night drop"
 and price-sensitive information 7.2
frustrating action
 amendment to Code (Rule 21.1) 1.4.4
 key Rules 1.6.4
 restrictions on
  hostile takeovers 7.2.8
  inducement fees 7.2.8.3
  shareholder approval 7.2.8.2
  Takeover Directive, impact 7.2.8.1
 Article 9 10.2.9
FSA (Financial Services Authority)
 Code of Market Conduct *see* **Code of Market Conduct**
 Disclosure Rules, pre-bid announcements 2.6.1
 Enforcement Manual 9.3, 9.5, 9.6.2
 inspectors, power to appoint 3.4.1.5
 market abuse regime, enforcement powers 7.1, 9.1
 Takeover Panel, referral to 9.6.2

FSMA (Financial Promotion) Order 2005
 exemptions 6.12.1
FSMA (Financial Services and Markets Act) 2000
 and CJA 1993 3.4.1.2
  share dealings 3.2.4
 effective from 3.2.4
 financial promotions 6.12.1
 market abuse regime *see* **market abuse regime**: FSMA (Financial Services and Markets Act) 2000
 misleading statements and practices (s.397) 3.4.2.1, 6.12.3
 standards of care 6.2.3
 Panel, effect on 3.4.2.5
 possible offer announcements 2.6.2
 share dealings, and CJA 1993 3.4.1.2
FTSE (Financial Times Stock Exchange) 100 3.5.1.1.3
Fuller, Smith and Turner
 George Gale & Co, offer for 5.2.1.1
fund managers
 dealings by 3.6.1
 disclosure 3.6.3.2
 restrictions 3.6.3.1

gatekeeper amendment
 market abuse regime 9.3
General Electric
 Amersham plc, offer for 2.7.2, 7.3.2
General Principle 1
 and Canary Wharf case 5.2.1.3.5
 equality of information to shareholders 7.2.5
 exemption from, and voluntary offers 4.3.1
 and mandatory offers 3.4.4.4, 4.2
 and Rule 16 of Code 5.2.1.3
General Principle 2
 offer documentation 6.2.2
 possible offer announcements 2.6.2
 and Rule 23 1.6.2
General Principle 3
 shareholder approval 7.2.8.2
General Principle 4
 holding statements 6.2.6

Index

possible offer announcements 2.6.2
pre-bid announcements 2.6.1
General Principle 5
offer announcements 2.4
General Principle 6
market abuse 9.3
General Principles (City Code)
Code amendments, Directive, implementation 1.4.4
contents 1.1
documentation 6.2.2
and interpretation of Code 1.3
Rules contrasted 6.2.1
and Section D of Code 2.1
see also individual principles, e.g.
General Principle 1
George Gale & Co
Fuller, Smith and Turner, offer by 5.2.1.1
Germany
minority shareholders in 10.3.6
GlaxoSmithKline
merger creating 2.7.2
Glazer family
approach for Manchester United plc 2.6.3
golden shares
and Directive 10.2.11
Goshawk Insurance Holdings
Matheson Lloyd's Investment Trust, offer for 5.2.1.2
GPG Group
De Vere, partial offer for 5.3
Granada
Carlton, proposed merger with 2.7.2
Forte bid 4.3.2, 8.1.5, 8.2
Grandmet
merger with Guinness 5.2.1.3.2
Grantchester Holdings
Dundonald Holdings, offer by 5.2.1.3.4
Great Southern Group
Service Corporation International, offer by 7.5
Great Universal Stores
Argos, takeover of 2.8.3, 6.9.2, 7.2.2

Groucho Club London
Zoo Hotels, partial offer by 5.3
Guinness
Distillers Company, bid for 3.2.3, 3.4.2.1, 4.3.1
GrantMet merger 5.2.1.3.2
and Rule 8 3.5.2.1

Hearings Committee
breach of Code, sanctions and remedies 1.12.2
disciplinary proceedings before 1.12.1
function/rulings 1.7.3
and Takeover Appeal Board 1.9
Hedley Byrne v Heller
and responsibility statements 6.2.4
Henson No. 1 Ltd
Peacock Group, acquisition of 5.2.1.3.4
Hiscox
offer for Hiscox Select Insurance Fund 5.2.1.2
holding statements
documentation (Rule 19.3) 6.2.6
home country rules
dual jurisdiction 2.2.6
home supervisory authority
Takeover Directive 10.2.4
host supervisory authority
Takeover Directive 10.2.4
hostile bids
acquisitions, timing restrictions 3.4.4.3
approach, notifying offeree 2.3.1
BIL International Limited/Thistle Hotels 7.2.2
Capital Management and Investment plc/Six Continents 3.4.4.2, 3.4.4.5, 4.3.3.1
Carnival Corporation/P&O Princess cruises 2.7.2
circulation of announcement 2.7.4
documentation
offeree circular contents 6.4
responsibility statements 6.2.4, 7.2.2

583

frustrating action, restrictions on 7.2.8
FSMA, and Panel 3.4.2.5
GPG Group/De Vere 5.3
Lafarge/Blue Circle 2.7.2
Lloyds TSB/Abbey National 2.7.2
Macquarie Group/LSE 2.6.3, 7.2.8.2, 7.4, 8.1.6
offer timetable (Day 42) 7.3.1.6
offeree circular contents 6.4
and responsibility statements 6.2.4, 7.2.2
Saint-Gobain/BPB 7.2.8.2
Wolverhampton & Dudley/Marston, Thompson & Evershed 7.2.1, 7.3.1.8, 8.2.2
Hoylake
BAT, offer for 4.3.3.2
HSBC Holdings
Midland Bank, bid for 7.2.7
Hyder
WPD and Nomura, bids from 7.3.1.12

identity
approach 2.3.2
Implementation of Takeover Directive – a Consultative Document **(DTI) (2005)** 1.2
inadvertent mistake
Rule 9, dispensations from 4.2.3.4
Income Tax (Earnings and Pensions) Act 2003
and equivalent options 5.2.1.2
Incorporated Society of Valuers and Auctioneers (ISVA) 8.2.1
independent advice
multi-service organisations 2.8.3
offeree company 2.8.1
offeror company 2.8.2
Indigo Capital
bid for Regus plc 3.4.4.2, 3.5.2.1
inducement fees
and documentation 6.8.3
frustrating action, restrictions on 7.2.8.3
information
and Directive 10.2.6

disclosure *see* **disclosure of information**
equality of
to competing offerors 7.2.7
to shareholders 7.2.5
financial *see* **financial information**
material confidential, and
independent advice 2.8.3
"material" new 7.2.6
price-sensitive *see* **price-sensitive information**
release of
advertisements 7.2.3.1
interviews/debates 7.2.3.3
telephone campaigns 7.2.3.2
responsibility for 7.2.2
sharing of, and confidentiality 1.13
sufficiency, key Rules 1.6.2
injunctions
FSA powers (market abuse) 9.5
inside information
market abuse regime 3.4.2.2.4
insider dealing
criminal offence 9.1
Insider Dealing Directive 9.1
dealing restrictions 3.4.1.1
insiders
mandatory offers 4.2.2.3
market abuse regime 3.4.2.2.3
inspectors, appointment
share dealing restrictions 3.4.1.5
Institute of Revenues Rating and Valuation (IRRV) 8.2.1
"interests in securities"
City Code 3.2.1
defined 1.4.1
and derivatives/options 3.2.1
and disclosure obligations 3.5.2.2
irrecoverable commitments 3.4.4.3
mandatory offers 3.4.4.4
Interim Regulations *see* **Takeover Regulations 2006**
International Securities Identification Number
securities in issue, bid announcements 2.7.6

Index

interviews
  and release of information 7.2.3.3
invoking conditions
  voluntary offers 4.3.4
irrevocable commitment
  defined 3.4.4.3
IRRV (Institute of Revenues Rating and Valuation) 8.2.1
ISVA (Incorporated Society of Valuers and Auctioneers) 8.2.1

James Reed & Partners
  Reed Executive, offer for 5.2.1.1
James Wilkes
  Petrocon bid 2.6.1
judicial review
  Panel and courts, relationship between 1.10
jurisdiction
  proposed changes 1.4.4
  shared 2.2.3
    complicated nature of 10.3.4
    transactions, range of 2.2.4

Kleinwort Benson
  Abbey National/Cater Allen offer 2.8.3
Kvaerner
  Amec, bid for 8.1.2

Lafarge
  Blue Circle, hostile offer for 2.7.2, 5.4, 7.6, 7.7.1, 8.2.2
lapse of offers
  circumstances 7.7.1
LASMO
  bid by Enterprise Oil 7.2.1
  cash offer by Agip Investment 5.2.1.2
Listing Rules
  Chapter 11, voluntary offers, acceptance condition 4.3.2
  documentation 6.11
  offer period, dealings prior to/during 3.4.4.2
  passport rights 6.11
  possible offer announcements 2.6.2
  profit forecasts 8.1.3

Lloyds TSB
  Abbey National, hostile offer for 2.7.2, 8.1.5
loans
  foreclosure on security for, Rule 9, dispensations from 4.2.3.2
London Stock Exchange plc
  Daily Official List 5.2.1.1
  Macquarie Group, hostile bid by 2.6.3, 7.2.8.2, 7.4, 8.1.6
  and market abuse regime 9.4
  misuse of information 9.6.1.1
  persons registered as market makers with 1.5.1
"look-through" principle
  identity of offeror 2.3.2
Luirc
  Merlin Properties, proposed offer for 2.4
LVMH
  Guinness/GrandMet merger 5.2.1.3.2

M&B *see* **Mitchell's & Butler plc**
McCorquodale, rival bids
  Datafin case 1.10
Macquarie Group
  London Stock Exchange, bid for 2.6.3, 7.2.8.2, 7.4, 8.1.6
Malins, Jonathan
  fining of 3.4.2.3
Mallett
  share buy-back authority sought by 5.4
management buy-outs (MBOs)
  equality of information, to competing offerors 7.2.7
  special deals with favourable conditions 5.2.1.3.4
  timing restrictions 7.5
Manchester United plc
  approach by Glazer family 2.6.3
mandatory offers
  acting in concert, persons deemed to be *see* **acting in concert**: persons deemed to be
  cash *see* **Rule 11**
  and Directive, Article 5 10.2.5

equitable price requirement 10.2.5
in Netherlands 10.3.7
offer announcements 2.4
partial offers 5.3
and recognised intermediary status 1.5.2
securities *see* **Rule 11**
share dealing restrictions 3.4.4.4
terms and conditions
  acceptance condition 4.2.1.3
  competition references 4.2.1.2
  consents 4.2.1.4
  material adverse changes 4.2.1.4
  price 4.2.1.1
  regulatory clearances 4.2.1.4
  Rule 9 provisions 4.2
30 per cent threshold 4.2.4.1, 4.2
see also **Rule 9 (mandatory offers)**
MANWEB profit forecasts (1995) 8.1.4
market abuse regime
background 9.3
categories of abusive behaviour 3.4.2.2.1
City Code
  operating together 9.6.2
  overlap with 9.6.1
as civil regime 9.1
Code of Market Conduct *see* **Code of Market Conduct**: market abuse regime
consequences 3.4.2.3
controversial aspects 9.2
defences 3.4.2.4
definitions 9.4
domestic markets 9.4
and ECHR 9.2
freezing of offers 9.5
FSA powers 7.1, 9.1
FSMA (Financial Services and Markets Act) 2000
  categories of abuse behaviour 3.4.2.2.1
  defences 3.4.2.4
  documentation 6.12.2
  inside information 3.4.2.2.4
  insiders 3.4.2.2.3

market abuse regime Directive *see* **market abuse regime Directive**
inside information 3.4.2.2.4
insiders 3.4.2.2.3
pre-bid announcements, failure to make 2.6.1
prescribed markets 3.4.2.2.2
qualifying investments 3.4.2.2.2
regular user test 3.4.2.1.1.1
Regulations 3.4.2.2
  prescribed markets and qualifying investments 3.4.2.2.2
restitutionary orders 9.5
state of mind 9.4
takeovers, impact on
  City Code 9.6.1
  market abuse regime/City Code 9.6.2, 9.6.1
  market manipulation limb 9.6.1.2
  misuse of information limb 9.6.1.1
territorial scope 9.4
market abuse regime Directive
implementation (2005) 3.2.4
market information defence
market abuse regime 3.4.1.6, 3.4.1.4
market makers
London Stock Exchange, persons registered with 1.5.1
share dealings by 3.6.1
market manipulation
criminal offence of 9.1
market abuse, definitions 9.4
Marks & Spencers
interest by Revival Acquisitions 3.3.1
Marston, Thompson & Evershed
Wolverhampton & Dudley's hostile bid for 7.2.1, 7.3.1.8
material change in circumstances conditions
mandatory offers 4.2.1.4
voluntary offers 4.3.3.3, 4.3.4
Matheson Lloyd's Investment Trust
Goshawk Insurance Holdings, offer by (1997) 5.2.1.2
MBA Bailey Associates
Metroyard, offer by 5.2.1.3.4

Index

MBOs *see* **management buy-outs (MBOs)**
meetings
  conduct during offer 7.2.6
merger benefits statements
  documentation 6.8.2
  need to report on 7.2.1
  profit forecasts 8.1.5
Merger Regulation (EC)
  mandatory offers 3.4.4.4, 4.4
mergers
  Boots/Alliance Unichem 7.3.2
  Carlton/Granada, proposed 2.7.2
  GlaxoSmithKline 2.7.2
  Guinness/GrandMet 5.2.1.3.2
Merlin Properties
  Luirc, proposed offer by 2.4
Metroyard
  MBA Bailey Associates, offer for 5.2.1.3.4
Midland Bank
  HSBC Holdings, bid by 7.2.7
Miller plc
  CALA plc, bid for 7.5
Minorco
  Consolidated Goldfields, bid for 4.3.2
misleading statements and practices
  FSMA (s.397) 3.4.2.1, 6.12.3
  standards of care 6.2.3
mistake, inadvertent
  Rule 9, dispensations from 4.2.3.4
misuse of information
  market abuse regime 9.4
  takeovers, impact on 9.6.1.1
Mitchell's & Butler plc
  BC Capital Partners' proposed offer for 3.5.2.1
mix and match offers 7.6
MMC (Monopolies and Mergers Commission) *see* **Monopolies and Mergers Commission (MMC)**
Mohammed, Arif
  fining of 3.4.2.3
Molins
  TKM, bid by 2.8.3

Monopolies and Mergers Commission (MMC)
  CalEnergy/Northern Electric takeover 3.4.4.1
Monsoon
  and partial offers 5.3
Morrison Supermarket
  Safeway plc, initial bid for 7.3.1.8, 7.7.1, 7.7.3, 7.7.1, 7.7.3
MSREF
  offer for Canary Wharf 2.6.4
multi-service organisations
  and financial advisers 2.8.3

Nabarro Wells, criticism 2.1, 2.6.1
National Westminster Bank plc
  bids for 2.6.4, 6.2.6, 7.3.1.8
Netherlands
  mandatory bid requirement 10.3.7
newco structures
  City Code 2.2.5
"no extension statements" 7.4
"no increase statements" 7.5
"no intention to bid" statements
  and "put up or shut up" regime 2.6.3
Nomura
  Hyder, bid for 7.3.1.12
North West Water
  NORWEB, bid for 4.3.3.1
Northern Electric
  CalEnergy, takeover by 3.4.4.1, 7.2.9, 7.3.1.8
  Trafalgar House bids 3.4.1.6, 4.3.4, 7.7.3
NORWEB
  North West Water, bid by 4.3.3.1
notifiable interests
  share dealing disclosure (Companies Act) 3.5.1.1.2
  relevant share capital 3.5.1.1.1
NTL
  Virgin Mobile, offer for 5.2.1.3.2

OFEX
  market abuse regime 9.4
"off-balance sheet" vehicle
  identity of offeror 2.3.2

587

offer announcements 2.4
  circulation 6.9.1
  possible 2.6.2
  pre-conditional 2.7.2
  side agreements, disclosure in 2.7.3
offer conditions
  document contents 6.3.1
offer document contents
  commercial issues, terms and
    conditions 6.3.1
  financial information
    cash offers 6.3.3.1
    non-UK listed offerors 6.3.3.3
    securities exchange offers
      6.3.3.2
    UK listed offerors 6.3.3.2, 6.3.3.1
  general information requirements
    6.3.5, 6.3.3.4
  shareholdings and dealings 6.3.4
  specific requirements 6.3.2
  see also **documentation**
offer period
  dealings prior to/during 3.4.4.2
  see also **Rule 8 (disclosure of dealings during offer period)**
offer timetable
  Day O (posting date) 1.6.2, 7.3.1.1
  Day 14 7.3.1.2
  Day 21 7.3.1.3
  Day 35 7.3.1.4
  Day 39 7.3.1.5, 7.4
  Day 42 7.3.1.6
  Day 46 7.3.1.7
    competing bids on 7.3.1.12
    no revision after 7.5
  Day 60 7.3.1.8
    Trafalgar House bid for Northern Electric 7.7.3
  Day 81 7.3.1.9
  Day 95 7.3.1.10
  extensions 7.3.2
  offeree company, requirement not to hinder for longer than reasonable 1.6.6
  posting date (Day O) 1.6.2, 7.3.1.1
    counting forwards from and excluding (Day 14) 7.3.1.2

  trigger date, compulsory acquisition of minority 7.3.1.11
offeree companies
  circular contents 6.4
  independent advice 2.8.1
  notifying 2.3.1
  requirement not to hinder for longer than reasonable 1.6.6
  rumour and speculation 2.6.1
offeree protection conditions
  voluntary offers 4.3.4
  withdrawal rights 7.3.1.6
offeror companies
  competing, equality of information to 7.2.7
  documentation *see* **documentation**
  identity 2.3.2
  independent advice 2.8.2
  joint 5.2.1.3.5
  liability, misleading statements and practices 3.4.2.1
  restrictions on exercise of control by 4.2.4.4
  share dealings by, Code restrictions 3.4.4.1
  see also **offeree companies**
offers
  acceptances, unconditional as to 5.2.2.2
  all, provisions applicable to
    administrative provisions *see* **administrative provisions (all offers)**
    equivalent treatment *see* **equivalent treatment**
  alternative 7.6
  and asset valuations 8.2.1
  cash *see* **cash offers**
  comparable, different equity classes 5.2.1.1
  conduct during *see* **conduct during offer**
  contents *see* **offer document contents**
  convertibles 5.2.1.2
  extensions of 7.4
  freezing of, market abuse regime 9.5
  increased 7.5

irrevocable offers to accept 3.4.3
lapse of 7.7.1
mix and match 7.6
partial 5.3
responsibility for making, Rule 9
   4.2.4.1
restrictions following
   delay of 12 months (Rule 35) 7.7.3
   lapsed offers 7.7.1
   target shares, freedom to sell 7.7.2
revisions 7.5
securities exchange 6.2.4, 6.3.3.2
timetable *see* **offer timetable**
unconditional as to acceptances
   5.2.2.2
Office of Fair Trading
acquisitions, timing restrictions
   3.4.4.3
Official List
cash offers, offer document contents
   6.3.3.1
securities exchange offers 6.3.3.2
shares admitted to, equivalent
   treatment 5.2.1.1
"open" auction process
and offer timetable 7.3.1.12
open-ended investment companies
Directive not applicable to 10.2.1
Operating Guidelines
share dealings
   market abuse regime 3.4.2.5
   rules and regulations 3.2.4
options
Code amendments/recent Rule
   changes 1.4.1
mandatory offers (Rule 9) 4.2.4.5
see also **derivative and option
   contracts, dealings**
Orb Estates
Alexanders Holdings Offer 2.8.3,
   3.4.4.4
orphan companies
and takeover regulation 10.3.5
Osmond, Hugh
Twigway, offer by 7.5
"out of the money" rights
and convertibles 5.2.1.2

Oxford Glycosciences
Celltech Group plc and Cambridge
   Antibody Technology plc, bids
   by 7.3.1.5

P&O Princess Cruises
Carnival Corporation, offer by
   hostile 2.7.2
   partial 5.3
   timetable extensions 7.3.2
"pac man" defence
and offer timetable 7.3.1.8
Panel on Takeovers and Mergers *see*
   Takeover Panel
Panther Securities
Elys (Wimbledon), two-tier offer for
   5.3
partial offers 5.3
Partridge Fine Arts
Amor Holdings, partial offer by 5.3
passport rights
Listing Rules 6.11
PCPs (public consultation papers)
acceptance levels, announcements
   (PCP 2005/2) 5.2.2.1
bid announcements, relevant
   securities in issue (PCP 2003/4)
   2.7.6
City Code amendments (PCPs 2005/5
   and 2006/1) 1.4.4, 1.4
   miscellaneous 1.4.5
dealing activities (PCPs 2005/1 and
   2005/2) 1.4.1
implementation of Takeover Directive
   (PCP 2005/5) 1.2
pre-conditional offer announcements
   (PCP 2004/4) 2.7.2
SARs, abolition (PCP 2005/4) 1.4.3
special deals with favourable
   conditions (PCP 2005/1)
   5.2.1.3
see also **RS (Response Statements)**
Peacock Group
Henson No. 1 Ltd, acquired by
   5.2.1.3.4
Permira
Debenhams, bid for 7.2.8.3

persons acting in concert 1.4.4, 4.2.2, 10.2.2
Petrocon
  bid for James Wilkes 2.6.1
Pizza Express
  offer by Twigway 7.5
Powergen
  bid for E.ON 2.7.2, 7.3.2
Practice Statements
  cash offers, financed by issue of offeror securities (No 10) 2.4
  holding statements (No 8) 6.2.6
  inducement fees (Nos 4, 14 and 15) 6.8.3
  meetings (No 9) 7.2.6
  misleading statements (No 19) 7.2.2
  offer timetable (No 8) 7.3.1.8
  pre-bid announcements (No 2) 2.6.1
  working capital requirements, cash and securities exchange offers (No 11) 2.4
  see also Executive
pre-bid announcements
  consequences 2.7.5
  possible offer announcements 2.6.2
  "put up or shut up" regime 2.6.3
  relevant securities in issue, numbers 2.7.6
  required when 2.6.1
  statement of interest by potential competing bidder 2.6.4
pre-bid period
  and Section D of Code 2.1
pre-conditional offer announcements
  and bid announcements 2.7.2
  see also **offer announcements**
pre-conditions *see* **offer pre-conditions**
prescribed markets
  market abuse regime 3.4.2.2.2
press announcements
  offeree, notifying 2.3.1
  variety of 2.1
Prevention of Fraud (Investments) Act 1958
  misleading statements and practices 3.4.2.1

price-sensitive information
  fair market preservation 1.6.4
  and "Friday night drop" 7.2
  share dealing restrictions 3.4.4.1
principal traders
  share dealings by 3.6.1
    dealing restrictions 3.6.4.1
    disclosures 3.6.4.2
private companies
  application of Code 2.2.2
profit forecasts
  assumptions 8.1.4, 8.1.8
  City Code 8.1.3
  definition 8.1.2
  documentation 6.8.1
  estimates 8.1.2
  evaluation 8.1.11
  exceptions 8.1.6
  format 8.1.7
  long-form report 8.1.9
    preparation 8.1.10
  merger benefits statements 8.1.5
  projections 8.1.2
  responsibility for making 8.1.9
  risks 8.1.4
  safe harbour rules 8.1.10
  and takeovers 8.1.1
  validity 8.1.4
  see also **asset valuations**
projections, profit 8.1.2
proof printing
  secrecy 2.5.3
Prospectus Directive
  and profit forecasts 8.1.3
proxies
  administrative provisions (Rule 18) 5.2.2.4
public companies
  application of Code 2.2.2
public consultation papers (PCPs) *see* **PCPs (public consultation papers)**
"put up or shut up" approach
  offeree company, requirement not to hinder for longer than reasonable 1.6.6
  possible offer announcements 2.6.2

Index

purpose 2.6.3
and statements of interest by potential competing bidder 2.6.4

qualifying investments
market abuse regime 3.4.2.2.2
Quebecor
Watmoughs, bid for 7.3.1.8
quotations
offer documentation 6.2.3
QXL Ricardo plc
competing bids for 7.3.1.12

Range Cooker Company
Britannia Living, offer by 5.2.1.3.5
Receiving Agents' Code of Practice
and acceptance verification 4.3.2
reciprocal action/reciprocity
and Directive 10.2.12
recognised intermediary status
background 1.5.2
dispensations 1.5.2
share dealings 3.6.2
derivatives and options 1.4.2
recognised investment exchange see RIE (recognised investment exchange)
Reed Executive
James Reed & Partners, offer by 5.2.1.1
regular user test
market abuse regime 3.4.2.1.1.1, 9.4
Regulatory Information Service see RIS (Regulatory Information Service)
Regus plc
bid by Indigo Capital 3.4.4.2, 3.5.2.1
Related Party Transaction Rules
voluntary offers, acceptance condition 4.3.2
relevant securities
defined 1.4.1
Rule 8 3.5.2.1
numbers in issue, announcement of 2.7.6
relevant share capital
Companies Act 3.5.1.1.1

remedies
breach of Code 1.12.2
Rentokil
unilateral offer for BET 2.6.1
rescue operations
Rule 9, dispensations from 4.2.3.3
residency test
abolition 1.4.4
application of Code 2.2.2
response statements (RSs) see RSs (response statements)
responsibility statements
directors 6.2.4, 7.2.2
restitutionary orders
market abuse regime 9.5
reverse takeovers
independent advice 2.8.2
Revival Acquisitions
interest in Marks & Spencers 3.3.1
RICs see Royal Institution of Chartered Surveyors (RICS)
RIE (Recognised Investment Exchange)
market abuse 9.4
RIS (Regulatory Information Service)
acquisitions 3.4.4.3
announcements in accordance with 6.6
roll-over relief
and share option schemes 5.2.1.2
Royal Bank of Scotland (RBS)
Nat West, bid for 2.6.4, 6.2.6, 7.3.1.8
Royal Institution of Chartered Surveyors (RICS)
Appraisal and Valuation Manual 8.2.2
valuations, and offers 8.2.1
RSs (response statements)
acceptance levels, announcements (RS 2005/2) 5.2.2.1
amendment of Code 1.4
definitions/timing (RS 2005/2) 1.4.1
derivatives and options, dealings in 1.4.1, 1.4.2
miscellaneous provisions (RS 2006/1) 1.4.5
SARs, abolition (RS 2005/4) 1.4.3, 3.2.2

circulation of announcement (RS 2004/3) 2.7.4
derivatives and options, dealings in
    control issues (RS 2005/3) 1.4.2
    disclosure issues (RS 2005/2) 1.4.1, 3.3.1
exempt principal trader status (RS 2004/3) 1.5.1
pre-conditional offer announcements (RS 2004/4) 2.7.2
recognised intermediary status (RS 2005/3) 1.4.2, 1.5.2
SARs, abolition (RS 2005/4) 1.4.3
share dealings 3.2.2
special deals with favourable conditions (RS 2005/2) 5.2.1.3
see also **PCPs (public consultation papers)**

Rule 1 (approach) 2.3
identity of offeror 2.3.2
offeree, notifying 2.3.1

Rule 2 (announcements: secrecy before, timing and contents)
bid announcements
    circulation 2.7.4
    consequences 2.7.5
    firm intention to make offer 2.7.1
    relevant securities, numbers in issue 2.7.6
circulation of offer announcements 6.9.1
consideration obligations, fulfilling 1.6.5
offer announcements 2.4
    possible 2.6.2
pre-bid announcements 2.6.1
publication of documents 6.6
"put up or shut up" rule 1.6.6
secrecy (Rule 2.1)
    advisors' obligations 2.5.2
    basic obligation 2.5.1
    employee consultation 2.5.4
    proof printing 2.5.3
voluntary announcements 2.6.3

Rule 3 (independent advice)
financial advisers 2.8.3
offeree company 2.8.1
offeror company 2.8.2
sufficiency of time, information and advice 1.6.2

Rule 4 (restrictions on dealings)
fair markets, preservation of 1.6.4
and market manipulation 9.6.1.2
offer period, dealings prior to/during 3.4.4.2
target shares, freedom to sell 7.7.2

Rule 5 (timing restrictions on acquisitions)
derivatives and options, control issues 1.4.2
share dealings
    applicability of rules 3.2.1
    disclosure 3.5.2.2
    prohibitions/restrictions 3.4.4.3
    rules and regulations, applicability 3.2.1
and Whitewash procedure 4.2.3.1

Rule 6 (minimum consideration, obligation to offer)
amendments, equality of treatment 1.6.1
compensation rulings 1.11.2
derivatives and option dealings, control issues 1.4.2
revisions 7.5
share dealings, prohibitions/restrictions 3.4.4.5

Rule 7 (consequences of certain dealings)
share dealing disclosure 3.5.2.2

Rule 8 (disclosure of dealings during offer period)
bid announcements
    circulation 2.7.4
    firm intention to make offer 2.7.1
    relevant securities, number in issue 2.7.6
definitions/requirements 3.5.2.1
fair markets, preservation 1.6.4
fund managers 3.6.3.2
misleading statements and practices 3.4.2.1
recognised intermediary status 1.5.2

Index

shareholdings and dealings 6.3.4
timing issues 1.4.1
Rule 9 (mandatory offers)
   acting in concert 3.4.4.4, 4.2.2.1
   amendments, equality of treatment, and protection of non-controlling shareholders 1.6.1
   chain principle 4.2.4.2
   Code amendments, Directive, implementation 1.4.4
   Code Committee, Notes on Dispensations from Rule 9 3.4.4.4
   compensation rulings 1.11.2
   concert parties 3.3.3
   convertible securities 4.2.4.5, 5.2.1.2
   derivatives and options, control issues 1.4.2
   dispensations from
      Code Committee notes 3.4.4.4
      inadvertent mistake 4.2.3.4
      non-acceptance by 50 per cent 4.2.3.5
      non-voting shares, enfranchisement 4.2.3.6
      redemption or purchase by company of own shares 4.2.3.7
      rescue operations, and Whitewash procedure 4.2.3.3
      security for loan, disclosure on 4.2.3.2
      Whitewash procedure, availability 4.2.3.1
   exempt principal trader status 1.5.1
   and General Principle 1 4.2
   insincere bids 4.2.4.7
   and lapsed offers 7.7.1
   offeror, restrictions on exercise of control by 4.2.4.4
   options 4.2.4.5
   and partial offers 5.3
   philosophy underlying 4.2
   practical effect 4.2.5
   pre-bid announcements 2.6.1
   provisions 4.2
   responsibility for making offer 4.2.4.1
   restrictions on freedom of action 4.1

share dealings
   applicability of rules 3.2.1
   disclosure 3.5.2.2
   prior to/during offer period 3.4.4.2
   prohibitions/restrictions 3.4.4.4
   redemption or purchase of own securities 5.4
   30 per cent threshold, crossing 4.2.4.1
   triggering during course of voluntary offer 4.2.4.3
   warrants 4.2.4.5
   Whitewash procedure
      availability 4.2.3.1
      and rescue operations 4.2.3.3
   yo-yo principle 4.2.4.6
   see also **mandatory offers**
Rule 10 (acceptance condition)
   restrictions on freedom of action 4.1
   voluntary offers 4.3.2
Rule 11 (cash and securities offers, requirements)
   amendments, equality of treatment 1.6.1
   compensation rulings 1.11.2
   derivatives and options, control issues 1.4.2
   restrictions on freedom of action 4.1
   revisions 7.5
   share dealings, prohibitions/restrictions 3.4.4.6
   voluntary offers, consideration requirements 4.3.1
Rule 12 (Competition Commission and European Commission)
   mandatory bids, terms and conditions 4.2.1.1
   restrictions on freedom of action 4.1
   voluntary bids 4.3.3.2
Rule 13 (pre-conditions, firm offer announcements and offer conditions)
   bid announcements
      consequences 2.7.5
      pre-conditional offer announcements 2.7.2
   restrictions on freedom of action 4.1

Rule 14 (all offers, provisions applicable to)
"comparable offer" 5.2.1.2
equivalent treatment 5.2.1
  comparable offers, different equity classes 5.2.1.1
  convertibles, appropriate offers for 5.2.1.2
Rule 15 (appropriate offer for convertibles etc)
documentation 6.10
equivalent treatment 5.2.1.2
and Rule 14 5.2.1.1
Rule 16 (special deals with favourable conditions)
asset disposals 5.2.1.3.2
Canary Wharf case 5.2.1.3.5
Code amendments, equality of treatment 1.6.1
equality of treatment 5.2.1.3
finders' fees 5.2.1.3.3
and General Principle 1 5.2.1.3
joint offerors 5.2.1.3.5
management retaining interest 5.2.1.3.4
Public Consultation Papers 5.2.1.3
share dealings, prohibitions/restrictions 3.4.4.7
top-ups 5.2.1.3.1
Rule 17 (acceptance levels, announcements)
administrative provisions
  all offers 5.2.2.1
  failure to announce 5.2.2.2
disclosure obligations 3.5.2.2
Rule 18 (proxies/other authorities, use of)
administrative provisions 5.2.2.4
Rule 19 (information)
advertisements 7.2.3.1
announcements, distribution and availability 7.2.4
approach, identity of offeror 2.3.2
conduct during offer (Rule 19.1) 7.2, 7.2.1
debates 7.2.3.3
fair markets, preservation 1.6.4

holding statements 6.2.6
interviews 7.2.3.3
merger benefits statements 6.8.2, 7.2.1, 8.1.5
offer documentation
  distribution and availability 7.2.4
  general responsibilities 6.2.2
  holding statements 6.2.6
  merger benefits statements 6.8.2, 7.2.1
  non-compliant documents, criminal liability for 6.5
  other parties, release to 6.2.7
  responsibility statements 6.2.4, 7.2.2
  specific standards of care 6.2.3
responsibility statements 6.2.4, 7.2.2
telephone campaigns 7.2.3.2
Rule 20 (equality of information)
competing offerors 7.2.7
fair markets, preservation 1.6.4
frustrating action, prevention 1.6.4
meetings 7.2.6
shareholders 7.2.5
Rule 21 (frustrating action, restrictions on)
bid announcements, consequences 2.7.5
and Directive 10.2.9
inducement fees 6.8.3
merits of bid, shareholders able to decide on 1.6.3
offer document contents, general information 6.3.3.4
prevention of frustrating action 1.6.4
shareholder approval 7.2.8.2
Rule 23 (general obligation as to information)
offer documentation, general responsibilities 6.2.2
offeree circular contents 6.4
possible offer announcements 2.6.2
sufficiency of time, information and advice 1.6.2
Rule 24 (offeror documents)
Code amendments, Directive, implementation 1.4.4

594

Index

content requirements 6.3.2
financial information 6.3.3
  cash offers 6.3.3.1
  non UK listed offerors 6.3.3.3
  securities exchange offers 6.3.3.2
  UK listed companies 6.3.3.2, 6.3.3.1
general information requirements 6.3.5, 6.3.3.4
offer announcements 2.4
shareholdings and dealings 6.3.4

Rule 25 (offeree board circulars)
Code amendments, Directive, implementation 1.4.4
contents of offeree circular 6.4

Rule 27 (shareholders, documents subsequently sent to)
documentation 6.9.2

Rule 28 (profit forecasts)
documentation 6.8.1
purpose 8.1.1

Rule 29 (asset valuations)
documentation 6.8.1

Rule 30 (availability of offer document/offeree board circular)
circulation of documents 6.7
employee consultation 2.5.4
offer timetable
  Day 0 7.3.1.1
  Day 14 7.3.1.2

Rule 31 (timing of offer)
acceptance condition
  subsequent documents 6.9.2
  voluntary offers 4.3.2
alternative offers 7.6
Day 21 7.3.1.3
Day 35 7.3.1.4
Day 39 7.3.1.5, 7.4
Day 42 7.3.1.6
Day 60 7.3.1.8
  Trafalgar House bid for Northern Electric 7.7.3
Day 81 7.3.1.9
Day 95 7.3.1.10
extensions to timetable 7.3.2
offer document contents 6.3.1

sufficiency of time, information and advice 1.6.2

Rule 32 (revision) 7.5
offer document contents 6.3.1
offer timetable 7.3.1.7, 7.3.1.8

Rule 33 (alternative offers) 7.6

Rule 34 (withdrawal rights)
offer timetable 7.3.1.6

Rule 35 (restrictions following offers/possible offers)
12 month delay 7.7.3

Rule 36 (partial offers)
and voluntary offers, acceptance condition 4.3.2

Rule 37 (redemption or purchase of own securities) 5.4
and mandatory offers 3.4.4.4

Rule 38 (restrictions on dealings)
principal traders 3.6.4.1

Rules of Code
application of, and Directive 10.2.4
consideration obligations, fulfilling 1.6.5
equality of treatment 1.6.1
fair markets, preservation 1.6.4
General Principles contrasted 6.2.1
interpretation 1.6
offeree company, requirement not to hinder for longer than reasonable 1.6.6
pre-bid period 2.1
shareholders, deciding on merit of bid 1.6.3
sufficiency of time, information and advice 1.6.2
see also individual Rules, such as **Rule 1 (approach)**

rumour and speculation
and pre-bid announcements 2.6.1

safe harbours
market abuse regime 3.4.2.5, 9.3
  misuse of information limb 9.6.1.1
profit forecasts 8.1.10

Safeway plc
Wm Morrison Supermarkets recommended offer 7.3.1.8, 7.7.3, 7.7.1, 7.7.3

Saint-Gobain
  hostile bid for BPB 7.2.8.2, 7.3.1.5
sanctions
  Directive 10.2.16
  fines *see* **fines**
SARs (Rules Governing Substantial Acquisitions of Shares)
  abolition 1.4.3, 3.1, 5.3
  background 1.4.3
  disclosure requirements 1.4.3
  share dealings, rules and regulations 3.2.2
schemes of arrangement
  Companies Act 4.3.2
Scottish Hydro
  offer by Southern Electric 2.7.2
"sealed bid" process
  and offer timetable 7.3.1.12
secrecy (Rule 2.1)
  advisors' obligations 2.5.2
  basic obligation 2.5.1
  employee consultation 2.5.4
  proof printing 2.5.3
Secretary of State
  inspectors, power to appoint 3.4.1.5
securities
  meaning 10.2.1, 10.2.2
  redemption or purchase of own 5.4
  relevant *see* **relevant securities**
  unenforceability of restrictions on transfer, Directive 10.2.11
Securities and Exchange Act (1934)
  dual jurisdiction 2.2.6
securities exchange offers
  financial information 6.3.3.2
  and responsibility statements 6.2.4
Securities and Investment Board
  and contracts for differences 3.4.1.6
"see-through" price
  convertibles 5.2.1.2
  offers to holders of 6.10
  inducement fees 6.8.3
Service Corporation International
  Great Southern Group, bid for 7.5
SETS (Stock Exchange Electronic Trading Service)
  and Companies Act 3.5.1.1.3

equivalent treatment 5.2.1.1
principal traders and fund managers, dealings by 3.6.1
Severn Trent
  Caird, bid for 4.3.4
share dealing disclosure
  City Code
    Rule 5 3.5.2.2
    Rule 7 3.5.2.2
    Rule 8 3.5.2.1
  Companies Act (Part VI) 3.5.1
    concert parties 3.5.1.1.4
    contravention, consequences 3.5.1.1.6
    "interests" for purposes of 3.5.1.1.3
    notifiable interests 3.5.1.1.1, 3.5.1.1.2
    relevant share capital 3.5.1.1.1
    Section 212 notices 3.5.1.1.5, 3.5.1.1.6
  fund managers 3.6.3.2
  principal traders 3.6.4.2
share dealing restrictions
  CJA 1993 (Part V) 3.4.1.1
    contravention 3.4.1.3
    and FSMA 3.4.1.2
  Companies Act 3.4.3
  contracts for differences 3.4.1.6
  FSMA 2000
    and CJA 1993 3.4.1.2
    market abuse regime *see* **market abuse regime; market abuse regime Directive**
    misleading statements and practices (Section 397) 3.4.2.1
    and Takeover Panel 3.4.2.5
    see also **FSMA (Financial Services and Markets Act) 2000**
  fund managers 3.6.3.1
  inspectors, appointment 3.4.1.5
  market abuse regime *see* **market abuse regime; market abuse regime Directive**
  principal traders 3.6.4.1
  Takeover Code
    competitive bid processes 3.4.4.8

Index

offerors and associates, dealings by 3.4.4.1
Rule 4 3.4.4.2
Rule 5 3.4.4.3
Rule 6 3.4.4.5
Rule 9 3.4.4.4
Rule 11 3.4.4.6
Rule 16 3.4.4.7
takeovers, consequences for 3.4.1.4
share dealings
by associates 3.4.4.1
Code amendments, Takeover Directive 3.1.1, 3.1
Companies Act
  disclosures 3.5.1
  prohibitions/restrictions 3.4.3
  rules and regulations 3.2.3
concepts
  associates 3.3.4
  concert parties 3.3.3
  dealings 3.3.2
  interests in securities 3.3.1
concert parties *see* **concert parties**
by connected market makers *see* **market makers, connected**
control
  definition 4.2
  derivatives and options, dealings in 1.4.2
  redemption or purchase of own securities 5.4
  regulation of changes 3.2.1
Criminal Justice Act 1993
  contravention 3.4.1.3
  and FSMA 3.4.1.2
  restrictions/prohibitions 3.4.1.1–3.4.1.6
  rules and regulations 3.2.4
dealings, concept 1.4.1, 3.3.2
disclosure of *see* **share dealing disclosure**
by fund managers 3.6.1
  dealing restrictions 3.6.3.1
interests in securities, concept 3.3.1
offer documentation 6.3.4
by offerors 3.4.4.1
by principal traders 3.6.1

prohibitions/restrictions *see* **share dealing restrictions**
recognised intermediary status 3.6.2
rules and regulations, applicability
  Code, application 3.2.1
  Companies Act 3.2.3
  SARs 3.2.2
  Takeovers Directive 3.1, 3.1.1
  30 per cent threshold 3.2.1
share option schemes
and roll-over relief 5.2.1.2
share price
"untoward" movement in 2.6.1
shareholders
equality of treatment 1.6.1
information 7.2.5
and frustrating action, restrictions on 7.2.8.2
merits of bid, opportunity to decide on 1.6.3
minority, and Directive 10.3.6
non-controlling, protection of 1.6.1
voting together, and acting in concert 4.2.2.1
Sharepeople Group
American Express, offer by 5.2.1.1
shares
equivalent treatment, comparable offers, different equity classes 5.2.1.1
golden 10.2.11
interest in, and mandatory offers 4.2
non-voting, enfranchisement 4.2.3.6
redemption or purchase of own 4.2.3.7, 5.4
target, freedom to sell 7.7.2
Shell Group
fining of 3.4.2.3
side agreements
pre-conditional offer announcements 2.7.3
Six Continents plc
Capital Management and Investment plc, hostile offer by 3.4.4.2, 3.4.4.5, 4.3.3.1
six-month average ratio 5.2.1.1

Societas Europaea
    and application of Code 2.2.2
    share dealings 3.2.1
Songbird Acquisition Ltd
    Canary Wharf Group, bid for 3.3.3
Southern Electric
    Scottish Hydro, offer for 2.7.2
Spain
    minority shareholders in 10.3.6
special deals with favourable
        conditions (Rule 16) *see* Rule 16
        (special deals, favourable
        conditions)
"squeeze-out"/"sell-out" rights
    Directive 10.2.15
    extensions of offer 7.4
    Takeover Regulations 3.4.4.7
    trigger date for compulsory
        acquisition of minority 7.3.1.11
standards of care, offer documentation
    general 6.2.2
    specific 6.2.3
standstill protections
    equality of information 7.2.7
Stead and Simpson
    Clayform Properties, offers by 5.2.1.1
Stock Exchange, London *see* London
    Stock Exchange plc
Substantial Acquisition of Shares,
    Rules Governing *see* SARs
    (Rules Governing Substantial
    Acquisitions of Shares)

T&N plc
    Federal Mogul, bid by 7.3.2
Takeover Appeal Board
    function 1.9
"takeover bid"
    meaning 10.2.1, 10.2.2
    see also bids
Takeover Code *see* City Code on
    Takeovers and Mergers
Takeover Directive
    Article 1 (scope) 10.2.1
    Article 2 (definitions) 10.2.2
    Article 3 (general principles) 10.2.3
        and Code amendments 1.4.4

Article 4 (supervisory authority)
    10.2.4
    and Code amendments 1.4.4
Article 5 (mandatory bid) 10.2.5
Article 6 (information on bid) 10.2.6
    employee consultation 2.5.4
Article 7 (acceptance period) 10.2.7
Article 9 (prohibition on taking
    defensive action to frustrate bids)
    10.1, 10.2.9
    opting out of/into 10.2.12
Article 10 (transparency) 10.2.10
Article 11 (unenforceability of
    restrictions on transfer of
    securities/voting rights) 10.1,
    10.2.11
    major impact 10.3.3
    opting out of/into 10.2.12
Article 12 (opting out of/into Articles
    9 and 11) 10.2.12
Article 13 (conduct of bid) 10.2.13
Article 14 (employees'
    representatives, information/
    consultation with) 10.2.14
Articles 15 and 16 (squeeze-out
    rights/sell-out rights) 10.2.15
Article 17 (sanctions) 10.2.16
Article 18 (committee procedure)
    10.2.17
Article 19 (Contact Committee
    appointment) 10.2.18
Article 20 (revision) 10.2.19
Article 21 (timing of implementation)
    10.2.20
background 10.1
and Companies Act 6.13.2
and Company Law Reform Bill 3.1.1,
    6.1, 7.1
concert parties 3.3.3
conduct during offer 7.1
employee consultation 2.5.4
equality of information to
    shareholders 7.2.5
EU takeover rules, impact
    Article 11, major impact 10.3.3
    increased protectionism across
    10.3.2

598

Index

minority shareholders 10.3.6
Netherlands, mandatory bid requirement 10.3.7
no level playing field for bids 10.3.2
no uniform set of rules 10.3.1
shared jurisdiction, complicated nature of 10.3.4
takeover regulation, all listed EU companies subject to 10.3.5
and frustrating action, restrictions on 7.2.8.1
future prospects 10.4
implementation in UK (2006) 1.1, 6.1
   Code amendments 1.4.4, 2.1, 2.2, 3.1.1, 3.4.4.4, 7.1
   management interest 5.2.1.3.4
   PCPs 1.2, 1.4.1
   share dealings 3.1.1
management interest 5.2.1.3.4
online version 10.2
share dealings 3.1.1
timing of implementation 10.2.20
transactions, range of, and Code 2.2.4
Takeover Directive (Interim Implementation) Regulations 2006 see **Takeover Regulations 2006**
takeover documentation see **documentation**
takeover offer
   definition 3.4.3, 10.2.1
Takeover Panel
   annual reports see **Takeover Panel annual reports**
   and Canary Wharf case 5.2.1.3.5
   case law 1.10
   composition 1.1
   and courts 1.10
   description 1.1
   disciplinary rules 1.12
   Executive see **Executive**
   exempt status obtained by application to 3.6.1
   FSA referral to 9.6.2
   FSMA, effect on 3.4.2.5
   functions 1.1, 1.7.1

   Hearings Committee 1.7.3
   jurisdiction changes 2.1
   mandatory and voluntary offers 4.1
   market abuse 9.3
   members 1.7.1
   new committee structure 1.4.4
   objectives 1.1
   partial offers, consent for 5.3
   powers 1.1
   proposed changes 1.4.4
   and Public Consultation Paper on Takeovers Directive (PCP 2005/5) 1.2
   and recognised intermediary status 1.5.2
   SARs, abolition 1.4.3
   and shared jurisdiction arrangements 2.2.3
   status 1.1
Takeover Panel Annual Reports
   1988
      pre-bid announcements 2.6.1
   1991
      mandatory offers 4.2
      offer announcements 2.4
   1995
      independent advice 2.8.3
   1996
      pre-bid announcements 2.6.1
   1997
      employee consultation 2.5.4
      offer announcements 2.4
   1999
      websites, and takeovers 6.14
   2000
      market abuse regime 3.4.2.5
   2001
      possible offer announcements 2.6.2
   2002
      application of Code 2.2.2
      independent advice 2.8.1
   2003
      pre-bid announcements 2.6.1
      pre-bid period 2.1
   2005
      possible offer announcements 2.6.2

Takeover Regulations 2006
  associates (Sch 2) 3.3.4
  and Company Law Reform Bill 7.1
  convertibles, appropriate offers for 5.2.1.2
  and Directive 7.1
  documentation 6.1
    non-compliant 6.5
  effective from 1.2
  scope 1.2
  share dealings 3.1.1
    Companies Act 3.2.3, 3.4.3
  squeeze-out provisions 3.4.4.7
takeovers
  approval in general meeting, Class 1 transactions 6.11
  and profit forecasts 8.1.1
  share dealing restrictions 3.4.1.4
  website use 6.14
talks announcement
  and bid announcement 2.7.1
  and circulation of offer announcements 6.9.1
target shares
  freedom to sell 7.7.2
telephone campaigns
  release of information 7.2.3.2
Tempus Group plc
  WPP Group plc, offer by 4.3.4
tender offers
  and dual jurisdiction 2.2.6
  and partial offers 5.3
Texas Utilities
  Energy Group, bid for 7.3.1.12
30 per cent threshold
  mandatory offers 4.2.4.1, 4.2
    EBTs 4.2.2.4
    foreclosure on security for loan 4.2.3.2
    inadvertent mistake 4.2.3.4
    Rule 9, triggering during course of voluntary offer 4.2.4.3
    yo-yo principle 4.2.4.6
  share dealings 3.2.1
Thistle Hotels
  BIL International Limited, hostile bid by 7.2.2, 7.3.1.6

TI
  offer for Dowty 5.2.1.2
"tie break" proposals
  and offer timetable 7.3.1.8
Tier 1 and II exemptions
  dual jurisdiction 2.2.6
timetable, offer *see* **offer timetable**
timing and revision
  Directive 10.2.19
  extensions of offer 7.4
  extensions to timetable 7.3.2
  offer timetable *see* **offer timetable**
  revisions and increases 7.5
TKM
  Molins, bid for 2.8.3
top-ups
  special deals, favourable conditions 5.2.1.3.1
Trafalgar House
  Northern Electric, bids for 3.4.1.6, 4.3.4, 7.7.3
transactions
  application of Code 2.2.4
  Class 1
    approval of takeover in general meeting 6.11
    and voluntary offers 4.3.3.1
  Class 2, announcement requirement 6.11
Transcomm plc
  Nabarro Wells, criticism 2.1, 2.6.1
transparency
  City Code amendment proposals 10.2.10
Treasury
  misuse of information 9.6.1.1
Triplex Lloyd
  and leak of confidential information 7.2
turnover tests
  competition law issues 4.4
Twigway
  bids by 7.5

UK Listing Authority (UKLA)
  Listing Rules *see* **Listing Rules**
  own shares, redemption or purchase 5.4

profit forecasts, exceptions 8.1.6
Related Party Transactions Rules 4.3.2
Unichem
Boots, pre-conditional offer by 2.7.2
United Kingdom
Takeover Directive implemented into *see* **Takeover Directive**: implementation in UK (2006)
UKLA *see* **UK Listing Authority (UKLA)**
United States
Securities and Exchange Act (1934), and dual jurisdiction 2.2.6

Virgin Mobile
offer by NTL 5.2.1.3.2
Virt-x Exchange Ltd
as RIE 9.4
"virtual bid" approach
possible offer announcements 2.6.2
voluntary announcements
"put up or shut up" regime 2.6.3
voluntary offers
acceptance condition 4.3.2
competition authorities, clearance condition from 4.3.3.2
consideration, particular form required when 4.3.1
invoking conditions 4.3.4
material change in circumstances conditions 4.3.3.3, 4.3.4
offer announcements 2.4
Rule 9, triggering during course of 4.2.4.3
specific action, conditions requiring 4.3.3.1

Ward White
Boots offer (1989) 4.3.2
warrants
mandatory offers (Rule 9) 4.2.4.5
Watmoughs
Quebecor and Webinvest, bids from 7.3.1.8

Webinvest
Watmoughs, bid for 7.3.1.8
websites
use in takeovers 6.14
Whitewash procedure
availability 4.2.3.1
redemption or purchase of own securities 5.4
requirements 4.2.3.1
rescue operations 4.2.3.1
Wickes/Focus Do It All bids 7.7.1
William Cook
competing bids for 7.2
Wm Morrison Supermarkets plc
recommended offer for Safeway plc 7.3.1.8, 7.7.1, 7.7.3
Winten Limited
and Derwent Valley Holdings
withdrawals
acceptances 5.2.2.2
general statements regarding 5.2.2.3
offeree protection conditions 7.3.1.6
Wm Low
Budgens, lapsed bid for 2.4
Wolverhampton & Dudley Breweries
Marston, Thompson & Evershed plc, hostile bid for 7.2.1, 7.3.1.8, 8.2.2
Worcester Group
offer by R Bosch
WPD
Hyder, bid for 7.3.1.12
WPP Group plc
Tempus Group plc, offer for 4.3.4

Xstrata (UK holding company)
and application of Code 2.2.1, 2.2.2

yo-yo principle
mandatory offers (Rule 9) 4.2.4.6

Zoo hotels
Groucho Club London, partial offer for 5.3